A. Walsh

FAREWELL ESPAÑA

*The World of the
Sephardim Remembered*

FAREWELL ESPAÑA

The World of the Sephardim Remembered

HOWARD M. SACHAR

Alfred A. Knopf
New York
1994

THIS IS A BORZOI BOOK
PUBLISHED BY ALFRED A. KNOPF, INC.

Owing to limitations of space, all acknowledgments of
permission to reprint previously published material will be
found following the index.

Library of Congress Cataloging-in-Publication Data
Sachar, Howard Morley.
Farewell España: the world of the Sephardim remembered /
by Howard M. Sachar.
p.   cm.
Includes bibliographical references and index.
ISBN 0-679-40960-2
1. Jews—Spain—History. 2. Sephardim—History. 3. Spain—Ethnic
relations. I. Title.
DS135.S7S23 1994
946'.004924—dc20   93-39501   CIP

Manufactured in the United States of America
First Edition

In memory of Shira
niece, radiant spirit, soldier of Israel

CONTENTS

My enduring memory of Cecil Roth is of a spare, angular figure, his expression somewhat quizzical behind dark-framed spectacles, his lips mildly pursed, gazing reflectively from the third-floor balcony of my apartment on Mevoh Yoram Street in Jerusalem. The flat lay in the Kiryat Shmuel quarter, and in the early 1960s it looked out on the United Nations Truce Supervision Headquarters on the demilitarized "Hill of Evil Counsel" between the Arab and Jewish cities. It was a building Roth remembered well in its earlier, mandatory-era incarnation, when it functioned as the British High Commissioner's Palace. In the 1920s and 1930s, he had been a frequent dinner guest there, and almost ideally in his element as he mingled with prominent figures of both the Zionist and British worlds. He much enjoyed reminiscing on the experience.

Cecil Roth was supremely an amalgam of those blended civilizations. London-born, he had earned his doctorate in general history at Merton College, Oxford, and then wrote and taught almost exclusively in the field of Jewish history. Even within that uniquely prismatic culture, Roth had become enamored early on of the Sephardic heritage. His cascade of scholarly works on the Jews of Spain, Portugal, Italy, and the Ottoman Empire, and their progeny in England, became more than the standard of Sephardic studies; for ensuing generations, it served as the wellspring of Sephardic historiography altogether. As the reading list even for this brief, impressionistic appraisal would suggest, no explorer in the field can yet presume to find his bearings without extensive exposure to Cecil Roth's magisterial volumes and articles on Sephardica. And surely no other scholarly works on that topic can begin to compare with his in sheer literary felicitousness.

Roth himself was the product of a Central European—Ashkenazic—

family, and little in his ancestral tradition prefigured an affinity for the Mediterranean strand in his people's mosaic. Yet his research was impelled by his temperament. Roth loved life. No theatrical or musical performance, no soirée, festive event, or intimate gathering, was too trivial for his delectation. Like others of his younger friends, I was drawn willy-nilly into the man's gravitational field. Whether recuperating from a long trip, an arduous writing project of my own, or even an illness, I would not be permitted a moment's self-commiseration. Cecil and Irene Roth were on the telephone to inform (not ask) me to prepare myself: we were going to attend this or that museum exhibition, so-and-so's birthday party, or such-and-such's public celebration. Only long after Roth's passing in 1970 did it occur to me that he had been drawn to the Sephardic world precisely for its own characteristic joie de vivre, its brilliance of plumage, its genial, accommodating, tolerant affection for life's pleasures and excesses, even its frailties.

Cecil Roth was a scholar, not a moralizer. Amidst a resurgent ideological zealotry that has tinctured elements of his own people (in common with those of not a few other nations), the vibrant, inquiring, pluralistic civilization that he more than any other scholar reconstructed and immortalized can be allowed to teach its own lessons. Meanwhile, the general reader may yet be intrigued by the achievements and vicissitudes of a protean, if demographically modest, subcommunity. There was a time when that fecund Sephardic leaven determined the cultural physiognomy of the Jewish people in their entirety.

In the preparation of this volume, I have benefited from the guidance and counsel of a number of eminent authorities. Professor M. Mitchell Serels, director of Sephardic Community Programs for Yeshiva University, generously opened out for me an extensive list of contacts overseas. Most of these individuals are cited in the text, but there are others whom I must also mention: For Portugal: Dr. Joshua Ruah and Mr. Solomon Marques, respectively president and former president of the Jewish Federation of Lisbon; Rabbi Avraham Assor of Lisbon's Sephardic Synagogue; and Mr. Narcisse Arié, also of Lisbon, businessman and distinguished historian of Portuguese Jewry. For Spain: Mr. Simon Hassan, engineer, of Seville; his brother, Mr. Ya'akov Hassan, curator of Judaica at the Arias Montano Institute in Madrid; Mr. Leon Sorenssen, executive director of the Jewish Community Center of Barcelona; and Mr. Alberto Hasson, businessman, of Barcelona.

France: Mr. Maurice Natif, executive director of the Centre Edmond Fleg in Marseilles, and Claude Maman, consistorial rabbi of Bordeaux. In

Italy: Rabbi Ernesto Colombo of Turin, and Rabbi Shimon Viterbo of Padua. For Yugoslavia: Dr. Lavoslav Kadelburg of Belgrade, president of the Federation of Jewish Communities of Yugoslavia; and Mr. Zvi Loker and Mr. Ze'ev Doron, historians, both currently in Tel Aviv. For Greece: Mr. Alberto Noar, director of public affairs for the Jewish Federation of Salonika; Mr. Raoul Sasportas of Tel Aviv, president of the Association of Greek Survivors of Concentration Camps in Israel; and Mr. Yitzchak Kerem (Charles Weingarten), scholar, also in Tel Aviv. For Bulgaria: Mr. Josif Levi of Sofia, president of the Central Israelite Religious Council; and Mr. Chaim Asher of Tel Aviv, former president of the Association of Bulgarian Immigrants in Israel. For Turkey: Mr. Tewfik Saracoglu, vice-president of the Quincentennial Foundation, Istanbul.

For the circumstances of contemporary Sephardim in these nations, readers may also wish to glance at an earlier volume of my own, *Diaspora* (1985). Its prologue lists numerous other resident authorities whose experience and expertise figured meaningfully in the preparation of the present book. Special mention should be made as well of Mr. Michael Grunberger of the Hebraica Division of the Library of Congress, and, at George Washington University, Ms. Tracey Valero of the Gelman Library and Mr. Sarandis Papadopoulos of the history department, for their solicitude in providing me with titles from near and far. By the same token, I extend my warmest thanks to Ms. Helena Koenig and the staff of that estimable Bethesda, Maryland, travel bureau, The Ticket Counter. Their integrity, resourcefulness, and dedication to each mile of my extensive itinerary far exceeded normal commercial considerations.

I am more indebted than I can express here to the distinguished colleagues and friends who perused, corrected, and commented on drafts of my chapters. For Moslem Spain: Professor Emeritus Majid Khadduri of Johns Hopkins University and Professors Dina Khoury and Robert Eisen (who also offered penetrating commentary on the kabbalistic period), both of George Washington University. For Christian Spain and its empire: Professor Angel Alcalá of the City University of New York. For Portugal: Professor Clea Rameh of Georgetown University. For France: Professor R. Emmet Kennedy of George Washington University. For North Africa: Professors Norman Stillman and Yedida Stillman of the State University of New York, Binghamton. For Italy: Professor Claudio Segre of the University of Texas and Professor Tommaso Astarita of Georgetown University. For the Ottoman Empire: Professor Avigdor Levy of Brandeis University, Professor Emeritus Roderic Davison of George Washington University (who also provided incisive commentary on modern Turkey), and Ms. Valya Shapiro of Brookline, Massachusetts. For Ottoman Armenia: Professor Richard Hovannisian of the University of California, Los Angeles, and Dr. Rouben Adalian of the Armenian Assembly of America, Washington, D.C. For Greece: Dr. Michael Matsas of Potomac, Maryland. For the Netherlands: Professor Ernst Presseisen of Temple University and Professor Robert Paul Churchill of George Washington University. For England: Professor Lois Schwoerer of George Washington University, president emeritus of the North American Conference on British Studies. For Yugoslavia: Professor Milan Vego of the United States Naval War College.

For evaluation of the manuscript in its entirety, I am indebted beyond measure to the venerated doyen of Jewish social science, Professor Raphael Patai. Once again, Ms. Jane Garrett and Mr. Melvin Rosenthal of Alfred A. Knopf, Inc., and my wife, Eliana, served as the most dedicated of collaborators. Not least of all, my late father, Dr. Abram L. Sachar, offered his own extensive counsel and commentary with a devotion that transcended his last months of grave physical suffering. As in my earlier books, his presence breathes in every page.

Kensington, Maryland
September 23, 1993

A NOTE ABOUT STYLE

Descriptive terms such as *converso* and *limpieza de sangre* in Spain become *convertido* and *limpeza de sangue* in Portugal. Personal names traditionally are spelled according to local usage: for example, Felipe (rather than Philip) in Spain; João (rather than John) in Portugal; Mehmet (rather than Mohammed) in Turkey. Yet nomenclature occasionally traverses national boundaries, as in the case of the popes of Rome, Emperor Charles V, or Hebrew names more commonly recognized by English-language readers as Isaac, Solomon, Jacob, Moses, and so on. A comparable eclecticism has been applied to place-names.

ENGLAND

DUTCH
NETHERLANDS

Altona
Hamburg

Emden

Haarlem
The Hague • Amsterdam
Rotterdam

Bristol ▲

London ▲

Ostend •
Antwerp •
Brussels •

SPANISH
NETHERLANDS

GERMAN
EMPIRE

• Paris

Nantes ▲

FRANCE

Bordeaux ◆

Lyons ▲

A L P S

Turin ■

Milan •

Padua •

Venice ◆

Mantua •
Parma •

Ferrara ◆
Ravenna ▲

Bayonne •
Peyrehorade •

Biarritz •

Genoa ■

Modena •

Bologna ▲

Pesaro

León •

Toulouse •

Montpellier •

Nice ▲

Pisa ▲

Ancona ▲

Oporto •

Zamora •

Burgos •

Narbonne •
Béziers •

• Lunel

Leghorn ▲

Siena •

PAPAL
STATES

PORTUGAL

Segovia •

Valladolid •

Tudela •

Marseilles •

Perpignan •

Florence •

ITAI

Belmonte ▲

Calatayud •
CASTILE

Zaragoza •
ARAGÓN

Lérida •
CATALONIA

Girona •

Rome •

• Lisbon

Madrid •

SPAIN
Toledo • Cuenca •

Guadalajara •

Teruel •

Barcelona •
Tarragona •

Tortosa •

Naples ▲

Ciudad Real •

KINGD
OF NAPI

Córdoba •

• Seville

Jaén •

MAJORCA ◆

Cádiz •

GRANADA

Cartagena •

Palermo •

Mes

Strait of Gibraltar
Tangiers •
Arzula ▲
Lareche ▲

Algeciras ▲
Tetuán ▲

Algiers ■

Tunis ■

Casablanca ▲
Mazagan

Rabat •
Meknès ▲

Fez ◆

ALGERIA

ALGERIA

TUNISIA

• Tlemcen

▲ Safi

MOROCCO

▲ Mogador

Marrakesh ▲

▲ Agadir

Sephardic Settlement

◆   15th Century

▲   16th Century

■   17th and 18th Centuries

▨   Spanish Lands

Boundaries as of 1648

0   Miles   300

0   Kilometers   500

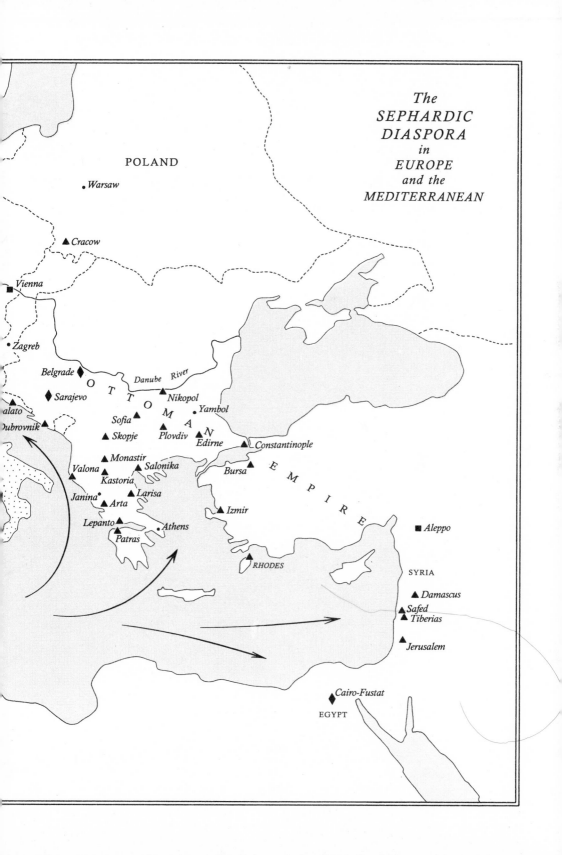

The
SEPHARDIC
DIASPORA
in
EUROPE
and the
MEDITERRANEAN

POLAND

• Warsaw

▲ Cracow

■ Vienna

• Zagreb

Belgrade ◆

O T T O M A N

Danube River

◆ Sarajevo

▲ Nikopol

alato

Dubrovnik

Sofia ▲

• Yambol

▲ Skopje

Plovdiv ▲

▲ Edirne

▲ Constantinople

▲ Monastir

Valona ▲

Salonika ▲

Bursa ▲

E M P I R E

Kastoria ▲

Janina •

Larisa ▲

Arta ▲

▲ Izmir

■ Aleppo

Lepanto ▲

• Athens

Patras ▲

▲ RHODES

SYRIA

▲ Damascus

▲ Safed
▲ Tiberias

▲ Jerusalem

◆ Cairo-Fustat

EGYPT

FAREWELL ESPAÑA

*The World of the
Sephardim Remembered*

CHAPTER I

UNDER ANDALUSIAN SKIES

The Moor Crosses the Strait

Córdoba meanders somnolently along the banks of the Guadalquivir River. A town of perhaps a quarter-million inhabitants, it is sustained by mercury and bauxite mined in a pine-clad sierra of neighboring mountains, by fruit and vegetables cultivated in an ochred checkerboard of enveloping farmland. We are in Spain's subtropical meridian, the apex of a triangle formed by Seville, ninety miles to the southwest, and Granada, a hundred miles to the southeast. Although each city in its time once served as the capital of Andalusia, it is Córdoba that best preserves the medieval legacy. Its Mezquita, or Great Mosque, defines that heritage. A Moorish phantasmagoria of striated marble pillars and garnet-and-ivory arches, the mighty edifice was begun by Caliph Abd al-Rachman I in the mid-700s and doubled in size by Caliph Abd al-Mansur I two centuries later. Even now, the Mezquita's crenellated walls and sculptured arcades overshadow, all but devour, a garish cruciform Renaissance cathedral fecklessly carved out of its viscera by later Christian conquerors.

With sublime impartiality, the Mezquita devours the legacy of its predecessors as well: four hundred years of Roman order and engineering, two hundred more of Visigothic rack and ruin. In administrative chaos by 711, the Iberian Peninsula was easy prey for an onrushing Moslem juggernaut. Then it was that Tariq ibn Ziyad, governor of Tangiers, led a mixed Arab-Berber army across the Strait of Gibraltar to establish Islam's initial beachhead on the European mainland. In ensuing years, with Western Christendom all but petrified in feudal immobility, the conquerors drew on a limitless hinterland of Arab power in North Africa and the Near East to engraft their Moslem civilization on a latinized population. As the first capital of al-Andalus—Andalusia—Córdoba under the Umayyad dynasty burgeoned into a metropolis of some half-million citizens by the ninth century, a commercial and administrative ganglion of nearly eight hundred mosques, a thousand ritual baths, a university, and a library encompassing four hundred thousand volumes.

It was a city, a realm, that proved uniquely congenial to its Jews. Dispersed in small enclaves throughout the southern and central regions of the peninsula, these Jews of *Sepharad* (the Hebrew term for Iberia) openly welcomed their new conquerors. Earlier, under the Christian Visigoths, the *Sephardim* had endured harsh conversionary pressures and intermittent physical abuse. Now they were quite prepared to offer their services to the invading Moors, even to organize their own Jewish militias for battle against the common enemy. It was a useful commitment. From the eighth century onward, ruled by the farsighted Abd al-Rachman and his heirs, the Umayyad Caliphate was preoccupied far less with religious orthodoxy than with economic prosperity. To be sure, the Jewish and Christian populations were to be regarded as *dhimmis* under Islamic law—that is, as nonheathen but still essentially second-class citizens. As such, they were subjected to discriminatory poll taxes, to residential and vocational restrictions, to social discrimination, even to demeaning badges of personal identification. Nevertheless, for the Jews, Moslem practice tended to eclipse theory. If Western regimes singled out Jews as the lone, stiff-necked infidel minority within reach, Islamic governments by contrast regarded Jews as merely one of several conquered dhimmi peoples, and in no sense the festering irredentist threat represented by the Christians. Indeed, for many years Jews remained by far the smallest of the non-Moslem communities, comprising less than 1 percent of the Iberian population. Sharing with the new conquerors a common Semitic origin, they fitted effortlessly into the ambience of the Arab elite, adopting their rulers' language, diet, and dress, and much of their folklore.

In consequence, the royal administration learned to trust the Jews. Even as it consigned them to their own residential quarters in Córdoba, Seville, and other captured cities, it ensured that they were decently accommodated—as a rule, within sight and under the protection of the royal palace—and suffered no limitations on their freedom of movement or economic activity. The arrangement was productive enough to attract Jews from other lands. During the eighth and ninth centuries, several thousand Moroccan and Egyptian Jews joined the far larger numbers of Moslem Berbers who migrated to Andalusia. Few were disappointed. In contrast to their circumstances in Christian Europe, where they were limited essentially to mercantile activities, Jews in Spain were allowed a far more diversified socioeconomic base. Some acquired modest plots of land and cultivated orchards and vineyards. Many others became leather-workers, tanners, dyers, jewelers, and silversmiths. To this day, former Jewish neighborhoods in Córdoba, Seville, Zaragoza, Málaga, and other southern Spanish cities bear such names as Plaza of the Tanners, Street of the Dyers, Lane of the Shoemakers, or Alcaicería de los Judíos—"Silk Market of the Jews."

Above all, the Sephardim were heavyweight merchants. As the diadem of a caliphate that linked the southern Mediterranean world in a network of standardized laws, weights, measures, and currency exchanges, Andalusia offered Jews an arena for commerce unparalleled since the glory days of Rome. Sailing the great Middle Sea, Jewish traders shared amply in the widening traffic. In Andalusia itself, they were the premier importers-exporters of silk, leather, textiles, grain, fruit, spices, and cattle, including the human "cattle" of slaves from the Balkans and western Russia.

Moreover, Islamic rule in Spain offered the Jews still another boon, one no less precious than physical and economic security. This was communal self-government. Through a council of their own notables, Jews assessed and taxed themselves. Their funds were applied both to the government's collective dhimmi poll taxes and to the Jews' own social, health, and educational services. The little community also operated under its own Jewish laws, administered its own Jewish courts, enforced its own sentences in its own jails, even occasionally turned over its criminals to the ruling authorities for execution. Although for many years these local Jewish courts depended extensively for their judgments upon responsa— legal opinions—issued by a "geniushood" of revered sages of the Talmud living half a world away in Baghdad, in every other respect Sephardic Jewry by the tenth century had become primus inter pares within the vast dispersion of their people. Numbering perhaps eighty thousand, they were emerging as a comfortable, middle-class population, sharing a collective security of existence all but unimaginable to their harried fellow Jews in Christian Europe.

Chasdai the Prince, Samuel the Exalted

In that same tenth century, even as the caliphate of Córdoba approached its zenith of economic affluence, one Isaac ben Ezra ibn Shaprut, a wealthy Andalusian merchant, moved to the capital city. Isaac's son, Chasdai, born there in 910, enjoyed every advantage of Jewish, Arabic, and Latin education, and doubtless could have excelled in any of several fields. He chose medicine. Soon, as a practicing physician, the young man began to win a name for himself by successfully applying ancient Greek drugs and treatments. Before long, he was appointed personal physician to Caliph Abd al-Rachman III.

With his refined and ingratiating personality, and his phenomenal linguistic skills, Chasdai over the years transcended his medical role to become the caliph's trusted personal confidant. In time, he came to function as Abd al-Rachman's principal adviser and negotiator even on complex political and diplomatic matters. As a mark of special favor, the caliph also turned over to Chasdai management of the department of customs, a concession that soon transformed this first Jewish courtier into a wealthy man. If Abd al-Rachman hesitated to confer the official title of vizier on a non-Moslem, he had a different honor in mind for Chasdai. It was to appoint him official leader of his own Jewish people, and thereby their spokesman to the court. The Jews of Andalusia were stunned. For them, henceforth, Chasdai would be the *nasi*—the prince—nothing less.

The title bespoke gratitude even more than awe. Chasdai was a river of personal generosity. Highly sensitive to his people's cultural needs, he dispensed a fortune to acquire Bibles, Talmuds, and books of Hebrew poetry and homiletics from all parts of the Jewish world. He imported a renowned Taranto scholar, Moses ben Chanoch, and lavishly endowed and staffed a talmudic academy for him that in one fell swoop established the Córdoba School, a collegium of scholarship that over the years achieved intellectual parity even with the "geniushood" of Baghdad. Like the broad-spirited Abd al-Rachman, a munificent patron of Islamic culture, the *nasi* also brought to his own "court" a galaxy of Hebrew philologists, poets, and other literary talents. He subsidized their families, provided them with audiences at his elegant soirées, and published and circulated their writings. By then, too, in his geniality and generosity, Chasdai ibn Shaprut functioned as paradigm as well as patron of his people. Sharing in the rewards of a secure and prosperous land, Andalusian Jews immersed themselves in their region's motifs and mores. Central among these was an accommodation of religious and cultural traditions to the newly accessible material pleasures and rewards around them. For if the tenth century in its widest ambit signified the onset of the Islamic Renaissance, it heralded no less an emergent "Golden Age" of Spanish Jewry.

Ironically, this plateau of self-assurance and self-indulgence was approached at the moment when its protective mantle, the Umayyad caliphate, was undergoing intermittent political upheavals. Soon, in fact, Moslem Andalusia fractured into a number of smaller and competing principalities. Córdoba became one of these. So did Seville. But it was

Granada, under the vigorous new Sinjadja dynasty, that emerged as largest and most durable of the successor realms. Indeed, as early as the original eighth-century Moslem conquest, the city of Granada itself had served as al-Andalus's eastern administrative center, for it was located between two mountain chains in the luxuriant Vega Valley and thus drew much of its wealth from surrounding gold, silver, copper, and iron mines, and from sugar and cotton plantations. Now, however, as capital of a newly independent kingdom, Granada developed even more impressively in size and affluence.

It had always possessed a sizable Jewish minority, as far back at least as the Visigothic era. But with its newly enhanced mercantile and bureaucratic inducements, Granada during the ninth and tenth centuries attracted still additional numbers of Jews, who swiftly won approbation as a loyal commercial element. By the late 900s, they numbered perhaps six thousand, very nearly equaling the ruling Moslem aristocracy in demographic mass. The Arab historian Achmad al-Razi wrote then that the Moors already were calling the city *Gharnatat al-Yahud*—Granada of the Jews. Another Arab chronicler observed that "whoever has not seen the splendor of the Jews in Granada, their good fortune and their glory, has never seen true glory, for they were great with wisdom and piety."

It was in Granada, too, early in the eleventh century, that one Samuel ben Joseph Halevi ibn Nagrela, youngest son of a local textile merchant, acquired a reputation as a precocious student of both Jewish and Arab law and literature, and as a talented calligrapher and stylist in the Arabic language. Soon the youth was taken on as secretary to the local vizier, Abu Abbas al-Arif. When later Abu Abbas was brought to the central Granadan court as minister of the treasury, Samuel accompanied him; and upon the older man's death six years later, Samuel was appointed his replacement. A vizierate was a signal honor for a Jew. For one thing, it assured Samuel an exponential growth of income as chief tax-collector of the realm. For another, the position gave him direct access to King Badis. So astute was Samuel's advice on a wide variety of public issues that in 1024, when he was thirty-one, the ruler appointed him grand vizier. If no Jew had ever before achieved such a position, no man ever more competently filled it. Samuel ibn Nagrela soon was adroitly negotiating alliances and counteralliances with neighboring Berber kingdoms, even with Christian kingdoms in the north. A grand vizier's duties in those days included warfare as well as diplomacy and politics, and Samuel thus was occasionally obliged to lead the Granadan army into battle. He did not shirk the challenge. Indeed, the Jewish diplomat proved a formidable commander. His Moslem officers admiringly described him as a warrior who confronted arrow and sword as if born to the role.

Among his fellow Jews, meanwhile, Samuel was revered as the *nagid*— the "chief" or "exalted." As in the case of the *nasi,* Chasdai ibn Shaprut, the title was more than an honorific. King Badis himself appointed Samuel leader of their *al-jama'a,* their official community. Among Granadan Jewry, therefore, every lawsuit of more than routine importance was brought directly before Samuel, and he personally issued final judgment according to the precepts and precedents of rabbinical law. In effect, Samuel functioned as chief rabbi of Granada, and he met this responsibility with a breadth of talmudic erudition that could hardly have been surpassed by professional scholars. More remarkable yet, however, were the nagid's achievements as litterateur, and specifically as Hebrew poet. His output was no mere facile versifying. In style, it was rigorous and polished. Its themes evoked a resonance among the most discriminating readers. Like other Arab and Jewish belletrists in Andalusia, to be sure, Samuel ibn Nagrela wrote of love, friendship, parting, aging, death. But the nagid also developed a motif that was unique in Hebrew poetry. It was the epic of battle, as he himself had experienced it. Except for the Bible, nowhere in Jewish literature can there be found an analogue to the nagid's commentary on warfare. Its mood shifts from humble piety to naked vengefulness. Thus, surrounded by the hosts of rival Seville, ibn Nagrela offers a heartfelt prayer: "Thou seest that I am in great need, hearken to my plea. . . . I am sunk in a deep abyss, the waters have reached my head. Stretch out Thy helping hand. Flame burns under my feet. . . . My tongue is silenced before the great danger, and my lips are closed. But all hearts are open before Thee. Hasten Thou to my help." The rabbi-warrior's supplication evidently is answered, for he triumphs, then offers "a great and splendid hymn of praise to a God splendid and great."

Victorious also in suppressing a local rebellion, ibn Nagrela dispatches the news in a lyrical message, a unique combination of delicacy and vituperation:

> Send a carrier pigeon,
> Though she cannot speak,
> With a tiny letter
> Attached to her wings,
> Sweetened with saffron water
> and perfumed with frankincense. . . .
> "My son, know that
> The cursed band of rebels had already fled,

> Scattered on the hills
> Like chaff from a windswept field."

And following a savage, decisive victory over the army of ibn Abbas, a neighboring Andalusian potentate, the nagid exults in a gasconade of raw vengeance:

> Their strong men lay on the battlefield, puffed up like bellows and pregnant women. All together they lay, slaves and lords, princes and servants together. With their king, the new Agag, they lay all around like dung on the field and were not brought to burial. Only one out of a thousand was saved, like single grapes in an abandoned vineyard. . . . The slain we left for the jackals, for the leopards and wild boar; their flesh we gave as a gift to the beasts of the field and the birds of heaven.

In 1056, Samuel ibn Nagrela died. It was a moment of abject despair for his people. Moslems passing near al-Qasaba, the Jewish quarter, could hear the wailing lament from thousands of voices, an explosion of grief so heartrending that Arab historians recounted the event generations later. Jewish communities beyond Granada shared in the sorrow. Yet none suspected that an era had closed with the nagid's passing. Indeed, as a matter of course, Samuel's son Joseph was appointed to succeed his father both as grand vizier and as nagid, and he filled these roles quite ably. Nevertheless, the young man over the years failed to recapture either the awe or the devotion evoked by his father—and this at a time when Jewish vulnerability was newly exposed.

Resentment of Jewish wealth and eminence was now suppurating in Granada. It was given early expression by Hunayn Abu Ishaq, a popular Moslem poet of the era. Addressing the Sanhadja, a confederation of Andalusian principalities, Abu Ishaq admonished the Granadans in the assembly:

> Your [king] has made a mistake
>   which delights malicious gloaters.
> He has chosen an infidel as his secretary when
>   he could, had he wished, have chosen a Believer.
> Through him, the Jews have become great and proud and arrogant—
>   they, who were among the most abject,
> And have gained their desires, and attained the utmost,
> and this happened suddenly, before even they
>   realized it.
> And how many a worthy Moslem humbly obeys the vilest ape
>   among these miscreants?

In 1066, Joseph ibn Nagrela displayed a certain tactlessness in opposing his king on a minor political issue. The ruler was not pleased. Perhaps a hint was dropped. Soon afterward, on December 30, as the vizier proceeded to synagogue on a Sabbath morning, a band of swordsmen waylaid him and his entourage and cut them down. The murders unloosed a wider orgy of violence. Rushing across the Daro River, an infuriated mob of several thousand Berbers and islamized native *musta'ribin*—former Christians—battered its way into the Jewish quarter. There the rioters set about disemboweling and beheading some fifteen hundred men, women, and children. Hundreds of Jewish shops and homes were looted and destroyed. Several days passed before the violence ebbed.

In ensuing months, the Jewish survivors only gradually ventured out of hiding. Timorously they set about rebuilding their homes and shops, and resuming their normal activities. If no longer intact, their critical mass still remained substantial; at least four thousand Jews resided in Granada as late as the twelfth century. Their economic role also remained preeminent. Nevertheless, in the hinterland, local Berber chieftains bullied and extorted from them. Bystanders jeered them in the streets. In retrospect, the "Black Sabbath" of December 30, 1066 augured a gradual erosion of Jewish fortunes in Andalusia. By the twelfth century, the Jewish "Golden Age" in Moslem Spain would register less in the realm of statecraft, or even of commerce, than in the world of culture.

A Synergy of Civilizations

During these same years of Islamic Renaissance and later political upheaval, both Jews and Arabs managed to produce intellectual elites of surpassing distinction. From the outset, ideas and attitudes cross-fertilized extensively between the two peoples. The Jews were entirely comfortable in Arabic, which had become their spoken vernacular and served them for writing as well, although in Hebrew characters. Yet, ironically, it was the very depth of the Jews' immersion in Arabic culture that revived their interest in Hebrew as a literary medium. For one thing, major developments in the study of Arabic grammar and usage impelled Jewish scholars to reexamine the structure of their own sacred tongue. The two languages were closely related, after all, and the methods developed by Arab scholars for Arabic studies seemed equally applicable to Hebrew. Thus, as early as the tenth century, the philologists Menachem ibn Saruq, Dunash ibn Labrat, and Judah ben David Hayyuj produced a series of lexicons and grammars that resurrected Hebrew as a contemporary literary vehicle.

A second factor in the new Hebraic sunburst was the historic role of poetry in Jewish tradition. If verse was the single Jewish literary genre for which Hebrew was used exclusively, there were decisive precedents. Hebrew was the language of the *piyyut,* the Jewish liturgical poem. More important, it was the language of the Bible. So it was that, as Jews acquired the model for a "pure" classical language from an Arabic rendered newly precise in structure and style, and celebrated love, nature, or wine in the Arab style, their lyrics were produced in the language of the Bible. Andalusia coruscated with these Jewish versifiers. In his *Thesaurus of Medieval Hebrew Poetry,* Israel Davidson lists over three thousand such poets and poetasters writing between the tenth and thirteenth centuries alone.

Today, it requires a leap of the imagination to resurrect the world that inspired their muse. Málaga, on the Costa del Sol, glitters enticingly in Spanish travel brochures. Its suburb of Torremolinos boasts lavish hotels, charming villas, powdery beaches. Málaga itself, however, is a rather shabby town. Its historic old port buildings and museums are peeling, dilapidated, understaffed. Its municipal park, seemingly lush in vegetation, upon closer inspection is bleached and neglected. More dispiriting yet for the visitor is the quest for the statue of Solomon ibn Gabirol. Commissioned by the municipality in 1959, the work has been declared the park's centerpiece. But even diligent exploration among its faded palm trees and cacti turns up no statue. Interrogation of policemen and benchsitters does not help. Few locals have so much as heard of the man.

Málaga's claim to Solomon ibn Gabirol is in any case tenuous. He was born there in 1021 but orphaned early and brought to Zaragoza as a child. Relatives provided him with a Jewish education at a local talmudic academy. Yet it was his native curiosity and omnivorous reading that gave him mastery of Arabic culture. From his early youth, literature was ibn Gabirol's passion, and Hebrew poetry his chosen métier. Indeed, his early success as poet was one of his rare consolations. He was desperately poor, and even more desperately tormented by a skin ailment, a mantle of pus-filled lesions that kept him in pain almost all his life. Ibn Gabirol's verses often echo that misery: "Sickness has wasted my body"; "I toss on my bed the whole night through, as on thorns and piercing reeds"; "My body is emaciated, a weak fly can carry it away on its wings." And, invoking his dead mother: "Ah, woe is me that you brought me into the world. How well it would have been had you remained barren." For ibn Gabirol, then, poetry was more than the expression of a dazzling literary talent. It was emotional therapy in every sense of the word.

It was also the vocation that earned him his bread. Initially, he ate it with affliction, reduced to churning out verses in praise of rich men for

their family celebrations. But later, by good fortune, a stipend was provided by Samuel ibn Nagrela, who brought ibn Gabirol to adorn his court
and sing his praises. It was a breathing space. Moreover, for the young
poet, his years under the nagid's patronage offered more extensive opportunity to study and adapt Arabic models. Beyond dutiful encomia to his
patron, therefore, ibn Gabirol's stanzas could range from descriptions of
radiant sunsets and gently descending nightfalls to occasional excursions
into humor, and even satire. Characteristic was his comment on a soirée
that ran short of wine:

> Old Moses of old caused the waters to flee,
> And led all his people dry-shod o'er the sea;
> But Moses our host at the precedent frowns,
> And us, his poor guests, he unflinchingly drowns
> In water, cold water.

But the interludes of playfulness and lyricism were brief. Rivals among
Samuel ibn Nagrela's entourage circulated false rumors of ibn Gabirol's
alleged disloyalty. In the end, the nagid turned against the young poet,
cutting off his stipend. Ibn Gabirol accordingly returned to a life of wandering and destitution, of singing for his supper at the homes of arrogant
Jewish effendis. His verses, once melancholy, became bitter. "How
should I sing," he protested, "when in our day every simpleton stretches
out his hand to the poet's crown?" In later years, as he moved from one
feckless patron to another, always in pain and in need, usually alone, he
fantasized a love affair. It was not with a woman—the notion was unimaginable for a man in ibn Gabirol's condition—but with God. His verse
now gained a new depth:

> At the dawn I seek Thee,
>   Rock and refuge tried,
> In due service speak thee,
>   Morn and eventide. . . .
>
> Pour out thy heart to the Rock,
>   Pour out thy inmost soul
> To the stronghold naught can shock,
>   As the mornings and evenings roll. . . .

Isolated from meaningful social relationships, ibn Gabirol gradually
transformed—sublimated—this vision of earthly love into a presumably
more enriching mystical religious fervor. Thus it was, in his mid-thirties,
and this time writing in Arabic, that the poet composed his single nonpo-
etic work, *The Fountain of Life*. Reflecting the neo-Platonism still current

in Andalusian intellectual circles, the book envisaged God's light passing outward through a hierarchy of divine "emanations" and ultimately suffusing all corporeal matter. Taut and precisely reasoned, *Fountain* is an intriguing philosophical document. In the twelfth century, translated into Latin under the title *Fons Vitae,* the work profoundly impressed Christian scholastics. William of Auvergne, Albertus Magnus, Bonaventura, and Thomas Aquinas studied *Fons Vitae* diligently, and Duns Scotus adopted its central argument into his philosophical system. Yet, inasmuch as the essay contained no specific reference to Judaism or Jews, after ibn Gabirol's death it was erroneously ascribed to an Arab philosopher, "Avicebron." It was not until the nineteenth century that the German-Jewish scholar Salomon Munk discovered the work's true origin.

Meanwhile, all but God-intoxicated in his last years, ibn Gabirol wove his adoration into his longest—and arguably his greatest—poem in Hebrew, *Keter Malchut* (The Royal Crown). Here the author himself traverses the universe beyond all terrestrial limits; surveys the life of man from birth to death; witnesses hosts of angels and demons, saints and sinners; and exults once more in the infinitude of God's wonders. As in others among his later poems, ibn Gabirol tends somewhat perversely to equate the human soul with the feminine gender, subject to "days of uncleanness."

> But if she hath been defiled,
> She shall wander to and fro for a space in wrath and anger,
> And all the days of her uncleanness
> Shall she dwell vagabond and outcast;
> She shall touch no hallowed thing;
> And to the sanctuary she shall not come
> Till the days of her purification be fulfilled.

All told, ibn Gabirol composed some three hundred religious and secular poems. Much of his religious poetry (with the exception of "The Royal Crown") has been incorporated into synagogue prayer and ritual, often with its authorship unrecognizable. In the words of his ablest translator, Israel Davidson, ibn Gabirol stands out in the history of Sephardic literature as a kind of tropical lungfish, capable of breathing in both air and water, of moving effortlessly between the sacred and the profane. In 1057, penniless and all but ignored, ibn Gabirol died, in Valencia, at the age of thirty-six.

The Golden Triad Completed

Moses ibn Ezra, born only two years before ibn Gabirol's death, offers a vivid contrast to his predecessor. For ibn Ezra, sheer love of life brimmed over almost uncontrollably. His father was a prominent merchant of Granada. The son, enjoying the luxury of a broad education and ample leisure, was able from the outset to devote himself almost entirely to poetry. His interests were unabashedly worldly. Indeed, ibn Ezra's greatest delight lay in celebrating the Andalusian landscape, its fields, vineyards, gardens, and fountains, its food, wine, and women.

> Why should I grieve? The purling of the brooks,
> The throstle's song, I hear. On couch of blooms,
> More brilliant than the weaving of Persia's looms,
> I lie beneath the myrtle's shade, and look
> On the bright necklace of the turtle dove—
> And dream—and dream, ah me, of my lost life!

> Dwell beside the beds of roses,
> Abide in the shade of the myrtles,
> And behold the dew of night upon their leaves,
> Like drops of bedellium and tiny pearls.
> Beside the flower beds thy lodging make,
> Nor hut nor palace for thy dwelling take;
> The dove, the throstle, all the woodland choir
> Shall sing thee music passing harp or lyre.

The idyll of self-indulgence did not endure beyond early middle age. An indifferent businessman, ibn Ezra suddenly lost the bulk of his inheritance and was reduced to employment as a clerk. The misfortune was compounded when he fell vainly in love with his niece, a passion "strong as death," as he acknowledged in letters to her. Her father—his brother—forbade the match; it fell under the scriptural ban of incest. When she married another, ibn Ezra was devastated. For nearly two years he could not bring himself to write. It was her death in childbirth that roused him to take up his pen, possibly as an act of self-therapy. He now brought a new depth, even a certain bitterness, to his work. Occasionally a cry of raw indignation surfaced. One of these poems, long since incorporated into the High Holiday liturgy as the "Tochechah," is a "Reproach" that echoes hauntingly each Yom Kippur eve:

> Ye deaf, hear from my lip of awes to be;
> Take thought to pierce the world's deep mystery;

And ye, O blind ones, look—that ye may see! . . .
Alas, how shall they hear,
That, wilful, stop the ear?
Or how shall ears with the world's tumult filled,
Heed wisdom's cry?

Ibn Ezra expired sometime after his eightieth year. "Tochechah" was his final lament.

The third member of Andalusian Jewry's "golden triad," Judah Halevi, surpassed ibn Ezra and arguably even ibn Gabirol in poetic genius. Born in Toledo of middle-class parents, Judah Halevi moved as a young man to Moslem Granada in 1095. The city's affluent and cultivated Jewish population offered a responsive audience for the young man's early poems. His subsequent verses reflected the genial, companionable mood of his surroundings. Although written in Hebrew, they were songs of wine, friendship, and love in the classical Arab tradition. Yet few of Halevi's Arab peers quite matched his delicacy of sentiment or the nuance of his language:

> Would that after my death unto my ears would come the sound of the golden bells upon your skirts. . . . From my grave I would ask of your love and your peace. . . . I ask not my share of time, but only the scarlet thread of your lips and the girdle of your waist. . . . I cannot hear your voice, but in the secret places of my heart I hear the sound of your footsteps.

Neither could Halevi's Jewish colleagues match his artistry in weaving biblical allusions even into his love songs:

> The sun is on thy face and thou spreadest out the night
> Over his radiance with the clouds of thy locks. . . .
> Sun and moon, the Plough and the Pleiades are zealous
> To be brothers and sisters of thine;
> Men and maidens think, ah! would they were but free
> To be thy slaves and thine handmaidens.

In contrast to ibn Gabirol and ibn Ezra, Judah Halevi did not find his ardor unrequited. He married well, the beauteous daughter of a wellborn family. For a while, he lived his dream.

In the early twelfth century, returning to his birthplace, Toledo, to improve his finances, Halevi entered the practice of medicine. His literary creativity did not flag; rather, it was the tenor of his poetry that changed. His beloved wife died in early middle age, as did his closest friend. In ensuing years, Halevi became preoccupied with the fragility of life, the eternity of God:

Lo, sun and moon, these minister for aye;
The laws of day and night cease nevermore;
Given for signs to Jacob's seed that they
Shall ever be a nation—till these be o'er.
If with His left hand He should thrust away,
Lo! with His right hand He shall draw them nigh.

Eventually, Judah Halevi would compose over three hundred poems of an intensely pietistic nature. Adapted to contemporary Arabic structure and meter, they nevertheless drew their inspiration from Lamentations, the Psalms, the Book of Job. Scores of these poems are incorporated into Jewish religious liturgy to this day.

It was also in the Toledan period that Halevi ventured to outline his commitment to his ancestral religion in a modest Arabic-language volume, *The Book of the Khuzari*. Taking as its starting-point the historic conversion to Judaism of the Tatar kingdom of the Khazars, the book consists of discussions between the Khazar ruler and four interlocutors: a Moslem, a Christian, a Jew, and a nonreligious scholar. Each of these explains to the king his beliefs and practices. Thus, the Jew insists that Israel, first to be vouchsafed the vision of the one true God, is still the Chosen People, and the Holy Land is still the land of prophecy. "But are you not like a dead body now?" scoffs the king. "Not dead but dangerously ill," replies the Jew, "and yet with a firm faith that the great miracle will happen."

The "miracle" Halevi had in mind was his people's return to Zion. In this respect, the *Khuzari* may be considered his admonition to the complacent Jews of Granada, Córdoba, Toledo, and other Spanish communities never to forget that their mother, Zion, the bondaged homeland, was crying out for them to return. It was a theme Halevi enmeshed even more persistently and poignantly in his *Zionides,* a series of laments that opened up a unique proto-Zionist vein in medieval Hebrew literature. The passion for the ravaged Holy Land achieved an almost unbearable intensity in the poet's single most widely quoted work:

My heart is in the East, and I in the uttermost West.
How can I find savor in food? How shall it be sweet to me?
How shall I render my vows and my bonds, while yet
Zion lieth beneath the fetters of Edom, and I in Arab chains?
A light thing would it seem to me to leave all the good things of Sepharad—
Seeing how precious in mine eyes to behold dust of the desolate sanctuary.

In its numerous transcriptions over the years, this untitled poem eventually was incorporated in the liturgy for Tisha b'Av, the fast day commemorating the destruction of the Temple in ancient Jerusalem. In our own time, a poignant image from another verse of this poem has appeared in an unanticipated context:

> To wail for thine affliction, I am like the jackals;
> but when I dream
> Of the return of thy captivity,
> I am a harp for thy songs.

In 1967, the Israeli composer-lyricist Naomi Shemer reinvoked that image—"I am a harp for thy songs"—in a haunting song, "Jerusalem the Golden," that in effect became the anthem of the Six-Day War.

In 1140, his children grown, Judah Halevi made the decision "to leave all the good things of Sepharad" and depart for his beloved Holy Land. In September of that year he sailed from Tarragona. Four weeks later, after reaching his initial destination of Alexandria, the poet boarded a second vessel, bound for Acre. But two days out of port, the ship encountered a storm and turned back. It was a mishap transformed by Halevi into surely the most indelible epic of the sea ever limned in the Hebrew language, a majestic vision of waves surging like lions, winds crawling like snakes through sails, decks trembling and quaking, sailors groaning, and then an evening calm mercifully descending

> . . . like an Ethiopian woman in raiment of gold
> And of blue inset with crystals.
> And the stars are confused in the heart of the sea
> Like strangers driven out of their homes;
> And after their image, in their likeness, they make light
> In the sea's heart, like flames of fire.
> The face of the waters and the face of the heavens, the infinity of sea,
> The infinity of night, are grown pure, are made clear,
> And the sea appeareth as a firmament—
> They are two seas bound up together;
> And between them is my heart, a third sea,
> Lifting up ever anew my waves of praise.

Judah Halevi died in 1141. Had he succeeded in reaching the Holy Land? There is scant evidence that he ever again departed Egypt. Yet romantics have chosen to believe the account offered by the nineteenth-century German poet Heinrich Heine, who fantasized "the fiery pillar of sweet song" meeting his death at the hands of an Arab horseman in Jerusalem.

An Andalusian Lifestyle

For all its political unrest, Moslem Iberia sustained its economic vitality well into the twelfth century. The Jews shared in that affluence. Heavily concentrated in Granada, they earned their livelihoods as brokers and distributors of the region's sugarcane and cotton; as exporters of marble, gold, silver, iron, and copper; as retail tradesmen, artisans, and physicians. Beyond Granada, Jewish enclaves were still to be found in Córdoba, the focus of the Jews' original settlement, and in Lucena and Seville. During periods of civil instability, additional thousands of Jews also migrated northward to the Christian kingdoms of Asturias, León, Castile, Navarre, Coimbra. Yet even in the north, Spanish Jews by and large preserved their Arabic language and nomenclature, and remained extensively integrated into the Arab cultural terrain.

Wherever they settled, too, the Jews continued to operate as a state within a state, exercising the widest measure of fiscal and juridical autonomy. For them, within that insular world, it was the synagogue that functioned as the communal omnium-gatherum. There were many hundreds of these, from public synagogues to synagogues erected by guilds of artisans to private synagogues attached to the homes of wealthy families. Córdoba and Granada, each with five or six thousand Jews, maintained at least two dozen synagogues. In Toledo, with barely four thousand Jews, there were eleven. Characteristically, Iberian (and North African) synagogues shared most of the architectural and decorative features of the mosque. Construction was in the shape of a rectangle. The Ark of the Torah, positioned in the center of the sanctuary, was encircled by cushions and mats. Inasmuch as Jews were forbidden to employ human likenesses, the synagogue, like the mosque, was adorned with the carvings of animals and vegetation, with plaster lobes, horseshoe bows, rosettes, and sacred verses filigreed in Hebrew lettering.

Plainly, the synagogue, in common with the mosque and the church, was first and foremost a house of prayer. For all of Andalusia's material pleasures, worship was a serious concern for its heterogeneity of Arabs, Moors, Jews, Slavs, Visigoths, and Lusitanians. But for Jews as well as for the others, the day of rest was also a convivial delight. Thus, after a Friday-afternoon visit to the neighborhood bathhouse, and its opportunity for gossip with friends, a middle-class Jew attended services on Saturday morning. Upon returning home, he and his family enjoyed an ample Sabbath meal, usually of spiced meat and flatbread, washed down with wine. A siesta followed. Afterward, the home was open to relatives and friends. The family ambience was tradition-bound.

It was sustained, as well, by self-satisfaction. Iberia's affluent Jews envisaged themselves as the aristocrats of the Diaspora. In its condescension, the assessment evinced at once economic success, superior education, and often a highly cultivated, characteristically Iberian elegance of personal demeanor. Appraising the Jews of *Ashkenaz* (the Hebrew term for Trans-Pyrenean Europe), a Sephardic intellectual could write:

> [The Ashkenazim] eat boiled beef, dipped in vinegar and garlic
> . . . and as the fumes . . . penetrate their minds, they then imagine that
> by these viands they have achieved an image of the Creator. . . . They
> have no fixed ideas except on rutting, eating, and drinking. . . . Stay
> clear of them and do not come within their embrace, and . . . let not
> your pleasant companionship be with any other than our beloved
> Sephardic brethren . . . for [the latter] have intellectual capacity,
> understanding, and clarity of mind.

Ironically, well-born Andalusian Jews experienced few similar concerns about "staying clear" of their Moslem peers. Relations between the two elites generally were equable. Although each of Spain's religious communities lived within its own quarters, well into the twelfth century, the mass violence that followed the assassination of Joseph ibn Nagrela in 1066 was uncharacteristic even of the restive Moslem lower classes. Among the affluent, business and professional contacts were extensive, and social visits between prosperous Moslem and Jewish families were by no means rare.

In the mid-1100s, however, a force majeure decisively shattered these placid multicultural relations. Led by Abd al-Mu'min al-Mohade, scion of a fundamentalist North African Berber dynasty that has traditionally been called the Almohades, a new wave of Islamic warriors swept down from Algeria's Atlas Mountains. Engulfing the North African littoral population, the invaders pressed across the Strait of Gibraltar to overrun central and southern Iberia. Decades of brutal Almohade persecution followed— of forced conversions equally of Jews, Christians, and "backsliding" Moslems. Thousands of Andalusian Jews accordingly fled to the Spanish Christian kingdoms of the north. The grim interregnum continued for over six decades, until 1212, when an alliance of Christian armies finally destroyed the Almohade minions at Las Navas de Tolosa, and with it Almohade rule in the Iberian Peninsula altogether.

In ensuing years, as local Moslem governments began reviving in Andalusia, large numbers of Jews returned to the south. But if they antici-pated resuming the former tempo of their lives, they were shortly un-deceived. Religious passions by then had been too widely stirred and diffused. Once again, Moslem rulers began enforcing the old sumptuary laws, and this time with a new rigor. Jews were obliged to wear badges or distinctively colored turbans. Jewish courtiers, physicians, and commu-nal officials faced new vocational restrictions. Jewish families were ex-posed to new refinements of social isolation. Jewish merchants were held responsible for bad harvests or food shortages, and often endured a gaunt-let of insults and petty humiliations in street and marketplace. By the latter 1100s, any lingering hope for Jewish revival in once-genial Andalusia seemed all but foreclosed. The departure of Jews northward, once tenta-tive and temporary, now gained momentum, swelling irretrievably from a rivulet to a stream.

A Rediscovery of Science

"The owl of Minerva flies only at twilight." In this same period of malaise and migration, the Hegelian adage fitted Andalusian Jewish cultural vigor almost precisely. If their political and economic glory was in decline, the Jews' intellectual élan had never blazed more brilliantly. That sunburst, of course, reflected the Islamic Renaissance itself, which reached its apogee in the twelfth and early thirteenth centuries. Long before, at the outset of its military campaign in the Middle East, the Arab host had overrun Syria and Egypt, where it took possession of many distinguished universities and libraries. From within their confines were recovered much of the literature of the Hellenic and Hellenistic eras. Among these were numer-ous Syriac translations of manuscripts by Plato, Aristotle, Euclid, Archi-medes, Hippocrates, Galen, and other giants among the ancient Greeks. In ensuing years, a significant number of these works, retranslated into Arabic, provided the basis for an upsurge of Islamic learning. So it was that Andalusia and Alexandria developed into major centers of Greco-Arab scholarship.

Mingling with the emergent elite of Arab intellectuals, Jews too were rapidly swept up by the new cultural effervescence. Indeed, they were uniquely qualified to share in it. As a law-based religion, Judaism histori-cally placed extensive emphasis upon learning. Even mathematics played a significant role in that tradition, for in their study of Bible and Talmud the Jews had long since become accustomed to the assignment of numeri-cal values to letters, and thus to mathematical thinking as a feature of their general literacy. A biblical scholar like Abraham ibn Ezra could write with equal proficiency on astronomy and astrology, and evoke respectful attention in the Moslem and Christian worlds. Ibn Ezra's rabbinical protégés Sahl ben Bishr, Sind ben Ali, and Abraham ben Chiyyat won even wider recognition for their astronomical calculations. Exposure to the rediscovered Greek mathematicians now further reinforced this Jewish vocation.

The passion of Jews for medicine appears to have been even more notable. In some degree, Islam itself encouraged the development. Unlike medieval Christianity, with its fixation upon the world to come, the religion of the Arabs had always placed much emphasis upon the healing arts. The recent discovery and translation of works by Galen, Hippocrates, and other Greek physicians simply fortified the image of medicine as a dignified calling, one deserving of appropriate remuneration. Influenced by this trend, as by parallel cultural developments in the Moslem world, rabbis living in Andalusia and other Islamic realms similarly devoted much of their responsa literature to questions of sickness and health. Indeed, a number of Sephardic talmudic academies included medicine in their curricula. It is recalled that Chasdai ibn Shaprut, the tenth-century "prince" of Córdoban Jewry, began his public career as physician to the royal court. Jonah ibn Bechlarish, court physician to the Sultan of Zaragoza, compiled the first known universal dictionary of drugs. Sheshet ben Isaac Benveniste, physician to the count of Barcelona, produced a famous treatise on gynecology. The poet Judah Halevi was a successful physician in Toledo.

It was, however, Moses ben Maimon, best known to posterity as Maimonides, who emerges as the transcendent physician of the medieval world. Born in Córdoba in 1135, the son of a rabbi-businessman, Maimonides fled the Almohade invasion with his parents when he was thirteen. For a decade, the family lived the life of nomads, wandering the peninsula with other refugee Jews. Crossing the strait, they resided for a while in Fez, capital of the Almohade empire, but still a rather quieter eye in the hurricane of Moslem fundamentalism. It was in Fez that Maimonides initially took up the study of medicine. Later, the family settled in Fustat, near Cairo, where it soon managed to gain a modest security as jewelry traders. Yet, at first, Maimonides himself was inactive in the business. Nor did he practice as a physician. His preference was for scholarship— reading, writing, corresponding, and commenting on issues of Jewish law and practice. But in 1166 his brother David, returning from a gem-buying journey to Persia, drowned when his ship foundered in the Indian Ocean. The jewels that sank with him represented most of the family's estate. Only then did Maimonides turn to medicine as a livelihood.

Fortunately for his parents, and his late brother's widow and children, whom he now supported, Maimonides proved an instant success as a physician. Indeed, his skill rapidly became the wonder of his peers. In 1170, Sultan Selah ad-Din ("Saladin") appointed him physician to the royal household—a post Maimonides held for the rest of his life, even while maintaining a full private practice. In common with other physicians of his time, he drew much of his information from ancient Greek and Arabic medical literature. Yet he depended even more extensively upon personal observation and experience. It was Maimonides's defining feature to accept no precedent on faith. Soon, then, he became a pioneer in the science of preventive medicine, advocating fresh air, sunshine, personal cleanliness, moderation in diet and in sexual indulgence. He was also the first medieval doctor to sense that the health of the mind depended extensively on the health of the body. Over time, Maimonides's achievements as a clinician became legendary among colleagues and patients alike. For centuries afterward, Jews visited the Cairo synagogue that bore his name less as a house of worship than as a shrine of healing.

Despite the burdens of his practice, moreover, and his widening responsibilities as a rabbi and communal leader (p. 24), Maimonides found time to produce ten important medical treatises. One of these was a huge compendium of some two thousand drugs. Others dealt with such pervasive afflictions as asthma, hemorrhoids, snakebites, melancholia, and sexual dysfunction (this last a matter of much importance to his royal patients). More impressive yet, Maimonides published a summation of all basic medical treatments, from Galen and other Greek authorities to his own day. It became the standard physician's handbook in the Moslem world. Translated into Latin, the work also was adopted as a basic teaching manual for European medical schools until well into the Renaissance. In his own lifetime, Moslem colleagues invariably referred to "Maimuni" (his Arabic name) as the "eagle of physicians." But Maimonides was simply the most vivid example of a dazzling Sephardic eminence in medieval science. The historian of science George Sarton has found that of eighty-five publishing scientists in Iberia between 1150 and 1300, at least thirty-five were Jews.

Faith and Reason

In the course of the Islamic Renaissance, the Arabs transmitted still another Greek treasure to the world. It was rational philosophy. The Jews were among its most avid students. This was an irony of sorts. In ancient times, Jews had feared Hellenistic thought, and only a few Greco-Jewish thinkers, such as Philo, were prepared to subject their faith to the risks posed by rationalism. It was not until nearly a millennium later, under Moslem rule, when Jews and Arabs began producing cosmopolitan urban elites, that both peoples adopted more forthcoming attitudes toward "Greek wisdom." Of the rediscovered ancients who influenced their common worldview, Aristotle was incomparably the most important. As early as the ninth century, Syriac translations of the great thinker were being retranslated into Arabic, then undergoing commentary by Moslem philosophers. Among the latter it was Avicenna, Alfarabi, and above all Averroës who fused Aristotelian logic and Islamic monotheism into an urbane and sophisticated theology.

The approach registered as well on an innovative minority of Jewish intellectuals. Entirely comfortable in their ancestral Judaism, these men nevertheless were deeply influenced by the Greco-Arabic passion for elegance of cognition and style. Like the Arabs, they too now sought to negotiate a reconciliation of faith and reason. The feat was not easily accomplished. Aristotle's vision of God was mechanistic rather than moral. It allowed little room for such Judaic tenets as creation, prophecy, providence, reward, or punishment. Even so, Abraham ibn Daud, a twelfth-century Córdoban, was the first to negotiate a modest doctrinal accommodation between Judaism and Greek philosophy. Although as a young man ibn Daud all but devoured the works of Avicenna and other Islamic philosophers of Aristotelianism, he waited until he was fifty before venturing any commentary of his own. Then, in a series of Arabic-language treatises, he developed his rather cautious hypothesis that both Aristotle and the Torah led to an identical goal, the attainment of moral truth. Yet, in ibn Daud's scheme, philosophy confirmed this moral truth only after many generations of seeking and groping, while the Jewish people had achieved their insights from the beginning, in the Prophets' divine revelation.

No Jew or Moslem, however, not even the great Averroës, succeeded in accommodating religious faith to Aristotelian rationalism quite as impressively as Moses Maimonides. In fact, Maimonides and Averroës were both born in twelfth-century Córdoba only a few streets and a few years apart. Tangible evidence of that proximity survives. Today, a marble figure of Averroës stands near a small entrance to the *al-jama'a,* the old Jewish community, on the Calle de la Luna. One passes then through the Puerta de Almodóvar and turns right down the Calle de los Judíos to the Rambam Synagogue, commemorating the sanctuary in which the great Maimonides worshipped as a youth. Characteristically, the structure is embellished with plaster fretwork, with Stars of David and Hebrew lettering interwoven in the Arab manner. The *al-jama'a* still breathes with the history of this people. In gleaming tile, each street name here is a whisper of their presence: Calle de los Judíos, Calle de la Sinagoga, Calle Juda Levi (Judah Halevi), Plazuela de Juda Levi, Calle Leifa Aguilar.

Nearby, too, are to be found the Plazuela Tiberides (after Maimonides's burial site in Tiberias), the Calle Maimonides, the Plazuela de Maimonides. The last, an elegantly tiled miniature square, is dominated by the august presence himself—a slim figure in life-sized bronze, robed, turbaned, goateed, his narrow, delicate face and hands sensitively imagined. On his lap, appropriately, rests a book. "Córdoba a Maimonides," declares the chiseled stone inscription on the pedestal, "en el 800 aniversario de su nacimiento 1135–1935." Maimonides may have fled Córdoba when he was only thirteen, but Arab historians invariably remember him as *al-qurtubi*, "the Córdoban," even as he himself tended to adorn his Arabic signature, Musa ibn Maimuni, with the embellishment *al-andalusi*, "the Andalusian."

It was during his early years of wandering and intermittent medical studies that Maimonides launched into his literary efforts. While still in his twenties, he produced an astonishingly learned commentary on the Talmud; a "Letter of Consolation" to his fellow refugees, eloquently entreating them to place their faith in God as the one "sure and certain source of hope"; and a "Letter Concerning Apostasy," eruditely citing Bible and Talmud to legitimize a Jew's right of tactical defection from Judaism for the "holy" sake of physical survival. Within barely a year of his arrival in Egypt in 1165, Maimonides's phenomenal command of Jewish texts and unique insights into their application won him unchallenged leadership of the Fustat Jewish community as rabbi and judge.

It was not an easy role. The local Jewry was convulsed in a debate between Karaites and Rabbinites. The former in effect were puritans who rejected the vast superstructure of postbiblical lore and literature. The latter were traditionalists who accepted as binding the Talmud, the responsa, and other expressions of the vast, evolving Oral Law. The two groups had diverged in such acrimony that neither would engage in business or social dealings with the other, or even bury each other's dead. Maimonides, although manifestly a traditionalist himself, displayed considerable tact in narrowing the schism between the two factions.

Perhaps of even greater importance, Maimonides was an incomparable source of guidance for rabbis abroad. In his replies to their unending stream of queries on matters of law and practice, he chose the approach of personal letters rather than the more formal and portentous responsa. These communications were invariably respectful and deeply human. "Peace be upon you, our dearly beloved master of all branches of learning," he would interpolate, "and upon our fellow scholars and all the common people, peace—peace like a shining light, 'an abundance of peace until the moon is no more!' Amen. Selah." Written in the master's own hand, often running seven or eight pages in length, the letters found their way to the minds and hearts of his correspondents.

With all these communal and professional burdens, Maimonides still managed in 1185 to complete a prodigious treatise, the *Mishneh Torah,* a "Code of the Law" which summarized the totality of Jewish jurisprudence, oral and written, as it had evolved over the centuries. The volume is a masterpiece of scholarly and literary elegance. A kind of rabbinical *Restatement,* it is divided into fourteen books and eighty-three subsections that range from commerce, industry, and property to taxation, penal law, and family relations. Maimonides's introductory synopses for each section were as practical and humane as they were lucid. Never before in their history, in fact, had the Jews produced so comprehensive and systematized a corpus juris. In short order, the *Mishneh Torah* became the standard reference on Jewish law. For centuries afterward, hardly a scholar would issue a pronouncement on Jewish legal tradition without first determining "what says the Rambam"—the acronym by which Rabbi Moses ben Maimon came to be known in the Jewish world. In his own time, and beyond all his contemporaries, the Rambam achieved universal recognition as the "Light of the Exile," the unquestioned successor to the Babylonian geniushood.

A Guide for the Perplexed

It was Maimonides himself who remained dissatisfied with that role. Thus far, his legal opinions and publications spoke only to the Jewish majority, to those who were unquestioning in their ancestral faith. Yet there was also an intellectual minority, a Jewish cultural elite who no longer could ignore the impact of Greco-Arab scholasticism. Although unquestioning in their loyalty to their people, these scholars manqués were disconcerted by the numerous anthropomorphisms and other palpable anachronisms they encountered in traditional Judaism. Such "perplexed" individuals, Maimonides felt, should not be forced to choose between religion and reason. It was to resolve their intellectual doubts, therefore, that he labored another five years, in an effort to harmonize the Written Law and the Oral Law with Greco-Arab rationalism. The result, *A Guide for the Perplexed,* completed in 1190, became the single most important philosophic work ever produced by a Jew.

In style, structure, and content, the *Guide* was unabashedly elitist. It made no concession to popularization. Written in the form of letters to Maimonides's devoted student and protégé Joseph ibn Aqnin, it explains in the introduction:

> I have composed this work . . . to promote the understanding of the real spirit of the Law, to guide those religious persons who . . . have studied philosophy and are embarrassed by the contradictions between the teachings of philosophy and the literal sense of the Torah.

Refusing, then, to take the reader by the hand, disdaining the clarity and system of his *Mishneh Torah,* Maimonides adopted a scheme that was almost intentionally discursive. The first half of Book I deals with words and expressions in the Bible; the second half, with divine "attributes" in the biblical text. Book II copes with the existence of God, creation, and prophecy. Book III commences with an allegorical explanation of the biblical story of the Chariot, then turns to discussions on Providence, the Book of Job, and religious precepts and rites.

By this apparent diffusion, which was actually a conscious dismantlement of traditional religious interpretations, Maimonides plainly was weeding out casual readers from intellectual purists. It was for the latter now that he reinterpreted biblical accounts which were obscure, primitive, or manifestly implausible. Mankind, explains the *Guide,* has undergone successive phases of development. Each phase requires its own language, from the simplistic to the sophisticated, to allow the committed Jew to grasp underlying spiritual meanings. Prophecy, too, for that matter, is to be regarded as an emanation from God's intellect ultimately to man's, but passing initially through man's rather more impressionable imagination. Thus, the essential function of the Prophets—including Moses, the greatest of them all—is to appeal to that imagination through the use of parables. It was a stunning, unprecedented rejection of biblical literalism. Yet the *Guide* went even further. It made clear that for Maimonides, as for Avicenna, Alfarabi, Averroës, and other giants of Greco-Islamic scholasticism, faith was but a preliminary to intellectual confirmation. Only the intellect can ratify faith. One does not merely worship God; one studies God in order to *know* God. Here was the very epicenter of Maimonides's theology; and so it was summarized in the book's final chapter: knowledge of God is man's highest goal. Faith and reason are inseparable—and compatible.

Maimonides wrote his *Guide for the Perplexed* in Arabic (although, typically, in Hebrew letters). Soon afterward, the work underwent translation—indeed, several translations—into Hebrew. The most elegant version was produced by a renowned Provençal linguist, Samuel ibn

Tibbon (pp. 34–35). Entitled *Moreh Nevuchim,* it was this masterful, precisely nuanced rendition that became authoritative in the Jewish world.
From Hebrew, the *Guide* then was translated into Latin, and thereby
circulated throughout Christian Europe. Its impact was extraordinary.
Apart from the Bible, this was the first theological-philosophical book of
Jewish origin to be incorporated into general culture. Even the most
eminent of medieval scholars gave respectful attention to the work,
among them Albertus Magnus, Thomas Aquinas, and Roger Bacon. Yet
it was perhaps inevitable that the *Guide* should evoke its widest resonance
in the Jewish world. With few exceptions, Jewry's intellectual and spiritual leadership greeted the book in a near-frenzy of enthusiasm. Once
again the mighty codifier, the "Light of the Exile,"·had responded to the
profoundest existential needs of his people. Henceforth, the *Guide* would
lie on the study table of virtually every educated Jew, and in consequence
would provide the greatest minds in Israel witlr their initial training in
rationalism.

As for Maimonides himself, the weight of his manifold duties, particularly his medical practice, began to tell on him. In 1201, in his sixty-sixth
year, he wrote to his friend and translator, Samuel ibn Tibbon:

> I dwell at [Fustat] and the sultan resides at [Cairo]; these two places
> are two Sabbath days' journey distant from each other. My duties to
> the sultan are very heavy. I am required to visit [the sultan] every day,
> early in the morning and when he or any of his children, or any of the
> [women] of the harem, are ill. . . . Normally . . . I do not return to
> [Fustat] until the afternoon. Then I am almost famishing of hunger.
> . . . I find the waiting rooms filled with people, both Jews and
> Gentiles. . . .
>
> I dismount from my animal, wash my hands . . . [eat a brief snack]
> . . . then set about ministering to my patients, and writing prescrip-
> tions and directions for their various afflictions. Patients go in and out
> . . . until two hours or later at night. I converse with them and
> prescribe for them while lying down from sheer exhaustion; and when
> night falls, I am so fatigued that I can barely speak. . . .
>
> In consequence of this, no Israelite can have any private meeting
> with me, except on the Sabbath. On that day the whole congregation
> . . . comes to me after the morning service, when I instruct them on
> their responsibilities for the entire week. We study together a little
> until noon, when they depart. Some of them return, and read with me
> following the afternoon service until evening prayers. In this manner
> I spend the day.

Maimonides actually was understating his schedule. He did not mention his extensive legal correspondence or his epic works of scholarship,

medical, theological, and philosophical. Never since the original Moses the Lawgiver had the Jews produced such a man.

Maimonides died in December 1204. The Jews of Egypt observed public mourning for three days. Upon learning of his death, the tiny Jewish settlement in Jerusalem proclaimed a day of general fasting. From Andalusia through North Africa to the Holy Land, Maimonides was eulogized as the "Prince of the East," the "Light of the Exile," the "Wonder of the World." In his testament, he had expressed the wish to be buried in Tiberias, one of Palestine's four "holy" cities, and that request was honored. On his grave in Tiberias the inscription is still readable:

> Here lies a man, yet not a man,
> And if a man, conceived by angels;
> By human mother born only in light;
> Perhaps himself a spirit pure—
> Not a child by man and woman fostered—
> From God above an emanation bright.

By the early thirteenth century, it had become plain that Andalusia, jewel of the Islamic Renaissance, was atrophying as a source of Arab vitality—and thus equally as a source of Jewish creativity. The axis of Jewish settlement was shifting to the Christian kingdoms of northern Spain. As that migration gained pace, Maimonides's writings became in effect the last significant Jewish literary contribution produced in the Arabic language. Nor in later years would the elegant poetry and prose that once had adorned the Jewish Golden Age survive amidst the primal zealotry of Christian Iberia, whether in Hebrew, Arabic, or the various Hispanic dialects. In his romantic thirteenth-century chronicle *Sefer Tachkemoni* (The Book of the Wise), Judah ben Solomon al-Harizi lamented the passing of the Andalusian giants, of Solomon ibn Gabirol, Judah Halevi, Moses ibn Ezra, Moses Maimonides:

> The fathers of poetry, Solomon, and Judah
> And Moses, as well—all shone in the West,
> And rich men were abundant then who purchased the pearls of their art.
>
> How sad is my lot now times have so changed!
> The wealthy have gone, and their glory hath diminished!
> The fathers encountered fountains—
> for me nary a fountain will plash!

It was a *kaddish* for a three-century incandescence now manifestly flickering out.

CHAPTER II

THE RISE AND FALL OF CONVIVENCIA

Revival in Christian Iberia

I am weary of roaming about the world, measuring its expanse;
    and I am not yet done. . . .
I walk with the beasts of the forest and I hover like a bird
    of prey over the peaks of mountains.
My feet run about like lightning to the far ends of the earth,
    and I move from sea to sea.
Journey follows journey, but I find no resting place, no
    calm repose.

The lament was uttered by Moses ibn Ezra. It was the mid-twelfth century, and the poet's genial Andalusian world had collapsed about him. Together with other non-Moslems, Jews were fleeing the murderous new Almohade regime by the thousands. Some departed for North Africa and Egypt. Others, like ibn Ezra himself, sought refuge in Spain's northern, Christian kingdoms.

The prospects for stability in the north at first seemed quite hopeful. Not long before, Castile had absorbed León to become the largest of the Spanish Christian principalities. Aragón had occupied the Balearic Islands, captured Valencia, and won the fealty of Catalonia to emerge as the dominant realm of the peninsula altogether. For the rulers of both Castile and Aragón, therefore, the priority henceforth was to stabilize their governments, revive their agriculture, and resettle their cities. With *mudéjares* (local Moslems) still extensively intermingled among Christians in the north—as Christians had been earlier among Moslems in Andalusia—and with each people dependent upon the other's economy, talents, and taxes, the Christian rulers of those years were inclined to a policy of *convivencia*, of mutual accommodation. Indeed, Fernando III of Castile actually found it appropriate in 1236 to style himself "King of the Three Religions."

The Jews of Spain numbered perhaps eighty thousand by the early thirteenth century. Of these, some forty thousand were settled in Aragón-Catalonia and possibly thirty thousand in Castile-León, with the rest scattered throughout Navarre, Portugal, and the Balearic and (later) the Canary Islands. Plainly, this was a less-than-substantial presence when measured against some two million Christians and nearly a million mudéjares. Yet it appeared to be a reasonably secure presence. To their rulers, the Jews were prized for their skills in handicraft and commerce, and their knowledge of the language and mores of the conquered Moslem peoples. Unlike the resentful mudéjares, too, these people, as a tiny and vulnerable minority, could be depended upon to serve their new masters loyally.

So it was that the Jews initially were assured a wider degree of royal protection in northern Spain than anywhere else in Christian Europe. As in the best days of caliphal rule in Córdoba or Granada, they were allocated their own local quarters, some of these even walled and barred against "alien" incursion. In Valencia, Jews were authorized to "keep closed all the gates" of their enclave, and no one could enter "against your will except Us [the royal family] and Our Household. . . ." In Barcelona, the *judería* lay in the center of town; in Tudela, hard by the central citadel; in Toledo, at the southwestern corner, where its encincture actually was known as the Jews' Fortress. And in whichever location, Jews continued to enjoy the fullest measure of communal autonomy. By royal or baronial authorization, they regulated their own affairs—juridical, fiscal, social, religious—as they had under Moslem rule, in full consciousness of their "sovereign" dignity.

In every other respect, however, Jews were integrated into the regional economy. Their role as merchants continued to be preeminent, yet they also produced numerous farmers and vintners. In thirteenth-century Castile, manufacturing rested largely in the hands of Jewish artisans. Jews were the leading producers of leatherwear, soap, parchment, and candles; the most skilled ironmongers, armorers, textile dyers, silversmiths, jewelers. In Aragón, they all but dominated the North African import-export trade. If Jews were shopkeepers and brokers, moneychangers and moneylenders, they also produced a disproportionate number of physicians, pharmacists, lawyers, and notaries. There were occasional Jewish professional gamblers, even Jewish lion-tamers. In at least two rural communities, there were Jewish bullfighters. Altogether, the economic base of Spanish Jewry was the most widely diversified in the Diaspora.

Its advantage to Christian monarchs soon became palpable. By 1284, Jews were contributing 22 percent of all direct taxes in Aragón-Catalonia, and possibly even more in Castile-León. More significant yet was the role fulfilled by Jews in royal and municipal government. Loyal, multilingual, experienced in financial matters, they served as personal secretaries, interpreters, bailiffs, political advisers, ambassadors, even military commanders. Samuel Menasseh, crown chancellor of Valencia, raised the armies that drove back a French invasion in 1269. Moses de Portella negotiated the surrender of Valencia's mudéjares in 1275, following a brief rebellion. In the thirteenth century, King Jaime I of Aragón entrusted the kingdom's entire land-division audit to Judah de la Caballería. As early as 1085, when Pope Gregory VII voiced dismay at this emerging Jewish prominence, Alfonso VI of Castile had to explain that "the Jews furnish our viziers, chancellors, and most of our officers of the army, and we simply cannot do without them."

Neither, for their part, could the Jews remain indifferent to the emoluments of office. In twelfth-century Castile, during the reign of Alfonso VII, Joseph Farisol and his nephew Solomon performed numerous diplomatic missions for the Crown. Their reward was the tax-farming concession for the entire Kingdom of Castile. Indeed, more than any other vocation, it was tax-farming—the purchase for cash of tax-collecting rights—that established the fortunes of such Jewish hidalgo families as Benveniste, Elazar, Abravanel, Abulafia, Caballería, Revaya, Shoshon, Vives, and Senior. As governmental and financial eminences, these notables were addressed by the honorific "Don," lived in spacious homes, and dressed and traveled as extravagantly as did other Spanish aristocrats.

In an age of convivencia, they also moved easily in the upper echelons of Aragonese and Castilian society. Christians, Moslems, and Jews attended one another's marriages and funerals. Wealthy Christian hidalgos often played at dice with Jews. Christian and Jewish women socialized extensively. At the royal courts of Castile and Aragón, in noble castles and public taverns, Jewish scholars and financiers, mudéjar balladeers and artists, intermingled with Paris-trained friars, Rome-trained canon lawyers, Genoese merchants, Provençal and Sicilian troubadours. Indeed, Jews and Moslems were stock figures in the popular culture of the age. *La dança general de la muerte,* a thirteenth-century ballad, begins with the pope and the emperor and ends with laborers, friars, hermits, "the bearded rabbi who always studied the Talmud," and the Moslem *alfaqui* (religious scholar) clinging to his wife. *El Poema de Alfonso XI* describes that Castilian ruler's early-fourteenth-century coronation at Burgos:

> The jongleurs were strumming
> Their instruments through Las Huelgas,
> Touching their beguiling lutes,

Plucking their viols,
The Rabbi with his psaltery,
The mountain guitar,
The Moorish flutes. . . .

Toledo, the capital of Castile, almost perfectly exemplified that Jewish presence. Travelers described a bazaar lined with scores of Jewish pavilions, their visibility all but defining the central business district. The judería itself was a ganglion of shops, offices, homes, and fully eleven synagogues. Indeed, Toledo was a city of synagogues. The best known of them, El Tránsito, can still be visited. It is located in the heart of the old judería, on the Calle de los Reyes Católicos. Built in 1357 by Don Samuel Levi Abulafia for his family and friends, it is a jewel of Moorish design, its floor inlaid with red tiles in herringbone patterns, an alabaster frieze and arcade of blind arches enveloping the sanctuary. On the east wall, two adjacent windows replicate the Tables of the Law, while interlocked Hebrew calligraphy and eight-pointed stars embellish the cedar rafters. The west wall, an immense plasterwork frieze with three lobed windows, is framed by side panels fretted with delicate green-and-red arabesques. In a meaningful touch, white bands serpentined with Hebrew inscriptions envelop the shield-shaped coats of arms of Castile and León. Don Samuel allowed no one to forget that he was a courtier, a personal adviser to King Pedro I ("the Cruel").

Even in its earlier incarnation as a Moslem city, ruled until the eighth century by the ibn Danqun dynasty, Toledo had encompassed a Jewish community of possibly four thousand. By the mid-thirteenth century, twice that many Jews lived there, out of a population of one hundred thousand. Their prominence was remarked upon by every observer. If commerce was extensively in their hands, so were textile manufacture, tanning, dying, weapons design, and other steelwork; and so, in large measure, was viticulture, for Jews owned the choicest grape orchards and the largest wine cellars and presses. As the hub of an expanding political and commercial network, Toledo drew to its midst some of the most distinguished Jews on the peninsula, among them the families of ibn Kamaniel, Shoshan, al-Fachtar, Halevi, Abulafia, Zadok, al-Barchilon, Farisol—renowned merchants, tax-farmers, mint-masters, customs-collectors, physicians, courtiers. Establishing ample demesnes, they settled in with elaborate retinues of kinsmen and friends, servants and slaves.

Jewish hidalgos emulated their Gentile counterparts not only in luxury and ostentation but often in the permissiveness of their lifestyles. There are accounts of Jewish courtesans flourishing in the judería of Toledo. In

Zaragoza, documents from Aragonese archives reveal numerous instances of carnal relations between Jewish men and Christian or Moslem women. Here, then, was the quintessential *Sepharad:* a sun-drenched land whose different communities preserved a relaxed spirit of mutual accommodation and a genial tolerance for worldly pleasures and foibles. Altogether, whether in self-satisfaction or self-indulgence, the Jews of Castile and Aragón enjoyed a plateau of economic and social well-being that had not been surpassed even in the earlier golden years of Moslem Andalusia. By the thirteenth century, they were more to be envied than Jews anywhere else in either the Christian or the Moslem world.

An Initiatory Renaissance

They also cast their shadow well beyond the Pyrenees. With their ancestral heritage of literacy and their prolonged recent exposure to the Islamic Renaissance, Jews who settled in the north emerged almost without competition as the intelligentsia of central-northern Spain. Although they continued to speak and write in Arabic well into the late 1200s, it was a pluralism that served their advantage. Under Christian rule now, and rather closer to the European world, this Eastern people suddenly found themselves with a unique role to fulfill. It was that of cultural intermediary between Orient and Occident. Through them, for one thing, the advances in both Arab and Jewish medicine were transmitted to the West. Indeed, from the twelfth to the fifteenth centuries, Jews served as physicians to virtually every royal court throughout the Iberian Peninsula, as well as to a host of lay and clerical officials. Even as late as 1460, when the climate of toleration had deteriorated all but irretrievably, Alfonso de Spina, a Franciscan monk, could bemoan the sheer number of these Jewish medical eminences:

> For many of the Jews, seeing how the Christians neglected the study
> . . . of medicine, worked with all their force to perfect the art, so that
> the temporal lords, nay—and that is the thing to weep over—the
> ecclesiastical prelates set great store by them, to such an extent that
> hardly one of them is to be found who does not harbor some devil of
> a Jew doctor.

Of greater significance even than the Jews' contribution to medical practice, however, was their role as translators of Arabic scholarship into European languages. Toledo was a major center of this activity. Here, as early as the twelfth century, a noted savant, the Archbishop Raimundo, engaged Jews, Christians, and Moslems to translate Arabic scientific and philosophic texts. The initial technique is explained in the prologue to the Latin verson of Avicenna's *De Anima*. Juan Hispano, a Jewish convert, translated orally from Arabic into Romance, and the Franciscan monk Dominicus Gudsalvi then translated by pen from Romance into Latin. By the thirteenth century, the translators were virtually all Jews, and the language of choice necessarily reflected this preponderance. It is recalled that even earlier, Jewish scholars had set about translating numerous Arabic scientific and philosophic treatises into Hebrew. Hebrew now served as the principal conduit between Arabic and subsequent translations into Latin, Catalan, Castilian, and other Western languages. Catalonia, Navarre, and Provence—just over the Pyrenees—henceforth became major staging grounds for these endeavors, even as the Jews, well versed in southern Mediterranean cultures, rapidly developed into the most prolific and esteemed translators of the late Middle Ages.

Possibly the best respected of them all was the ibn Tibbon family. Judah ben Saul ibn Tibbon, the patriarch, was an Andalusian, born in Granada in 1120. His birthplace has not forgotten him. Today, the University of Granada boasts an ibn Tibbon Institute of Semitic Languages. At the entrance to the Calle de los Reyes Católicos, a statue of the man is displayed in oriental garb, robed and turbaned, holding a scroll. Like the Maimonides sculpture in Córdoba, the ibn Tibbon likeness is all dignity, the figure slim, the features chiseled and elegant. "Granada to its distinguished son, Judah ibn Tibbon," declares the inscription on the pedestal, "Patriarch of Translators, Doctor, Philosopher, Poet." He was all of these. After departing Granada as a youth, ibn Tibbon settled in Lunel, in southern France, where he practiced medicine as a livelihood and translation as an intellectual passion. Among his best-known efforts were Judah Halevi's *Book of the Khuzari,* into Hebrew, and ibn Gabirol's *Fountain of Life,* into Latin, as well as the writings of other poets and thinkers of the Andalusian Golden Age. Early on, the "patriarch of translators" laid down guidelines for his discipline. They ordained a thorough knowledge not only of Arabic, Hebrew, and Latin but of the subjects under translation.

The characterization "patriarch" is entirely accurate. Judah's son, Samuel ibn Tibbon, exceeded even his father in the breadth and precision of his literary interpretations. These included scientific works, among them Ali ibn Ridwan's famed commentary on Galen's *Ars Parva* and several of Maimonides's best-known medical treatises. It was Samuel ibn Tibbon too who produced the *Moreh Nevuchim,* the definitive Hebrew version of Maimonides's Arabic-language *Guide for the Perplexed.* Through correspondence, he and Maimonides achieved a perfect symbiosis of content and style. Samuel's protégés later retranslated the *Guide* into Latin, ensuring its wider dissemination throughout Christian Europe. Moreover, in an extraordinary reach of linguistic erudition, Samuel and the "Tibbonides" also translated into Hebrew, and afterward into Latin, the Moslem philosophers Avicenna and Averroës, as well as treatises subsequently produced by renowned Arab physicians and astronomers.

Still others of the Tibbonides included Samuel's son, Moses ben Samuel ibn Tibbon, whose translations into Hebrew and Latin included the writings of Aristotle, Euclid, and Hunayn ibn Ishaq. Moses's son, Jacob ben Machir ibn Tibbon, whose career extended into the early fourteenth century, rendered into Hebrew, and occasionally Latin, numerous books of philosophy, mathematics, and astronomy. It was a formidable clan, but not uncharacteristic of that remarkable Jewish galaxy scattered throughout central-northern Spain and southern France, whose lexicological virtuosity transmitted the Greco-Arabic heritage direct from Iberia into the very heartland of Western Christendom.

A Defender of the Faith

Girona is a modest Catalonian town of some eighty thousand, located an hour's train ride northeast of Barcelona and a half-hour's from the Costa Brava. To this day, it preserves tangible memorabilia of its medieval Jewry. Dating back at least to the ninth century, Girona's settlement of Jewish artisans, farmers, and merchants flourished almost uninterruptedly into the fourteenth. Its medieval judería, now bounded by the Calle Força on the west and the Calle Clavería on the east, is a ziggurat of cobbled lanes and flat-faced brick-and-stone houses and shops. Its doorposts still bear notches of long-vanished Torah parchment. On the Calle de Sant Llorenc, the aging Isac el Cec Synagogue, named for the town's last rabbi, who departed in 1492, is all but overgrown with ivy. The synagogue courtyard encloses a wood-block circumcision table and a tiled ritual bathhouse for women. A terrace then divides the building from a stone-and-stucco villa. Currently occupied by a local Catalan, the house belonged in the thirteenth century to Rabbi Moses ben Nachman, better known to posterity as Nachmanides. The sobriquet, accorded as a gesture of near-equivalence to the immortal Maimonides, evinced the man's preeminent role in confronting the first in a series of grave ideological crises in Spanish-Jewish history.

As it happened, the infusion of Greco-Arab rationalism into classical Judaism begat social as well as intellectual transformations. The Jewish upper classes, particularly those of affluent Catalonia and Languedoc, embraced "Maimunism" as a doctrine likely to distinguish them even further from the Jewish majority. For their part, the Jewish middle and lower classes reacted irascibly to this intellectualization of their comfortable folk-religion, with its plainspoken list of prayers and regulations. In truth, the threatened schism between Maimunists and anti-Maimunists paralleled a gulf opening in the surrounding Christian world. By the late thirteenth century, as the church's Augustinian theologians negotiated their own scholastic accommodation to Aristotelian rationalism, the sophisticated clerics and aristocrats of Languedoc and northern Italy cordially welcomed the effort. Not so these regions' simple peasants and townsfolk, or such humble friars as Francis of Assisi and other monkish purists. Very close to mysticism by then, the "antischolastics" launched a vigorous countercampaign against the "gnostics" of Languedoc.

The reaction was duplicated by the Jewish anti-Maimunists of southern France—of Montpellier, Narbonne, Béziers, Lunel, and Perpignan. In the late thirteenth century, these traditionalists adopted a comparably zealous stance against Averroism, Maimunism, and liberal-minded Jews altogether, whom they suspected of ridiculing the Sages or the Commandments, or of interpreting biblical and talmudic narrative allegorically. For ideological support, they turned now to their soul mates in the Spanish kingdoms. One of these was Solomon ibn Adret, chief rabbi of Barcelona. Ibn Adret normally was a gentle and tolerant man. But in 1305, after several years of pressure from his constituents, he felt impelled to proclaim a series of bans against "renegades" who "undermined the faith" of the Jewish people. "From this day on," declared one proscription, "and for the next fifty years, no member of our community shall study the 'Greek' works on science and metaphysics, either in the original [Arabic] or in translation, before he will have reached the age of twenty-five." Ibn Adret exempted only the study of medicine.

A second ban was rather harsher. It flatly excommunicated the allegorists and "Maimunists," and interdicted their teachings:

> They preach blasphemous nostrums and mock the words of the sages. . . . They say that the biblical account from Genesis to the divine revelation on Mount Sinai is all allegory. . . . They even speak critically of Moses and argue that the Torah is not of divine origin. . . . These are mortal sins, and all Israel are duty-bound to ban and excommunicate these sinners. . . . We proclaim the books they have written to be works of heresy and their possessors to be heretics, and like their authors they are subject to this decree of excommunication, until they burn these books.

In an age of social and intellectual flux, however, the prohibition could not be sustained. Averroism and Maimunism were challengeable only by effective counterargument. Yet here, too, as it developed, the task had been well launched, even decades earlier. The champion of the counter-campaign was Moses ben Nachman—Nachmanides.

Born in 1194, scion of a prosperous mercantile family, Nachmanides lived nearly all his seventy-six years in his native Catalonian town of Girona. In his case, geographic provincialism did not bespeak intellectual parochialism. So vast was his talmudic erudition that by his early twenties Nachmanides already was issuing responsa well beyond Catalonia-Aragón, and even the Iberian Peninsula. When the Maimonidean contro-versy first erupted, therefore, in Montpellier in 1232, Nachmanides was regarded as the logical authority to resolve it. In this crisis, despite his own ideological literalism, he evinced a touching forbearance, and displayed a genius that was tactical no less than intellectual. On the one hand, he warned the Jewish communities of Navarre and Languedoc, as those of Catalonia, Aragón, and Castile, to guard against the Maimunists, the "seducers into sin," and, if necessary, to "use the shepherd's rod." On the other hand, in a second letter to his followers, he rejected the very notion of a ban on Maimonides's writings. The Rambam (Maimonides) had performed numerous great services for his people, Nachmanides re-minded them—he had written the *Mishneh Torah,* codified Jewish law, and used his vast influence to drive the puritan Karaites from the Egyptian court. It was Nachmanides's suggestion, rather, to establish a middle ground, a policy of allowing a limited measure of secular learning, but in a manner that was gradual and thereby not threatening to traditional pieties. The farsighted approach would be heeded by both sides only intermittently. Even so, Nachmanides's evident nobility of character, to-gether with the sheer breadth of his knowledge, made him acceptable to both groups later in a far graver confrontation. This one, however, was not among themselves but against a common enemy—the zealots of the Christian Church.

By the latter thirteenth century, the emergence of Christian fanaticism in Spain was impelled by a confluence of factors. One was the evident waning of Islamic power throughout the entire Mediterranean, and spe-cifically in the Iberian Peninsula. The more the fractious Moslem dynas-ties of Andalusia lashed out at one another, the greater waxed northern Christian enthusiasm for *reconquista.* The ardor for reconquest gained a new dimension following the Castilian-Aragonese victory over the Al-mohade army at Las Navas de Tolosa in 1212. Subsequently, in all of former Moslem Andalusia only the fragmented little kingdom of Granada maintained a precarious, vassal-like independence. During these same years, too, the Crusades were infusing a new ideological dynamic into the Christian-Moslem relationship altogether. In Iberia, the vision of reconquest was nurtured with particular ardor and eloquence by monks of the Dominican order, the ideological doyens of the Spanish church. Under their influence, the older tradition of convivencia, of pragmatic accommodation with non-Christians, began to give way.

As it mounted, Christian xenophobia perhaps inevitably turned also against the Jews. Indeed, the new religious fervor exploited a wellspring of quite tangible anti-Jewish resentments. Beyond their older, folkloristic suspicion of Jews as deicides and well-poisoners, Christians rich and poor alike nurtured a growing animus against Jewish tax-farmers and money-lenders. Even Alfonso X of Castile, for all his goodwill toward the Jews, could not ignore this undercurrent of hatred. On occasion, he succumbed to it himself. In 1279, when funds were lacking to complete the siege of Moslem Algeciras, the king in his frustration had several of his most prominent Jewish tax-farmers dragged to their deaths through the streets of Seville. At his orders, too, in 1291 the wealthy Jews in Seville and even Toledo were locked in their synagogues until they agreed to come up with 4 million gold maravedís. For the next two years, the little group of Jewish courtiers hovered on the verge of ruin, until Alfonso finally relented and eased his terms. Yet by then Jewish circumstances in Castile had become generally precarious. Neither Jewish financiers nor simple Jewish shop-keepers knew from year to year what the political climate would be. In neighboring Aragón, uncertainty was equally a fact of Jewish life. Jews gradually were displaced from the provincial administrations. Under Alfonso III, the entire Aragonese Jewish population became a sponge to be squeezed dry, and by the beginning of the fourteenth century several middle-sized Jewish communities faced total impoverishment.

In the end, however, the extortions signified more than royal opportunism, or economic jealousies, or even the passions aroused by reconquista. Xenophobia against non-Christians involved a clerical animus directed specifically and unreservedly against Jews. By the late thirteenth century, during the Easter season, as townsmen engaged in random attacks on local juderías, they could depend on church approbation at the highest level. Pope Nicholas III himself had issued a bull in 1279 ordering an intensified campaign of proselytization among the Jews. Dominican friars in Castile harangued mobs with incendiary anti-Jewish accusations. In both Castile and Aragón, the Dominican order focused on the Talmud as a source of particular danger to Spanish Christianity, and anti-Talmud agitation soon became virtually a clerical obsession. On occasion, Jewish *cals* (communities) were intimidated into attending conversionary sermons—sometimes delivered in their own synagogues.

Apostates and Disputants

If forced exposure to proselytization was humiliating to the Jews, even more galling was the vindictiveness of Jewish apostates. There were not a few of these. It is idle to speculate on the fratricidal sources of their resentments, except to note that their bitterness appeared to generate its own self-fulfilling continuum. Moreover, given their familiarity with Hebrew religious literature, some of these converts were able to formulate lethally inimical versions of talmudic and other classical texts. Two noteworthy examples of this filial vindictiveness were Nicholas Donin and Pablo Cristiani of Provence. Through relentless goading, it was Cristiani who succeeded eventually in manipulating even the great Nachmanides into a public disputation.

The episode might almost have been lifted from Judah Halevi's *Book of the Khuzari*. It is recalled that King Jaime I of Aragón-Catalonia, a principled advocate of convivencia, by and large was solicitous of his Jews. Yet so tenacious was Cristiani's ideological crusade that in 1263 the ruler finally approved a religious disputation, even agreeing to preside over it himself. Nachmanides, in turn, acceded to the pleas of his followers to present the Jews' case. Several weeks of procedural negotiations followed. The confrontation began then in the episcopal chancery of Barcelona on July 20 and continued in four sessions until the end of the month. The church delegation, led by Cristiani, included important Dominican and Franciscan clerics. Nachmanides was the lone spokesman for the Jews. Indeed, no other Jew was so much as seated in the audience.

The scene can be only partially reconstructed from medieval woodcuts. The participants' features are unclear. Yet in the dank stone receptorium, King Jaime appears enthroned on the dais. Flanking him are court and church dignitaries. The written account is somewhat more detailed. Following Cristiani's lead, the clerics drew extensively from the Talmud's own narrative passages, then argued that the Messiah already had appeared, that he was "both human and divine," that he had died as atonement for the sins of mankind, and that Judaism as a consequence had lost its validity. Nachmanides riposted with vigor. As he did so, interestingly enough, he chose to ignore his own earlier, anti-Maimunist strictures against "allegorism." It was the rabbi's argument now that Jews were free to deviate from a strict construction of the Talmud's nonlegal passages.

The principal issue between Judaism and Christianity, in any case, related not to belief in the Messiah but to belief in one God. Moving to the offensive, Nachmanides then straightforwardly attacked the Trinitarian doctrine itself as an affront to human intelligence. Worse yet, the entire creed was a hypocrisy. Christianity as a religion of love and kindness? "From the time of Jesus until the present," Nachmanides reminded his listeners, "the world has been filled with violence and injustice, with the shedding of more blood than by the followers of any other creed." Here the rabbi concluded with a frontal assault of almost unimaginable daring. Christian "civilization" would not survive, he predicted, for even the Roman Empire had declined after embracing this faith, "and now the servants of Mohammed have a greater realm than they." The assembled churchmen were stunned.

By the fourth session, on July 31, sensing that matters had gotten out of hand, Cristiani asked that the disputation be "interrupted." King Jaime acquiesced. Yet the ruler would not depart without delivering a valedictory sermon of his own. The setting was Barcelona's largest synagogue. Arriving with his entourage the following Sabbath, Jaime ceremonially ascended the podium to invoke the wisdom and blessings of the New Testament. If the episode was without precedent in the Christian world, so was its immediate sequel. Once the ruler concluded his remarks, Nachmanides was permitted to issue a reply in defense of Judaism. This he did briefly, but with his typical spirited eloquence. The king was not affronted. Rather, he graciously informed the congregation afterward that "I have never seen a man defend a wrong cause so well." The following day, moreover, Jaime sent Nachmanides a purse of three hundred sólidos, with assurances that the rabbi was free to return to Girona in safety.

The disputation's farther-reaching consequences were by no means as positive. Angered by the outcome of the debate in Barcelona, Pope Clement IV issued a new directive to the Franciscans and Dominicans of Aragón-Catalonia. It was to collect all Jewish religious books in order that Pablo Cristiani might "examine" them personally. Indeed, King Jaime himself now belatedly cooperated in the "examination." Jews henceforth were obliged to expunge from their copies of the Talmud any passages suspected of vilifying Jesus and Mary. Copies of Maimonides's *Mishneh Torah,* reputed to contain barbed references to Jesus, were to be burned outright. In 1266, finally, three years after the fact, King Jaime was persuaded that Nachmanides had blasphemed Jesus in the Barcelona disputation. Reversing his traditional policy of sufferance, Jaime ordered the Girona rabbi banished from the realm for two years, although with a six-month grace period before departure. Nachmanides chose not to wait.

Within six weeks, he had embarked for the Holy Land. He would not return.

During these same years of the early fourteenth century, Jew-hatred was similarly on the increase in neighboring Castile. Here, too, much of the animus was rooted in economic jealousy. Yet, as in Aragón-Catalonia, religious passions added fuel to social resentments. Moreover, they were consciously inflamed by King Alfonso XI, who was engaged in an ongoing military offensive against Moslem Andalusia. Like his contemporaries Louis IX of France and Edward I of England, Alfonso was intent on achieving cultural homogeneity. But the Castilian monarch faced a dilemma. He was not prepared to jeopardize the convivencia that supplied his economy with Jewish funds and talent, and his administration with Jewish tax-farmers. His hope, rather, was to achieve uniformity without social disruption—that is, by intellectual consensus. In the effort, such Jewish apostates as Pablo Cristiani had fulfilled a useful role in Aragón-Catalonia. In Castile, Abner of Burgos proved an even more effective collaborator. Abner, in fact, emerges as one of the most fascinating éminences grises in Jewish history.

Little is known of his origins except that he was born in 1270 in southern Castile and evidently was reared as a devout Jew. As a young practicing physician in Burgos, however, Abner suddenly experienced a vision, a dream. Later, he wrote of a tall man "who said to me . . . prepare thyself against the appointed season; for I say unto thee that the Jews have remained so long in captivity for their folly and wickedness and because they have no teacher of righteousness through whom they may recognize the truth." On awakening, Abner fasted, scoured himself in fire and water, then set about intensively reevaluating his ancestral faith. For the while, he evidently held firm. But three years later, the apparition returned, in a second dream. "How long, O sluggard, wilt thou slumber?" the figure rebuked Abner. "Upon thy back rest all the sins of the Jews and their sons throughout their generations." When he awoke, Abner found his robe imprinted with crosses, "like the seal of Jesus of Nazareth." Twenty more years of spiritual wrestling would follow. Then in 1321, Abner, now middle-aged, produced a Hebrew-language volume (later translated into Castilian), *The Wars of the Lord*. In this account, drawing extensively from Jewish sources, he traced his long and painful spiritual odyssey to Christianity. Upon undergoing baptism, Abner adopted the Christian name Alfonso de Valladolid.

Subsequently, through the 1320s and 1330s, Abner produced several additional books and pamphlets, each attacking Jews and Judaism with progressively growing spleen—and greater ingenuity. Thus, in addressing

Jews of the rationalist, Maimunist persuasion, Abner was able to make an erudite case on Aristotelian premises. In arguments with Jewish tradition-alists, he drew on his limitless command of talmudic and midrashic (homiletic) sources. It was accordingly this curious, inscrutable figure, steeped in Jewish and Moslem philosophy, who now all but single-hand-edly buttressed the intellectual case for mass conversion as the one accept-able basis for a Jewish presence in the realm. In later years, well after Abner's death, as the proposition filtrated the consciousness of church-men, laymen, and even a significant minority of Jews, it would bring unimaginable rack and ruin to this little people in their peninsular Eden.

A Beating of Wings

Royal attitudes toward Jews and Moslems were not yet fixed in stone. In fourteenth-century Castile, Alfonso XI remained unwilling to dispense with Jewish funds and talent. In Aragón, Jaime II actually opened his kingdom to Jewish refugees from France and permitted local Jews to migrate to his overseas possessions. Indeed, Majorca (Mallorca), largest of the Balearic Islands and a major crossroads of Mediterranean com-merce, ultimately developed into Aragón's single wealthiest Jewish com-munity. Some five hundred Jewish families were settled here. Their cargoes and brokers were known throughout Spain and North Africa, and as far east as southern Italy. As shall be seen (p. 331), the community also produced several generations of renowned Jewish cartographers and astronomers.

Barcelona, the largest city in Aragón-Catalonia, also remained a thriv-ing center of Jewish commercial and intellectual activity. Here in the fourteenth century lived Rabbi Chasdai ibn Crescas, a renowned poet-philosopher of Judaism. Although an antirationalist, Crescas was a thinker of great depth and originality. His essay *Ohr Adonai* (The Light of God) adopted Aristotelian logic specifically to make the case against Maimunist "allegorism." In his defense of Judaism against Christian proselytization, moreover, Crescas was not a man to limit himself to mere apologetics. Forthrightly, he laid out a tenet-by-tenet, line-by-line compar-ison of Judaism and Christianity to make the case for the former's superi-ority. By his erudition and fearlessness, he emerged as a culture hero to his people, and as possibly the most venerated Spanish Jew of his genera-tion. It was in recognition of his stature, and of his great personal dignity, that the Crown appointed Crescas senior judge in the Jewish court system, and even rewarded him with a munificent tax-collectorship. Plainly, then, royal protection in Aragón-Catalonia continued strong. Despite widespread xenophobia among the lower classes, violence against Jews still appeared only a remote possibility in this kingdom.

In the south, meanwhile, Andalusia seemed the unlikeliest terrain of all for a new outbreak of fanaticism. Even today, the pace of life in the once-quintessential Moorish community of Seville remains "comfortably" Mediterranean. Spain's third-largest city, Seville is also its loveliest. Orange trees shade its mosaicked sidewalks, its plashing fountains and tessellated plazas. The exteriors of restaurants, hotels, and shops are embellished with Moorish arabesques and brilliantly striped awnings, with simple white-walled, beam-ceilinged interiors. Here the mighty Giralda, adjacent to one of Seville's principal cathedrals, survives as a remnant of the largest mosque in Andalusia. From its 322-foot rhomboid-brick bell tower a muezzin once called the faithful to prayer.

Yet it is the site of the old judería, in the Barrio de Santa Cruz, that offers an even more poignant return excursion to the world of convivencia. Still within view of the Giralda, the network of flagstoned streets and alleyways—Calle de Cal, Calle de Cal Mayor, Judería Vieja, Calle de los Tintes—encloses pastel villas adorned with floral trellises, with discreetly barred courtyards offering glimpses of miniature fountains, intricately tiled wall patterns, and cages of exotic birds. The Plaza de Santa Cruz, hub of the judería, is the setting for a monumental wrought-iron cross, filigreed in metallic vegetation and encircled by a delicate iron-grillwork fence and ornamental lanterns. Nearby, the Plaza Doña Elvira is a mosaic of inlaid-tiled walks and pebbled benches. A flanking stone barrier proclaims the entrance to "La Susana," the tiny passage in which a Jewish girl once inadvertently betrayed her people to the Inquisition (p. 67). Smaller block letters identify the site as "Calle de la Muerte."

There can be no doubt under whose protection this medieval quarter once functioned. A connected archway, the Arco y Torreón de la Judería, links the barrio to the vast crenellated rampart of the Alcázar (al-Qazar) citadel. Whether under Moslem or Christian rule, these were the king's Jews. They lived and thrived by his sufferance. If the Almohade period blighted their vitality, the interregnum was brief. Fernando III of Castile recaptured the city in 1248. The Jews celebrated the event. In Seville's Great Cathedral, directly across the hall from the tomb of Columbus, an extensive collection of treasures includes two decorative keys to the city, each with the identical Hebrew inscription: "The King of Kings will open; the King of Earth will appear." Apparently he did for a revived Jewish population. By the late fourteenth century, the Jews numbered seven thousand in this city and maintained fully a score of large and small synagogues.

Yet by then, too, Dominican fanaticism had revived, and refocused on the policy of convivencia. Archdeacon Ferrant Martínez, canon of the Great Cathedral, was systematically preaching fire and brimstone against the Jews. They should be carried to the baptismal font on pain of death, he exhorted his listeners; their synagogues should be destroyed. Martínez's incendiarism was rather much for King Juan I, who still favored accommodation. He admonished the canon to stop. The warning was ignored. Indeed, Martínez riposted by counterwarning against royal interference with the church's "holy" mission. In 1389, then, upon the death of the local archbishop, Martínez emerged as senior prelate of Seville. Shortly afterward King Juan was killed in a riding accident, leaving only an invalid son to succeed him. Dissension immediately broke out at court, and effective government soon was all but paralyzed.

The vacuum of leadership gave Martínez his opportunity. In March 1391, while celebrating Ash Wednesday in Seville's public square, the canon loosed a particularly venomous sermon against the Jews—whereupon the crowd, roused to a fury, set off for the judería. There it launched into an orgy of beating, rape, and pillage. Calm was not restored until nightfall. But Martínez was not appeased. Neither would he confine himself any longer to polemics. Three months later, at dawn on June 6, thousands of Sevillanos armed with pikes and axes suddenly poured out of their homes. They were led by Martínez himself. As the mob descended on the judería, it embarked upon yet another orgy, this time of unrestrained killing. In a single day, four thousand Jews were slaughtered. Others averted death only at the last moment by accepting baptism. Still others fled the city. They found no respite. In ensuing months, a chain reaction of massacres swept through at least seventy Castilian towns and cities. In Córdoba, mobs demolished the Jewish quarter, hacked and clubbed men, women, and children, and left two thousand corpses rotting in the streets. On August 5, 1391, Toledo's judería of nearly ten thousand, the largest on the peninsula, similarly was looted and gutted, with the loss of three thousand lives.

By late summer, the frenzy had become uncontainable. It now extended to Aragón-Catalonia. In Girona, the Feast of San Lorenzo was celebrated by wholesale atrocities against Jews. In the Aragonese province of Valencia, terrified Jews from smaller towns and villages began flocking into the port city itself, seeking refuge in the local judería. It proved no haven. Using battering rams, Valencia's rabble broke through the ghetto's wooden gates, then launched into the now-characteristic cycle of murder, pillage, and burning. Six hundred Jews died; another thousand saved their lives by accepting baptism. Flaring from city to city, the horror evidenced a complete breakdown of public order. Indeed, in Barcelona it burgeoned into a kind of class revolution. When the local governor arrested some forty ringleaders, the mob turned against the governor's councilors, killed several of them, then broke into the jail to free their comrades. Soon the neighboring peasantry joined in the assault. Storming the city hall, the rioters torched its tax records. Afterward, they directed their attack on Barcelona's fortress-castle, where the governor had given refuge to nearly a thousand Jewish inhabitants. The latter resisted tenaciously, but in the end the fortress was breached. Again, numerous Jews saved themselves by undergoing baptism. The four hundred who did not were cut down without mercy.

One of the Barcelona victims was the son of Rabbi Chasdai ibn Crescas. With the riots gaining in savagery, Crescas approached the Aragonese court (sitting then in Zaragoza) to implore intercession for the young man and his wife. Immediately Queen Violante sent a message to the governor: the couple must be protected as "royal favorites," she insisted. The dispatch arrived too late. Later, describing the calamity in a letter to the Jewish leadership of Avignon, Crescas allowed himself a brief, poignant allusion to "my only son, a bridegroom, a lamb without blemish . . . [who] was become Isaac, a sacrificial offering." Elsewhere in the Aragonese kingdom, in Girona and Tortosa, the fate of the Jews was sealed. So extensive was the horror that it extended even to the Balearic Islands, to the vibrant Jewish community of Majorca. Here some three hundred Jews were killed, and possibly twice that many accepted baptism. The rest fled to North Africa.

Four months passed before the mass slaughter ebbed. By then, perhaps thirty thousand Jews had perished. A famed apostate, Solomon Halevi, now a prominent Christian theologian (p. 53), discerned the hand of God in the massacres: "God inspiring vengeance for the Blood of Christ, a multitude of the people rose up against [the Jews]." The view was shared by others, who perceived "a signal miracle" in the forced baptisms. In fact, numerous devout Jews similarly grasped God's hidden design in the atrocities. Yet for them the portent was hardly Christological. As a renowned Jewish astronomer, Abraham Zacuto, was to describe the holocaust nearly a century later: "According to our tradition, these sufferings were the just punishment of divine wrath. For many [of the victims] had taken Gentile women into their homes, children were born of these illicit unions, and they later killed their own fathers."

A number of modern historians regard the massacres as a delayed consequence of the wider social unrest shaking Western Europe between 1378 and 1385. In Barcelona and Majorca, after all, the lumpenproletariat who had attacked the judería turned later against nobles and merchants. In Girona, the rampaging peasantry had demanded the abandonment of sales taxes (which fell more heavily on the poor) in favor of direct taxation. Indeed, the Jews themselves sensed how thoroughly Gentiles despised Jewish tax-collectors, as well as the luxury in which many Jews lived. "We have received measure for measure," acknowledged the religious essayist Solomon Alami. "Because we arrayed ourselves in [Christian] apparel, they have clothed us in different garments."

But religious zeal invariably transcended social resentments. Gestating throughout the latter fourteenth century, the passion was evident in the sheer ferocity of Dominican and Franciscan proselytization, a fanaticism directed far more specifically against Jews than against Moslems. Indeed, Moslems still were treated with a certain respect in the popular Hispanic literature of the time. On a day-to-day basis, relations between Christians, mudéjares, and professing Moslems generally were pacific in Aragón and Castile alike. Economics unquestionably played a role in this disjunction. Simple farmers and artisans rather than prosperous merchants or tax-collectors, local Moslems aroused little resentment. Yet even more significant, these people rarely were defined as sorcerers or devils, while Jews almost invariably were. Ferrant Martínez diabolized Jews not as economic leeches but as deicides and antichrists. Thus, except in Barcelona, violence tended to abate once the surviving Jews accepted baptism. On the Iberian Peninsula, as in England and France earlier, pressure was growing for a homogeneous Christian civilization. Still another century would pass before this fixation prevailed over the accommodationist instincts of Aragón's and Castile's rulers, but in 1391 a major shift plainly had occurred in the direction of "spiritual unification."

Even Chasdai ibn Crescas, for all his sensitivity to the vicissitudes of his people, failed for many years to discern the approaching crisis of Iberian Jewry. Instead, he anticipated a period of collective rehabilitation and revival. The court of Aragón evidently had that purpose in mind as well when it appointed Crescas to select individual families from hard-hit smaller Jewish communities for resettlement in Barcelona and Valencia. Crescas dutifully accepted the task. Indeed, he sought also to rehabilitate his own family. In 1393, seeking royal consent to take a second wife, twenty-six years younger than he, Crescas reminded Aragón's King Juan I: "Sire, I have lost my only son. My wife is an old woman who can no longer conceive. Unless I am blessed with a second son, my family name will not continue." Crescas received his permission. In the ensuing decade, too, his literary output remained extraordinarily fecund. These were the years when he produced *Ohr Adonai*, his trenchant analysis of

Averroist and Maimunist rationalism. It was not the progeny he wanted most, however. "Each night I hear the beating of the wings of the angel of death," he lamented in correspondence with his friend Rabbi Joseph Arabuena of Navarre. "Shall not my seed yet continue in this land?" For at least a decade before his death in 1412, as he lay half-paralyzed in his Zaragoza sickroom, Crescas must have foreseen the answer.

CHAPTER III

THE LONG GOOD-BYE

The Arm of God

O may their perfumed incense now emit
A repugnant stench befouling it, and all
Their bread become serpentlike; their wine, vinegar;
Their honey, wormwood and gall.

It was the poet Solomon da Piera who offered this sulfurous valedictory
to the Christians of his native Aragón. The year was 1392. Seven months
had passed since the inferno of mass slaughter, and Piera had just witnessed yet another group of ruined Jewish neighbors departing Zaragoza
for North Africa. Thus far, a majority of the survivors had chosen to
remain behind. Yet the once-fecund juderías of Aragón and Castile were
manifestly failing to revive. If many Jews continued on in the cities, the
majority dispersed to smaller towns and villages, where they anticipated
a wider measure of security from volatile urban mobs. Jewish tax-collectors and physicians still were not lacking, to be sure. Nevertheless, most
Jews now earned comparatively modest livelihoods as shopkeepers and
artisans. The circumstances of Castilian Jews were "altogether changed,"
lamented Rabbi Moses Arrangel in 1422, "for we are in great misery and
poverty." Jewish tax records in fact confirm a sharp economic decline,
even as Jewish business correspondence reveals a profound underlying
malaise. There are accounts of Jewish *cals* occasionally mortgaging their
communal lands and even pawning their Torah crowns.

The distress was a consequence not only of the 1391 massacres but of
their aftermath in a vast upsurge of conversionary pressure. Valencia was
the initial breeding ground of that fanaticism, and its underlying cause by
then far transcended economic jealousy. Today, journeying to Valencia
by slow train from Zaragoza, one passes from scrub landscape to near-

instant prosperity. The region draws its sustenance from a rich alluvial *huerta,* a plain irrigated according to a complex system perfected by the Moors at least twelve centuries ago. Now as then, it remains hardly less than an agricultural paradise, blanketed with millions of orange trees, with ubiquitous market gardens, flower nurseries, nut-tree orchards. The city of Valencia, with its diaphanous sunlight and ripe colors (the inspiration equally for the painter Sorolla and the novelist Blasco Ibáñez), appears even less likely a focus for religious hatreds than does Seville. Indeed, throughout the twentieth century Valencia has been all but synonymous with Spanish liberalism. During the 1936–39 Civil War, its population valiantly supported the Loyalist cause, wringing crops from the overworked *huerta* to feed the starving inhabitants of Madrid. Afterward, the city's renowned permissiveness survived even the years of Francoist repression.

Nowhere is that vibrant bohemianism more evident than in the Plaza de la Reina. An entanglement of churches, the square is dominated by the Cathedral, a structure that literally was grafted onto a captured mosque in the thirteenth century, and whose octagonal Miguelete tower commands a view of possibly three hundred additional church belfries. It is a strange combination of medieval sacramentalism and contemporary permissiveness. On a Sunday morning, as scattered handfuls of congregants observe Mass in the Cathedral and surrounding churches, the Plaza de la Reina is deluged with swarms of visitors. We are in Valencia's flea market. Here dozens of stalls offer coins, stamps, articles of clothing, tools, electrical appliances, bric-a-brac, toys, videotapes (many of them pornographic). On the steps of the Cathedral, meanwhile, perhaps a dozen moneychangers declaim the going price for Western currencies: *"quinientas pesetas," "mil pesetas," "dos mil pesetas."*

Inside, as if trapped in a time warp, the priest sermonizes (first in Valencian, then in Castilian) on the episode of Jesus driving the moneychangers from the Temple. After the spectacular vista from the Miguelete, the Cathedral's interior is an anticlimax. There are Goyas and Velázquezes and several handsome metalwork grilles enclosing crypts and adjoining chapels, yet the sanctuary's walls and ceilings are bone-gray and all but devoid of ornamentation. Even its most frequently visited crypt projects an identical mood of fractured austerity. On the western arm of the nave, guarded by an elaborate wrought-iron gate, the bier lies under a richly hued Velázquez. By contrast, several of the windows are missing their stained-glass alembic, and the light is harsh, uncompromising, stark. This is the tomb of a canonized monk, as it happens, San Vicente Ferrer, and the effect of macabre disjointedness is entirely appropriate.

He was born in this town in 1350, the son of a scrivener. Even as a youngster, he was said to have borne a pietistic afflatus—hectoring other children for profane behavior, fasting twice a week. As a youthful Dominican friar, he experienced visions. San Antonio appeared to him in dreams, exhorting him to leave the shelter of the monastery. At last, Vicente Ferrer went out into the world as a Savonarolaesque evangelist, inveighing against the evils of the time, graphically reminding his audiences of the hellish torments awaiting those who "abandon themselves to the fetid delights of the flesh." If Ferrer relied less on sophisticated oratory than on body language and sheer lung power, his declamations were shatteringly effective. Over the years, as he traveled from town to town, a miracle-hungry rabble thronged after him in solemn procession, carrying banners, crosses, icons of saints, and other holy relics, and chanting religious and penitential hymns. His sermons were delivered in public squares or fields, and usually at night when people were returning home from work. Great flambeaux were lit, creating an unearthly effect among crowds that grew to eight or ten thousand. As Ferrer preached, threatening to whirl away a corrupt society in an instantaneous dance of death, he reduced his audience to weeping, babbling, pleading for salvation.

By the turn of the century, the millennialist crusade turned increasingly against the Jews, whom Ferrer characterized as "the worst enemies" Christianity had ever known, more "devilish" even than Moslems or pagans, veritable antichrists who dared not be allowed beyond the pale of the true faith. For their part, Jews learned to dread the arrival of this tonsured monk as he moved from city to city. Local councils now admonished them to attend his sermons. In some towns, they were actually obliged to give over their synagogues to Ferrer's harangues and to lodge his entourage in their homes. Dissatisfied with mere "persuasion," however, the fiery Dominican eventually sought harsher measures against the "diabolical people." In Valladolid, he admonished the municipal authorities to cordon off the Jews. Later, in Ayllón, he visited with Doña Catalina, queen mother of Castile and tutor of the child king Juan II. Regaling the dowager with horror stories of Jewish satanism, Ferrer entreated her to ghettoize Castilian Jewry altogether. "Just as prostitutes should live apart," he insisted, "so should Jews." It was a dire proposal. Until then, congregating in their juderías largely for reasons of communal self-protection, the Jews otherwise were free to come and go for business or social activities. But now the queen mother, aged and intensely devout, succumbed to Ferrer's appeals. In 1412, she issued a *pragmática* imposing a formal quarantine against Jews throughout Castile.

The *pragmática* in fact evinced more than an old woman's pietistic vulnerability. Its concept was endorsed that same year by the Spanish antipope Benedict XIII and in 1415 by the royal court of Aragón-Catalonia, in language almost identical to that of the Castilian *pragmática*. For both realms, the provisions were unequivocal. Henceforth Jews were confined to walled ghettos, forbidden to leave the country or even to change residence from one town to another. They were barred from every form of public office—from tax-farming and customs-collecting to notarizing and petty clerking—from several of their traditional arts and crafts, even from the exercise of their former communal juridical and fiscal autonomy. They were forbidden as well to hire Christian employees or personal servants, to work in Christian homes, to minister to Christian patients. All Jews over the age of twelve were obliged to attend conversionary sermons three times a year. As a final indignity, Jews were restricted in their outer clothing to black coats adorned only by a red "Jew badge." Solomon Alami wrote from his self-imposed exile in Portugal:

> They barred us from commerce, agriculture, and crafts. They forced us to grow our beards and our hair long. Former palace dwellers were driven into wretched hovels and ill-lit huts. Instead of the rustle of silk, we were compelled to wear miserable clothing that only drew further contempt and revulsion upon us. Hunger looked everyone in the face, and children died at their mothers' breasts from exposure and starvation.

A Community of Conscience

Increasing numbers of Jews chose apostasy. By the early 1400s, possibly thirty-five thousand had become *conversos* out of a Jewish population approaching two hundred thousand. Initially, it was the massacres that hounded them into baptism. But Ferrer's lurid harangues, his incensed crowds of listeners, and the maze of legal restrictions all now added their own inducements. To be sure, the motivations of Jewish apostates were far from uniform. Samuel Abravanel of Seville, descendant of an ancient and affluent Castilian family, was a man long honored among Christians and Jews alike for both his business acuity and his Jewish learning. As minister of finance to Enrique III of Castile, he often forthrightly defended his people's interests before the royal court. Yet when Vicente Ferrer's minions descended upon Seville, Abravanel immediately underwent baptism and assumed the name Juan Sánchez de Seville. Here, plainly, the decision was taken in extremis. Indeed, shamed by his moral collapse,

Abravanel let it be known that he would resume his ancestral faith the moment the wave of hatred ebbed. Fleeing to Portugal later with his wife and children, he kept his word.

Still other fifteenth-century New Christians, like Pablo Cristiani and Abner of Burgos before them, were driven by self-contempt into paroxysms of displaced rage. Bonafus (formerly the converso Pedro) de la Caballería, in his treatise *The Zeal of Christ Against Jews, Saracens, and Infidels,* argued that Christianity's very survival required extermination of the "synagogue of Satan." There were yet other apostates, swept up in the recriminative frenzy, who fiercely avowed that Jews were murdering Christian children, torching Christian homes, cursing churches, stabbing communion wafers, flogging crucifixes, abominating holy images, vomiting ritual blasphemies on Christ and the Apostles.

Yet oscillation between self-abasement and projected fury was not typical of most conversos. If some quietly accepted their new Christian identity, others wavered for years even after baptism, maintaining a fearful, secretive allegiance to Judaism, awaiting the moment when they might return openly to the ancestral faith (p. 61). Nor was it uncommon for individual Jewish conventicles to be divided on the possibly redeeming Jewishness of *anusim,* pro forma converts who had apostatized to save their lives, and *meshumadim,* those who had accepted baptism for less urgent reasons of moral expediency, or even, heaven forfend, of intellectual conviction.

A more traumatic ideological confrontation pitted a small number of genuinely obsessed apostates against the rather larger group of equally stiff-necked Jewish loyalists. Indeed, the developing polemic between ex-Jews and professing Jews, carried on intermittently throughout the fifteenth century, was unparalleled for its literacy, passion, and dialectical exploitation of every weapon in both the Jewish and Christian intellectual armories. An early and spirited debate of this nature occurred between Solomon Halevi of Burgos and Joshua Halorki of Alcañiz. The two men were of approximately the same age. Both had enjoyed almost identical advantages of economic security, education, and travel. Halevi's provenance may have been fractionally more distinguished. His family had produced government tax-farmers for generations, and he himself had served as Castile's ambassador to Aquitaine. The man's Jewish credentials were equally impressive. Talmudic scholars, marveling at the breadth of his erudition and his grasp of Maimunist philosophy, granted him the honorific "Rabbi."

Then, in 1390, in his fortieth year, encountering the avalanche of anti-Jewish violence, Halevi led his wife and five sons to the baptismal font.

He himself was christened Pablo de Santa María. At the time, it was the most consequential act of apostasy in Spanish-Jewish history. Not satisfied with a pro forma ritual conversion, moreover, the renowned hidalgo then continued on to Paris and became a priest, a doctor of theology, and eventually an intimate of Cardinal Pedro de Luna, who would become the antipope Benedict XIII. With these connections, the brilliant new Christian eminence was dispatched back to Castile in 1406, where he assumed the bishopric of his native Burgos. There, too, he fully supported Vicente Ferrer's conversionary campaign. Was the man a rank opportunist? Halevi's extensive writings hardly convey that impression. Tightly reasoned in the best scholastic tradition, they evince a profound conviction that the messianic prophecy had been fulfilled in Jesus.

The most important of those writings, in fact, were the consequence of Halevi's extended literary debate with Joshua Halorki, from 1406 to 1412. Halorki was not a man to be intellectually intimidated. A physician, an ordained rabbi, and a Maimunist, Halorki could hold his own in any competition of reason. Corresponding with his old acquaintance Halevi, he went immediately for the jugular. "Did you convert because you wanted these riches and honors?" he sneered. "To gaze into the countenance of Gentile women?" Yet, in the end, Halorki had to face the painful likelihood that Solomon Halevi—Bishop Pablo de Santa María—might genuinely believe. And as he grappled with that awesome prospect, Halorki found that he himself no longer could evade the Christological implications of Jewish suffering. Was Israel, he wondered, then expendable after all? Only a hint of this emotional turmoil is revealed in his cryptic notation of March 1412: "Perhaps, perhaps Christianity is truth, perhaps all of the proof texts they have been trying to show us in the Bible to demonstrate [their own] . . . allegories are correct." In June, Rabbi Joshua Halorki was baptized as Jerónimo de Santa Fe. The blow to Castilian Jewry was shattering. *Kaddish* services were intoned in synagogues throughout the peninsula. But if Joshua Halorki was dead to the Jews of Castile, the Jews of Aragón-Catalonia would soon learn that Jerónimo de Santa Fe was very much alive.

A Disputation at Tortosa

The man wasted little time in striking out at his ancestral faith. As physician to Benedict XIII during the latter's frequent return visits to Aragón, Halorki was strategically located to press for a renewed Christian-Jewish "disputation." Yet the notion was as much Benedict's brainchild as his own. In 1394, during the period of the "Great Schism," with its rival claimants to the pontifical throne, this Spanish-born cardinal was elected to the papacy. If elsewhere in the Christian world he was disdained as the "antipope," Benedict was determined at least to fortify his pontifical credentials on his native soil. Success in orchestrating a Jewish mass conversion would be an impressive step toward that goal, and all the more at a moment when factions of the sundered church were negotiating a reunification at the Council of Constance. At Benedict's initiative, therefore, and with the approval of Aragón's rather pliant ruler, Fernando I, letters were dispatched to the various Jewish *cals* throughout the realm, "inviting" them to send emissaries to the papal court in Tortosa by February 1413.

Present-day Tortosa can be reached by direct rail journey north from Valencia, some two-thirds the distance to Barcelona. It is a handsome, smallish town of modern villas, nestled in a green-and-brown saddle of hills, extensively steepled with churches. Despite its modest population of some thirty thousand, Tortosa carefully preserves its numerous historic treasures, and the judería is one of these. A characteristic apiary of winding lanes and side streets, the little enclave once enjoyed a certain affluence. Indeed, when Ramón Berenguer IV, count of Barcelona, first captured Tortosa from the Moors in 1158, he encouraged Jews to settle by offering them numerous evacuated houses and vineyards, together with assurance of full communal autonomy. But here as elsewhere in the peninsula, the barometer of toleration fell in ensuing years, and by the fifteenth century the Jews of Tortosa were restricted effectively to ghettos, forced to wear distinctive clothing and identifying badges, and exposed to mounting physical harassment. As the temporary court of a Spanish pope, moreover, Tortosa offered an even less congenial setting for a disputation this February 1413.

Nevertheless, the *cals* of Aragón-Catalonia dutifully appointed ten representatives, nine of them rabbis. The Christian delegation, twice as large and composed almost entirely of Dominican friars and priests, was led by Jerónimo de Santa Fe—Joshua Halorki. Benedict XIII welcomed both groups courteously, if with a backhanded swipe at the Jews. "Although rejected [by God] for your sins," he explained to them, "[you] will meet with no guile or wrong . . . [and] will be suitably lodged and . . . given . . . of whatsoever food [you are] permitted to eat by [your] religion." The formal proceedings began the next day in a papal courtyard filled with nearly a thousand persons, most of them clerics. Benedict himself presided. It was also he who stunned the Jews by informing them that the event would not after all be a disputation between two equal parties but rather an "examination" of Judaism, which they, the Jews, would have an opportunity to "defend."

Hereupon Joshua Halorki assumed the role of prosecutor. In his opening address, the renowned converso launched into an extended disquisition "proving" from authentic Jewish sources (which he cited at length, from memory, in Hebrew and Aramaic) that Jesus was the true Messiah. The Jews, in turn, although angered and discountenanced by the turn of events, were obliged in their response to avoid even the faintest hint of reproach for Christian doctrine. The effort was difficult, and all the more so as the proceedings continued, day after day. Argumentation tended to revolve largely about the Messiah: the time of his arrival (Christian past or Jewish future), his attributes (Christian divine or Jewish mortal). Halorki was unrelenting. With his case based squarely on talmudic and midrashic passages, he rejected all Jewish explanations of context or allegorization. Moreover, Benedict himself occasionally intruded to press home a point or to rebuke the Jews for stubbornness. The atmosphere at Tortosa was palpably more ominous than in the straightforward, intellectually resilient Barcelona disputation of a century and a half earlier. As the weeks passed, then, the ordeal gradually drained the Jews' emotions and energies. Refused leeway for the orderly development of their ideas, they often faltered, contradicted themselves, experienced lapses of memory.

The "debates" continued into 1413—March, April, May—and into the sweltering months of summer. By then, however, the Jews finally had developed the technique of adverting to written memoranda, even to clue-words. The tactic at least permitted them to gain a second wind and formulate a certain consistency of intellectual stance. Refuting the notion of a messianic death atoning for the sins of mankind, they now provided the classical Judaic interpretation of the Messiah as a righteous man and prophet, entirely mortal in his personal qualities, who someday would redeem the Jews from political bondage, thereby allowing them freely to observe the Law of Moses. It was an impressive recovery. Faced with this adamance, Halorki was obliged gradually to shift his argument to the Talmud's "errors, heresy, villainy, and abuse of the Christian religion." Discussions on the talmudic issue then extended intermittently over additional months. And here, too, notwithstanding the pressures of intimidation and exhaustion, the assembled rabbis in their erudition and imagination proved a match for their prosecutor. Indeed, their responses—as transcribed in Solomon ibn Verga's Hebrew text of the disputation, *Shevet Yehuda* (The Tribe of Judah)—comprised a rather masterful précis of Judaism at its medieval apogee.

An impasse had been reached. In November 1413, Halorki informed the pope that the Jews manifestly had been "defeated" and he was prepared to rest his case. The Jews in turn appealed to the pope's humanity. They had been in Tortosa for ten months, they reminded Benedict, and their confinement had cost them dearly. Some of them had exhausted the entirety of their savings and had gone into debt. Others had lost wives and children in the interval. Their communities, too, had suffered irreparable harm by their absence. Could men faced with such sacrifices be regarded as "defeated"? The appeal was eloquent, and it registered on the pope. Yet the political stakes were too high for Benedict to allow the disputation to end inconclusively. His single concession, in January 1414, was to order the proceedings abridged. Nonetheless, they meandered on through the winter and into spring.

Finally, in May 1414, in a gesture of elementary compassion, Prince Alfonso of Aragón interceded with Benedict. He suggested an adjournment at least until the Jewish delegates could visit their families and attend to their needs. The pope acquiesced. But in the early autumn he summoned the rabbis back for yet another desultory series of meetings. These extended into mid-November 1414. It was then too that Benedict issued a bull condemning (without actually banning) the Talmud for its "hateful and blasphemous" aspersions on Christianity, and proclaiming the disputation a triumph for the true faith. And now, at last, the participants were allowed to depart. With all its recesses, the production had consumed twenty months and had all but devoured the Jews' economic and emotional resources.

The cost for the wider Jewish community was graver yet. Inflamed by the anti-Jewish diatribes of church and state, local populations intensified their harassment. In smaller towns, mobs occasionally terrorized Jews (and some Moslems) into flight. Like their kinsmen in Castile, exposed to legal restrictions and proselytizing coercion, the Jews of Aragón-Catalonia sensed that they were on the verge of economic ruin. Additional thousands of them now gave up the ghost and accepted baptism. The ranks of these defectors included not a few renowned Jewish communal leaders and intellectuals. Indeed, one of these, Don Vidal Benveniste de la Caballería, actually had participated in the Tortosa disputation. Cut to the heart by this act of "treason," Don Vidal's friend and fellow poet Solomon Bonafed lamented:

> Wake and stir, O silent flute,
> Singing harp become so mute.

All the army drive away
Of our sorrow and dismay.

The aged Hebrew poet Solomon da Piera (p. 48), who reluctantly underwent baptism at almost the same time, quoted passages of the Talmud to rationalize his decision. And again Bonafed voiced his anguish:

Yet, I remember them their company, I recall them not in parting,
   for ever since my heart and soul are lost!
Their names are engraved upon my brow! How now,
   that they are gone, shall I erase these pleasant names from my doorposts?

Bonafed sought his consolation in the quality of his friends—intellectuals, physicians, lawyers—who apparently still held steadfast as professing Jews. But the numbers of these, too, were shrinking. Conceivably, Vicente Ferrer's sermons may have impressed some of this elite group. Others doubtless were confused by the church's proclaimed "victory" at Tortosa. In any case, few among the converso upper class appeared tormented by a genuine spiritual crisis, or even by the inner furies of an Abner of Burgos or a Joshua Halorki. As sophisticated men of the world, usually of a rationalist bent, they had long since become detached intellectually from the Jewish common folk. From his Portuguese refuge, Solomon Alami addressed himself to these careerists, "whose wives and daughters dressed like great ladies," who "despised religion and humility. . . . O worm of Jacob! They who were brought up in scarlet now embrace dunghills!"

The Rise of a Converso Hinterland

The asperities of history move in fits and starts. For the Jews, a momentary breathing space accompanied political changes in Spain's royal and clerical courts. In Aragón, Alfonso V became king in 1416; in Castile, Juan II attained his majority in 1419. Preoccupied with economic concerns, the two young rulers evinced little interest in religious zealotry. Their pragmatism was additionally fostered by the accession to the pontificate in 1417 of Martin V, a man of moderation. In ensuing years, kings and pope alike countenanced a certain discreet relaxation of the proselytizing campaign. Ghetto curfews and the harsher vocational restrictions no longer were enforced. Self-government was restored to the *cals.*

At all times, a small number of Jews maintained their influential roles at the upper levels of government. Abraham Benveniste served as Juan II's treasurer, doubling as chief rabbi of Castile. In later years, Abraham

Senior would become chief tax-farmer for the Castilian throne. It was under Senior's tutelage that one of Iberian Jewry's most illustrious families briefly resumed its eminence. As far back as the fourteenth century, the Abravanel clan of Seville had achieved standing among Castile's principal royal tax-collectors. In 1391, we recall, Samuel Abravanel, chief tax-collector for the province of Andalusia, had undergone an expedient baptism and fled soon afterward to Portugal, where he and his family then reverted to Judaism.

In Portugal, too, the Abravanels—father, son, and grandson—were swiftly elevated to comparable positions as royal tax collectors and financiers. Indeed, the grandson, Don Isaac Abravanel, born in 1437, succeeded his father as treasurer to Portugal's King Afonso V, and managed also to become a distinguished scholar of Judaism. Yet the family's period of tranquillity in Lisbon ended with Afonso's death in 1481 and the accession to the Portuguese throne of his son João II. Suspecting—unjustly—that Abravanel was disloyal, King João placed his Jewish treasurer under sentence of death. By ingenuity and much good luck, Abravanel managed at the last moment to escape over the Castilian frontier, and later to smuggle other family members out of Portugal (p. 159). Once again, in 1484, he found himself called into royal service, this time to the throne of Castile, under Isabel I. His patron was Abraham Senior. Well apprised of Don Isaac's vast experience, Senior arranged for his appointment as tax-farmer for Castile's central and southern provinces. In 1491, then, it was Senior and Abravanel who collected the revenues that funded the joint Castilian-Aragonese military expedition against Moslem Granada. Blessed, too, with an ingratiating personality, Abravanel emerged as a particular favorite of young Queen Isabel. He became her personal financial adviser.

So it was that the Jews maintained their visibility in Spanish life well into the 1400s. Beyond their role as government financiers, there were eminent Jewish court physicians. In the private sector, more than a few Jews continued as landowners, prominent wholesale and retail merchants, importers-exporters, and investment bankers. In the larger cities, business contacts between Jews and Christians remained functional. Nevertheless, after the shock of 1391, and the next quarter century of emotional trauma, it was the social relationship between the two peoples that failed to revive. Nor would the Jews recover in their critical mass. During the fourteenth century, they had lost perhaps thirty-five thousand of their people to violence, and at least that many to apostasy. Estimates have placed the entire (identified) Jewish population of Castile in 1474 at thirty thousand families; of Aragón, at six thousand. In both realms by then, the combined figure could not have exceeded 150,000 souls, in a surrounding population of six million. Altogether, the glory had faded in such formerly dense areas of Jewish habitation as Seville, Toledo, Burgos, Barcelona, and Girona. The Jewish locus continued to shift to smaller towns. Wherever they lived, most Jews were businessmen and artisans of so modest a scale that their annual tax payments by 1480 comprised less than half of 1 percent of total revenues.

As it shrank in demographic and economic weight, Spanish Jewry also began to atrophy culturally. Hebrew verse, once the pride of the Jewish Golden Age, continued its dignified decline. Responding to the anguish of their times, poets tended now to write hymns of penitence and supplication. Talmudic scholarship still was produced in this last Iberian twilight, but intellectual schisms reflected the little community's widening social disjunctions. "Averroism" and "Maimunism" continued to hold sway among the rearguard of affluent laymen. In the aftermath of Ferrante Martínez, however, of the 1391 pogroms, of Vicente Ferrer, and, later, of Tortosa, Spanish Jewry's rabbinical leadership execrated ideological resiliency as a mortal threat to communal survival. Don Abraham Benveniste, rabbi and chief judge of Castilian Jewry, issued uncompromising strictures against "philosophism" in any shape or form. In Aragón, journeying from town to town, Rabbi Isaac Arama warned the Jewish *cals* that Averroism was spreading the "gall of heresy throughout the world." Arama's listeners were essentially the poorer and more devout shopkeepers and artisans. They may have lacked the influence of the well-born, yet by the fifteenth century they were the Jewish majority. For these simple people, a disavowal of Averroism, indeed, of intellectualism altogether, was the reaction of terror. They were beleaguered, and not alone in their Judaism. By then, they sensed that they were losing their very lifeblood to the Gentile camp.

In the 1420s, ironically, even as the proselytizing campaign appeared to be easing, the number of conversos approached perhaps a third of the entire Jewish population. These former Jews essentially continued in their traditional vocations as artisans and small tradesmen. But there were also those who exploited the open terrain before them to advance in public life. Frequently, their ascent was much more rapid than that of "Old Christians." Here it was that their superior literacy, often the talmudic training they remembered from their youth, stood them in good stead. Conversos assumed key positions in the financial administration and the judiciary; in municipal councils, provincial assemblies, and universities; even in the church. By midcentury, these "New Christians" or their children were represented in almost every public office of importance in Castile and

Aragón-Catalonia. A century later, in 1507, Juan de Anchías of Zaragoza, an inquisitional secretary, amused his friends by drawing up a genealogy, the *Libro verde de Aragón,* demonstrating the precise Jewish antecedents of a significant proportion of the nation's aristocracy.

The progress of the Santángel family is instructive. Noah Chinillo of Calatayud produced five sons. One of them, Azariah, was converted early in the fifteenth century under the impact of the Vicente Ferrer rampage. Adopting the name of a saint, he became Luis de Santángel. Eventually, as a lawyer, he attained high office at the court of Aragón and was raised to the nobility. His nephew Pedro de Santángel was appointed bishop of Majorca. His son Martín became a magistrate in Zaragoza. A Luis de Santángel of a later generation was financial agent to the Aragonese court.

More impressive yet was the rise of the Caballería family. Already prominent in Catalonia as early as the thirteenth century, Judah de la Caballería acted as bailiff for King Jaime I. Many of Don Judah's descendants assumed comparably high positions. It is recalled that one of these, Don Vidal Benveniste de la Caballería, participated in the disputation at Tortosa. By the mid-fifteenth century, eight of the nine sons of Don Solomon de la Caballería (Don Vidal's brother) had been baptized. Their lineage by then was so ancient and honorable that they did not bother even to change their surname. The eldest son, Bonafus, was comptroller general of Aragón and a favorite of Queen María. Bonafus's son Alfonso was appointed vice-chancellor of Aragón. Another son, Luis, became a counsellor to King Juan I. Still another, Jaime, served as a trusted adviser and companion of King Alfonso V. Bonafus's brother Samuel rose to high office in the church; another brother, Isaac, was vice principal of the University of Zaragoza; another, Luis, became treasurer of the Kingdom of Navarre; and all Luis's sons amassed fortunes as tax-farmers. Characteristically, the family intermarried among several of the proudest and wealthiest "Old Christian" dynasties of Aragón.

In Castile, meanwhile, the converso families of González, Chinet, and Coloma similarly attained exalted estate. Hernando del Pulgar was secretary to Queen Isabel I. Alfonso de Cabrera, governor of the Alcázar of Segovia, married the queen's favorite, Beatriz de Bobadilla. Don Juan Pacheco, the marquis of Villena and Grand Master of the Order of Santiago, was a descendant on both sides of the former Jew Ruy Capón. His brother, Don Pedro Girón, was Grand Master of the Order of Calatrava, while the archbishop of Toledo was their uncle. By the late fifteenth century, at least seven of the chief prelates of the kingdom were of Jewish extraction, not to mention the treasurers. Hardly an office of importance in state or church, for that matter, was not occupied by descendants of some converted Jew, or by members of Old Christian families intermarried with those of New Christians. Much of Iberia's intellectual elite similarly reflected this converso penetration. They included a significant minority of writers and humanists who set the cultural tone of fifteenth-century Spain, among them Alvarez Gato, Rodrigo de Cota de Maguesque, Juan de Valladolid, Juan de España *el Viejo*, Juan de Mena, Anton de Montoro, and Alfonso de la Torre. Two of Castile's most widely admired prose works in the reign of Isabel the Catholic were produced by New Christians: Diego de San Pedro's *La cárcel de amor* and Fernando de Rojas's *La Celestina.*

During the 1391 horror and its aftermath, nevertheless, possibly the largest numbers of conversos still regarded their apostasy as a temporary aberration that one day could be reversed. Whether members of the upper classes, who were the first to save their skins and fortunes, or of the tradition-oriented middle and lower classes, Jewish apostates by and large espoused Christianity as a simple marriage of convenience. Socially, they remained closer to their converso kinsmen and friends than to "ethnic" Christians. Artisan conversos formed their own guilds. Converso merchants did business with one another, granted one another credit, patronized one another's shops and offices, and married one another's womenfolk. For many years, in fact, only the wealthiest and most exalted among them, such hidalgos as the Caballerías and the Santángels, aspired to marry into Old Christian families.

Were, then, the conversos "judaizers" after all—that is, individuals who privately still maintained their identities as Jews? Many in fact were, particularly among the middle and lower classes. They shared courtyards with Jewish families and friends, participated with these kin in Jewish festivals, refrained from working on the Sabbath, observed Jewish rules and regulations, employed their own Hebrew teachers and ritual slaughterers. At the least, there existed among New Christians and professing Jews a kind of unspoken, intermingled emotional community. The fact could hardly have been a secret to the government or the clergy, or surely to the population at large. Yet, unable to cope with the sheer extent of the mass conversion, Spanish Gentiles watched glumly as these conversos, emancipated from legal restraints, continued to ascend the hierarchy of government, church, and economy. At times, Old Christian grandees and businessmen vented their resentment in petitions and letters to the royal government. Solomon ibn Verga quotes a typical fifteenth-century protest to the court of Castile:

It is of no use to your Majesty to pour holy water on Jews and to call them Peter or Paul, while they cling to their religion like Akiba or Tarfon. There is no advantage in their baptism except to make them arrogant against true Christians, since outwardly they are accepted as Christians. The royal tribute, which they used to pay when they were Jews, they pay no more. Know, Sire, that Judaism unquestionably is one of the incurable diseases.

It was in Castile that popular hatred of the conversos first boiled over, in 1449. The provocation was King Juan II's decision to impose heavier taxes on the city of Toledo. The revenue agents were conversos, and the amalgam of New Christians and new assizes was simply too much for the harassed locals. They exploded in mob demonstrations and stonings of converso homes and shops. Two weeks passed before the government managed to restore order. Afterward, to avert additional unrest, the Crown felt it politic to dismiss several dozen converso tax-collectors, notaries, and judges. By then, however, the issue of New Christians already had touched off a lengthy polemical war in public and private circles alike. For the church, universalism was a cardinal tenet, and the Vatican thus flatly rejected the very notion of treating New Christians as second-class citizens. In 1449 the humanist pope Nicholas V went so far as to issue a bull, *Humani Generis Inimicus* (Enemy of the Human Race), that threatened to excommunicate anyone demanding *limpieza de sangre*—purity of blood—in short, racism. Nevertheless, many even within the clergy now also began shifting their stance, assuming precisely a secret ideological Jewishness among those lacking "purity of blood."

At this point the Crown, too, began to equivocate on the converso issue. Fearful of jeopardizing his precarious relations with the nobility, King Juan induced Pope Nicholas to suspend his threat of excommunication in 1450, only a year after issuing it. Fifteen years later, following a renewed outburst of street fighting in Toledo between Old and New Christians, King Enrique IV banned conversos from holding any public office in the city. Spanish Gentiles were not placated. In ensuing years, they erupted in violence still again, in Córdoba, Jaén, Carmona, and other Andalusian cities. Their hostility was evident as well in propaganda against "false" or "fair-weather" Christians. Literary attacks ran from satirical tracts to vulgar ditties. In the late fourteenth century, a threshold had been crossed in relations between Christians and Jews. By the late fifteenth century, a threshold plainly was being approached in relations between Old and New Christians.

The Catholic Monarchs

By then, too, Spain's two largest kingdoms were entering a new political configuration. In 1469, Prince Fernando of Aragón married his cousin, the Castilian heiress Isabel. Five years later, Isabel ascended her country's throne. It was a formidable alliance, both of personalities and of political destinies. Although intensely pious, Isabel was described by her contemporaries as a "mistress of dissimulation and simulation," a woman capable of pursuing her goals without scruple or sentiment. Fernando, in turn, although a dynamic and attractive figure, a brave soldier and respected commander, could be as ruthless and duplicitous as his wife. When informed that Louis XI of France complained of having twice been deceived by him, Fernando protested: "The king of France lies. I deceived him not twice, but ten times."

Isabel and Fernando operated from a base of promising strength. By law, Castile and Aragón remained separate and independent. In actual fact, the linked resources of their kingdoms enabled the "Catholic Monarchs" to transform Spain into a major European empire. During the 1470s and 1480s, the two rulers conducted a vigorous, unrelenting campaign to break the power of the nobility. To that end, they shrewdly discerned the political advantage implicit in a joint campaign of *reconquista*. By pressing the onslaught against Granada, Islam's last foothold on the peninsula, Fernando and Isabel might harness the support of the church and the religious passions of their subjects, including the fractious nobility, on behalf of "Christian civilization." At the same time, under the mantle of reconquest, a second goal might be achieved. This was an expedient and unifying crusade against heresy within the Christian community itself.

For the Jews, the new royal strategy was a matter of grave moment. On the one hand, such men as Abraham Senior and Isaac Abravanel held important positions under Fernando and Isabel and enjoyed the warm esteem of their rulers. Indeed, it was specifically the queen's political ambition that revived their historic fiscal talents, and those of other Spanish Jews. "All the Jews in my realm," Isabel declared as late as 1477, "are mine and under my care and my protection and it belongs to me to defend and aid them and keep justice." Yet by then, her "care and protection" hardly could be reconciled with the royal intention of manipulating the nation's religious fervor. Within the frontiers of Christian Spain, the issue of conversos was fast becoming an inflamed public lesion. To treat that wound, and to foster their subjects' ideological unity, Isabel and her husband turned to a mechanism of vast latent potential. It was an "Inquisition" into heresy and backsliding.

As early as the thirteenth century, the church itself had established an Inquisition to deal with Christian schismatics. These were Albigensians, Waldensians, and Pasagians, most of them in southern France. Finding precedent in Roman law, the church's investigative machinery during those years was administered by individual diocesan bishoprics. Dominican and Franciscan monks acted as the principal inquisitors. If the operation was ill-coordinated, the threat of heresy was not particularly serious then. But now, in fifteenth-century Castile and Aragón, suspected heretics no longer were isolated Christian apostates or Christian deviants but large masses of former Jews, individuals in the tens of thousands who appeared to be clinging suspiciously to their ancestral traditions. Popular sentiment no longer would tolerate the anomaly, and the question therefore arose of the appropriate means to correct it. An Inquisition based on the practice of intermittent diocesan inquiries seemed incapable of rooting out this vast Jewish netherworld. Equally unfeasible was an Inquisition centrally directed from Rome; Fernando and Isabel were not prepared to forfeit royal control.

To resolve the issues of both the structure and the authority of the Inquisition, the Catholic Monarchs thereupon entered into protracted negotiations with the Vatican. Finally, in 1478, they reached an agreement with Pope Sixtus IV. To begin with, an Inquisition would be limited initially to the diocese of Seville, embracing much of Castilian Andalusia. Here a large and still affluent converso population lived directly adjacent to the Moorish kingdom of Granada. Indeed, it was fear of this lingering Moslem enclave that induced Pope Sixtus to accept the Spanish Inquisition's new and unique status. Its personnel, although clerics every one, would be answerable not to Rome but to royal, secular authority. Thus, the first inquisitors were two Dominican friars, Miguel de Morillo and Juan de San Martín; but it was the Crown of Castile that confirmed their appointment, as it would those of all other inquisitors.

The rationale for the new enterprise was the need to root out heretics who "daily return to the superstitious and perfidious sect of the Jews. . . . Not only have they persisted in their blind and obstinate heresy, but their children and descendants do likewise." To achieve this goal of doctrinal cleansing, the Inquisition in the years after 1478 gradually developed a set of procedures. It allowed a brief state of "grace" for backsliding Christians—that is, former Jews—to turn themselves in. By the same token, all others who possessed knowledge of secret judaizers were obliged to transmit their information forthwith, on pain of excommunication. Once the identity of the accused individuals was established, they would be seized, thrust into inquisitional dungeons, interrogated (occasionally under torture), and sentenced to a variety of punishments, ranging from terms of penitential service to imprisonment or to "relaxation," that is, death. Thus, even in its earliest phase, between 1479 and 1481, in a ferocious reign of terror, nearly four hundred individuals were burned at the stake for heresy in the city of Seville alone. Throughout Castilian Andalusia, some two thousand persons were burned alive, seventeen thousand others were "reconciled," that is, spared the death penalty but subjected to such punishments as imprisonment, confiscation of property, and debarment from all employment, public and private. Their wives and children faced destitution.

Once it had proved its efficacy in Andalusia, the Inquisition was extended step-by-step into the towns of central Castile, including Toledo and Ciudad Real. No one was safe from the frenzy of denunciations. Protected by anonymity, informers often implicated alleged *marranos* (the Spanish pejorative for secret judaizers) to satisfy private grievances. An army of inquisitional spies remained on the lookout for "suspicious" behavior. Those conversos who actually observed Judaism in private had not yet become adept at maintaining secrecy. A single careless remark could endanger an entire extended family. In Aragón, too, during these same years, King Fernando gradually was introducing his own Inquisition, adopting precisely the methods developed in Castile. In both kingdoms, the price of those methods often was high. Numerous smaller towns were virtually depopulated by the converso trials and the terrified flights, the imprisonment of key economic figures, and the impoverishment of their families. Yet no mitigation of procedure or punishment was deemed acceptable. By the mid-1480s, the great inquisitional machine was all but running on its own—and the worst of its depredations still lay ahead.

The Royal Inquisitor

Its efficiency owed much to consolidation under unified direction. In 1483, the Catholic Monarchs appointed Tomás de Torquemada as inquisitor general for the combined territories of Castile and Aragón. The choice was an inspired one. No individual could more perfectly have suited a regime of unrelenting fanaticism. Educated in a Dominican monastery near Valladolid, his birthplace, Torquemada as a young man displayed a religious ardor so ferocious that he literally wore a hair shirt, refused linen even for bedclothes, and abstained from all meat and sweets. Later, as prior of the monastery of Santa Cruz at Segovia, Torquemada served as confessor to the young Princess Isabel. The unique intimacy of the relationship determined his future career. He became Isabel's personal choice as one of the original Castilian inquisitors and, in 1483, the appointee of both monarchs as inquisitor general. It was accordingly this joyless zealot who brought the vast juggernaut of inquiry and vengeance to its eeriest perfection.

From a purely administrative viewpoint, the Inquisition was a formidable achievement. It represented the first all-Spanish institution on the peninsula at a time when state authority itself still was officially divided between Castile and Aragón. The Suprema, or inquisitional Supreme Council, became one of only five royal councils attached to the combined thrones, and its operation permitted the Catholic Monarchs additional leverage in their drive toward centralization and absolutism. But at what a price! For long intervals, the economies of such major commercial centers as Barcelona, Zaragoza, and Valencia were gravely disrupted. The number of executed victims mounted so rapidly that in several of the larger cities allocation had to be made for a *quemadero,* or special burning site. No one was immune to the horror. The entire family of Vice Chancellor Alfonso de la Caballería was arrested, imprisoned, and tried in a proceeding that continued for twenty months. Eventually both parents and all the grown sons were burned alive. By 1490, the competitive delirium of arrests and trials approached the threshold of the previous century's indiscriminate mass violence. In the eighteen years of Torquemada's ministry alone, over two thousand conversos were burned, nearly three thousand condemned and burned in "effigy" (normally a posthumous sentence), and thirty-seven thousand "reconciled" to the church by dint of various terms of imprisonment and penance. The thousands of orphans left behind cannot be estimated.

Neither can the vast sums confiscated from the victims' estates. Indeed, a defendant's funds and businesses were sequestered from the moment he was imprisoned, well before actually facing trial, and these "preliminary" incarcerations often stretched on for years. Confiscated, too, was the property of individuals who had died years earlier but had been convicted posthumously. Their descendants instantly were stripped of their legacies, creditors denied access to debt payments, savings expropriated, families left impoverished. All funds escheated to the Crown. Financial greed thus soon became a major factor in the inquisitional crusade. The Catholic Monarchs had negotiated a threefold division of spoils among the royal treasury, the Holy Office, and the inquisitional clerics engaged in each trial. These last therefore possessed a vested interest in broadening the scale of arrests, convictions, and confiscations.

As for the New Christians, their own reactions to the terror varied widely. The more affluent and educated among them generally had maintained only nominal links with the Jewish religion even before baptism. They had not found it difficult to apostatize for reasons of financial expediency, and if they were seized afterward by the Inquisition, many were quite prepared to degrade themselves, even to invent details that incriminated others, to save their lives and fortunes. There were instances of husbands, wives, and parents testifying against one another, although usually under torture. Other conversos simply fled the country with their families. In 1489, as the first inquisitors arrived in the Balearic Islands, at least two thousand Majorcan Jews—a community that only lately had been reviving in the aftermath of the 1391 massacres—did not wait for the proceedings to begin. They quit their principal city of Palma de Majorca en masse and departed for North Africa or France.

It was the converso lower-middle classes that sustained the warmest communal links with their identified Jewish kinsmen. Many were marranos or near-marranos. Confronted now by the Inquisition, not a few of these secret judaizers were consumed by paroxysms of belated martyrdom. "I rejoice," declared one converso prisoner in Torrelaguna to his fellow defendants, "for as soon as the measure of our torments and oppression is full, the Messiah, whom we all await, will speedily appear. Happy the person who will see him!" Among those caught up in the sacrificial euphoria were even a number of converso monks, including three friars in Toledo's monastery of San Jerónimo. Arrested as marranos in 1485, they were imprisoned and tortured. None would give evidence against the others. Rather, with the unfocused millennialism that doubtless had attracted them initially to a religious order, several of the prisoners experienced visions of Arthama and Moses, and fantasized their impending death as redemption to the Land of Israel on the backs of clouds or on angels' wings. Approaching the stake in a fever of exultation, they joyously intoned their Hebrew prayers.

There were instances of converso resistance as well. In 1480, with the establishment of the first inquisitional tribunal in Seville, a handful of New Christians met secretly at the home of a wealthy merchant, Diego de Susán. Among the group were the governor of Triana, the royal financial agent of Castile, even several church dignitaries. Together they made plans for an armed attack on the "interlopers." At the last moment, however, the plot was shattered by Don Diego's daughter. A famed beauty, "La Susana" had a Christian lover, and inadvertently divulged the plot to him. He promptly informed the authorities. Don Diego and his accomplices then were seized, tried, convicted, and executed. As an "accessory," La Susana herself was condemned to life in a convent. Escaping some years later, she became a prostitute. Eventually she perished in destitution. On her deathbed, La Susana left instructions for her skull to be placed over the door of her hovel as a testament to her shame. There, in an alley known ever after as the Calle de la Muerte, the skull remained for centuries. Folklore had it that in the middle of the night, cries of grief occasionally issued from its fleshless grinning jaws.

Five years after the Seville episode, in 1485, converso resistance also surfaced in Aragón, where the economic disruptions caused by the Inquisition had aroused widespread opposition among middle-class elements. It was believed that an act of defiance might touch off a popular uprising. The plot was laid in Zaragoza, where an inquisitional tribunal was soon to conduct hearings under a renowned chief judge, Pedro Arbués. At first the conspiracy went according to plan. The converso assassins caught Arbués off guard in church and stabbed him to death. No uprising followed, however. Instead, the plotters were hunted down and sentenced. The killers had their hands amputated and were left to bleed to death. Other plotters were similarly mutilated, then burned alive. One of the condemned was Francisco de Santa Fe, a grandson of Jerónimo de Santa Fe—Joshua Halorki. The young man hurled himself from his prison tower to avoid execution. With the failure of the Zaragoza plot, all further resistance to the Inquisition in Spain ended.

Convivencia's Last Rites

Iberia's last remaining Moorish palaces are girdled by the Alhambra, Granada's mile-wide stone fortress. Behind its rufescent walls survives a royal city. Its third, and inner, palace encompasses the famed Court of the Lions, whose central fountain, a basin supported by twelve gray marble lions, possibly represented the months of the year. Water once was reputed to have issued from the mouth of a different lion each hour of the day. Directly across the courtyard is the lavishly domed Sala de las dos Hermanas, a pavilion built for the sultana and her daughters and for the mother of Boabdil, Granada's last sultan. In a sumptuous royal bathhouse nearby, the nineteenth-century American poet Washington Irving rented furnished rooms and set about writing the book, *Legends of the Alhambra,* that in 1832 introduced the fortress-city to the outside world.

Throughout 1491, it was from the Alhambra's steep heights that the Moors staved off the combined armies of Fernando and Isabel. In January 1492, however, overwhelmed numerically and racked by famine, they surrendered to the Christian invaders. So ended an offensive that had begun eleven years before—and an even more fundamental campaign of *reconquista* that had originated three centuries earlier. Exultant in their triumph, the Catholic Monarchs now were inclined toward generosity. They allowed the defeated Moors to keep their lands, homes, chattels, and mosques. All wishing to emigrate were free to do so. Sultan Boabdil and his family were among these. Leaving Granada, he mounted the last hill with a view of the Alhambra, cast a longing glance backward over the scene of vanished glory, and wept. The promontory was thereafter to be known as "El último suspiro del moro"—The Moor's Last Sigh.

The war had cost Fernando and Isabel dearly as well. The entire population had contributed its full share of revenues; yet, as always, the Jews paid most heavily of all. Despite their shrinking demographic and economic base, they contributed 58 million maravedis in special taxes between 1482 and 1491, and another 20 million in forced "loans." There was additional money yet to be squeezed from the Jews, as it happened, but only through outright confiscation. That recourse, in turn, was linked to the more fundamental issue of converso "trustworthiness." As Inquisitor General Torquemada and other zealots long had argued, the lurking marrano peril could be excised only by dealing with the source of its encouragement and inspiration—namely, the far larger surrounding hinterland of professing Jews. Over the years, Fernando and Isabel had twisted and turned in evading this conclusion. They had sought to be just, to protect "their" Jews. But now the atmosphere of religious crusade forced an issue that financial need might have raised only later.

Indeed, on their own, the municipalities of Toledo, Madrigal, and Burgos already were passing ordinances against their local Jewries—restricting, ghettoizing, expelling. As early as 1482, inquisitional courts similarly ordered a partial expulsion of Jews from a number of Andalusian cities and towns; two years later, the Jews were driven from the entire dioceses of Córdoba, Seville, and Cádiz. None of these measures was carried out under royal imprimatur. Nevertheless, the Catholic Monarchs this time voiced only perfunctory objections. They sensed that the djinn of *reconquista* and Inquisition was out of the bottle. The fall of Granada might even be interpreted as a sign of divine favor. Perhaps the time had come to consolidate and fortify Spanish Christianity—and, in a single decisive stroke, simultaneously augment the treasury's financial reserves.

By the spring of 1492, the royal court was reestablished in the captured city of Granada. The place was alive with rumors and counterrumors of imminent Jewish departure. Yet when the actual Edict of Expulsion was jointly signed by Fernando and Isabel on March 31, it came like a bolt out of the blue. The preamble stated:

In our land there is no inconsiderable number of judaizing and
wicked Christians who have deviated from our Holy Catholic Faith.
This has been effected above all by the intermingling between Jews
and Christians . . . whereby the latter have been led astray and made
to believe in the damnable beliefs and . . . ceremonies of the Jewish
law . . . [leading] to the undermining and humiliation of our Holy
Catholic Faith.

The declaration then noted that expulsion had been put off several times
in the hope that the Jews might yet reform their ways "without the need
of sterner measures." But the postponements apparently were in vain.
"We have, therefore, decreed to order all Jews of both sexes to leave the
confines of our lands forever."

The reference to "our lands" was no mere literary flourish. The edict
applied to Jews in all Spanish dominions, including Sicily and Sardinia,
and would come into effect on July 31. Within that four-month grace
period, Jews would have the opportunity to sell their homes and take with
them all their movable property. All except their money. Access to Jewish
funds was obviously a decisive inducement for the royal households.
Indeed, it belied the decree's tone of moral sanctity.

Stunned and horrified, the tax officials Isaac Abravanel, Abraham Senior, and Meir Melamed immediately sought an audience with King Fernando. The experience was unnerving. They found the ruler cold, implacable. They turned then to friends at court. A few were prepared to
intercede, but their efforts were to no avail. In a second royal audience,
in mid-April, Abravanel and Senior again entreated Fernando, with even
greater passion. Abravanel recalled later:

I pleaded with the king many times. I supplicated him thus: "Save,
O king. Why do thus to thy servants? Lay upon us every tribute and
ransom, gold and silver, and everything that the Children of Israel
possess, they shall willingly give to their father. . . ." [But] like an
adder which stoppeth its ears, he remained deaf to our appeals. The
queen, also, was standing by his side, but she would not listen to our
plea.

Three weeks later, on behalf of his constituents, Abravanel was able to
come up with a stupefying ransom offer of three hundred thousand gold
ducats—a sum that would have repaid the entire cost of the recent Granadan campaign. The Catholic Monarchs held firm.

Abravanel's one remaining hope was his personal influence with the
queen. His relations with Isabel had always been close. He understood her
mind, her intense religiosity and impressionability. The Jewish courtier

invoked no further financial arguments with her, therefore, only mystical ones. He alluded to the eternity of the Jewish people, their ability throughout history to survive all enemies. And the queen responded in equally pietistic terms: "Do you believe that this comes from us?" she pronounced. "The Lord hath put this thing into the heart of the king." Plainly, the decision was Fernando's. Convinced at last that the realm no longer could absorb its Jews, the Aragonese monarch had reached a firm and final conclusion to liquidate their presence to maximum financial advantage.

An Iberian Leave-Taking

On April 29, 1492, in Toledo's central municipal square, an officer of arms, flanked by three trumpeters, two local magistrates, and two bailiffs, read out a proclamation. It commanded:

> All Jews and Jewesses, of whatever age they may be, that live, reside, and dwell in our said kingdoms and dominions [of Castile] . . . shall not presume to return to, or reside therein, or in any part of them, either as residents, travelers, or in any other manner whatever, under pain . . . of death. . . . And we command and forbid any person or persons of our said kingdom . . . [to] presume publicly or secretly to receive, shelter, protect, or defend any Jew or Jewess . . . under pain of losing all their property, vassals, castles, and other possessions.

A subsequent addendum to this royal decree warned against false compassion after the—now—three-month grace period had passed. Under pain of excommunication, all Christians were forbidden "to converse and communicate . . . with Jews, or receive them into your homes, or befriend them, or give them nourishment of any sort for their sustenance. . . ." An identical edict of expulsion was issued for Aragón-Catalonia.

No sooner had the decree been made public than the clergy launched an intensified last-minute conversionary offensive among the Jews. Proselytization hardly was needed this time. Clients were waiting. In a major coup for the church, these included none other than Abraham Senior (now christened Fernando Pérez Coronel) and his son-in-law Meir Melamed (christened Fernando Núñez Coronel). Of the privileged group of Jewish courtiers, Isaac Abravanel was among the very few to reject baptism. In truth, perhaps as many as a third of the remaining Jews in Aragón and Castile rushed to yield themselves up to a process that already had been wreaking havoc among them for over a century. How many Jews clung to their faith and accepted expulsion? Historians have steadily revised the estimates downward. It is possible that some one hundred thousand initially departed, although as many as thirty thousand may secretly have returned in ensuing years (p. 168). At least that many remained as longstanding or recent conversos.

Once the shock of the decree registered, a burning issue for the impending fugitives was the estate they could take with them. The Catholic Monarchs had not intended that the Jews should depart in abject destitution. The edict permitted them to "barter, alienate, and dispose of all their movable and immovable property, freely and at will . . . to export their wealth and property, by sea or land, from our said kingdoms and dominions. . . ." Yet there was a caveat: "provided they do not take away gold, silver, [or] money." In theory, the Jews could mitigate the restriction by disposing of their homes and lands in exchange for movables, then by selling those possessions in their new lands of asylum. But the prospect was hardly realistic. In Aragón, King Fernando ordered a partial confiscation of Jewish real estate and chattels as security for revenues "owed" the Crown. Where homes and other possessions were allowed to be put on sale, they could be auctioned off only at distress prices. Landlords extorted from their Jewish tenants, demanding rent payments three months in advance. In some towns, local authorities barred Jews from leaving their neighborhoods to seek out buyers. As the weeks passed, therefore, and the deadline approached, people in their desperation would exchange an entire vineyard or an orchard for a donkey to carry their children or their aged and ailing parents. Some paid a thousand maravedis for a horse or gave away their homes for a bag of coins.

Where would they go? With the French border closed to professing Jews, there existed only two possible havens by land. Consequently, ten to twelve thousand of the exiles made their way into the northern border kingdom of Navarre. A far larger group, perhaps sixty to seventy thousand, journeyed toward the Portuguese frontier. Most of the remaining thirty thousand refugees continued on to southern ports, intending to embark by sea for North Africa, Italy, or (eventually) the Ottoman Empire. Among these, a small number managed the departure with a protected nest egg. Don Isaac Abravanel and his brothers Joseph and Jacob negotiated a private arrangement with the Catholic Monarchs. Writing off the funds they had advanced the rulers against uncollected tax revenues, each was allowed one thousand gold ducats and an unspecified quantity of jewels. With this remnant of their fortune in hand, the Abravanels then set sail from the port of Valencia for Italy.

But for the Jewish majority, the final stages of departure were unalleviated misery. Refugees choked the highways. At seaports, they were cursed, stoned, often beaten and robbed. Local merchants cheated them. Ship captains squeezed them dry. A contemporary observer, the priest Andrés Bernáldez, recalled:

> They went out from the lands of their birth, boys and adults, old men and children, on foot, and riding on donkeys and other beasts and in wagons. . . . They went by the roads and fields with much labor and ill-fortune, some collapsing, others getting up, some dying, others giving birth, others falling ill, so that there was no Christian who was not sorry for them. . . . The rabbis were encouraging them and making the women and boys sing and beat drums and tambourines, to enliven the people. And so they went out of Castile.

On August 2 and 3, 1492, the last professing Jews on Spanish soil clambered aboard ship in Seville and El Puerto de Santa María. At the smaller, nearby harbor of Palos de la Frontéra, three small caravels were waiting to hoist sail. Their commander, Christopher Columbus, noted with interest the departing procession of refugee vessels, a "fleet of misery and woe," as he described it in his log. The Jews would have agreed. For generations afterward, they would exalt their people's role as statesmen, physicians, and philosophers during eight hundred years—eight centuries!—of the Jewish presence in Spain. Lamenting the departed glory of an idealized race of Jewish hidalgos, they would manage also to embellish and romanticize their former homeland as an alembic of vibrant civilizations, each endlessly infusing the other. But that evaluation was for the bejeweled and enameled Spain of folklore, not for the rapacious zealots who had left them deracinated, plundered, and broken in mind and heart. August 2, 1492 by coincidence was the ninth day of the Hebrew month of Av, the fast day commemorating the destruction of the Temple in Jerusalem, and the Children of Israel were setting out yet again into the featureless limbo of exile.

CHAPTER IV

OTTOMAN DAWN

A Byzantine Legacy

In the year 1160, Benjamin ben Jonah, a gem-dealer of Tudela, set forth on a journey that would take him from his little Pyrenean kingdom of Navarre through northeastern Catalonia and southern France to Italy and Sicily, then on to the Near and Middle East, until his return home thirteen years later, in 1173. The purpose of this extended odyssey may have related to the gem trade. Benjamin of Tudela does not say. Of his voyage by land and sea, however, he tells us much. In medieval Hebrew, he provides a terse, fascinating description of the lands he visits, and specifically of their Jewish communities.

Nowhere is Benjamin more forthcoming than in his portrait of Constantinople. He devotes three pages to the great Byzantine capital, acclaiming its wealth and amplitude, its natural and architectural beauty. Yet his account of the local Jewry is rather more subdued:

> No Jews live in the city itself, for they have been located behind an inlet of the sea. . . . No Jew there is permitted to ride horseback . . . for their status is very low, and there is much hatred against them. . . . The tanners . . . throw out their dirty water in the streets before the doors of the Jewish houses and defile the Jews' quarters. So the Greeks hate the Jews . . . and subject them to great oppression, and beat them in the streets, and in every way treat them harshly.

The description was apt. Under Christian rule, the Jews of the Eastern Roman Empire had been reduced over the centuries to poverty and debasement. Whether in the capital or in the hinterland of Asia Minor or the Balkans, these Romaniotes, or Greek-speaking Jews, would have welcomed almost any change in their status.

That transformation in fact began early in the fourteenth century. A thousand miles to the east, in Central Asia, a succession of dynamic Turkish-warrior tribes were making their way southwestward. One of them, under the Osmanli (Ottoman) dynasty, managed to extend its sway over much of Anatolia. In later decades, infused by a crusading Islamic zeal, the Ottoman Turks pressed on as far as the European side of the Bosphorus, and even deep into the Balkan Peninsula. By the mid-1400s, large segments of the Byzantine Empire were in their hands. In turn, the modest Jewish settlements of Asia Minor and the Balkans sensed new opportunities for security and dignity. The demise of the hated Greek Christian regime also came at a propitious moment for Jews elsewhere. As far back as 1290, Jews had been driven from England. They had been evicted twice from France, in 1306 and in 1394, and intermittently from Central Europe throughout the fourteenth century. Emigration from Spain had gained momentum well before 1492. If most of the Ashkenazic Jews—those living in trans-Pyrenean Europe—found sanctuary in the newly rising Kingdom of Poland, the much larger populations of Sephardic and Romaniot Jews needed a refuge closer at hand, in their own Mediterranean world.

That asylum was offered by the Ottoman sultans. Although by no means untutored in the arts of administration, these rough-edged Asian warriors were quite prepared to leave the task of self-government to their *rayahs,* or non-Turkish communities, provided the latter accepted political subservience and paid their collective taxes. In fact, the Ottomans granted an even wider degree of toleration and solicitude to Jews than to other non-Moslems. Here was a people that had suffered bitterly from Christian oppression, whose animus toward the Byzantine and other Western Christian governments fully matched that of the Turks themselves. They could be trusted. And the Jews, for their part, responded gratefully to that confidence and benevolence. From Edirne (Adrianople), in Asia Minor, Rabbi Yitzchak Tsarfati in 1420 dispatched an open letter to colleagues in Germany:

> Your cries and laments have reached us. We have been told of all the sorrows and persecutions which you suffer in German lands. Listen, my brothers. . . . If you . . . knew even a tenth of what God has blessed us with in this land, you would give heed to no further difficulties. You would embark at once to us. . . . Here the Jew is not compelled to wear a yellow hat as a badge of shame. . . . You will be free of your enemies. Here you will find peace.

Well apprised, then, of this promising new Ottoman haven, European and Iberian Jews in the fifteenth century began migrating toward the Balkan Peninsula and Asia Minor in growing numbers.

Their presence was further augmented by an epochal event. This was Sultan Mehmet II's final, successful onslaught on Constantinople in 1453 and the transformation of the once-mighty Byzantine stronghold into the capital of a new Ottoman successor empire. Initially, the captured metropolis was a desolated shell of a city, shrunk by prolonged siege and starvation to barely fifty thousand inhabitants. Somehow it would have to be revitalized, and for that task vigorous and enterprising settlers were needed. Plainly, "Mehmet the Conqueror" was not interested in using Christians for this purpose; but neither did an influx of Turks appear a useful solution. However reliable as fellow Moslems, these hardy farmers and soldiers were not the people to generate a commercial revival. The importation of Jews seemed a more logical answer. To that end, in 1456, the sultan ordered the Romaniot Jews of Anatolia and the Balkans transplanted en masse to Constantinople.

The ordeal was painful, even traumatic. To ease the Jews' suffering and resentment, therefore, Mehmet offered his personal assurance of security:

> Who among you of all my people that is with me, may his God be with him, let him ascend to [Constantinople], the site of my royal throne. Let him dwell in the best of the land, each beneath his vine and fig tree, with silver and gold, with wealth and cattle. Let him dwell in the land, trade in it, and take possession of it.

Within the year, the number of Jews in the capital rose to seven thousand. Slowly, their economic circumstances improved. True to his word, Sultan Mehmet defended the Jews against their perennial enemies, the Greek Christians. He encouraged them to resume their vocation of tax-farming and welcomed Jewish financiers and physicians to his royal court. Manifestly, the ruler's promise was as valid as Rabbi Tsarfati's: "Here you will find peace."

A Sephardic Inundation

In the latter fifteenth century, far larger waves of Jews began migrating to the Ottoman world. This time most of the newcomers were refugees from Spain. Their flight to Ottoman territory was by no means the consequence of blind hope. Like their predecessors, they were assured of welcome. Bayezid II, who succeeded to the Ottoman throne in 1481, grasped no less astutely than had Mehmet II the value of a sophisticated commercial people who shared the Turks' distrust of the Christian world. Upon learning of King Fernando's expulsion decree in 1492, Bayezid allegedly exclaimed: "Can you call such a king wise and intelligent? He is impoverishing his country and enriching my kingdom."

So it happened. The newcomers settled in Constantinople and in towns throughout the Balkans and Asia Minor. In the process, they replenished Jewish communities that had been all but denuded by Mehmet II's earlier transplantation of Jews to the capital. Thus, Sephardic *cals* were established in Edirne, Izmir (Smyrna), Salonika, Kastoria, Bursa, Gallipoli, Tokat, Patras, Lepanto, Lárisa, Valona, Monastir (Bitola), Skopje, Janina, Siris, Corfu, Chios, and a necklace of smaller villages. Most of the newcomers were artisans or modest merchants. Some were peddlers. But a wave of later-arriving Portuguese marranos brought an even wider commercial experience. Soon, these former New Christians proved all but indispensable to the empire as assessors and collectors of taxes on salt, fisheries, sheep, candles, and wines; as minters of coins and moneylenders. As early as 1547, a French observer, Pierre Bellon de Mans, commented: "[The Jews] have taken over the traffic and commerce of Turkey to such an extent that the Turk's wealth and revenue is in their hands. [Their tax-farmers] set the highest price on the collection of tributes from the provinces and harbor dues from ships. . . ." Jews almost immediately filled the vacuum of Ottoman medicine. From their midst came the empire's most respected physicians. Virtually all Turkish courtiers and wealthy private citizens depended on their ministrations.

As far back as 1453, meanwhile, Sultan Mehmet had favored the appointment of a single leader to represent Ottoman Jews before the throne. In the manner of the Greek Orthodox patriarch, this spokesman would function as communal liaison for his people, as the eminence responsible for their collective tax payments and civic behavior. Initially, Mehmet's choice for the role was Moses ben Elijah Capsali, a prominent Romaniot rabbi in Constantinople. Yet apart from his title of "chief rabbi" and his ceremonial place at the royal *diwan,* Capsali acquired little of the authority of the Greek patriarch. The Sephardic newcomers maintained their own *cals,* their own rabbinical courts, their own tax-collectors, their own communal leaders. They would not accept a Romaniot as their spokesman.

In the provinces, those spokesmen tended to be rabbis. But in Constantinople, Jewish laymen increasingly were assuming this responsibility. The government did not object, so long as the Jewish *cals* administered themselves peacefully and met their fiscal responsibilities. For a while, these lay eminences even tended to be the sultan's physicians. Mehmet II himself unwittingly established the pattern. After his indifferent experience with Rabbi Capsali, the sultan turned to a young immigrant doctor from Italy, Ya'qub (Jacopo) of Gaeta. Serving as the sultan's physician and as his confidential adviser, Ya'qub in effect became Mehmet's finance minister, and thereby his de facto Jewish liaison. The practice continued in later years under Selim I and Suleiman I. Even so, no Jew ever achieved a spokesmanship for his people comparable to that of a renowned Sephardic immigrant family, the "House" of Nasi.

Beatriz da Luna—Doña Gracia

Its founder was a woman, Beatriz da Luna Mendes, better known to posterity as Doña Gracia Nasi. The lady's arrival in Constantinople in 1553 was noteworthy. Her caravan of four magnificently gilded coaches, pulled by a train of sleek horses and flanked by three dozen uniformed bodyguards, thundered into the city with an elaborate entourage of family members and retainers. Doña Gracia, forty-four years old, handsome, regal in bearing, entirely suited her times. Indeed, the sixteenth century was an age of famous women: Elizabeth, Mary, and Mary, Queen of Scots, in Britain; Lucrezia Borgia, Isabella d'Este, Caterina Sforza, and Vittoria Colonna in Italy; Catherine de Médicis in France; Esther Handali in Constantinople.

Born in Portugal in 1509, "christened" Beatriz da Luna, the new arrival was descended from a family that had fled from Spain to Portugal in 1492, there to undergo King Manoel's forced conversion five years later (p. 161). In Portugal, Beatriz was married to Francisco Mendes, the marrano owner of a prosperous diamond-importing firm. When Mendes died in 1536, leaving Beatriz with a young daughter, she moved on to the Spanish Netherlands, where her brother-in-law Diogo Mendes operated the company's branch in Antwerp. Joining him, Beatriz Mendes worked with Diogo in building the House of Mendes into one of Europe's greatest luxury trading enterprises.

Still nominally Catholic, the Mendes family all the while remained intensely Jewish in their private lives. They observed the Sabbath and other holidays as well as the dietary laws. Indeed, for them residence in Antwerp was only a transitional stage in the Jewish odyssey that originally had taken the family from Spain to Portugal. Even now, the House of Mendes directed an elaborate underground rescue organization for marrano refugees. From its headquarters in Antwerp, the firm's network of agents moved throughout Italy and the Balkans, sending back information on promising escape routes to the East, the location of "safe" inns and private homes. Ironically, it was the House of Mendes's very wealth that threatened this clandestine operation. Emperor Charles V, intent on preserving the firm's vast assets intact within his Habsburg realm, ordered the family kept under tight supervision. On two occasions, the ruler had Diogo placed under house arrest; both times, he was released at the intercession of Antwerp's mercantile community. Meanwhile, throughout the late 1530s the Inquisition was reviving in the Spanish Netherlands. Suspected judaizers were being arrested in growing numbers. For the House of Mendes, time plainly was running out in Antwerp.

By 1542, Diogo Mendes had devised elaborate arrangements for the secret transfer of family funds to Italy. But that year he died suddenly. It was his sister-in-law Beatriz who was left now to complete the operation. For help, she turned to her nephew João Migues. Despite his youth, João had already developed useful contacts in government circles. Shrewdly, he set about buying time by distributing "gifts" among influential court officials. Then, in November 1544, Beatriz suddenly departed with her daughter, her widowed sister, and her niece, ostensibly to "take the waters" at Aix-la-Chapelle. The women actually were crossing the Alps en route to Italy. They carried with them a significant portion of company assets in the form of jewels. Upon being informed of this development, Charles V, furious, ordered the residue of the Mendes estate impounded. Yet even for the Habsburg emperor, there were legal constraints against outright seizure. Judicial proceedings dragged on for over a year. In the meantime, João Migues succeeded in negotiating the conversion of still additional assets into bills of exchange on Italian banks. And then one day, even before the case was resolved, João himself disappeared, to follow his aunt's secret route across the Alps. Half the Mendes estate was left in Antwerp, but the family now had ample—even prodigious—reserves in their new haven.

That haven was Venice. Beatriz, João, and the other family members rented a luxurious mansion in the heart of the city and soon made their home a favored gathering place for other marranos. It was never an entirely secure existence, even in a comparatively tolerant republic. In 1551, coveting the Mendes fortune, the Venetian government placed Beatriz under house confinement as a suspected judaizer, and impounded nearly a third of her liquid assets. Fortunately, the family already had taken the precaution of secretly transferring funds abroad—in this instance, to Constantinople. Here they were able to count on the help of Moses Hamon, physician to Suleiman I. Hamon had raised the issue of the Mendes estate with the sultan. Suleiman and his advisers in turn were not dense in smelling a potential bonanza for the imperial economy. They swiftly devised a formula. It was to proclaim the Mendes family Ottoman subjects *in posse,* and thus under royal protection. The government of Venice in turn procrastinated for yet another six weeks but finally released a sizable portion of the impounded Mendes estate. It was more than enough to allow the family to move on.

The next way station was Ferrara. In this duchy, under the enlightened rule of the House of Este, former marranos could live as professing Jews. Here, then, Beatriz immediately resumed her original family name of Gracia Nasi. It was characteristic of the woman, too, that she gave generously of her time and money to patronize Jewish culture in Ferrara and to subsidize the translation of numerous Hebrew works into Spanish and Portuguese for other returning conversos. One of Doña Gracia's protégés was Samuel Usque, whose magnificent Portuguese prose-poem *Consolaçam as tribulaçoens de Israel* was written to fortify marranos in their lonely vigil against Christian oppression (p. 166). Significantly, Usque included a lengthy panegyric to Doña Gracia in the *Consolaçam:*

> With her golden hand and angelic purpose, she lifted the majority of our people in Europe from the abyss of this hardship and countless others where poverty and sin had hurled them. She continued to guide them until they were in safe hands, and until she had returned them to the obedience and precepts of their ancient God.

Others shared that evaluation. The author and former marrano Imanuel Aboab wrote of Doña Gracia's "excellent virtues and noble deeds." Amatus Lusitanus, a renowned marrano physician, described her as "adorned by all the virtues." For Moses Almosnin, a famed Salonikan rabbi, she was the "crown of the glory of goodly women."

In August 1552, with all financial transfers at last completed, Doña Gracia and her vast retinue set off for Turkey. It was a cautious, deliberate journey—through Italy to the Adriatic coast, then by sea to Ragusa (Dubrovnik), then by old Roman roads to Salonika. João Migues temporarily remained behind, but at his direction all passage rights had been negotiated in advance, all movables stored in warehouses en route. And so it was, after a voyage of six months, that the convoy made its unforgettable entrance into Constantinople. Doña Gracia's choice of residence was equally magisterial. Not for her the city's impacted Jewish quarters in Hasköy. Instead she settled among the European colony in Galata, just beyond the Golden Horn, where she supervised the construction of a palatial home for the family overlooking the Bosphorus (eventually this quarter, too, would become partially Jewish). Here the grande dame was attended to night and day by an elaborate train of servants and supplicants. She had a clear vision of her role in Constantinople. While her nephew eventually assumed responsibility for the family's business activities (pp. 84–85), Doña Gracia for the next dozen years gave herself over almost exclusively to the cause of her people. She lavishly supported hospitals, synagogues, talmudic academies, and schools; patronized scholars and writers; rescued hostages. Altogether, through her largesse, she dominated her community to an extent unparalleled by any Jewish woman in the history of the Diaspora.

Nowhere was Doña Gracia's devotion more evident than among the Jews of Ancona. The town itself was a modest Adriatic port under the jurisdiction of the Papal States. In 1555, when the fanatical Cardinal Gian Pietro Carafa ascended the pontifical throne as Paul IV, one of his first actions in launching the Counter-Reformation was to inaugurate the Inquisition in his own realm (pp. 228–29). Until then, the Jews of Ancona had thrived as barely disguised marranos. Now they were early victims of papal reaction: twenty-six were condemned and burned, and far greater numbers suffered imprisonment and confiscation of property. Tremolos of horror swept through the entire Mediterranean Jewish world. Among those most deeply affected was Doña Gracia. She knew some of the victims personally. Moreover, this time she was in a position to intercede on their behalf. Promptly arranging an audience with Suleiman I, Doña Gracia explained the heartrending circumstances of the Jews of Ancona, then entreated the sultan to assume a protectorate over them as he had earlier over her own family. Suleiman agreed on the spot. Although he limited that protection to victims who had resided on Ottoman soil, the qualification was easily finessed. Most Ancona Jews at one time or another had done business in Ottoman Balkan cities. Grand Vizier Rustem Pasha then summoned the papal consul and demanded the release of all Ottoman "protectees" in Ancona, together with their property. If this was not done, the vizier suggested, their losses would be made good from Anconan agents and merchants trading in the Balkan Levant.

Unfortunately for the Jews, Paul IV was not a man to be intimidated by a Moslem potentate. He refused to stay the Inquisition's hand—even when Ottoman customs officials duly boarded Anconan vessels and auctioned off the cargoes. At this point, Doña Gracia and her nephew pressed Jewish shippers and importers to organize their own boycott of Ancona. The proposal won acceptance throughout the empire. In one Ottoman city after another, local rabbis even agreed to enforce the embargo by decreeing a *cherem,* a ban of excommunication, on any Jew violating the boycott. Led by the House of Nasi, all Jewish business with the Italian Adriatic soon was shifted from Ancona to the smaller anchorage of Pesaro. The Ottoman government cooperated by encouraging non-Jewish traders similarly to direct their maritime operations elsewhere. Never before in the history of the Diaspora had Jews fought back against oppression with such collective vigor.

At first, the boycott proved remarkably effective. Ancona's economy was driven to the verge of paralysis, and several of its most important mercantile houses went bankrupt. The quarantine might quite possibly have brought the papal regime to heel, if the Jews of Ancona themselves had not fractured the common front. More than other merchants, they warned, it was their own who were facing ruin. Who, after all, were the major traders in Ancona? Whereupon, sobered by the warning, the Jews in Edirne broke ranks, then in Bursa, Izmir, Yambol, and finally Salonika. The blockade crumbled. Ancona's economy slowly revived.

It was a painful defeat for Doña Gracia. Over the next few years, she withdrew into herself. Although remaining an endless source of generosity, she now allowed her nephew to assume the spokesmanship for Jewish causes. Then, in 1569, Doña Gracia died of congestive heart failure, at the age of sixty. Twenty thousand persons attended her funeral. Indeed, memorial services were held throughout the Jewish world. In Salonika, the poet Saadia Lungo declaimed:

> Every mother town in Israel
> Weeps for the fate of those in anguish left.
> Gone is the brilliance;
> My mourning is unspeakable,
> And broken is my heart.

Not since the days of Salome Alexandra, the Hasmonean queen of Judah, had a woman's death been so profoundly mourned by the Jewish people.

The Wealth of Empire

If Doña Gracia spoke for a community at the pinnacle of its fortunes, a decisive factor in her influence was the power and wealth of the Ottoman realm itself. Sultans Selim I and Suleiman I added Syria and Egypt to the Ottoman state, then Mecca and Medina, then Belgrade, Buda, Baghdad, and much of North Africa. The sheer breadth of the empire's territorial conquests measurably influenced Ottoman Jewish life. For several decades, it provided them a wider ambit of law and order. As in earlier centuries of Islamic grandeur, a unified political entity also opened out broader opportunities for commerce. Indeed, a tangible consequence of the Jews' revived affluence was the sheer increase of their numbers. Constantinople's Jewish settlement numbered eight thousand by 1478, eighteen thousand by 1524, and reached possibly thirty thousand by 1570—thus becoming the single largest Jewish community in the world. Salonika in that same year encompassed a Jewish population of approximately twenty thousand. Baghdad, whose Jewry had shrunk to fewer than two thousand at the time of the Turkish conquest, approached fifteen thousand in the latter sixteenth century. By then, the empire's Jewish population totaled possibly three hundred thousand altogether.

A community this large in effect generated its own economic momentum. For one thing, it produced an uncommonly large number of artisans. As early as 1555, a German visitor, Hans Dernschwam, an employee of the Fugger banking house, noted: "The Jews of Constantinople . . . have goldsmiths, lapidaries, painters, tailors, butchers, apothecaries, physicians, surgeons, cloth-weavers . . . barbers, mirror-makers, dyers . . . silk-workers, gold-washers, . . . assayers, engravers." Nicholas de Nicolay, accompanying the French ambassador to Constantinople in 1557, observed: "[The Jews] have among them superb workmen of all arts and crafts, and especially of the [marranos] recently . . . driven out of Spain and Portugal, who to the great detriment and damage of Christianity, have taught the Turks . . . to make artillery, harquebuses, gunpowder, shot and other ammunition. They have also set up printing, never before seen in these countries. . . ."

Beyond this talented pool of artisans, the Jews produced a far larger proportion of businessmen than did any other subjugated nation. Most of their merchants remained modest shopkeepers. Yet the classical Jewish roles of tax-farmer, moneylender, and importer-exporter were established here as early as the fifteenth century. In the following decades, Jews once again emerged as a preeminent mercantile elite in many sectors of commerce. "There are no wares which the Jews do not carry about and trade in," observed Hans Dernschwam. "Just as soon as a foreign ship comes in from Alexandria, Jaffa, Venice, and other places, the Jews are the first to clamber over the side. They [also] import all the goods that come to Constantinople from India. . . ." And in the seventeenth century an unfriendly critic, Michel Febre, acknowledged that "[The Jews] are so adroit and diligent that they make themselves indispensable to everybody. One cannot find any well-to-do family among Turks and foreign merchants which does not employ a Jew in its service, be it for appraising merchandise and its quality, for serving as interpreter, or for giving advice on any other occurrence."

As elsewhere in the Sephardic Diaspora, these talents were applied with particular effect in international trade. Nicolay was impressed that "[the Jews] have in their hands the most and greatest traffic and merchandise and ready money that is in the Levant. And likewise the . . . warehouses, the best furnished with all sorts of merchandise, which are in Constantinople, are those of the Jews." In his magisterial economic history of Europe, Fernand Braudel describes a vast sixteenth-century Jewish trading network based in Constantinople, Izmir, Salonika, and Edirne. Each of these four cities in turn produced satellite Jewish communities. Sarajevo, Monastir (Bitola), and Uskub (Skopje) linked Salonikan Jewry to the Adriatic and Venice. The Jewish settlements of Philippopolis (Plovdiv), Sofia, Nikopol, and Widdin dotted the overland trade route from Constantinople via Edirne to the Danubian Basin, and thence to Central Europe. Izmir was the terminus of the major trade routes from Asia Minor into Anatolia, and also linked the smaller Anatolian Jewish communities of Aydin, Tyre, Manisa, and Bergama. Wherever Ottoman Jews did business, moreover, they were able to conduct their trade almost entirely with their fellow Sephardim. They spoke the same language, after all, operated within their own commercial codes, resolved their disputes within their own judicial system. Few Gentiles could match these advantages.

Don Joseph Nasi

As matters developed, Jewish influence within the empire eventually was reflected less in the person of the redoubtable Doña Gracia than in the person of her nephew. Like her, João Migues was born to *convertido* parents in Lisbon, one of two sons of Gracia's late brother. Both youths fled with their aunt from Portugal to the Spanish Netherlands in 1536. Both grew up among the marrano haute bourgeoisie in Antwerp and attended the University of Louvain. Subsequently, João Migues enrolled in the Spanish army for a brief stint as a cavalry officer, then joined the House of Mendes. Upon Diogo Mendes's death not long afterward, João assumed direction of the firm. As we recall, it was he who persuaded his aunt to begin transferring her funds out of the country, then to depart Antwerp for a "vacation" in Aix-la-Chapelle. Two years later, in 1546, João himself managed to rejoin Doña Gracia during her stay in Venice, and in 1553 he followed in the family's wake to Constantinople. Indeed, his arrival in the Ottoman capital by armed coach-convoy produced the identical sensation created by his aunt some months earlier. In April 1553, João Migues underwent circumcision and became Joseph Nasi. In June, he married Doña Gracia's daughter, Reyna, thereby becoming the great lady's son-in-law as well as her nephew.

Building a sumptuous mansion for himself and his bride overlooking the Bosphorus, Don Joseph set about augmenting the family fortune. This he did by distributing "loans" to Sultan Suleiman I and government ministers, thereby winning in return numerous lucrative government tax-farming and other concessions. With his network of Jewish business agents in Europe, moreover, Nasi became privy to vital political information in foreign capitals. As the French ambassador Jean de la Vigny recalled, Don Joseph possessed "the best means of hearing about anything happening in the West, better and earlier than anyone in the world." These insights he shared with the government, becoming "the true mirror in which [the sultan] saw all the developments in Christendom."

At the same time, Don Joseph grew especially close to Prince Selim, who in 1566 ascended the throne as Selim II. Although something of a playboy (cruelly remembered as "Selim the Sot"), the new sultan was shrewd enough to depend extensively on the advice of Don Joseph, whose influence at court soon became all but unprecedented. Even the Greek patriarch frequently sought his intercession. Foreign governments obsequiously invoked his goodwill. Eventually, it was Joseph Nasi who played the central role in negotiating the empire's peace treaty with Austria and its commercial treaty with Poland. "Illustrious prince and beloved friend," a grateful King Sigismund II of Poland wrote Don Joseph in 1570, "most welcome to Us is the demonstration of Your Excellency's great good will toward Us. . . . Your Excellency must be assured that We in our turn . . . will be prepared to render similar good will to your Excellency, whensoever the opportunity may offer." Altogether, Jewishness was the marque of Ottoman diplomacy by then. The original versions of seventeenth-century Ottoman trade treaties often were formulated in Hebrew, to accommodate the numerous Jewish agents and dragomans employed by both sides.

As for Selim II, his esteem for his Jewish friend seemed limitless. In one of his first acts of government, he created Nasi "Duke of Naxos." The title was no mere honorific; it signified the enfiefed overlordship of the island of Naxos and the surrounding Cyclades. Owned until recent years by Venice, this Aegean archipelago lay just west of Asia Minor, between the Greek mainland and the Dodecanese islands. Naxos alone encompassed some four hundred square miles and possessed valuable coastal inlets, as well as rich marble deposits and extensive olive, orange, and pomegranate orchards. It was an impressive coup for a man who only thirty years earlier had been a suspect New Christian in Portugal. Never before had a Diaspora Jew ruled over a territory and its people. Joseph Nasi well appreciated the distinction. Although he left the administration of the island duchy to others, he abandoned nothing of the dignity and pomp inherent in his new rank.

At the same time, Don Joseph's unique influence at court enhanced his status as "prince" of his people. So did his munificence. Like his aunt, he funded synagogues, libraries, printing presses, and orphanages, patronized rabbis, scholars, bibliophiles, writers, and mendicants. They came and went from his mansion in an endless stream. Rabbinic documents addressed him with the formula reserved for royalty—"May his glory increase." Perhaps Nasi's single best-remembered effort for the Jews was inspired by a dream of Doña Gracia's. It was to establish a permanent grave for her late husband, Francisco Mendes, in the Holy Land. According to Jewish tradition, bodies interred in sacred soil would be resurrected earliest. Each year, therefore, shiploads of Jewish bones arrived in Palestine for reburial; and in 1559, Doña Gracia arranged for Francisco Mendes's remains to be exhumed and transported from Lisbon to Tiberias. Revered in Jewish memory, this ancient Galilean town had sustained Jewish learning for centuries after the fall of Jerusalem. Much of the Palestinian Talmud had been written in Tiberias. Maimonides was buried there.

In fact, by the sixteenth century Tiberias was desolate and all but deserted. Yet this was Doña Gracia's opportunity. In 1559, it was a simple matter for her to win the permission of Suleiman I to colonize the town with Jews. As an inducement, she offered to pay taxes to the Ottoman treasury far exceeding those currently generated by Tiberias's impoverished handful of inhabitants. The sultan promptly allocated Doña Gracia a tract in the "holy city," including land reputed to be suitable for silkworm cultivation. As an additional gesture of goodwill, Suleiman put Joseph Nasi in charge of the project. Don Joseph, in turn, assigned a friend, Joseph ben Ardit, as his deputy. When Selim II ascended the throne, he appointed Nasi "lord" over Tiberias and its neighboring villages, then ordered the district pasha "to do everything that [Joseph ben Ardit] would ask for." Immediately, the pasha set about recruiting Arab workmen for new construction projects in Tiberias.

Eventually, in 1564, under harsh Turkish prodding, Arab workmen erected a modest security wall, and several buildings were completed later as an incipient town center. A few dozen Jews arrived then, some from the Ottoman Empire, others from Europe. Under Ardit's direction, mulberry trees (for silkworms) were imported from France, merino sheep (for wool) from Spain. In the latter 1560s, a modest number of Italian Jews immigrated there as refugees from papal persecution. Learning of Nasi's project in the Holy Land, these fugitives had lauded "the crown and glory and grace of the prince, the lord and noble . . . Don Joseph." Their gratitude was well placed. Nasi was bringing them to Palestine at his own expense. In 1569, his convoy of four vessels arrived at the Italian port of Cori and seven hundred Jews embarked. Two months later, they reached Tiberias.

Unfortunately, the living and working conditions awaiting the refugees were more oppressive even than in their native Italy. The heat was enervating. Malaria and typhoid decimated the newcomers' ranks. Soon, Jewish immigration to the Holy Land came to a halt. The Tiberias enterprise was never actually abandoned, however. A small Jewish nucleus remained. Neither did the government officially revoke the scheme. Indeed, the venture would continue even after Nasi's death, when a new sponsor appeared, in the form of Alvaro Mendes. A former Portuguese convertido (apparently not related to the House of Mendes) who had settled in Constantinople as a re-identified Jew, Mendes adopted the name Solomon ibn Ya'ish. He played a moderately important role afterward in Ottoman diplomacy, and, like Nasi, he was appointed a duke—in this case, of Mytilene (ancient Lesbos). In the late sixteenth century, ibn Ya'ish similarly took an interest in the Tiberias project and dispatched his son Jacob there to revive it. But upon reaching the Holy Land, Jacob became a student of mysticism and displayed no further concern for worldly affairs. When Solomon ibn Ya'ish died in 1603, the colony lost its final influential protector. It subsequently expired.

During the 1570s, meanwhile, at the height of his power, Joseph Nasi became obsessed with a pet scheme of his own. It was to conquer the island of Cyprus, a Venetian dependency he regarded as the key to the eastern Mediterranean. The plan encountered resistance among Nasi's rivals at court. Led by Grand Vizier Mehmet Sokolu, these opponents preferred diplomacy to a military expedition. But Nasi persisted and eventually won over Sultan Selim. In June 1570, therefore, a vast Turkish armada carrying some fifty thousand troops passed through the Dardanelles; two weeks later, it reached Cyprus. Within a month, the Turkish expeditionary force captured Nicosia, then set about massacring all twenty thousand of the city's inhabitants. This act of wanton brutality achieved nothing beyond stiffening the resistance of other Cypriot communities. Famagusta managed to hold out a full year; and although the town finally was overrun, the cost for the Turks was ten thousand lives. At sea, Turkish casualties were even heavier. In 1571, a combined Spanish-Venetian fleet destroyed the Ottoman navy in the Gulf of Lepanto, with the loss of eighteen thousand Turkish lives. Two years later, Venice signed a peace treaty that relinquished Cyprus to the Turks. But the exhausting campaign had brought no glory to Joseph Nasi.

Don Joseph's influence thus began to wane following the death of Selim II in 1574. Although he was permitted to keep his revenues and dignities, otherwise he soon was reduced to little more than a gilded obscurity. In 1579, he died. The Duchy of Naxos did not continue in the

Nasi family; there was no son and heir. Yet Don Joseph's most enduring
accomplishment, in retrospect, may indeed have been the conquest of
Cyprus, painful as it was. The island remained in Ottoman possession for
the uncommon span of three centuries, until it was taken over for Britain
by still another Jew, Benjamin Disraeli. Otherwise, Don Joseph's reputation as an éminence grise transcended his actual achievements as a
statesman. Reaching as far as England in garbled form, it inspired Christopher Marlowe in 1589 to write his famed drama *The Jew of Malta*. Its
theme was

> The story of a rich and famous Jew
> Who liv'd in Malta.

In Marlowe's version, the Jew Barabas, maddened by persecution and
intent on wreaking horrible vengeance on the Christian world, plots with
the Turks but ultimately is destroyed by his own conspiracy. With his vast
wealth, overweening ambition, anti-Christian bias, Machiavellian scheming, and hispanicisms of speech, with his rise to the governorship of Malta
(read Naxos) and intimacy with "Selim Calymath, son to the Grand
Seignior"—Marlowe's Jew could only have been one man.

After Nasi's death, Jews continued to figure prominently in Ottoman
politics and commerce, but exalted figures among them were rare. Two
physicians, Solomon Nathan Ashkenazi and Moses Benveniste, advised
Sultan Murad III on foreign policy. Solomon ibn Ya'ish was well rewarded for his useful European intelligence contacts (p. 87). In the late
sixteenth century, Esther Handali became the secretary-confidante of
Suleiman's and Selim's sultanas and daughters, and acted as intermediary
between the harem and the Jewish community. Esther held the position
until she was well into her eighties, and her influence-peddling at the
seraglio made her a wealthy woman. But in 1593 she dabbled in politics
once too often, supporting her own nominee for a billet that had been
promised to another. Angered, the rejected candidate persuaded Sultan
Murad III of Esther's "treachery." At the sultan's orders, she was stabbed
to death in the seraglio courtyard. Horses then dragged her corpse to the
public square, where dogs ate it clean.

The late sixteenth century ended a unique era of Jewish preeminence
in Ottoman affairs. Joseph Nasi's widow, Reyna, witnessed the transition.
Surviving in lonely grandeur in her Bosphorus mansion, Reyna nurtured
memories of a furtive marrano existence in Lisbon, a cloak-and-dagger
journey of escape across Europe, acquaintance with royalty (in Antwerp,
the queen mother Marie actually had sought to negotiate a match for her),
and eventually flight to Constantinople, where she reigned as duchess of

Naxos until her death in 1599. Nearly three centuries would pass before another Jewish "dynasty," the House of Rothschild, achieved comparable power and splendor in public affairs.

Ottoman Jewry at Efflorescence

The Jews were still a heterogeneous community. Dispersed widely throughout the empire, separate congregations of Romaniotes, Ashkenazim, Sephardim—even Sephardic subcommunities from various Iberian towns—functioned separately, each with its own rabbis, rituals, and liturgical variations; each with its own schools, cemeteries, abattoirs, courts, and assessors. This extensive intramural diversity notwithstanding, Jewish self-government functioned remarkably well. At all times, it enjoyed official Ottoman approbation. While other Turkish and non-Moslem peoples also maintained their own institutions, the Turks felt particularly comfortable with the Jews in their shared distrust of Christians and in the complementarity of their economies. As in the case of the Arabs, moreover, both peoples evinced common Eastern origins and even a certain intermingled folklore. As in Andalusia, the Ottoman synagogue bore a close architectural similarity to the mosque. With few limits on their construction, synagogues of all shapes and sizes went up by the hundreds in cities and towns throughout the empire. Within their premises, Jews worshipped, transacted community affairs, educated their children, conducted litigation, assessed taxes.

Communal "sovereignty" was reflected as well in physical and social separation. Each *rayah* people was strictly demarcated from the Moslem majority, and from each other. Those Jews who arrived in Constantinople during the reign of Bayezid II (1481–1512) were settled along the southern shores of the Golden Horn, between the Greek quarter of Phanar and the walls of the city, in an area known as Balat. Comparably delimited Jewish quarters were established in the other major cities of Turkey. But whether in Izmir, Bursa, or Edirne, the Jews were on their own. In common with other religioethnic communities, their cultural life was essentially inner-directed. The role of Jews in Ottoman medicine remained preeminent, to be sure, both as practitioners and as contributors to medical literature. Disproportionate, also, was the Jewish contribution to the performing arts, especially drama. As late as the seventeenth century, theatrical performances in the principal Turkish cities were mounted almost entirely by Jews. Printing, too, was essentially a Sephardic contribution, although less in the Turkish language (whose Arabic script was forbidden to non-Moslems) than in Hebrew, Spanish, and Portuguese. But otherwise, so thoroughly were Jews—and some Christians—excluded from Turkish social and cultural life that it was not until the late nineteenth century that they mastered the Turkish language. The lacuna entirely characterized the stratified mosaic of Ottoman society.

A specifically Jewish cultural life, on the other hand, was a much more fully developed phenomenon. Indeed, in their growing numbers the Sephardic newcomers transformed their Ottoman enclave into the world center of Jewish scholarship for much of the sixteenth century. Constantinople even became known briefly as the "city of scholars and scribes." Its seminaries, like those of Salonika, Safed, and Jerusalem, took the place of the once-renowned academies of Córdoba, Toledo, and Girona. One of these, directed in Constantinople by the eminent scholar Joseph Levi, was underwritten by Doña Gracia and Don Joseph Nasi. Another, supported by Solomon ibn Ya'ish and his sons, produced the largest number of rabbis in all the Ottoman Empire. Still other academies operated in Izmir, Edirne, Bursa, Angora (Ankara), Nikopol, Tiriya, and Corfu.

It was also in Turkey that Joseph ibn Verga completed his father Solomon's celebrated chronicle of persecutions, *Shevet Yehuda* (The Tribe of Judah), and the former Lisbon rabbi Jacob Tam ben David ibn Yahya published his revered consolatory work *Yossifun*. Other Sephardic literary figures included the mystic Abraham ben Eliezer Halevi, who found in the Book of Daniel assurance that the redemption would begin in 1524 and that the Messiah would reveal himself in Upper Galilee in 1530. To fortify his people's hearts meanwhile, Rabbi Halevi produced a remarkable homily, *Megilat Amrafel* (The Testimony of [King] Amrapal), a flaming apotheosis of martyrdom based on the Song of Songs. These messianic-mystical works would figure increasingly in Jewish religious life from the sixteenth century on, although their principal source no longer would be Constantinople but Safed and Salonika (chaps. VI–VII).

Poetry, too, experienced a brief afterglow in the sixteenth-century empire. It was based largely on the old Hispanic meter-structure, a form that actually was taught at a Jewish academy of poetry in Constantinople. Within its premises, one scholar translated from Latin into Hebrew; another from Castilian into Hebrew; a third rendered the poetical books of the Bible into Greek; a fourth translated Italian-Jewish poems into Castilian. Among the refugee literati from Spain and Portugal, however, few were stars of the earlier Andalusian magnitude. Perhaps the single lyricist of quality was Solomon ben Mazal Tov, whose best collections were "Zionides," laments to Zion, and were specifically adapted to the forms and meters of Turkish and Arabic folk songs.

Altogether, the Ottoman Jewish sunburst was a mixed heritage, a com-

bination of royal benevolence and bureaucratic callousness, of economic
vitality and cultural inconsistency. It began, after all, with the enforced
transplantation of Romaniot Jews to the capital and was followed by
recurrent fiscal extortions, intermittent arrests, and occasional executions.
Even under such comparatively permissive sultans as Bayezid, Suleiman,
Selim I, and Selim II, Jews were periodically reminded of their status as
dhimmis (*dhinnis* in Turkish), forbidden to employ indentured servants, to
dress "immodestly," to ride horses. But whatever the inconvenience or
even harshness of these constraints, Ottoman Jews invariably were thank-
ful, and usually obsequious, to their royal masters. How could any Jew be
indifferent to the sanctuary granted them after the Iberian nightmare of
Inquisition and Exile? In the responsa literature and homiletics of the
time, that gratitude is all but overwhelming. As austere a rabbinic scholar
as Samuel de Medina could write:

> He who is not concerned with honoring our king, the great and pious
> sultan (may his glory increase), would be better off if he had not come
> into the world, for it is an obligation . . . to pay solemn heed to his
> pronouncements and obey his orders and decrees as it is an obligation
> to obey the laws and commandments of the King of the World.

The resplendent empire had produced a new breathing space for its harried stepchildren. They would not forget. Nor, in the centuries to follow,
would an ever harsher reality be allowed to occlude a progressively utopi-
anized memory.

CHAPTER V

TURKISH SUNSET

Stepchildren of the Sick Man

The jeweled Old City of Istanbul, Europe's peninsular last gasp at the threshold of Asia Minor, remains intact within a triangle of Byzantine walls, a Marmaran coastline, and a Golden Horned maritime inlet off the Bosphorus. Its mightiest icons—the Aya Sofya, the Topkapi Palace, the Edirne and Great Golden gates, the Suleymaniye, Mihrimah, and Blue mosques—all survive in pristine and profitable splendor. In a headlong race for the twenty-first century, it is modern Istanbul that has undergone rampant, uncontrollable growth. Municipal squares, intended as settings for prized monuments, are desolations of tarmac. The new commercial center of Beyoglu, with its luxury hotels and airline offices, camouflages a shantytown of lean-to retail shops and jerry-built housing. Malodorous tanneries divide the castle of the Seven Towers from the garden suburbs along the Marmara coast. It is "progress," of course, and here as elsewhere in Turkey its momentum seems unstoppable. Amidst the chaos, multistory buildings are going up from district to district, together with new schools, hospitals, bridges, airport terminals. A girdle of elegant villas has all but preempted the once-verdant Bosphorus coast and the Marmara's floriant Princess Islands. Restaurants, theaters, concert halls are filled. Turkey is still a developing nation, but hardly any longer a third-world country.

The revival has proceeded far more rapidly than the long, slow malaise and deterioration of the parent empire. It was the six-decade reigns of Selim I, Suleiman I, and Selim II, ending in 1574, that marked the apogee of the Ottoman golden age. Afterward, Turkish military expansion in Europe foundered against stiffening Habsburg resistance. Even the army's conquest of the Arab Middle East and the North African littoral proved dysfunctional in the long run. Vast and dispersed, the new territories seriously overextended the imperial administration. Almost simultaneously, a gradual shift of historic maritime trade routes from the Mediterranean toward the Atlantic threatened the Ottoman economy. With its customs stations bypassed and its cash coffers depleted, the Turkish government soon was reduced to accepting its funds wherever it could find them. Increasingly, it found them in bribes—indeed, in bribery at every level, from local officials to the royal harem and royal court itself. The *ulema,* the Moslem religious hierarchy, conceivably might have fostered a spirit of reform. But by the seventeenth century Ottoman Islam had calcified, and its ideological fundamentalism in turn tinctured the empire's juridical and educational systems, virtually its entire popular culture. By the early 1700s, the very structure of the Ottoman realm appeared to be succumbing to political and social enervation.

Those years of imperial enfeeblement and religiocultural atrophy were somber ones for the Jews. In part, the decline in their status reflected the decline of the empire itself. Yet Jewish economic and cultural attrition was far more extensive than among other non-Moslem communities. It was exacerbated by a virtual cessation of Jewish immigration from Europe, the traditional reservoir of Sephardic artisans and merchants. In turn, Ottoman Greeks, favored by the solicitude and rising power of Christian Europe, began to preempt the Jewish role in the imperial economy. The Greeks dispatched their sons to European universities and encouraged their young men to acquire the Western skills and sophisticated trading connections that the Jews previously had all but monopolized.

The reversal of roles was accompanied by a widening Greek campaign of violence against Jewish neighborhoods in Constantinople, Bursa, Izmir, Edirne, and other Ottoman cities. Ostensibly the pogroms were linked to blood-libel accusations. But in fact, they were rooted in economic competition. More ominously yet, they exploited an emergent vacuum of royal protection. Indeed, fearful of offending the Greeks' European patrons, the government now also permitted Greeks and Armenians to supplant Jewish tax- and customs-collectors. By the early eighteenth century, as a result, the French consul in Alexandria could report that the loss of the Egyptian customs monopoly had "completely ruined the Jewish nation." Elsewhere in the empire, the government similarly replaced Jews as imperial agents and dragomans. Then, in 1826, Sultan Mahmud II disbanded the perennially rebellious janissary corps. This professional military caste had long been a mainstay of the Jewish middle class. For nearly two centuries, Jews had functioned as its quartermasters, purveyors, and textile suppliers (p. 134). The loss of the janissary connection soon

proved devastating for the wider Jewish economy. By the late 1700s and
early 1800s, Jews were reduced increasingly to marginal vocations, as
petty shopkeepers and housepainters, even as porters, peddlers, bootblacks, and ragpickers.

As far back as the sixteenth century, too, the incorporation of millions
of Arabs into the empire produced a Moslem majority for the first time
under Ottoman rule. Reflecting that predominance, the government in
later years began enforcing the dhimmi laws with a new vigor. This time,
the Jews suffered far more than did the Christians. Without European
"brother" governments to intercede on their behalf, they were subjected
once again to humiliating sumptuary regulations on clothing, limitations
on synagogue construction and repair, painfully segregated residential
quarters. In 1728, a government decree uprooted several hundred Constantinople Jews from their traditional neighborhoods in the Balat district;
their presence evidently defiled a nearby mosque. The Jews' successor
neighborhoods, warrens of congested interlocking courtyards, deteriorated into shabby slums and thus became the objects of still further
Moslem contempt and intimidation. Rabbinical responsa of the eighteenth century provide despairing accounts of robberies, assaults, even
killings. At a time when Jews in Western lands were inching toward
emancipation, the status of Jews in Constantinople was described by
Charles MacFarlane, a British business agent, as "the last and most
degraded of the Turkish rayahs . . . loaded with the concurrent and utter
contempt of Frank [European], Turk, and Armenian. . . . Throughout the
Ottoman dominions, their pusillanimity is so excessive that they will flee
before the uplifted hand of a child."

Spiritual Infirmity, Linguistic Transformation

The collapse of the Jews' economic and political circumstances was inevitably reflected in their communal and cultural life. Fully alert to the
venality of the Ottoman judicial system, Jews too now resorted to bak-
sheesh to overrule or evade the judgments of their own courts. Bribery
then also began to infect the Jewish fiscal structure. Payoffs to communal
assessors gradually shifted the tax burden from the affluent to the poorer
classes. Still another factor in this Jewish "spiritual" debilitation was the
belated impact of the millennialist hysteria that had been aroused, then
dashed, by the seventeenth-century false messiah Shabbatai Zvi (chap.
VII). Afterward, fundamentalism reigned uncontested within the Jewish
community. Local rabbis functioned increasingly as watchdogs of communal morality, even of social minutiae. Regulating Sabbaths and other

holy days on an hour-by-hour basis, they monitored the precise length of men's beards and the shape of their headgear, and forbade women to appear in public unless veiled. Schoolchildren learned their daily lessons exclusively under obscurantist religious teachers.

The ossification of seventeenth- and eighteenth-century Islamic culture compounded this Jewish malaise. Although Jews in Turkey and other Moslem provinces resided in their own quarters, they could not avoid exposure to many of their neighbors' customs and superstitions: their incantations, conjurations, and amulets; their homeopathic remedies and dietary proscriptions against physical afflictions; and an omnipresent "evil eye" (p. 196). Jewish family life also became a microcosm of Near Eastern sociology. Like the Moslems, Jews living in joint courtyards often intermarried with second or even first cousins, frequently producing off-spring whose physiological and intellectual characteristics over the generations were at best unlovely, at worst dysfunctional.

A particularly interesting feature of this inbred existence was the emergence of a unique Judeo-Spanish dialect, Ladino, a tongue that evolved century by century, with regional variations, throughout the Ottoman Empire. Ladino was not to be confused with the pure Castilian or Portuguese spoken by Sephardic Jews in Western Europe. These latter often were former conversos, Jews who had continued to live under Spanish and Portuguese rule well into the 1500s and 1600s. Even upon reaching Holland, England, or the Americas, where they later reverted to Judaism, "Western" Sephardim maintained contact with Iberian civilization in its Golden Age and proudly spoke and wrote its languages. Not so the loyal and observant Sephardic majority that had departed Spain in the fifteenth century to rebuild their lives in the Ottoman Empire. In spoken form, their tongue was heavily penetrated by Hebrew words; in written form, either for religious texts or for business or personal correspondence, the vernacular was transliterated into "Rashi," a modified version of Hebrew script or (later) Hebrew voweled lettering. Subsequently, the patois was further leavened with Turkish and Slavic words adapted from the communities of Jewish settlement—Constantinople, Salonika, Sarajevo, Sofia, and others. So it was, over the centuries, that this petrified pre-Cervantes, pre–Golden Age Spanish evolved into Ladino, a lingua franca unique to the Sephardim of the Ottoman world.

In the eighteenth century, moreover, Ladino gradually began to nurture its own literature. The Jerusalem-born Jacob Culi gave the development its early momentum. After settling in Constantinople in the early 1720s, Culi produced a number of treatises on the Bible. His masterpiece was *Me'am Lo'ez* (From a Strange-Tongued People), a multivolume thesaurus of biblical, talmudic, and midrashic literature. Written in simple, popular Ladino, *Me'am Lo'ez* for the first time transmuted an essentially oral dialect into a literary vehicle. Over the years, then, a modest secular literature also began to emerge in Ladino. Much of it was based on *romanceros*, popular medieval Spanish ballads. These folk epics and folk songs varied slightly from one Ottoman community to the next, but a common feature was their de-Christianization, the tendency to adapt the structure and meter of Spanish romanceros to purely Jewish themes. Thus, in the "Song of Death," a ballad of Salonika, a Moorish chieftain and Christian maiden of medieval Andalusia are transformed into a Christian monarch and a Jewish woman:

> Seven sons had Hannah,
> Hannah the good Jewess.
> The king he sent for them
> All on the same day.
>
> "Come here, son of Hannah,
> Hannah the good Jewess,
> Come take my crown
> And on my throne sit down."
>
> "Your crown I do not need,
> On your throne I shall not sit.
> I'll not reject my Holy Law
> Or idolatry heed. . . ."

But there were also ballads taken directly from Iberian Jewish folklore. The epic *Poema de Yosef,* an anonymous fifteenth-century work, retells the story of Joseph and his brothers:

> Of him our Holy Scriptures the following relate
> In words of witnesses who were so fortunate
> That they saw his face so gentle and stature great,
> For in truth a giant was he and his name was Joseph.
>
> Joseph always feared the mighty Lord of Hosts
> And was with his brothers a shepherd of the flocks.
> At that time it was that he sinned one of the sins,
> Causing them to quarrel with their father over Joseph. . . .

Most of these ballads evolved from semispontaneous recitations given at festive events, only later making their way to the written page.

In the twentieth century, interest in Ladino revived among Hispanicists, who found it a gold mine of medieval Spanish words and entire phrases frozen in a kind of etymological amber. In Israel, three universities offer courses in Ladino. In Madrid, the Arias Montano Institute of Hispanic Civilization has published compilations of Ladino writings (p. 371). In his book *Sefaradita* (1928), the Catalan poet-philosopher Miguel de Unamuno poignantly acknowledged his respect for this durable tongue, speaking through a Jewish protagonist:

> Ladino, noble language
> In which we lamented Zion,
> And mourned the loss of Spain,
> Land of our consolation.

Tanzimat: *Promise and Nonfulfillment*

In the early nineteenth century, with its European empire crumbling and its ramshackle administration faltering, the Ottoman regime embarked on a belated effort at "Tanzimat"—of political reform and economic modernization. Launched by Sultan Mahmud II in 1826 with the destruction of the janissary corps, the program gained momentum under Mahmud's successor, Abd al-Majid I. One of Abd al-Majid's most radical decrees, the "Rescript of the Rose Chamber" of 1839, ordained nothing less than full legal equality for the empire's non-Moslem communities. In ensuing years, a series of royal firmans officially terminated dhimmi poll taxes, the inferior standing of non-Moslems before state courts, and the humiliating restrictions imposed on their clothing, housing, and government employment. Military service henceforth was opened to Moslems and non-Moslems alike. (In fact, both Jews and Christians tended to shun the "boon" of conscription; as before, they continued to pay taxes as a kind of surrogate service.) By the mid-nineteenth century, the empire's three hundred thousand Jews were not dissatisfied with the new "liberalization." Following additional constitutional improvements in the 1860s, several Jews were appointed to minor government positions, to district and municipal councils, and a few even to the Council of State. During the reign of Abd al-Hamid II (1876–1909), a sultan otherwise notorious for corruption and brutality, occasional Jewish notables were awarded decorations and honorific titles.

Nevertheless, the Jews' integration into Ottoman society remained quite superficial. Except for a modest nucleus of bankers and merchants, their economic position continued to decline throughout the nineteenth century. Even an alteration in their communal "rank" brought only mixed blessings. As an integral feature of Tanzimat, the government in

1839 officially anointed the Jews a *millet*—an autonomous, self-governing community, a status they had enjoyed only informally in earlier years. The chief rabbi of Constantinople became the *haham bashi,* a designated Ottoman official on a level with the Greek and Armenian patriarchs. The post, however, assumed a purely honorary character. Over the years, with the Jewish court and tax systems becoming institutions of the past, the haham bashi's purview was confined to the narrowest limits of religious and cultural affairs. Even within this shrunken rabbinical ambit, religious observance and education remained incorrigibly fundamentalist.

By the mid-nineteenth century, as a result, a number of middle-class Jewish families began to bypass the parochial Jewish school system. They preferred to enroll their children in the developing network of Protestant and Catholic mission schools. These at least offered a modern, secular curriculum. So, increasingly, did local Greek and Armenian schools. To the incipient Jewish bourgeoisie, it was becoming clear that their own educational system hardly dared offer less, if their people were to survive economically. The decisive initiative for change came from the West. It was the powerful French Jewish philanthropy, the Alliance Israélite Universelle, that accepted responsibility for educating Jews living in the Near East and North Africa. By no coincidence, this was terrain long regarded as within the French sphere of imperialist influence. As the acculturated Westerners saw it, plain and simple French patriotism dictated an effort to "enlighten"—in effect, to gallicize—the unfortunate Sephardim.

To that end, in the 1860s and 1870s the Alliance opened a series of pilot schools, first in Constantinople, then in Izmir, Edirne, and several other Turkish cities. The network widened in ensuing decades to include Syria, Egypt, the Balkans, and North Africa. Initially, the teaching staff were nearly all French Jews. But in later years the instructors tended to be native Sephardim who themselves had been Alliance-educated. The curriculum still offered religious and Hebrew studies, but courses now ranged from mathematics and the natural sciences to history, geography, and "useful" languages. Predictably, instruction was itself carried out in the "useful" language of French. Turkish was relegated to third place in these schools, after French and Ladino (Hebrew came last).

As envisaged by the patriarchs of the Alliance and their Sephardic allies, the program emphasized still another goal, this one "moral." For Narcisse Leven, secretary general of the Alliance network, it was to "combat the bad habits . . . widespread among oriental populations, of egotism, arrogance, exaggerated expressions of feelings, insipidity, blind respect for fortune and the violence of petty passions." For Nissim Behar, principal of the Alliance "mother" school in Constantinople, the Jews of the Galata district were "irascible, loud, self-seeking, none too scrupulous about the means of earning money, enemies of all work." Other teachers described the Jews of Constantinople as simply "amoral." Of Bursa, one wrote: "Profound ignorance, dirtiness, vulgarity in language and manners, total absence of dignity, reluctance to do any hard work—here are the characteristics of our coreligionists in Bursa." The self-contempt was at once poignant and provocative. The Alliance teachers were not, after all, describing Turks or Arabs or Gentiles at large; nor were they characterizing "uncouth" Ashkenazim. It was their own kinsmen they were identifying, the descendants of hidalgos, poets, and philosophers; of Judah Halevi, Moses Maimonides, Isaac Abravanel.

In Turkey and the Balkans alone by 1908, some forty thousand students were attending Alliance schools. By then too the lockstep of Jewish parochial education had been broken. Growing numbers of Alliance graduates were beginning to make their way into the imperial economy, to augment the nucleus of an emergent Jewish bourgeoisie. Their model henceforth was the West, the heartland of commerce, prosperity, culture. The very transformation of their names signified the new Eurocentrism. As an Alliance teacher noted: "One would be loath today to be called Moshe, Shabbatai, Salo, Simul—[instead] one is called Moïse, Charles, Caroline, Eugénie." For Ottoman Jewry, France had emerged as the central referent for economic modernization, for cultural and social enlightenment, for "progress."

Revolution and War

Within the Ottoman Empire itself, the momentum of change was becoming irreversible. In 1908, the issue of political transformation was forced when the corrupt and ineffectual Hamidian regime was overthrown by the Committee of Union and Progress. The latter was a collection of "Young Turk" army officers and business and professional men who were joined in a common dedication to imperial liberalization. As it happened, no community welcomed the prospect of a revitalized empire more enthusiastically than did the Jews. Indeed, several Jews played rather significant roles in the Committee of Union and Progress and in the ensuing Young Turk government. Among these were Abraham Galanté, Albert Fua, Nissim Russo, Samuel Israel, Vitali Stroumsa, Nissim Mazliah, Albert Asseo, and Emmanuel Carasso. Carasso, a Salonika-born attorney, later was elected a deputy to the new Ottoman parliament and served as senior legal adviser to the foreign ministry. It was in fact the prominence of Jews, and of Moslems of Jewish origin (pp. 154–55), that convinced Sir Lewis

Mallet, Britain's ambassador to Constantinople, that the Young Turk revolution was nothing less than a Jewish "conspiracy," a private cabal intent upon maneuvering Turkey into war against the Anglo-Russian Entente, "because the Jews hate the Russians." The notion was spurious. However much Jews "hated the Russians," Moslem Turks at all times dominated the party and government.

Indeed, the new regime soon would generate its own fulminant Turkish xenophobia. The 1908 coup, after all, was fueled not merely by revulsion at Sultan Abd al-Hamid's brutality and ineptitude but by outrage at his failure to protect the realm against the encroachments of Europe. No sooner was the Committee of Union and Progress itself in office, however, than it confronted a new onslaught of European imperialism. In 1909, Austria-Hungary annexed Ottoman Bosnia-Herzegovina, and Bulgaria proclaimed its final independence from Turkish rule. In 1912, Ottoman Crete declared its union with Greece, and Italy annexed a large portion of Ottoman Tripolitania. In the ensuing year and a half, Greece, Bulgaria, and Serbia devoured Ottoman Macedonia, reducing Turkish rule in Europe to a thin buffer zone on the very doorstep of Constantinople. With its hopes of territorial revival all but dashed, the revolutionary government began to vent upon the empire's non-Moslem peoples its own emergent, and frustrated, Turkish ethnocentrism.

The Jews encountered the full fury of that chauvinism in the early winter of 1914–15, almost immediately upon the government's decision to enter the World War. It was not a reaction they had anticipated. The moment hostilities broke out, Jewish spokesmen had proclaimed their community's unstinting devotion to the imperial cause. Unlike the Greeks and Armenians, Ottoman Jews entirely favored hostilities against tsarist Russia. Their bankers made financing available to the government. Their young men, conscripted into the army, served on every front. Even so, in Palestine, an active battle zone, government suspicion of Jews—and of Arabs and other non-Turkish peoples—soon escalated into overt antipathy. In December 1914, Beha-a-Din, the aged and irascible Ottoman governor of Jaffa, ordered an immediate expulsion of the six thousand Russian Jews living in his port city. Most of these civilians eventually were shipped off to internment in Egypt.

Some twenty-five hundred other young Palestinian Jews were even less fortunate. Drafted into special "labor" battalions, they were set to work building roads or quarrying stone, and reduced to starvation rations. Their community's ordeal, in fact, was only beginning. Djemal Pasha, commander of the Ottoman Fourth Army, returned to Palestine in February 1915 following an unsuccessful expedition against the Suez Canal. In a black mood, determined to intimidate the country's non-Turkish population into a state of terrorized submission, Djemal ordered Zionist newspapers, schools, and financial and political institutions closed. More ominously yet, Jewish land titles were called into question, and local Bedouin tribes were not discouraged from pillaging Jewish villages. The fate of the Jewish "labor" battalions was particularly grim. Several hundred of these young men were marched off to prison in Damascus; others were dispatched to a living death in the granite pits of the Taurus Mountains. Few returned.

Elsewhere in Palestine, the Fourth Army set about confiscating livestock and foodstuffs, reducing thousands of Jewish and Arab families to maize grits as the staple of their diet. In 1916 and 1917, some thirty-five thousand inhabitants of Syria and Palestine died of starvation or hunger-induced disease. Perhaps eight thousand of these were Jews. In the winter of 1917, the final remnants of Jewish security in Palestine collapsed. Turkish soldiers, many of them deserters, were running amok, looting Jewish and Arab settlements, foraging, raping, killing. By the time the Ottoman government sued for peace, in October 1918, the Jewish population in the Holy Land had declined from its prewar figure of eighty-five thousand to less than fifty-five thousand.

The wartime ordeal of Ottoman Jewry was not limited to Palestine, nor did it end with the October 1918 armistice. Five months later, the Allied Powers authorized the Kingdom of Greece to "administer" southwestern Asia Minor, a sector extensively inhabited by Ottoman Greeks. At first, in common with the Turks, Jews living in the city of Izmir suffered the pillage of their homes and shops by occupying Greek military units. Then, in 1922, a revived Turkish army soundly defeated the Greek forces and forced their ignominious evacuation. The development brought little relief to the Jews, as it happened. Under terms of the 1923 Treaty of Lausanne, the surviving Greek minority in Turkey's Izmir region and the beleaguered Turkish minority within the Kingdom of Greece were to be permanently exchanged and resettled among their kinsmen in each's respective "motherland." The economic shock was severe on both sides. For the Jews, settled in the heaviest zones of repatriation both in Turkey and in Greece, the trauma added thousands of their own people to the transfer of populations (p. 155).

Well before 1923—indeed, since the turn of the century, as they fled the despotism of Abd al-Hamid, then the upheaval of the 1912–13 Balkan Wars, then the carnage of the World War, and finally the Greco-Turkish war of 1920–22—as many as twenty-five thousand Ottoman Jews migrated to Europe and the Western Hemisphere. In Latin America, the immigrants were known as *turcos,* and virtually all of them started out as peddlers, accommodating their Ladino tongue to the local Spanish and Portuguese speakers. Yet the largest majority of formerly Ottoman Sephardim made their way to the United States. By 1930, their population on American soil approached thirty thousand.

Of these, three or four thousand settled in the Midwest and Far West, particularly in Los Angeles, San Francisco, and Portland. But most of the newcomers remained in New York. Few of them possessed marketable skills. Congested in the wretchedest of Lower East Side tenements, they tended to eke out their existence as bootblacks, candy and ice-cream vendors, cloakroom attendants, or waiters. Their women, all but illiterate, found occasional employment in the garment industry but more commonly worked as maids or laundresses. And thus it was, for mainstream American Jewry, that the encounter with these hapless Near Easterners was their first introduction to the once-luminous and venerated Sephardic "aristocracy."

In the Republic of the Gray Wolf

The fate of that historic remnant was determined rather more frontally and forcefully in Turkey itself. It was here that Moslems, Christians, and Jews alike were exposed to a thunderous new personality and ideology. Possibly no other figure in the modern Balkan world, not even Yugoslavia's Josip Broz Tito, so charismatically embodied the spirit of nationalist resistance and renewal as did Mustafa Kemal, the "gray wolf" of Turkish modernism. Kemal was thirty-nine in 1921, a professional officer with fifteen years' hard military service. Notwithstanding the ravages of drinking and wenching, the man's dynamism and imagination were unprecedented perhaps since the days of the original Mehmet the Conqueror. In 1915, it was Kemal, as the Turkish area commander, who shattered the British expedition at Gallipoli. In September 1921, it was this same elemental force who rallied a tatterdemalion army, survivors of the defeated host in the recent World War, to block the advance of the Greek army at the very threshold of Ankara. Less than a year later, in August 1922, Kemal launched his ragtag soldiery on a daring counteroffensive that within a single month drove the Greek expeditionary force out of Turkey. Over a million Ottoman Greek civilians followed in their wake.

The achievement, brutal as it was, represented merely the first act in the nation's resurrection. The following year, Kemal's personally inaugurated Grand National Assembly declared Turkey a constitutional republic, then elected the incomparable "gray wolf" himself as its first president. To some degree, the mantle of constitutionalism was a façade. Kemal functioned as virtual dictator of his nation, and he gave his people no rest. Soon after taking office, he enlarged the former imperial program of economic autarchy, establishing government monopolies for such basic industries as tobacco, salt, wine, matches, and munitions. The policy reflected ethnic nationalism as much as economic pragmatism. Until the war, Turkish industry and commerce depended heavily on networks of Greek and Armenian businessmen, and on a minority of Jewish financiers and importers. Most of the Greeks and Armenians were gone by now, but some one hundred twenty thousand Jews remained. Could they function, or even survive, under an aggressively nationalist regime, under leadership committed to the overriding objective of turkification?

It was an issue the Jews confronted as early as 1923. The Treaty of Lausanne extended to the Kemalist republic's non-Turkish communities the identical guarantees provided minority peoples in other postwar successor states. These included the prerogative of maintaining distinctive communal and social institutions and languages, including separate educational systems. No sooner was the ink dry on this document, however, than the nationalist government ominously suggested that the Jews "reconsider" whether they truly wished to be regarded as a minority, and thereby the subject of possible foreign interference in domestic Turkish affairs. The intimation in fact was all but explicit that the Jews were risking exposure to the fate of the Greeks and Armenians. At this point, several younger Jewish intellectuals hurriedly advocated forgoing the protected status of a minority. Chief Rabbi Haim Bejerano acquiesced, and so did Turkish Jewry's lay spokesmen. Taking their chances on the republic's new Swiss-based civil code, the Jews in 1926 also relinquished their former guaranteed millet seats in Parliament.

The accommodation went unrewarded. Once aroused, Turkish ethnocentrism would not be limited to the country's remaining pockets of Greeks and Armenians. Economic jealousy was always a factor. In 1934, with Turkey languishing in the world depression and unemployment rampant, Moslem crowds stormed Jewish homes in Thrace and the Chanak peninsula, looted Jewish property, and sent three thousand of the region's thirteen thousand Jews fleeing to Istanbul. The Jews of Edirne faced a comparable upsurge in violence. Two of their synagogues were razed. When pressure mounted on the Jews of Gallipoli to depart, their spokesmen ventured a complaint to President Mustafa Kemal himself. He brushed them off. It is doubtful that Kemal personally was antisemitic. Yet his regime's militant nationalism would not spare any minority. Although, together with all Turkish citizens, Jews were recruited into the army, few managed to attain the rank of officer. Virtually no Jews remained in the civil service by the late 1920s. In the 1930s, several German-Jewish (and non-Jewish) refugees were taken on as faculty members at the University of Istanbul, but only in slots for which competent Turks were unavailable. Meanwhile, the government moved relentlessly to shift commerce from Jews and Christians to Moslem Turks, who invariably were given preference in import and export licenses.

During the 1920s, too, determined to root out the last vestiges of religious obscurantism, Kemal waged an unrelenting campaign against clerical influence in public life. At his instigation, the caliphate was abolished, Islam was dethroned as the state religion, and the Moslem ulema was stripped of its lingering jurisdiction over civil litigation and the nation's school system. Here the nationalist regime displayed an unexceptionable evenhandedness. With indiscriminate severity, it purged religious education from the schools of all the non-Moslem communities: Jewish, Greek, Bulgarian, Armenian. Henceforth, with Turkish the sole language of primary instruction, Hebrew lessons ended in Jewish communal schools. So did French as the primary teaching language in Alliance schools. In common with other citizens, Jews were barred from affiliation with non-Turkish organizations. None, therefore, could participate in the World Zionist Congress, the World Jewish Congress, or even Orthodox religious federations.

In their vulnerability and insecurity, most Jews now felt obliged to work overtime to prove themselves loyal Turks. Even as their children rushed to master Turkish, Jewish lay and rabbinical leaders encouraged the older generation to mount a comparable effort. The results were significant. In 1927, 80 percent of Turkish Jews registered "Yahudice"—that is, Ladino—as their mother tongue. Eight years later, the percentage had dropped to 54. In a poignant throwback to the "salon Jews" of early-nineteenth-century Germany, two prominent Jewish intellectuals, Albert Samwil and Moïse Cohen-Tekinalp (the "Tekinalp" a recently adopted addition), urged their fellow Jews to define themselves as "Turks of the Mosaic religion."

The extent of the Jews' integration into Turkish society was exposed decisively in World War II. On the one hand, the government had displayed considerable goodwill toward Jews during the latter 1930s in opening the nation's doors to refugees from Nazi Europe. But once the war began, in 1939, Ankara's policy shifted. An impoverished people, the Turks were singleminded in their determination to recover from the trauma of their earlier struggles, and at all costs to avoid taking sides in this latest conflict. As a consequence, they fended off every German effort to revive the military partnership of 1914–18. By 1942, however, plainly intimidated by the sheer magnitude of Germany's recent victories and the looming proximity of the Wehrmacht in the Balkans and southern Russia, President Ismet Inonu and his government set out to placate Berlin in every fashion short of actually entering the war. They provided the Reich with vital supplies of manganese and mercury, even allowed the German embassy to become a hotbed of Nazi espionage and propaganda. They also adopted a policy of thinly disguised hostility toward Jews and other minorities. Once again, Jewish military recruits were concentrated in special "labor battalions." Even more ominously, Jewish refugees no longer were given asylum en route to Palestine, even on a temporary basis.

In December 1941, the S.S. *Struma* dropped anchor in Istanbul harbor. It was a rickety little schooner of less than a thousand tons. Several weeks earlier it had departed the Romanian port of Constanţa, bound for Palestine. Carrying 767 Jews, the overloaded vessel had limped along the Black Sea coast. Now, with its engine malfunctioning and its hull leaking, the *Struma* had no alternative but to dock in Istanbul. The refugees implored the Turkish government for sanctuary. The appeal was rejected. At this point, incapable of proceeding and barred from returning, the passengers were confined to shipboard in Istanbul harbor. As the weeks passed, they suffered from hunger, overcrowding, and mounting panic. The British sent word that they would not accept the Jews in Palestine. The Turks would not permit them to disembark even for purposes of internment— although the American Jewish Joint Distribution Committee guaranteed the entirety of their expenses. At last, in late February 1942, declaring its patience exhausted, the Turkish government ordered the *Struma* to weigh anchor. Five miles out at sea in the Bosphorus, the ship sank, with the loss of 428 men, 269 women, and 70 children.

The local Turkish-Jewish population also experienced the effects of minority vulnerability. In 1942, the wartime blockade was imposing grave economic hardship on the nation. To help resolve its budgetary shortfall, the government began characterizing as profiteers certain "mercantile elements." These turned out, in effect, to be the traditional minority communities of Greeks, Armenians, and Jews. In December of that year, Ankara moved to impose a capital levy on them. Known as the *Varlik Vergisi,* the impost was as savagely vindictive a tax as any inflicted by the most tyrannical Ottoman sultan. To determine its application, mixed commissions of government officials and local Moslem businessmen divided taxpayers into two lists: the "M" list for Moslems, and the "G" for *gayrimuslim,* non-Moslems. The latter were obliged to pay up to ten times as much as the former. In some instances, taxes exceeded the entirety of individuals' capital assets. Additionally, to ensure payment, the government escrowed the debtors' property. Businesses, homes, furnishings, artifacts—all were confiscated and auctioned off for "reimbursement." In June 1943, under severe criticism from liberal quarters, President Inonu acknowledged that the *Varlik Vergisi* was being paid essentially by "non-Turks," but he insisted that the asymmetry was only "reasonable" inasmuch as "all the real estate and sources of wealth are in their hands." Under this rationale, individuals whose confiscated property failed to cover the bill were sentenced to punitive labor.

Ultimately, ten thousand "defaulters" were carried off to road-building camps in the hinterland. More than half the victims were Jews. Work conditions were brutal. Accommodations were leaking tents; food and even water were in short supply. Illness was frequent, and there were occasional deaths. Berlin praised the sentencing. The Allies condemned it. Indeed, the United States ambassador in Ankara, Laurence Steinhardt, hinted at possible diplomatic complications with Washington. By the late summer of 1943, the tide of war had turned against Germany, and Nazi influence in Turkey began to fade. The Turkish government now felt it prudent to allow such organizations as the American Jewish Joint Distribution Committee, the United States War Rescue Board, and the Jewish Agency to conduct their operations from offices in Istanbul. In Nazi-occupied Europe, several Turkish consuls interceded in behalf of Jewish victims. Yet it was not until March 1944 that Turkey's parliament abolished the *Varlik Vergisi,* and an additional seven months after that before the last of the prisoners was released. The tax had raised 315 million Turkish liras. In the process, it had also shaken the nation's business world and pauperized fully a third of Turkish Jewry.

In his 1991 volume *The Jews of the Ottoman Empire and the Turkish Republic,* an eminent Turkologist, Professor Stanford Shaw of UCLA, has offered a noteworthy interpretation of Turkish wartime behavior. Both Moslems and non-Moslems suffered from the *Varlik Vergisi,* he observes, and those Turkish Jews who were not affected by the tax "continued their lives normally":

> One interesting comment received from more than one source was that the *Varlik Vergisi* helped the Jews of Turkey by showing Turks that the Jews were suffering so much that they should not give in to the Nazi demands to deport their Jews to the death camps. The deprivation of their wealth by the government drained what resentment there might otherwise have been among Turks against Jewish

wealth while the mass of the population was suffering because of the war.

If Shaw, himself a Jew, was prepared in this fashion to cosmeticize Turkish behavior toward his own people, one must speculate on his reaction, and that of other American Turkologists, to the fate of the Armenians, a people that in earlier years had suffered far more cruelly at Turkish hands. In fact, the campaign to rewrite the ordeal of both minorities was linked to a fascinating venture in communal politics. Here, too, the author begins a periodic intrusion into our narrative.

The Armenian Genocide: The Invention of a "Non-happening"

In the spring of 1971, as a guest at the Washington conference of the Armenian Assembly, I was struck by a curious sense of ethnic juxtaposition. This could as easily have been a Jewish conference. The resemblance was not a matter of physiognomy alone. For Armenians, as for Jews, the wellspring of memory was a holocaust, the maceration of a third of a people's demographic substance. For both minorities, a throbbing wound had become the focus of an entire communal agenda.

The Armenians were an old civilization, hardly less venerable than the Jews. Concentrated principally in the eastern districts of Anatolia, the little people here numbered approximately 1.8 million on the eve of World War I. They were Christians, and hence dhimmis. In the latter nineteenth century, under the oppressive rule of the Hamidian sultanate, the Armenians became increasingly susceptible to irredentism, and specifically as it was preached by ideologues among some two million of their people living directly across the border in Russian Armenia. In February 1915, therefore, as a tsarist army penetrated Ottoman soil, several thousand local Armenians enthusiastically greeted their "liberators." It was not a widespread reaction. The vast majority of the Armenian population was mortally fearful of the war, and particularly of Turkish retribution. Nevertheless, in March, Constantinople issued instructions to "resolve" the Armenian question on a permanent basis.

Throughout the spring and summer of 1915, hundreds of thousands of Armenian men, women, and children were rounded up and brutally marched off to the Syrian desert—and eventual death. By winter, the "deportations" had largely been completed. Wartime estimates differed on the number of victims; the most thoroughly documented was that of Dr. Johannes Lepsius, a German Protestant missionary in Turkey, who calculated a total of 1,396,000 dead. By any evaluation, it was a racial annihilation unprecedented until that time in modern history.

Over the ensuing decades, survivors of that horror kept its memory alive. Enshrined in books, journals, institutes, religious services, and annual commemorations, the genocide of a people remained fulminant and dominant in the Armenians' folklore. It was a reaction the Jews shared. Yet in the case of the Jews, the Nazi holocaust ceased to be a political issue. By word and deed, the post–World War II Bundesrepublik acknowledged the magnitude of Nazi Germany's crime against the Jewish people and offered significant financial restitution to survivors. Not so the Republic of Turkey. Neither publicly nor privately were the Turks prepared to accept the burden of guilt for the Armenian tragedy. In their frustration and rage, then, Armenian nationalist underground groups in the 1970s and 1980s set about "executing" Turkish diplomats and family members in Europe and the United States.

Ankara's response to the campaign of Armenian recrimination and violence was a countercampaign, one of propaganda. Its purpose was to dissuade friendly nations from giving credence, or even acknowledgment, to the Armenian genocide. In recent years, the public relations effort has been notably intense in the United States. American politicians, newspaper columnists, teachers, clergymen, and others venturing so much as an allusion to the Armenian tragedy have been barraged with official Turkish "explanatory" material denying the very notion of a genocide, or, at times, even of a significant historic Armenian presence in Turkey.

Finally, in 1985, a denouement of sorts was reached when the Armenian Assembly and other Armenian-American groups focused on the United States Congress. They persuaded the House Foreign Affairs Committee to place on its agenda a resolution commemorating the seventieth anniversary of the Armenian tragedy. The Turkish government in turn riposted with a stern warning to the State Department. The threat registered. Testifying before Congress, Secretary of State George Shultz reminded the legislators that Turkey was a NATO partner and the site of vital American air force bases, and warned that this strategic relationship would be threatened if the Turks were provoked. The resolution was defeated in committee. Reintroduced in 1987 and again in 1990, it was turned back each time. On both occasions, too, the State Department endorsed Ankara's proposition that the 1915 slaughter of Armenians was unproven, or at worst should be regarded as the inevitable consequence of war between two peoples.

In May 1985, the Turkish argument was imaginatively buttressed by an open letter to the *New York Times*. It was sponsored by the Association of Turkish-American Associations, a body unofficially but extensively funded by the Turkish government, and signed by sixty-nine American academicians, among them a number of eminent Jewish scholars of the Middle East including Bernard Lewis of Princeton and Stanford Shaw of UCLA. The statement objected to the use of the term "genocide" and repeated the longstanding Turkish contention that the 1915 tragedy was the "inevitable consequence" of wartime conditions (Shaw's book *A History of the Ottoman Empire and Modern Turkey,* co-written with his Turkish-born wife, Ezel, neglected even to describe the fate of the evacuated Armenians). It is of interest that either directly, by personal subsidy, or indirectly, by grants supplied to their academic programs, many of the professors had received generous financial support from the Institute for Turkish Studies, a body founded and underwritten by the Turkish embassy in Washington.

For a number of years, the wider Jewish response to the Armenian genocide issue was somewhat ambivalent. In 1985, a majority of Congress's Jewish senators and representatives initially favored a pro-Armenian resolution. A few drew specific parallels between the fate of the Armenians in 1915 and that of the Jews in World War II. But soon these legislators, and Jews elsewhere, came under heavy Turkish pressure. Indeed, three years earlier, Ankara had similarly protested to the government of Israel. An international symposium on genocide then under way at Tel Aviv University included several Armenian scholars among its participants. The Turks got wind of the conclave and protested. The Israeli government then intervened and academic sponsorship was revoked. Afterward, however, the event continued, although under "private" auspices.

Yet if the Jews would not abandon their wide-ranging exploration of genocide, neither would the Turks relinquish their campaign of intimidation. The following spring, in April 1983, two officials of the United States Holocaust Commission in Washington, Dr. Barbara Abramowitz and Rabbi Seymour Siegel, dropped by my home to discuss a vexing problem. The commission had tentatively formulated plans for an Armenian "section" in the impending Museum of the Holocaust, but lately had faced stiff Turkish warnings to drop the proposal. Was there truth, my visitors queried, to the Turkish argument that the Armenian genocide was a non-happening? In reply, I offered a personal and unambiguous evaluation, then suggested appropriate reading material. But the episode was troubling. As I learned afterward, it was but the tip of the iceberg of a triangular Armenian-Turkish-Jewish crisis.

While Congress's mandate to the Holocaust Commission in 1980 ostensibly was to memorialize all victims of genocide, there was little question that the principal emphasis would be laid upon the Six Million of World War II. Nevertheless, the commission's Jewish members at the outset assured their Armenian colleague, Set Momjian, that his people's tragedy would be "substantially" integrated into the exhibit. That pledge failed to materialize in ensuing years. The Turkish government had learned of the proposal, and reacted with characteristic spleen. In the summer of 1980, Ankara dispatched a sharp protest to Washington. If Armenia were so much as mentioned in the Holocaust exhibit, it warned, there would be repercussions against NATO bases in Turkey. The State Department passed on the warning to the Holocaust Commission without comment.

Three years later, in June 1983, the Turkish cultural attaché in Washington invited several of the Holocaust Commission's staff members to an "educational" session at his office. Waiting with him were four or five American scholarly authorities on Middle Eastern history, among them Richard Chambers, Justin McCarthy, and Heath Lowry, executive director of the Institute for Turkish Studies. Virtually on cue, these men proceeded once more to attack the notion of an Armenian genocide, invoking the familiar arguments of Turkish self-defense and of extensive killings on both sides. After approximately an hour of this edification, the group broke for cocktails and lunch with Ambassador Sukru Alekdag. At the luncheon table, the ambassador, equable and gracious until then, suddenly became a man transformed. "If the Armenians are so much as mentioned in your holocaust museum," he threatened, "it will go badly for the Jews in Turkey. Also for Jewish refugees from Iran. We permit them to cross into our territory, you know, even without passports. That could all stop."

Soon after this discussion, a full-page statement was published in ten or twelve leading American-Jewish newspapers. This time the signatories were the principal rabbis and communal spokesmen of Turkish Jewry. The text was imaginative. It emphasized the warm hospitality Turkey had extended the Jews over the previous five centuries and the Jewish community's heartfelt gratitude. The choice of the American-Jewish press for the declamation was by no means a scattershot tactic. Beyond its rather poignant display of Turkish-Jewish insecurities, the statement bore witness to a widely shared Turkish assumption that Jews in the United States were authentic movers and shakers on the American landscape. Perhaps, then, at the initiative of the Turkish-Jewish community, the American-Jewish community could similarly be mobilized to produce a more "balanced" understanding of Turkey's record of "tolerance and love" (in the words of a Turkish Information Office brochure). In the process, Jewish influence might similarly be exploited to help bury the unrequited ghost of the Armenian people.

The Quincentennial Foundation

One of those who contested the perennial Armenian-genocide resolution, both in published statements and in direct testimony before the House Foreign Affairs Committee in 1989, was an eminent Turkish-Jewish industrialist, Jak Kamhi. Upon returning to Istanbul following his appearance before Congress, Kamhi gave more intensive thought to a potential Jewish role in making Turkey's case. As he acknowledged later to an Israeli journalist, "Some newspapers [here] complained that we Jews are not doing anything in this matter of defending Turkey's image." Evidently, it was not enough simply for local Jews to cooperate in Ankara's public relations campaign; their cooperation had to be visible. To that end, Kamhi and other prominent Jews set about organizing a "Quincentennial Foundation." Its purpose was to mount an extensive series of events to commemorate the five-hundredth anniversary of Sultan Bayezid II's historic welcome to Sephardic Jews in 1492.

Kamhi was both the driving force and the principal financial benefactor of the undertaking. Estimates of his personal contribution ranged up to $5 million. He could afford it. One of the richest men in Turkey, Kamhi was chairman of the Profilo Group, a vast industrial–real estate conglomerate. Doubtless much of his enterprise depended upon official licenses and favorable tax assessments, and upon a general atmosphere of public and private approbation. Moreover, after the recent Jewish vicissitudes in the Turkish Republic, other local Jewish businessmen would similarly find it useful to remain on the qui vive for official goodwill. As Kamhi explained patiently to his interlocutors, the Quincentennial Foundation "is just a way to say thank you, to honor the remarkable spirit of tolerance the Turks have shown toward their Jewish compatriots." And the foundation's charter would add, in language that was all but a road map: "This spirit is not an isolated instance of humanitarianism. Throughout its history, Turkey has welcomed people of different creeds, cultures, and backgrounds. The Jewish community in Turkey is part of this tradition." And so, one was left to assume, were the Armenians.

Kamhi and his associates projected an extensive agenda for the foundation, especially in the United States. They opened an office in New York. Under its direction, a speakers' bureau made available to Jewish organizations a wide selection of lecturers and artists, of music, dance, and other folklore groups, all offering "authoritative" insight into Turkish-Jewish life. A documentary film on Turkish Jewry was prepared for public television, as well as text material, audiovisual aids, articles, fact sheets, human-interest stories, and photo essays for Jewish schools, synagogues, adult-education courses. The foundation also underwrote scholarly symposia on Turkish Jewry at selected American universities.

The largest of these programs, in November 1992, took place at UCLA, and its organizer was Stanford Shaw. Indeed, it was the foundation that sponsored the publication of Professor Shaw's *The Jews of the Ottoman Empire and the Turkish Republic* in 1991. Although densely textured and engaging, the book was essentially prefigured in a background paper Shaw had whipped up earlier for foundation distribution, intended for a more popular readership. Its summary established the theme for Shaw's—and the foundation's—enterprise in the United States:

> In secular Turkey there has been no place for the separate . . . millets, since all citizens have equal rights and equal legal status regardless of religion. . . . Jewish Turks have participated in all areas of life in Republican Turkey . . . and almost every area of the economy. . . . Jews remain extremely comfortable with their lives in the Turkish Republic and secure in their Turkish patriotism and loyalty to the Turkish Republic.

The high-powered media campaign was an unqualified success. American Jews were won over almost without reservation. Local Jewish communities participated enthusiastically in programs the foundation organized and often partially funded. At its Chicago convention in September 1990, the American Sephardi Federation adopted a resolution of "gratitude to the people and government of Turkey," and encouraged all members and friends to participate in the 1992 "celebration in Turkey." B'nai B'rith passed an identical resolution at its international convention in Dallas in August 1990. The goodwill—American and American Jewish—was powerfully enhanced in the ensuing year, as the Turkish government proved a steadfast and valuable ally in the Persian Gulf campaign against Iraq.

The "celebration in Turkey" of 1992 was the apotheosis of the foundation's two-year program. It encompassed a sequence of elaborate guided tours; visits to synagogues, schools, and cemeteries; scholarly symposia with papers offered by Turkish, American, and Israeli academicians (whose expenses from the latter two countries were generously underwritten); communal conclaves; drama and music festivals; government receptions. The extravaganza culminated in early August 1992 with a series of performances by the Israel Philharmonic, under the baton of Zubin Mehta, in a concert hall in Istanbul and later at the Roman amphitheater of Ephesus. Turkish Airlines assigned five special jets to fly the Ephesus passengers to and from Istanbul. The visiting thousands of American Jews were overwhelmed. Kamhi and his associates doubtless were relieved. The Turkish government could not have been less than gratified.

I decided to anticipate a possible American-Jewish tourist crush. Yet even in the summer of 1991 I could not preempt the Israelis. Turkey swarmed with them. They came in organized tourist groups, and one heard them before seeing them. Izmir might not have seemed the likeliest item on their agenda. It was Turkey's principal Aegean port, to be sure, a rather more elegant version of Haifa, with its refreshing sea breezes, its broad, palm-lined avenues, and its villa-dappled hills. As late as the 1700s, Izmir had sustained a population of nearly fifty thousand Jews, most of them packed into the city's Karatas section, where they were principally engaged in wool manufacture. The community maintained nine synagogues and two renowned talmudic academies. But in the nineteenth century the animus of Izmir's Greek-speaking majority, as well as a series of typhoid epidemics, eroded the Jewish presence. The pillage and fire of Turkish reconquest in 1922 further reduced the numbers of Jews, to barely fifteen thousand. Finally, in 1949, crippled by the wartime *Varlik Vergisi,* the shrunken little community gave up the ghost and departed almost en masse to Israel. Today, fewer than two thousand Jews remain. Each year, nevertheless, twenty times that many Western Jews and Israelis visit.

The contact with Jews from abroad would have been unacceptable in the earlier, hair-shirt years of Turkish nationalism. But the birth of Israel in 1948 made a difference. With their own lingering resentment of Arab "treachery" in World War I, a dislike exacerbated by later Syrian claims on the port of Iskenderun (Alexandretta), the Turks envisaged the new Jewish state as a potential buffer against Arab irredentism. In 1949, Turkey established a legation in Jerusalem, thus becoming the first Moslem state to recognize Israel. It was prepared even to countenance the emigration to Israel of Turkey's poorer, "redundant" Jewish citizens. By 1954, some forty-five thousand of these people had packed their meager baggage, paid out a few liras for deck space on Turkish coastal steamers, and sailed off to Israel.

Relations between the two countries underwent fluctuations. In 1981, when the Menachem Begin government offended even Israel's closest allies by flamboyantly proclaiming "united" Jerusalem as the nation's capital, the Turks reduced their official representation in the Jewish state to a second secretary. The diplomatic freeze might have continued but for the failure of Arab regimes to display the gratitude the Turks expected. Ankara had anticipated a flood of Arab investments. These did not materialize. Nor did the Arab League support Turkey in its lingering dispute with Greece over Cyprus. Then, in September 1986, even as the Turks were reassessing their Middle Eastern policy, two Palestinian Arabs burst into Istanbul's stately Neve Shalom synagogue, where a large number of worshippers had congregated for Rosh HaShanah services, and raked the sanctuary with machine-gun fire. Twenty-two people were killed. It was not the first act of Arab terrorism on Turkish soil; in 1970 Israel's consul-general was shot down by Arab gunmen. But this latest atrocity, committed against local Jews—Turkish nationals—was too much for the Turkish government and people alike. Several months later, Ankara made the decision to exchange ambassadors with Israel. Since then, trade between the two countries has sextupled, and cooperative ventures are under way in agricultural research and irrigation technology.

For the Quincentennial Foundation, however, the principal concern at all times was to reconfirm Turkish goodwill toward the country's native Jewish population. I was reminded of that priority upon visiting the foundation office in Istanbul. It was located on one of the top floors of a gleaming downtown skyscraper. The building was owned by Jak Kamhi's Profilo Group, and the Quincentennial Foundation suite was merely an extension of Kamhi's own executive headquarters. It was an impressive setup—commodious, well staffed, equipped with the last word in electronic office equipment. My host in the Profilo executive dining room was Tevfik Saracoglu, a foundation vice president. Saracoglu, a Moslem Turk, was a retired former ambassador to the Common Market. Multilingual, he was every inch the courteous diplomat. Evidently, Kamhi found it useful to flaunt this establishment figure. He took Saracoglu with him on every visit to the United States, to every city, banquet, and reception there. In so many words, too, Saracoglu delicately acknowledged that his role was to ensure the foundation's "pansectarian" credentials. It was he who had recruited its thirty-eight prominent Moslem trustees (among sixty-seven eminent Jews) and who served as the foundation's intermediary with the government.

After lunch, Saracoglu ushered me into his employer's presence. Then sixty-six years old, Kamhi was a saturnine, mustached gentleman of middle height, elegantly dressed in a shantung silk suit and moccasins. We settled on French, and in the next two hours he responded to my questions unhurriedly and expansively. His family had provenance, all right. A Kamhi had crossed over from Aragón to settle in Montpellier as far back as the twelfth century. In the sixteenth century, the family migrated to Constantinople. They became importer-exporters. It was the vocation of Kamhi's own grandfather and father. They did well, living in comfortable homes in the city's fashionable Tepache quarter. Kamhi himself attended an Alliance grammar school before continuing on at the French-speaking St. Michel lycée. These were the World War II years. Did Monsieur Kamhi not experience antisemitism in that period? Very little, he insisted. "Mustafa Kemal always protected the Jews, and so did Kemal's successors. The Turkish people are not antisemitic." After the war, Kamhi journeyed to France to earn a polytechnical degree as a metal engineer, then acquired his first professional experience in several French factories. Upon returning to Istanbul, he joined his brother and brother-in-law in a series of industrial projects, manufacturing electrical appliances under license from General Electric, Westinghouse, Thomson, and other Western companies. By the early 1970s, Kamhi had built one of Turkey's great industrial empires. Indeed, he vastly augmented his fortune by shrewd real estate development. The man plainly had a stake in the country.

Besides the current Quincentennial project, had Monsieur ever been actively involved in Jewish affairs? Here Kamhi became vague. In pro-Israel activities? Here he became explicit. A Jew overtly engaging in pro-Israel activities would endanger the entire Jewish community, he explained: "We dare not do it." I raised the issue of the *Struma,* the refugee vessel that had been turned away in 1942 to sink in the Bosphorus. Once again Kamhi refused to impute antisemitism to Turkey. The government had been placed under heavy German and British pressure, he emphasized. It had no choice but to force the *Struma* out. And the *Varlik Vergisi?* Kamhi remained unruffled. The tax was not directed "specifically" against Jews or other minorities. It was aimed only at the rich, against those who had "exploited" the Turks. If the tax fell heavily on Jews, "who else had liquid capital?" If some Jews were ruined by that capital levy, they were people "without roots" in the country.

Finally, there was the issue of the Armenians. "It's very simple," Kamhi replied, with a speed and fluency suggesting that he had been through this catechism earlier (and he had, in 1989, before the congressional committee). "They were traitors. They were agents of the Russians." The great "exodus" of 1915 was carried out to "protect" Turkey. "I don't approve of the methods used against the Armenians," he explained, "but we must blame Armenian agents provocateurs themselves for causing this tragedy."

We chatted amiably for a few more minutes, and I took my leave.

"The Land of Tolerance and Love"

The Neve Shalom synagogue is to be found in Istanbul's aging Shishane quarter, a densely populated commercial-industrial zone enveloped by smoke-stained office buildings and shabby storefronts. The edifice is non-descript on the outside, but its interior was reconstructed following the 1986 Arab terrorist attack. Its gates now are of solid steel, its doors paneled in bulletproof glass. At least this is one synagogue that remains in use. Most have been abandoned, together with their neighborhoods. In Banat and Yambol, once major enclaves of Jewish settlement but now decrepit warrens of tiny offices and workshops, the synagogues have been vacant for decades.

What has put the kiss of death on this community, a Jewry that only a century before exceeded one hundred thousand souls? The *Varlik Vergisi* was a decisive factor, of course. Probably it was as responsible as Zionist idealism for the initial mass exodus of Jews to Israel after 1949. And in 1956, an outburst of violence was provoked by the Cyprus crisis. Rumors circulated that Greeks had destroyed the Salonika house in which Mustafa Kemal had been born. Within days, a mob raged through the streets of Istanbul, attacking Greek shops and homes. The violence then spilled over to the Armenian quarter, and finally to Jewish commercial and residential neighborhoods. Business establishments with non-Turkish names were pillaged and burned. The Pera district, where virtually all the shops were Jewish, was gutted. Shaken to their depths, another fifteen thousand Jews pulled up stakes then and there and departed for Israel and Western Europe. In Turkey's internal political crises of the 1960s and 1970s, possibly ten thousand more Jews left the country.

Fewer than eighteen thousand remain. These tend to be a fractionally more affluent group than their predecessors. Except for perhaps a thousand professionals, they are businessmen. Most still function as retailers, but an important nucleus has won a foothold in the nation's revived import-export trade, in textile and automobile-parts manufacturing, in chain-store merchandising. Unwilling to pull up roots, these middle-class elements live comfortably today in fashionable apartments in Galata and Cadde Bostan, and many own seaside villas along the Bosphorus and in the Princess Islands.

Yet the tenor of their Jewishness has been profoundly diluted by the Kemalist legacy. The chief rabbinate's jurisdiction is narrowly confined to matters of ritual. Istanbul's once-famous rabbinical seminary is closed.

There are no Jewish archives, no kosher restaurants. Only two Jewish parochial schools are left in the country, and these follow the official state curriculum. Most Jewish students attend private French- or English-language institutions. Their language of daily discourse is Turkish. A Turkish-language newspaper–communal bulletin, *Shalom,* enjoys a decent circulation, but only one Ladino newspaper survives, with a readership of less than two thousand. The aged worshippers who manage to turn up on the Sabbath and Jewish holidays often can barely read the Hebrew prayer book. In recent years, the Turkish government has eased its restrictions on membership in international Jewish organizations. Nevertheless, few local Jews appear to be well informed on their people's affairs elsewhere in the world.

Fewer yet are willing to flaunt their ancestry. Concern for Arab terrorism is a factor. As late as February 1992, Istanbul's Neve Shalom synagogue was targeted once again, by a small—presumably Arab—bomb, which exploded outside the main entrance, injuring a Turkish passerby. Several days later, a much more powerful car-bomb killed an official of the Israeli embassy in Ankara. Even more frightening, however, is the simmering threat of Turkish chauvinism. No one who lived through World War II or the riots of 1956 can ignore that danger, or the threat of Moslem fundamentalist and other right-wing parties that lately have won substantial followings. In 1991, the Israeli journalist Yoav Karmi described a conversation with Shevket Kazan, a former minister of justice and vice chairman of REFA, Turkey's Islamic orthodox party. "In the days of the Ottomans," declared Kazan, "we let the Jews rule our community for over five hundred years. Our entire economy was in Jewish hands. And even now all the prime commercial areas still remain in their hands." The charge—entirely false—was repeated by other REFA notables, among them the mayor of Urfa, a middle-sized town near the Syrian border. Visiting Germany that same year, the mayor placed a wreath on the grave of "the heroes of the SS" and publicly declared his regret that Hitler had failed to complete his mission. The party did not repudiate the mayor's remarks. It is a minority party, of course, by no means characteristic of the nation's political mainstream. But neither was the nation's latent xenophobia a distant memory for the country's Jewish remnant.

"No problems remain," Chief Rabbi David Asseo blandly assures his foreign visitors. "We live here tranquilly." Questioned on the punitive tribulations of the war and the riots of the postwar period, Rabbi Asseo insists that "those are times past." Jacob Schreiber, an Israeli correspondent who visited the Neve Shalom synagogue in 1987, evoked a more subdued reaction. "As we shuffled out the door, someone grasped me firmly from behind." It was Panache, the *haham,* the reader of services, a man reputed to be a collateral descendant of the incomparable Don Joseph Nasi. " 'Take off your skullcap before going outside,' " warned Panache. Other congregants needed no reminder. For them, at least, the ghosts of "times past" would not be that easily exorcised.

CHAPTER VI

THE MYSTICAL LAND

An Intermittence of Return

Embarking by sea from Constantinople, our redoubtable twelfth-century traveler Benjamin of Tudela made his way through the Aegean archipelago to Cyprus, then on to the Syrian littoral. From the coast Benjamin traveled south by mule to the Holy Land. It was 1169, and Palestine had been transformed into the Latin Kingdom of Jerusalem—terrain ruled precisely by those Crusading zealots who had butchered Jews in the thousands en route to this sacred soil. Nevertheless, Benjamin gives no sign of trepidation in his memoirs. His diary entries are characteristically straightforward, even flat. Accounts of geography and architecture are interspersed with descriptions of a minuscule Jewish presence: two hundred Jewish families in Galilee, forty in Jerusalem, twelve in Bethlehem, two in Jaffa:

> Six parasangs from [Haifa] is Caesarea, the Gate of the Philistines, and here there are about two hundred Jews and two hundred . . . Jews of Shomron, who are called Samaritans. . . . [Jerusalem] is a small city, fortified by three walls. It is full of people whom the Mohammedans call Jacobites, Syrians, Greeks, Georgians, and Franks, and of people of all tongues. . . . There are about two hundred Jews who dwell under the Tower of David in one corner of the city.

For Benjamin, the precarious status of his people in the Holy Land was a simple fact of life, rather like the weather.

Nearly three centuries would pass before this skeletal Jewish enclave began to stir. In 1517, Sultan Selim I wrested Syria-Palestine from the Mamelukes, who themselves had wrested it from the Crusaders, and extended Ottoman sovereignty over the entire Levant. Henceforth, Turkish improvements in security and communications encouraged a substantial upsurge of Jewish immigration. From neighboring Egypt, the journey to Palestine now became safe even for pregnant women and old people. During the sixteenth century, therefore, a recognizable Jewish nucleus developed in the Holy Land for the first time in a millennium. In Jerusalem, the Turks supplied the protection of high walls, a decent underground water system, a caravansary for pack animals, and a covered bazaar. The city's Jewish population grew to some one thousand by 1530, to three thousand by 1600. Living in their own quarters of Risha, Sahraf, and Maslach, these turbaned and often Arabic-speaking Sephardim rarely experienced molestation of any kind. As elsewhere in the Ottoman Empire during those years, they governed their own communal affairs and pursued their customary vocations of artisanry, petty trade, moneychanging, and occasional tax-farming for the district government.

Yet it was not Jerusalem but Safed, a mountain community in Upper Galilee, that became the cynosure of revived Jewish settlement. This was an irony. When Benjamin of Tudela visited Safed in the twelfth century, he did not record a single Jew living there. The site was hardly more than an overgrown Arab village. Not until two hundred years later, in the mid-1300s, did it begin to attract Jewish settlers. By then, under the Mamelukes, and later the Ottomans, Safed had been transformed into a regional administrative center. Moreover, with its location almost midway between Tyre, Jaffa, and Jerusalem, the town also intersected Syria's principal southern trade routes. Jews and Arabs alike then began to gravitate toward the lofty fastness. Among the former, Sephardim made up the majority well before 1492. It was they who developed a thriving textile industry in Safed. By the mid-sixteenth century, their population here may have reached five thousand. An Italian Sephardi, David de Rossi, who had first visited Palestine in 1525 and returned a decade later, noted in astonishment that "whoever saw Safed ten years ago and sees it again now is amazed, for the Jews are constantly coming in and the clothing industry is expanding daily."

With its new demographic base, Safed began to generate a Jewish religious and intellectual vitality unknown to the Holy Land for a thousand years. Throughout the sixteenth century, dozens of rabbis settled here. Subsisting as part-time merchants or market gardeners, they managed to devote their principal energies to study and writing. Indeed, some of their religious poetry was austere enough to make its way into the Sabbath prayer book. Other rabbis established talmudic academies and concentrated exclusively upon learning and teaching. By the late 1500s, Safed maintained thirteen synagogues, four seminaries, and a distinguished collection of resident scholars.

By far the most eminent of these intellectuals was Joseph ben Ephraim Caro. Born in Toledo in 1488, Caro had departed for Lisbon with his parents in the great 1492 exodus. Five years later, the family took refuge in Turkey, where Joseph Caro remained for the next forty years, principally in Constantinople and Edirne. It was in Edirne that he came under the influence of Solomon Alkabez. A talented poet, author of the beloved Sabbath hymn "Lechah Dodi," Alkabez was also a renowned talmudic scholar. It was at his suggestion that Joseph Caro set about preparing an analytic compilation of Jewish law. In the late 1530s, still at work on the project, Caro followed Alkabez to Safed. There he was formally ordained. There, too, his astonishing erudition won him the chairmanship both of Safed's largest talmudic academy and of its local "Sanhedrin," a council of rabbinical sages. Within a few years, Caro's responsa on legal issues were accepted as authoritative throughout much of the Jewish world.

It was also in Safed, in 1542, that Caro finally completed his mighty juridical compilation *Beit Yosef* (The House of Joseph). Encompassing four volumes, the book was a detailed systematization of the vast moraine of codes and rabbinical dicta that had evolved over the previous three centuries. Indeed, so encyclopedic was this magnum opus that Caro entertained few illusions about its usefulness for everyday purposes. Consequently, with almost superhuman discipline, he spent an additional fourteen years summarizing its conclusions in a straightforward, readable format that limited itself to basic rules and regulations. Appropriately enough, he entitled the terse conspectus a *Shulchan Aruch,* a "Prepared Table." Almost immediately, the volume became the single most consulted source book in the Jewish world—perhaps even more widely than the Bible. Indeed, the *Shulchan Aruch* became the first universally revered code of Jewish law since the time of Maimonides, and among ultra-Orthodox Jews it remains so to this day.

Living to the great age of eighty-seven, Caro might easily have been content to preside as Jewry's senior jurisconsult. But in his last decades he abandoned the exposition of classical rabbinical law for a more exotic avocation. By then it had become the métier of virtually all scholars who congregated in Safed during the 1500s. This was the study and practice of *kabbalah.*

The Lure of the Kabbalah

As far back as the thirteenth century, we recall, thousands of devout Jews and Gentiles alike were conscientiously rejecting the "rationalist" approach to God. In scorning the coldly transcendentalist theologies of

Averroës and Maimonides, fundamentalists of all backgrounds often preferred to turn away even from biblical or koranic literalism in search of a direct, or theosophical, communion with God. As these pietists saw it, God's revelation was a continual, intricate, and mysterious process, one that could be evoked as much by the efforts of a reverential mortal as by the Almighty Himself. In the Islamic world, theosophy was favored by the proponents of Sufism, a form of mysticism that survived in Andalusia and North Africa, and later in the conquering Ottoman Empire.

Jewish mysticism similarly gained its initial momentum in medieval Iberia and Provence. Among its early practitioners in the thirteenth century, the best known may have been Abraham Abulafia. Born in Zaragoza in 1240, Abulafia moved extensively with his family throughout Catalonia and Navarre. In his late teens he was suddenly possessed by a "calling," and felt impelled to depart on his own for the Holy Land to seek out the "Ten Lost Tribes and the river Sambation." On his first voyage, however, young Abulafia got no farther than the port of Acre. With characteristic impulsiveness, he made the decision instead to sail back to Europe in order to marry. It was in later years, as he wandered with his bride throughout Italy and Greece, that Abulafia took up the study of kabbalah, or theosophy. Persuading himself that he had acquired prophetic insight, he soon began preaching his doctrine of mystical ascension to a small group of disciples.

Abulafia also published extensively. One of his early works, *Sifrei Nevuah* (Books of Prophecy), projected a series of exotic, even arcane formulas for communion with God. It was in the aftermath of one of his own communions, in 1280, that Abulafia declared himself summoned by God to help redeem His people. To fulfill that obligation, he departed for Rome. His intention was straightforward. It was to admonish Pope Nicholas III for the sufferings of the Jews and to exhort the pontiff to ameliorate their lot. Upon arrival and making his intention known, however, Abulafia was promptly clapped in prison and scheduled for burning. Only the sudden death of Nicholas a month later won Abulafia a reprieve and release, under a general amnesty proclaimed by the incoming pope, Martin IV. Shaken by the experience, Abulafia confined himself thereafter to more sedentary theorizing.

Yet if the man was rather less than a prophet, he was unquestionably a precursor of the single most influential figure in medieval Jewish mysticism. For between 1275 and 1291, even as Abulafia was proclaiming his otherworldly nostrums in Italy, a book was being written in Castile that was destined ultimately to overshadow all other kabbalistic texts. It was the *Sefer HaZohar* (The Book of Splendor). Consisting of twenty-four hundred tightly inscribed pages, the *Zohar* within two centuries would be ranked by much of the Jewish world as equivalent in prestige to the Talmud and even the Bible. Its author, Moses ben Shem Tov de Leon, born in 1240, the same year as Abulafia, spent the better part of his life in the middle-sized Castilian town of Guadalajara. Evidently much of his youth was devoted to the study of Maimonides and the Greco-Moslem philosophers. But in later years, Moses of Leon turned decisively from Aristotelianism to neo-Platonism, a philosophy that projected man's supreme goal less as a rational search for truth than as an ongoing struggle to emulate the perfection of God. It was this neo-Platonic approach that informed virtually every page of the *Zohar*.

Moreover, in a fascinating abnegation of scholarly ego, Moses of Leon chose to conceal his role as author and instead attribute the *Zohar* to Simon Bar-Yohai, a saintly teacher who lived in Roman Palestine in the second century A.D. In midrashic fashion, the volume proceeded discursively, taking the form of a series of conversations on the Bible conducted among Rabbi Simon, his son Eliezer, and a group of friends and disciples. The unlikelihood of Simon Bar-Yohai's authorship soon becomes apparent to the modern critic. Its mixed Hebrew-Aramaic text is ungrammatical; its geographic descriptions accord far better with thirteenth-century Castile than with second-century Palestine. Even so, for generations the legend persisted that the book actually was written by the beloved Simon, and it accounted for the veneration accorded his burial plot in Meron, Palestine. It explained as well the growing migration of kabbalists to the Galilean mountain village of Safed. Beyond its prestige as a focus of rabbinical scholarship, the town was only half a day's journey from Meron and the tomb of "Simon the Righteous."

The *Zohar*'s principal doctrines were essentially an elaboration of thirteenth-century ideas that developed almost simultaneously in Spain, southern France, and northern Italy. Foremost was the conception of God as the ultimate "Infinity." As the *Zohar* explained it, mortal man seeking communion with the Infinity could aspire at best to penetrate the "godhead," that is, the distilled reflection of the Infinity's attributes in the outer world. Thus far, in its emphasis upon refraction and obliqueness, the notion was characteristically neo-Platonic. Yet the *Zohar* went further, suggesting that perception of the godhead could be attained by reading the Torah as a vast corpus symbolorum, with each word and letter offering clues to the Infinity's hidden attributes. In later years, acceptance of this concept signified the beginning of the word-jugglery and numerological divination that became a favorite pastime of the medieval Jewish mystic. So did espousal of the *Zohar*'s rather libidinous formula of transmigration, the process by which the soul ascended after death from the nether regions into the godhead's "chamber of love."

Until the fifteenth century, the conflux of these exotic beliefs—the godhead, Torah-symbolism, reincarnation—was still the doctrine of a fringe element of theosophists, essentially limited to Castile, Catalonia, and southern France. But in 1492 the Spanish Expulsion Decree radically altered the functions and usages of kabbalah. Now, suddenly, the fate of the Jews was reinterpreted in the perspective of a transcendent apocalypse, as the final catastrophe before the "End of Days," that is, the redemption of the People of Israel in their own homeland, and ultimately of each among them in the Garden of Eden. The expulsion, then, apparently portended the advent of the Messiah. Isaac Abravanel, himself a victim of the Spanish expulsion (p. 72), was the first to stress in his exegetical writings that the tragedy of the Jews was purposeful—a manifest prelude to the arrival of the messianic age, which he calculated would begin in 1530.

Numerous other authors followed Abravanel's path, most of them producing various exegetical and homiletical treatises that interpreted the Spanish expulsion as the "birth pangs of the messianic age." It was this fusion of theosophy with messianism that would become the distinguishing characteristic of the "new," sixteenth-century kabbalah. The doctrine would be fashioned largely in Safed, by the sages and scholars who converged on this alluring mountain town in anticipation of the End of Days. Indeed, Safed's very air was redolent of once and future miracles. It was shared by the venerated Simon Bar-Yohai, whose grave lay in nearby Meron; the prodigious Maimonides, interred in Tiberias, only a day's journey away; the monumentally erudite scholar Joseph Caro, presiding in Safed over a "Sanhedrin" of fellow geniuses. Here, then, the wondrous event would soon occur, the apocalypse predicted by the "calculators of the End."

Most recently, Joseph Caro had verified the certainty of this occurrence. The great man was not simply a codifier and systematizer; he also shared in the mystical-messianic tendencies of his generation. In Edirne, he had come to know the talented young Solomon Molcho (p. 164), who was among the first to introduce him to kabbalistic theosophy. Some years later, after completing his *Beit Yosef,* Caro acknowledged that a messenger periodically appeared to him at night, identified himself as a heavenly spokesman for the godhead, and promised him that "you will fathom the depths of the wisdom of kabbalah. You will surpass the great kabbalist of Meron [Simon Bar-Yohai], and he will learn Torah from you." The promise was not quite fulfilled. Unquestionably, Caro was the greatest rabbinic authority of his time, and a man who now was lending his own vast prestige to theosophy. But in the mysteries of kabbalah he was soon to be much surpassed by several others among his colleagues in Safed.

The best known among these included Moses Alsheikh, David ben Solomon ibn abi Zimra, and Solomon Alkabez, the poet. In Edirne, Alkabez similarly communed with "heavenly messengers." After moving to Safed, he too began producing numerous mystical works, laying much emphasis on piety and prayer, on the importance of "cleaving to God" through passionate enthusiasm, even ecstasy. Over time, however, the seemingly endless pilgrimages of disciples to Alkabez's home aroused irritation among his Arab neighbors. One day, taking it upon themselves to end the annoyance, they stabbed him to death, then buried the body in his own courtyard.

With Alkabez gone, it was another of his disciples who eventually emerged as an even more renowned figure in the Safed school of mysticism. This was the Jerusalem-born Moses ben Jacob Cordovero. In his best-known work, *Pardes Rimonim* (Pomegranate Orchard), and in a profusion of later treatises, Cordovero adapted a selection of contemporary mystical ideas and reformulated them into a messianic-oriented theosophy more characteristic of the "new" kabbalah. In sheer output alone, Cordovero was legitimately to be compared to the intellectual giants of earlier centuries. By the time he died, in 1570, he had produced a voluminous series of commentaries and theses, many of these also works of considerable depth and originality. It became clear only later, in fact, that Cordovero was the profoundest theoretician of kabbalah since Moses de Leon himself.

It was still another mystic of Safed, however, Isaac Luria, a man of uncommon charisma, who proved far more successful in popularizing Cordovero's ideas. Luria was not a Sephardi. Rather, he had been born in Jerusalem of a Central European father, a background so atypical of the early mystics that later he was dubbed "Isaac Luria the Ashkenazi." Reared in Egypt, the young man studied kabbalah in a village on the Nile, and returned to Palestine only in 1569, at the age of thirty-five. This time he made his home in Safed, where he earned his livelihood as a dealer in pepper and other condiments. In Safed, too, characteristically, and despite the pressures of business and a growing family, Isaac Luria found time to synthesize and articulate his basic theosophic concepts.

They were essentially Cordovero's doctrines. Yet Luria was able to gather about him, as Cordovero never had, a substantial group of disciples, young rabbis who marveled at the range and depth of his vision, the lucidity of his expression. Luria actually wrote comparatively little in his lifetime and once observed, apparently without vaingloriousness but also without false modesty: "If all the oceans were ink, and all the bullrushes were pens, and all the heavens were paper, it still would not suffice for the transcription of my knowledge." His works have been passed down to us from notes transcribed by his students, Joseph ibn Tabul and Cham Vital, and these records make plain how, among all the giants of sixteenth-century Safed, Isaac Luria remained without peer as an interpreter and popularizer of kabbalah. The contraction of the initials of his best-known appellation, the "Ashkenazi Rabbi Isaac," gave him a fitting title, HaAri, "the Lion," the acronym by which he has since become renowned to posterity.

The Lion vastly amplified all previous kabbalistic teachings. One of the essentials of his system was his notion that the Infinity's luminescence, or, in Luria/Cordovero's interpretation, the "divine sparks" cast off at the moment of Creation, proved so formidable that the cosmic receptacles holding them suddenly broke, allowing them to blaze forth at random and thus to become contaminated by the impurities of the outer world. The process of redemption, that is, the achievement of the messianic age, was thus to be equated with the restoration of those divine sparks to the Infinity. It was the Lion's (and Cordovero's) revolutionary concept, more-over, that man played an active role in bringing the redemption to pass. In addition to contemplating the hidden symbols of sacred script, mortal man—by ardent prayer, by good deeds, by meditation upon God—was capable of actively projecting his soul into contact with the godhead. Even more, if enough men prayed with this fierce dedication, fasting and ob-serving penitence for the corruption of the world, then the holy sparks ultimately would be redeemed from their bondage on earth and, in turn, would release the godhead from exile. At the moment this came to pass, the messianic age would have arrived, and redemption would have been completed. For each individual who shared in the process, his soul, too, in the End of Days, would be released from its exile and transmigrate into the Garden of Eden.

The "Lurianic Kabbalah"

If there had been a certain linkage of kabbalism with messianism in earlier years, the union never achieved a fervor as intense as in sixteenth-century Safed, or a discipline as rigorous. In the hallucinatory atmosphere of this Galilean aerie, asceticism became a central feature of Jewish mysticism for the first time. Moses Cordovero adjured his followers against eating meat and drinking wine on weekdays, for "these foods endow [Satan] with strength." The "heavenly messenger" cautioned Joseph Caro "not to enjoy your eating and drinking and marital relations. It should be as if demons were compelling you to eat that food." As for Isaac Luria, the Lion prescribed ritual immersions in the winter, sleeping on the ground, rolling naked in the snow, rubbing dust in the eyes, walking barefoot over rocks. Chaim Vital recommended sackcloth and ashes, self-flagellation, sexual abstinence. In sum, the ultimate goal of religious life for the Safed kabbalists was a total withdrawal from terrestrial pleasures and a concentration upon prayer of an all-but-unbearable intensity.

Yet another characteristic emerged as integral to Safed mysticism. It was the prominence of conventicles of masters and disciples, and specifically those led by Cordovero, Eliezer Azikri, Chaim Vital, and, above all, Isaac Luria himself. Indeed, in the Lion's final years, and still more after his death in 1572, a rich tapestry of legend was woven around him. Immersed in the labyrinth of kabbalah, he was presumed to be endlessly catching glimpses of the outer spheres. While strolling with his disciples (the "Lion's Whelps"), he would blandly point out to them the graves of pious ancients with whose souls he held uninterrupted discourse. He understood not only the mysteries of *Zohar* but the chirping of birds, the rustling of leaves, and the speech of angels. Even while he slept he studied Torah with the souls of the saints in the Garden of Eden.

Numerous paintings by the renowned twentieth-century Israeli artist Moshe Castel are based on the Lion-legends. In *The Lion and His Whelps Greet the Sabbath,* a bearded and turbaned Isaac Luria, precociously white and gaunt (he died when he was thirty-eight, of cholera), leads a procession of equally white-bearded "students" along the brow of Mount Atomon. Beneath them, the rooftops of Safed are visible, while above hover two winged angels, becountenanced as women. The moon, stars, and two Sabbath candles gleam from a single cloud. So does the hand of the godhead, extending, supplicating, palm outward. The work interprets a particularly famous Lion-legend. One night, it was said, the wind of the Infinity crossed Isaac Luria's face. Inspired, the Lion remarked to his students: "Come, let us depart for Jerusalem to receive the Sabbath." We must assume that he expected to fly, for Jerusalem was a four-day journey from Safed. Most of the students promptly agreed. But one of them was more cautious. "Let us talk it over first with our wives," he suggested. Thereupon the Lion observed sadly: "The wind of the Almighty has already passed, for you have hesitated. Had you been of a single mind, the Messiah would already have come."

Chaim Vital Calabrese, of Italian Sephardic descent, was one of the few locally born members of Isaac Luria's original circle. Surviving the Lion by forty-seven years, Vital became the principal disseminator of his teachings. Indeed, Vital came to envision himself not merely as the authentic interpreter of the Master but as his lineal successor. Something of an "operator," he allowed it to be known that to him alone the Lion had vouchsafed his secrets, and he elaborated upon his bona fides in a self-serving autobiography, *Etz Chaim* (The Tree of Life). In it Vital declared that three years before his birth, a holy spirit prophesied to his father that a son would be born who would "not be less than the Messiah" and "would undoubtedly rule over all Israel."

In fulfillment of that worshipful destiny, Vital set about formulating a tortuous matrix of "practical" rules and regulations. These were devoted to the "cleansing" of the heavenly receptacles through release of the "holy sparks"; the assurance of transmigration for repentant sinners; the proper use of "concentrated" prayer for intercession in the "upper" regions. Under Vital's heavy hand, Isaac Luria's quite tentative use of *gematria,* the transposition of letters into symbolic numbers, was debased into quackery. So was the emphasis now placed on alchemistic prescriptions for physical illness and "soul" disease, on incantations and exorcisms of demons, dybbuks, destroyers, devils, and the "seven torments of hell." It was this "practical" kabbalah, then, trumpeted by Vital as the authentic "Lurianic" version, that emerged in ensuing years as a manual of ritual often as compelling as Joseph Caro's *Shulchan Aruch.*

First by oral tradition, then in works printed in Hebrew, Spanish, Portuguese, and Ladino, the "practical," "Lurianic" kabbalah transfused the largest part of the Sephardic world. From the seventeenth century on, moreover, its inroads were particularly far-reaching among oriental Jews, those living in the midst of vast Moslem majorities throughout the Near East and North Africa. Tactile and simplistic in its altered focus on talismans, icons, amulets, and sheer devotional rapture, kabbalism appeared tailor-made for these non-European communities. In the synagogues of Morocco, Algeria, and Tunisia, fraternities of *Zohar* readers (usually older men known for their piety and wisdom) were engaged to recite and offer commentary on kabbalah. In the backward Jewish enclaves of the Atlas Mountains, relays of kabbalists would chant from the *Zohar* on a twenty-four-hour-a-day basis during the week preceding major Jewish holidays. Like their audiences, these conventicles possessed only a dim understanding of the Aramaic texts. It hardly mattered, though; the process offered emotional release. So did the recipes and prescriptions intended to ward off devils and the evil eye, to assure health and fertility, and eventually to speed the arrival of the Messiah and the pietists' own ascent into the Garden of Eden.

So it was, by the seventeenth century, as the tidal wave of kabbalah swept from east to west, overflowing the Mediterranean littoral and penetrating the continent of Europe, that an exiled and traumatized people was engulfed by a fervor of mysticism that almost imperceptibly resolved itself into a euphoria of messianism.

The Mystical Light Fades

Well before then, ironically, the vigor of kabbalism in Palestine itself was beginning to ebb. The Ottoman Empire had swooned into its long, slow prostration, and nowhere was that enfeeblement more apparent than in the Holy Land. The communications network of the Levant began to deteriorate. So did public security. Commerce atrophied. Officials and military garrisons turned increasingly to extortion. In Jerusalem, Jewish immigration slowed, then halted, then reversed, until by 1600 fewer than a thousand Jews remained. The community in Safed held out a bit longer, then also began to shrink. By the end of the century, barely a half-dozen of its synagogues and academies survived.

Nor were these congregations predominantly Sephardic any longer. It was in the late 1700s that as many as two thousand Ashkenazim arrived in the Holy Land from Central and Eastern Europe and proceeded to make their homes in Safed. The newcomers were Chasidim, members of a subcommunity destined in future years to encompass a significant portion of East European Jewry. The Chasidim, who also were oriented toward mysticism, selectively modified a number of kabbalistic precepts. They rejected the Lion's emphasis upon penitence and suggested rather that the holy sparks cast out by the Infinity, far from being contaminated by evil, simply purified the world around them. The Chasidim insisted, moreover, that the pietist in search of communion with God should live his life in a rictus not merely of purposefulness but of joy, even ecstasy.

Yet there were other features of kabbalistic lore that the Chasidim of Safed enthusiastically accepted. For them, too, souls were continually in flight or in the process of reincarnation. For them, too, the letters of Scripture were freighted with secret and symbolic meanings. Chasidim and Sephardim alike regarded the venerated early kabbalists of Safed as wonder-workers, exalted Masters of the Good Name, chosen intermediaries between man and the Infinity. In every respect, Ashkenazic pilgrims matched their Sephardic counterparts in exalting these renowned holy men and in visiting, lamenting, and worshipping at their graves. And of all the interred pietists, none was adulated more than Simon Bar-Yohai, whose resting place was the focus of the original Sephardic presence in

Safed. For the Chasidim, Simon's tomb in nearby Meron became a shrine exceeded as an object of reverence only by those of the Patriarchs. Each Lag b'Omer, the eighteenth day of the Hebrew month of Iyar, in the midst of the "days of counting" between Passover and Pentecost, and the reputed date of Simon's death, the Chasidim visited his grave. There they gave themselves up to transports of mystic frenzy—dancing, shrieking, even, in the manner of Sufi dervishes, leaping through fire.

Guidebooks today list Meron as a "mere" three-mile drive from Safed. In fact, the trip is almost uninterruptedly perpendicular. Mount Meron looms nearly four thousand feet above sea level, one thousand feet above Safed. The town itself is inhabited by a few hundred Chasidim, essentially caretakers for the tomb. The resting place of Simon the Righteous is a spare, even stark, gray catafalque. Its chrysalis is the waxen residue of innumerable generations of memorial candles. A crude shelf attached to the neighboring walls bears the anguished petitions of equally numberless generations of Chasidim. The surviving appeals, on crumbling yellow parchment, seem to have been written almost exclusively by women. "Oh, Master of the Good Name," reads one, "five years now have I lain with the same husband, a gentle and pious man. But for the days of my uncleanness, he has known me without interruption. Still there is no issue. Diligently have I recited from the holy literature [presumably kabbalistic] all known remedies and prescriptions. Yet my womb is empty. Blessed saint, *ten li siman* [give me a sign—a rare Hebrew phrase in the Yiddish-language petition] so that I may do what is necessary to preserve my husband's name and the name of his revered father, the Rabbi Avner Mordecai the Ashkenazi." Another entreaty seeks relief from an illness, presumably trachoma, "woeful and melancholy affliction that curses my every waking hour. If I cannot see I cannot read the prayer book and make the pilgrimage to thy resting place except as a burden to my children. *Ten li siman.*"

The gravitational field of Simon's shrine and of later renowned kabbalistic grave sites accounted for the fitful migration of Ashkenazic Jews to Safed during the 1700s and 1800s. Many of the newcomers remained dependent upon charitable contributions from their European communities of origin, while others earned their livelihoods as tinkers, shoemakers, or spice merchants. During these same years, nevertheless, Safed's original sixteenth-century population of approximately five thousand diminished by at least half. Lawless Arab bands roamed the Galilee unchecked and periodically ravaged the little Jewish enclave. In 1838, an earthquake struck the district, killing many hundreds of people in Safed and shattering the economic base of the town's remaining Jewry.

For the mystics, however, even this natural catastrophe was not without an inner logic. In his celebrated historical novel *The Enchanted City* (1949), the Israeli author Yehoshua Bar-Yosef describes the earthquake's ominous approach, the "unbearable silence that envelops the town from all sides. It seems as if the mountains are whispering dread secrets to each other. Birds rush by in terror, screeching piteously. Vultures swoop down on the smaller birds. And all the while Rabbi Avrom Dov the Chasid silently observes the frightful slaughter of the upper regions, and trembles inwardly. . . ." Soon unearthly colors blaze through gray clouds, and the earthquake strikes. The rabbi watches helplessly as "a mighty thunderclap splits the air, and the mountain roars its response." In an instant, houses, people, and animals are gone. Only Rabbi Avrom Dov, his little synagogue, and its congregants inexplicably are saved.

Months later, Avrom Dov sits with his fellow worshippers late on a Sabbath afternoon, seeking an augury in the recent horror, and in their own unaccountable survival:

> The group is suffused with the pious mood of the Sabbath, and their half-closed lips breathe a quiet melody of hidden longings, of devotion to the godhead and the Infinity. The rabbi himself is lost in a hallucination of confused thoughts and images. Suddenly he visualizes himself dressed entirely in white, partly walking, partly flying over a wide field from whose sacred fruits rise scents of the Garden of Eden, saturating the air. Then, directly before him, he encounters none other than the venerable Lion, and the Lion's Whelps sitting at his right and left hand. They all raise their eyes heavenward, and behold! the blue sky is instantly inflamed by a spectrum of bright lights and joyous hues. Something is revealing itself in heaven. It is a splendid flower, a rose, unfolding its petals. And within the petals appears a gracious smile of ineffable beauty. The eyes of Avrom Dov have perceived the radiant face of the godhead.

The rabbi's vision portended no reversal of Jewish fortunes in Safed. Fifteen hundred souls had perished in the earthquake. The community was doomed. The majority of the survivors carried themselves off to Jerusalem or Jaffa. Those who remained were essentially aging mendicants, content to persevere on donations sent from abroad. Bar-Yosef informs us that dried twigs served as their winter fuel. Grits, peas, and goat's milk were their standard fare.

An evil spirit assailed this hapless remnant. Ashkenazic and Sephardic leaders quarreled among themselves over the trickle of charitable donations. World War I was their coup de grâce. The British naval blockade cut Palestine off from imports, including philanthropic remittances. Another thousand of Safed's Jews perished of hunger and typhus. By the time the State of Israel was born, fewer than five hundred remained. Hopelessly impoverished, evoking only the scorn and pity of their Arab neighbors, they wandered aimlessly between home and synagogue in a ruined dreamworld of their own.

CHAPTER VII

THE MESSIAH
OF THE AEGEAN

The Jerusalem of the Balkans

Salonika shimmers in an Aegean mirror. It is more than the luminescence of sea and sky that warms the visitor's heart. The streets are clean and wide. Scrupulously manicured parks and gardens compete in floral delectation. A magnificent stone-pebbled esplanade places the seaside within reach of Everyman. Parasoled waterfront cafés might have been transplanted from Capri or Amalfi, Torremolinos or Marseilles. Charming old villas, imaginatively trellised and landscaped, gaze down from the surrounding hills.

Traffic signs offer a clue to this unanticipated amalgam of order and aesthetics. We are only a few score miles from the Yugoslav and Bulgarian frontiers. This is not the Peloponnesus. This is Macedonia, well removed from the torpor of meridional Hellas, and Salonika is its crown jewel. The Greeks laid hands on the city only in 1912, after five centuries of Ottoman rule. Remarkably, they have not yet managed to ruin it, to wreak havoc on its natural grandeur or its treasury of Byzantine shrines, to deface the elegant urban face-lift achieved by engineers and architects of the occupying Allied armies in World War I. Yet Salonika's municipal authorities have perpetrated one unforgivable transgression: they have built their handsome, modernistic University City on the site of a Jewish cemetery that once was the second-largest in Europe, that bespoke a Jewish community which in size and luster was universally renowned in earlier years as the "Jerusalem of the Balkans."

In the Middle Ages, there would have been little intimation of that future eminence. Visiting Salonika in 1169, during the Byzantine period, Benjamin of Tudela encountered a harassed and straitened minority of not more than five hundred Jews. It was the Turkish conquest in 1430 that transformed their circumstances. In the years that followed, Salonika came to be inhabited by Jews of all backgrounds, but here as elsewhere in the Ottoman Empire the principal influx was of refugees from Spain. Indeed, they hispanicized the city. By 1530, Salonika's twenty thousand Jews—half the city's population, and by then the second-largest Jewish population in the world—spoke Ladino and dressed, cooked, and built their synagogues in the Sephardic manner. As late as 1904, Angel Pulido, a visiting Spanish senator, was astonished and overjoyed to discover that he could converse freely in his mother tongue virtually from one end of Salonika to the other.

The Jews brought their crafts and mercantile skills with them. It was the aggregation of expert Jewish weavers and dyers that developed the textile industry in the Turkish Empire. Their looms clacked ceaselessly in Salonika, producing vast quantities of sheets, carpets, and pile blankets. Some of this material was consigned for export, but most went to fulfill the Jews' fiscal obligations as dhimmis. Indeed, from the latter sixteenth century on, Salonikan Jews paid their poll taxes essentially in lengths of cloth to the Ottoman janissary corps. Even more than manufacture, however, it was commerce that became a virtual Sephardic monopoly here. The international Jewish network plainly stood the community in good stead, as did the preeminence of Venice as the trading entrepôt for the central Mediterranean, and thus the clearinghouse for Balkan traffic. Jews were leading importers and exporters both in Venice and in Salonika, as in numerous Adriatic way stations. In Salonika, their warehouses dominated the harbor skyline. Sephardic names appeared on every major shop in the town's commercial districts. By the seventeenth century, the Jewish mercantile role in Salonika was so overwhelming that all business, Jewish and non-Jewish, halted on the Sabbath.

Jews lived where they worked. Their homes were near the port, in the Francomahalla, the "quarter of the Francos," where elite Jewish agents for European companies operated under the protection of the European consuls; and near the Hippodrome, on the edge of the Greek quarter, where scores of shops and ateliers bore titles in Hebrew lettering. In whichever section, the Sephardim preserved their institutions and traditions. Subcommunities of Jews from Aragón, Catalonia, and Castile, from Portugal, Sicily, and Italy, all maintained separate and distinctive *cals,* each with its own skein of activities and services. Moreover, in their affluence and communal vigor, Salonikan Jews generated a cultural vibrancy second to none in the Diaspora. So numerous were their schools and academies that Jewish Salonika acquired the aura of a university city. Education was all-pervasive here. Every household was familiar with the Bible, the Talmud, the Lurianic kabbalah. Printing presses made this literature available at modest prices. Students came here from all parts of the empire, and even from Italy. If the sixteenth and early-seventeenth centuries were the golden age of Balkan Jewry, it was Salonika, endlessly renewed by infusions of marranos from Portugal and Italy, that glowed in the vortex of that creativity.

Then, in the 1620s, the sunburst began to fade. Marrano immigration slowly dwindled as Amsterdam emerged as an alternate sanctuary. With commerce shifting increasingly to the Atlantic, Venice too faded as a major trade center, and Salonikan Jewry's unique connection there declined in importance. Worse yet, the government's dhimmi taxes were becoming extortionate. Twice, Sultan Murad IV actually imposed a huge capital levy on the Jews. Throughout the latter 1600s, social despair among Salonikan Jewry evoked protests, even occasional riots. The Turks responded with imprisonments and occasional executions. So it was that frustration and hopelessness evoked an upsurge of kabbalism among Ottoman Jews. Salonikan Jewry shared in that compensatory passion. Mystery literature now was studied everywhere in schools, seminaries, homes. In their passion to hasten the coming of the Messiah, the faithful turned increasingly to nostrums prescribed in the Lurianic kabbalah, undergoing lengthy fasts and periods of self-flagellation. By the same token, emissaries from the Holy Land were received now with an excitement that bordered increasingly on hysteria. Surely, it was believed, these visitors would bring news of some decisive transformation in the Jewish condition.

The Man of Illuminations

To some degree, the messianic concept had worked its way into the Sephardic tradition even before its joinder with the Lurianic kabbalah. Following the 1492 expulsion, numerous Jewish émigrés threw themselves into a wave of apocalyptic speculation. Don Isaac Abravanel, it is recalled, went so far as to predict the Messiah's arrival in 1530. When the momentous year came and then went, eschatological tensions abated only temporarily. Intermittently, they were revived by self-proclaimed "messengers." In 1532, one David Reuveni appeared in Rome to proclaim himself emissary of the "lost tribe of Reuben" (supposedly in the Arabian Peninsula), whose king now wished the support of the pope and the European monarchs in reconquering the Holy Land. Could Reuveni be the Messiah? Jews were given little time to reflect on the possibility; after a few years of posturing and pronouncement-issuing, Reuveni was clapped in a Spanish prison, where he eventually died. His protégé, the former marrano Solomon Molcho, who echoed his patron's messianic fantasies, similarly met death, in his case at the hands of the Holy Roman emperor (p. 166). The tragedy traumatized Molcho's friend, the renowned scholar Joseph Caro. His "beloved Solomon" had been among the first to introduce him to the mysteries of kabbalah. Later in Safed, Caro would intensify his commitment to messianism as an integral feature of his theosophy.

By then, Lurianic kabbalism was shaping the religious consciousness of Jews everywhere. The movement's emphasis upon redemption of the "holy sparks," and thus redemption of the people of Israel, came to be suffused with an almost breathless expectancy of the arrival of a redeemer. Moreover, by the seventeenth century messianism gained an additional measure of urgency. In the Ukraine, a series of massacres annihilated tens of thousands of Jews. In the West, additional thousands were systematically being forced into ghettos. And in the Ottoman Empire too now, the deterioration in Jewish circumstances so affected the "Jerusalem of the Balkans" that Salonika's academic circles came to base their study of the Bible almost exclusively on kabbalistic tenets.

From the mid-1600s on, as it happened, those expectations coalesced about an unlikely messianic pretender, one Shabbatai Zvi. The man's origins are uncertain. His father, a merchant, apparently departed the Greek peninsula for Izmir about 1630. It was there that Shabbatai received a conventional religious training and was ordained a rabbi at the age of eighteen. Like others of his generation, he immersed himself in kabbalism. Even more than others, he developed an acute presentiment of the messianic age, a sense of impending apocalypse that was manifested increasingly in his personal behavior. Although Shabbatai evidently was incapable of sustained intellectual effort, his curious otherworldly demeanor and his soulful countenance, which appeared to be gazing endlessly upon a kind of inner vision, won him a group of disciples, who studied Talmud and kabbalah with him.

Possibly these were the characteristics that had attracted his wife. Shabbatai married her when he was twenty, then refused to touch her and divorced her a few months later. Soon afterward, he married a second time, again without consummation, and within the year again divorced. More bizarre yet were Shabbatai's "illuminations." These were convulsive withdrawals, either manic-depressive or, more likely, epileptic, that convinced observers he was either a madman or a prophet. A friend recalled: "He would retire to the mountains or caves without his . . . family knowing his whereabouts. At other times he would withdraw to a miserable little room where he locked himself in and from which he emerged only occasionally. . . . His brothers were grieved by his behavior and greatly ashamed, but could not prevail upon him to change his ways."

It was in the midst of one of these seizures, in 1654, that Shabbatai Zvi allegedly heard a voice proclaiming: "Thou art the savior of Israel. . . . I swear by my right hand and by the strength of my arm, that thou art the true redeemer, and there is none that redeemeth besides thee." When he recounted the episode and the claim, his listeners were scandalized. Indeed, the local rabbinate banished him from Izmir.

Shabbatai thereupon set off on an extended odyssey, wandering through the empire, subsisting on modest family allotments. His first port of call was Salonika, in 1655. Here, for the next two years, he achieved a certain tranquillity. But in 1657 Shabbatai suddenly went out of control. Upon undergoing a new series of "illuminations," he invited the Jewish communal leaders to a banquet, erected a bridal canopy, and performed a "marriage ceremony" between himself and the Torah. Horrified, Salonika's rabbis immediately pronounced a *cherem* on Shabbatai, a ban of excommunication, and expelled him from the city. He resumed his wandering. In 1658, the "redeemer" arrived at Constantinople. Here his spells became more frequent. During one of them, he purchased a large fish, dressed it as a baby, and explained that the redemption of Israel would occur under the astrological sign of Pisces. The reaction of the local rabbis was to have him lashed publicly by a court bailiff, then driven out of the city. Before departing Constantinople, however, the undaunted savior of Israel rejected Mosaic law in favor of a "higher law and new commandments." Henceforth, he would answer only to this "higher law."

Passing through Rhodes and Syria, Shabbatai eventually made his way to the Holy Land. For a year he stayed put in Jerusalem, where he organized a small talmudic academy. Notwithstanding his occasionally erratic behavior, here at least he evoked little more than pity. Jerusalem's skeletal Jewish population had known too many crazed pietists to be fazed by this latest eccentric. The interlude in any case was a brief one. In 1663, Shabbatai departed for Cairo. He remained there for two more years, preaching, praying, occasionally "illuminating"—and deciding to marry yet a third time. His bride, Sarah, was an Ashkenazi, a survivor of the 1648 Ukrainian massacres. She had made her way through Europe to Egypt by working as a prostitute. In Cairo with his new wife, Shabbatai entered into a period of relative stability. Although overweight and easily tired, apparently he experienced no further illuminations.

The Prophet and the Messiah

During his last months in Jerusalem, in 1663, Shabbatai may briefly have met a student, one Abraham Nathan ben Elijah Chaim Ashkenazi. Known simply as Nathan, this son of Polish-born Jews proved so astonishing an intellect that at the age of twenty he was married off to the daughter of a wealthy Sephardic merchant of Gaza and allowed to pursue his studies free of material concerns. Those studies were almost entirely in kabbalah. From his earliest adolescence, Nathan was all but overwhelmed by the world of mysticism. Soon he was consumed as well by the accounts he began hearing of Shabbatai Zvi. In March 1665, "Nathan of Gaza" himself underwent a vision. He wrote later:

> I was fasting in the week before [the holiday of] Purim. . . . [Upon] reciting the penitential prayers . . . with many tears, the spirit came over me, my hair stood on end, and my knees shook . . . and I saw visions of the [godhead] all day long and all night, and I was vouchsafed true prophecy . . . as the voice spoke to me and began with the words: "Thus speaks the Lord." And with the utmost clarity my heart perceived toward whom my prophecy was directed, that is, toward [Shabbatai Zvi].

From that moment on, Nathan emerged as a John the Baptist to the new messiah. In truth, he was a far abler figure than the stricken and confused Shabbatai, who on his own probably would have been dismissed as one of many quasi-messianic Jewish dreamers and misfits of the time. Now, in turn, rumors of Nathan's vision began reaching Shabbatai. Puzzled, the older man traveled from Cairo to Gaza to appraise this unknown admirer. The meeting evidently was cautious. But in ensuing weeks of intensive discussions, the two men drew closer. Together, they visited the graves of the Patriarchs in Jerusalem and Hebron, and Simon Bar-Yohai's tomb in Meron. Shabbatai recounted the circumstances of his life, his illnesses, dreams, and illuminations. Fascinated and moved, Nathan soon fitted these details into a pattern that fortified his vision of Shabbatai as the Messiah. Shabbatai's manic episodes were to be interpreted as the struggle of his soul, itself one of the "divine sparks," to wrest free from the forces of evil. Both men now underwent a final trauma of fantasizing and fainting. At last, in May 1665, Shabbatai openly declared himself "the anointed of the God of Jacob."

Remaining in Palestine, surrounded by a growing coterie of acolytes, the fat, middle-aged epileptic almost miraculously was transformed into a man of action. Indeed, Shabbatai even began devising mystical allusions to himself through *gematria*. Preaching repentance, he imposed heavy fasts and mortifications on visiting pietists. He also expanded upon his earlier practice of eliminating selected Jewish holy days and changing certain dietary rules. With Nathan's help, Shabbatai now won to his side a majority of the rabbis of Gaza and Hebron, and even a number of those in Jerusalem. Nathan meanwhile set to work devising a recognizable kabbalistic framework for Shabbatai's messiahship. With considerable ingenuity, he managed further to define the older man's illuminations as a process of capturing the "divine sparks" before they fell into the abyss. Bit by bit, he trimmed, adjusted, and manipulated the ingredients of Lurianic kabbalism to match the trajectory of Shabbatai's paroxysms and pronunciamentos.

Indeed, Nathan's charisma and showmanship fully complemented Shabbatai's. The younger man displayed both qualities in imputing to Shabbatai the power to redeem "even the greatest sinner, and . . . whoever entertains doubts about him . . . [Shabbatai] may punish with great afflictions." More portentously yet, Nathan assured his correspondents that the Messiah soon would painlessly take the crown from the Turkish sultan himself and make the ruler his servant. As he explained afterward in a letter to a Cairo rabbi:

> Our Messiah will come to Jerusalem with Moses our teacher and the people of Israel, [and] the Almighty will let down from the heavens the Temple, constructed of gold and precious stones that will illumine the whole city. . . . Then our Messiah will bring sacrifices to the Almighty, and the resurrection of the dead will take place over the whole world. . . . I inform you of this that you may know that you will soon have the privilege of being redeemed. Thus saith Nathan Benjamin Ashkenazi.

The Messiah Revealed

People were listening. Thoroughly infused by the prevailing mood of kabbalistic mysticism, the Jews of Jerusalem acclaimed Shabbatai with unalloyed hysteria in July 1665, as he proceeded in an escorted carriage on a self-proclaimed "missionary" tour. His destinations were first Aleppo, then Tripoli, then Izmir. Upon reaching the last community, and still in one of his tranquil interludes, the Redeemer charmed his listeners with a pacifying display of kindness and tact. In December, however, Shabbatai was seized again by illuminations. Rising in the middle of the night, he performed several ritual immersions in the sea, then appeared in the

Portuguese synagogue at dawn garbed in a gold-braided robe and carrying a silver fan as a kind of scepter. At the lectern, speaking now through his own mouth rather than Nathan's, Shabbatai for the first time declared publicly that he was indeed the Messiah, and he invited the assembled worshippers to come forward to "kiss the hand of the king." Most of the congregants did so. From this point on, Shabbatai began issuing a series of decrees, changing the dates of Jewish liturgical practices, even declaring Monday rather than Saturday as "his" Sabbath.

The Izmir rabbis were profoundly divided. Aaron Lapapa, leader of the Portuguese congregation, set about organizing resistance to the "madman." But Lapapa and other rabbinical skeptics had not reckoned with their own congregants. Some of these now threatened to break down the doors of any synagogue that denied Shabbatai recognition as the "son of David" and "Redeemer of Israel." Shabbatai himself promptly set about rousing the community to a frenzy. In a synagogue ceremony, he proclaimed the date of imminent redemption as 15 Sivan 5426, that is, June 18, 1666. Soon afterward, he ordered an end to the tradition of fasting on Tisha b'Av, the Hebrew date commemorating the destruction of the ancient Temple. Plainly, lamentation and mourning no longer were appropriate now that the Messiah had arrived. Wherever Shabbatai so much as appeared in public by then, worshippers pressed forward to touch his cloak, kiss his hand, invoke his blessing.

News of this transfiguration circulated rapidly. Izmir was an important port city. Its population included a substantial colony of English, Dutch, and Italian traders; their incredulous accounts of the messianic craze reached far beyond the Ottoman Empire. A Dutch merchant wrote home:

> At that time there appeared . . . over two hundred "prophets and prophetesses" upon whom there fell a mighty trembling so that they fainted. In this condition, they babbled that Shabbatai Zvi was the Messiah and King of Israel who would lead his people safely to the Holy Land, and that ships of Tarshish, that is, with Dutch crews, would come to transport them. . . . Even little children four years old and less recited psalms in Hebrew.

By late 1665, the mass hysteria was extending throughout Asia Minor, from Izmir to Bursa to Edirne. In Gallipoli and the Aegean islands— Rhodes, Crete, Cyprus—the reaction was the same flood of emotion and mass prophesying. The frenzy engulfed not only untutored common people but more than a few rabbis, men renowned for their scholarship and wisdom. In Salonika, the rising exultation brought trade nearly to a standstill as Jews engaged in banqueting, dancing, torchlight processions.

Meanwhile, in a breathtaking act of lèse majesté, Shabbatai went so far as to abolish the traditional synagogue prayer for the sultan and applied its text instead to the "new king of Israel." In December 1665, compounding the sacrilege, he distributed among his followers "kingdoms" selected at random from Ottoman territory. It was this final effrontery that provoked Izmir's local Turkish authorities to expel Shabbatai Zvi on the spot. Yet the Messiah remained unfazed. Sailing out of Izmir, he projected as his next destination the largest Jewish community in the world, the thirty thousand Jews of Constantinople itself.

They awaited Shabbatai in a state of almost unbearable excitement. But emotions were mixed. For many rabbis and communal elders, tension was infused with dread. They feared the consequences of Shabbatai's "royal" bestowals. Indeed, their first instinct was to denounce him. But the Jewish masses would have none of it. They were seized in a delirium of imminent redemption. Chroniclers have left accounts of people dropping in the streets, twitching uncontrollably, foaming at the mouth. Letters of homage to Shabbatai were arriving from other parts of the Jewish world, acknowledging him as ruler, placing their lives in his hands, entreating him to restore the Kingdom of Israel, to redeem the spirits of their loved ones. Evidently too much time had passed for the rabbis of Constantinople to turn back the tide.

It was Grand Vizier Ahmed Koprulu who first took preemptive action. On his orders, Shabbatai's vessel was intercepted as it entered the Dardanelles, and the Messiah himself was brought to the capital under guard. There he was placed in detention, well removed from the Banat area, the principal Jewish quarter. Koprulu, one of the great statesmen of Ottoman history, was not a cruel man, and he was entirely uninterested in making a martyr of Shabbatai Zvi. But Shabbatai could not be allowed to disrupt the normal life of the capital, as he had of Izmir and Salonika. If thousands of Jews were to abandon their business activities, or, worse yet, depart for the Holy Land, the economic losses for Constantinople would be grave. Within three days of his arrest, the Messiah was escorted to the Great Diwan, presided over by Koprulu. Yet by then Shabbatai apparently had entered into a stable interlude once more. He impressed the grand vizier and other ministers with his charm and moderation, and his professions of loyalty to Sultan Mehmet IV. Accordingly, Koprulu ordered Shabbatai confined for the time being, but in quarters of reasonable comfort. He was even permitted to receive visitors, as long as he exercised restraint.

Shabbatai's followers, however, had been worked into an uncontrollable redemptionist hysteria. Foreign merchants encountered paralysis in the markets and warehouses. Without their customary Jewish interlocutors, these visiting businessmen were unable so much as to change money or unload their produce. After two months of this agitation, the government ordered Shabbatai removed to the fortress of Gallipoli, on the European side of the Dardanelles. Thereby opened an entirely new chapter in the Shabbatean movement.

Shabbateanism in Europe

It was a movement, we recall, that drew its earliest impulsion from the Holy Land—from Safedian mysticism, the Lurianic kabbalah, and Nathan of Gaza. As a result, it generated its principal momentum in the oriental world. The upheaval affected Europe only in late 1665. Italy was its likeliest venue. A half-century earlier, as their legal and economic status deteriorated under the impact of the Counter-Reformation (pp. 228–29), the Jews of Naples, Rome, Venice, and other peninsular cities had been among the first to be swept up in kabbalism. For them now, Shabbatean messianism represented essentially a continuation of that initial theosophic release. It drew also from the Lurianic tradition of mass penitence. A traveler in seventeenth-century Casale noted that a scheduled local Purim carnival had been canceled, as there would be no time for such merriment in the hysteria of anticipated departure. Rabbis exhorted their congregants to restore all ill-gotten gains before the Redemption. In Ferrara, reports circulated of individuals expiring as a consequence of week-long fasts.

From Italy, the wave of excitement surged westward. Ironically, even prosperous Amsterdam offered a favorable climate for Shabbateanism. In contrast to Turkey, where Shabbateanism soon would be regarded as tantamount to political rebellion, or to such Catholic cities as Rome or even Venice, where clerical suspicions had to be taken into account, cautionary measures were less important in this Protestant city. Secure and protected, Jews here were freer to respond to messianic tidings as they chose. Accordingly, Shabbateanism was embraced by communal leaders and simple Jews alike, the wealthiest and the poorest. In the Esnoga, the main Portuguese synagogue, Shabbateans who joined in wild dancing around the Ark of the Torah included the kabbalist Isaac de Fonseca Aboab, the grandee Abraham Pereira, the learned philologist Benjamin Mussafia. Pereira and Isaac Na'ar, dean of Amsterdam's talmudic academy and a friend of Spinoza, actually set out with their households for Turkey to greet the "king of kings," the "Messiah of the God of Jacob," "our king and redeemer." Rabbi Aaron Tsarfati of Amsterdam, writing to a friend, described a people "whose fervor is beyond description. . . . If you were here, you would behold the world upside down."

In 1665, Amsterdam Jewry adopted a new calendar, beginning with the "Year of the Deliverance of Israel." Letters and even books were dated from "the first year of the renewal of the prophecy and the kingdom." Jews now began selling their homes and lands as they prepared for departure to the Holy Land. Some pietists anticipated literally being carried off on clouds, and they awaited the decisive moment on their rooftops. Many Jews arranged to disinter the bones of family members for transport to Jerusalem. Young and old alike gave breathless attention even to the faintest rumors of Shabbatai's odyssey. News of the Messiah's confinement in Gallipoli early in 1666 infused them with still greater anticipation. Shabbatai, it was claimed, had passed through the locked doors of his prison. He had broken chains and bars alike. He had levitated over water. He had resurrected the dead.

From Amsterdam, the craze spread throughout Western and Central Europe. In England, non-Jews commented on the pandemonium reigning in London's tiny Sephardic community. Samuel Pepys described "a Jew in town, that in the name of the rest do offer to give any man £10 to be paid £100 if a certain person now at Smyrna [Izmir] be within these two years owned by all the Princes of the East, and particularly the grand Signor, as the King of the World . . . and that this man is the true Messiah." The "good news" reached even the Americas. In Boston late in 1665, Increase Mather sermonized that "the Israelites were upon their journey towards Jerusalem . . . and they [have] written to others in their Nation, in Europe and America, to encourage and invite them to hasten to them, this seemed to many godly and judicious [people] to be a beginning of that Prophesie [Ezekiel 37:21]." In France and Germany, meanwhile, there was much excitement among Sephardic and Ashkenazic Jews alike. In Hamburg, a gathering of communal elders resolved to offer the entirety of their congregation's real estate for auction to pay off the community's debts "and prepare ourselves for the journey which we soon hope to make with God's help."

And so it was, through late 1665 and much of 1666, that the messianic delirium reached its apogee. When Nathan of Gaza decreed the issuance of new Shabbatean prayer books, the Hebrew printing presses of Constantinople, Salonika, Amsterdam, Mantua, Frankfurt, and even Prague and Cracow worked overtime to meet the demand. Everywhere, worshippers took lengthy ritual baths, fasted up to a week at a time, lay naked in the snow, scourged themselves with thorns and nettles. Commerce was extensively interrupted. Thousands of Jews continued to sell their businesses,

homes, and chattels in anticipation of the journey to the Holy Land. No
Jewish community remained untouched by the Shabbatean epidemic.

From his confinement in Gallipoli, meanwhile, the Messiah began
signing his pronouncements as "first-born son of God," "your father
Israel," "the bridegroom of the Torah," even "I am your Lord Shabbatai
Zvi." A swelling pilgrimage of devotees made its way to his quarters.
Upon completing their audiences with the great man, the visitors would
return wonder-struck with tales of his "court" and his "royal" manner.
Leib ben Ozer, an Ashkenazi of Cracow, described Shabbatai lounging at
his ease on red cushions, the walls of his room hung with gold tapestries,
the floor covered with red and silver carpets:

> It was a princely chamber. [Shabbatai] sat at a table made of silver
> and [covered] with gold, and the inkstand on the table was made of
> gold and jewels. He ate and drank from gold and silver goblets en-
> crusted with jewels. . . . All day long he was singing hymns of praise
> to God . . . and whoever went in, left him with great joy and great
> consolation.

In the late summer of 1666, Shabbatai reissued a "decree" that he had
proclaimed from Izmir nearly a year before. It was abolition of the fast of
Tisha b'Av. Plainly, then, the redemption of Zion was at hand. Jews in
the Ottoman Empire and Europe alike now launched into a new round of
penances and mortifications. They fell into trances and spoke in tongues.
In fact, the crescendo of preparations foreshadowed less a deliverance
than a denouement of the Shabbatean movement. Rumors that the Holy
Land was about to devolve into the hands of Israel took on a rather more
sobering character for Sultan Mehmet IV.

A Salonikan Interlude

No city should be judged by its commercial center. Salonika's today is
comparable to the downtown of any middle-sized European city.
Crowded thoroughfares and drably functional office buildings and shops
offer few surprises. The little Sephardic synagogue does. Its entrance, in
the heart of this congestion, on Vassileou Irakliou Street, is one of a
succession of rather nondescript doorways in a shopping gallery. Inside,
however, the chaste sanctuary is a delight of pastel understatement and
minimalist ornamentation. In the summer of 1991, Rabbi Moshe Halegua
blended with the restrained decor. Small-boned, fair-skinned, balding,
wearing a summer shirt, he sat inconspicuously in one of the pews,
chatting softly with a congregant of his own generation. Both men had
numbers tattooed on their forearms.

Halegua was born in this city in 1918, one of seven children of a kosher-wine salesman, Yitzhak Halegua, and his wife, Flor. The family's, and community's, language was Ladino. Residing on Frangolepoulou Street, a lower-middle-class Jewish quarter, the Haleguas shared with neighboring families a labyrinth of interlocked apartments and joint cooking facilities. The communal life Moshe Halegua remembered was highly organized and as intensely ethnocentric in its Jewish ceremonialism as the public and family activity of Greeks, Bulgars, Turks, and others among Salonika's heterogeneity of peoples. By tradition, the rabbi governed as undisputed leader of the *cal,* presumably serving as the fount of piety and wisdom.

As late as the mid-nineteenth century, this mosaic of cultures functioned within an empire that was still in a condition of apparently terminal paralysis. The Jews had shared in that malaise. Over the years, they, too, had declined from wealthy capitalists into petty shopkeepers and artisans, and even into a substantial proletariat of fishermen, stevedores, carters, and porters. By the latter part of the century, however, there were tentative intimations of economic revival. In 1889, a major new harbor was completed for Salonika, providing wharfage for more extensive shipping traffic. At almost the same time, the city was connected to the new Trans-Balkan Railroad, linking it more efficiently to the mercantile centers of the West. European technology and European ideas similarly began to make their way into the port community. The Jews, numbering then about ninety-five thousand—still almost half Salonika's population—once again began to generate the nucleus of a vibrant middle class. Indeed, by the early twentieth century, they appeared to be regaining direction of the city's commercial life, in shipping, import-export, tobacco manufacturing and distributing, not to mention retailing. So thoroughly by then was the rhythm of Salonika attuned to its Jewish plurality that, as in the 1600s, all business came to a standstill on the Sabbath and Jewish holidays.

Here as elsewhere in the Ottoman Empire, the establishment of a network of Alliance Israélite Universelle schools fortified this tentative Jewish embourgeoisement. So did the growing number of young Jews who journeyed to France for their higher education. "The century was drawing to a close," Leon Sciaky remembered in his *Farewell to Salonica* (1946). "Stealthily the West was creeping in, trying to lure the East with her wonders. She dangled before our dazzled eyes the witchery of her science and the miracle of her inventions. We caught a glimpse of her brilliance, and timidly listened to the song of the siren." Responding to that allure, Salonikan Jewry by the early 1900s had embarked upon a modest cultural and political renaissance. From their midst they generated a new spate of newspapers and journals, of drama, music, literary, and political-party activities. The sunburst also reflected a "higher" intellectual familiarity with the French language and its literature. With their solid ethnic roots, Salonikan Jews were developing an impressive multilingual ethnicity in Hebrew, Ladino, and French, if only marginally in Turkish and Greek.

Perhaps the most prominent feature of that renewed vitality was Zionism. Nowhere in the world was passion for the Holy Land more full-orbed than in Salonika. In the immediate aftermath of World War I, at least twenty Zionist societies of various ideological hues were functioning in the city. Every synagogue and parochial school had its little blue-and-white Jewish National Fund box. By 1939, seventeen thousand Salonikan Jews had emigrated to Palestine. Among them was Moshe Carasso, scion of a distinguished political family (p. 99), who developed numerous import-export, automobile, and real estate enterprises in Palestine. The financier Yehuda Recanati settled in Palestine in 1935 to help found the Discount Bank, eventually to become the largest private Jewish bank in the country and one that contributed massively to the growth of the Israeli economy. Most of the immigrants, to be sure, were people of limited means, among them several hundred stevedores who helped to build the new port of Haifa. But whatever their economic circumstances, the vision of a redeemed Jewish National Home reflected the deepest emotional instincts of a profoundly, irredeemably ethnocentric community.

That Zionist vision also bespoke a growing sense of political vulnerability. In 1912, the first of two Balkan Wars drove the Turks from Macedonia and established Greek rule over Salonika. The government in Athens wasted little time consolidating its grip on the great Aegean port. To shift economic advantage to the local Greeks, it imposed a punitive series of taxes upon such traditional Jewish vocations as textile manufacture and retailing. World War I compounded the Jews' difficulties. No sooner had British and French troops occupied Salonika in 1917 than an epic inferno gutted the city's principal commercial districts—again, essentially the Jewish business areas. In the longer run, the devastation enabled Allied engineers to redesign and virtually rebuild Salonika as a paradigm of municipal efficiency and aesthetic elegance, but the interregnum was traumatic. Worse was to come. The postwar Greek regime was determined to hellenize Salonika, to purge it of its "cosmopolitan," that is, Sephardic, ambience. Ironically, the man who offered the government its best chance was Mustafa Kemal, who himself had been born in Ottoman Salonika. Yet as the architect of postwar Turkish revival, it was the selfsame Kemal who drove the Greek army out of Asia Minor in 1922, sending over a million "Smyrniot" Greeks—citizens of Izmir and its surroundings—fleeing into the Kingdom of Greece. Ultimately, more than one hundred thousand of the fugitives were resettled in Salonika.

The arrival of this Smyrniot tidal wave doomed Jewish preeminence in the city. Offered every financial and tax benefit, the Greek-speaking newcomers soon achieved decisive control over local trade and industry. In 1923, moreover, the government of Prime Minister Eleutherios Venizelos banned all commercial activity in Greece on Sunday. Jews who observed their own Saturday sabbath were thus obliged to close their businesses for an extra day. New education laws similarly required the Alliance schools to drop French, even Ladino, as the language of instruction in favor of Greek. Well into the 1930s, the Venizelist press engaged in thinly veiled antisemitism, editorializing against "those interlopers who suck the blood of our people, who are in the forefront of communism." Fascist political and paramilitary groups sprang up. In 1930, when a congress of Balkan Jewish sports organizations gathered in Sofia, a Bulgarian Jew inadvertently parroted Bulgarian nationalist claims to Macedonia. Greek newspapers immediately seized upon the comment, and right-wing elements then attacked the Salonika Jewish suburb of Campbell, razing some three hundred homes while the police stood by. In the 1920s and 1930s, the earlier trickle of Jewish emigration grew into an uninterrupted stream. Even then, as seventeen thousand Jews sailed off to Palestine, nearly that many also departed for France and the Americas. By 1939, the Jewish population of Salonika had dropped to approximately sixty-five thousand.

They were still a dynamic community. Yet if Zionism gained momentum among Salonika's Jews, so now did socialism, even communism. "We understood their bitterness," explained Rabbi Halegua. "A majority of our people were intensely Jewish. Anyone will tell you that. Even the Jewish Communists published their newspapers in Ladino. But with the rise of fascism in Greece, radicalism was the one political protest left to us." As for Halegua himself in those years, he continued his education in a talmud torah, in preparation for entering the local rabbinical seminary. Then, in October 1940, a force majeure obtruded. Mussolini launched his army against Greece.

Adiós, Salonika

The Italian campaign failed. Greek resistance proved unexpectedly fierce. On April 6, 1941, however, Adolf Hitler came to Mussolini's rescue. The German Wehrmacht invaded Greece and overran the country within a month. Soon afterward, the nation was partitioned into zones of occupation. The Italian salient encompassed western Greece, including Athens, the Peloponnesus, and the Dodecanese islands (already under Italian administration). Thrace and eastern Macedonia were delivered over to the Bulgarians. Germany reserved central Greece and Salonika for itself. Indeed, in mid-April 1941, even before hostilities ended, the first German motorized columns entered the great port city. Moshe Halegua, then twenty-three, remembered the moment. Almost immediately, the Jewish hospital and a number of Jewish private apartments were sequestered for Nazi use. The Jewish community council was shut down. In early May, Dr. Zvi Koretz, the chief rabbi, was taken into custody.

Koretz was an Ashkenazi. Not long before, the Jews of Salonika, Sephardim almost to the last soul, had broken from tradition to elect him. Presumably, his superior education justified the choice. In his late forties, tall, fluent in German, with a beautifully manicured goatee and courtly manner, Koretz now seemed the ideal person to deal with the Nazis. Yet at this moment, just when his presence had become crucial, he was unaccountably under detention. Several days later, the Germans took Koretz off to Vienna. Weeks passed and the rabbi's fate remained a mystery. Was he interceding on behalf of the community? Was he being intimidated? Brainwashed? Abused? "We were almost breathless awaiting news of him," Halegua recalled. And then, a month later, Koretz suddenly returned. He would say nothing of his experiences in German hands. If pressed, he became evasive and simply assured his congregants that "all will be well with our people, now that I am back." Indeed, in ensuing weeks, when no additional anti-Jewish measures were introduced, the community began to breathe more easily.

In late June 1941, the Wehrmacht launched its assault on the Soviet Union. Almost simultaneously, an SS unit arrived in Salonika and began requisitioning additional Jewish homes. Accompanying the SS troops were academic specialists from the "Institute for Jewish Studies" in Frankfurt, an antisemitic think tank that now set about cataloguing and carrying off valuable synagogue artifacts, together with thousands of volumes and manuscripts from Jewish libraries. "We queried Koretz about these developments," Halegua remembered. "He would say nothing except that all would be well, that we must not protest German actions." By the autumn, however, as maritime traffic dried up, the population of Salonika experienced growing privation. Gentiles as a rule had access to kinsmen in the surrounding farm country who could provide them with occasional foodstuffs. The Jews did not. In the winter of 1941–42, their death rate from malnutrition reached sixty a day.

Thus far, at least, no explicit racial laws had been introduced. "The chief rabbi was with us," explained Halegua. "We regarded him as our shield." Koretz seemed even more than that. The Germans actually exalted his role. They appointed him president of a reestablished—puppet— community council, and thus virtually as ruler of Salonika Jewry. The man acted the part. He demanded strict obedience from his constituents. "I had been married for a year by then," Halegua recounted. "My wife, Daisy, was expecting. I was prepared to grasp at any straw that promised us security, even when Rabbi Koretz declared that Hitler was doing a number of good things in Europe. I swallowed that. We all did."

In the spring of 1942, yet another SS commission arrived. This one compiled a detailed census of Salonika's Jews. Then, three months later, on July 11, lightning struck. The Nazi commandant ordered some nine thousand male Jews between the ages of seventeen and forty-five into Liberty Square, the city's main plaza. There they stood for hours in the blazing sun as the SS queried each of them. Finally, in mid-evening, they were released. Three days later, however, the SS rounded up two thousand of these men and boys and loaded them onto cattle trucks. Carried off to work camps in the hinterland, the Jewish prisoners were assigned to swamp-clearing. Hundreds died of exposure and malnutrition. Within Salonika itself, Jews were forbidden by then to use public transportation, to own telephones or radios, to appear in the streets after dark. In a particularly sinister new development, the Germans ordered all the remaining fifty-five thousand Jews transplanted to a compact slum area near the railroad station. Housing facilities here totaled a bare six hundred rooms. The congestion was surrealistic. The human beehive soon was fenced off from the rest of the city. Searchlights and machine guns were installed on towers outside.

Koretz had been assured complete autonomy for his Jewish "government." He now exhorted his "subjects" to fulfill all SS orders punctiliously. On March 13, 1943, the chief rabbi transmitted yet a new German directive, this one ordering Jews to turn over all their remaining movables to central depots, except for household goods and the simplest personal necessities. In theory, they would be given cash payment. In practice, their money would be deposited in banks, in a special account to be "supervised" by the SS. To ensure swift fulfillment of these orders, the Germans seized one hundred prominent Salonika Jews as hostages. It is all but certain that Koretz himself drew up the list. At the same time, locomotives and freight cars began pulling up on newly laid rail spurs outside the ghetto. The likelihood of "relocations" no longer could be ignored.

Moshe Halegua by then was caring for his widowed mother and six younger brothers and sisters as well as his wife and infant daughter. He decided to visit Koretz's office. "The Germans want additional laborers for their special work camps," he reminded the rabbi, alluding to the grim penal compounds. "If I volunteer, can you assure me that my family will be spared from harm?" Koretz radiated confidence. "You couldn't make a better move," he promised the young man. "The Germans react well to that kind of cooperation." And so Halegua departed for his labor incarceration that very week.

More rolling stock arrived at the ghetto. "These trains will be carrying our people to Cracow," Koretz explained to a meeting of Jewish representatives on March 15. "The great Jewish community of Cracow will welcome you and ensure that you are properly cared for. Everyone will be given work according to his ability and preference. I urge you to cooperate." The chief rabbi then distributed a quantity of Polish zlotys among the group. Despite their grave misgivings, the representatives accepted the currency and disbanded. As Salonika's Jews prepared for collective departure, some of them managed to contact Gentile acquaintances and barter their last personal possessions for warm clothing. During the next weeks, they were boarded on a succession of departing trains. Not everyone cooperated. Several dozen younger Jews attempted to flee the city, intending to join the partisans. Most were caught and shot. By late summer, the largest numbers of Salonika Jewry were duly carried off to Poland. Their destination was not Cracow, of course, but Auschwitz.

As for Moshe Halegua, laboring on a road gang in Thebes, his own status was not altogether unbearable. He was tattooed and confined in a verminous barracks. His rations were marginal. But his supervising officer, an overage Austrian supernumerary, took a liking to him and protected him from terminal "resettlement." In June 1943, Halegua was even selected out and shipped back to Salonika. Koretz still reigned there as king of the Jews. But in fact, only a few thousand of his subjects were left. It was then Halegua learned that his own wife, daughter, mother, brothers, and sisters were among the missing. They had been deported. In his horror and grief, the young man barged into Koretz's office. He accused the chief rabbi of betrayal. "Hold your tongue," warned Koretz. "Another word out of you and I'll summon the Germans." The threat was not idle. On earlier occasions, Koretz had telephoned SS officials in outlying towns and identified Jewish escapees. As he had explained to his staff, the measure was necessary to save the "bulk" of the Jewish population. It was in any case one of the last threats the chief rabbi uttered. In late August 1943, he himself was arrested with his family and carried off to Bergen-

Belsen. His wife and son survived. Koretz held on until the Allied liberation but died one week afterward.

Throughout the spring and summer of 1943, German trains had carried off nearly fifty thousand Salonikán Jews. Only twelve hundred returned —a killing rate of 97 percent. When Halegua now describes these events (in perfect, near-literary Hebrew), he does so without emotion. Shlomo Reuven, who lost his mother, a sister, two brothers, and eight nieces and nephews, chooses to express himself formally in poetry. Reuven lives in Tel Aviv and writes of Salonika's vanished Jewry in a Ladino-language newspaper:

> No. This is not the city where I first saw light.
> These are not the men I knew in my infancy.
> This is not the sun that shone then,
> Nor this the sky that intoxicated me. . . .
>
> So the shadows pass in a long file and I hear
> The steps on the asphalt and their lips palpitate,
> And their terrifying laments mix with the wind,
> The wind that is powerless to drown out the groans.

The wind that was powerless as well to drown out the curses against him who had collaborated in Salonikan Jewry's last martyrdom.

The Great Betrayal

It was not the Sephardic world alone that waited breathlessly throughout August 1666 for the impending redemption. From distant Lvov, there now arrived in Gallipoli one Nechemia Hacohen. On behalf of the Council of Polish Jews, Hacohen had made the trip to learn from the Great One the precise date for the mass return. Yet, upon being admitted to the celestial presence, and engaging in three days of extended conversations, Nechemia discerned certain incongruities in Shabbatai's claims. He was particularly troubled by Shabbatai's rejection of a key scriptural injunction, namely, that the Messiah should be preceded by a "messenger" from the House of Joseph. The discussions ended in acrimony. Distraught, Nechemia secured an audience with the local Turkish aga and denounced Shabbatai to this official as a fomenter of "sedition"—although without specifying whether against Jewish or Ottoman authority.

By then the government had had its fill of Shabbatai. In September he was carried off to Edirne and brought to one of the royal palaces. There he was interrogated by the Great Diwan, which was sitting in the provinces that month. Sultan Mehmet IV himself was present, observing the interrogation from a latticed alcove. Shabbatai apparently sensed that royal toleration for his messiahship had expired; he had fallen into a near-catatonic despondency. Accused now of fomenting sedition, he could only mumble his denial. Hereupon the assembled ministers offered the prisoner a choice: he could become either a live Moslem or a dead messiah. On the spot, Shabbatai agreed to embrace Islam. For a circumcised Jew, the procedure was a simple one. He had only to discard his Jewish headgear, don a Moslem turban, and pronounce the credo: "There is no God but Allah and Mohammed is the messenger of Allah." Soon afterward, as "Aziz Mehmet Effendi," Shabbatai graciously consented to accept a royal pension in his honorific new position as *kapici bashi*, "keeper of the palace gates." His wife was brought from Gallipoli, where she joined him in his Moslem faith as "Fatima."

When the Ottoman government proudly announced Shabbatai's apostasy, the first reaction among his followers was stunned incredulity. As the weeks passed, disbelief was replaced by stupefaction, then by demoralization. For nearly two years, tens—possibly hundreds—of thousands of Jews had entered a new dimension in their spiritual lives. Now they were asked to accept that it had all been in vain, that their redeemer was an imposter. Many could not. To preserve some degree of collective equilibrium, therefore, even rabbis of anti-Shabbatean bias now reacted circumspectly, preferring simply to hush up the entire affair, to restore the Jewish condition to its "normal" state of exile. Thus, in the years that followed, a rather eerie silence on the Shabbatean episode descended upon Jewish communal life. It became a non-happening. Denied access to synagogues and to publishing facilities, surviving conventicles of Shabbateans were consigned to silence—in effect, to oblivion.

But there were some who could hardly be exorcised as non-persons. Nathan of Gaza was one of these. Upon learning of Shabbatai's volteface, he, too, initially swooned into near-speechless despondency. Earlier than most, however, he managed to recover, and informed his circle that the Messiah's behavior was a deep theological mystery that he, Nathan, would seek to resolve. The Prophet then departed for Turkey to meet with Shabbatai. En route, he set about developing an ingenious rationale for the recent thunderbolt. As Nathan saw it, the act of conversion actually signified redemption of the "holy sparks," emanations of the Infinity that until then had been widely dispersed among the Gentiles and therefore contaminated by the "outer impurities." These sparks could be redeemed only by the Messiah personally, and thus Shabbatai was obliged to immerse himself in the Moslem world in order to destroy the "outer impurities" from within.

So it was, by formulating the paradox of an apostate Messiah, a tragic but still legitimate redeemer, that Nathan laid the foundations for a new ideology. Shabbatai then "affirmed" this interpretation when he and Nathan met and conferred over the next weeks. Within the lineaments of the new formulation, the objectionable acts of biblical heroes, the incongruous tales of scriptural narrative, the heretofore indecipherable passages of *Zohar*—all were reconcilable. And, indeed, in the next years this convoluted "theology" would be accepted by a small group of loyalists and kept in underground circulation throughout the Balkans.

As for Shabbatai, he continued openly, even flagrantly, to maintain his Jewish connections. Receiving intermittent delegations of followers, he presided over services at a "Shabbatean" synagogue in Edirne. Sometime in 1672, however, he began also to establish connections with several ultramystical Moslem dervish orders. At this point, a number of former devotees turned on him in outrage, execrating him for duplicity, even for sexual license. Nor did they hesitate to convey these denunciations afterward to Grand Vizier Koprulu. Thoroughly exasperated by then, Koprulu promptly exiled Shabbatai to the remote Albanian town of Delvine. There the Messiah was allowed no further contact with his followers. In seclusion, he began to fantasize again, to succumb to his former illuminations. During one of these, he divorced Sarah, his third wife, and took yet a fourth bride, Esther. But several months later, on Yom Kippur 1676, Shabbatai suddenly died at the age of fifty. Upon learning of his death, Nathan immediately circulated the proposition that Shabbatai had merely entered an "occultation," that he had been absorbed into the "supernal lights." Then, in January 1680, Nathan himself died, while attending a Shabbatean conventicle in Skopje, Macedonia.

The False Apostates

In the years immediately following the demise of the Messiah and the Prophet, a new sect emerged, nominally Moslem but developing gradually its own peculiar amalgam of kabbalistic, Shabbatean, and crypto-Jewish practices. Its adherents were not to be confused with the larger minority of Shabbateans who remained within the Jewish fold for another century or so, espousing a number of Shabbatai's bizarre preconversionary rites. Rather, in 1683, only three years after Nathan's death, some three thousand Jewish families of Salonika followed in Shabbatai's footsteps by apostatizing to Islam and adopting the hybrid Judeo-Islamic practices he himself had embraced. Later this nucleus was joined by three or four thousand additional Jews.

Leadership among these "true believers" initially devolved upon the family of Shabbatai's fourth wife, Esther, and particularly to her father, Rabbi Joseph Filosof. In Turkish, the little sect was known as the Donmeh (false prophets), those who professed Islam in public, who even participated in the *hajj,* the pilgrimage to Mecca, but who otherwise adhered privately to a mixture of traditional and Shabbatean Judaism, with special emphasis on study of the *Zohar.* Yet in no sense was it a secret that the Donmeh were observing a private variant of Judaism in tandem with their public observance of Islam. The two versions, Shabbatean Jewish and Moslem, were simply two equal components of a single intricate creed. The group's sociology was no less complex. The members worshipped exclusively in their own "mosque" and lived, intermingled, and married only among their own little comminution.

In the early 1700s, the Donmeh splintered into two subsects. Of these, the larger was founded by a charismatic, rather impenetrable figure, one Baruchia Russo. It was Baruchia's notion that the new, messianic Judaism entailed a complete transposition of the Torah's thirty-six prohibitions into "positive" commandments. These reversals included all previously forbidden sexual unions, including incest. In future years, the bizarre little group was continually replenished by adherents from Izmir—whence their popular sobriquet, "Izmirlis." The males were outwardly distinguished from other Donmeh by their tarbushes, long beards, and delicate physiques (they, too, married only among their own). Over time, most of the Donmeh families in Turkey emigrated to Salonika. It was here, in the mid-eighteenth century, that yet another Shabbatean offshoot developed, clustered around one Darwish Effendi, who professed to be both a mystic and a social reformer. Darwish's conception of social reform, as it happened, also related exclusively to sexual behavior, including annual orgies and other forms of debauchery.

By the late nineteenth century, the Donmeh may have numbered fifteen thousand, with most of their adherents clinging to the Baruchia version. Hebrew survived among them for prayer purposes, but Ladino, and eventually Turkish, became their language even in matters of religion. As long as they remained concentrated in Salonika, their institutional framework survived intact. There, too, several upper-middle-class Donmeh became active in the Salonika branch of the Committee of Union and Progress— the Young Turk movement. After the 1908 revolution, the first Young Turk cabinet actually included several Donmeh members, among them Djavid Bey, the minister of finance. The British ambassador in Constantinople had Djavid in mind as much as Emmanuel Carasso when he encouraged the fascinating motion that the Young Turk revolution was Jewish-inspired (p. 99).

In the 1923–24 exchange of populations following the Greco-Turkish war, the Donmeh, listed officially as professing Moslems, suddenly were confronted with the agonizing prospect of being uprooted from Greek Salonika and transplanted en masse back to Turkey. Bitterly, they protested that they were not "true" Moslems, but rather Shabbatean Jews. Their objections were ignored. The Venizelos government wanted all "nonauthentic" elements out. And thus, in common with the vastly larger enclave of four hundred thousand Thracian and Macedonian Turks, the little Donmeh minority was carried off to Asia Minor, where they sought to recultivate their ancestral roots in Izmir and Istanbul. They were luckier than they knew. Had they been allowed to remain in Salonika, they would almost certainly have shared the fate of the city's professing Jews during the Nazi occupation of World War II. By now, in any case, under the pressures of Turkish nationalism and acculturation, the Donmeh have intermarried extensively with Moslem Turks and have all but given up their dual existence. Even Mustafa Kemal would have accepted them as "authentic."

Farewell Salonika

"The Jerusalem of the Balkans," recalls Moshe Halegua, "had become a Jewish desert by 1945." Its renowned Sephardic community was destroyed. Unwilling to remain on, its few hundred survivors prepared to join the illegal refugee immigration to Palestine. Halegua was eager to accompany them. But the Joint Distribution Committee asked him to remain in Salonika as director of its tiny religious school. A small number of children had survived in hiding with their parents, and they needed schooling. Halegua could not refuse. Later the Joint sent him to Paris to complete his rabbinical studies. Upon ordination, he returned to Salonika, in 1948. The Jewish remnant by then had stabilized at approximately two thousand. Halegua was entreated to serve as community rabbi. With much reluctance he agreed, on a "temporary" basis. But he has never left. Eventually he found a new wife, a widow who had survived Auschwitz with a small daughter. The daughter, Flor, now lives in Israel with her own family. So does Alegre, the daughter Halegua and his new wife produced after the war. "They are both my daughters," he observes matter-of-factly. He turns then to the minyan of aged men and a few women seated in the little synagogue on Vassileou Irakliou Street. "And these are my brothers and sisters."

In the whole of Greece after liberation, not more than eleven thousand Jews remained alive—15 percent of their number in 1939. Confronting the additional hardships of the Greek civil war, their numbers in ensuing years shrank even further, to six thousand. Two-thirds of them lived in Athens. As earlier, however, it was Salonika that remained the cradle of Zionist devotion. Of the twenty-six thousand Jews of Greek background currently in Israel, perhaps 40 percent trace their origins to the "Jerusalem of the Balkans." Admittedly, those among them who reached Israel after the Holocaust included no Carassos or Recanatis, no legendary statesmen or entrepreneurial millionaires. Rather, living on rooftops or in laundry rooms or workroom basements in the slums of Cholon, Jaffa, and Bat Yam, the Salonika refugees performed the least rewarding of the young nation's "black work," from road-paving to sewer-cleaning. But if the Salonikans generated no Maecenases, neither did they produce "Black Panthers" or Sephardic "blocs" or other variations of political and social protest movements. They simply persevered, grimly working their way up the economic ladder. Their children now live in decent neighborhoods and their grandchildren attend university.

Historians have speculated on the impulsion that sustained this cruelly mutilated people in their tenacity. I am reminded of their élan upon visiting Israel's Association of Greek Survivors of Concentration Camps. The office is on Levinsky Street, in a south Tel Aviv slum. Access is roundabout, via a side alley. I enter a hall filled with aging men. They sit at tables, playing cards, drinking Turkish coffee or ouzo, barking to each other in a jargon that turns out to be a proletarian Ladino. In an anteroom the president, Raoul Sasportas, discusses new variations in the German restitution law with a group of fellow officers. Like the cardplayers in the hall, they are all products of Salonika—and Auschwitz. All of them bear tattooed arm numbers. All of them are gruff men, these scions of the "Jerusalem of the Balkans." They mutter, growl, curse, drink, and gamble.

And in 1945, they were the first Jews in the world to crack Britain's naval blockade of Palestine. For these veteran stevedores and fishermen, the sea held no terrors. To survivors of Nazi death camps, the trek from Allied displaced persons camps to secret Italian coastal inlets meant nothing. Stolidly and phlegmatically, they packed themselves into four leaking steamers and hurled themselves against the worst the Royal Navy could offer. One of the refugee vessels was intercepted, and its passengers were transported for internment in Cyprus. The second and third slipped through the British dragnet to unload their human cargo on Palestine's beaches. And in November 1945, a fourth, the *Berl Katznelson,* engaged in a full-scale ramming confrontation with two naval frigates. Crowding the decks, the Salonikans glared across the rails at a boarding party of British marines. Iron pipes and crowbars were in the refugees' fists, the implacable promise of death in their faces. After ninety minutes of tense standoff, the warships suddenly reversed course. The *Berl Katznelson* then proceeded toward the coast. Its passengers had awaited no further assurance of messianic deliverance. Achieving the Holy Land on their own, this time they were redeeming themselves.

CHAPTER VIII

AN IBERIAN EPITAPH

An Initial Portuguese-Jewish Confrontation

Stepping from the inferno of Lisbon's afternoon sunlight into even the minutest reticle of adjoining shade, one is instantly refreshed, revived, redeemed. Lusitanians, Romans, Visigoths, Moors, Jews, and others early on mastered the art of carving shadow out of a blistering solarium. They kept their streets narrow, their roofs and ledges wide, their walls and gates high, their courtyards enclosed, the filigreed skin of their dazzling ornamental tiles refracting the sun up, out, away. Present-day residential and even mercantile neighborhoods conscientiously replicate the character of the Alfama, that medieval Lisbon still nestled within walled hills. It is a labyrinth, some of its passageways so constricted that pedestrians must walk in single file. Guidebooks do not exaggerate. The little enclave is still overhung with balconies ablaze with scarlet geraniums and lined with hole-in-the-wall taverns festooned with strings of peppers, garlic, cheeses. By day, caged canaries trill on balconies. By night, wrought-iron lamps relay their flares, alley to alley, gateway to gateway. It is style more than structure that has been preserved. The sun is tamed here.

In the Alfama, traces of old Jewish and Moorish habitation can still be found. The clues are occasional street names, the *judiarias* and *mourarias,* the streets of Dyers, Goldsmiths, Jewelers. But do not search local faces for evidence of Semitic ancestry. In Portugal, Jews were a belated presence, with roots far shallower than in the neighboring Spanish kingdoms. Although a Jewish nucleus can be identified in Roman times, Lisbon did not emerge as a major port until the thirteenth century, and only then began attracting substantial numbers of Jewish merchants and artisans. Characteristically, the newcomers made their homes on the edge of the Alfama, in their own judiaria, with its own network of lanes and culs-desac. Here as elsewhere they governed themselves, administering and enforcing their own laws, assessing and collecting their own taxes. Here, too, a significant minority of Jews achieved eminence as financiers, revenue-collectors, and physicians. By the late fourteenth century, their circumstances were distinctly preferable to their kinsmen's in riot-torn Castile and Aragón.

It was thus in 1391 that Don Samuel Abravanel, royal treasurer and recent converso, departed Castile to resume his career as financier and professing Jew in Lisbon. His son, Don Judah Abravanel, subsequently became personal banker to Prince Fernão, the heir apparent. And in 1461, Don Judah's son, the twenty-four-year-old Isaac Abravanel, was brought to court to become King Afonso V's finance minister and chief tax-collector. The young man's precociousness and charm swiftly made him a royal favorite. It was not a status shared by his people at large. Even as the number of Jews in Portugal grew to perhaps fifteen thousand, their economic achievements evoked popular resentment. A typical petition to a local municipality complained:

> We saw Jews made knights, mounted on richly caparisoned horses and mules, and clothed in fine gowns and hoods, silken doublets, gilt swords, and masks and turbans, so that it is impossible to know what race they belong to. . . . It is a travesty that Spanish Jews, having been driven from their own country on account of their perverse heresies, find welcome and protection in this kingdom.

As early as 1449, an anti-Jewish riot erupted in Lisbon, consuming nearly two hundred lives and wreaking extensive property damage. Shocked by the depth of this hostility, King Afonso felt obliged to restrict Jewish trading privileges.

Isaac Abravanel's fate in a sense paralleled that of his coreligionists. For two decades, in addition to his responsibilities at court, the talented financier had managed the personal estate of the House of Bragança, the nation's most powerful noble family. The relationship ultimately proved his undoing. In 1483 Duke Fernão da Bragança launched an insurrection against the new king, João II. It was crushed, and Fernão was executed. Anticipating the same fate, Don Isaac Abravanel made the instant decision to abandon his vast holdings and flee to Castile. He and his family traveled light, carrying with them only several bags of gold, silver, and jewelry. Moving always by night, the little group at last negotiated a hairbreadth escape (p. 58). From exile, Don Isaac could not resist a final letter to his king: "Why have you done evil to your servant?" he protested.

"Why have you cast me out?" The responsive silence was thunderous. For the House of Abravanel, the Portuguese chapter in their odyssey had ended.

A Crossing of Iberian Frontiers

For the great majority of Jews in Aragón and Castile, a Portuguese chapter would soon begin. Only nine years later, the Expulsion Decree sent between sixty and seventy thousand of them fleeing to the smaller neighboring kingdom. Indeed, for Portugal, a nation of fewer than one million inhabitants, the influx threatened a demographic revolution. At first, João II's reaction was passionless—and mercenary. For payment of a thousand cruzados per family, he offered the refugees an eight-month residence permit. Few could accept the offer; most were penniless by the time they reached Portugal. Instead, the Jews tended to follow back roads and make their way into Portugal's mountainous northern interior. Here they established shantytowns and subsisted initially as hired laborers. Exploited by ruthless employers, they were soon reduced essentially to slave laborers.

The Jewish presence was not a secret to the royal court. Yet, with or without the eight-month grace period, King João was unwilling simply to expel the fugitives. Sensing their potential usefulness to his nation's backward economy, he chose to "amalgamate" the little people through proselytization. Moreover, upon João's death in 1495, his successor, the rather kindlier Manoel I, dropped the limitations on Jewish settlement altogether, including pressure for their conversion. In growing numbers, the northern fugitives thereupon made their way down to Lisbon, where they gradually resumed their commercial and professional vocations.

For all his tolerance, however, King Manoel was a ruler of distinctly imperial ambitions. He had long cherished the dream of an "Iberian Union" with Castile-Aragón, and thus for several years aggressively pursued a marriage agreement with María, eldest daughter of Fernando and Isabel. There was a price on the match, as it happened; neither parents nor daughter would consent unless Portugal was "cleansed" of the Jewish presence as thoroughly as their own realm had been. After some hesitation, Manoel finally agreed. In November 1496, the marriage contract was signed and a week later the king issued a royal decree of banishment. The Jews now had ten months to clear out.

Yet, even then, Manoel was loath to forfeit these talented and productive refugees. He preferred to explore an alternate solution. If Jews living in the mountainous northern region were still largely invisible, the majority of this people now resided in Lisbon and were accessible. It was accordingly the king's intention to bring them to Christianity en masse in a single decisive stroke. Thus, as the date of scheduled evacuation approached and the Jews of Lisbon dispiritedly converged toward the harbor, royal guards suddenly ordered twenty thousand adult males into the Rossio, the great public square. Here they were informed that the king had "softened his heart." They would be allowed to remain, provided they underwent conversion. As a gentle inducement, the Jews were obliged to continue standing in the Rossio for hours, racked by thirst and pain. Within the day, virtually all of them agreed to undergo baptism together with their families.

The ordeal in fact merely hastened a move the largest numbers of Jews almost certainly would have taken in any case. For one thing, by remaining on, they were assured the same privileges enjoyed by other inhabitants of the kingdom. Moreover, these instant convertidos differed significantly from the conversos of Spain. In Portugal, they did not experience the slow, debilitative process of erosion suffered by New Christians in Aragón and Castile between 1391 and 1492. Their Jewish loyalties remained more or less intact, as did their traditional social and communal bonds. King Manoel did not press his *novos cristãos* to abandon those ties. Indeed, in May 1497, four months before the expiration of his deadline, he had assured his new subjects of exemption from all discrimination. For the next twenty years, they would be spared queries into the authenticity of their faith—spared, in short, a Spanish-style Inquisition. Later, the grace period would be extended to 1534.

The inducement proved decisive. The convertidos now had time to accommodate to new conditions, to devise viable forms of crypto-Judaism, to function essentially as Jews in everything but formal religious affiliation. So it happened. In a dispatch to Vienna in 1528, the Austrian envoy to Spain, Martin Salina, expressed his wonderment:

> A Jew has been permitted to sermonize in Portugal in favor of the religion of Moses, and against our Christian faith. He has also written letters to this kingdom of Spain, which have induced many of his [fellow Jews] to abandon their homes and fly to that country. . . . I cannot predict how the affair will end, but fear that God in the end will punish the king [of Portugal] who tolerates such evils in his realm.

King Manoel was no philanthropist. As early as 1499 he formally banned New Christians from emigrating. His purpose at all times was to keep this talented minority at work in his undeveloped and largely illiterate realm. In that objective he was successful. Within a few years the Sephardim began to make their mark again, particularly in their former vocations as merchants, tax-farmers, financiers, importers-exporters, and physicians. By the latter sixteenth century, a sizable element among them was flourishing mightily. As New Christians, they enjoyed access to a unique chain of Sephardic business correspondents worldwide. It was with these advantages that such renowned convertidos as Rodrigues de Evora, Ximenes Aragão, and Duarte da Silva purchased their spices, brazilwood, silver, sugar, tobacco, diamonds, and slaves in India, Africa, and Brazil, and exported them to Europe at great profit. Indeed, Silva may have been the most opulent Portuguese merchant of the seventeenth century. Well connected at court, he lent the monarchy vast sums and provided ships, food, uniforms, and munitions for the midcentury expedition against the Dutch in Brazil (p. 354). Little wonder that during the 1600s Portuguese official and private correspondence used the term *novos cristãos* interchangeably with *homens de negócios*—"businessmen." In international mercantile circles, the term "Portuguese" in effect became synonymous with "Jew," unqualified even by the euphemism "New Christian" or "convert."

A comparable interchangeability applied to the words "physician" and "Jew." As early as the twelfth century, Yahya ibn Ya'ish was appointed physician to the Portuguese royal family. So later were Yahya's grandson and great-grandson. Throughout the fourteenth and fifteenth centuries, four generations of Navarros served as royal physicians. Afterward, as convertidos, Jews in Portugal maintained their domination of the medical profession. Tomaz da Veiga was physician to Afonso V and João II; his son Rodrigo, to kings João III and Sebastião, and to Cardinal Henrique, the brother of João III. Abraham Zacuto, a renowned sixteenth-century astronomer-mathematician, was also a distinguished physician, and a distant relative of Amatus Lusitanus, who would become the single greatest medical figure of the Renaissance (p. 221). In these same years, New Christian physicians were acclaimed as pioneers of medicine in the Portuguese Empire in both Asia and Brazil. Altogether, King Manoel's decision to hold on to "his" Jews seemed an inspired investment.

As in fifteenth-century Castile and Aragón, however, the tangible evidence of this convertido upward mobility unsettled the native Portuguese. As early as 1507, during Easter week, a Dominican friar preached an inflammatory sermon against Jews "masquerading" as Christians. Other monks and priests then set about haranguing crowds with anti-convertido abuse. Within days, mobs were raging through Lisbon, massacring New Christians, then roping and dragging their corpses to the Praça da São

Domingos for burning. Even sailors from Dutch, French, and German ships lying at harbor gleefully joined in the murderous chivaree. Before the week ended, nearly a thousand convertidos had been slaughtered, often after undergoing torture or rape. Large quantities of their property had been looted. The Lisbon Massacre of 1507 must be ranked as one of the great pogroms in European history—and it was not directed even against professing Jews.

King Manoel was deeply shaken. Forthwith he ordered the hanging of numerous perpetrators, and afterward remained sternly watchful against further excesses. But in 1521 Manoel died. His son, João III, a weak, intensely pious young man, did not inherit his father's solicitude for the captive New Christian minority. Sensing the new ruler's equivocation, the clergy then began prodding him to establish an Inquisition along Spanish lines. At last, after nearly a decade of indecision, João agreed to begin negotiations on the subject with Pope Clement VII. The pontiff in fact shared the king's initial uncertainty. He happened to be short of funds, and the Portuguese convertidos were not. Indeed, throughout the 1530s and well into the 1540s, they plied Clement with substantial "gifts" that repeatedly forestalled papal approval for a local Inquisition. But in 1547 King João produced a sweetener of his own. He offered Paul III, Clement's successor, administration of the revenues from the vastly wealthy See of Viseu. It was a prodigious inducement, one the convertidos could not match. In July of that year, therefore, Paul issued a bull, *Meditatio cordis,* finally and formally establishing a Spanish-style Inquisition in Portugal.

It was a dire moment for the New Christian minority. In Italy Samuel Usque (p. 80), a marrano fugitive, recalled the inquisitional machine that had driven him to flee, initially from Castile, and then from his Portuguese refuge:

> This monster, with its devilish countenance and terrible mien . . . has cast a lethal terror over all of Europe. . . . It is wrought of iron and stone, saturated with poison and snake venom, and armored with the strongest steel. It has enveloped the earth with its thousands of wings heavy as lead. . . . This monster is like the dragon of the African desert. . . . Rivers of sulfur and fire issue from its mouth. It preys on thousands of human victims. Wheresoever it turns, all perishes and decays, all the grasses are withered, all the blossoms of the trees are shriveled, and the most fruitful land is become a desolated wilderness.

Responses to the Monster

By the thousands, convertidos sought the alternative of flight. Ironically, had they been spared inquisitional pressures, most if not all would have chosen to remain in Portugal. They had learned to become comfortable with their hybrid existence and its often substantial financial rewards. Now, however, they were confronted with a machine that functioned with cold indifference to their true religious preference. They asked themselves: Had the effort been worthwhile all these years? The struggle to maintain at least a vestige of their ancient faith?

It was in 1524, when the issue of a Portuguese Inquisition first was raised, that a dark-skinned, elaborately bejeweled little man appeared in Rome to offer his own alternative to the Jewish condition. Mounted on a white horse and surrounded by a retinue of attendants, the exotic visitor announced himself as David Reuveni, a "prince" whose brother ruled the "Jewish tribal kingdom of Reuben," deep in the Arabian Desert. With his colorful oriental costume and even more flamboyant demeanor, Reuveni dazzled the Jews of Rome, and all the more when he proclaimed his mission. It was nothing less than the reconquest of the Holy Land from the Turks. But for that purpose, he and his brother required extensive military help from the pope and the Christian rulers of Europe.

The improbable David Reuveni not only secured his audience with Pope Clement VII but actually managed to win the pontiff's blessing for his extravagant project. He also elicited substantial cash donations from the Jews of Rome, which he used to purchase and lavishly appoint a vessel bearing his name and flying his Jewish flag. Thus ornamented, Reuveni sailed off with his entourage to Portugal, where King João III, much impressed by the prince's grandiloquent entrance into the port of Lisbon, received him with all the honors due a foreign ambassador. The city's marrano community was agog. Indeed, they discerned in this exalted, dark-skinned apparition the thrilling promise of Redemption. Among those swept up in the messianic euphoria was a young convertido and government secretary, Diogo Pires. Overwhelmed by Reuveni and the apparent imminence of a mass return to the Holy Land, Pires now full-heartedly resumed his ancestral faith. Secretly he circumcised himself (almost dying from loss of blood), discarded his Christian name in favor of Solomon Molcho, then devotedly attached himself to Reuveni's enterprise. Reuveni, however, persuaded Molcho to leave Portugal without delay, lest he bring harm on himself. This Molcho did, embarking surreptitiously for Turkey.

In Edirne during the next two years, Molcho was inducted into the hidden mysteries of kabbalah. New worlds were revealed to the young man, including prophetic visions (which he shared with Joseph Caro). As he subsequently declared to rapt and growing audiences, a heavenly messenger had visited him, disclosing that the cruel, persecuting world of Christendom would itself soon be destroyed. There had been unmistakable portents lately. The catastrophe experienced by Rome in 1527, when invading Austrian and Spanish troops violated local churches, surely signified the beginning of the End of Days, when the Kingdom of Esau, that is, Christianity, would fall and the Messiah would appear in all his glory. Molcho left few doubts that the Messiah was none other than himself.

From Edirne, the young man set out for other major centers of kabbalism—Salonika, Izmir, Safed—and then eventually made his way back to Rome. There he was received by adoring throngs of Jews and respectful multitudes of Christian onlookers. Yet, rather than adopting a triumphant stance, Molcho confounded his admirers by wrapping himself in rags and joining the company of beggars and cripples on a Tiber bridge opposite the Vatican. He remained there for thirty days. His purpose, he explained, was to approach a mystical threshold to the godhead. Evidently he succeeded. During his ordeal, Molcho experienced visions that suggested an impending disaster, a vast earthquake that would begin in Portugal and lead directly to the Apocalypse of Redemption. Whereupon, impelled by this omen, Molcho approached the Portuguese ambassador in Rome and presented him with a letter for King João III elaborating upon his recent auguries.

Calamitous events now actually began to occur. In October 1530, the Tiber overflowed its banks and inundated the capital. A month later, Flanders also suffered a major flood. Soon after that, Molcho's predicted earthquake did indeed rend Lisbon and numerous other Portuguese cities. At the same time, a "fiery, wondrous sun"—in fact, Halley's Comet—appeared in the skies above Rome. Nevertheless, in 1531 the response of the Roman Inquisition to this bizarre conjunction of prediction and fulfillment was simply to arrest Molcho and convict him of blasphemy. And once again, sheer personal charisma protected the young Jew. So impressed was Pope Clement VII by this remarkable clairvoyant that he arranged to substitute another man, a condemned criminal, to die at the stake in Molcho's place.

By then, however, the hallucinating messiah was tempting fate. A year later, in 1532, united once more with Reuveni, who had lately returned from Provence, Molcho sought and secured an audience with Emperor

Charles V in Ratisbon. The interview was a fiasco. Molcho pressed his views with such vigor and lèse majesté that he offended the ruler. A man of little patience, Charles had the messiah summarily led to the public square and burned alive. Reuveni, for his part, was carried off to Spain in chains. There, six years later, he died in prison.

Molcho's reputation was not easily eradicated. Among his pertinacious followers, the legend grew that he had arisen from the fire. Some insisted that he had departed for Safed, where his bride was awaiting him. Hope died hard among a distraught people. In later years, there were periodic aftershocks of messianism among Portugal's convertido minority. In 1546, a New Christian physician, known simply as Mestre Gabriel, proceeded from house to house seeking converts back to Judaism. Another erstwhile New Christian, in Coimbra, ventured to open a school for Hebrew instruction. These and other initiatives were easily quashed. For most *novos cristãos,* the residual faith in Judaism was ebbing. Their perseverance in the ancient faith had brought little in the way of tangible advantage. How, then, could they ignore the claim of Portuguese churchmen that God had abandoned the Jews when they rejected Jesus, that Jewish suffering attested to the truth of the Christian faith? Even then, as growing numbers of convertidos fled Portugal for safer havens, they hesitated to embrace Judaism openly. Frequently, they still preferred to be identified at least as titular Christians.

Could this Portuguese remnant yet be saved for Judaism? One of the émigrés, Samuel Gomez, was convinced that it could. He adopted the pseudonym Samuel Usque to protect relatives in Portugal, and in 1553 addressed a stirring message to his people entitled *Consolaçam as tribula-çoens de Israel* (A Consolation for Israel's Tribulations). Our knowledge of the author is less than extensive. Apparently he was born in Castile, joined his family in 1492 as a refugee in Portugal, then shared in the forced baptism of 1497. It is certain that Usque was a man of rich culture, for he displayed familiarity not only with Jewish sources but with classical Greek authors. When the likelihood of an Inquisition began to surface, he proceeded first to Italy, in 1531, then to Constantinople, then to Salonika. Twenty years later, an aged man, Usque settled for good in Ferrara. It was there that he came to know Beatriz Mendes—the incomparable Doña Gracia—whom he praised extravagantly in the *Consolaçam* (p. 80). Indeed, Doña Gracia funded the publication of this great prose-poem. It appeared in 1553, two months after Usque's death.

The work is composed in the form of a pastoral dialogue, a common neo-Platonic device in Renaissance Italy. Three shepherds, Jacob, Nahum, and Zechariah, are discussing the history of the Jews. Jacob is doleful as he recounts the sufferings of Israel. "How long must I moan and sigh and slake my thirst with my tears?" he laments. Christian polemicists had long since formulated their own answer, of course, insisting that the Jews' tribulations would never cease, in punishment for their sin in rejecting Jesus. To rebut these arguments, Nahum and Zechariah turn to the Bible for confirmation that the Jews have suffered not for their abandonment of Jesus but for their sin of assimilation with Gentile peoples, thereby leading Israel to apostasy, idolatry, and marriage with non-Jews. It is the *Consolaçam*'s central and recurrent theme. All that now is required of the Jews—whether professing, marrano, or other New Christian—is rededication to their ancient faith and trust in God's endless concern for them. If this feat can be managed, all yet will be well.

To buttress their case, Nahum and Zechariah recall the fate of other nations that have persecuted Israel: Egypt, Babylon, Persia, Greece. These peoples once ruled their world, but where are they now? In lyrical, poetic language, Usque's dialogue concludes with assurance that Israel's fortunes are about to change. As a consequence of their latest ordeal in Spain and Portugal, "the people [of Israel] have run the entire gauntlet of misfortunes and have reached the end of [their] tribulations." Already the Seed of Abraham can be seen returning to the Holy Land. It follows that Israel's remaining lost tribes soon will be found, her dead resurrected, her unity restored under the House of David.

The treatise underwent several translations, and by the late 1500s it had achieved an extensive readership in the Sephardic world. But was it, in fact, a source of hope and rededication? There appeared pitiably meager evidence of Usque's anticipated halcyon age. Rather, for the New Christians of Portugal, faith appeared an uncertain response to the mounting inquisitional crisis. Departure offered a more promising alternative.

Between Scylla and Charybdis

A return trek across the Spanish frontier was the initial exit route. It was not always an easy operation; a royal decree had closed the frontier. Yet bribery speeded the process. Flight to the very epicenter of religious persecution may retrospectively have appeared suicidal. In the decades since the original Expulsion Decree of 1492, however, important political changes had occurred in Spain. Upon the death of Fernando the Catholic in 1516, the whole country came under the governance of Fernando's grandson, Charles I. Better known as Emperor Charles V, the new ruler inherited not only his grandfather's possessions in Spain and Italy but the vast terrain of the Habsburg monarchy in Austria, the Netherlands, and the New World. Charles's son, Felipe (Philip) II, who ascended the throne in 1556, was intrigued by the notion of adding Portugal to this wide-flung inheritance, thus unifying the entire Iberian Peninsula. Accordingly, in 1580, Felipe dispatched a great army into Portugal under his ablest general, the duke of Alba. Resistance collapsed immediately. Some months later, Felipe journeyed to Lisbon to be crowned king. Yet he undertook to maintain Portuguese autonomy and to appoint only Portuguese citizens to that nation's administration. The promise was generally honored.

This unexpected peninsular unification profoundly affected the destinies of New Christians in both countries. In Portugal, the full machinery of the Inquisition remained in force. There soon followed an exodus of perhaps twenty thousand Portuguese New Christians into Spain. The convertidos were impelled by awareness that the Spanish and Portuguese Inquisitions were separate operations. No provision for extradition existed between the two countries—or the two Inquisitions. A fugitive from Portugal at least would arrive in Spain with a "clean" record. More important, with its growing empire, Spain had developed one of the largest economies in Europe. Even as a temporary way station to other havens, it would offer New Christians a certain respite to recover financially.

Indeed, the gamble already had proved worthwhile to a number of earlier returnees. By the mid-sixteenth century, Spanish government officials were reappraising the cost to the national economy of the initial departure of Jewish international traders. Few native Christians thus far appeared qualified to fill that gap. In recent years, too, Charles V's and Felipe II's military campaigns and Felipe's elaborate building program had begun to devour the nation's currency reserves, including even the vast bullion imports from the New World. From the middle of the century on, therefore, and well before the Iberian Unification, the Spanish court placed no serious barriers in the way of gradual, unobtrusive New Christian reimmigration from Portugal. Even the Spanish Inquisition tended to concentrate on earlier, "veteran" conversos. Later-arriving Portuguese convertidos did quite well in Spain. If most earned their livelihoods as artisans or small merchants, others emerged as a dynamic minority of importers-exporters, fiscal agents, tax-collectors, army contractors. Some actually matched their predecessors, reaching high estate in government, nobility, military orders, clergy.

But there were other, less felicitous parallels. Like their forebears, the immigrant conversos aroused intense resentment among Spain's Old Christian establishment. Eventually the Inquisition took notice. In perspective, then, the Suprema devoted two major time-frames to its anti-judaizing activities. The first, we recall, launched as early as 1481 and continuing to 1530, was devoted to New Christians of essentially Spanish provenance. Even this earlier period was characterized by grave excesses. A classic example was Luis de la Isla, a Jewish youngster who was eight years old in 1492, when he and his family departed Cádiz. Somewhere in the littoral of North Africa, Luis became separated from his parents. Searching for them, he embarked on a lifetime of wandering. For two months, the boy traversed the North African coast without success. Finally he slipped into a refugee ship bound for Italy. In Genoa, Luis accepted baptism and joined a pack of other starving Jewish street urchins who were rewarded with bread for their apostasy. After four years, Luis began to hear rumors of a group of Jewish stragglers from Fez who had made their way back to Spain. Clinging frantically to the hope that his parents might yet be among this remnant, the twelve-year-old wangled passage as a cook's helper on a returning Spanish vessel. Over the next decade, he moved from one Spanish city to another, working on and off as an itinerant textile weaver, endlessly in quest of his family. At last, in despair, Luis returned to Italy.

In Venice, the young man hired himself out as an indentured servant to a company of Portuguese merchants and sailed with them across the Adriatic to Ottoman Albania. En route, his employers inadvertently divulged their own Jewish origins. Luis in turn joyously revealed himself to them and even adopted the name Abraham. Subsequently, as an identified Jew, he attached himself to yet another fraternity of Jews, this one bound for Asia Minor. Stopping off in Salonika, Luis by chance encountered several former neighbors from Cádiz—evidence, again, of the astonishing ebb and flow of Jewish refugees in that tormented era of flight and refuge. They informed him that, to their knowledge, his parents had migrated to Egypt with a group of other refugees and might yet be alive there. Instantly, Luis departed for Alexandria. While at sea, he fell deathly ill. Weeks later he recovered, but was left totally blind. At this point, Luis decided to go "home" for good, to Spain. In 1512 he was back in Toledo, a sick, blind, frail man of twenty-eight. And not long afterward, he was seized by the Inquisition as a *relapso*. The records of Luis de la Isla's trial break off in 1514, when he was languishing in a dungeon, but it is almost certain that he was burned.

The initial phase of the inquisitional nightmare ended in 1530, with the "relaxation" of 107 persons in Córdoba. Although some forty thousand New Christians had remained on in Spain after 1492, nearly four decades later any lingering Jewish identity among this remnant was all but extinguished. The long campaign to obliterate Spanish Judaism, a "crusade" that had begun with the massacres of 1391, appeared to be completed. Integrated and acculturated as identified Catholics, most of the conversos and their descendants evidently had vanished altogether from the ken of Jewish history.

The Spanish Inquisition at Full Crescendo

Then, suddenly, with the Iberian Unification of 1580, an unanticipated influx of possibly twenty thousand additional conversos flowed into the country from Portugal. Less than a century after the original Expulsion Decree, Spain was confronted with a substantial New Christian population, and once again this Catholic nation found itself obsessed with a Jewish problem that it imagined had been long since exorcised. In Spain, the word "Portuguese" now became virtually synonymous with "Jew" (or, as a vulgar Castilian gibe had it, "a Portuguese is born of a Jew's fart"). So it was that the Spanish Inquisition was galvanized into revived activity. This time it enjoyed the fullest approbation of Felipe II. The Counter-Reformation was in full swing, and as its leader and champion in zealotry the Spanish ruler was not prepared to tolerate even the faintest deviation from his empire's religious homogeneity.

More than a little "deviation" was to be found among the influx of Portuguese New Christians. Unlike their Spanish counterparts, the immigrants nurtured a substantial minority of crypto-Jews—that is, marranos. Their "judaizing" may have been less than knowledgeable. More often, it was expressed in a confused sequence of prayers, fast days, or dietary traditions passed down through the generations. Besides shunning "forbidden" foods, the marranos slaughtered their own fowl according to their vague, if selective, memory of ancient practice. For the Sabbath, they cleaned their homes, changed their linen. The Passover Seder was more or less observed, if disjointedly. The one ritual marranos dared not observe was circumcision, which would instantly have given them away. It was their consolation, rather, that they "circumcised their hearts with good deeds."

However disoriented and inauthentic, the new judaizing peril was an intolerable provocation to the Spanish Inquisition. Under Felipe II, the awesome machine in its second phase rapidly developed a self-sustaining momentum. No other institution of the time could exceed it in relentless efficiency. As before, one of its ugliest procedural features was its reliance on secret informers. By the late sixteenth century, there was a veritable army of these *familiares,* all of them competitively, even frantically, volunteering their services, whether out of private grievance or genuine suspicion. Arrests, isolation, interrogations similarly followed precedent. Far more than in the era of Torquemada, however, it was torture that now became the Inquisition's single most defining characteristic.

Among the more commonly used methods of "persuasion" were the *potro,* the *strapado,* the *toca,* and the *garrote.* The *potro,* or rack, was a triangular frame on which the prisoner was bound and stretched. Cords were attached to the wrists and ankles, then connected to a windlass that, when turned, dislocated the joints. The *atrapado* was a vertical rack. With shins tied behind the back, the prisoner was lifted by a rope attached to the ceiling, then allowed to fall with a jerk to within a few inches of the ground. The procedure was repeated several times. Occasionally, weights were tied to the victim's feet to increase the shock of the fall. The *toca* was water torture. The prisoner was bound to a trestle with sharp-edged rungs. The head was positioned lower than the feet in a hollowed-out trough and kept there by an iron band around the forehead. Cords, biting into the flesh, were twisted around arms, thighs, and calves. The prisoner's mouth was opened and a strip of linen thrust into the throat. Water from a jar was poured through this tissue, blocking throat and nostrils and inducing a state of semisuffocation. In the *garrote,* the prisoner was swung off the ground by a belt with arms tied together across the chest and attached by cords to rings in the wall. Each turn of the cord sliced through skin and muscle.

These techniques were applied indiscriminately to prisoners of both sexes. Thus, a forty-two-year-old mother, Elvira del Campo, was accused before the inquisitional tribunal of Toledo of abstaining from pork and of donning fresh linen on Saturdays. The woman admitted these actions, but denied heretical intent. Torture then was applied to compel her to acknowledge that intent. A verbatim transcript of the proceedings appears in H. C. Lea's classic history of the Spanish Inquisition:

> She was carried to the torture chamber and told to tell the truth, and she said that she had nothing to say. She was ordered to be stripped and again admonished, but was silent. When stripped, she said: "Señores, I have done all that is said of me and I bear false witness against myself, for I do not want to see myself in such trouble. Please God, I have done nothing." . . . The tying of the arms was commenced. . . . She was told to tell the truth, and replied, "I have told the truth and have nothing to tell." One cord was applied to the arms and twisted. . . . Then she screamed and said, "I have done all they say. . . . Tell me what you want, for I don't know what to say." She was ordered to tell what she had done . . . and another turn of the cord was ordered. She cried, "Loosen me, señores, and tell me what I have

to say. I do not know what I have done. O Lord, have mercy on me, a sinner." Another turn was given. She said, "Loosen me a little that I may remember what I have to tell. . . . I did not eat pork, for it made me sick. . . . Loosen me, and I will tell the truth." Another turn of the cord was ordered, when she said, "Tell me what I have to say. I did it, I did it. They hurt me, señores. Loosen me, loosen me, and I will tell it. . . . Ay! Loosen me, loosen me, take me from here, and I will tell it when I am taken away—I say that I did not eat it." . . . Another turn was ordered, and she said, "Señores, I did not eat it because I did not want to—release me, and I will tell it. . . . I don't remember—tell me what I have to say—oh, wretched me!—I will tell all that is wanted, señores—they are breaking my arms—loosen me a little—I did everything that is said of me."

The notion of double jeopardy did not exist in Roman, canon, or inquisitional law. Thus, a certain Isabel Dalos of Ciudad Real was first tried by the Valladolid tribunal in 1608 when she was twenty-two; subsequently she was arraigned five more times—twice at Llerena, twice at Cuenca, and finally at Toledo. Altogether, eighteen years of Isabel's life were passed in inquisitional dungeons. The last trial began in 1665, when she was eighty, and continued until 1670. In this final proceeding, the aged woman was subjected to torture three times, until eventually she died of her ordeal. Even then, the tribunal claimed its revenge; Isabel Dalos was posthumously declared guilty, and her corpse was burned.

Sentences were pronounced at the *auto de fe*, the so-called "act of faith." Over the years, the ceremony was transformed into an increasingly elaborate production. It began with a cortege that included the plenum of the city's clergy and public officials. Behind these eminences followed the prisoners, carrying lighted tapers. Each wore a *sanbenito*, a long yellow robe bearing a black cross, and a miter, a tall peaked head-piece. When the column arrived at the public square where the auto de fe was to be "celebrated," a ranking cleric would preach a sermon, directing a torrent of insults on the heads of the prisoners. The accused would be ushered then one by one before the pulpit to learn their sentences. The recitation began with "moderate" judgments and continued up to pronouncements of death. Quite often, confiscation of property accompanied the harsher sentences, and was retroactive to the date of the original heresy—thus stripping families of all their possessions. There were occasional mitigations of punishment. By tradition, even a last-minute acknowledgment of repentance would secure a less draconian end for a prisoner condemned to death. This "merciful" alternative was execution by garroting, with only the corpse consigned to the flames. It was accordingly not rare for innocent victims, sentenced to the pyre, to make a factitious act of contrition simply to win the "mercy" of the slow twisting of an iron collar around their necks.

Whether by garroting or burning, the execution of heretics, like the auto de fe itself, was one of the great public spectacles of early modern Spain, exceeding even the bullfight in popularity. Distinguished royal and clerical personages often attended these events. A series of death sentences carried out in June 1680 in Madrid was graced by the presence of King Carlos II and his young bride, Marie-Louise d'Orléans. Before fifty thousand onlookers, the auto de fe, then the executions, continued for fourteen hours, from early morning until nightfall. Fifty-one conversos were "relaxed," either in person or in effigy. Among those dispatched to the *quemadero,* the public burning ground, was a beautiful girl of seventeen who cried out in despair for the queen to save her. Marie-Louise paled but remained silent. King Carlos himself was given the honor of igniting the pyre. Horrified, the marquise de Villars, one of the queen's entourage, turned her eyes away (much to the annoyance of the Spaniards around her). "The cruelties that were witnessed at the death of these poor wretches," she declared later, "are impossible for me to describe."

In Quest of "Purity of Blood"

The inquisitional terror halted for a brief interlude. Felipe II died in 1598 and was succeeded by his marginally less fanatical son, Felipe III. In 1601, the New Christians of Spain and Portugal paid the king 200,000 ducats for permission to settle in the overseas colonies. A year later, the conversos opened negotiations with the Crown to help secure a papal general pardon for alleged judaizers. For this intercession, the New Christians offered a "gift" of 1.8 million ducats, plus 50,000 cruzados to the duchess of Lerma (the king's mistress), and 40,000 and 30,000 cruzados, respectively, to two members of the Suprema. The result of this vast financial exertion was Clement VIII's papal pardon of 1604, a document countersigned by King Felipe the following year. Extended to all conversos of the realm, it allowed them two years' grace to receive forgiveness, and thereafter to be spared indignities, property confiscations, or any form of corporal punishment. But in 1610, the pardon was withdrawn. The machinery of the Inquisition ground steadily on.

At no time did it lack for "clients." Nor was there ever a corner of Spain in which smaller or larger minyans of Portuguese crypto-Jews were not discovered and ruthlessly prosecuted by the Holy Office. In 1630, a judaizing cell was ferreted out at a private home in Madrid on the Calle de las

Infantas. Its members were sentenced and burned in the great auto de fe of July 1632. Three years later, a group of one hundred fifty Portuguese was tracked down in Badajoz, not far from the western border and a natural hiding place. These captives too paid a grim price, as did other, smaller conventicles in Llerena. In Seville, in 1667, eighty-one accused judaizers were sentenced at a vast auto de fe. Eight died at the stake; the rest served varying terms of imprisonment. Otherwise, by the late seventeenth century, the Portuguese "infection" was effectively cauterized. The rare pockets of conversos who nurtured faint, nostalgic memories of the ancestral religion hardly regarded themselves as Jews any longer.

Yet the ordeal of the New Christians did not end with their assimilation. As early as the sixteenth century, an "objective" factor had come to stigmatize even the most thoroughly acculturated converso. This was the critical absence of limpieza de sangre—"purity of blood." Without the cachet of that "purity," a New Christian was endlessly suspect of harboring clandestine Jewish allegiances. Over the years, one municipality after another enacted ordinances based on limpieza de sangre, barring persons tainted by Jewish ancestry from vocational associations, universities, the military, or monastic orders. In Córdoba, applicants for church choirs were obliged to take an oath denying so much as a scintilla of Jewish or Moorish ancestry, then list for investigation the names of parents and grandparents and their places of birth. The Inquisition, too, then gradually came to regard absence of blood purity as prima facie grounds for investigation.

Under these guidelines, no one was safe, not even the doyens of Hispanic culture. In the sixteenth century, Fernando de Rojas, a lawyer by training, emerged as Spain's outstanding novelist-dramatist; Juan Luis Vives, as its most brilliant humanistic essayist (although he spent most of his life outside Spain). Neither man could protect family members from arrest, or occasionally from prosecution, even execution. These arrests were based on no objective evidence whatever, frequently not even on the testimony of witnesses. More often, they were invoked exclusively by the stigma of "impure" blood. The dragnet sent a wave of terror through every echelon of the intellectual community—which may well have been the Suprema's intention.

At least one intellectual succeeded in mocking the racist obsession. A typical plebeian like Sancho Panza gloried in his credentials as a limpio, a man of pure blood, simply because no one could prove the contrary. Could the author of Don Quixote have nurtured a vested interest? Critics have speculated that Miguel de Cervantes may himself have been a converso. His father, Rodrigo, was a surgeon, a profession extensively identified with New Christians. In his plays, Cervantes did not disguise his contempt for distinctions between "Old" and "New" Christians. Although reticent about his own background, he was known to have been influenced by the *Dialoghi d'amore* of Leone Ebreo (Judah Abravanel) (p. 225). When he referred in *Don Quixote* to "a better and older language [than Arabic]," Cervantes presumably was alluding to Hebrew. In any case, he was flying in the face of contemporary mores. Throughout the sixteenth and the early seventeenth century, Spain's "Golden Age" of letters entirely shared the obsession with purity of blood. Satirical references to the alleged physical imperfections of the Jew, his hunger for social position, his pernicious beliefs and practices, appeared repeatedly in literature. Names suggestive of Jewish ancestry were ridiculed.

Whether as public policy or popular culture, the fixation on limpieza de sangre spared few New Christians the terror of scrutiny. Who could be certain of his blood purity "since time immemorial"? Limpieza de sangre ultimately became a qualification negotiated through bribed witnesses, shuffled genealogies, falsified documents. By the late 1600s, the Inquisition itself had assumed responsibility for issuing "authoritative" certificates of limpieza. The Suprema's personnel were kept almost as busy issuing these documents as prosecuting alleged transgressors. Separation of Old and New Christians became an article of faith. It is probable, too, that Iberian notions of racial superiority fortified the already well developed "ethnic" haughtiness of Sephardic Jews. Unwittingly, they themselves gradually came to internalize the current mythos of pedigree and ancestry (pp. 381–82).

Notwithstanding persecution and isolation, there remained one sector of the kingdom in which Jews for many years still found it possible to sustain their loyalty and vitality. It was the Balearic Islands, less than one hundred miles off the eastern coast, and specifically the island of Majorca. Although today its capital, Palma de Majorca, is a rather somnolent middle-sized tourist city of some 235,000, as late as the eighteenth century it remained an extraordinarily vital Mediterranean community. So did its Jewish population. These people had endured much, including the ravages of the 1391 massacres and the 1492 Expulsion Decree. Nevertheless, an influx of several hundred Portuguese marranos in the seventeenth century helped to revive at least a portion of their original demographic base. Nominally Catholic, they were in fact judaizers almost every one, and they sustained each other through every vicissitude, financial and moral. In the process, too, they maintained a secrecy that was all but impenetrable. Living and working as artisans and merchants of silver and jewels, the newcomers managed ingeniously to avoid revealing their private crypto-Jewish rituals and dietary habits.

But for all their mutual support, these marranos very nearly met their nemesis in the Majorcan Inquisition. With its secret army of *familiares*, the tribunal here became more remorseless and inventive than possibly anywhere else in Europe. No other inquisitional panel could match its record in hunting down marranos, harassing anyone of remotest converso background, and confiscating New Christian property. Throughout the 1670s, Majorca's inquisitional bailiffs swooped down on suspects almost weekly. One massive auto de fe seemed to follow another in the Balearics, with each sequence of human tragedy more agonizing than its predecessor. Instructive was the fate of Jacobo López, a boy of sixteen. In 1667, together with other Jews en route from Oran to Leghorn, Jacobo was dragged off a ship that had anchored at Majorca for reprovisioning. As identified Jews, the captives in fact had broken no laws. Thus, after a week of detention, they were released on orders of the governor. The vessel departed. But one passenger was held in Majorca—the youth Jacobo.

Information had reached the local Inquisition that the boy's parents, who once had lived in Madrid as conversos, in practice remained secret judaizers, as did their son. In Majorca, Jacobo was tortured to confess, and did. Yet no threat or torture would induce him to forsake the Law of Moses. Finally, he was burned alive in the great auto de fe of January 1675 together with six Portuguese marranos, four of them women. Over thirty thousand persons had gathered in the Plaza del Borne to witness the spectacle, among them the viceroy, the archbishop, and other resident state and clerical dignitaries. The inquisitional transcript also noted that precisely at the time Jacobo and others were blazing on their pyres, the bishop and his entourage were "served ices and chocolates." By then, the resistance of Majorca's lingering conversos had been entirely broken. Well before the end of the seventeenth century, judaizing even of the most superficial variety was a closed chapter.

Then and later, nevertheless, descendants of the Majorca conversos remained objects of suspicion and disdain. Indeed, their little circle of some four hundred families would labor under the obloquy of "tainted blood" down to the 1900s. The local term for these people was *chueta* (derived from *xuhita*, an old Majorcan word for Jew). In no sense were the chuetas other than practicing Catholics. But they could not escape the sin of impure ancestry. If their plight in Majorca was no longer one of clandestine existence or fear, they remained pariahs. From the 1700s on, social pressure confined these people to a restricted *chuetería*, essentially the neighborhood near La Calle, the downtown center of their silverware and jewelry shops.

During the Napoleonic Wars, the chuetas were accepted into the Spanish army on an emergency basis to resist the French, and after several decades the ban even on their routine military service was lifted. But in every other respect, the little group remained in quarantine. Periodically, government and intellectual circles debated the status of the chuetas. In the early twentieth century, one of those who took their side was the renowned novelist Vicente Blasco Ibáñez, whose 1916 novel *Los muertos mandan* (The Dead Command) expressed warm sympathy for them. Legal restrictions against this group finally ended with the inauguration of the Spanish Republic in 1931. In Majorca, however, two distinct chueta communities survived into the Franco era, and even beyond. Numbering approximately three thousand, descendants of conversos to this day make their homes in their chuetería. Lately, they have been in contact with Jewish emissaries from the West and Israel, and several dozen actually have returned to formal identification with Judaism.

Otherwise, in the amberized medievalism of Spanish society, institutional change remained a grudging process. The Inquisition continued to function well into the eighteenth century, even under a new Bourbon dynasty. "Relaxations" may have been less frequent by then, but arrests and interrogations of suspected Jews—and Protestants and blasphemers—continued until the era of the French Revolution. Abolished in 1808 during the brief reign of Joseph Bonaparte, the Inquisition was resuscitated by Fernando VII in 1815 and survived in law until 1820, when it was formally terminated. Even after that, King Fernando suspended his decree of termination intermittently to confront "heretical emergencies." As late as 1826, a suspected marrano was burned alive and a Protestant schoolmaster was garroted. Finally, in 1833, Queen Regent María Cristina ended the Inquisition for the third and last time.

Since its inception in 1478, the "monster" had taken a grim toll: 31,912 prisoners "relaxed"; 17,649 burned in effigy; 29,401 imprisoned or reconciled *de vehementi*—under harsh and punitive scrutiny. A majority of the victims were conversos. For its champions, in any case, the Inquisition had amply fulfilled its promise. By the 1800s, no country in Europe was more thoroughly purged of its Jews than Spain.

The Inquisition as Infection

Three centuries earlier, the Inquisition in Portugal overcame its somewhat hesitant beginnings to assume the lineaments of its Spanish prototype. The most intensive phase of its activities coincided with Felipe II's accession to the Portuguese throne in 1580. Although each Inquisition remained separate, there was little to distinguish between them in arrogance, murderousness, or corruption. Soon the fate of New Christians became virtually identical in Spain and Portugal. Between 1651 and 1673 alone, Portugal's three inquisitional tribunals at Évora, Coimbra, and Lisbon "relaxed" one hundred eighty-four victims in person and fifty-nine in effigy. Confiscations proceeded with similar rapacity in both countries.

Frantic for self-protection, a number of affluent New Christian spokesmen then offered the Portuguese Crown a substantial gift to stay the inquisitional terror. A precedent, after all, had been established in the payoff to Felipe III of Spain and Clement VIII, resulting in the papal pardon of 1604 (p. 173). In Portugal, the effort succeeded in 1674, when Pedro II accepted a bribe of twenty thousand cruzados and duly suspended the Inquisition. But the respite endured only seven years; the monster resumed its operations in 1681. Afterward, autos da fé and "illuminations" became increasingly spectacular, Coimbra vying with Lisbon, Lisbon vying with Évora in pageantry and ferocity. In 1705, an auto da fé in Lisbon convicted sixty-six victims and burned eleven of them. A particularly gruesome upsurge of Portuguese autos da fé claimed one hundred eleven victims in 1706 and one hundred thirty-eight in 1714. The nation's population was barely a third of Spain's, yet between 1547 and 1765 its Inquisition prosecuted no fewer than forty thousand cases. As in Spain, a majority of the defendants were of New Christian background. At the Suprema's orders, eighteen hundred persons were garroted or burned at the stake, and thirty thousand more were "reconciled" with sentences of varying length. Innumerable thousands of other victims expired or went mad in their prison cells without ever having been sentenced.

For many of these victims, their fate was played out in the Rossio. Officially known as the Praça Dom Pedro IV, the Rossio today is Lisbon's central municipal square. Inlaid with superb mosaics, the plaza encompasses a towering bronze statue of King Pedro IV, two soaring fountains, and a profusion of brilliantly hued flower pavilions. In earlier centuries, the Rossio was the site of the nation's most elaborate autos da fé and burnings. Its current National Theater once functioned there as the inquisitional "Palace." When the building first was opened to public inspection in 1821, the Portuguese *Annual Register* reported in shocked tones:

> The edifice . . . is three stories high, and encompasses several vaulted galleries, along which are located a number of dungeons of six, seven, eight, and nine feet square. Those on the ground floor and on the first floor are windowless, and thus are deprived of both air and light when the door is shut. The dungeons on the next floor possess a breathing hole of sorts in the form of a chimney through which the sky may be seen. . . . The doors of certain dungeons, which had not been used for many years, still remained shut, but the visitors soon forced these open. In nearly all of them, human bones were found. . . . In some of these dungeons, the chimney-shaped airhole was walled up, which is certain evidence of the murder of the prisoner. In such cases, the unfortunate victim was thrust into the airhole, the lower extremity of which was immediately sealed by masonry. Quicklime was afterwards dumped on him, which extinguished life and destroyed the body.

Notwithstanding these congenialities, several thousand New Christians evidently underwent a final crisis of conscience in the seventeenth century and decided to take their chances as marranos. They settled largely in the mountainous north, isolated from all Jewish sources, and were thus compelled to develop innovative new patterns of Jewish living. Some managed the feat. Most could not. The Inquisition focused on the judaizing menace beyond all other threats to Catholic homogeneity, and pounced like a hawk on all suspected marrano conventicles. By the end of the century, as a result, crypto-Jews had all but vanished from the Portuguese social topography.

During these same years, *novos cristãos* lived under a cloud that transcended religious identity. As in Spain, ethnic assimilation was fostering its reciprocal antisemitism. Indeed, in a nation as small as Portugal, the ratio of "intermingling" was far more extensive—perhaps as high as 8 or 10 percent even as early as the mid-sixteenth century. Yet the "amalgamation" was shorter-lived than in Spain. Here, too, as the doctrine of *limpeza de sangue* gained acceptance, it was infused by the escalating passion of the Counter-Reformation. Felipe II lent the campaign of purgation his unique brand of missionary zeal. But even after separation of the two countries in 1640, the notion was widely accepted that neither baptism nor the practice of Christian virtue could change a person's Jewish "character." The infection had to be rooted out at the core—within the convertido hinterland itself.

Throughout the 1600s and 1700s, therefore, persons of New Christian origin (in some instances to the seventh degree) were officially excluded from government and ecclesiastical posts, from military orders, municipal councils, and university faculties. Legal and medical guilds no longer would admit convertido lawyers and physicians. The restrictions were not evenly enforced. Some *novos cristãos* managed to infiltrate closed vocations and organizations, particularly in the overseas empire (p. 348). But otherwise, the doctrine of limpeza de sangue came to be incorporated into the very public policy of the realm, and the Inquisition's post-factum scars in consequence endured far longer than the "relaxations" or imprisonments themselves. Convertidos were to be regarded henceforth as irretrievably contaminated by their Hebrew blood, and so were their families. They were outcasts, economically redundant, socially untouchable.

Yet Portugal was not to be indefinitely resistant to the new spirit of European Enlightenment, no more than was Spain. By the eighteenth century, both the inquisitional danse macabre and the pretensions of limpeza de sangue came under rising attack. No one articulated the new rationalism more pungently than did Sebastião José de Carvalho e Mello, Marquis of Pombal. As prime minister to King José I, from 1756 to 1777, Pombal regarded his nation's lingering medievalism as a mortifying burden, and not only for honorable Portuguese of New Christian ancestry. It had convinced foreigners that Portugal was a nation pullulating with judaizers—indeed, a nation composed essentially of Jews. Even the great Erasmus had petulantly dismissed the Portuguese as "a race of Jews" *(illud genus judaicum)*. Pombal had spent his earlier years as ambassador to London and Vienna, and was thoroughly aware of these legends. He was equally aware that the stigma of limpeza de sangue would leave virtually no Portuguese untainted. On one occasion, King José's morning agenda included an inquisitional demand that *novos cristãos* be limited to white hats for headgear as badges of their ancestry. The next day, Pombal allegedly turned up before the royal cabinet holding three white hats. He had brought one for the king, he explained, one for the grand inquisitor, and one for himself.

With his characteristic blend of dispassion and decisiveness, the prime minister focused initially on liquidating the Inquisition. In 1768 he stripped the Suprema of its power of censorship, and in 1771 he forbade it to conduct public autos-da-fé. Two years later, Pombal finally sold the king on legislation that eradicated limpeza de sangue as a condition for officeholding. Later, the measure also was applied to the private sector, both in Portugal and in its overseas empire. By then, in any case, few convertidos remained, even of the "seventh degree." Like Spain, Portugal now evidently was purged of its Jews as thoroughly in race as in creed.

In Search of Barros Basto

Lisbon's original judiaria is to be found in the Alfama quarter. Like its counterparts in Mediterranean Europe, the labyrinth of cobblestoned alleyways and three- and four-story rabbit-hutch favelas is of interest principally to antiquarians. Today, Lisbon's approximately six hundred Jews live in fashionable middle- or upper-middle-class surroundings. One of these is a spacious old apartment on the elegant Rua Rodrigo da Fonseca. My hostess, Senhora Hannah Sequeira Marques, is a fair-skinned, delicate-featured lady in her midfifties. She speaks perfect English. So, presumably, did her grandmother, who was born in British Gibraltar, where she married her Sequeira cousin from Faro. Eventually the couple settled in Lisbon, and Grandfather Sequeira prospered there as an importer-exporter. "We were a devout family, and still are," Senhora Marques assures me. "Our lives revolve around our community, our people." Can she feel comfortable in this land? "Only to some degree," she acknowledges. "I still have my folk-memories of the terrible things that happened in Portugal. To this day, I cannot go to the National Theater at the Rossio. They burned our people there, you know." Senhora Marques's artless, "integral" Jewishness is touching. "But I was born here," she continues, "in this very apartment. It has been our family home for three generations."

Altogether, the revived Jewish presence in this land dates back hardly more than four generations. It was not until the early nineteenth century that identified Jews were discreetly permitted entrance. Those like the Sequeiras from Gibraltar, who possessed British citizenship, were the first to venture the return. If most came without "legal" permission, none was molested. Indeed, the vanguard soon was joined by others, principally Moroccan Jews from Tetuán and Tangiers. In 1818, a second Jewish community was established, in the Azores, and in 1830 still another, in Faro, on the mainland. Over the years, cemeteries were chartered, congregations founded, each with the usual communal welfare and educational facilities.

Portugal's minuscule Jewish revival was never entirely unshadowed. In 1926, following decades of political turmoil, a right-wing military cabal assumed power in Portugal, and six years later Dr. António de Oliveira Salazar, a professor of economics at Coimbra University, became prime minister–dictator of a harshly repressive administration. Even then, however, the nation's two or three hundred Jews managed to conduct their affairs in reasonable security. Several of them even rose to economic and

professional eminence. It is a fact that the Salazar government supported
Franco during the Spanish Civil War. Yet in World War II it was also
Salazar who assured protection for his nation's tiny Jewish community,
then gave sanctuary to thousands of Jewish refugees on a temporary
transit basis. Perhaps a hundred of these Ashkenazim remained on after
the war, although neither they nor the Sephardic majority have generated
a particularly vigorous communal life. They are simply too few.

The Sephardic synagogue on Rua Alexandre Herculano, in Lisbon's
central commercial district, is an aged wooden building, virtually invisible
behind a twenty-foot steel gate. Its rabbi wears a large bowler. His white
beard accentuates his dark complexion. "Hardly any of us are 'Western'
Sephardim," he observes forthrightly. "I myself came from Tetuán, over
forty years ago. Nearly all my congregants are of Moroccan background,
except for possibly a hundred from Gibraltar." He smiles. "And I'm not
so sure about them." He is even less certain that there is a future for
Portuguese Jews. They are not replenishing their numbers, and few attend
synagogue except on the High Holidays or involve themselves even in
Jewish secular affairs. The rabbi's own children now live in Israel. Other
people's children are building careers for themselves in Latin America or
the United States. In their parochialism, too, the Jews of Lisbon are riven
with factional jealousies. A former president of the Jewish community,
Dr. Joshua Ruah, an eminent urologist, speaks for the "true," "refined"
Sephardic minority. A current president, Solomon Marques, the
Moroccan-born husband of Hannah Sequeira Marques, speaks for the
North African "traditionalists." The two groups vie for the approbation
of the Israeli ambassador, whose dicta usually are accepted as authoritative. It is touching.

Is there no hope for a wider demographic revival? In fact, once there
was. In 1917, Samuel Schwartz, a Polish-born mining engineer on contract
to the Portuguese government, set up his base of operations in the northern mountain town of Belmonte, near the Spanish border. One day, an
acquaintance cautioned Schwartz to avoid a certain neighborhood shop.
"The proprietor is a Jew," he warned. Then and there, Schwartz visited
the store. When he attempted to query the owner, the man at first em-
phatically denied any Jewish connection. But when Schwartz identified
himself as a Jew, and even recited a prayer in Hebrew, the shopkeeper
responded in delight. Within hours, he notified local friends and relatives.
Their excitement matched his own. These isolated Portuguese villagers
had believed themselves the last Jews on earth.

Schwartz's discovery was not limited to a neighborhood marrano conventicle, as it turned out. He had stumbled upon a pocket of crypto-Jewish

communities that extended throughout the northern provinces of Trás-os-Montes, Beira Alta, Alto Douro, and Minho, comprising perhaps as many as eight thousand individuals. Living in the towns of Belmonte, Fundão, Castelo Branco, Idanha-a-Nova, Penamacor, Guarda, Bragança, and Monsanto, these rustics were descendants of convertidos who had fled the Inquisition in the late seventeenth century. They clustered along the old Aragonese frontier in the event flight might be required to the more densely inhabited Spanish hinterland. Since then, twisted by secrecy and ignorance, their religion had mutated into an eccentric parody of classical Judaism. Hebrew was all but unknown among them. Their ceremonies were entirely misshapen. Although they observed the fast on Yom Kippur, the marranos also fasted on Purim, a holiday traditionally reserved for merriment. They conducted their equally inauthentic Sabbath and holiday prayers exclusively in nuclear-family groups, not in congregations. Like the chuetas of Majorca, they married exclusively among their own.

Schwartz wasted no time in reporting his discovery to Jewish organizations in Europe. They shared his excitement. Indeed, no sooner had the war ended than relays of Western rabbis hurried off to Portugal to investigate the situation for themselves. Their descriptions of the crypto-Jews soon were lavishly embellished by rumors that as many as twenty thousand marranos were champing at the bit to return to authentic Judaism. Meanwhile, in 1924, the tiny Jewish community of Lisbon, confused and limited in its resources, turned for advice to Jewish leaders in England. Whereupon a prominent Anglo-Jewish activist, Wilfred Samuel, funded a commission of inquiry. Its chairman was Lucien Wolf. A mandarin of Central European pedigree, Wolf in his distaste for Russian Jews had made himself something of an authority on Sephardic history. Once in Portugal, he mingled extensively with the northern marranos and soon was persuaded of their bona fides. Brimming with enthusiasm, Wolf then hurried back to London to help organize a Pro-Marrano Committee. During the latter 1920s, branches were established in France and the United States.

The committee's objective quite simply was to guide these lost sheep of Israel back into the Jewish mainstream. To that end, it underwrote a Portuguese-language newspaper to supply information on modern Jewish life and religious practices. Ironically, the newspaper's explanations of basic prayers and ceremonies were lifted almost verbatim from the *Thesouro dos Dinim,* compiled in the seventeenth century by Menasseh ben Israel for the Sephardim of Amsterdam (p. 307). But the committee also translated Sabbath and holiday prayer books into Portuguese. Most useful of all, it sponsored visitations by English and American rabbis to conduct model services for the northern marranos. In 1928, it rented premises for religious worship on the main street of the town of Bragança.

The principal revivalist effort, however, was directed to Oporto, Portugal's second city and gateway to the crypto-Jewish communities of the north. Here a distinguished judiaria had thrived in medieval times. And here, in 1928, the Pro-Marrano Committee of London decided to build its largest synagogue. In 1933 the project gained momentum when it was underwritten by the sons of Elie Kadoorie, a renowned Iraqi-Jewish merchant-prince. Five years later, the building was completed. Its dedication was attended by Jewish leaders from throughout the world, as well as by some one hundred of the marranos themselves. Located on Rua Guerra Junqueira, in an upper-middle-class residential quarter, the Mekor Chayim synagogue is imposing in size but simple and dignified in its classical Sephardic design (pulpit in the center of the sanctuary, wooden pews arranged in an open square). Today, the building lacks only a rabbi—and a congregation. Within a decade after its construction, most of the "rediscovered" Jews had vanished into obscurity.

Several factors torpedoed the marrano revival. For one thing, responding to church pressure, the government had issued a veiled warning of limited employment opportunities for Catholics who "defected" to Judaism. The hint registered. But so, even more conclusively, did the fate of the marranos' preeminent champion. His photograph is framed on the wall of the Kadoorie synagogue. Middle-aged, somewhat overweight, smiling modestly, he wears the uniform of a Portuguese army captain, replete with epaulets and a double row of medals. His name was Artur Carlos de Barros Basto. When I first heard Solomon and Hannah Marques allude to him as the "Portuguese Dreyfus," the characterization struck me as Latin and grandiose. I was premature.

It was Max Azencot who first set me right. An elderly gentleman of mixed Sephardic-Ashkenazic parentage, Azencot received me at his law offices in downtown Lisbon. Little of the Barros Basto experience was unknown to him; the two men were brothers-in-law. Indeed, the case of the "Portuguese Dreyfus" lay in Azencot's files. Its details were stark. Born near Oporto in 1887, Barros Basto was a descendant of convertidos. Although his own parents were practicing Catholics, he had vague childhood memories of grandparents lighting candles on Friday evening. It is not unlikely, too, that he inherited a certain ancestral proclivity to overachievement. Without funds to pursue a legal education, the young man won acceptance at the national military academy. His academic record there was brilliant. So was his "extracurricular" record. Early on, he became a dynamic figure in the revolutionary movement. When the monarchy was overthrown in 1910, it was Barros Basto who hoisted the republican flag over the Oporto town hall.

"But something was missing in those early years," Azencot explained. "Much later, Artur told me that he felt a vague sense of spiritual emptiness. During his trips to Lisbon, he would occasionally visit our synagogue to sit in on Sabbath services." Nothing came of these intermittent contacts. Nor did the local Jewish population encourage them; it was best not to revive Catholic suspicions of judaizing. Meanwhile, the Great War had begun. Portugal entered the conflict on the side of the Entente, and in 1916 Barros Basto was dispatched to the European front. Commanding a squadron of infantry, he saw action in Flanders, endured a gas attack, was several times decorated. In Flanders, too, one Friday evening, Barros Basto happened to stroll into the tent of his French liaison officer and found him lighting candles. "It is a Jewish Sabbath tradition," the Frenchman explained. For Barros Basto, the dim memory of his grandparents' ritual suddenly locked into focus. "From that moment he knew what he was," Azencot observed, "and where he belonged."

A captain when the war ended, Barros Basto was appointed garrison commander in Oporto. It was a sedentary billet, offering ample leeway for outside activities. Barros Basto used his free time to engage in an intensive study of Judaism. By 1920, he was passionate in his desire to convert. But who would complete his instruction and perform the ceremony? He consulted with Professor Moses Bensabat, rector of the National Technical University and president of the Lisbon Jewish community. Bensabat directed Barros Basto to Tetuán, in Spanish Morocco. There the local rabbinate fulfilled the captain's wish. In 1921, he returned to Oporto a formally and officially identified Jew. A year later, he met Azencot's sister Leah and they married. At the same time, he was giving his every free moment to a cause he now regarded as sacred. It was to win back to the Torah people like himself, descendants of marrano families who had abandoned their ancestral traditions. Henceforth, publishing and distributing an extensive circular literature, Barros Basto entreated these compatriots to emerge from hiding and ignorance, and make themselves known to him.

In his missionary zeal, the captain found an important ally. It was London's Pro-Marrano Committee. Learning of Barros Basto's campaign, the committee swiftly embraced it, funded it, and supplied it with prayer books, Hebrew grammars, and other literary material. By the early 1930s, moreover, Barros Basto was operating out of the formidable new Kadoorie synagogue. Calling himself "Ben-Rosh," he gave the name

"Rosh Pina" (Cornerstone) to the talmud torah, the Hebrew secondary
school, he operated for marrano youngsters in the synagogue's classroom.
By 1935, Barros Basto had enrolled some fifty students, and appeared likely
to ignite a modest Jewish renaissance among these children and their
families.

A reaction was not long in coming. One phase of the church's counterattack was oblique, and was exerted through pressure on the government.
A second phase was directed against Barros Basto himself. In 1935 a local
priest, Tomaz Correia da Luz Almeida, prior of the monastery of Al-
furada, awaited Barros Basto's students each day as they walked home
following their afternoon classes. Gently but persistently, Frei Tomaz
won the confidence of several youngsters. Through skillful, manipulative
questioning, he was able to fabricate a case against the captain. Soon the
cleric convinced the police that Barros Basto was a "degenerate," that he
was engaging in unnatural practices during circumcision ceremonies,
under the pretext of sucking blood from the infants' incisions. Whereupon
the Oporto municipal prosecutor immediately brought criminal charges
against Barros Basto. The captain was unperturbed. He had anticipated
church opposition and knew that his own devoted constituency of students and colleagues would decisively repudiate the libel.

But here Barros Basto encountered a shattering surprise. One of those
"colleagues," Isaac Cassuto, had immigrated to Portugal several years
earlier from Hamburg, where his father had been president of that city's
tiny Sephardic community. It later developed that Cassuto had departed
under a cloud; evidently he had "appropriated" rare Hebrew incunabula
from the Hamburg talmudic academy. In Portugal, as an equally slippery
dealer in rare books, Cassuto did well enough to maintain a luxurious villa
in the seaside resort of Estoril. Barros Basto, in turn, had sufficient information about the man to block his repeated overtures for congregational
office. It was as a gesture of revenge, therefore, that Cassuto now volunteered to serve as a police witness against the accused captain. His testimony was devastating. Barros Basto's dossier then was turned over to the
army, which instituted its own court-martial. With extended interrup-
tions, the case dragged on from 1935 to 1937. Eventually it was dropped for
lack of conclusive evidence. Yet the damage was done. By the mid-1930s,
parents had withdrawn their children from the Rosh Pina school, and
Barros Basto had become persona non grata among his once-devoted
marrano followers. With equal timorousness, the established Jewish community also now distanced itself from the case. Finally, in 1943, the
ministry of defense revoked Barros Basto's officer's commission for reasons of "good and welfare." He was a ruined man.

His daughter would never forget. The wife of a successful bank director, Senhora Miryam Barros Basto Teixeira da Silva received me cordially in her spacious apartment on the Rua António Garcia in Oporto. She was in her late fifties, a handsome woman, her silver coif framing a high complexion and turquoise eyes. Over tea, Senhora Teixeira da Silva proceeded in animated French to describe the aftermath of her father's dismissal. "For two years he sat in a daze," she recalled, "unable to work or even to think. We were also in a state of economic paralysis. There was no income." She was obliged to abandon her plans for law school. Her mother baked pastries for a caterer. Eventually, a French-Jewish admirer, Marcel Goldschmidt, engaged Barros Basto as the local agent for his Lyons silk factory. It was not a productive arrangement. Barros Basto ate his bread with affliction. In 1961, he died. His wife followed soon after.

Although comfortably married by then, with family responsibilities of her own, Senhora Teixeira da Silva never abandoned hope of redeeming her father's good name. And in 1974, following the revolution that overthrew the last remnants of the Salazar government, she thought she had found her chance. Her uncle, Max Azencot, helped to prepare her appeal. To the consortium of politically liberal officers now operating the ministry of defense, Senhora Teixeira da Silva resubmitted the Barros Basto file of over thirty years before. The evidence of her father's innocence and of the conspiracy against him was overwhelming. The officers were impressed. On their advice, she appealed directly to the new president, the Socialist general Francisco Costa Gomez. Two months passed before an answer arrived from Costa Gomez's chef de cabinet. "He conveyed the president's fullest sympathy," Senhora Teixeira da Silva recalled, her eyes brimming, "but explained that it was impossible to resuscitate the case after so many years." There the matter remained, and remains to this day.

What of Senhora Teixeira da Silva since then? She has devoted herself to her family. Her husband is Catholic. Her two children have chosen the path of Catholicism, and both have married Catholics. And she herself? "I attend both church and synagogue," she explains straightforwardly. "It was a choice I made many years ago." At that, it was a more forthright option than the one selected by the eight thousand crypto-Jews of the brief marrano "renaissance." By the latter 1930s, they had returned to their secret conventicles in Trás-os-Montes, Beira Alta, Alto Douro, and Minho. Once burned, they did not seem prepared to be lured into the open again.

A Converso Legacy

The converso émigrés of the sixteenth and seventeenth centuries displayed vast ingenuity, both in negotiating their routes of passage to a wide variety of destinations and in fulfilling a historic Diaspora role in the lands of their resettlement. They functioned as the indispensable yeast in their host societies' trade and commerce. Throughout Europe, after all, as well as North Africa and the Balkans, from west to east, the Sephardic dispersion was informed by a shared social culture. Conversos might travel from Hamburg to Bordeaux, from Bordeaux to Leghorn, from Leghorn to Izmir or Constantinople, without a wrenching sense of change. They maintained their correspondence over half the civilized world in a common language. They operated within commercial rules and regulations according to a common tradition.

With no corner of the trading world beyond the Sephardic ambit, therefore, certain branches of trade rapidly devolved almost entirely into their hands. New Christians dominated the import of gems into Europe from the East Indies and the New World. The coral industry was their monopoly. So was the traffic in sugar, tobacco, and other colonial agricultural products. From the 1600s on, converso financiers established several of Europe's great national banks. Indeed, as conversos, marranos, or identified Jews, the emigrating Sephardim in their economic activities vindicated Joseph Addison's late-seventeenth-century "Essay on the Jews": "They are . . . so disseminated through all the trading parts of the world, that they are become the instruments by which the most distant nations converse with one another, and by which mankind are knit together in a general correspondence."

Hardly less significant than their economic role, however, was the conversos' impact upon their own people. The Jews who sailed off directly to the Ottoman Empire or Italy during the late fifteenth and early sixteenth centuries were for the most part individuals of private Jewish loyalties who turned for asylum specifically to lands where they might safely revert to Judaism. By contrast, the New Christians who remained behind on Iberian soil were people of somewhat feebler Jewish conviction. Even the marranos among them might have been content to accept Catholicism, had they been allowed quietly to do so. It was not the Inquisition alone but rather the constraints of limpieza de sangre that forced conversos apart from Old Christians and into their own self-contained vocational, social, and marital networks. Thus, in the end, it was less the tenacity of Jewish ideology than the quest for sheer economic survival that impelled these New Christians belatedly to pull up stakes and depart.

Unlike the 1492 exodus of professing Jews, moreover, few New Christians of the Renaissance and early modern era traveled to the Ottoman Empire or Morocco or other lands in which they might openly profess Judaism. Rather, their initial ports of call were such Christian entrepôts as Flanders and the overseas Spanish and Portuguese empires, where they still were obliged to maintain at least an outward Christian identity. Even later, when these emigrants occasionally declared themselves as Jews—in Ferrara, Venice, Mantua, Ancona, Leghorn—they were by no means announcing a fidelity long nurtured in their hearts. Again, it was convenience, often a web of Jewish trade connections, that determined their choice.

But whether as expedient New Christians or as expedient returnees to Judaism, the migrating Sephardim were left with cruel psychological scars. Even beyond Spanish or Portuguese terrain, they lived painfully involuted lives in one country after another, posing occasionally as Christians, occasionally as Jews, sometimes believing they were one, then the other. In Brian Pullen's discerning simile, they operated in a netherworld of uncertainties, here wearing the Jewish badge, there the Christian hat. What impact could this dissimulation have had on their children, who remained unsure of their true identity, changing like chameleons from country to country, circumstance to circumstance, bereft of anchorage or certitudes? It was their good fortune, at least, upon finally arriving at havens of identified Jews abroad, that most of these communities were willing to extend them a fraternal reception—on the Maimonidean premise that "a Jew, even if he sins, remains a Jew." With few exceptions, the awaiting kinsmen knew what these repentant defectors had undergone and were prepared to forgive them and their parents any earlier tactical apostasy.

Yet the gesture of forbearance did not always evoke a reciprocal accommodation. Either as secret or as reverting Jews, the marranos had internalized the classical Iberian penchant for aristocratic self-esteem (p. 175). Their tombstones, often chiseled with the names of their Iberian cities of origin, bore haughty Spanish and Portuguese coats of arms. The gesture represented more than a poignant, emulative fixation with limpieza de sangre, or even an ill-disguised social contempt for their "uncouth" Ashkenazic cousins. As Yosef Yerushalmi has astutely observed, it proclaimed a cultural and intellectual equality with Christians. Unlike Jews of Central European ancestry or identified Jews of Sephardic background (each community linked into its own matrix of economic restrictions and social quarantine), the conversos dressed in the same manner as high-born Gentiles and spoke a pure language, either Castilian or Portuguese. They also managed the social graces and thus often were positioned to secure political benefits for their people that could never have been negotiated by professing yet ghetto-bound parochial Jews.

After having studied at respected universities—Coimbra, Salamanca, Alcalá, Toulouse, Montpellier, Paris, Padua, Ferrara, among others—the conversos were also the first Jews since the apogee of Moslem Spain to be exposed to the cultural and scientific accomplishments of the wider host society. As matters developed, that cultural provenance often functioned as a two-edged sword. Unquestionably, it helped carve a path to vocational achievement in the Gentile world. Yet at the same time it provoked sharp ideological repercussions once the conversos, feeble in their Jewish loyalties, resumed their ancestral identity. The threat of intellectual dissension was accurately stated in seventeenth-century Amsterdam by Baltasar Orobio de Castro, himself a returning New Christian. While acknowledging that some of his fellow returnees unreservedly embraced traditional Judaism, Castro noted:

> Others come to Judaism who, while in idolatry, had studied various profane sciences such as logic, physics, metaphysics, and medicine. These arrive no less ignorant of the law than the first, but they are full of vanity and pride . . . convinced that they are learned in all matters, and that they know everything. . . . They enter under the felicitous yoke of Judaism . . . [but] their vanity and pride do not permit them to receive instruction so that they emerge from their ignorance . . . to contradict that which they do not understand, even though it be all true, all holy, all divine.

The behavior described by Castro could not be attributed to "vanity and pride" alone. The returning conversos experienced a severe culture shock, one that compounded their earlier psychological ambivalence. They were obliged to undergo a "crash" education in a vast, unfamiliar reservoir of Jewish skills and knowledge. The need could only partially be served by a virtual translation-industry of classical Jewish texts into Portuguese and Spanish, from prayer books to the *Shulchan Aruch* (p. 121). In truth, the effort of Jewish reacculturation failed more often than it succeeded. Intellectual exhaustion was not the explanation. As Castro suggested, intellectual skepticism was now the predominant motif. The returning conversos brought a new ideological dimension to their understanding of religion altogether—their own as well as others'. Culturally fructified by immersion in a broader world of secular information and ideas, these emigrating sophisticates were less prepared to accept any creed, even ancestral Judaism, on faith alone. Reason and knowledge had a role to play. Five centuries before, the lesson had been taught by the great Maimonides. It awaited the return of the lost sheep of Israel for that message to be revived and decisively revitalized.

CHAPTER IX

THE POISONED EMBRACE

A Questionable Sephardicization

In the eighth century, at the height of Islamic conquest, the North African littoral was a bleak, subequatorial poorhouse of herdsmen and village laborers. At no time did its heterogeneity of races and tribes permit of effective, centralized government. Although unified under Moslem rule, the vast subcontinent eventually fractured into a succession of dynastic principalities loosely corresponding to present-day Algeria, Tunisia (including Libya), and Morocco. Their governments were hybrid regimes of Middle Eastern Arabs and indigenous Berbers.

A significant minority of those natives were Jews. Concentrated in the Atlas Mountain range of Morocco and Algeria, and in several desert oases, their clans apparently had been judaized in earlier centuries by traders or refugees from the Holy Land. Berber in race, in language, and in many of their folk traditions, these *moghrebim* (from Maghreb, the Arabic term for the North African massif) somehow remained Jewish in religion even following the islamization of the surrounding majority population. They were an impoverished element, possibly even more than their non-Jewish neighbors. In the twelfth century, the Almohade dynasty in its zeal consigned them to the lowest rank of dhimmi inferiority, and later rulers institutionalized that status. Execrated by the Moslem natives, reduced to distinctive clothing and badges, numerous moghrebim fled deeper into the interior or into the fetid ghettos of the cities. There, in ensuing years, these backwater Jews gradually swooned into a long era of economic and spiritual atrophy.

In the fourteenth century, however, numbers of rather more affluent and educated Jews from Castile, Aragón, and the Balearic Islands began making their way to the North African littoral. Virtually all of them arrived as fugitives from the escalating fanaticism of the *reconquista*, and particularly from the trauma of 1391 and its aftermath. Gravitating initially to the more developed port cities of Oran and Tunis, some of the newcomers later moved on to Miliana, Constantine, Fez, and to other inland towns. They were not unacquainted with this hinterland, as it happened. North Africa had long played a central role within the Iberian trading orbit, and Sephardim traditionally had been the masters of that commerce. The Farisols, Manduels, and other important Jewish trading families maintained branch offices and warehouses in the ports of Bougie, Algiers, and Tunis. Others functioned as translators, dragomans, brokers, and commercial agents between European and North African ports. Among North African Jews, the economic and social status of the Sephardic minority even then contrasted vividly with that of the Maghreb Jewish majority. Although most of the *berberiscos* (as the Sephardim contemptuously described these native-born Jews) in fact were city-dwellers who spoke Arabic rather than local Berber dialects, they eked out their livelihoods essentially as small artisans, shopkeepers, and peddlers. The two communities had little in common.

It was the Spanish Expulsion Decree of 1492, and its Portuguese counterpart in 1497, that permanently transformed the demography of Maghreb Jewry. Perhaps as many as fifty thousand Sephardic refugees made their way across the Strait of Gibraltar to North Africa. Their ordeal was a cruel one. In Morocco, the least developed of the littoral states, thousands of these fugitives were plundered and slain by local tribesmen. Others decamped in open fields and perished of hunger and exposure. Still, remarkably, perhaps two-thirds of the refugees managed to survive the initial trauma. These were the exiles who made their way to Fez, Marrakech, Meknès, and Shafshawan, in the interior; to the Atlantic coastal cities of Asilah, Larache, Azemmur, Mazaghan, Safi, and Agadir; and to the Mediterranean ports of Ceuta, Tetuán, and Velez. It was in these cities that they at last were offered the protection of Sultan Muhammad al-Sheikh al-Wattasi. Thoroughly apprised of Sephardic Jewry's commercial and professional skills, the ruler discerned value in these people.

Yet for all their usefulness to the Moroccan economy, the newcomers were consigned to the same urban ghettos inhabited by the older, Berber Jewish community. They were also subjected to the identical legal restrictions imposed on the lowly berberiscos, to the poll taxes, the distinctive apparel, the ban on the construction of new synagogues or the repair of old ones. There were occasional personal exemptions. These included the vocational and professional elite—important merchants, court physicians, financial advisers. Indeed, almost every Moroccan ruler had his Jewish counselor, his Jewish doctor, and at least one Jewish ambassador to a foreign land. Joseph and Samuel Pallache served as Morocco's commercial and diplomatic representatives in the Dutch Netherlands from 1609 until their deaths, negotiating vital military and economic treaties between the two governments. In neighboring Algeria, a later-arriving wave of Sephardim from Leghorn proved so rich in experienced tax-farmers, merchants, and commercial envoys that it managed to win en bloc immunity from the ghetto.

Nevertheless, in Morocco, the densest area of Jewish habitation in North Africa, most Sephardim remained confined to walled *mellahs* and *casbahs*. They had of course lived in their own juderías in Castile and Aragón for centuries, and thus physical ghettoization by itself was not an unendurable humiliation. Enforced domicile in the same quarter with berberiscos was. Assiduously, therefore, the newcomers continued to speak and write in their own Castilian or Portuguese rather than adopting the hybrid Ladino of their Balkan and Turkish kinsmen. Arabic and Judeo-Berber, for many years, they disdained altogether. They made a point, too, of wearing the *caperon,* or cape headdress, as distinguished from the turbanlike headgear of the older group. For that matter, the Sephardim shunned contact of any sort with the Arabic-speakers. In their autonomous communal government (functioning here as elsewhere in the Diaspora), they maintained their own synagogues and liturgies, their own communal schools and welfare institutions.

Even so, the sultan held his Jews collectively responsible for their poll taxes, and negotiations between Sephardim and Arabic-speakers as a result became inevitable. The former accepted the fact grudgingly. With their greater wealth and intellectual sophistication, their extensive government and overseas trading connections, they felt entitled to leadership at least within the Maghreb Jewish world. And, in truth, they swiftly coopted that leadership. It was they who appointed the principal communal judges and tax assessors. In each city, the *nagid,* the chief or official spokesman, was a member of a prominent Sephardic family.

Over the years, too, the berberiscos paid the Sephardim the ultimate tribute of emulation. Increasingly, they tended to feign Sephardic lineage for themselves. If it was not possible to change their Berber or Hebrew family names, they gave their children Sephardic first names. Their girls, particularly, flaunted such Iberian appellations as Donna, Bella, Perla, Fortuna, Gracia, Alegra, Reina, Estrella, and adopted the Spanish *mantón,* the fringed shawl. Their Judeo-Arabic dialect incorporated numerous Castilian words and phrases. In this fashion, Berber Jews came to fantasize a kind of honorary sephardization for themselves. They also sold their questionable Iberian ancestry to European Jews, who in future years tended indiscriminately to categorize all of North African Jewry as Sephardic—much to the discomfiture of the real article.

A Chimera of Redeemers

During the early sixteenth century, meanwhile, the largest part of the North African littoral came under Ottoman rule. Only little Morocco, a kind of Iberian hinterland, succeeded in fending off Turkish occupation. But whether in Morocco or in the Turkish-administered regions, the lack of an effective central government took its toll. Gradually the entire south Mediterranean world reverted to political fractiousness and economic dysfunction. For North African Jews, those years represented a nadir of humiliation unparalleled elsewhere in the Islamic world, and surely in the eastern Ottoman Empire. They were confined by and large to vocations that were prohibited to Moslems, such as gold- and silversmithing, or to others held in contempt by the Berber majority, such as shoemaking, dying, weaving, petty shopkeeping. Their isolation remained absolute. Even when venturing out of their mellahs, Jews were obliged to wear distinctive straw sandals, or to go barefoot altogether when passing a mosque.

In European travel literature of the early modern era, a uniform picture emerges of Maghreb Jewish debasement. Germaine Mouette, a French visitor, wrote in 1683:

> [The Jews] are exposed to suffering the blows and wounds of every-one, without daring to say a word even to a child of six who throws stones at them. If they walk before a mosque, no matter what the climate or season may be, they must remove their shoes, not even daring in the royal cities, such as Fez and Marrakesh, to wear them at all, under penalty of five hundred lashes and being locked in prison, from which they would be released only upon payment of a heavy fine. . . .
>
> If they speak up too much before a governor in defense of their rights . . . he has the guards slap them in the face. When they bury one of their own, the children bedevil them with a thousand maledic-tions. . . . These, briefly, are the miseries which this people, formerly so dear to God, endure, and who are today the laughingstock and scum of all nations.

Visiting Marrakesh late in the eighteenth century, the British traveler William Lempriere noted that "The Moors display more humanity to their beasts than to the Jews. I have seen frequent instances where [Jews] . . . were beaten so severely as to be left almost lifeless on the ground. . . ." Well into the nineteenth century, the government assigned Jews the degrading chore of personally gathering up the heads of executed criminals or rebels fallen in combat, then salting the remains and hanging them on city gates for public display. In smaller towns, the repugnant obligation continued into the twentieth century.

It was inevitable under these conditions that Maghreb Jews should become uniquely susceptible to kabbalism, Shabbateanism, and other varieties of mysticism and messianism. Although their communities still managed to produce a number of learned rabbis and several distinguished Hebrew poets, the Jewish majority tended to share the superstitions of their Moslem neighbors. They, too, resorted to amulets and incantations against demons and the "evil eye" (p. 128). Some took so ardently to drink that travelers commented upon widespread alcoholism among Moroccan Jews. Nevertheless, by the nineteenth century, as physical assaults on their neighborhoods increased in frequency and destructiveness, emotional palliatives no longer sufficed. A more tangible assurance of security was becoming urgent.

Europe provided it. In 1830, France established its protectorate over Algeria; later it incorporated this largest of the Maghreb nations directly into the administration of the metropolitan homeland. Tunisia became a French protectorate in 1881, as did Morocco between 1905 and 1912. Under French rule, then, North African Jews were at last assured a certain physical safety, and even release from their ghettos. Moreover, as Jewish children began to attend French public and private schools and the widening network of Alliance Israélite Universelle schools throughout the Maghreb, virtually every Jewish family became an *aspirant* to French culture—indeed, to modernization altogether. Algerian rabbis now delivered their sermons in French, and in later years the Torah crown in the main Algiers synagogue actually was fashioned in the shape of the Eiffel Tower.

In 1870, impressed by Maghreb Jewry's poignant gallicization, and well aware of this little people's usefulness as clients of French imperialism, Paris bestowed full citizenship on the fifty thousand Jews of Algeria (their numbers would more than double in subsequent decades). The boon of instant equality was not without its cost, to be sure. It provoked deep resentment among Algeria's Moslem majority, themselves forever beyond the pale of the exalted French circle. In their frustration and vindictiveness, local Arab mobs began tearing through Jewish neighborhoods—in Temcen in 1881; in Algiers in 1882, 1897, and 1898; in Oran and Sétif in 1883; in Mostaganem in 1897. Despite the best efforts of French security services, hardly a town of any size escaped the orgy of looting and synagogue-sacking, and even occasional killings.

By the late nineteenth century, too, Jew-hatred was burgeoning with comparable malevolence among Algeria's substantial enclave of European settlers. Typically insecure expatriates, these *colons* discerned in their Jewish "fellow citizens" a useful target for their own minority chauvinism. Thus, in the 1890s, the Dreyfus Affair in metropolitan France touched off an unprecedented explosion of colon antisemitism. As their delegate to the French Chamber of Deputies, Algeria's Europeans elected a professional Jew-baiter, Edouard Drumont. Max Régis, another xenophobe, became their choice for mayor of Algiers. For a while, the collapse of anti-Dreyfusardism in France slowed the racist momentum in Algeria. So did the performance of Algerian Jews in the French army during World War I—a display of battlefield valor so manifestly infused with patriotic gratitude that it evoked admiration on both sides of the Mediterranean. But in 1936, when Léon Blum assumed the premiership of France at the head of a Popular Front government, Algeria's Europeans again erupted in outrage. Focusing their animus on a Jewish minority that by then had grown to nearly one hundred thousand, the colons launched widespread attacks on Jewish shops, offices, homes, and synagogues, and on individual Jewish men, women, and children. Nearly fifty died.

For the two hundred thousand Jews of Morocco and the one hundred thousand of Tunisia, French rule evoked even more painfully mixed results. In neither protectorate did Jews enjoy the Algerian bloc privilege of French citizenship. In neither country, by the same token, did they experience the worst of colon resentment. Nevertheless, dispersed widely throughout the countryside, Jews also became surrogates for a Berber xenophobia that was unable to challenge the French occupation head-on. Intermittent native pogroms claimed scores of Jewish lives. In 1934, an Arab mob attacked the Jews of Constantine, looting and burning homes and massacring thirty-three people. Outnumbered, the French police intervened only at the last moment. When the Jews of the *bled*—the hinterland—fled for protection to Casablanca and other large cities, their presence simply exacerbated the congestion of Jewish neighborhoods, the economic redundancy of the Jewish lower-middle class.

As late as the 1930s, therefore, despite centuries of intermingling between "pure" Sephardim and berberiscos, the typical Moroccan and Tunisian Jew still was likely to be a shoemaker, a leatherworker, a silversmith, a greengrocer, a sidewalk vendor of costume jewelry and knicknacks, a dealer in secondhand clothing, even a porter or a bootblack. In their frustration, these stepchildren of the Maghreb continued to drink, to gamble, to maltreat their women. Whether a majority or a minority among their own kind, nowhere in the world had the proud descendants of Andalusian Jewry fallen to so low an estate. And nowhere else, as a result, did they continue to invest more poignant hopes in the redeeming mantle of French solicitude.

A Meridional Aristocracy

The Talgo, Spain's proud bullet train, crosses into France at the medieval border town of Perpignan. Here the squad of heavily armed Spanish police disembarks and boards an armored personnel carrier to return home. Spared interception by Catalan terrorists, the Talgo races on through Languedoc, through a patch-quilt of farmland, hewn-stone villas under red-tiled roofs, double-spired churches, and occasional ramshackle châteaux. The train flashes by Narbonne, once a major terminus on Aragonese Jewry's escape route across the Pyrenees, now a provincial backwater. Minutes later, Béziers, hardly more than a whistle-stop, appears briefly as a disjointed entanglement of barns, houses, gentle hillsides.

Benjamin of Tudela traversed this route, too, proceeding from Zaragoza to Tortosa, from Tortosa to Barcelona, then from Barcelona on a three-day ascent through Pyrenean mountain paths to Béziers, and from Béziers on to Montpellier, to Lunel, to Posquières, to Arles, to Marseilles. In each town, our traveler-diarist punctiliously recorded the two dozen Jews here, the three dozen there, the presence or non-presence of rabbis, of synagogues, of ritual baths and kosher abattoirs. In those years, most of southern France's fifteen or eighteen thousand Jews were artisans, shopkeepers, moneylenders, traders in wheat, wine, spices, textiles. There was little here to distinguish them from their Iberian kinsmen.

For a long while, too, with Provence, Languedoc, and other southern provinces under extensive Catalan cultural influence, French talmudic academies were staffed almost entirely with scholars from Barcelona and Girona. Journeying through the trans-Pyrenean chain of Jewish communities, Benjamin of Tudela encountered scores of these learned rabbis instructing hundreds of equally diligent students. In Arles, Béziers, Lunel, Marseilles, Narbonne, Nîmes, and Perpignan, treatises were produced on biblical exegesis, Hebrew poetry, lexicography, grammar. In Lunel and Montpellier, the ibn Tibbon family maintained a veritable cottage industry for the translation of Hebrew and Arabic writings (including those of Maimonides). Indeed, during the thirteenth century, these two modest towns became nothing less than the principal conduit of Arabic scholarship into the European world at large. They served a comparable purpose for Jewish medicine. The University of Montpellier to this day preserves a marble inscription in its central entrance hall citing "the Masters of the University of Medicine at Montpellier 1200–1220." The honor roll commences with "le Rabbin Samuel Yehoudah ben Tibbon de Lunel 1199," and includes more Jews than Christians. In 1300 the university appointed Jacob ben Mahir as its dean.

Then, in 1481, Provence was formally united with the Kingdom of France, whose own Jewish population had been expelled a century earlier. Whereupon Louis XI, the "spider king," duly applied that original edict of expulsion to Provence and its neighboring southern provinces. Most of the region's Jews accordingly departed, while only a tiny comminution underwent baptism and remained on. Nevertheless, throughout the sixteenth and seventeenth centuries, augmented by periodic rivulets of Sephardic fugitives, the little enclave of Provençal conversos began to regain something of its former demographic vitality. Bordeaux served as its initial nucleus. Long the commercial center of southwestern France, the city had attracted Iberian Jews as far back as the eleventh century, when references first appear to a "Mont-Judaïque" outside the walls, between the present rue Dauphine and rue Mériadec, the site of the Jewish cemetery. At the foot of this hill lay Jews' Street, known as Arrua Judaea in the thirteenth century, and now as rue Cheverus. The current Porte Dijeaux then was Porte Judaea. Successive acts of expulsion in the twelfth, fourteenth, and fifteenth centuries eventually terminated this Jewish presence. Yet, in Bordeaux as elsewhere in southern France, an indeterminate scattering of conversos remained behind. And after 1481, the Sephardic remnant was quietly enlarged by an uninterrupted infusion of New Christians from Spain and Portugal. Virtually all of them were judaizers—marranos.

It was this minority's good fortune that the church in France was vigorously Gallican. Here the Inquisition had never been particularly active. Moreover, in 1483 Louis XI, who only two years before had expelled the Jews of Provence, accorded a wide array of residential and trading privileges to foreign merchants settling in Bordeaux. Most were conversos, and King Louis could not have been unaware of their identity. But neither could he ignore their potential role in fostering the city's commercial development. The king's sufferance was amply vindicated in future years. By the eighteenth century, some fifteen hundred conversos were settled in Bordeaux. Most were small businessmen, but an important minority fitted out ships, traded with the colonies, established banks. One

Bordeaux banker, David Gradis, opened branches in Canada and the French West Indies. During the Seven Years War, Gradis's nephew, Abraham Gradis, outfitted thirteen French frigates. These and other affluent Bordeaux conversos lived in dignified luxury and maintained spacious estates and country houses.

Later, an even more important New Christian port of call emerged far to the southwest, in Bayonne, on the Bay of Biscay. Its suburb of Saint Esprit and the surrounding communities of Biarritz, Bidache, Peyrehorade, and Saint Jean-de-Luz ultimately nurtured a Sephardic population of some twenty-five hundred. Like the marrano community of Bordeaux, this trans-Pyrenean cluster of settlements became a major focus of crypto-Judaism in southern France. "The Portuguese conversos come in troops, by foot and by coach," lamented a chagrined commissioner of the Inquisition in Pamplona, a neighboring way station in Navarre. Indeed, the Provençal marranos barely troubled to disguise their Jewish identity. Over the years, their Sabbath and holiday prayer observances, their Jewish burials, their Jewish schools and philanthropies were all but openly acknowledged. A Bordeaux merchant, Isaac Mendès-France, declared in his will of September 1685: "I desire and intend that my said legatees hereinafter named shall pay and distribute on the day of my death the sum of one hundred livres to the poor of the Portuguese nation and a month thereafter a further hundred livres for the use of the little synagogue which I established in the rue des Augustins." By the eighteenth century, in any case, there was no further need for dissemblement of any kind. Reconfirming Sephardic domicile privileges, Louis XV in 1723 alluded specifically to "Jews of the Portuguese Nation," although permission was limited essentially to the Bordeaux area. And in 1776, when Louis XVI reconfirmed the authorization yet again, there was no mention this time of geographical limitations. Four years later, the Prince de Condé and the Prince de Bourbon were guests at a Friday-night service in Bordeaux's largest synagogue, on the rue Bouhault.

In the late 1700s, the Sephardim of France, still concentrated essentially in the south, numbered possibly five thousand. Yet by then they comprised barely one-sixth of the nation's Jewish population. The majority of Jews in France were German-speaking Ashkenazim. A lower-middle-class element of artisans and petty tradesmen, the "northerners" were congested in the recently annexed border regions of Alsace and Lorraine. Neither Sephardim nor Ashkenazim were particularly beloved of the French rank and file. But the Enlightenment was in full radiance, the mood of bourgeois economic pragmatism and political egalitarianism all but irresistible. By the later eighteenth century, too, more than a few

Sephardim were themselves conscientiously immersing themselves in the new spirit of Gallic rationalism—joining Masonic lodges, anointing their children with French names, inscribing their tombstones with French as well as Hebrew dates.

In their passion to acculturate, moreover, these veteran Jewish Provençals resented a widespread Gentile unwillingness to distinguish between them, the "honorable, refined" Sephardim, and the "uncouth" Ashkenazim of the northern provinces. In 1763, stung by Voltaire's rancorous literary defamation of Jews, Isaac de Pinto of Bordeaux took pains to cite the numerous differences between "his" people and the "others." The divergences related not only to customs and rituals, insisted Pinto, but to moral standards: the Sephardim produced wealth and culture; the Ashkenazim, usury and swindling. Petitioning for renewal of their residence permits, in 1765 and in 1777, other Sephardic advocates drew the same invidious contrast. Jacob Rodriguez went so far as to publish an open letter in the press berating a Gentile lawyer, Jean-Marie Goulleau, for stigmatizing the "Portuguese nation" in terms more appropriate for the Ashkenazim.

From the same patrician vantage point, Salomon Lópes-Dubec and Abraham Furtado, appearing before the Royal (Malesherbes) Commission, which conducted hearings on the issue of Jewish disabilities in 1788, limited their appeal for "freedom of residence, property, and economic activity" to members of the "Portuguese Nation"—essentially the five thousand Jews in the south. Nothing, of course, was said of "German Jews," the thirty thousand Ashkenazim of Alsace and Lorraine. The following year, a Sephardic delegation led by Abraham Rodrigues again pressed the Estates General for Jewish equality, and once more on a selective basis. The legislators were receptive. In its initial emancipation decree of January 1790, the National Assembly (successor to the Estates General) affirmed that "all Jews known in France under the name of Portuguese, Spanish, and Avignonese Jews . . . shall enjoy the rights of citizenship." But twenty-one months later, in September 1791, the same body was unwilling to risk qualifications of any kind upon the still-fragile experiment in rationalist liberalism. Thus, overriding both Sephardic and Gentile reservations, the assembly extended political emancipation to the entirety of French Jewry—some thirty-five thousand souls.

Even then, however, within the Jewish world the Sephardim continued vigorously to protect their elitist status. During the Napoleonic era, they ensured themselves the decisive role in their people's initial representative bodies, the Assembly of Jewish Notables in 1806 and the Sanhedrin of 1807, both summoned by Napoleon to elicit a full-orbed Jewish identification with *la patrie*. In the Jewish Consistory—Napoleon's device for "galli-cizing" synagogues and rabbis—it was Abraham Furtado who became the first chief rabbi. The regional Consistory of Bordeaux was extended to encompass fully ten *départements*, far more than its modest, essentially Sephardic demography warranted; and in 1845, the Consistory of Algiers, Oran, and Constantine was linked to that of Bordeaux. In 1860, Jules Carvallo became the first president of the new Alliance Israélite Univer-selle, soon to become the most powerful Jewish philanthropy in the world.

Nor, for that matter, were Sephardim prepared to go quietly into the night in French society at large. During the French Revolution, Abraham Furtado and Salomon Lópes-Dubec represented the Gironde in their region's Popular Commission. Early in the nineteenth century, the broth-ers Emile and Isaac Péreire established the Crédit Mobilier, destined for many years to reign as France's largest private mortgage investment bank, and financier of the nation's earliest railroads. Both Péreires eventually sat as members of the Chamber of Deputies and were awarded the Legion of Honor. Olinde Rodrigues, principal disciple of the Utopian Socialist Henri de Saint-Simon, taught the virtues of capital and labor functioning in idyllic collaboration within a social republic. Camille Pissarro, born in the West Indian colony of Saint Thomas, was a leading figure in the impressionist school of French painting. In these and other areas of na-tional life, the venerable Sephardic community maintained its creativity and visibility well into the nineteenth century, and long after their hubris, like their critical mass, was swallowed up in an Ashkenazic sea.

La Patrie: Illusion and Reality

A century later, they mounted an unlikely revival. A visit to Marseilles attests to the fact. The city's physiognomy has been transformed beyond recognition since World War II. Like most international harbors, this one had been a polyglot even earlier, a magnet for thousands of Corsicans, Sicilians, Indochinese, black Africans, and Maghreb Berbers. Today as well, these and other distinctly non-Gallic elements crowd the lower port area around the rue d'Aix and the rue Sainte-Barbe. As recently as the early postwar years, however, few observers would have anticipated the presence among them of eighty thousand Jews.

They were not the issue of prewar France. Indeed, the fate of the "vet-erans" is symbolically recorded on a stone tablet mounted on the boule-vard Charles Livon, a splendid panoramic vista overlooking the recon-structed Vieux Port. It is a memorial to fallen heroes of the anti-Nazi underground in Marseilles. Twenty-two names appear on the tablet. Like the designation of the site itself, "Place Léon Schapiro," all the names are Jewish. They are an intermingling of Ashkenazim and Sephardim, from Schapiro and Wajsbrod to Fontano and Salvedo. The inscription begins:

JARDIN MISSAK MARRO
1906–1944
CHEF D'UN GROUP DE RE
EN FRANCE
FUSILLÉ PAR LES

Although the names remain, all allusions to *"résistants"* and *"allemands"* have been surgically amputated by the stroke of an electric saw. Who could have committed this desecration years, decades, after the collapse of Nazi Germany?

During the war, Marseilles had fallen within the Unoccupied—Vichy—Zone. Here the Pétain-Laval regime in its Fascist insularities drew upon historic wellsprings of Gallic nativism. The Jews knew. With the surrender of June 1940, they had begun flocking there. By the end of the year, some two hundred thousand of them were dispersed throughout this Unoccupied southern region. It proved an insecure haven. In July 1940, the Pétain government began issuing a series of decrees that stripped French citizenship from the many thousands of recently naturalized Jews, disqualified all Jews from government employment, "aryanized" specific Jewish enterprises and property holdings, and incarcerated over ten thousand "stateless" Jews in grim internment camps.

Then, in November 1942, the Wehrmacht suddenly poured across the demarcation line into the Vichy Zone. The SS established its southern headquarters in Marseilles, in a former apartment building on the rue Paradis. From this nerve center, a manhunt was launched for Jews of all backgrounds and origins. The search continued methodically and implacably over the ensuing two years. Marseilles' local Jewish community of twelve thousand souls became the first victims of the roundup. The Great Synagogue on the rue de Breteuil offers testimony of their fate. Restored after extensive wartime damage, it is a spacious, dignified edifice, crenellated by a handsome fanlight window and clock, flanked by elaborately carved stone columns supporting a massive stone arch. Above the curvature, a marble tablet commemorates "le jour," January 24, 1944, when two thousand local Jewish inhabitants were herded into the synagogue sanctuary, then marched off for deportation.

Was it then the Germans or the French who liquidated this congested Jewish enclave? The presence of the Wehrmacht and the SS was the catalyst, of course. Yet the Vichy authorities cooperated in the dragnet as fully as the local police in Occupied France. In advance, it was they who prepared a detailed census of Jews. It was with their help in late 1942 that forty-three thousand refugee Jews were deported to the Occupied Zone, and then on to Auschwitz, and another thirty-four thousand in 1943 and 1944. The collaborative record of horror and shame has yet to be confronted by the French people. And now, almost half a century later, a monument is desecrated on the boulevard Charles Livon. In the summer of 1991, walking the length and breadth of the Vieux Port, I could only speculate on the transgressors' identity as I confronted the grinning visage of Jean-Marie Le Pen on a succession of oversized placards announcing rallies of his racist party, the Front National. Fourteen months later, in the French Senate elections of November 1992, the Front National won an alarming 15 percent of the vote nationwide, a percentage nearly equaled even in Marseilles, with its bouillabaisse of racial and religious communities.

The eighty thousand Jews in today's Marseilles are a substantial feature of that teeming heterogeneity. Only the smallest minority are Ashkenazim, essentially survivors of the veteran group whose kinsmen are memorialized at the Great Synagogue on the rue de Breteuil. Others, a rather larger element, are "older" Sephardim, a number of them descendants of the original Provençal conversos but the majority representing an infusion of more recent, fin-de-siècle immigrants from Salonika, Egypt, and Turkey. Several blocks away, their rather drab little Ozar Danim synagogue contains its own Holocaust memorial plaque. The names are classically Sephardic: Ozariah, Sellam, Ezrati, Vitalis, Pep, Carasco, Behar, Cordova, Zambetta, Palombo. An aging sexton requests a donation. "Parle Monsieur espagnol?" I inquire. Smiling, the factotum replies in Ladino. He, too, speaks for a minority.

In overwhelming numbers, the Jews of Marseilles are postwar immigrants from North Africa. As late as 1940, a half-million of them were concentrated in the Maghreb—285,000 in Morocco, 135,000 in Algeria, 105,000 in Tunisia. Following the surrender of France that year, the North African empire was consigned to the rule of Vichy, and with it the future of this vast Jewish archipelago. The Pétain-Laval regime was unable to ship its Maghreb Jews across the Mediterranean to Nazi-occupied France. But at least Vichy could subject them to the mainland's racial laws—strip Algerian Jews of their French citizenship, purge their breadwinners from the administration, their children from French lycées. The colons entirely favored these measures. It was not surprising, then, that the Algerian anti-Vichy resistance consisted almost exclusively of Jews. In November 1942, on the eve of "Operation Torch," the American invasion of North

Africa, it was specifically the leadership of the Jewish underground—José Albouker, Jean Gozlan, Roger Jaïs, Roger and Pierre Carcassonne—who entered into secret contact with United States intelligence to arrange the seizure of Algiers' telecommunications centers. The plans were carried out meticulously on November 8 by some two hundred Resistance fighters. All but a score of them were Jewish. The ensuing information blackout all but neutralized the capital at the very moment American troops were landing on the coast.

Yet the Allied invasion did not immediately relieve the plight of Algerian and other Maghreb Jews. Indeed, the opposite was true. Commanded by General Henri Giraud, the new Free French administration in North Africa chose to postpone indefinitely the restoration of Algerian Jewry's prewar civil status. Several hundred stateless Jews even were left in their former Vichy detention camps. The Americans raised no objections. Felix Cole, the United States consul in Algiers, urged Washington to refrain from intervening, lest "we almost entirely alienate the active and passive sympathy now felt by the Algerians of French nationality for the great democratic powers and thus provide an additional obstacle to the anti-German cause." President Roosevelt did not demur.

Indeed, at the Casablanca Conference of January 1943, Roosevelt personally approved the plan, formulated by the Free French regime, to restrict the number of Jews authorized to resume their professions. "[The] plan would further eliminate the specific and understandable complaint which the Germans bore towards the Jews in Germany," Roosevelt observed, "namely, that while they represented a small part of the population, over 50 percent of the lawyers, doctors, schoolteachers, and college professors, etc., in Germany were Jews." As for the internment camps, the president did not intercede until October 1943, almost a year after the initial invasion. At that, it required a succession of appeals from American Jews to force his hand. The delay was a cruel psychological blow for Maghreb Jewry. Even longer-lived, however, were the economic scars of their wartime ordeal. For the next six or seven years, the Joint Distribution Committee was obliged to provide food and clothing for tens of thousands of North African Jewish families.

In the end, the Jews departed North Africa altogether. Throughout the 1950s, a chain reaction of Moslem insurrections doomed the likelihood of continued French rule in the Maghreb. Ironically, until then the Jewish population had chosen selectively to ignore the wartime Vichy betrayal. They preferred to remember an imperial presence that had guaranteed their security before and after the "interregnum" of 1940–43. But now the risk of staying on no longer could be taken. By 1965, their era in North

Africa was a closed chapter. Approximately 200,000 Jews departed for Israel, most of these poorer elements from Morocco and Tunisia. The remaining 300,000, including a majority of the Tunisians and almost the entirety of the Jews of Algeria, settled in France. Their arrival in the metropolitan homeland transformed the physiognomy, the very character, of the Jews of France. For one thing, it nearly doubled their presence, from 350,000 in 1952 to 650,000 in 1965. For another, it dispersed that presence. Paris remained the Jewish focus, to be sure, with some 340,000 Jews, while perhaps a tenth that number remained in Alsace-Lorraine. But newer Jewish communities, or moribund older ones, now unexpectedly burgeoned out in Toulouse, Bordeaux, Lyons, Nice, and, above all, in Marseilles. Indeed, within the space of a generation, Marseilles' Jewish population of eighty thousand became the third-largest Jewish community in Western Europe.

The influx of these Maghreb fugitives effected still another transformation. It "judaized" French Jewry. The newcomers' heritage of Jewish ethnocentrism proved far more substantial than the rather pale "cultism" of veteran, nativized French Jews. By now, even France's "spiritual" leaders are of North African origin. In Marseilles, the consistorial rabbi, Jacques Ouaknin, smilingly acknowledges that he can deal with every variety of Jew. "After ordination, I assumed my first pulpit in Metz, in Alsace," he explains, "an Ashkenazic community if ever there was one. I ministered according to 'their' liturgy. No problem. In America, Orthodox rabbis deal only with their fellow Orthodox. They feel no obligation to be flexible. In France, a consistorial rabbi must deal with Jews of all backgrounds and traditions. We quickly learn to be tolerant." In truth, the genial Rabbi Ouaknin has not "quickly learned" this approach; rather, he has inherited it from his forebears. A relaxed, pragmatic, "Mediterranean" attitude in matters of doctrine and observance has long since evolved as the hallmark of Sephardic Judaism. Centuries of immersion in Islamic and Christian host societies, of furtive marranism and intellectual accommodation to alien cultures, have taught these people a thing or two.

Have the painful consequences of Vichy-style fascism taught the French people any lessons? The inroads of Le Pen's Front National are worth taking seriously. So is the mutilated stone tablet on the boulevard Charles Livon. Yet a contrasting image seemingly emerges from photographs in Rabbi Ouaknin's album recording his consistorial inauguration of several years earlier. Present for the occasion at the Great Synagogue on the rue de Breteuil was a galaxy of public notables, all of them uniformed, besashed, bemedaled to within an inch of their lives. They included the mayor of Marseilles, the presidents of the Marseilles local council and the Rhône departmental council, the commander of the southern regional army, the admiral of the Mediterranean fleet, the cardinal of the Catholic Church's Provençal regional diocese.

Still another talisman of that apparently cordial embrace surfaced earlier, in the cult of "Mendèsism" that flourished in the 1950s and 1960s. The son and grandson of decorated war heroes, Pierre Mendès-France was trained in the law, then elected to the Chamber of Deputies in 1932. He held his seat until the outbreak of World War II, when he promptly enlisted as an air force officer. Although Mendès-France evaded Nazi capture in 1940 by making his way to North Africa, the Vichy regime there arrested and imprisoned him for "desertion." Once again he managed a dramatic hacksaw-and-bedsheet escape and eventually reached England, where he joined the Free French air force. During the next two years he flew some forty missions over Europe. In September 1944, a war hero in the family tradition, Mendès-France returned to France to serve as minister of national economy, then as a perennial in the Chamber of Deputies. It was in those postwar years, too, that he rose swiftly to leadership of the "progressive" wing of the Socialist party, and eventually, in 1954, to the premiership.

Forty-seven years old, trim, dark, square-jawed, at the height of his intellectual powers, the new premier moved swiftly to introduce a disciplined program of Keynesian reforms. In record time, he succeeded in jump-starting his nation's sluggish economy. Even more impressive was his 1955 success in extricating his nation from its war in Vietnam, a conflict that had raged for eight years and sapped France's manpower and wealth. Operating under a tight deadline at the Geneva Conference, Mendès-France negotiated a compromise—de facto partition of Vietnam into Communist and non-Communist sectors. The formula permitted a face-saving French withdrawal from the Indochina quagmire. Earlier, the premier had devised similarly acceptable terms for French withdrawal from Morocco and Tunisia. By these accomplishments, Mendès-France won the respect of every major political group in the country, even becoming something of a national icon.

Yet one may speculate whether this battle veteran and widely admired statesman, a descendant of Sephardim who had lived in France for six centuries, was a figure of truly universal acceptance. Years later, receiving an honorary doctorate at Brandeis University, Mendès-France confided his doubts to his hosts. With a tight, cryptic smile, he recalled a comment made in the immediate aftermath of his diplomatic achievements in North

Africa and Asia. Maurice Bourgès-Manoury, one of his closest political allies and oldest (non-Jewish) friends, a philosemite and great ally of Israel, remarked to him: "How fortunate for the nation, Pierre, that you were in office when the dismantlement of our empire became necessary. An authentic Frenchman could never have gone through with it."

CHAPTER X

THE JEWS OF
RENAISSANCE

An Evolving Peninsular Oasis

Don Isaac Abravanel, a renowned casualty of the Spanish Exodus, sailed
off from Valencia in July of 1492. The journey was a nightmare of overcrowding, avaricious crewmen, racking illness, uncertainty of destination.
For nearly six weeks, Abravanel's refugee flotilla of nine caravels was
denied entrance at one Mediterranean port after another. The passengers
were turned back, wrote one eyewitness, "as if they were plague-ridden
animals." Not until reaching the Bay of Naples, on August 24, were the
fugitives permitted at last to disembark. By October, nine thousand other
Jews would find asylum here. Local Neapolitans were shocked at their
condition. "You would have thought they were masks," wrote one observer. "They were bony, pallid, their eyes sunk in the sockets, and had
they not made slight movements, it would have been imagined that they
were dead." Abravanel shared that enervation. At the age of fifty-six, he
looked and felt himself an old man. Only a decade earlier he had fled for
his life from Portugal to Castile. Now in exile again, his wealth and power
gone, he was all but shattered in spirit.

Rescue was at hand. King Ferrante I of Naples had long been aware of
the Jews' mercantile acumen. He was prepared to admit them, even to
allow them the fullest measure of residency and trading privileges. The
Jews were overwhelmed by this godsend. Within the year, therefore, some
twenty thousand of their people arrived in Naples and its dependencies of
Calabria and the Dodecanese islands. It seemed at first that the neighboring Kingdom of Sicily would accept nearly as many. Yet this island-nation
was an Aragonian principality, and King Fernando the Catholic was not
prepared to countenance Jews in his overseas territories. In late 1492, they
were forced to move on. It was accordingly the Kingdom of Naples,
augmented by refugees from west and south, that soon encompassed the

largest Jewish population in Western Europe, numbering at least forty thousand by the early 1500s. As Ferrante had anticipated, moreover, the immigrants proved to be a vibrant community, displaying all their traditional commercial skills, from shopkeeping to merchant banking.

Isaac Abravanel was among those sharing in this congenial haven. Indeed, he was tendered a personal reception by King Ferrante himself, who offered the distinguished financier appointment as supervisor of tax and customs collections. Grateful and relieved, his spirits almost manically soaring, Don Isaac promptly characterized Ferrante and the latter's son, the future Alfonso II, as veritable "princes of mercy and righteousness." Both men in fact were notorious Renaissance despots—"bloody, wicked, inhuman, lascivious," in the words of the French ambassador. Nevertheless, finding Abravanel an able and trustworthy courtier, they compensated him well for his efforts. His personal fortune revived immediately and immensely. Soon he was joined by his brothers, Jacob and Joseph. With his help, they built impressive estates of their own as grain brokers. And Isaac's own three sons similarly did not fail to make their mark: Judah became a physician, an eminent writer, and a philosopher (pp. 221–25); Joseph also was a physician; and Samuel as a broker and banker achieved a financial status comparable to his father's, and eventually succeeded him as *nasi* of Neapolitan Jewry.

It was also in Naples that Don Isaac Abravanel, upon replenishing his estate, returned to his cherished vocation of scholarship, to his commentaries on the Bible. Eventually, he transferred his principal financial responsibilities to his son Samuel. Taking up residence in Monopoli, an attractive little Adriatic port halfway between Brindisi and Bari, the elder Abravanel spent the next few years on the terrace of his seaside villa, giving himself over exclusively to writing. From time to time, King Ferrante sent word that "we hold dear" Don Isaac, and would "cherish" his return. But Abravanel now was committed to the intellectual life. In any case, the region's chronic political and military unrest was not for him.

From 1494 on, the French, under Charles VIII and then Louis XII, launched repeated assaults against the Kingdom of Naples, as did Aragón's Fernando the Catholic. In 1500, the Treaty of Granada ostensibly divided the realm between France and Aragón. But in later years, Fernando gradually manipulated Louis out of his share of the booty, then consolidated his presence in the rest of the kingdom. So it was that Neapolitan Jewry again fell victim to the zealotry that had driven them from Spain, and afterward from Sicily. At last, in 1510, the Sword of Damocles fell: the official expulsion order was issued from Spain. To be sure, the decree required a certain time for implementation, for southern

Italy did not lend itself to efficiency. As late as 1533, at the initiative of Samuel Abravanel, a group of "exception" Jews was permitted to remain on. But their numbers were reduced each year, and by 1540 all professing Jews had departed the realm, most of them for the Ottoman Empire. From then on, the south would remain exclusively Catholic.

An older beachhead was available on the peninsula. "If there is now in Rome any institution more ancient than the Papacy," Cecil Roth once observed, "it is the Synagogue." Jewish settlement in the ancient capital actually traced back to the original first-century captives of the destroyed Jewish Commonwealth. It survived without interruption into the early modern era. If no longer slaves, Roman Jewry remained a pariah community. Confined to the malarial trans-Tiber area, to small-scale retailing and peddling, to gold- and silversmithing or pawnbroking, they were an insular and inbred group, and often quite poor. Neither did they revive demographically. Benjamin of Tudela, visiting Rome in the 1160s, estimated the Jewish population at less than a thousand. By the late fifteenth century, infusions of Central European Ashkenazim raised their number to perhaps four thousand.

It was the arrival of Sephardic refugees in the 1500s that doubled the Jewish presence. Many of these people still were reduced to marginal vocations. But others, dispersed in smaller communities throughout the Papal States—the wide band of central Italy under the pope's direct rule—began to venture more extensively into silk and cotton production, into importing and exporting, paper and distilled-water manufacture, tobacco processing and distributing. It was their good fortune too that the Renaissance popes, more worldly and materialistic than their predecessors, were not ill-disposed toward their industrious Jewish minority. In 1493, Alexander VI personally ordered his officials to shelter the Sephardic fugitives who were camped in the open on Rome's Appian Way. Twenty years later, Pope Leo X insisted that Jewish refugees arriving in Rome "not be vexed through undue exactions." Under Adrian VI and Clement VII, a qualified moderation remained Vatican policy. Although an Inquisition of sorts functioned in the Papal States, autos de fe and burnings were rare, and the victims as a rule were non-Jewish "blasphemers." The Sephardic newcomers, meanwhile, developed autonomous communities independent of the earlier *scuola*—"school"—of veteran Italian Jews, and the several *scuole* of the less numerous Ashkenazim. As elsewhere, they governed and taxed themselves, maintained their own courts, their own schools, synagogues, and rituals, and occasionally even fractured into separate scuole of Castilians, Aragonese, and Catalans, and later of Portuguese, Provençals, Sicilians, and Neapolitans.

A Jewish presence similarly was growing outside the papal domain. As early as the twelfth century, our ubiquitous Benjamin of Tudela described scattered handfuls of Jews in the principal northern Italian cities. Most were Ashkenazim, who were allowed residency only under severe vocational constraints. Yet here, too, medieval religious passions eventually cooled. Intent on fostering economic growth, the peninsula's northern republics and duchies by and large were prepared to tolerate the presence of Jewish brokers, of secondhand-commodities dealers, moneylenders, and importers-exporters of Near Eastern goods. Indeed, by the time of the Sephardic influx, the Republic of Florence, affluent and cosmopolitan under the rule of the Medicis, had become a particularly likely focus of Jewish revival. Here as elsewhere in Tuscany the numbers of Jews slowly increased, possibly reaching two thousand by the mid-sixteenth century. By 1575, nearly that many had settled in Lombardy, although essentially dispersed in the hinterland rather than gathered in the capital city of Milan. In these years, too, the Duchy of Mantua extended its hospitality to Jewish merchants and bankers. By 1600, under the benign House of Gonzaga, approximately fifty Jewish communities of varying size and encompassing perhaps three thousand individuals flourished throughout the realm.

In the north-central peninsula, Ferrara's ruling House of Este all but provided the Jews an embossed invitation. In 1492, Duke Ercole I personally welcomed a group of twenty-one Sephardic refugee families that had been turned out of Genoa and granted them communal autonomy on the spot. Among those who later settled in the duchy were Samuel Abravanel, the son of Don Isaac. For some years afterward, the Abravanel clan maintained its headquarters here. Moreover, in 1550, the Ferrarese government issued comprehensive letters of protection to all "business" refugees. By the late sixteenth century, therefore, with a Jewish population approaching four thousand, Ferrara had developed into a major center of Jewish religious and communal life in Italy, the home of the peninsula's first Hebrew printing press and of several distinguished Jewish literati.

Altogether by then, in the principalities of the north, from the Alps to the Adriatic, Jews were cotton-broking, moneylending, paper- and textile-producing, spice-, gem-, and tobacco-importing. They were also worshipping in their own synagogues, maintaining their own courts, schools, and other communal institutions, each with its own "rite" and in its own language. In Italy, the Sephardim once again emerged as the preeminent group within this constellation of subcommunities. Yet it is of interest that their scuola would not become quite as dominant in Italy as elsewhere in the Mediterranean Jewish world. Once refugees from Portugal and Spain dispersed throughout the peninsula, settling cheek by jowl beside older communities of Italian and Ashkenazic Jews, they were taking up residence precisely in the heartland of the Renaissance. Indeed, it was a time when Italian culture was becoming a model for the entire European world. Italy's veteran Jewish scuole already had become well acculturated to that humanistic ambience. Here, as a result, the pattern was not one of native Jews accommodating to the proud descendants of Iberian Jewry but of the Sephardim coming to terms with the vitality and fecundity of the natives. In common with Italian and Ashkenazic Jews, the newcomers functioned at best as equal members in a triad of *tre nazioni.*

A Venetian Gun Foundry

The paradigm of this genial Renaissance multiculturalism was Venice, destined to surpass Ferrara and Mantua as the locale of the single most vital Jewish community on the Italian peninsula. The city's éclat has still not faded altogether; dozens of freighters still anchor each week in its spacious Adriatic harbor. Yet four centuries ago, when Venice was the web-center of Mediterranean trade, its docks were hardly less than a forest of masts, a rainbow of pennants spanning occidental and oriental ports of origin. Even now, gliding in a *vaporetto* beneath the city's perpetuum of bridges, one may fantasize at the markets that thrived along its banks when the Rialto functioned as the pulse of European commerce.

The water-bus lets travelers off at the Lido San Niccolò. A bobbing cluster of fishing boats and three or four docked motor launches represent the local traffic. Behind the walled enclosure, mottled with verdigris, lies Venice's old Jewish cemetery. Its main entrance passes between Gigi's Trattoria and a pharmacy on the Fondamente de Cannaregio. After a sharp turn left, a rather dank tunnel leads into a narrow alley of cadaverous old houses, many with bricked windows and empty sentry boxes. Another minute by foot brings visitors to a modest cobblestoned square flanked by two aged synagogues. We have reached the Ghetto Vecchio (Old Ghetto). Linked by a network of passageways and bridges, the site actually is one of three encinctures: the Ghetto Vecchio, the Ghetto Nuovo (New Ghetto), and the Ghetto Nuovissimo (Newest Ghetto). Together, the three comprised Venice's historic Jewish quarter.

There is an Ashkenazic synagogue here, and it is available for immediate inspection. Built in 1529, not long after the ghetto was established, its sanctuary glows in dark walnut and red velvet. Next door, the scuola of native Italian Jews is not to be outdone. Completed only three years later, it offers an identical contrast between dark paneling and ruby-and-gilt cloth tapestries. Jerusalem, the Red Sea, the River Jordan, and other biblical scenes appear as carved reliefs. The Ark of the Torah is elaborately interwoven with carved floral patterns, while the prayer rostrum, framed by spiraled stairways, is crowned in an arch of intertwined olive branches. How the coruscation must have befitted the setting, this aqueous jewel of a city at the full radiance of its wealth and power! Even in earlier centuries, Venice had attracted Jewish traders from across the Alps, from the Balearic Islands, the Morean Peninsula, and Constantinople. Yet few had been admitted into the city proper. The Serenissima, Venice's governing body, confined these newcomers to Mestre, a shantytown across the Great Lagoon on the mainland. In 1509, however, during the War of the League of Cambrai, invading Spanish troops sacked and burned Mestre. The Serenissima then cautiously allowed the Jewish squatters to make their way into the city, to open modest offices and shops, even discreetly to organize their religious and communal affairs.

One of those who briefly shared in this initial settlement was Isaac Abravanel. In recent years, his little Monopoli retreat had ceased to serve as a haven for quiet scholarship. It too was threatened by rival French and Spanish armies. In 1503, then, Don Isaac's son Joseph suggested that Venice might offer a more congenial atmosphere. It did. The elder Abravanel's reputation as a financier preceded him, and almost immediately the Serenissima co-opted the great man's talents to negotiate a commercial treaty with Portugal—and paid him well for his efforts. In Venice, Abravanel managed also to finish his scholarly commentaries on Jeremiah, the Minor Prophets, and the Torah. But in 1509 he was obliged to interrupt his writings once again, this time to join the migration from Mestre across the Great Lagoon to Venice itself. Possibly the strain of these repeated wanderings took its toll. Don Isaac died that same year, at the age of seventy-three.

Throughout the Sephardic world, Isaac Abravanel was lamented as the "great eagle," as "a man wise as Daniel," as "a fortress and shield to his people." At his funeral, members of the Serenissima joined in tendering him honor.

> A tower of strength to his people was he,
> A buckler and shield in their need;
> Repairer of branches, restorer of paths,
> Consoler in word and in deed.
>
> In counsel profound, in station supreme,
> The captain, his hand at the helm.

The princes came daily to seek his advice;
The nobles and chiefs of the realm.

The verses, written by Abravanel's son Joseph and inscribed on his monument, are not to be found in Venice. No Jewish cemetery existed in the city when he died. He was buried in neighboring Padua.

Under intense pressure from church officials, meanwhile, the Serenissima in 1516 coped with the rising influx of Jews by assigning them their own quarter, well distant from the city's major residential neighborhoods. The choice fell on a warren of disheveled apartment houses near an abandoned gun foundry, a *giotto,* a term that later gave way to the jargonized "ghetto." The Jews who settled here initially were local Italians and some Ashkenazim. But within less than a decade they were joined by still another group, the "Levantines," that is, Sephardic merchants from the Ottoman Empire. For these newcomers, the ghetto settlement in fact was intended less as quarantine than as the equivalent of a mercantile compound, the kind other foreign traders—German, Greek, English, Dutch—traditionally inhabited in Venice. Several years later, as Ottoman Jews arrived in still greater numbers, the Serenissima was obliged to allocate yet additional space for them. The logical choice was the Ghetto Vecchio, an adjacent block of decrepit flats that in spite of its "old" title functioned as a new, extended site of Jewish settlement.

Ironically, as the years passed, it became an open secret that most of these Sephardim had never so much as set foot in the Ottoman Empire. Rather, the majority had arrived as New Christians directly from Spain and Portugal, or had lived as marranos briefly in Naples, or in Rome, or in other Western centers, before deciding to return openly to Judaism. Under the constraints laid down by the Vatican, local authorities were obliged to seek out and arrest suspected apostates. But the Venetians were a pragmatic race. If the "Levantines" remained in their ghetto and behaved as Jews, the city gave little heed to their origins, or to their possible backsliding. In time, the Serenissima turned a blind eye to the infusion of conversos. Most were permitted entrance into the ghetto, where they quietly melted into the Jewish mainstream. And in 1589, with the arrival of an unusually large group of "Ponentines"—by then the Venetian term for directly arriving "Western" Sephardim—the Serenissima authorized the establishment of a Ponentine scuola. It also granted additional space for Ponentine residential needs. This was the Ghetto Nuovissimo, a connected extension of the original Ghetto Nuovo. Upon learning of the decision, the Vatican blustered and threatened. The Serenissima ignored the protests.

As the Ponentines then set about organizing their institutions, their synagogue, their "Scuola Grande Spagnola," characteristically became the diadem of the Sephardic presence, and the crowning achievement of Jewish settlement in Venice altogether. Designed by Baldassarre Longhena, a renowned architect of the sixteenth century and a Gentile, the structure is restrained and unobtrusive on the outside, except for a rather bulbous bay-style window overhanging the street. The interior, by contrast, glows in a typically Renaissance polychrome of Carrara marble pillars, Corinthian capitals, oiled walnut paneling, gold-leaf ornamentation, pilaster molding, velvet drapery. More even than in the scuole of the Italians, Levantines, or Ashkenazim, the Ponentine sanctuary is a shimmering webwork of intricate wrought-iron lamps and crystal chandeliers.

For all their radiance, the Scuola Grande Spagnola and its three companion synagogues functioned in a Jewish rabbit hutch. The Serenissima's "Jewish" committee, upon first establishing this isolated enclave, assumed that existing apartments in the original Ghetto Nuovo were "most spacious" and capable of sheltering the city's approximately seven hundred Jews. But as that population multiplied and remultiplied over the years, even successive annexations to the ghetto complex proved inadequate. The quarter became almost surrealistically impacted. People often were reduced to sleeping in shifts. Fortunately for the Jews, they had not come this far without developing a certain talent for adaptation. In Venice, they learned to compartmentalize their lodgings. In warehouses, the process could be accomplished horizontally, with new floors inserted between existing storeys and ceilings. If the ghetto dwellers' makeshift flats were dark, extra windows were cut. These improvisations can be seen even today, ascending irregularly up the walls of old buildings. Beyond all other techniques, however, Jews dealt with their congestion by adding tier after tier to their buildings, until the ghetto came to resemble an agglomeration of ramshackle towers. Occasionally, wealthier individuals found ways of attaching cantilevered balconies or rooftop "belvederes" and patios to their apartments. In this fashion, within the perimeter of their three linked neighborhoods, as many as six thousand Jews of all backgrounds managed somehow to adjust to ghetto life.

Nor was it by any means an insupportable life, not in sixteenth-century Venice or in other Italian cities where Jews similarly were consigned to their own quarters. Rarely were these people treated as sinister or even exotic aliens. Over time, they adopted the prevalent Italian vernacular and managed to communicate easily with Gentiles. Moving without hindrance through the city in daytime hours, doing business in every commodity and with every interlocutor, often prospering, Jews acquired the relaxed, easygoing ambience of the local Venetians. Manifestly the ghetto, with its congestion, its high walls, its gates locked and guarded against exit at nightfall, was less than a garden of delights. But with its powerful communal and philanthropic life, its extensive network of self-help institutions and dazzling synagogues, neither was it a sinkhole of misery. In a published journal of his trip to Venice in 1607, Thomas Coryat, an English visitor, was particularly taken by the occupants of the women's gallery in a ghetto synagogue,

> . . . some of whom were more beautiful than any women I have ever seen, and so elegant in their dress, adorned with gold chains and rings ornamented with precious stones, such that certain of our English countesses would have difficulty in rivaling. They wear wonderful low trains, like the trains worn by princesses who have lady's maids whose whole function is to look after them. This shows the great wealth of some of these Jews.

It also suggested the instinct of former conversos, upon reaching Venice, to rejoin the Jewish fold. Men such as Antonio Días Pinto, Francisco Jorge, or Duarte Pereira, all once eminent judges of canon and secular law in Florence and Pisa, migrated to Venice specifically to return to Judaism. So did Immanuel Aboab, great-grandson of the last Sage of Castile; and Jacob (Rodrigo) Mendes da Silva, formerly historian-royal at the court of Aragón. These and other eminent conversos did not hesitate to identify with the new world opening to their people on the Adriatic. So it was, within the space of barely three decades, that the ghetto of Venice became all but synonymous with entrepreneurial dynamism and with intellectual and cultural vitality, and functioned as a glowing microcosm of Renaissance Jewry at the apogee of their fortunes.

A Humanistic Benevolence

It was the hallmark of the quattrocento that individuals of culture drew their role models extensively from classical Greece. Entering Western consciousness for the first time, the Hellenic intellectual heritage was embraced now with vast enthusiasm by Renaissance Italy's emerging new capitalists. Often of nonaristocratic lineage, these men shared the characteristic Hellenic idea that a person's worth should be judged by his accomplishments, not his birth, by the breadth of his knowledge and culture, not that of his estate. Or of his religious tradition. Here was an apparent incongruity. During the same years in which Jews were confined to the Venetian ghetto—and, soon, to an even more constricted Roman ghetto—

they were attending Italian universities together with Christians and engaging in friendly correspondence with Italian colleagues (pp. 220–21). The Vatican's anti-Jewish edicts and restrictions by and large remained unenforced in Renaissance Italy, even within the Papal States. Indeed, Pope Leo X and other members of the Medici family were on cordial terms with the Volterras, a family of affluent Florentine Jewish bankers. Lorenzo de Medici welcomed to his court such Jewish literary figures as Elijah del Medico, Jochanan Alemanno, and Abraham Farisol. Ottaviano Farnese, duke of Parma, maintained a warm friendship with the financier Joab da Rieta. The duke also accepted the magnificent private hospitality of his fellow ballet lover, Isachino Massarano.

The fifteenth and sixteenth centuries' widely diffused adulation of talent could also produce substantial material rewards. Pope Sixtus V granted Meir Mangano the concession for a new and improved method of silk manufacture in Rome. Also in Rome, the physician Bonet de Lattes invented an instrument for calculating the altitude of the sun. Another physician, Raphael Mirami of Ferrara, published an ingenious treatise on the refraction of light. Both men were awarded handsome cash prizes by the papal government. In Mantua and Ferrara, Jews displayed much inventiveness in producing improved gunpowder and were compensated accordingly.

No Jewish talent was more valued, however, than the little people's historic vocation of translation. As in Spain, it was a two-stage process, from Arabic into Hebrew, then from Hebrew into Latin. Eventually their works numbered in the thousands. If Catalonia and Provence nurtured the earliest prototypes of these famed translators, southern Italy followed rapidly in the 1400s. Here numerous Jewish scholars were welcomed for the specific purpose of translating Greco-Arabic classics. Their ranks included Jacob Anatoli of Naples, Judah ben Solomon ibn Machta of Taranto, Moses ben Solomon and Faraj de Girgenti of Salerno, Samuel ben Jacob of Capua.

During the Renaissance and baroque eras, the profession extended into central and northern Italy. In Padua, the Jewish physician "Maestro Bonacosa" rendered Avicenna's famed medical treatise directly from Arabic into Latin, a version that became a classic of scientific literature for decades afterward. In Ferrara, Nathan Hameati with his son and grandson functioned as a virtual cottage industry for the translation of Arabic medical works. Hillel of Verona translated both Arabic medical and philosophical treatises. While pursuing his medical studies at the University of Perugia, Moses Alatino discovered several ancient Hebrew versions of formerly unknown works by Aristotle and other Greek thinkers. Over the next twenty years, retranslating the documents into Latin, Alatino produced a collection of immense importance for Italian Renaissance scholarship. The Spanish-born Jacob Mantino achieved eminence both as personal physician to Pope Clement VII and as translator of Arabic medical books and articles. Indeed, Montino's innumerable renditions of Arabic scientific and philosophic works established him as the single most prolific Jewish translator of the fifteenth century. Altogether, there was no profession more highly esteemed in Renaissance Italy, and none whose practitioners were more respected or better compensated than were these Jewish polymaths.

The Renaissance fascination with the classical world encompassed the languages as well as the scholarship of antiquity. Hebrew was one of these. To unlock its resources, Christian students turned increasingly to Jewish scholars for the production of Hebrew-Latin and Hebrew-Italian grammars, dictionaries, and primers. Moreover, with the sacred literature of the Jews the very *Ursprung* of Christianity, Renaissance interest in Hebrew extended inevitably to the Bible and Talmud, even to kabbalah. Here it was that the improved quality of Hebrew printing became critical. In fact, of all Jewish communities, those of Italy were the first to employ Johannes Gutenberg's recent invention. As early as 1450, two Hebrew presses were founded in Reggio di Calabria and Pieva da Saca; twenty years later, full-length books in Hebrew were coming off the presses in Padua. "I am the art that is the crown of all arts," declared an exuberant publisher's addendum to the first of these works (Rabbi Jacob ben Asher's *Arba'ah Turim* [Four Columns]). "I myself am hidden, but in me all secrets are concealed. Without pens, my script is clear to all." Ultimately, it was the Soncino family of Lombardy that elevated "the crown of all arts" to its memorable apogee. Beginning in the northern Italian town of Soncino, the physician Israel ben Nathan de Soncino established his first printing press in 1483. In later years, Israel's son and grandson moved the press successively to other cities and eventually to Venice. Each of the family members displayed exemplary taste in composition and artistic embellishment. Later branches of the firm were established in Salonika and Constantinople.

It was the growing availability and legibility of classical Hebrew texts, in turn, that enabled Fra Ambrogio Traversari, general of the Calmodensian order in Florence, and his pupil, the great scholar-statesman Gianozzo Manetti, to launch the serious study of Hebrew in Italy. Under their influence, enthusiasm for the Hebrew language reached Rome, where the subject became a favorite of priests and laymen alike. By 1514, Hebrew was a required subject at the Sapienza, the Vatican university. Sharing this fascination with the ancient language, the Medicis, in and out of the Vatican, set about assembling superb collections of Hebrew manuscripts for their private libraries. Cosimo de Medici engaged a Jew as his Hebrew librarian. Fra Egidio da Viterbo, general of the Augustinian order in Rome, employed four Jewish scholars to build his own immense Hebrew library. The duke of Urbino kept thirty *scrittori* at work, five of them Jews and the rest trained by Jews, producing copies of Hebrew texts. By the early sixteenth century, many of Italy's wealthiest families were seeking out Jewish scholars for personal instruction in Hebrew.

By then, Jews were moving almost everywhere in humanist circles, establishing contacts with Gentile intellectuals not only in libraries but in universities, even in private salons. Noteworthy was the Jewish relationship maintained by Giovanni Pico, son of the ruling prince of Mirandola. Pico attended the University of Padua at a time when four Jews were teaching Hebrew and philosophy there. One of these was young Elijah del Medigo, regarded as a particularly brilliant intellect. Pico studied Hebrew with Elijah, then brought him to Florence to translate the Mirandola library's extensive collection of Hebrew philosophical writings. Among these were versions of Averroës's initial paraphrase of Plato's *Republic* and Aristotle's *Logic*. Soon other humanists gathered around the dazzling young Jew, listening with fascination to his lectures at the Mirandola home. Jews sat with them, participating in the soirées on an equal basis with Gentile colleagues.

A forty-minute train journey from Venice brings me to Padua. It is now a much larger city than the jewel of the Adriatic. Time and patience are required to negotiate the old Jewish quarter's cobblestoned streets. Via San Martino-Solferino is hardly more than a lane, yet its synagogue is ample in breadth. If less than a Renaissance chrysalis in the Venetian manner, the sanctuary resonates warmth and dignity. It is Sabbath morning. Assembled for prayer are perhaps twenty men, a tenth of Padua's minuscule Jewish community. I am called to the reading of the Torah. Upon reciting the Hebrew blessings in my American accent, I am rewarded with a dutiful *"chazak!"* ("strong," "well done") from the congregants.

Services are brief. As we file out, a middle-aged gentleman greets me in English. He is Dr. Feruccio d'Angeli, professor of chemistry at the University of Padua. Later, d'Angeli gives me a tour of the university. Its superbly preserved oaken lecture halls and gilded escutcheons evoke the gravamen of possibly the most esteemed academic institution in Renaissance Italy. Assuredly, Padua's medical school was the successor to

Montpellier's as the very best in Europe. D'Angeli guides me through an amphitheater, its gradations of wooden benches encompassing a narrow wooden declivity. In the pit stands a dissecting table. Grave-robbers brought cadavers here by water, sliding them down a chute to the chopping block. At Padua, students acquired hands-on training.

At least one hundred fifty Jews were among them in the 1500s and 1600s. Notwithstanding religious suspicions, the *ebrei* continued to fulfill their historic medical vocation in Italy. Indeed, they acted as personal physicians to popes, cardinals, princes, dukes. As early as the thirteenth century, Pope Nicholas IV availed himself of the services of Isaac ben Mordecai, known as Maestro Gajota. In the fourteenth century, Boniface IX appointed as his physician and *familiar* Angelo, son of Manuele the Jew. In the fifteenth century, beyond the Vatican, Immanuel ben Solomon in Rome was the city's most admired "society" physician, as was Hillel ben Samuel in Ferrara. For patients of affluence and eminence, Jewish doctors were de rigueur. And with the fifteenth- and sixteenth-century influx of Sephardim, the numbers of these physicians increased dramatically. Among them, Saladino Ferro d'Ascoli became the leading pharmacologist of his time. Rabbi Bonet de Lattes served as physician to Popes Alexander VI and Leo X; David de Pomis, to Pope Pius IV; Philotheus Eliajus Montalto, to Grand Duke Ferrante of Florence; Rabbi Jacob Zahalon, a renowned medical scholar, to Ferrara's House of Este.

Possibly the single most renowned medical figure of the Renaissance era altogether was João Rodrigues de Castelo Branca, known to sixteenth-century Europe as Amatus Lusitanus. Born in Portugal to marrano parents, Amatus studied medicine at Salamanca, returned to Portugal for private practice, then fled the Inquisition to Antwerp. In 1536, he achieved instant fame with the publication of his first book, the *Index Dioscorides,* a treatise on medical botany. It was a pathbreaking work. Indeed, Amatus was forthwith summoned by Ercole II, duke of Ferrara, to become lecturer in medicine at the University of Ferrara. Proficient in many disciplines, the young scientist won comparable fame as an anatomist, as a peerless dissector of corpses and author of numerous articles and three books on dissection. Translated into several languages, his works swiftly became international classics. In 1555, however, as the climate of toleration shifted in Rome (pp. 228–29), Amatus moved on yet again, settling eventually in Salonika. There at last he returned openly to Judaism. Years later, ironically, it was Portugal that assumed credit for this blazing meteor of European science. Amatus's bust appears above the main entrance of the University of Coimbra Medical School, his portrait in the Tableau of Portuguese Medicine at the University of Lisbon Medical School.

The Jews of Humanism

In addition to the widening range of cultural interests they shared with educated Italians, Renaissance Jews were particularly exhilarated by new opportunities to immerse themselves in the lifestyle of humanism. Here they emulated the great Italian masters in the arts, producing in their turn an impressive minority of painters, engravers, sculptors. Emulating the age's passion for collecting, affluent Jews became enthusiastic accumulators of art and fine books; employed skilled craftsmen in their households, their offices, their synagogues (the Scuola Grande Spagnola included works by Benvenuto Cellini). Jewish parents, intent on providing their children with a broad secular as well as Jewish education, scoured Italy for the ablest tutors.

The impact of the Renaissance was by no means limited to Jewish patricians. The fashions and social habits of the Italian middle classes found imitators in the ghetto. Like their Gentile counterparts, Jews in Venice and other northern Italian cities dressed in the height of fashion and adapted regional fairs and masked balls to their own religious holidays. Beyond the charmed circle of elegant humanists, Jews and Christians periodically visited, traveled, and drank together. They transgressed together, too, not infrequently sharing in the less attractive features of Renaissance worldliness. Their most typical vices were gambling at dice and cards, but there were also Jewish bandits, informers, looters, even Jewish contract murderers. Jewish women shared in the relative freedom of Renaissance society. Like their Italian counterparts, they traveled about unescorted in the marketplace and on social visits. Several were quite well educated, for affluent families provided their daughters with tutors in Hebrew and general studies. A few Jewish women even played important roles in community life. The era of Lucrezia Borgia, Isabelle d'Este, Caterina Sforza, and Vittoria Colonna would also produce a Doña Gracia Nasi and a Benvenida Abravanel.

Benvenida's father was Jacob Abravanel, brother of the estimable Don Isaac. Her husband was Samuel Abravanel, son of Don Isaac, and thus her own cousin. Doña Benvenida in fact was a formidable personality in her own right. Don Pedro de Toledo, Spanish viceroy of the Kingdom of Naples, thought so highly of her when the Abravanels briefly lived in his capital that he consulted her in the education of his daughter Leonora, who called her "mother" and turned to her for advice even after becoming grand duchess of Tuscany. When disaster overwhelmed Neapolitan

Jewry in late 1540, Samuel and Benvenida Abravanel moved to Ferrara. There they lived in high style, with prominent Christians and Jews alike visiting their mansion. Upon Don Samuel's death in 1547, Benvenida took over the family's thriving import-export business and directed it to even greater success. At all times, too, she remained a devoted Jew. When David Reuveni arrived in Italy, she prepared with her own hands the magnificent gold-and-silk banner that the exotic charlatan carried on his fabulous travels. Immanuel Aboab, the renowned chronicler, described her in his *Nomologia* as "one of the noblest and highest-spirited matrons who have ever existed in Israel since the time of our dispersion . . . [a] model of chastity, of piety, of prudence and of valor."

For well-born Renaissance Jews of both sexes, the social arts were as important as a sound education. Knowledge of music and dancing was obligatory. Some Jews also ran their own schools of music and singing, and these were attended by Jew and Gentile alike. Indeed, Jewish dancing-masters were highly esteemed, and enjoyed a wide Italian clientele. Jewish composers and instrumentalists were prized guests and performers at several distinguished courts, including Lorenzo de Medici's in Florence. Jacopo di Sansecondi, a concert violinist, was a favorite of Pope Alexander VI (Rodrigo Borgia) and performed at Lucrezia Borgia's wedding in 1502. Late-sixteenth-century Mantua produced such famed instrumentalists as Abramo del'Arpa and Isacchino Massarano; the composers David Città, Allegro Porto, and Anselmo de'Rossi. Salomone de'Rossi collaborated in numerous compositions with Monteverdi. His sister Rachele was a widely popular vocalist who sang under the name "Madame Europa."

Nowhere in Jewish intellectual life, finally, was Italian humanism more vivid than in literature. For Jews as for Gentiles, it was poetry that evoked the most appreciative audiences. Each Jewish community had its versifiers who greeted every festival or public event with a flood of rhyme. Initially, the medium of expression was Hebrew. The papal physician Moses da Rieti actually composed a renowned Dantesque epic poem in Hebrew, *Mikdash M'at* (The Lesser Sanctuary). Moses ben Jacob published Hebrew verses on such contemporary events as the siege of Florence in 1529–30. Giuseppe Sarfati, son of the papal physician Samuel Sarfat, introduced the drama into Hebrew by adapting a popular Spanish comedy, *La Celestina* (written by a marrano, Fernando de Rojas). So elegant was the Hebrew of these Jewish belletrists that they did not begin turning to literary Italian until the early sixteenth century. By then, however, it was in Italian that Leone da Sommi Portaleone wrote Italy's first treatise on stage production. Besides producing and directing, he crafted plays that often were staged at the court of the duke of Mantua. Guglielmo da Pesaro published extensively on the aesthetics of ballet.

The Dialogues of Love

By far the most distinguished Jewish literary figure of the Renaissance era, however, was Judah Abravanel, eldest son of the mighty Don Isaac and known to posterity as Leone Ebreo—Leon the Jew. Born in Lisbon about 1460, Judah Abravanel was thoroughly trained by his father in Jewish and Arabic studies. Later, he studied medicine and became a practicing physician. His professional career in Lisbon was brief. When Don Isaac fled Portugal in 1483 (p. 159), Judah followed. Castile was the family's initial haven, then the site of their expulsion in 1492. It was thus in 1492 that Judah Abravanel secretly dispatched his one-year-old son (also named Isaac) back to Portugal with a nurse, anticipating a reunion elsewhere in Europe. The secret was discovered. Vindictively, Portugal's King João II had the child seized, baptized, and reared in a monastery. The tragedy weighed heavily on the father. Years later, in 1503, Judah Abravanel's poem "Tlunot al HaZman" (Laments Against the Time), revealed the immeasurable depth of his grief:

> O how I long and yearn to see thee,
> My darling precious, young gazelle!
> At thought of thee, my sleep departeth,
> The day from night I cannot tell.
>
> My darling child, a word to thee;
> Be no more my sorrow, care;
> Thou art a scion of the wise,
> And to wisdom thou art heir.
>
> Fritter not away thy youth,
> Acquire learning, knowledge, wit!
> Study zealously, my child,
> The sacred tongue and Holy Writ.

It was unlikely that these hopes were realized. The father never saw his son again.

Upon departing Spain, Judah Abravanel initially earned his livelihood practicing and teaching medicine in Naples. Yet his favored avocation, like his father's, was literature. It was thus in Naples that the younger Abravanel began composing his earliest poems. Written in Italian (his fourth language, after Hebrew, Portuguese, and Castilian), they evoked immediate critical attention. In ensuing years, however, Abravanel devoted his principal effort to a long, gracefully written philosophical disquisition. The work was published in Rome in 1535 under the title *Dialoghi d'amore.*

As its title suggests, Abravanel presented his ideas in the form of dialogues, a style much favored by Italian humanists, who tended to downplay Aristotle in favor of Plato. The book's central premise similarly was neo-Platonic—namely, that love, like God, functioned as the ideal of all existence. Abravanel expounded upon the nature of this motive force, tracing its operation in the planets, in the terrestrial world, in the private universe of man's own senses, intellect, and soul. Ultimately he reached the striking conclusion that the purpose of life was nothing less than a union of all creatures in the very epicenter of love—God. With sublime artistry, Abravanel filigreed this theme into one realm of knowledge after another, from religion and ethics to astronomy and astrology, from biblical and rabbinical dicta to Greco-Islamic and Maimonidean scholasticism. The *Dialoghi* altogether was a spectacular feat of erudition and style, one of the truly distinguished intellectual accomplishments of the Italian Renaissance and very possibly its most enduringly popular philosophical work. Within sixty years of publication, it was translated from Italian into French, Spanish, Latin, and, eventually, Hebrew. Its fascinating version of love permeated the lyric poetry of Michelangelo's *Sonnets* and Torquato Tasso's *Minturno,* the metaphysical treatises of Giordano Bruno and Baruch Spinoza.

Notwithstanding the impact of Abravanel and of other talented Jewish intellectuals, in the end it was Renaissance Italy that exerted a far more substantial impact upon its tiny Jewish minority. The imbalance was unavoidable. Numbering barely twenty thousand—the southern Italian expulsions were never made good—the Jews of Italy for the first time in Christian Europe were allowed unprecedented, voluntary access to a rich and diverse majority culture. In contrast to their circumstances in Spain or Portugal, the price of accommodation to Italy's enveloping host culture was rarely apostasy. Italian Jews thus managed to sustain their ancestral tradition not by the wrenching convolutions of marrano dissemblement but through a harmonization of classical Judaism with Renaissance style. That synergy was a matter, first and foremost, of aesthetics, of adapting to Jewish religious and community expression the Italian flair for music, art, and literary elegance.

Yet the little minority also shared with Italian Gentiles a revived classical fascination with the Bible and antiquity. Abraham Portaleone, an eminent physician and medical writer, published a series of extensively researched Hebrew-language treatises on the biblical period. In sixteenth-century Mantua, Azariah ben Moses dei Rossi, arguably the most important Jewish scholar of the Renaissance era, published numerous learned commentaries on Jewish history and Hebrew literature. The grammatical and lexicographical works of Elias Levità, Solomon d'Urbino, Abraham de Balmes, and David de'Pomi laid new foundations for Hebrew linguistic purity. Italian Jews soon became famous throughout the Diaspora for the perfection of their Hebrew usage and diction. In this fashion, sharing the humanist/classicist absorption with Bible and antiquity, "aestheticizing" their Judaism with the emollients of music and art, the Jews of Renaissance Italy at all times remained comfortably identified with their ancestral tradition.

If there was a lurking peril in the symbiosis of the Renaissance and Jewish traditions, it may have been epitomized in the career of one Leone da Modena, a bird of paradise who flashed brilliantly, if briefly, across his people's sixteenth-century ghetto world. Born in Venice in 1570, Leone was reared in Ferrara, where he won instant recognition as a prodigy in Bible and Talmud. His education in fact characteristically extended beyond Jewish studies to the humanities, to Latin and Italian literature. After accepting the position of associate rabbi at Venice's Scuola Grande Spagnola in 1593, Leone soon won acclaim for his ability to interpret rabbinic Judaism within the context of a broader humanism. As an adroit and prolific versifier, a facile interpreter of both Jewish and classical Greek philosophy, he became a welcome colleague and soul mate of Gentile intellectuals.

But in the end, it was "facility" that may have defined Leone da Modena altogether. As a rabbi, he was both a kabbalist and an anti-mystic, a traditionalist and a rationalist, a defender of Orthodoxy and a champion of doctrinal flexibility. Discarding the skullcap, Leone favored ball-playing and other amusements on the Sabbath. A compulsive gambler—and loser—at dice and cards, he adopted numerous expedients to avoid destitution, and subsisted variously as investment broker, translator, scribe, amulet-composer, marriage broker, choirmaster, comedy writer, play director. He dabbled in alchemy, too, a vocation that led to the death by lead-poisoning of his infant son. Nor did Leone offer much in the way of inspiration to his two older sons. Like their father, they mingled in often-disreputable circles, and eventually one was killed in a drunken brawl. The other was a deadbeat and roué who emigrated to Brazil and never communicated with his father again. Leone's two sons-in-law and one of his daughters died quite young, and his wife lost her mind and was institutionalized while still comparatively young.

It is not improbable that the career of this strange, charismatic man anticipated that of his fellow Venetian Jews both in explosive talent and in poignant vulnerability to worldly temptation. They had undergone so many vicissitudes in their odyssey across the Mediterranean world that now, with a foothold on the Italian peninsula at last, they could savor the ebullience of a prosperous and uniquely tolerant society. Yet even as they luxuriated in that memorably genial ambience, they were exposed simultaneously to a precocious acculturation as humanists and a belated ideological disorientation as Jews. In all their future career, it was a dilemma that would never cease to bedevil this little people.

CHAPTER XI

ITALIAN TWILIGHT

The Jews of Counter-Reformation

Still known today as the ghetto, Rome's Lungotevere quarter along the Porto d'Ottavio, on the west—Trastevere—bank of the Tiber River, has become the "in" quarter for young marrieds. Its ancient houses, renovated and fashionably exotic by current standards, have been leased out to media personalities, businessmen, diplomats. Even the decrepit old synagogues give the location a certain panache. For all intents and purposes, the half-mile enclave has been restored to its original Renaissance configuration. So has its relaxed and genial ambience. As late as the 1500s, when the Jews of Rome congregated about their scuole in their own neighborhoods, the choice of residence was essentially still theirs, and the Porto d'Ottavio was nothing more nor less than an ethnic community.

It was the Counter-Reformation that ended Lungotevere's role as a focus essentially of communal gregariousness. Confronted by the widening ideological schism in Christendom, the latter-sixteenth-century popes abandoned their predecessors' earlier role as enlightened patrons of literature, science, and the arts and thereafter acted as uncompromising guardians of doctrinal probity and canon law. The transformation became particularly evident in the zealotry of the Neapolitan cardinal Gianpietro Caraffa, who ascended the papal throne in 1555 as Paul IV. In July of that year, the new pontiff issued a bull, *Cum nimis absurdum* (For inasmuch as it is absurd . . .). It was absurd, the document explained, that Jews, condemned by God to eternal slavery for their offense of deicide, should be permitted to live among Christians in the same neighborhoods. Corrective steps would have to be taken immediately. From then on, Jews were to be banned from owning real estate, employing Christian servants, attending Christian universities, treating Christian patients, evading the obligation (largely disregarded until then) of wearing special badges and hats. Rigid controls now should be imposed on Jewish banking, retailing, and other mercantile activities. Henceforth, the only Jewish livelihoods to continue essentially unrestricted were peddling and the secondhand trade in clothing and other household goods.

Above all else, *Cum nimis absurdum* institutionalized the ghetto as a matter of law. Wherever they lived in Rome, Jews were driven from their often comfortable homes to the dank and malarial Lungotevere. While similarly bleak Jewish compounds were mandated in other towns and cities throughout the Papal States, Rome's was to become by far the most oppressive. Beyond physical congestion, and the humiliation of distinctive badges and hats, the transfer inflicted grave financial loss on the Jews. They had been obliged to sell their property elsewhere under distress conditions. Many were reduced to instant destitution. In extremis, a significant minority now accepted baptism.

Still their ordeal was not over. In 1569, the incoming pontiff, Pius V, issued still another bull, *Hebraeorum gens* (The Jewish People), which uprooted Jews from smaller, outlying villages in the Papal States to the larger towns. Here they could be quarantined more effectively. The bulk of this population thus was transplanted into the squalor of the Roman ghetto itself, which in one fell swoop became the largest and most congested in Italy. By the seventeenth century, ten thousand people were compacted into some one hundred thirty apartment houses. The atmosphere was rancid. Periodically, the Tiber overflowed its banks, leaving a residue of slime in the narrow streets and market areas. Gravely impoverished, confined for the most part to the old-clothing and ragpicking trades, the Jews of Rome were subjected to conversionary sermons on Christian holy days and at all times to popular contempt and obloquy. Indeed, with the passing of the years, they were transformed into a hangdog presence, the most reviled and spiritless Jewish community in all of Europe. Under pressure from the Vatican, the duchies of northern Italy introduced comparable ghettos in their own major cities—in Florence, Turin, Siena, Mantua, Ferrara, Padua. All, including their predecessor in Venice, were tightly shuttered and rigorously guarded at night.

As early as 1542, meanwhile, Cardinal Caraffa revived the Inquisition in the Papal States. It was never as all-pervasive or systematic as in Spain or Portugal. Yet its operation at least was more flagrant and frontal than anywhere else beyond the Pyrenees, and soon produced its own measurable share of human tragedy. Thus, a group of Portuguese marranos in Ancona who had settled there a half-century before, attracted by the city's flourishing Levant trade, believed themselves safe enough to practice Judaism openly. In 1556, however, the Vatican suddenly ordered the inauguration of inquisitional proceedings against all "relapsed heretics." In the spring of that year twenty-four men and one woman were burned alive. Nearly three hundred others were sentenced to the galleys. It was this horror that evoked Doña Gracia's retaliatory boycott of Ancona (pp. 81–82). In 1571, seven "relapsed" conversos in Naples were tried and burned. A decade later, Pope Gregory XIII persuaded the normally moderate House of Este to allow the Inquisition into Ferrara, a prominent center for returning conversos. Soon numerous members of the Portuguese "nation" were arrested, imprisoned, and tortured into professions of repentance. In these same years of the mid- and late 1500s, finally, suspected marranos were arrested and executed in Modena, Siena, and Parma. If the numbers of victims were minimal by Iberian standards, they were unprecedented by those of Italy.

Even in this grim post-Renaissance era, however, there were occasional redeeming oases. The Mantua ghetto experienced a modest cultural revival late in the sixteenth century, particularly in theater. In Padua, Jewish medical training survived the papal ban well into the 1600s. And the Adriatic port of Leghorn (Livorno) for many years flourished as the single most vital and prosperous Jewish community in Italy. In 1548, Cosimo de Medici, who ruled the surrounding Duchy of Tuscany, set out to transform Leghorn from a mosquito-infested coastal village into a port that would function as an alternative to Pisa, whose harbor was now silted up. To that end, proclaiming his intention of establishing a free port, Cosimo offered important new tax concessions to prospective settlers. He also offered assurance of complete religious freedom. The duke's invitation was transparently directed to the Jews, whose commercial acumen he had long admired. Over the next years, therefore, small family groups of Sephardim did indeed make their way to Leghorn and on their own began transforming the little community into a substantial Mediterranean entrepôt, a port that linked into the Sephardic trade network operating throughout the Near East and North Africa.

Soon greater numbers of Jews were flowing into Leghorn. Many arrived from elsewhere in Italy, others from Morocco, Turkey, and the Balkans. Several hundred marranos even arrived directly from Portugal and Spain. Indeed, the latter often were greeted at dockside by local Jews calling out poignantly—and, occasionally, successfully—for relatives and friends. By the eighteenth century, the Jews of Leghorn, veterans and newcomers alike, numbered six thousand and comprised the second-largest Jewish community in Italy. By then too they had produced their own share of notables, including Moses Cordovero, renowned mystic and eventual Lurianic precursor in Safed; David Azulai, another famed kabbalist, who also lived the last years of his life in the Holy Land. The family of England's great philanthropist-statesman Sir Moses Montefiore (pp. 326–29) originated in Leghorn, as did that of Sabato Morais, rabbinical scholar and founder of America's Jewish Theological Seminary.

Above all else, the Jews of Leghorn were merchants and industrialists. The Mediterranean coral trade, the manufacture of silk and soap, were almost entirely in their hands. So powerful an influence did Leghorn exert in Mediterranean commerce that in Tunis the Livornese (Leghorn) Jewish trading colony maintained its own synagogue, the largest in the city. In their affluence, too, Leghorn Jewry soon generated an appropriately vibrant community life, endowed with famed rabbis, seminaries, and printing presses. Their principal synagogue was regarded in its time as the most elegant in all Italy. Residing in the city's finest neighborhoods, Jews here occasionally financed out of their own pockets such popular municipal festivals as "Mercury's Chariot" and the "Car of the Cuccagna." Relations with Gentile neighbors were equable. As a popular saying had it, "If you harm a Jew, you harm Leghorn."

Elsewhere in Italy, however, the Inquisition sustained its implacable campaign against heretical doctrines and literature. The Talmud it regarded as a particularly invidious source of Jewish obduracy. Thus, in 1555, the Inquisition dispatched its officers to make a room-by-room search among the Jews of Rome, seizing every copy of the Talmud they could find. On Rosh HaShanah, the Jewish New Year, hundreds of volumes of this vast corpus juris were burned in a public square. Similar burnings were organized in other cities. In Cremona, in 1559, twelve thousand Jewish religious books of all varieties were incinerated in a great public ceremony. At the same time, the interdiction on Jewish publishing of any sort remained in force, decade after decade, well into the eighteenth century. As late as 1753, thirty-eight wagonloads of "forbidden" Hebrew books, including Sabbath prayer *siddurim,* were carted off and destroyed. Since 1555, too, all talmudic academies had been closed in the Papal States, thus stripping the Jews of Rome and other Romagnese cities of rabbinical leadership. In the years that followed, banned from secular as well as religious education, the Jewish community underwent a slow but decisive attrition of its once-vaunted intellectual acuity.

Not once in this bleak period, meanwhile, did the church ease its relentless conversionary pressure on the Jews. At times, the campaign resorted to tactics that were harshly eccentric, even grotesque. In Reggio, during the plague of 1630, a barber presiding over an extemporized infirmary took it upon himself to "christianize" eighteen small Jewish children by shaving their heads, thus rendering them unrecognizable to their parents.

Condoning the deed post-factum, the local bishop then "appropriated" the youngsters, and arranged for them to be reared under Christian auspices. Thereafter, in the mid-1700s, Benedict XIV institutionalized the practice by officially decreeing that even a Jewish child baptized without the knowledge or permission of his parents henceforth would be regarded as Christian, and the church accordingly was obliged to rear him in the True Faith. In formerly cosmopolitan Venice, the Jewish community was obliged to pay a stiff fine for refusing to disclose the hiding place of the wife and children of an apostate husband.

It was inevitable, therefore, that mysticism should begin to make inroads among Italian Jewry as early as the sixteenth century. By the end of the century, it had acquired irresistible force. Indeed, it was the ban on the Talmud that helped divert Jewish attention to the legally permissible literature of kabbalah. As we recall, one of the paladins of Safed's Lurianic school was Chaim Vital Calabrese, himself of Neapolitan Sephardic ancestry. Later it was Vital's role in popularizing the Lurianic kabbalah, with its doctrine of redemption, that helped mysticism obtain its extraordinary hold upon Italy's distraught and insular Jewry. Kabbalistic prayer groups were formed throughout the peninsula. Special kabbalistic fast days and liturgies fostered a stark penitential religiosity that served only to exacerbate the Jews' cultural and psychological malaise. By the mid-1600s, no Jewish population in any other land could have been more susceptible to the Shabbatean movement. Even in prosperous Leghorn, whence the false messiah imported his fourth bride (p. 153), the entire congregation was seized with a frenzy of expectation. Mahalel Civitanova, rabbi of Ancona, composed a synagogue hymn in Shabbatai Zvi's honor. Nor was the spell entirely broken by Shabbatai's apostasy; the movement lingered on in Italy for decades.

All the while, intellectual atrophy was compounded by debasement in vocational and communal life. Jews were locked even tighter into such marginal retail trades as ragpicking, peddling, and hawking; denied the right to form processions for their funerals, to erect headstones for their graves, to travel except to other ghetto communities. Rarely were they exposed to violence, except that of the Inquisition. Yet on the threshold of the modern era they had markedly deteriorated in status from their earlier Renaissance incarnation. By the eighteenth century, the Jews of Italy had become superstitious, neurotic, timorous. Year by year they were reduced to the uncouth and furtive ghetto caricature that, for Europeans, had become synonymous with the Jews as a people. Physically, they appeared to have lost inches off their stature and to have acquired a perpetual stoop. Demographically, their base was shrinking. In Venice, the Jewish population declined from seven thousand in the mid-sixteenth century to two thousand by the mid-eighteenth century; in Rome during the same period, from ten thousand to six thousand; even in Leghorn, from six thousand to three thousand. Italy, it seemed, was a closed chapter for the Jews.

Enlightenment and Risorgimento

Napoleon Bonaparte reopened it. Crossing the Alps in 1796–97, the French commander overran the peninsula's Habsburg garrisons, then transformed much of northern Italy into a French satellite republic. In the process, he shrewdly exploited France's revolutionary promise of equality and fraternity to win over local "progressive" elements. Jews were among these. Earlier, their circumstances already had been improving in Habsburg Venetia. But now other communities were being emancipated from their ghetto servitude. Indeed, the Jews of northern Italy were extended full and equal treatment under French protection. It was an exhilarating moment.

It appeared to be a fragile one, however. In the wake of Napoleon's departure and demise, the Congress of Vienna in 1815 seemingly wrote finis to all hopes of Jewish emancipation. Local governments reinstituted many of the old ghetto constraints. Nevertheless, the calendar could not be turned back everywhere. There were oases of improvement. In Ancona and Ferrara, Jewish vocational opportunities broadened significantly; in the liberal principality of Piedmont-Sardinia, Jews were allowed to take up residency in Turin, Nice, and other large towns; in Leghorn, they had always been free to utilize their commercial talents.

Indeed, for Jews as for Christians, the distinction in the post-Napoleonic condition was essentially between north and south. In prosperous, enlightened Piedmont, in Lombardy, Venetia, and in other areas of Austrian domination or influence, the worst of the anti-Jewish decrees gradually lapsed. Only in Rome and elsewhere in the Papal States did the ghetto survive intact. So did the old vocational and educational restrictions, and the ban on Jewish publishing. There were instances even of infringement on personal security. Thus, in Bologna, on the night of June 23, 1858, a contingent of papal police burst into the home of a well-established Sephardic family, the Mortaras, and abducted their six-year-old son, Edgardo. Five years before, evidently, when the child was severely ill, the Mortaras' Christian servant girl had arranged for him to be secretly baptized "to save his soul." Only now did she reveal her deed to her confessor, and the priest immediately notified the papal authorities, who in turn ordered Edgardo seized. Carried off to Rome, the youngster was placed in the House of Catechumens, a traditional way station for recent converts. In their shock and horror, the Mortaras appealed to the Vatican for their child's return. To no avail.

Within weeks, the case provoked a universal outcry. Protestant nations were outraged. Catholic France was embarrassed. The Jews in their consternation mounted frantic protest meetings in Vienna, Berlin, London, Paris, New York. Sir Moses Montefiore, a renowned Anglo-Jewish leader, a veteran of successful earlier interventions in behalf of his people (pp. 326–27), departed immediately for Rome to seek a personal audience with Pope Pius IX. He was rebuffed. The Vatican secretary of state, Cardinal Antonelli, made plain to Montefiore that ecclesiastical policy was specific and immovable on issues of baptism. Edgardo Mortara would be kept from his parents, reared as a Catholic, and allowed to choose his religion for himself only upon reaching the age of eighteen.

The ramifications of the Mortara Case were far-reaching. Within the Jewish world, it fostered the growth of major defense and philanthropic organizations, including the Board of Delegates of American Israelites in the United States and France's Alliance Israélite Universelle. In Protestant and liberal Catholic circles, indignation eventually became vocal enough to give even Pius IX serious pause. Although he would not relent, the pontiff confessed years later that he had "saved this Jewish soul, but at the expense of the papacy." Few objections were raised even in Catholic nations when the Kingdom of Italy annexed the city of Rome in 1870, and the pope was stripped of his secular authority. Yet this development brought little consolation to the Mortaras. Although Edgardo by 1870 was free to return to his parents, during the preceding twelve years he had taken the name Pius and lately had become a novitiate in the Augustinian order. Far from wishing to return to his ancestral tradition, he became so ardent a proselytizer that Pope Leo XIII granted him the title of Apostolic Missionary. Conversant in six languages, Edgardo/Pius eventually became a canon and professor of theology at the Sapienza, the Vatican university. He died in 1940 at the Abbey of Bouhey near Liège, shortly after the Nazi invasion of Belgium.

As early as the 1820s and 1830s, fortunately, political change was stirring in Italy. In the northwest, Piedmont's King Carlo Alberto introduced constitutional government in his realm. Then, to rally other Italians to his flag and its constitutional blessings, the king in 1848 launched his army across the frontier into Habsburg-ruled Lombardy. The effort was premature, as it happened; the Austrians crushed the invasion. Yet spontaneous outbursts of liberalism elsewhere on the peninsula exerted their impact.

One duchy after another eased its political limitations. As in the preceding Napoleonic era, the Jews shared in the relaxation. Except in the Papal States, they were no longer physically incarcerated in ghettos or denied the right to travel.

Indeed, a number of Jews were themselves becoming active in the *Risorgimento,* Italy's "resurgence" toward liberal unification. During the chain reaction of political uprisings in 1848, Giuseppe Finzi, a close associate of the great nationalist ideologue Giuseppe Mazzini, was entrusted with command of the revolutionary forces in Mantua. Later, Finzi participated in Garibaldi's 1860 expedition to liberate Sicily. Isaaco Artom served as private secretary to Prime Minister Camillo Cavour, statesman-father of the Risorgimento, while Giacomo Dina edited Cavour's official publication, *Opinione.* In Venice, the revolutionary republic of 1848 was actually proclaimed by the half-Jew Daniele Manin, a fiery political activist. Numerous Jews fought in Venice's Republican Guard. Three were elected to the province's first legislative assembly, seven to the second. In the first Venetian provisional cabinet, Leone Pincherle became minister of agriculture and commerce, Isaaco Pesaro Maurogonato minister of finance. And when a republican government briefly was formed in the Papal States in 1849, Jews enlisted by the hundreds in the revolutionary Civil Guard. Three Jews were elected to the Rome National Assembly, three to the Rome city council.

Ten years later, Piedmont-Sardinia's Savoyard dynasty revived its campaign for unification. This time, with the help of the French army, the effort succeeded. For the Jews of Italy, and specifically those of the Papal States, the emergence of a united kingdom represented their moment of political deliverance. Piedmont's renowned 1848 constitution had included civil rights for non-Catholics and Catholics alike. Now this freedom was extended to Italy as a whole, including the Papal States. In one papal city after another, enthusiastic crowds of citizens and soldiers encouraged Jews to leave their restricted shantytowns and settle in the neighborhoods of their choice. To Italians of all backgrounds, these anomalies were the very incarnation of the detested ancien régime. At last, in 1870, Piedmont's King Vittorio Emanuele II invested the city of Rome and transformed it into his national capital. Only then, and later than anywhere else in Italy, were the gates opened in the single foulest and most reactionary ghetto in all Europe.

The Jews of Acculturation

As recently as midcentury, no Western nation had inflicted more galling restrictions on Jews than had the states of peninsular Italy. Only thirty years later, no European country offered Jews a wider degree of religious and political freedom. Nowhere in Europe, for that matter, were Jews becoming more rapidly acculturated. The Renaissance pattern was revived. As "Mediterranean" in their physical appearance as other Italians, the Jews now rushed again to dress, speak, behave indistinguishably from their Gentile neighbors. Indeed, the speed of their frenetic, all but obsessive mastery of the Italian idiom both reflected and accelerated the pace of their political emancipation.

In 1861, three Jews were elected to the first parliament of a united Italian kingdom. In 1870, seven Jews sat as deputies. In 1870, as in 1849, almost from the moment the Roman ghetto was opened for the second and final time, two Jews were elected city councillors. In 1907, Ernesto Nathan was elected mayor of Rome. In 1891, Luigi Luzzatti, member of a prominent Venetian Jewish family, was appointed minister of finance in the national government. Luzzatti held the position in two later cabinets, and in 1910 was elected prime minister. Salvatore Barzilai of Trieste sat in the cabinet before and during World War I, and served as a member of the Italian delegation to the Paris Peace Conference. Baron Sidney Sonnino, the Protestant son of a Tuscan Jewish landowner, served as finance minister, as foreign minister, and twice as prime minister (in 1908 and 1910). Giuseppe Ottolenghi, appointed Italy's first Jewish general in 1888, became minister of war in 1902. Among the thousands of Jews who served in World War I, fifty-one were generals. One of them, Emanuele Pugliese, was the single most decorated general in the Italian army.

In business, the professions, the arts, Jews within a generation became as vibrant a presence as in public life. Graziado Isaiah Ascoli was the nation's most eminent philologist; Alessandro d'Ancona, its most prestigious literary critic; J. B. Supino, its most respected art historian; Tullio Levi-Cività, its most renowned mathematician. It was in Italy, too, that Cesare Lombroso founded the science of criminology and Pio Foà the science of modern pathology. Jewish intellectual prowess burgeoned out further yet during the interwar years. Comprising one tenth of 1 percent of the Italian population in 1930, Jews provided 8 percent of the nation's university professors.

As much as in any field of expression, it was in belles lettres that Italian Jews evinced the passion of their acculturation. Sabatino Lopez of Milan, author of over seventy plays (none profound but all entertaining), emerged as the best-known figure in Italian theater during the early twentieth century, and served for years as president of the Italian Society of Authors. Italo Svevo was possibly the nation's most esteemed novelist of that era. Born Ettore Schmitz in Habsburg Trieste, Svevo chose the language of his Italian-born mother for his literary career. His first major success, *Senilità* (translated as "As a Man Grows Older"), was praised enthusiastically by his close friend James Joyce. Later, collections of Svevo's writings achieved wider audiences yet. His masterpiece, *La coscienza di Zeno* (The Confessions of Zeno), appearing in 1928, won rapturous acclaim for its "Proustian" technique of interior monologue through dream and vision. Lopez and Svevo in turn prefigured a virtual explosion of Jewish literary talent. In Rome, Alberto Moravia (born Alberto Pincherle), son of a Venetian Jewish father and a Slovene Catholic mother, achieved his widest audience in the 1930s and 1940s with some two dozen novels of contemporary Italian social and sexual tensions. Enzo Levi, born in Modena twenty years earlier than Moravia, also lived through two world wars, producing a series of highly admired novels, short stories, and autobiographical essays.

It was Levi's account of his lonely Jewish boyhood, moreover, and his eventual drift from Judaism to immersion in the "wider" Italian culture, that evoked the life experience of an entire generation of Jews who similarly reached maturity in the 1920s and 1930s. Their headlong assimilation was confirmed by a soaring intermarriage rate of at least 30 percent, and possibly even higher in middle-sized and smaller communities. If, then, exposure to secular humanism was foreshadowed in the problematic Renaissance career of Leone da Modena (p. 226), the process was all but completed in the twentieth century. By the post–World War I years, the largest numbers of Italian Jews maintained an "intermediate" stance of vague, if inchoate, Jewish identification, one that normally was rooted in social far more than in religious tradition. Years later, in 1962, Giorgio Bassani recalled of his own middle-class Jewish childhood in Ferrara:

> The fact that we were Jews . . . inscribed in the registers of the same Jewish community, in our case hardly counted. Because what on earth did the word "Jew" mean? What meaning could terms like "community" or "Israelite universality" have for *us,* since they took no account of the existence of that more basic intimacy . . . derived from the fact that our two families, not from choice, but through a tradition older than any possible memory, belonged . . . to the same scuola.

Carlo Levi confirmed this evaluation. Born in 1902, emerging from an identical milieu, in this case the acculturated Jewish middle class of Turin, Levi was trained as a physician but successively became a painter, a Socialist political activist, and the author of the renowned post–World War II memoir *Christ Stopped at Eboli.* Together with a colleague, Natalia Ginzburg, he also later described the "secret complicity" between Italian Jews as one totally devoid of religious identity.

In any case, it was by no means yet a painless "complicity." Well after the fulfillment of Risorgimento, Italian society had not altogether purged itself of lingering prejudices. In 1873, when a prominent Venetian Jew, Senator Isaaco Pesaro Maurogonato, was nominated as minister of finance, an obscure deputy, Francesco Pasqualigo, protested that Jews were bound by a "double nationality" and hence were unqualified to serve in a government cabinet. Maurogonato, in turn, fearful of arousing the sleeping dog of antisemitism, immediately declined the appointment. It was a circumspection quite typical of other Jews in Italian public life. In their deference to the Catholic majority, they tended also for several decades to gravitate toward a moderate, centrist liberalism rather than follow the more common European Jewish identification with the radical Left. Not until World War I and after did Jewish political activists achieve a wider prominence in Italian socialism. Until then, their discretion on issues of Catholic clericalism reaped important rewards, including the friendship of the new pope, Pius X. By 1914, religion-based antisemitism in Italy was all but moribund. Neither did economic jealousy figure meaningfully in national life. Jewish financial eminence here in no sense matched that of Jews in Germany. Keeping a low profile, Italian Jews were rather admired for their quiet, dignified manners and modest bearing. By 1914, no Jewish community in Europe appeared more socially respected—or more politically secure.

The Jews of Fascism

Benito Mussolini's rise to power in 1922 produced little discernible alteration of Jewish status. Indeed, an important minority of Jews were themselves drawn early to the Fascist movement. This was a middle-class community, after all, one that shared the widespread fear in Italy of mounting syndicalist and anarchist violence. More than a few Jews also admired Mussolini's fiery irredentism: between 1922 and 1933, some five thousand were enrolled in the Fascist party, almost 9 percent of the Italian Jewish population. Aldo Finzi, a wartime fighter pilot, became an early member of the Fascist Grand Council. Dante Almansi served as vice-chief of the national police; Guido Jung, as minister of finance; Maurizio Rava, as governor of Italian Somaliland; Ludovico Mortara, as president of Italy's supreme court; Ugo Foà, as a magistrate of the Rome court of appeals; Giorgio Del Vecchio, as rector of the University of Rome. The Jewish-born Margherita Sarfatti was one of the Duce's early mistresses, and an influential adviser.

At all times, however, far many more thousands of Jews supported the nation's anti-Fascist parties and movements. The brothers Carlo and Nello Rosselli were perhaps the most forthright of these resistants. Members of an affluent Tuscan Jewish family with a long and distinguished career of patriotic service (a younger brother was killed in combat in 1916), the Rossellis were ardent Socialists. As late as 1926 they published a vigorously outspoken anti-Fascist newspaper. In that year, however, Carlo Rosselli was arrested and sentenced to five years on the desolate prison island of Lipari. He did not complete his sentence. In 1929, a boatload of rescuers daringly picked him up on the beach and spirited him away to France.

It was in France, afterward, that Carlo and Nello founded the Justice and Liberty Party, the principal coordinating body for all émigré, non-Communist, opponents of Italian fascism. Segre Amar and Leone and Natalia Ginzburg were early members. So was Carlo Levi. In his autobiographical novel *The Watch* (1951), Levi poignantly evoked the warm comradeship and idealism of these young Jewish anti-Fascists. During the mid-1930s, several of the group characteristically organized an "Italian Column" for the Spanish Civil War. It was the first international unit of anti-Fascist volunteers to reach Spain, and Carlo Rosselli was himself a member of the group. Seriously wounded in August 1936, he was invalided back to France. In June 1937, Carlo and Nello left their small hotel in Normandy for an afternoon drive. Waiting in ambush was a band of French *cagoulards*—right-wing strong-armers—in the pay of the Italian government. The gang intercepted the brothers on an isolated country road and murdered them.

Curiously enough, Mussolini in the 1920s was willing to overlook the Jews' propensity for social protest. He himself displayed little personal interest in antisemitism. Moreover, his party-controlled press, eager to court Jewish goodwill both in- and outside of Italy, continually invoked the maxim: "The Jewish problem does not exist in Italy." In 1931 a comprehensive "Law on the Jewish Communities" even restored much of the religious and educational autonomy Jews had exercised in the pre-Risorgimento years. Earlier, in 1923, the government bestowed full Italian citizenship on the nearly two thousand Jews of Rhodes (under

Italian rule since 1912), and five years later established a rabbinical seminary on the island. These gestures plainly were intended to foster Italian
influence among Sephardim throughout the Mediterranean world, and to
some degree they succeeded. The Rhodes seminary attracted students not
only from the Dodecanese islands but from Turkey, Egypt, the Balkans,
and Palestine. At the same time, Mussolini played an active role in
ensuring appointment of an Italian rabbi in Alexandria and endowing a
chair in Italian literature at the Hebrew University of Jerusalem.

Nor would the Duce allow the complex issue of Zionism and Palestine,
or his government's rivalry with Britain in the Mediterranean, to affect his
forbearing approach to the Jews. In 1930, he denounced antisemitism as
"unworthy of a European nation . . . stupid and barbarous," and two
years later he dismissed Hitler's racial theories as "nonsense." In 1934,
incensed at the Nazi role in assassinating Austria's Chancellor Dollfuss,
Mussolini loosed a particularly harsh blast at Hitler's Aryan theories,
making distinctions between his own "responsible" policies and those of
a "racial megalomaniac." As a matter of "principle," the Duce then
opened Italy's gates wide to German-Jewish refugees.

Yet by the mid-1930s the congruence of Italian and German territorial
revisionism drew the two Fascist nations closer together. It was in the
spring of 1937, with Italian forces bogged down in the Spanish Civil War
and increasingly dependent on German support, that Rome launched a
farrago of press attacks on "Jewish bolshevism" and "Jewish dual loyalties." And in the summer of 1938, genuflecting even more obsequiously
before the mighty German Reich, Mussolini felt obliged to shift to flagrant
Nazi-style racism. In July of that year, *Il Popolo d'Italia,* organ of the
Italian Fascist party, published the notorious "Manifesto of the Racial
Scientists." Invoking the usual jargon of racial pseudoscience, the document concluded that the Italians, like the Germans, were of pure Aryan
origin, and the Jews "do not belong to the Italian race." The signatories
were ten academicians, none of them a scholar of reputation. The declaration in turn was followed almost immediately by establishment of a new
government agency, the "Office of Demography and Race." In November 1938, it was this bureau that formulated a list of anti-Jewish rules and
regulations—in effect, a modern-day version of Paul IV's sixteenth-
century bull *Cum nimis absurdum.*

Under terms of the manifesto, Jews suddenly found themselves banned
from the management of companies engaged in military production, and
from all companies employing over one hundred fifty workers. They were
expelled from their positions in party and government, in the arts,
sciences, universities, and, eventually, in the armed services. Jewish chil-

dren were barred from the public schools. Marriages between Jews and Gentiles were prohibited; and to close all loopholes of expedient "passing," baptismal certificates were accepted only if issued before October 1, 1938. Finally, some ten thousand refugees from the Third Reich, whom Mussolini earlier had welcomed to Italian soil, were now ordered to leave the country within six months.

In his novel *The Garden of the Finzi-Continis* (1962), Giorgio Bassani movingly portrayed the trauma these measures inflicted on the venerable and intensely acculturated Jewish minority of his native Ferrara, and specifically on the haughty Finzi-Contini clan, with its dense network of relatives and friends. Whatever their earlier economic affluence and social snobberies, the aristocratic Finzi-Continis now instinctively join their fellow Jews in presenting a common front to the world. "We're all in the same boat now," the old patriarch acknowledges. Yet, as Bassani and other observers recalled of that era, the pain of exclusion was virtually inexpressible. They had been the best of Italians, after all. It particularly grieved them that King Vittorio Emanuele III had let them down. The monarch's father and grandfather, and he himself in his younger years, had stood loyally by the Jews. But now, in response to Jewish appeals, the frightened little king simply offered a platonic invitation "to recognize the merits of those who have distinguished themselves by their patriotism." Pope Pius XI displayed even less moral fortitude: the pontiff's single formal protest against the racial laws in 1938 concerned its ban on Gentile marriages to converted Jews. His successor, Pius XII, upon ascending the papal throne the following year, evinced a comparable reluctance to challenge Mussolini's new racial policies. Terrified of bolshevism, the incoming pope favored any agenda that would bind Italy and Germany in close friendship.

From its very outset, however, the antisemitic program was highly porous. Lower-middle-class Jews faced ruin, to be sure, and even affluent Jews were seriously affected. But all Jews still received their government pensions and at least partial compensation for any confiscated industrial or commercial properties. Jewish professionals were allowed to function within the Jewish economy, many of them as teachers in segregated Jewish schools (thus producing the best-educated children in Italy). Families of Jews who had been killed, wounded, or decorated in the World War often managed to negotiate "exceptions" for themselves and their families, as did Jews whose public accomplishments defined them as persons of "special merit." In typical Mediterranean fashion, decisions were made on a case-by-case basis, and bureaucratic arbitrariness played its traditional role. So did venality.

With the help, too, of numerous church officials, baptismal certificates could be backdated, thereby instantly transforming Jews into Christians. In this fashion, during the next three years more than six thousand Jews underwent an expedient conversion in a poignant effort to salvage at least their children's future. Another six thousand emigrated, although most of these were already fugitives from the Reich, and even they were almost immediately replaced by seven thousand additional refugees. At no time did antisemitism achieve the kind of solid popular base in Italy that characterized Eastern or Central Europe. Rather, the opposite was the case. Historians agree that it was the racial laws more than any other factor which eroded the popularity Mussolini had won earlier in 1935 with his conquest of Ethiopia. The typical Italian family could neither understand nor emotionally accept the gratuitous persecution of the Jewish family next door.

Italy at War

As late as 1938, the Italian census recorded a Jewish population of forty-seven thousand (including seven thousand refugees). With Mussolini's declaration of war in June 1940, the status of these people immediately deteriorated. On June 14, the government froze all Jewish bank accounts. Vocational restrictions were tightened so drastically that one-third of the nation's Jews were subsisting on charity by the end of the year. Even grimmer at first were the circumstances of the foreign refugees. Nearly half of them were arrested and confined in fifteen "internment" camps scattered around the country. Nevertheless, as the war progressed, the treatment of these people often was softened in practice. Many eventually were allowed to reside in neighboring towns and villages, although under surveillance and subject to curfew. Jewish communal representatives were permitted to assist them. Nor would Mussolini's government give even the remotest thought to deporting Jews back to German-occupied Europe. As the German foreign ministry official Dr. Carl Theo Zeitschel reported after a late autumn visit to Rome: "It is unthinkable . . . for [our] embassy in Rome to touch such a burning subject as the Jewish question in Italy."

The Jews themselves made every effort to care for their own. Their principal relief organization was the Delegazione Assistenza Emigranti Ebrei—"Delasem"—and its mandate first and foremost was to help refugee Jews, those in most imminent danger of arrest. Delasem funds were not local. They arrived circuitously, via Switzerland, from the American Jewish Joint Distribution Committee. It was Delasem's national chairman, Lelio Vittorio Valobra, a Genoese Jewish lawyer, who then put the money to immediate use. The rescue effort was efficient and ingenious at all times. In the spring of 1942, Valobra, learning that forty-two Yugoslav Jewish children who had escaped the German-Croatian massacres were hiding in the Yugoslav countryside around Ljubljana, within the Italian zone of occupation, traveled there and managed to shepherd the terrified youngsters into the city of Ljubljana, where he arranged temporary lodgings for them. Over the next two months, Valobra negotiated permission from Italian officials to move the children into Italy proper. Jewish community representatives found shelter for the refugees in an old villa in the village of Nonantola, about six miles from Modena. In the spring of 1943, the group was joined by some fifty additional Jewish children, also in flight from Croatia's Ustasha Fascist regime. Working closely with other Delasem representatives, Modena's non-Jewish residents provided food, clothing, and schooling for the youngsters. One citizen took several of the children into his own home. A local physician gave them free medical care. By the time the Germans occupied northern Italy (p. 245), the refugees were thoroughly dispersed among Modena's townspeople. Not one was ever caught. Similar rescue efforts were taking place throughout Italy.

In midsummer, 1943, however, the danger suddenly intensified. The war was going badly for the Axis. Allied troops were fighting their way up the peninsula from the south. For the Italian people, the conflict had become both pointless and unendurable. Then, on July 25, leading a conspiracy joined by the king and the Duce's enemies in the Fascist party, Marshal Pietro Badoglio and a group of fellow officers overthrew the government and placed Mussolini himself in custody. As the cabal saw it, the priority now was to extricate the nation from the war. For the Jews, the coup promised a decisive liberation. Indeed, as the nation's racial laws became almost immediately inoperative, refugees began to emerge from hiding. Local Jews slowly returned to their homes and businesses. Like other Italians, they gave hardly any thought to the six German divisions remaining on the peninsula in the north. None was aware that ten additional German divisions soon would join this host.

But on September 12, as the Badoglio regime intensified its armistice negotiations with the Allies, German glider troops swooped down to rescue Mussolini from his confinement outside Rome. He was carried back to Salò, on Lake Garda, within German-occupied territory. Three days later, the Germans proclaimed Mussolini dictator of the "Italian Social Republic"—essentially the area from Rome northward. In practical fact, the Duce was now a German puppet. Assuredly he was in no position to block any draconian plans the Nazis might have for the area's

Jews. Otherwise, September 1943 remained a month of deadly quiet. German troops continued to flood into northern Italy, proceeding down toward Rome itself but making no overt move against the Jewish minority.

By then, however, the Führer himself had issued orders "to wipe the slate clean in Italy." SS Lieutenant General Karl Wolff was appointed "security adviser" to the Mussolini puppet government. Indeed, SS detachments soon quietly embarked on a hunt for Jews who had taken refuge in the collection of northern summer resorts around Lake Maggiore. The operation was small-scale, and never publicly reported; the much larger Jewish population of Rome remained virtually unaware of it. Meanwhile, SS detachments in the Italian capital were taking up their positions, anticipating that the city's twelve thousand Jews could first be "squeezed," then deported.

On September 26, 1943, General Wolff's deputy, Commandant Herbert Kappler, summoned Ugo Foà to his office. Foà was a prominent former magistrate and current president of the Rome Jewish community. It was to him that Kappler now made a chilling announcement. The fate of the Jews was all but sealed, the German declared bluntly. They might yet spare themselves deportation, however, if they could manage to pay fifty kilograms of gold or its equivalent within the next thirty-six hours. Kappler then dismissed his visitor with the observation that "the clock is ticking." Immediately, Foà and his terrified associates set about organizing a "contribution" center in the city's largest synagogue, at the Lungotevere former ghetto, and alerting as many of their fellow Jews they could reach. In his desperation, Foà also approached his Vatican contacts on September 27 in the hope of securing a loan. The hope was vindicated: within hours, Pius XII sent back word that he was prepared to lend the Jews any amount of gold they needed. As it developed, none was required. Local Jews deluged the synagogue with their contributions of jewelry and silverplate and the collection campaign reached its goal without the pope's help. By the morning of September 28, the treasure was delivered in cartons to Kappler's office. Although physically and emotionally exhausted, Foà and his colleagues began to breathe easier.

They were premature. The SS had taken over the Fascist archives and was studying its lists of Jewish names and addresses. From Berlin, then, Adolf Eichmann dispatched his personal aide, SS Captain Theodor Dannecker, to supervise a decisive *judenrazzia* in Rome. Two and a half weeks later, on the night of October 16, the roundup began. Without warning, SS troops and accompanying Italian Fascist police surrounded the eight-block Lungotevere enclave. Approximately four thousand of the city's twelve thousand Jews still lived here. Of these, the SS now collected twelve hundred men, women, and children in their nightclothes, loaded them into trucks, and summarily carried them off for rail shipment to extermination camps in Poland. Eventually, another eight hundred Jews were tracked down in Rome and deported.

Thus far, the anti-Jewish campaign elsewhere in Italy had been somewhat disjointed and on a far smaller scale. But in November 1943 Captain Friedrich Vosshammer replaced Theodor Dannecker as Wolff's assistant. It was Vosshammer who promptly set about coordinating the hunt for Jews. By then, Jews living in the north were thoroughly apprised of their danger, particularly after the Rome *judenrazzia*. Yet thus far their efforts to escape were only intermittently successful. In Milan, the Germans managed to seize and deport over eight hundred victims. Another four hundred were carried off from Siena, Florence, and Bologna. Raids and roundups were similarly conducted in numerous smaller towns. By December 1943, four deportation trains already had left Italian soil, one carrying three hundred refugees who only lately had arrived from France, the others carrying two thousand Italian Jews. Their destination was Auschwitz.

Ironically, the eight thousand foreign Jewish refugees in Italy, with their earlier experience of the Nazis in their own lands, were the first to grasp the full magnitude of the German danger. Upon learning of the German takeover in September 1943, therefore, several hundred Yugoslav Jewish refugees, in hiding north of Turin, decamped immediately to Switzerland. In the south, beyond the area of direct German occupation, other isolated groups of Yugoslav Jewish fugitives made haste to reach the advancing Allied armies (p. 148). But notwithstanding their premonitions and precautions, foreign Jews usually did not fare as well as Italian Jews. Few possessed money, documents, contacts, or the linguistic ability to pass themselves off as Italian Catholics. As a result, a far larger proportion of these fugitives eventually were seized and relocated. Unlike Italian Jews, their destination was not Auschwitz, but La Risiera, a particularly gruesome concentration camp established on the site of a former rice-refining factory near Trieste. To operate this facility, the Germans imported SS agent Erwin Lampert, a crematorium expert from Sobibór. Lampert's subsequent replacement was Franz Stangl, the actual former commandant at Sobibór. For the hundreds of Jews captured in northern Italy, it was La Risiera in Trieste, not Auschwitz in Poland, that became the end of the line.

Rhodes, too, came under German occupation almost the same day that the Nazis moved against the Badoglio government in Rome, September

12, 1943. In the next months, a series of harsh new regulations kept local Jewish inhabitants under tight curfew and even tighter rations. Finally, in July 1944, the Germans ordered all Jews in the island's main city (also named Rhodes) to assemble with their baggage in Commercial Plaza. So it was that the entire remaining Jewish population of seventeen hundred men, women, and children gathered in the fiery summer sun, relinquished their valuables, and then were escorted under guard to the port of Leros. Here they were packed into three small freighters and carried off. After an agonizing four-day journey in which scores of older people and infants perished, the flotilla anchored at the Greek port of Piraeus. The survivors were loaded on trains and dispatched immediately to Auschwitz.

As late as September 1943, thirty-seven thousand Italian Jews and eight thousand foreign Jews had remained in integral Italy. Of these, nearly seven thousand were deported in the ensuing nine months. Rather poignantly, their communal leaders had counted on the vast influence of the Vatican to shield them. That act of faith was unwarranted. Pius XII, after all, was the pontiff who had declined to condemn Mussolini's racial laws, who had not lifted a finger to protect Jews in other European countries. Yet in Rome, at least, the local Jewry believed that personal contacts would make the difference. In earlier years, Dante Almansi, national president of the Union of Italian Jewish Communities, and Ugo Foà, president of the Rome Jewish community, had been high-ranking officials under Mussolini. Since then, both men had developed useful ties with the Vatican. On a case-by-case basis, moreover, the papal court displayed sympathy, providing employment within the Vatican for Jews who had lost their jobs, helping Jewish families emigrate, authorizing backdated baptismal certificates.

Yet from the outset Pius XII and his advisers were unwilling to take seriously rumors of the Holocaust, or to risk provoking the Germans. It was only in late 1942 that a secret warning was delivered by SS Colonel Kurt Gerstein, who personally had witnessed mass gassings of Jews at Belzec; and the following August, in 1943, additional confirmation was provided by Baron Ernst von Weizsäcker, Germany's ambassador to the Vatican. Even then, Pius XII refrained from issuing so much as a discreet, private protest to the Germans, or a warning to the Jews to move swiftly in organizing their escape plans. There would have been time. The Rome *judenrazzia* did not take place until October 16. Mass arrests of Jews in Florence, Genoa, Venice, and elsewhere did not begin until November. During late September and early October, many Jews in those communities remained unaware of the impending danger. If they had known, they might have taken measures to save themselves. For that matter, had the

Vatican issued a threat of papal interdiction or excommunication, numerous Italian Fascists, and possibly even a few German Catholics, might have hesitated to cooperate in the Holocaust. The pontiff's single, belated gesture in late September 1943, agreeing to lend gold to the Jews of Rome, came much too late to have much effect one way or the other.

Meanwhile, following establishment of the German-controlled "Italian Social Republic," local Italian officials were left without authority to block the Nazi extermination program. Within their own ranks, too, there were more than a few personnel who actively collaborated in the Final Solution. Some were racist fanatics. Others were pro-Nazi toadies. Most were simply venal informers. Among these elements was the police chief of Rome, Pietro Caruso, who in 1943 and 1944 instructed his men to "proceed urgently with the arrest of pure Italian and foreign Jews." Private individuals occasionally divulged the hiding places of Jewish neighbors. One non-Jewish wife even revealed the whereabouts of her Jewish husband, then despaired when her son was also arrested. Other victims were caught by private Italian bounty hunters who developed a knack for tracking down Jews. Primo Levi, the future great author, was among those ferreted out by collaborators.

But if some Italians displayed the uglier side of human nature, the survival of no less than four-fifths of Italian Jewry would suggest a far more compassionate reaction. To be sure, the Jews themselves were uniquely equipped to evoke that help. They were comparatively few in numbers and thus easier to hide. They looked, spoke, and "acted" Italian. Unlike the Jews of Eastern Europe or the Balkans, whose Yiddish or Ladino accents gave them away, these people blended in easily. Moreover, in the Mediterranean tradition, Italian Jews tended also to be lackadaisical about obeying government orders to report for internment (in contrast to the punctilious, law-abiding Jews of Central Europe). They displayed a regional ingenuity at evading labor conscription, in negotiating on the all-pervasive black market. But in the final analysis, no minority, however resourceful, could have survived without active help. The Italians supplied more of that help than did any other nation in Europe, except the Danes. As SS Commandant Herbert Kappler noted ruefully, in the aftermath of the October 16, 1943, roundup in Rome:

> The behavior of the Italian people was unalloyed passive resistance, which in some individual cases amounted to active assistance. . . . [A] great mass of people . . . even tried to cut off the police from the Jews.

Beyond all other factors, then, the attitude of the Italians toward their Jewish neighbors emerged from the absence of a modern antisemitic tradition in the country—indeed, from plain and simple kindliness of heart.

That substratum of compassion was evident in the sheer multitude of hiding places the Italians supplied. In rural areas, Jews were taken in at pensions and private farms. When the countryside became too dangerous, cities provided the alternative of anonymity. Here Jews moved in with Gentile friends, or rented private rooms or apartments in distant neighborhoods. Entirely typical was the experience of Carlo Milano, who lived with his wife and two daughters in a Rome apartment for six months. The family possessed no identification papers or ration cards; these were supplied by a friendly policeman. The owner of the building, aware that his tenants were Jewish, said nothing. The bank in which Milano kept his account also knew his identity, yet illegally cashed his World War I pension checks. There were thousands of such episodes. Almost no one could have survived without the help of non-Jews.

That assistance was more vital yet in the case of foreign Jewish refugees. Here priests and nuns often provided the initial asylum. They housed and fed fugitives, usually in convents and monasteries. By June 1944, even after nine months of German occupation, a rescue network organized by the Capuchin Father Mario Benedetto was sheltering some fifteen hundred Jewish refugees in north-central Italy. In Genoa, Father Francesco Repetto worked closely with Cardinal Pietro Boetto, and with Delasem representatives, to shelter nearly a thousand Jews. Before the war ended, at least one hundred seventy of these clerics were executed for treason and several hundred others were imprisoned. Physicians, evincing a comparable solicitude, hid refugees in hospitals and clinics. A number of mayors and other bureaucrats played a decent, courageous role. In Fiume, Giovanni Palatucci held the position of "commissioner of foreigners" at local police headquarters. When German troops initially flooded into northern Italy, Palatucci destroyed all police files and lists of Jews, alerted Jews of pending SS and police searches, even helped Jews embark secretly from Fiume to Bari, behind Allied lines. In September 1944, Palatucci was arrested and deported to Dachau, where he perished.

Everywhere, too, there were simple farmers, maids, janitors, and other private citizens who hid Jews in attics or cellars, or saved their possessions. Near Lugano, Giuseppe Tiburzio convinced a Belgian Jewish father that his nine-year-old daughter would not survive the winter in an open mountain hut at five thousand feet. He offered to take the child himself, promising to rear her in the Jewish faith. The father agreed. Tiburzio then brought the girl to his parents in Venice, who cared for her. The father subsequently was caught and died in Auschwitz. The daughter survived, and the Tiburzio family, despite their love for her, gave her up after the war to an aunt living in England. Meanwhile, from other towns and villages throughout northern Italy, perhaps six thousand Jews managed to evade capture and reach Switzerland. Their escape also was due largely to workaday Italians who helped them negotiate the mountain routes near Lakes Maggiore, Lugano, and Como. Altogether, the survival of nearly thirty-eight thousand Jews out of a 1943 population of forty-five thousand was almost unique for Nazi-occupied Europe.

As a community, they did not survive unscarred. The wound to Italian Jewry's communal and cultural ethos was grave. The SS had looted synagogues and Jewish libraries of their richest artifacts and manuscripts. If a Jewish élan had been faint before 1940, it was all but moribund for many years afterward. On an individual basis, Jews swiftly resumed their former importance in the nation's economic, academic, and professional life, but few since the war have offered their talents to Jewish culture. Community leadership still remains very weak. In Milan, encompassing the nation's wealthiest Jewish population, the rabbi of its Great Synagogue, Giuseppe Laras, is privately despised as a pompous mediocrity. In Rome, the learned and respected chief rabbi, Dr. Elio Toaff, has retired in favor of less-prepossessing talents. In the last decade before the war, approximately 30 percent of Italian Jews married out of the faith. Since then, the ratio has approached 50 percent.

Yet the choice of the Jews' cultural destiny at least remains entirely in their own hands. The Italian people continue as forbearing and benign as in earlier years. They esteem Jewish history, respect the Jewish presence. Today, many streets and squares are named for Jews who played illustrious roles in Italian history, including Cesare Lombroso, Daniele Manin, Sidney Sonnino, and Luigi Luzzatti. Public sites are also named for Jews who performed gallantly in the anti-Fascist cause: Via Fratelli Rosselli in Florence, for Carlo and Nello Rosselli; state high school Eugenio Colorni in Milan, for a Jewish anti-Fascist hero killed in Rome; memorial column Angelo Finzi, a reformed Fascist and later fallen Jewish resistance hero. There are perhaps two dozen such memorials and monuments in Italy, some named for Italian Gentiles who helped Jews.

During the postwar years, Jewish organizations and communal leaders have been singled out for honor. In 1966, the Union of Italian Jewish Communities was awarded the Italian Republic's Gold Medal for Merit. The Jewish community of Milan received the municipality's gold medal in recognition of its welfare and educational work, and its "great dignity of sacrifice" during the years of racial persecution. On the occasion of the republic's twentieth anniversary, in June 1966, President Giuseppe Sarragat named Astorre Mayer, president of the Milan Jewish community, a Knight of Labor, the nation's highest public service award.

In bestowing these honors and encomia, erecting these monuments, dedicating these streets and public squares, the nation of Italy at least subliminally has projected a mirror image of itself as one of modern history's unforgettable case studies in immemorial humanity.

CHAPTER XII

A BALKAN SEPHARAD

On the Riviera

Cradled by the Maritime Alps and the Mediterranean, Nice is Miami Beach with elegance. Not every hotel is the patrician Negresco, or every street the dignified Promenade Anglaise, but the city luxuriates in manicured parks and powdered beaches, effulgent floral displays, decorous tiled villas, ornately fenestrated boutiques. On a July twilight, I am beset by the strains of marching bands. Each summer, the municipality of Nice stages weekly "happenings" as tourist attractions. This week's event is an international folk dance festival, and the calvalcade is an appetizer for the evening performance. In a delectation of color and melody, the gaily costumed young performers flaunt their national flags and quickstep to the beat of drums, trumpets, tambourines. Mexicans parade by, Circassians, Macedonians, Turks, Peruvians, Tyroleans, Estonians. Dancers wave to onlookers. Onlookers respond with cordial applause. In Yemenite costumes, an Israeli delegation struts its stuff, pirouetting and swaying to the tune of "Eretz Zavat Chalav u'Devash" (Land Flowing with Milk and Honey). Spectators smile benignly, clap, wave back.

For me, the moment evokes only disorientation, a synaptic failure to bridge the gulf between these exuberant young Israelis and a distraught Jewish influx of only fifty years before. The "visitors" of 1940 and 1941 were fugitives from Occupied France. Nice lay within the Non-occupied zone. The place was no Eden then, not under Marshal Pétain's collaborationist Vichy regime. For French Jews, it was second-class status. For foreign or even recently naturalized Jews, it was penal internment, and often selective deportation back to Occupied France, then to Auschwitz. In November 1942, however, the German Wehrmacht suddenly poured across the armistice line to invest "Non-occupied" France altogether. The entirety of the sector's two hundred thousand Jews thereupon became fair game for the SS.

Yet, even within this newly opened hunting-and-killing ground, an enclave of sanctuary remained. The Maritime Alps—in essence, the French Riviera—were part of the Italian zone of occupation. In peace-time, approximately fifteen thousand Jews had lived here, most of them Sephardim. But with the fall of France in 1940, and specifically with German investiture of the Vichy Zone in November 1942, some thirty thousand Jews of all backgrounds crowded into the Italian-administered sector, and nearly half of these into the city of Nice, its military headquar-ters. One month later, the Vichy district prefect ordered this refugee colony to make ready for departure to Occupied France. It was a death warrant. Learning of it, Tullio Calisse, the Italian consul-general in Nice, appealed to Rome for help. The response from the Italian foreign ministry was unequivocal: "It is not possible to permit . . . [the Jews] to settle in areas occupied by the German troops. Measures to protect the Jews, both foreign and Italian, must be taken exclusively by our officials." They were. Not a single Jew was turned over to the Vichy administration. Pierre Laval, Vichy's foreign minister, twice wired Rome to protest. It was wasted effort. The fugitives soon learned that they were entirely safe in Italian-occupied territory.

So were refugee Jews from other parts of Europe. The Italian adminis-tration even requisitioned several Nice hotels for them. When the Vichy police occasionally sought to raid these Jewish "cells," Italian military personnel turned them back. Reporting to Berlin in December 1942, Dr. Werner Knochen, director of the German Sicherheitdienst in France, noted angrily that "[t]he best of harmony prevails between the Italian troops and the Jewish population. The Italians live in the homes of the Jews. The Jews invite them out and pay for them." In a later message to Berlin of February 1943, Knochen added:

> We must . . . record the fact that because of the Italians it has been
> completely impossible to enforce the legislation which was enacted by
> the French government against the Jews. By forbidding arrests, the
> Italians again have taken the foreign Jews under their protection.

The complaint was followed by another, in April, from Klaus Barbie, SS Obersturmführer for Lyons. At least four hundred Jews were lodged in "special hotels" under Italian occupation, noted Barbie, who added then, with much indignation, that "[t]here are among the Jews twelve [children] for whom the French police have been searching for a long time, yet the Italians refuse to hand them over."

Repeatedly, the Nazi command interceded with Rome, seeking an end to this "intolerable state of affairs." Foreign Minister Galeazzo Ciano was entirely uncooperative. So was Mussolini, although the Duce preferred the technique of dissembling. After promising German Ambassador Hans Georg von Mackensen to "correct the sentimental humanitarianism of my generals," the following day he gave his staff instructions directly to the contrary. German protests were unavailing. Even Foreign Minister Joachim von Ribbentrop's personal appeal to Mussolini achieved no results. By early 1943, the Duce had been informed of the mass murders in Poland. He entirely agreed with Ciano that "no power, not even Germany, could make Italy a partner to such crimes, for which the Italian people would one day have to pay the reckoning." By May 1943, Carl Zeitschel in Berlin (p. 242) confirmed in a dispatch to the Sicherheitdienst in Vichy that "the Italian government simply is not interested in the Jewish question, for there hardly is in Italy a Jewish question as such. We cannot expect any assistance from this side."

Mussolini fell in July 1943. In August, the successor Badoglio government, embarking on armistice negotiations with the Allies, prepared to withdraw Italian troops from their former zones of occupation. Upon learning of this development, the Jewish refugee group in the Riviera frantically sought permission to accompany Italian units back to Italy. On August 20, Rome gave its authorization in principle. In practical fact, transport was lacking for civilian evacuation. Urgent three-way negotiations followed then among the Delasem (the Jewish relief organization), the Italian government, and the Allies. Finally, the Badoglio regime agreed to provide four ships. The Allies would permit the Jews haven in North Africa. The American Joint Distribution Committee would finance the undertaking.

Even as these arrangements neared completion, however, the Wehrmacht suddenly crossed into the Italian occupation zone. On September 9, even as the Badoglio government was putting final touches on its armistice negotiations with the Allies, German troops entered Nice. Following in their wake, SS units promptly rounded up some two thousand Jews and carried them off to Drancy, outside Paris. Their final destination was Auschwitz. Jews hiding in the Riviera countryside fared somewhat better, but eventually nine thousand of these also were hunted down and deported. The rest managed to disperse successfully throughout France. Nine hundred other fugitives made their way over the rugged passes into Italy itself. Here they were immediately taken in by the Italian people, who hid, fed, and protected them in seminaries, monasteries, convents, and private homes. It was a poignant climax to an otherwise flawed rescue effort.

A Greek Odyssey

The cradle of democracy and Periclean culture, Athens today ranks as the most squalid capital in the European Community. Walking through the commercial heart of the city, I sidestep garbage cans and unboxed merchandise overflowing shop and warehouse entrances. Melidoni Street, my destination, is vintage Balkan provincial. Flanked by cubelike private homes, the synagogue here is whitewashed and drab. Is Athens airport the prototype of security negligence? Try the Melidoni Street synagogue. Its sentry box is deserted. The policeman has strolled off for his morning coffee-break. Its gate is wide open. So is the door to the rabbi's office. Characteristically, the room is disheveled. The telephone is ringing. There is no one to answer.

Ten minutes later, the rabbi wanders in for our appointment. David Amar, mercifully, is a warm and outgoing man. He answers all questions straightforwardly, in perfect French. Although himself of Sephardic ancestry, Amar was born in Larissa, a bailiwick of Romaniot—Greek-speaking—Jewry. During the German occupation, as he and his family moved from village to village, it was not simply absence of the telltale Ladino accent that helped save their lives. EAM-ELAS partisans offered their protection to Jews. So did the Greek Orthodox clergy, by providing false baptismal certificates. But upon returning to Larissa in 1944, the Amars and other surviving Jews encountered desolation. Their homes had been picked clean by looters. Throughout Greece, barely ten thousand Jews had survived out of a prewar Jewish population of some ninety thousand. Now they were stripped of subsistence and often of elementary lodgings.

The Joint Distribution Committee played a major role in keeping this remnant alive. The survivors also eked out a living by selling off their parents' real estate. Most would have no further use for it; in the next few years, at least half of them departed for Israel or the West. A decade after the war, by the time of Amar's ordination (at Paris's Ecole Rabbinique), not more than four thousand Jews remained in Athens itself. In the years that followed, to be sure, the little community slowly regained its economic solvency and political security. Today, its relations with government, church, and public at large are satisfactory. The police protection at the synagogue is against Arab terrorists, not the locals. Nevertheless, this is even by post-Holocaust standards a dying minority. The attrition is not in numbers alone. Most Jewish children shun the Jewish schools. Synagogue attendance is minimal. Intermarriage is rising.

The war determined the character as much as the demography of these survivors. The initial invasion, in October 1940, was entirely an Italian enterprise, and a failure. It took the Germans to do the job properly. Once the Wehrmacht overran the country in April 1941, Greece was divided administratively into three zones. Bulgaria, an Axis partner, was awarded most of Thrace and a large share of Macedonia. Germany retained eastern Thrace and the great Macedonian port of Salonika, encompassing the nation's largest Jewish population. The Italian sphere included the rest of the Old Kingdom—pre-1912 Greece—with its capital, Athens. Approximately six thousand Jews lived in the kingdom, two-thirds of them in Athens. Most were Romaniotes.

Under Italian rule, this modest Jewish enclave conducted its affairs without molestation, apparently sealed off from the Nazi terror in Salonika. The Germans were incensed. With growing vehemence, they pressed the Italians for information on the number of Jews in the Old Kingdom. The Italians agreed to conduct a census, then reneged on the promise. Instead, they transformed their zone into a kind of free port for Jews escaping German and Bulgarian rule, and supplied refugees with lodgings and false identity papers. Soon, the Jewish population of the Old Kingdom climbed to twelve thousand. Even in German-occupied Salonika, during the acutest period of Nazi deportations, the local Italian consulate interceded repeatedly for Jews of "Italian origin." On their behalf, it fabricated several hundred documents of "nationality." The vice-consul, Rosenberg (not a Jew, despite the name), and the military liaison officer, Captain Merci, were the heart of the rescue effort. Over many months, the "Rosenberg Rescue Brigade" interpreted the term "Italian subject" broadly. An Italian-sounding name was enough to qualify. Among a Sephardic community, there were not a few of these.

Yet no sooner had the Badoglio government formulated its armistice offer to the Allies, on September 9, 1943, than the Wehrmacht flung itself upon the entire zone of Italian occupation in Greece. Late that month, the SS began a systematic registration of Jews. During the spring and summer of 1944, over three thousand Jews in the Dodecanese islands were shipped off to Auschwitz, including seventeen hundred Jews from Rhodes (p. 246). At the same time, the Germans intensified their reign of terror among the twelve thousand Jews of Athens, Preveza, Arta, Agrinion, Patria, Chalkis, Volos, Larissa, and other mainland towns of the Old Kingdom. Most of these people were well integrated into Greek life, spoke mainly Greek, had access (through Greek contacts) to a certain advance warning of German plans. Their rabbis and communal leaders had carefully destroyed all address lists. Fleeing to the mountains, then, families like those of David Amar were sheltered by local villagers and actively protected by the partisan resistance. Even so, at least six thousand native and refugee Jews in the Old Kingdom fell victim to the Nazi dragnet, most to perish in death camps.

Sephardic Island, Slavic Sea

Like the Association of Greek Survivors of Concentration Camps, the Association of Bulgarian Jews in Israel is located in south Tel Aviv, bordering Jaffa. The street is characteristically nondescript. Yet the Association's little suite of offices upstairs is functional and tidy. The executive secretary, Mrs. Lily Avrahami, is a middle-aged lady, refined and cordial. It is the summer of 1991 and Mrs. Avrahami is quite busy. In recent months, there has been an unexpected influx of nearly a thousand Bulgarian immigrants. A half-dozen of the newcomers are sitting in the reception room now, smoking and chatting. They are young men, lean and rather good-looking. I slowly take in their blond hair and high cheekbones. Mrs. Avrahami appraises my skepticism. "They're half-and-halfs," she acknowledges, "products of mixed marriages, almost every one." So much for East European Jewry in the past forty-five years.

Although Bulgaria's prewar Jewish community of some fifty thousand was among the few in the Balkans to survive the Hitler epoch, it did not survive intact. As a wartime ally of Nazi Germany, the Sofia government had left these people spoliated and desperately impoverished. The postwar Communist regime was not prepared to return their confiscated homes and shops. The Jews then were not prepared to remain on in Bulgaria. In their thousands, they applied for exit visas. The Communists were not having it. Every skill was needed for reconstruction. But in 1948 representatives of the Jewish Agency held a friendly series of conversations with the party chairman. An understanding was reached. In exchange for a substantial Agency payoff in dollars, Bulgarian Jews would be allowed to depart en bloc for Israel. Most did. By late 1949, only five thousand remained. In Israel, subsequently, the newcomers were lodged in the abandoned Arab towns of Jaffa, Bat Yam, Cholon, Lod, Ramle. Their early years were as impoverished as those of their Salonikan cousins. Nevertheless, slowly, painfully, they worked their way to lower-middle-class status. And that, presumably, was the end of the Bulgarian story.

Until the implosion of the Communist empire in 1989–90, and the collapse of the Marxist economies along with it. These were not congenial circumstances for the Jews who had stayed on in Bulgaria after 1949, maintaining their status during the intervening four decades of socialism as elitist professionals and managers. Like their predecessors, then, this tiny residual group was prepared to pick up stakes and depart for Israel. No obstacles were placed in their way. Indeed, in 1991, Bulgaria restored diplomatic ties with Israel for the first time since the Six-Day War of 1967. Some twelve hundred Bulgarian Jews have arrived in Israel to date (although less than half have remained). Initially, the process was not advertised. The emigrants flew out of Sofia each week at 2:00 A.M. on Bulgarian Airlines. The ungainly Tupolevs promptly unloaded their passengers at Ben-Gurion Airport and took off again before the light of day. But since 1992, flights have increased to three a week, with El Al participating. Traffic is free and open.

The Jewish world the newcomers have left behind is a shell. The Great Synagogue of Sofia remains the largest Sephardic synagogue in the world. Much of its past grandeur also survives, its Byzantine-style cupolas and bell turrets, its immense chandelier descending from a one-hundred-foot ceiling. Yet only a dozen or so worshippers appear on the Sabbath. At Plovdiv, Bulgaria's second-largest city, with an even older synagogue, assembling a minyan of Jews is difficult even on Yom Kippur. Both in Sofia and in Plovdiv, Jewish councils maintain a thin substructure of community events and publish monthly bulletins. The Jewish rank and file display little interest.

It was not always so. This is an old Jewry. Its descendants bear such Romaniot names as Politi, Roditi, Canetti, Kalo. Not until the Ottoman conquest were the Jewish Greek-speakers inundated by a wave of Sephardic refugees. The later arrivals made their homes in Sofia, Janina, Nikopol, Plovdiv, and in a few smaller towns. In Bulgaria, as elsewhere in the Ottoman Balkans, they resumed their essentially mercantile vocations. Trade and industry flourished in their hands. The production of woolens in Plovdiv became their monopoly. It was they who founded and developed the leather, fur, and dyeing industries. In their communal autonomy, moreover, the Sephardim laid down strict rules governing business affairs. Gentile merchants learned to accommodate to these regulations.

By the mid-eighteenth century, Jews comprised fully a tenth of the populations of Sofia and Plovdiv. Theirs were stable communities, if rather less brilliant than those of their kinsmen in maritime Salonika or Constantinople. Literacy was universal. Even the poorest children attended Jewish schools. In Nikopol, the local talmudic academy was established by Joseph Caro, who lived there for several years before continuing on to Edirne and Safed, and it sustained its intellectual eminence well into the 1700s. Here, above all, Jewish culture remained proudly Sephardic down to the twentieth century. In his autobiographical *The Tongue Set Free,* the Bulgarian Jewish Nobel laureate Elias Canetti (who may actually have been of Romaniot ancestry) recalled his youth:

> The first children's songs I heard were Spanish, I heard old Spanish *romanceros;* but the thing that was most powerful, and irresistible for a child, was a Spanish attitude. With naive arrogance, the Sephardim looked down on other Jews; a word always charged with scorn was *Todesco,* meaning a German or Ashkenazi Jew. It would have been unthinkable to marry a *Todesca,* a Jewish woman of that background.

Equally unthinkable for the Sephardim would have been intimate relations with the "primitive" Bulgars. Thus, in the latter nineteenth century, they regarded with foreboding the emergence of nationalism among their Slavic neighbors. Their concern appeared warranted, moreover, when a "liberating" Russian army in 1878 actively encouraged pogroms against the Jews of Sofia and Nikopol. Fortunately, local chauvinism subsided with the early departure of the Russians. In newly independent Bulgaria afterward, the Jews resumed and even augmented their commercial and professional eminence. Rather, it was their participation in the nation's cultural and political life that lagged. Jewish children bypassed Bulgarian schools for their own network of Alliance institutions. They knew the Bulgarian language only as a street patois. Their own first language at all times remained Ladino. It was more than a vernacular of home and business. Bulgarian Jewry produced over one hundred Ladino-language newspapers and journals. As in Salonika, theirs was an intensely separatistic culture, maintaining a virtually identical skein of choirs, drama groups, libraries, philanthropies, as well as "Israelite" economic syndicates, banks, credit societies, partnerships, corporations. Numbering forty-three thousand by 1914, the Jews of Bulgaria functioned as a self-contained island within a Slavic ocean.

It was a world of ethnicity far more than of religiosity. Zionism was its ultimate expression. Every rabbi in Bulgaria preached the redemption of the Holy Land. Indeed, political Zionism in Bulgaria actually anticipated Theodor Herzl's pathbreaking volume *Der Judenstaat.* When Herzl passed through Sofia in 1897, returning from an exploratory visit to the Turkish government in Constantinople, some two thousand cheering Jews were waiting at the railroad station to lift him from his carriage and onto their shoulders. Later, as the dominant force in Bulgarian Jewish life, Zionism produced a dense network of clubs, drama groups, Hebrew-language journals, sports and gymnastic associations. Here the principal Jewish holiday was not Yom Kippur but Yom HaShekel, Zionist membership day. It was a gala production, an extended weekend of bands, dancing, public parades.

The community put its money and human resources where its ideology lay. Emigration to Zion was a serious option here. As early as 1895, Bulgarian Jewry established an agricultural training school for prospective emigrants, then dispatched its vanguard of pioneers to the Holy Land. In Palestine, they organized a farm settlement, Hartuv, the first of an eventual half-dozen to be founded by their community, as well as a Palestine-Bulgarian Bank for Immigration and Settlement. By 1939, thirty-five hundred Bulgarian Jews had departed for Palestine, nearly a twelfth of their population.

The Wages of Revisionism

It was a commitment that for years evinced pride far more than insecurity. Bulgaria fought at the side of the Central Powers in World War I, and the Jews shared fullheartedly in that effort. Their military performance evoked only admiration, and specifically their heroism at the battles of Drenova, Glava, and Tutrakan. Nevertheless, in the aftermath of defeat and extensive territorial amputation, the nation's mood became increasingly embittered and xenophobic. A collection of right-wing parties and paramilitary associations sprang up, focusing on Bulgarian losses in Macedonia, on the perceived failures of democratic government. The most avowedly antisemitic of these groups was the Ratnik (Warrior) party, lower-middle-class in membership and pro-Nazi in the dreams it shared with Germany of territorial revision. By the mid-1930s, as the Nazi Reich began to flex its muscles and draw Bulgaria into its economic orbit, German political and racist ideology gained wider acceptance among the Bulgarian people.

With the outbreak of World War II, moreover, Hitler was able to woo the Sofia government into his anti-Comintern Pact of Fascist solidarity. In February 1940, responding to the Nazi gravitational field, King Boris III selected as his prime minister an undisguised Germanophile, Bogdan Filov. During the spring and summer of that year, following the Wehrmacht's conquest of France, the time appeared ripe for a formal diplomatic and political alliance with Berlin. Accordingly, in April 1941, Filov signed the "Pact of Vienna," allowing German troops access to Bulgarian territory; and two weeks after that, Bulgaria became the springboard for Hitler's devastating invasion of Greece and Yugoslavia. As a payoff for this help, the Führer then awarded the Bulgars extensive areas of Greek and Yugoslav Macedonia, and portions of Greek Thrace.

So it was that thirteen thousand Macedonian and Thracian Jews, most of them veteran Romaniotes, now fell under the rule of an avowedly pro-Nazi regime. Almost immediately, too, Bulgarian Fascist Legionnaires in these territories launched themselves on the pillage and destruction of synagogues and other Jewish communal institutions. Far worse was to come. That same April, Theodor Dannecker, formerly special SS representative in Vichy France and later in Italy, was attached to the German embassy in Sofia, once again as "special adviser" on the Jews. Under Dannecker's remorseless prodding, the Bulgarian regime promised its active cooperation with the Germans on "racial" matters. Indeed, even earlier, it had adopted a particularly brutal policy toward several hundred naturalized Jewish citizens. Depriving these families of their passports, the government in December 1940 had forced them onto three aged, unseaworthy vessels and shipped them out of the Black Sea port of Varna in the direction of Palestine. Only one of the leaking hulks, the S.S. *Salvador,* got as far as the Sea of Marmara. Caught in a storm there, it sank less than a mile from the Turkish coast. Twenty-two passengers managed to swim ashore. Two hundred four drowned, including sixty-six children.

Over the next months, the Filov cabinet developed a more systematically punitive approach to the nearly fifty thousand Jews of integral Bulgaria. Its special "commissar" for Jewish affairs, Aleksandur Belev, had visited Germany, studied Nazi racism in action, then formulated specific proposals to offer his government. In November 1941, these were accepted. Initially, Jews were excluded from all commercial and professional associations, from the civil service and the army. In January 1942, a far broader program was adopted. Henceforth, Jews were obliged to "sell" their real estate to a government corporation at 40 percent of the 1932 market price. With payment to be spread out over twenty years, the scheme was tantamount to confiscation. The number of Jewish doctors, lawyers, university faculty members, and other professionals allowed to practice was limited to the ratio of Jews in the general Bulgarian population. In effect, their careers were foreclosed. Jews were prohibited from owning automobiles, telephones, radios. Their children were denied admission to Bulgarian schools and universities. Jewish-Christian marriages were banned. The badge now became mandatory, together with identifying signs on all Jewish residences. Food rations for Jews were reduced below those for other Bulgarians.

Harshest of all, however, was the order dispatching all Jewish males of military age to road-building camps, with the physically unfit obliged to pay a crippling indemnity tax. By June 1942, under the supervision of Belev's commissariat, nearly six thousand Jewish men and boys were living in penal compounds. Working fifteen hours a day, they suffered freezing weather, malnutrition, illness, periodic beatings.

The Wages of Collaboration

The circumstances of Jews in Bulgaria were intimately related to the even more dire fate of Jews in Bulgarian-occupied Macedonia and Thrace. In October 1942, Theodor Dannecker, Germany's SS "adviser" in Sofia, made plain to Commissar Belev that the Reich expected a mass deportation of all Bulgarian Jews to German-controlled territory in the "east"— that is, Poland and the Soviet Union. Belev personally raised no objections. Nor did Prime Minister Filov. Privately, however, Filov understood that the king, and important personages in the church and even the government, would balk at the likely extermination of their Jewish fellow citizens. He procrastinated, noting in a memorandum to German Ambassador Beckerle that the Jews were needed on road-building projects. For the moment, Beckerle and Dannecker accepted the explanation. But if they postponed their claims on the Jews of integral Bulgaria, they were unrelenting on the issue of Jews in the occupied territories of Thrace and Macedonia.

By then, Berlin was pressing the matter directly. Adolf Eichmann, in the Reich Main Security Office, even offered to supply the Bulgarians with personnel to administer Jewish deportations. Once matters were finished in the territories, Eichmann assumed, the liquidation of Jews in integral Bulgaria would follow as a matter of course. Even then, the Sofia government hesitated. It was entirely aware of the connection the Germans were making. Ambassador Beckerle for his part divined with equal precision the source of Bulgarian misgivings. In a January 1943 dispatch to Berlin he noted: "Raised partly among Greeks, Armenians, Gypsies, and Turks, the average Bulgarian does not fathom the significance of the fight against the Jews, especially since he is not too concerned with racial issues." But in February, as the presence of German military units in Bulgaria became increasingly flagrant and intimidating, Prime Minister Filov offered Dannecker half a loaf. He agreed finally to deport the thirteen thousand captive Jews in Macedonia and Thrace. Indeed, upon ratifying this agreement, on March 2, the cabinet placated the Germans further with a promise that eight thousand Jews from integral Bulgaria would also be included later, specifically those of leadership status "who keep the Jewish spirit alive."

The first "territorial" deportations began the next day, March 3. Victims were forty-three hundred town and village Jews in occupied Thrace.

Dragged from their beds, they were hustled off to local tobacco ware-houses and locked in. Three days later, famished and frozen, the captives were transported to Drama on the old Greco-Bulgarian border and impris-oned in temporary compounds. Late in the month, the Jews who survived exposure and starvation were loaded again into freight cars and dis-patched to Lom, a village on the Danube. Here they were force-marched onto barges. In midstream the barges were deliberately capsized. Not a single prisoner survived. That same March, seventy-three hundred Jews in Yugoslav Macedonia, now in the Bulgarian zone, also were rounded up, packed onto freight trains, and carried off to makeshift holding pens in open fields. Several weeks later, this entire uprooted humanity was reloaded onto trains and transported directly to Treblinka in Poland. There they were gassed to the last soul. Another fifteen hundred Jews, in hiding throughout the countryside, perished of hunger and exposure. The liquidation was accomplished in near-total secrecy. Of the handful of government figures privy to the "relocations," only King Boris protested. Filov recorded the conversation in his diary entry of March 11:

> [The king] asked where [the Jews] were going and I said "to Poland." "This means that they are going to their deaths," he remarked. I answered that this was an exaggeration, that they would be used as a labor force, as we use them here. [The king's] reply was that the situations were not identical and that the Jews were being treated inhumanely.

Yet Boris did not prohibit the extermination.

Meanwhile, further to placate the Germans, Prime Minister Filov au-thorized Aleksandur Belev, the commissar for Jewish affairs, to complete arrangements for the promised deportation of eight thousand Jewish "un-desirables" from integral Bulgaria. Well beforehand, the lists had been prepared, the concentration camps earmarked, the railroad schedules ad-justed, the freight wagons collected. On March 9, 1943, the intended victims were gathered at predetermined sites. And then the unexpected occurred. After four days of terrified waiting, the assembled Jews were informed that deportation was being "postponed." Whereupon several hundred older people and women fainted dead away.

The facts behind the "March trauma" emerged only years later. At the end of February 1943, it appears that Minister of the Interior Grabovsky summoned to his office Chayim Bechar, a member of the Jewish Federa-tion. Venal even by Balkan standards, the minister now unblushingly offered to sell Bechar and his fellow Jews "valuable information" for the price of five thousand leva. Bechar wasted no time haggling. He rounded up the funds and paid the bribe. It was then that he learned of the impending disaster. Immediately Bechar alerted other Federation members, and with their approval he contacted the district governor, Lyuben Mitenov, and promised this official a one-million-leva "gift" for the latter's intercession with the cabinet. Mitenov agreed. Once the Jews raised the money—with much difficulty, given their parlous economic situation—Mitenov duly put them in touch with a "reachable" cabinet official, Nikla Zakhariev. It was Zakhariev, in turn, who revealed the content of the Belev-Dannecker agreement of February 22, with its focus on the Jews of the occupied territories rather than of integral Bulgaria.

Apprised of this crucial loophole, the Jewish leadership rushed to alert their Bulgarian liberal contacts. Several of these were members of Parliament. Within hours, the shocked legislators raised the issue of Jewish deportations in the assembly. Forty-two members of parliament actually signed a protest, warning that the deportation of Jews could gravely jeopardize Bulgaria's "future international relations." It was an unmistakable allusion to the likelihood of Allied retribution, at a time when the tide of battle was shifting against the Axis. Indeed, the British and American governments already had raised the prospect of war-crimes trials. On March 10, moreover, Archbishop Kiril of Plovdiv telegraphed the king that he, Kiril, was prepared to lie down on the railroad tracks in front of any trains carrying Jews off for extermination. Other members of the church synod issued similar warnings.

At long last, King Boris began to assert himself. On that same March 10, he held an extended discussion with Filov. The prime minister later noted in his diary: "I had an audience with the king from 4:30 P.M. to 6:30 P.M. We discussed primarily the Jewish question. His Majesty insists on a firm stand on this score." Boris now flatly rejected the notion of mass deportations from integral Bulgaria. So it was that the eight thousand "undesirables" were spared. At the end of the month, the king made a previously scheduled trip to Berlin. There evidently he reiterated his position, for Ribbentrop informed the German embassy in Sofia that "the king declared that he had given his consent for the deportation to eastern Europe of the Jews of Thrace and Macedonia only. . . . The balance of twenty-five thousand will be concentrated in camps inside Bulgaria, because they are needed for highway construction."

The threat to Bulgarian Jewry was far from over. It was indeed Filov's and Belev's intention to dispatch not less than twenty-five thousand Jews to the provinces for penal servitude; later, from these distant reaches, they might yet be secretly shipped on to German-occupied territory. In anticipation of the first "dispersals" on May 24, rolling stock actually was accumulated and new internment camps prepared. But on May 14 the Jewish community got wind of the impending horror. Nine days later, with only hours to spare, a private message reached King Boris from Bulgarian Chief Rabbi Daniel Tsion. The note implored the monarch to save his own soul, which was in mortal jeopardy. Although a learned Hebrew scholar, Tsion also shared much of the centuries-old Balkan susceptibility to mysticism. Some Jewish purists even suspected the chief rabbi of flirting with the popular mystical sect of Dunovism. If he did, that connection was their good fortune. King Boris, like his father, Ferdinand I, may himself have been a secret Dunovist. His mother, Euxodia, surely was, and so was the king's intimate adviser, Liubomir Lulchev. Moreover, Rabbi Tsion and a group of ten other Jews took the precaution of visiting and alerting the Bulgarian Orthodox primate, Metropolitan Stepan, who also gravitated toward a characteristically Eastern occultism. Profoundly shaken, Stepan in turn dispatched a personal letter to the king. In the style of Ecclesiastes, the prelate repeated the warning that Boris's immortal soul was at risk.

The intercession was at least partly effective. It was not possible to delay the scheduled relocation to the camps of some twenty thousand Jews. Yet as a consequence of urgent royal and clerical intercession, the government now dropped all plans for additional deportations to German-occupied territory. The king had sent down word through his adviser, Khanzhiev: "His Majesty . . . will do everything in his power to alleviate the lot of our compatriots of Jewish origin." Today, in Tel Aviv, Lily Avrahami still has vivid recollections of German tanks and troop-carriers rumbling by her suburban Sofia apartment, of German troops billeted in nearby farms and schools. But the Jews were not touched. By the summer of 1943, plainly losing the war, the Nazis also had lost their final leverage with the Bulgarian government.

On August 28, 1943, in the aftermath of a secret visit to Berlin, Boris III suddenly died. Two weeks earlier, according to Filov's diary, the king had been summoned by Hitler himself. Visibly suffering from depression, Boris had departed for the German capital in a Luftwaffe transport. He returned the next day after responding evasively to the Führer's request that Bulgaria enter the war. Then, on August 23, Boris experienced palpitations, and five days later he expired under mysterious circumstances. Rumors immediately circulated that the Germans had poisoned him. There was even speculation—rather farfetched—that he was murdered for his refusal to authorize mass Jewish deportations. Whatever the circumstances, Bulgarian Jewry mourned the king's death profoundly. Recalling his earlier, cordial relations with them, they regarded him as the man principally responsible for saving the largest numbers of their people.

In the autumn of 1943, the Allies launched a series of massive air raids over Sofia. Terrified, the government anticipated even more dire Allied retribution in the near future. The following April, therefore, it closed the two largest Jewish internment camps and allowed the prisoners to return home. Then, in the summer of 1944, as the Red Army drew nearer, an internal coup suddenly overthrew Filov and his pro-German cabinet. The new government thereupon rushed to enact a series of anti-Fascist measures. All remaining Jewish captives were set free. Their confiscated homes were returned to them, although most of their chattels had been pillaged. They were permitted also to return to their vocations, even though, again, their recent ordeal had left them penniless. Indeed, a substantial number of Jews did not return at all. Beyond the thirteen thousand victims in Macedonia and Thrace, as many as five thousand Jews of integral Bulgaria may have perished of mistreatment and deprivation. Nevertheless, the great majority of Jews, forty-five thousand, remained alive at war's end.

Surely a key factor in their survival was the absence of a deep-rooted antisemitic tradition in the nation at large. Ambassador Beckerle's evaluation was accurate. Racism, by and large, was alien to the Bulgarian mentality. Few citizens lifted a finger to help Jews—indeed, hardly any objected to the notion of occupying "disposed" Jewish homes and businesses—yet few also were prepared to cooperate actively in a program of extermination. Crucial, too, was the vigorous intervention of the Bulgarian Orthodox Church. And even more so, ironically, was Bulgaria's formal alliance with the Reich, in contrast to the subjugation experienced by other European peoples. Here the Nazis could lay their hands on Jews only through persuasion and diplomacy, not by force. And, in time-honored Balkan tradition, the Sofia government preferred to hedge its bets on the outcome of the war rather than commit an act of mass genocide and risk Allied retribution. As for King Boris, the Jews were rather too inclined to lavish gratitude on this archtemporizer and opportunist. Had there been no danger of retribution, it is possible, even likely, that the king would have collaborated in Jewish deportations, as he had in Thrace and Macedonia. Yet the myth of Boris as their savior remained intact among Bulgarian Jews, year in and year out, and with it the legend that the Nazis poisoned him, or deprived him of heart medications, or actually induced a fatal heart attack by engaging in dangerous aerial maneuvers during his return flight from Berlin.

In 1988 Kardam of Saxe-Coburg—grandson of King Boris and son of former King Simeon—who had been born and raised by his émigré parents in Madrid, paid a visit to Israel. A hydraulic engineer by profession, Kardam was interested in studying Israeli irrigation techniques. He arrived as a private person and alerted no one to his family background. But during his visit his identity somehow was discovered, and the Association of Bulgarian Immigrants insisted on mounting a reception for him. The affair was held in a pavilion of a Ramat Gan apartment complex, and some fifteen hundred guests arrived from every corner of Israel, many wearing Bulgarian folk costumes. Officials of the association presented their honored guest with bread and salt, intoned blessings on him in Bulgarian, Ladino, and Hebrew. Kardam spoke no Bulgarian or Hebrew, and understood only snatches of the remarks in Ladino. But when the guests lined up for the privilege of kissing his hand, he burst into tears, and continued weeping intermittently until the reception ended. "I wept, too," recalled Lily Avrahami drily, "but, believe me, it wasn't in memory of his grandfather."

A Sephardic Strand in South Slavia

During the Six-Day War in June 1967, urgent radio communication periodically was necessary between General Chaim Bar-Lev, Israel's deputy chief of general staff, and General David Elazar, commander of Israel's northern (Syrian) front. To save precious time, the two commanders spoke on open, uncoded radio frequencies. There was little chance of interception by enemy intelligence. Their language was Serbo-Croatian.

Elazar was born in 1925 into a comfortable mercantile family of Sarajevo. His forebears had settled in this picturesque Bosnian mountain town in the sixteenth century. With other Sephardic refugees, they discerned Sarajevo's potential as a way station on the east–west overland trade route from Constantinople and Salonika to the Adriatic. The city's oldest synagogue, Il Kal Grandi (The Great Congregation), dated back to 1581. Nearby, in the old Jewish quarter, a new synagogue, Il Kal Nuevo, was constructed soon afterward to accommodate an overflow of Sephardim from other parts of the Ottoman Empire. Each was constructed in the Islamic style of Moorish cupolas and filigree latticework. Almost half a millennium later, in 1930, when a modern synagogue was erected (also Il Kal Grandi) on the bank of the Miljacka River, its architects were careful to preserve the Near Eastern decor. Meanwhile, smaller Jewish communities gradually developed in other Bosnian-Herzegovinian towns, in Travnik, Banja Luka, Bijeljina, Mostar, Zenica, Tuzla.

Bringing with them their renowned skills as artisans and merchants, the Sephardim rapidly found their place amid Bosnia's heterogeneous population of Slavs, Turks, and Greeks. Here as elsewhere in the empire the local Turkish aga permitted them the fullest autonomy. Indeed, as a special mark of favor to this industrious people, the governor of Sarajevo allowed their women use of the Turkish *hammam* for ritual bathing purposes. Most Jews tended to congregate around their synagogues, but a number of wealthier families chose to live in Sarajevo's more affluent and prestigious neighborhoods. Some achieved even greater visibility. In the late nineteenth century—the era of *Tanzimat*, of Ottoman constitutional reform—Yaver Effendi Baruch was Bosnia's delegate to the imperial parliament. Isaac Effendi Shalom served on the governor's advisory council, and upon his death his place was taken by his son Solomon, who also sat in the Ottoman parliament. By 1908, the Jews of Sarajevo, secure and respected, had become a substantial community of seven thousand, 12 percent of the city's population. If most were not affluent by Western standards, they played a central role in Sarajevo's economy. Indeed, the city's commercial life slowed visibly on the Sabbath and Jewish holidays. Nor did a transformation of sovereignties erode the Jews' status. It happened that 1909 was the year of Austria's annexation of Bosnia-Herzegovina; and, together with their Moslem and Christian neighbors, the Jews suddenly found themselves citizens of the Habsburg Empire. They did not suffer thereby. Except for a series of bureaucratic restrictions on their communal autonomy, and an inflation that affected all inhabitants in common, no threat developed to their political or economic freedom.

There was a rough parallelism in the circumstances of Jews in neighboring Serbia. Here, too, their settlement was overwhelmingly Sephardic. As early as the seventeenth century, at least two thousand of their people had settled virtually en bloc in the Dorcal quarter of Belgrade. Several blocks square, the enclave consisted initially of three huge interconnected apartment buildings. The largest encompassed 103 rooms, 49 kitchens, 27 cellars, and a single enormous courtyard. Two adjacent smaller buildings were comparable Jewish beehives. However unprepossessing, this congested quarter became in effect the nerve center of Serbian international trade.

That classical entrepreneurial role survived even a radical political transformation. In 1803, the Serbs embarked upon a revolt that by midcentury achieved full independence. At the outset, to be sure, replacement of a benign (if corrupt) Turkish administration by a fulminantly nationalist successor regime proved an unsettling experience to the Jews. For several decades, they were subjected to intermittent restrictions on their choice of residence, and discriminatory taxes on their shops and offices. Yet these vexations gradually were eased. By the turn of the century, Jews enjoyed the fullest measure of political equality. On a day-to-day basis, too, their relations with non-Jews remained as equable as under the Turks. Their demography bespoke that underlying security. In 1830, the Jews in Serbia numbered two thousand; in 1894, five thousand; in 1912, seven thousand; in 1921, thirteen thousand.

As in Bosnia-Herzegovina, they clung tenaciously to their group identity. Here, too, they bore such proud family names as Altarac, Papo, Levi, Abinum, Albahary, Attias, Danon, Kabiljo, Kamhi, Maestro, Elazar. Upon their sons they bestowed such forthrightly Jewish first names as Avram, Isak, Jakov, Haim, Solomon, Isser, Aron, Samwil, Daniel. Until late in the nineteenth century, their language and literature remained overwhelmingly Ladino. Their children attended their own Alliance primary schools. It was not until World War I that Jewish parents, caught up in the fierce nationalism of their fellow citizens, consented at last to send their sons and daughters to Serbian secondary schools. On their own, Jewish youngsters in Sarajevo and Belgrade by then were lapsing increasingly into Serbo-Croatian for conversation. It was the language in which David Elazar was reared. When his mother died in his sixth year, he composed a childish poem to her memory in Serbo-Croatian.

In truth, Bosnian and Serbian Jews over the centuries had become quite fond of their fellow countrymen and grateful for their evident casual goodwill. For that matter, they learned more from their non-Jewish neighbors than Serbo-Croatian. From these hardworking, rather stoical Slavic workers and farmers, Jews imbibed an artless, straightforward patriotism. There was no question that they would do their duty in good times and bad. Thus, during the Balkan Wars of 1912–13, and the Great War of 1914–18, sixteen hundred Jews, virtually every able-bodied male among them, volunteered for the Serbian army. Of these, four hundred were killed, including three highly decorated brothers for whom Amar Brothers Street is named in Belgrade.

Yugoslav Pluralism, Jewish Nationalism

In 1937, when David Elazar was twelve, his father made the decision to send him to Zagreb, in Croatia, to study in that city's respected science gymnasium. It was then that the youngster began a lifelong friendship with another Jewish student, a local Ashkenazi boy, Chaim Bratizlavski, whose name subsequently would be hebraized to Bar-Lev. The relation-

ship in fact was less than characteristic of the arm's-length reserve functioning among other South Slav religioethnic elements—Serbs, Croats,
Slovenes, Dalmatians, Bosnians, Montenegrins. In 1918, all these communities were jerry-built into a makeshift nation, eventually to be known as
the Kingdom of Yugoslavia. Within that variegation of peoples, the Jews
alone, the perennially exposed minority, transcended regional and cultural divergences.

Those dissimilarities were not trivial. The minuscule Dalmatian Jewish
communities in Split and Dubrovnik (Ragusa) were largely of Sephardic
origin. With few exceptions, the Jews of Croatia, Slovenia, and Vojvodina
were German-speaking Ashkenazim, most of whom had arrived in the
eighteenth and nineteenth centuries from Habsburg Hungary. By 1918, it
was the latter who constituted three-fifths of Yugoslav Jewry. Disparities
in education and income compounded those of geographic origin. Ashkenazim, living in the northern, urbanized parts of the country, tended to
be more affluent and secular. Sephardim, concentrated in the under-
developed south, in Bosnia and Serbia, remained somewhat less prosperous, more tightly ethnocentric, even more pietistic. Yet they needed each
other. The Jews' entire critical mass in 1921 Yugoslavia did not exceed
71,000—17,000 in the Vojvodina, 13,000 in Bosnia-Herzegovina, 13,000 in
Serbia, 19,000 in Croatia, 7,000 in Macedonia, 2,000 in Dalmatia. The
sum total comprised less than one-half of 1 percent of Yugoslavia's eighteen million inhabitants.

The Jews' equality of status and communal freedom remained almost
fully intact in the early postwar years. Serbs and Bosnians had long
evinced friendship for "their" Jews, who had fought bravely in the Balkan
Wars and in World War I; and it was the Serbs who controlled the
Yugoslav government during the entirety of the interwar period. Indeed,
the royal household itself set the tone of cordiality; King Alexander I often
granted audiences to Jewish delegations and bestowed numerous decorations and honors on prominent Jews. As a matter of state policy, too, the
government provided subsidies for the nation's host of varied religious
and communal institutions. Among these were synagogues, Jewish
schools, and Jewish orphanages. Even rabbis received salaries from the
state. During religious holidays, Jewish children were excused from
school, Jewish civil servants from work, Jewish soldiers from military
duty.

Enjoying this civil and cultural latitude, Yugoslav Jewry would have
seemed unlikely material for a viable Zionist movement. Yet no other
Diaspora community, not excluding Bulgaria's or Salonika's, was ever
more passionately enmeshed in Zionist activism. For the Sephardim, here

as elsewhere in the Balkans, attachment to Zion remained a compulsion of essentially mystical significance, intimately related to the messianic upheavals of the sixteenth and seventeenth centuries. Even the movement's later transition to political nationalism was pioneered by a Bosnian rabbi, Yehuda Alkalai (1798–1878). Born in Sarajevo, Alkalai was called in 1825 to serve the tiny Sephardic community of Semlin (Zemun), near Belgrade. Not far away, the Greeks recently had won their war of independence. Others of the Balkan nationalities were beginning to stir. The idea of national freedom and restoration thus came easily to Alkalai's mind. So did the messianic influences he remembered of Jerusalem, where he had spent four years of his youth.

As early as 1834, therefore, in a Hebrew-language booklet *Sh'ma Yisrael* (Hear, O Israel), the Semlin rabbi invoked the ancient Jewish myth, well embroidered by the kabbalists, of the Messiah eventually conquering and restoring the Holy Land. The idea became rather more pragmatic for Alkalai in 1840 with the Damascus Blood Libel, the imprisonment of a dozen Syrian Jews on charges of ritual murder. Indeed, the episode convinced him that his people must look to a life exclusively of their own, secure in their own ancestral home. Driven by this obsession, the Semlin rabbi then embarked upon a succession of Hebrew booklets that developed his thesis of self-redemption. In the most important, *Minchat Yehuda* (The Offering of Judah), published in 1843, Alkalai contended:

> [A]s the initial stage in the redemption of our souls, we must cause at least twenty-two thousand [Jews] to return to the Holy Land. This is the necessary precondition for a descent of the Divine Presence among us; afterward, He will grant us and all Israel additional signs of His favor.

Much of Alkalai's appeal was directed to such Western Jewish notables as Sir Moses Montefiore, Lionel de Rothschild, and Adolphe Crémieux. Had he been able to secure appointments with these eminences, he might have won their sympathy, if not their active support. Fair-skinned, delicately featured, a man of gentle charm and rich erudition, Alkalai was esteemed by his constituency as were few other rabbis of his generation— and far beyond the borders of tiny Semlin. Even so, neither Montefiore, Rothschild, nor Crémieux was available to him, and Alkalai was obliged instead to resort to essay and letter. His proposal, admittedly, was not trivial. It was for these Jewish "grands seigneurs" to commit themselves to the actual "purchase" of the Holy Land from the Turks. Alkalai was nothing if not imaginative. One of his schemes was for a revival of the Great Sanhedrin, a body that in turn would establish a national fund to buy up land in Palestine, and also to issue a national loan. These were all ideas that anticipated those of Theodor Herzl. The Semlin rabbi also prefigured Herzl by journeying frequently to Western capitals to organize several Zionist circles. But their careers were brief. With his exertions seemingly in vain, then, Alkalai in 1878 finally ended his days in his beloved Jerusalem, convinced that he was a failure. His despondency was unwarranted. Simon Loeb Herzl, Theodor's grandfather, had become an admirer and disciple of Alkalai. David Alkalai, a lawyer, the rabbi's nephew (and son-in-law), was among the delegates to the First Zionist Congress in 1897, and later served as president of the Yugoslav Zionist Federation. In his novel *Altneuland* (1902), Theodor Herzl himself memorialized David Alkalai as the Sephardi activist Aladin.

Among Yugoslav Jews, the vision of a redeemed national homeland would remain imperishable. By the 1930s, in fact, Zionism had emerged as the single most powerful organized force in each of their communities, Sephardic or Ashkenazic, Bosnian, Serbian, or Croatian. The largest numbers of their children (David Elazar and Chaim Bar-Lev among them) belonged to the Shomer HaTzair Zionist youth movement. By then, the zeal of the movement was infused not simply with ideology but with a mounting survivalist anguish. The Croatian Peasant party and the Slovenian People's party were flirting with antisemitism as a feature of their anti-Serbianism. So was the Ustasha, a league of Croatian Fascists that operated mainly in exile in Italy, where it was subsidized by the Mussolini government. It was the Ustasha, in 1934, that hired and trained the Macedonian gunman who assassinated Yugoslavia's King Alexander I. To compound the factional xenophobia, Nazi Germany's vigorous campaign of economic imperialism was drawing Yugoslavia increasingly into the German trading orbit. In turn, genuflecting toward Berlin, the pro-Fascist government of Milan Stojadinovic felt obliged to support the German revisionist program in Europe—and, increasingly, to implement a program of domestic antisemitism. In September 1939, therefore, following the German invasion of Poland, Belgrade set about expelling Jewish children from the nation's secondary schools and simultaneously establishing a tight numerus clausus for Jews in Yugoslav business and professional life.

It was in the course of these developments, in 1937, that Shlomo Elazar, David's father, visited Palestine on business. Upon returning to Sarajevo, he discussed with friends the option of dispatching their children to the Zionist homeland. None demurred. Indeed, in Zagreb, Chaim Bar-Lev's sister was sent to Palestine in 1938, and a year later Chaim himself followed to complete his high school education at the Mikveh Israel Agricultural School. Other Jewish families now hurried to make their own arrangements. It was not a simple matter; the British mandatory administration in Palestine allocated a tight quota of immigration certificates. Although David Elazar was one of those to secure approval, in the spring of 1939, another year passed before all formalities could be completed. At last, in November 1940, the fifteen-year-old departed with a group of other selected teenagers. Shepherded by Jewish Agency representatives, they skirted the rim of Axis Europe, journeyed south by train via Bulgaria, Turkey, Syria, and Lebanon, and reached Palestine only in January 1941. After an additional six weeks' internment in a British holding compound, the youngsters finally were released to the Jewish Agency, which immediately placed them in several Shomer HaTzair kibbutzim. Neither David Elazar nor Chaim Bar-Lev would see his family again.

A Balkan Inferno

Cardak Hill, in the suburb of Pancevo, is the site of Belgrade's largest Jewish cemetery. Here stands a vast stone tablet honoring the four hundred thirty Jewish soldiers killed resisting the Germans in 1941. Nearby appears a second shrine, a pair of huge stone wings, crowned by a menorah and enclosing an altar. Jointly erected in 1962 by the government and the local Jewish community, it honors the civilian victims of Nazi genocide.

It was on March 27, 1941, that a Serbian general, Dusan Simovic, led a bloodless coup that overthrew Yugoslavia's pro-German cabinet. The deed was gallant but suicidal. A week and a half later, in a coordinated series of offensive thrusts, the German Wehrmacht struck at Serbia at the same moment the Italians attacked Dalmatia. Hungarian and Bulgarian troops then joined the invasion. Overwhelmed, the Yugoslav armed forces surrendered two weeks later. At Berlin's direction, the spoils were divided immediately. The Germans occupied Serbia, northern Slovenia, and the Banat. Hungary was allocated a portion of the Vojvodina, a territory Budapest had lost to Yugoslavia after World War I. Bulgaria, in turn, took over Yugoslav Macedonia (lost in the Balkan War of 1913), while Italy assumed responsibility for Dalmatia. The remainder of Yugoslavia, encompassing Croatia, Bosnia, and Herzegovina, was reconstituted as the Independent State of Croatia, a collaborationist regime directed by Ustasha Fascists and their prime minister, Ante Pavelic.

The fate of Serbian Jews under German rule was predictable. At the outset, they were ghettoized. In the weeks that followed, all of Serbia's eight hundred Jewish institutions—synagogues, schools, community offices—were pillaged and destroyed. Then, in July and August 1942, the SS rounded up four thousand Jewish males in Serbia and the Banat and transported them to penal compounds. In October, those who survived exposure and starvation were put to work digging mass graves. There they were shot and buried. Soon afterward, under the direction of a collaborationist Serbian general, Milan Nedic, six thousand Belgrade Jewish women and children were collected and dispatched to a concentration camp in Kakomco, near Semlin. During the winter and spring of 1943, they were asphyxiated in gas vans built over the exhaust pipes of captured Soviet tank engines. Another three thousand Jews, hiding in the countryside, evidently perished of debilitation. Serbia and northern Slovenia henceforth were essentially judenrein.

Still another Jewish war monument can be seen in a handsomely tended park in Monastir, in Slavic Macedonia. It commemorates civilians. Under Bulgarian occupation, seventy-three hundred Jews from Monastir, Skoplye, and other, smaller Macedonian towns were ghettoized, then shipped off in three massive truck convoys to Treblinka, where they were annihilated (p. 262). In the Hungarian-occupied regions of the Vojvodina, two thousand Jews were shot to death in January 1942. Over the next year and a half, nearly six thousand other Jews were mobilized into labor units and dispatched to Serbia's Bor copper mines, by then under Hungarian administration. Once the Germans assumed control of the Hungarian zone in March 1944, most of the survivors were deported to Auschwitz and the gas chambers.

The largest of Yugoslavia's public monuments, an immense stone statue, has been erected not to war victims but to a renowned public eminence, Moshe Pijade. It stands on Moshe Pijade Square, in the heart of Belgrade. Born in the city's Dorcol (Sephardic) quarter, Pijade began his career as an art teacher, then joined the outlawed Communist party in 1920. The following year he was briefly imprisoned for several months, released, then imprisoned again in 1925, this time for fourteen years. One of Pijade's cellmates was Josip Broz, later known as Tito. They became more than devoted friends and comrades. In future years, sharing dangers and the most intimate thoughts and plans, the two men became alter egos. Following the German conquest, Pijade helped Tito organize the Communist partisans and displayed great personal bravery in battle. In the postwar years, upon assuming power, Tito appointed Pijade to the dual role of president of the Serbian Republic and chairman of the Yugoslav National Assembly. When Pijade died in 1957, he became one of only five citizens to be buried in the Crypt of National Heroes. Altogether, the Jews here were a people who shared the military tenacity of their Yugoslav fellow citizens. Forty-five hundred Jews served in the partisan resistance, of whom one-third died in combat. Fourteen Jews achieved the rank of general. Eleven of these subsequently were designated National Heroes.

It was a tradition Yugoslav Jews carried with them. David Elazar in these same war years was spending his adolescence in a Palestinian kibbutz, Sha'ar HaAmah. Without parents, he was making his adjustment to a new land and language, to a Socialist society that was the antithesis of the patriarchal, conservative community of his boyhood in Sarajevo. But if the process was difficult, there was at least one activity in which he, and Chaim Bar-Lev, performed as impressively as did any native-born *sabra*. It was the rugged Zionist program of Haganah underground military training. In 1946, David Elazar left Sha'ar HaAmah to enlist in the underground's elite shock units. Here the muscular, square-jawed young Sarajevan found his métier. His ascent through the ranks was swift. Two years later, in Israel's War of Liberation, the twenty-three-year-old Elazar became deputy commander of the brigade charged with defending Jerusalem. In the bitterest period of the Arab siege, his courage and ingenuity defined his entire future military career. Almost without conscious volition, Elazar emerged as a professional soldier. "It never occurred to me then," he confessed long afterward, "that twenty-six years later I would still be in uniform."

Nineteen years later, in fact, during the 1967 Six-Day War, it was Elazar, as Israel's northern-front commander, whose divisions accomplished the virtually unimaginable feat of scaling the Golan Heights, a dragon's nest of powerful Syrian artillery emplacements, and capturing the entire fortress-region for Israel. A year later, Elazar's friend and comrade, Chaim Bar-Lev, then deputy chief of staff, was promoted to chief of staff. And four years later yet, Elazar himself would succeed Bar-Lev in the same role. The timing of the appointment proved ironic. It came only months before the outbreak of the Yom Kippur War in 1973. Elazar's intelligence branch was caught short in that conflict, and the heavy costs to Israel in manpower and equipment would oblige him later to resign his command. Yet during the actual period of battle it was characteristic of Elazar that he held fast under the weight of a massive Egyptian-Syrian offensive, preserved his army with fierce tenacity, then launched the counterattack that placed Israel's armies less than twenty-five miles from Damascus and ninety miles from Cairo.

Whether in the mountains of Yugoslavia or the deserts of Israel, these people asked only a chance to fight. In wartime Croatia and Bosnia-Herzegovina, the opportunity hardly existed. The Germans, upon first occupying these provinces in April 1941, marked their entrance into

Sarajevo by setting fire to the city's exquisite Kal Grandi synagogue. It was soon afterward that they turned over Sarajevo and the rest of Bosnia-Herzegovina to the "Free State of Croatia," Ante Pavelic's Ustasha regime. Throughout the breadth of this combined territory, then, Ustasha terror bands launched into one of the most frightful chapters of the war. Massacring Serbs by the tens of thousands, the Ustasha had resources and more to spare for the Jews.

In Sarajevo, during the summer of 1942, the Ustasha anti-Jewish campaign began initially as random shooting and rape. Then, in the autumn, Jews were herded into concentration camps at Jasenovac, Djakovo, and Alojzije. The Croatian guards at these compounds doubtless resolved the prisoners' fate less efficiently than in Nazi death camps, but they were more sadistic in the widespread use of torture. Father Bozidar Bralo, the Catholic priest representing the Croatian government in Sarajevo, replied to questioners: "Do not worry about the Jews. I saved their souls"—by having them baptized before their deaths. Other priests actually participated in concentration camp executions. These were the gruesome circumstances under which eleven thousand of Bosnia's thirteen thousand Jews died by the end of 1942. In integral Croatia, the somewhat more dispersed Ashkenazic Jewish community enjoyed a brief respite. Yet here, too, in January 1943, roundups began in Zagreb. By the spring, approximately two thousand Jews had expired in the infamous torture camp of Jasenovac. The majority of Croatia's Jewish population, some eleven thousand souls, were delivered over to the Germans and deported to Auschwitz for gassing.

Ultimately, through executions, starvation, exposure, as well as death in combat, fifty-seven thousand Yugoslav Jews perished in World War II, approximately 80 percent of the prewar population. Thirteen thousand Jews remained alive. In the early postwar years, at least half these survivors applied for departure to Israel. As Tito's closest associate, Moshe Pijade was the logical intermediary. Pijade in no sense nurtured any residual Jewish loyalties, yet he discerned a certain usefulness for Yugoslavia in establishing equable relations with Israel. The Tito government lately had broken with Moscow, and the Zionist nation was regarded as a possibly useful connection to the West. Through Pijade's intervention, then, Yugoslavia's Jews were allowed to leave freely during 1949–50. Between six and seven thousand remained. These were divided fairly evenly among Sarajevo, Belgrade, and Zagreb, and in almost the identical ethnic ratio as before the war: two-thirds Ashkenazim, one-third Sephardim. As in other ravaged Jewish communities, their postwar birthrate was low, their death rate high. In ensuing decades, their numbers stabilized at barely five thousand, with intermarriage the norm. Yet their physical circumstances at least appeared to be not uncomfortable. Even in Zagreb, with its inferno of wartime memories, the Jewish remnant played an important role in the economic and cultural life of the nation. Jews held secure positions as administrators, businessmen, professionals.

By contrast, their Jewish life remained as enfeebled as their demography. Belgrade's last rabbi died in 1969, and synagogue services were attended only by skeletal congregations. The Jewish Federation, itself partly funded by the American Joint Distribution Committee, maintained an old-age home and several rather decrepit Jewish libraries. It published a communal bulletin and sponsored a few lecture and other cultural programs. As much as any other factor, it was public goodwill that at least helped keep Yugoslav Jewry's élan flickering. From 1948 on, travel between Yugoslavia and Israel remained open and uninterrupted, even after the diplomatic rupture following the Six-Day War. With full government approval, too, the Jewish Federation in 1985 sent a team to participate in the Twelfth Maccabia in Israel, the only East European Jewish community to secure this permission. Two years later, Tel Aviv and Zagreb even initiated a twin-city relationship.

Approbation was not a matter of official policy alone. When monuments were dedicated to Jewish fighters and martyrs, it was significant that religious and veterans delegations invariably were present, together with government representatives. The four-hundredth-anniversary celebration of Jewish settlement in Bosnia-Herzegovina was entirely characteristic of this widely diffused public benevolence. Assembled for the event in 1984 was an extensive array of foreign and local Jewish spokesmen. Their presence was matched, even outshone, by non-Jewish dignitaries. The mayor of Sarajevo, Salki Lagundjia, was a Moslem. Dedicating the city's new Jewish museum, Lagundjia lavished praise on his Jewish fellow citizens and dwelt at length on their illustrious contributions to Bosnian economic and cultural life. Music and dance programs then were presented, with performances by the Sarajevo Opera and Philharmonic Orchestra. The climax of the week's festivities was at the old Jewish cemetery. From early morning, thousands of visitors—Jews, Christians, Moslems—poured into the site. Numerous speeches and benedictions followed. Government and veterans groups laid wreaths at the foot of the Monument to the Martyrs. As long as the Yugoslav Federation itself survived, and with it that venerable paradigm of multiculturalism, Sarajevo itself, these people somehow remained locked together in a fellowship of honor. A bittersweet interregnum, it was also a proleptic valedictory.

CHAPTER XIII

A CALVINIST JERUSALEM

The Jews of Mercantilism

In 1556, Felipe II succeeded his father, Charles V, as ruler of the Spanish Empire. Intensely pious, the young monarch was committed to religious homogeneity as a tenet of both moral and political certitude. The principle in fact was tested within a decade of his accession, as Felipe confronted a suppurating epidemic of imperial unrest. The focus of the infection was the northern, Dutch-speaking provinces of the Spanish Netherlands. Protestantism was taking root there. The heresy was by no means confined to the region's burgeoning middle class of industrialists, merchants, and agricultural magnates. Incited by their Calvinist preachers, simple townsfolk and country-dwellers now also launched into a frenzy of violence. Attacking Catholic churches, they smashed images and altars, then enlisted in their thousands for militia-service to resist government retaliation. Eventually Felipe was obliged to accept the challenge head-on. In 1568 he dispatched a powerful military force to the Lowlands under the command of his ablest general, the duke of Alba. Alba's vengeance was harsh. Over the next four years, his troops laid waste to a broad swath of Dutch towns and villages, executing thousands of men, women, and children alike.

Here it was that Prince Willem of Orange, wealthiest and best equipped of the Netherlands' *statthalters*—provincial barons—set about organizing an army and navy for the territory. His efforts were almost immediately successful. Indeed, the makeshift Dutch navy proved a devastating surprise to the Spaniards. Functioning as a hodgepodge of shallow-draft privateers, these "Sea Beggars" by 1573 managed to carve out a sizable enclave for themselves along the Scheldt River. Success generated a self-sustaining momentum. Even as Alba's troops continued their implacable massacre of civilians, decimating the residents of Zutphen, Malines, Haarlem, and other towns, the Dutch were consumed by a messianic delirium of religiopatriotism. In their ferocity and self-sacrifice, they opened their homeland's dikes, inundating their own farmlands and homesteads to force a Spanish withdrawal before the onrush of floodwaters. At this point, sensing that the battle was moving their way, the statthalters of Friesland and Zeeland united under Prince Willem's leadership, pledging their material and military resources to the common cause. Willem in turn felt sufficiently emboldened to shift his strength to the Catholic south, even to threaten an offensive into Flanders.

Seeing the handwriting on the wall, King Felipe signaled his willingness to accept a compromise. The agreement, reached in November 1573, was to be known as the Pacification of Ghent. By its terms, the Dutch provinces remained under the nominal sovereignty of the Habsburg Crown but were free henceforth to determine their own religion. In the event, the agreement was honored more in the breach than in the observance. Skirmishes and pitched battles continued to break out intermittently. But thirty-six years later, in 1609, still another negotiated armistice granted the Dutch Netherlands equal trading privileges with the Spanish Empire overseas. For all practical purposes, then, the rebels were launched as an independent state among other European states. Indeed, as far back as 1579, under the Union of Utrecht, the Dutch had formally proclaimed their nation an autonomous confederation, the United Provinces.

It was significant that Article XIII of the proclamation declared that no inhabitant of the realm was to be persecuted for religious reasons. With vivid memories of the Catholic oppression that had driven them to revolt, provincial statthalters manifestly had in mind freedom for Protestants of all persuasions. It is unlikely that Jews so much as entered their thoughts. Yet not far away, in Antwerp, queen city of the southern, Catholic Netherlands, there existed an enclave of conversos. By the sixteenth century, this mighty Belgian port, the largest in Western Europe, was fulfilling a vital role for the Spanish Empire as its principal entrepôt for international trade. Accordingly, as many as a thousand New Christian merchants already were living there. The most eminent of these, of course, was Diogo Mendes, who operated the local branch of the great import-export house established by his family in Lisbon.

Mendes and a great many of his fellow New Christians were marranos. Indeed, their judaizing was so thinly disguised that Felipe II later complained of conversos actually gathering in their synagogues and observing their rites publicly. "There they perform these ceremonies very boldly," he insisted, "and . . . [are] making a mockery of our Holy Catholic Faith and observances." In 1549, still during the reign of Charles V, the government had moved to expel those conversos who had recently arrived from Spain and Portugal. Only New Christians who had lived in Antwerp at least five years were permitted to remain. And, at the same time, the inquisitional campaign against suspected judaizers gained momentum. By the 1570s, in Felipe's time, even the residual group of "veterans" felt impelled to look increasingly toward Amsterdam. It was a logical focus. The Dutch Provinces had won their de facto independence. More important, Amsterdam was beginning to forge ahead of Antwerp as a thriving port city. Thus far, some nineteen thousand Protestants had departed Antwerp for the north.

Whether traveling from Antwerp, however, or directly from Portugal and Spain, the conversos who joined the migration to Amsterdam tended at first to settle in rather cautiously. Often they maintained the façade of professing Christians, even disguised their names. Their concern actually was less for the Protestant Dutch than for the safety of families and business associates they had left behind under Spanish rule. None dared be identified. Thus, from the outset, Rabbi Menasseh ben Israel operated his printing press in Amsterdam under his original family name of Manuel Dias Soeiro; Joshua Habilo ran his business as Duarte Fernandes; Joseph de la Vega, as Joseph Penso Felix *alias* Alvaro Felix *alias* Philiberto Fortunato *alias* Alvaro Bommelman. Francisco Rodrigues Gutierres and Antonio Gutierres Gómes carried on their businesses under no fewer than fifteen different names. These precautions notwithstanding, the disguises intermittently were penetrated by Habsburg informers, some of them doubling as commercial agents. Instances of retribution against Spanish and Portuguese New Christians were by no means rare.

Among the Dutch, however, dissemblement soon proved gratuitous. In 1598, a dozen or so conversos were arrested on suspicion of engaging in Catholic religious services. The day was Yom Kippur. Fortunately, one of the members, Jacob Tirado (né Manuel Rodrigues Vega), could express himself in Latin. He made clear that the gathering was not one of papists but of worshippers whose suffering under the Inquisition exceeded even that of Protestants. Upon acknowledging that he and his fellow worshippers were Jews, Tirado then took the initiative: he described the likely commercial advantages to the Dutch Netherlands if his people were encouraged to settle there. It was a compelling argument. The prisoners were released to complete their Yom Kippur services, and in ensuing months the physical security of Amsterdam's Jewish refugees no longer was called into question. On occasion, local merchants protested Jewish trading privileges. Yet the Calvinist Dutch by and large were uninterested in harassing non-Catholics. In 1607, under Jacob Tirado's auspices, a group of Jews ventured to organize a congregation in rented facilities, even to engage a rabbi from Venice. In later years, as the little Jewish settlement continued to grow, it began establishing other tiny congregations.

From the outset, however, economic inducements drew the Sephardim to Amsterdam far more than religious ones. Throughout the 1590s, the Dutch tightened their control over the outlet of the Rhine, Europe's largest inland transportation route. At the same time, Amsterdam's emerging reputation as a deep-draft harbor accelerated the shift in continental traffic outward from the Mediterranean to the vast new Atlantic frontier. These logistical advantages were further enhanced by Protestant literacy and Dutch capitalistic aggressiveness. By the seventeenth century, as a result, the Netherlands was all but exploding with energy and enterprise. Its dockyards were building a thousand new ships a year and transforming the nation into the world's single largest maritime carrier. Pouring into Amsterdam, too, was the wealth of the continent and overseas empires, from Baltic grain and timber to Middle Eastern fruits and silks. The great city already outstripped Hamburg, Antwerp, even London, as Europe's principal emporium for spices, sugar, and most of the products of the West and East Indies.

It was ironic that the largest quantities of these imports, except for grain and timber, actually came from Holland's perennial enemies, the Spanish and Portuguese. Cargos were imported almost entirely on Dutch ships, which loaded at Iberian ports in greater numbers than the vessels of any other nation. Indeed, by the early 1600s, Holland virtually monopolized the carrying trade between the Iberian Peninsula and Northern Europe. Here, then, Jews had a unique role to play. The pragmatic, acquisitive Dutch needed no reminder that Spain's and Portugal's international commerce was overwhelmingly conducted by New Christians, who transacted their import-export business in other lands with fellow conversos. Thus, even as Dutch shippers widened their own access to the Iberian imperial trade, they found in the Sephardim a group capable of serving them in an identical mercantile role.

The Jews more than fulfilled that expectation. Even earlier, in Spain and Portugal, New Christians had developed the commercial land route over the Pyrenees, linking Madrid to Bayonne. From Bayonne, Dutch vessels chartered by other conversos transported silver and merino wool to Holland. Once reaching Amsterdam, these products in turn were taken in hand by still additional Sephardic importers, who purchased the merchandise outright or exchanged it for locally produced cloth or for spices imported by their fellow Sephardim from the East Indies. The multifaceted commerce burgeoned out more dramatically yet after the signing of the Treaty of Münster in 1648, when Spain and the Dutch Republic formally and officially terminated their state of war. By midcentury, the trading network operating among the Jews of Holland and their converso kinsmen in Portugal and Spain throbbed with a vitality unprecedented since the heyday of the Italian city-states.

The Jews of Calvinism

Could the Jews have found life tolerable even among the Protestant Dutch? The Netherlands was still a Christian nation, after all, presumably with its own traditions of anti-Jewish suspicion. An answer of sorts may be found at Amsterdam's Museum Het Rembrandthuis. In this building, from 1639 to 1658, Rembrandt van Rijn made his home, using the ground floor as his lodgings, the sunlit upper floor as his studio. The address, Joodenbreestraat 4 (Jewish Quarter Street 4), places the house directly on the edge of the city's old Jewish section. Here Rembrandt came to know many of his Jewish neighbors. Two of these, Ephraim Hezekiah Bueno and Menasseh ben Israel, became his friends and models for his portraits. Some two dozen other local Jews, a number of them old and bearded, similarly appear in the great man's etchings and paintings. He portrayed them in the street, in their homes, in their synagogues, at work, at prayer, at ritual ceremonies, at leisure. He also reproduced their features in his paintings of biblical patriarchs. None is demonized.

Nor was Rembrandt's pluralism a special case. Amsterdam's Jewish quarter was hardly a ghetto. No walls or gates confined its inhabitants. No Jew was obliged to wear a badge. To be sure, Jews were not yet objects of warm benevolence. The *Classis*—the Council of the Dutch Reformed Church—had opposed their initial admission. In resisting the later enlargement of their civic privileges, the church *predikanten* not infrequently indulged in crude antisemitism. Yet it was the same Calvinist clergy who unwittingly helped lay the psychological groundwork for Jewish toleration. The Dutch had inherited the Renaissance fascination with the classics, including the Hebrew language. Moreover, that passion was religion-based to a far greater extent than in the Italy of the quattrocento.

Scriptural exhortation was the common idiom of all Calvinist culture. Disdaining ritual and clerical intercession, Calvinists and other radical reformers engaged in endless reading and exegesis of the Old Testament, a text that functioned as a sourcebook of current history, its every chapter offering an analogue to contemporary events. Simon Schama, in his majestic account of seventeenth-century Dutch culture, *The Embarrass-*

ment of Riches (1987), has unforgettably described the "cascade of rhetoric" crashing down from the pulpit each Sunday morning, invoking the destiny of the Hebrews as though the congregation were itself a tribe of Israel. In the *credenda* of the Reformed Church, the United Provinces were the new Zion, and Willem of Orange was an anointed captain of Judah. The war against the Spanish enemy was the struggle of the ancient Hebrews against the Philistines, Amalekites, and Midianites. Like the Children of Israel, the Dutch had entered into a covenant with the Lord. The sacred Gedenck-Klanck, the oath of loyalty to the Republic, palpably reflects this sense of a special relationship:

> O Lord . . . even as You led the Children of Israel from their Babylonian Captivity, the waters receded before us and You brought us across dry-shod even as the people of antiquity, with Moses and Joshua, were brought to their Promised Land. . . . You have not held the sins of Your people against them but have emancipated us from the thrall of the Moabites.

In Italy, the Renaissance humanists had offered prefigurations of this Bible-centeredness in their depictions of patriarchs, kings, and a host of other major and minor characters. But it was the Hollanders who gave that Renaissance pageantry a uniquely filiopietistic treatment. Abraham de Koning's portraits of *Esther* (1618) and *Samson* (1619) made transparent allusions to the fortunes of ancient Zion and the Calvinist new Israel. Jacob Revius's play *Haman, A Tragedy* (1630), Nicolas Foneyn's *Esther, or the Picture of Obedience* (1638), Johannes Serwouter's *Esther, or the Deliverance of the Jews* (1659)—all drew analogies between the scheming iniquity of a bloodthirsty counselor (Haman/duke of Alba) and the vindication of a blameless patriotic hero (Mordecai/Willem of Orange). Jerusalem, too, appeared endlessly in these scriptural parallelisms as a Hebrew Leiden or Amsterdam.

As for the approximately fifteen hundred Jews then living in early-seventeenth-century Holland, the Dutch Christian attitude toward them was one of mild toleration. Indeed, Jews were almost routinely absorbed into the standard modes of Dutch culture. Johann Leusden's and Jan Luiken's engravings of Jewish circumcision rites, Passover celebrations, or mourning receptions contained no forbidding overtones of sinister practice. In popular references, Jewish customs no longer were envisaged as antitheses to the Christian mysteries, or the synagogue as an incarnation of the "false church." In this essentially casual atmosphere, Jews little by little made their way into seventeenth-century Amsterdam.

Their unremarked status was given its first "official" evaluation only in

1615. They had petitioned to construct synagogues for public prayer. Almost at the same time, as it happened, a quarrel had arisen between two factions of the Dutch Reformed Church, the Remonstrants and the Counter-Remonstrants. The former had complained to the States General that the Jews, who denied Jesus, already enjoyed more freedom than did they, "decent" Christians. The dilemma was an awkward one for the provincial aristocrats. To resolve it, they appointed a special commission on the issue of Jewish privileges. Its chairman and presiding eminence was none other than the renowned international jurist Hugo Grotius. With characteristic scholarly thoroughness, Grotius promptly launched into a study of the Jewish religion, even of the Hebrew language, invoking the help of both Christian Hebraists and several Jewish writers. After five months of painstaking research and discussion, Grotius and his colleagues finally submitted their *Remonstrantie* in the autumn of 1615.

The report suggested that the States General, in effect, were presented with three alternatives: to compel the Jews to adopt Christianity; to allow them to practice no religion whatever; or to tolerate Judaism. The first option was morally repugnant for a nation that owed its very existence to the struggle for religious freedom. The second option, atheism, was far worse than Judaism. Toleration, then, was the only valid approach. The reasons were principally humanitarian. Here Grotius cited the medieval expulsions of Jews, the blood libels against them, and contrasted these atrocities with the humanity demanded by the Reformed Church for all mankind. In the spirit of that reverential scripturalism, the *Remonstrantie* added:

> With respect to the Jews, there are special considerations that are not applicable to other non-Christians. They are the children of Abraham, Isaac, and Jacob, the Israelites who . . . are to partake of the glory, the covenants, the laws, the religion, and the promises; theirs are the forefathers from whom Christ Himself descended in the flesh. . . . As the Apostle says, they should be our enemies as regards the Gospel, but beloved for the sake of the forefathers, who are especially chosen of God.

In Grotius's view, these theological considerations transcended economic ones as a basis for extending religious freedom to the Jews.

Yet even the *Remonstrantie* suggested a number of constraints on toleration. They included a limitation of Jewish numbers to one hundred families in any one city, a Jewish obligation still to attend an annual Christian sermon, a ban on intermarriage between the two faiths, and a restriction of Jews to wholesale commerce and a limited number of retail trades and crafts. Finally, in an intriguing caveat that later would exert much influence on Jewish religiocommunal life (p. 292), Grotius recommended that the Jews themselves be compelled to adhere closely to their own faith.

The *Remonstrantie* essentially determined national policy. Persuaded by its arguments, the States General now left the matter for individual provinces and municipalities to decide, and virtually every one of these accepted most of the proposals. On the one hand, limits were imposed on the number of Jews in retail trades. Jews were admitted to citizenship only "insofar as they are merchants of importance." Jews were forbidden to marry with "daughters of the land," or to blaspheme against God or Christianity. Yet, on balance, these constraints were modest. Jews were spared conversionary sermons. They were free to live where they chose, to develop their own religious and communal institutions. Indeed, for its time the legislation represented the single most far-reaching step toward Jewish emancipation ever taken in the Christian world. Soon, the Esnoga, the Great Synagogue of Amsterdam, became well established, even something of a tourist attraction. In 1639, royal guides conducted Queen Mother Marie de Médicis of France through the building. Three years later, the congregation was honored with a formal visit by Frederick Hendrick, statthalter-in-chief of the Netherlands, who was accompanied by Queen Henrietta Maria, consort of Charles I of England. If Amsterdam was emerging as a new center of European prosperity, so now was that city's comfortably ensconced Jewish minority.

The Wages of Prosperity

As the Dutch people luxuriated in their seventeenth-century affluence, they had little doubt that the unrestrained play of talents offered the key to their economic dominance. In 1650, during his exile in Holland, a persecuted English "Leveller," William Walwyn, enviously described the freedom of political expression he encountered among this highly literate population. Even the most controversial issues were discussed in pamphlets and debated publicly, he noted. Walwyn was particularly impressed that toleration was extended to Jews and atheists. "It is more than evident by the prosperity of our neighbors in Holland," he wrote, "that the severall wayes of our brethren in matters of religion hinder not, but that they may live peaceably one amongst another . . . unite sufficiently in the defense of their common liberties and opposition of their common enemies. . . ."

For several years even following Grotius's *Remonstrantie*, Jews remained excluded from a number of guilds, banned from office or from voting in municipal elections. Nevertheless, their preeminence in the burgeoning Spanish-Portuguese trade had become so palpable that the States General was now eager to foster their business activities. Thus, in 1657, the legislative body proclaimed to the world that Dutch Jews traveling abroad for business must be regarded and treated as citizens of the United Provinces. In 1680, it instructed its consuls to protect the safety and security of Dutch Jews as forcefully as those of Dutch Christians.

It was an unprecedented mantle of diplomatic solicitude, and the Jews were not slow in exploiting it. Descriptions of Amsterdam harbor in the early seventeenth century provide an insight. Virtually every month, arriving vessels unloaded scores of conversos from Spain and Portugal. As the inquisitional terror intensified, entire arriving shiploads of fugitives were not unheard of. By 1617, some one hundred marrano families had settled in Amsterdam. By midcentury, the Jewish community totaled four hundred families—perhaps seventeen hundred souls in all. By the end of the century, the Sephardic population would reach three thousand, with an additional three thousand Ashkenazic Jews, most of them refugees from the Ukraine. If these numbers were not large by the standards of Salonika or even Venice, the economic influence of Amsterdam Jewry was unprecedented in all of Jewish history until then. That apotheosis of course reflected the diversion of international trade beyond the older Mediterranean sea-lanes to the wider oceans, and specifically the Netherlands' burgeoning new commerce with the Spanish and Portuguese empires. So it was, in the Sephardic world, that primacy shifted from Venice, City of Lagoons, to Amsterdam, City of Canals. Dutch Jewish trade with the Spanish Indies may have remained exclusively in the hands of conversos. Portugal would not countenance foreign, professing Jewish traders in its overseas empire until 1640, when it regained its independence from Spain. But under whichever identification, New Christian or professing Jewish, the Sephardim of Amsterdam emerged as senior figures in the Netherlands' commercial network.

As much as any factor, it was the imperial sugar trade that accounted for that economic vitality. Raw sugar arrived in Holland from Brazil via the Dutch West India Company. There it was refined and sold as a finished product elsewhere in Europe. No industry in the Netherlands was quite as profitable. Nor was any group of businessmen involved in it quite as extensively as the Jews. Indeed, Amsterdam's first sugar refinery was established in 1665 by Abraham and Isaac Pereira. Other early refiners included Solomon and Isaac del Pina, Isaac Mocado, Abraham Davega, David d'Aguilar, and perhaps a score of middle-sized entrepreneurs. They marketed the finished product in Germany, Scandinavia, England,

France. Other Jews, meanwhile, wasted little time developing additional New World resources. It was conversos in Brazil and the West Indies who were the first to ship tobacco leaves back to Europe. In Amsterdam, their kinsmen moved with alacrity to establish their own tobacco-spinning plants. Importing, spinning, distributing, Jews soon dominated the Dutch tobacco market as thoroughly as they controlled the sugar trade. They maintained that eminence until late in the seventeenth century.

By the eighteenth century, too, the exploitation of Brazilian mines had dramatically opened up the supply of gems. In 1728, when Portuguese sailors first brought their stones to Amsterdam, Sephardic merchants were waiting to negotiate with them in their own language. Afterward, these entrepreneurs wasted little time mastering the art of stonecutting and polishing, not to mention brokering and marketing. Throughout the mid-1700s, approximately six hundred Jewish families earned their livelihood from the diamond trade, ensuring Amsterdam's status as the gem capital of Europe. "The Jews are necessarily in the most lucrative transactions in the precious stone business," noted a Dutch author. "It appears as if they control the market." They did. They also established Amsterdam's first silk mills in Antwerp, dominating the field until the early eighteenth century.

The publishing industry was by no means a Jewish monopoly in the Netherlands. In a literate, Protestant country, some thirty thousand Dutchmen were employed in this vocation, manufacturing more books than were produced by all other European nations combined. Yet, early on, Jews developed a powerful printing industry there and, by the mid-1600s, their community surpassed even Venice as the world center of Hebrew publishing. By then, too, Jewish printers were turning out works, mostly Bibles, in four languages: Dutch, Portuguese, Spanish, and English. "For several years I have myself printed more than a million Bibles for England and Scotland," proudly declared Joseph Athias, in an introduction to an edition of the Scriptures he issued in 1687. "There is no plowboy or servant girl there without one." So elegant was the quality of Athias's work that the States General honored him with a gold chain for issuing "the most correct and exact edition of the Bible that has ever been published." By the end of the seventeenth century, over three hundred Jewish printers were plying their craft in Amsterdam, and a fourth of these were producing books for the general market.

In their prosperity, Jews shared with other businessmen the need for investment of surplus capital. Yet here they were only peripherally involved in the money trade. Holland in the thriving 1600s was entirely capable of supplying its own bankers; as non-Catholics, its citizenry faced no doctrinal injunctions against moneylending. Thus, for Jewish venture capitalists, the great overseas trading corporations seemed likelier outlets. Indeed, Jews soon formed a substantial minority bloc of shareholders in the Dutch West and East India companies. Their presence was equally noteworthy in the fledgling Amsterdam stock exchange. The guild of stockbrokers, by chance, was one of the few trade associations open to Jews, provided they limited their transactions to other Jews. The qualification was no impediment. By 1657, of four hundred thirty brokers on the exchange, fifty were Jews; and their Jewish clients traded vigorously in the booming shares market. It is uncertain that Jews proved more astute as financiers than did the canny, acquisitive Dutch. But with their network of Sephardic connections, they were unexcelled in their grasp of international finance. As early as 1618, a French diplomat in Amsterdam remarked on "the cleverness, commercial energy, and communal solidarity of the Jews":

> [T]hey acquire their information from the other Jewish communities . . . with which they are in close contact—[with] Venice . . . [with] Salonica . . . with the secret [marrano] communities of England and France. In this fashion, the Jews in Amsterdam are the best informed about foreign commerce and news of all people in the world.

As in virtually every other area of their Diaspora, too, the Sephardim of Amsterdam produced more than their share of physicians. It was not rare to encounter entire families of doctors, as in the Pharer family (father and two sons) or the Bueno family (grandfather, two sons, six grandsons). Excluded they may have been from the guilds of surgeons and pharmacists, but Jews were entirely free to practice among their own Jewish community. And soon they managed to ignore guild constraints altogether. In 1625, Joseph Bueno was summoned to the sickbed of the Statthalter, Prince Maurits of Nassau.

By midcentury, then, the Jewish presence in the Netherlands transcended visibility and approached eminence. Sephardic millionaires, among them such renowned mercantile families as the Pereiras, the Pintos, and the Barrios—all marranos before settling in Amsterdam—entertained in grand style, became intimates of Dutch aristocrats and other non-Jewish notables. It is of interest that several of these personages were not citizens of the United Provinces. Thus, the brothers Samuel and Joseph Pallache, serving as diplomatic envoys from Morocco, attached themselves so permanently to Amsterdam society over the years that their origins became irrelevant. Moreover, the brothers' role in negotiating trade agreements between Holland and Morocco proved of such extraordinary benefit to both countries that they soon became favorites of the Dutch government. Upon Samuel's death, Prince Maurits marched behind the bier at his funeral. In later years David Mesquita, Chaim Toledano, and David Schalom d'Azevedo successively represented Morocco in the Netherlands, and also became semipermanent fixtures in the Dutch Jerusalem. So did Louis and Henrico d'Azevedo later yet, and Isaac Sasportas and David Torres, who negotiated trade agreements in Holland on behalf of Algeria. But whether Dutch or merely "resident" Sephardim, these affluent Jews observed social customs virtually identical to those of the wealthiest Christian patricians. They entertained lavishly, dressed in expensive silks and satins, devoted much time to plotting matrimonial alliances, just as in the best aristocratic circles.

Plainly, the largest numbers of Dutch Sephardim were neither eminent capitalists nor distinguished professionals. Most were small merchants and artisan-shopkeepers—tobacconists, gold- and silversmiths, tailors, fishmongers, vintners, greengrocers. Nevertheless, by the standards of the time, the little people did well. Their economic influence mattered. In 1653, a telling clue was the Dutch government's reaction upon learning that Rabbi Menasseh ben Israel was campaigning for admission of the Jews into England (p. 314). The Hague then sent out queries to ensure that a mass Jewish exodus from Amsterdam was not imminent. For all its lingering restrictions against Jews, the United Provinces had learned to value this talented minority.

The Inner Sanctum

Today, Amsterdam's Visserplein tract is a rather drab collection of modest shops and aging houses. Yet in its former Joodenbreestraat enclave the Joods Historisch Museum evokes a rich past. The structure is a reincarnation of four once-thriving synagogues. In 1607, we recall, the tiny nucleus of Sephardic newcomers conducted its religious services privately, at the home of Jacob Tirado (who thereupon dubbed his congregation Beth Ja'acob—Casa de Jacobo). A year later, still another arriving group of conversos resumed its identity as Congregation Neve Shalom. In 1638, both congregations united in the Esnoga, the Great Synagogue. By 1675, after further additions, it would become the largest Jewish house of worship in all Europe. Indeed, the Esnoga later served as a model for the synagogue in London's Bevis Marks, as well as for eighteenth-century synagogues erected in Curaçao and in Newport, Rhode Island.

From the outside, the Esnoga seems hardly more than a cube of functional rust-colored brick with windows. It springs to life within, its sanctuary embodying a graceful amalgam of styles. The walls are emblazoned in dark Italian wood. Rows of huge cylindrical stone columns line the three principal aisles, while twelve smaller columns (symbolizing the Twelve Tribes of Israel) demark the women's galleries in the side aisles. Windows are square. Hanging lamps emerge from plaster sunflower medallions in the ceiling. The Ark, containing no less than fifty Torah scrolls, vaguely recalls the functional stepped gables of Amsterdam's canal-side houses. By contrast, the pews are decorated with Gobelin tapestries—nearly a thousand of them. The sheer amplitude, multiformity, and extravagance of this mighty synagogue fittingly evoke a community that in its turn once briefly evoked awe as the jewel of the Diaspora.

So it was, on the banks of the Amstel, along the Joodenbreestraat, that a kind of miniature Lisbon or Madrid arose, with Portuguese and Spanish the tongues of official and private discourse. Nowhere in the world was religioethnic vitality more evident than in the Joodenbreestraat's extensive network of synagogues, schools, and communal offices. Its talmud torah—secondary school—was renowned for the scope of its curriculum and quality of its teaching. Its largest talmudic academy, established by the munificent Pinto family, ordained more rabbis than did any seminary in Western Europe. The literature turned out by Amsterdam Jewry's unsurpassed printing presses, whether in Dutch, Portuguese, Spanish, English, or Hebrew, included liturgical material for virtually every Sephardic community in existence.

From the outset, too, the States General granted Jews their traditional prerogative of communal autonomy. Such religious matters as marriage, divorce, and burial continued as always under rabbinical jurisdiction. As elsewhere in the Diaspora, civil cases among Jews were submitted exclusively to Jewish courts. Indeed, the authority exercised by rabbis and *parnassim*—lay presidents—was virtually omnicompetent. Any Jew presumptuous enough to challenge their jurisdiction risked a severe fine, or even the cherem, the dreaded ban of excommunication, and these penalties were enforced by the state itself. In their uncompromising obdurateness, too, rabbis and parnassim evinced more than a little of the inquisitional spirit of their former Spanish and Portuguese homelands.

Neither officiousness nor fanaticism alone impelled this rigidity. The Jews were fighting to save their very identity. The earliest conversos, arriving in the Netherlands at the end of the sixteenth century, normally lacked even the faintest recollections of their ancestral religion. Those who resumed their Jewish allegiances now often did so with considerable uncertainty and lack of enthusiasm. A minority of immigrant conversos actually opted to reemigrate to Portugal and Spain, to the "lands of idolatry," in the rabbis' withering description. Of the defectors, a small number later returned yet again to Amsterdam, essentially for mercantile purposes. The Inquisitors of Jewish Amsterdam took a harsh view of these *relapso* opportunists, as it happened, and in 1644 felt obliged to issue an injunction, declaring

> [that] from this day onwards, a circumcised Jew who shall abandon Judaism and go to any land belonging to Spain and Portugal . . . if he shall return to this Holy Congregation, he shall not be received in it . . . without beforehand, from the altar, publicly, before the whole congregation, begging for forgiveness from the blessed Lord and His holy Torah. . . . And until four years shall have passed since his return he shall not be able to be called to the Torah or be honored with any commandment in the synagogue.

Between 1644 and 1724, eighty-two *relapsos* were punished in this fashion, and forty-nine were denied burial in the congregation's cemetery. For the Amsterdam rabbis, it was vital to intimidate returning conversos against regression, at any cost, any penalty.

As the Jewish elders saw it, there existed beyond the transgression of backsliding the more subtle but more pervasive lure of humanism, and thus of secularism. Among the New Christians who arrived in the seventeenth century, we recall, significant numbers lacked religious commitment of any kind, Jewish or Christian. If anything, it was their passion for Spanish and Portuguese culture that remained vibrant, and specifically their fascination with literary and philosophical developments in the Iberian world. And upon settling in Holland, among a Gentile nation palpably more tolerant than the one recently left behind, the Sephardim resonated to the wider vistas opening out for them—economic, social, intellectual. Soon the ambience of wealth and culture traversed ethnic lines. In their mutual prosperity and literacy, well-born Jews and Dutchmen came to visit and know each other. Increasingly, therefore, Jewish religious and intellectual life was marked by an underlying tension between the strict Orthodoxy of rabbis and parnassim on the one hand and the skeptical, individualistic rationalism of lay intellectuals on the other. To former New Christians, religious loyalties under Catholic rule had long been tangled in a confusing thicket of dissemblement. Now, at last, in the freer air of Amsterdam, issues of doctrinal Orthodoxy could be evaluated more openly.

Uriel the Blasphemer

An initial crisis of testing the intellectual waters was the affair of Uriel
Acosta. Born in Oporto, Portugal, in 1585, Gabriel da Costa—his Christian name—was the product of an affluent convertido family. His father
was a devout Catholic; his mother observed a few disoriented marrano
traditions. Years later, in his terse autobiography, *Exemplar Humanae
Vitae,* written in Latin, Acosta acknowledged that

> religion has brought unbelievable misery into my life. . . . I was
> educated in Roman Catholicism. When I was a mere youth the terror
> of eternal damnation made me anxious to observe all its doctrines
> meticulously. I employed my leisure time in reading the Gospels, the
> Breviaries . . . and other religious literature. But the more time I
> devoted to them, the more confused did I become. . . . Reflection led
> me to the belief that . . . absolution by the confession of sins and the
> fulfillment of all that the Church required was impossible.

Thus far, the young man had given little thought to his Jewish antecedents. During one Easter-Passover season, however, becoming aware of a
shortage of bitter herbs in the marketplace, he suddenly experienced an
intuitive glimpse of a world apparently honeycombed with a tenacious
and enduring Judaism. His interest whetted, Acosta then discreetly took
up the study of the Old Testament. Eventually he was moved by its
prophetic message of social justice. "Hence," he recalled, "I decided to
become a convert to the Law of Moses." Acosta's widowed mother and
brothers joined him in the commitment.

They joined him as well in the decision to embark for the "Dutch
Jerusalem." It was not a simple venture. New Christians and their descendants were forbidden to leave Portugal. Nevertheless, secretly trans-
mitting their funds to the Netherlands, Acosta and his family managed to
elude detection and set sail for Amsterdam. "At the end of our voyage,"
Acosta wrote, "we arrived at Amsterdam where we found the Jews professing their religion with great freedom. . . . [My brothers and I] immediately fulfilled the precept concerning circumcision." Purchasing a large
home and investing their substantial capital in local import-export companies, Uriel, Isaac, and Joseph Acosta (the brothers changed their names)
began taking instruction with rabbis and faithfully attending synagogue.

But very soon Uriel Acosta was puzzled by Amsterdam Jewry's complex rabbinical rules and regulations. It mystified him that he had abjured
one body of ritual only to replace it by a regimen even more austere. More

disconcerting yet, "I observed that the customs and ordinances of the modern Jews seemed quite different from those commanded by Moses." They were. Acosta was exposed for the first time to rabbinic Judaism as it had evolved over the centuries, with its layers of talmudic responsa and individual dicta. His mother and brothers accepted these accretions unquestioningly. He did not. Where was the simple Mosaic creed of reason and righteousness he had sacrificed so much to find? Gnawing away at Acosta, in fact, was the identical corrosive principle that had undermined his Catholicism, the criterion of "right reason."

In his anguish and disorientation, Acosta soon began haranguing shocked groups of Jews outside the synagogue, insisting that their rabbis and parnassim had betrayed them and the "true" Mosaic law. Within the week, communal elders summoned the possessed young man before a *bet din,* a solemn, black-robed rabbinical tribunal. There he was charged with heresy. Acosta bitterly recalled the experience:

> The modern rabbis . . . are an obstinate and stiffnecked race of . . . Pharisees . . . and in their vanity are covetous of prestigious seats in the synagogue and respectful greetings in the marketplace. . . . They insisted that I strictly obey their rules and regulations or else suffer . . . the full sentence of excommunication.

But Acosta had endured too much for his principles to recant. The court accordingly imposed a cherem on him, a ban that henceforth placed him beyond the pale of his fellow Jews. None was permitted to have any contact or so much as speak with him. "Even my own brothers . . . dared not take any notice of me as they passed me in the streets, for fear of the rabbis," Acosta lamented. In the Joodenbuurt, the Sephardic quarter, children threw stones at his window.

Nevertheless, unbudging, Acosta vigorously broadened his attack on rabbinic Judaism, this time in a trenchant Portuguese-language essay, *Tradado da immortalide.* This time he pressed much further than in earlier critiques, insisting that within the Jewish religion it was impossible even to find justification for the immortality of the soul. The accusation was a grave one, for it appeared to subvert the essence not only of Judaism but of Christianity. Indeed, Acosta had fallen precisely into the trap Hugo Grotius had anticipated in his *Remonstrantie,* when the great jurist had urged that the Jews be obliged to adhere closely to their own faith. Nor were the parnassim oblivious to the political explosiveness latent in Acosta's charges. Hence, the communal elders now hurried to register a preemptive complaint against him before the public magistrate. They were not acting simply against a Jewish blasphemer, after all; they were making an indispensable gesture of theological and civic respectability before the government of the Netherlands. Well aware of that fact, the magistrate in turn dutifully ordered Acosta imprisoned for ten days, then fined three hundred florins. Also, copies of the "heretical" tractate were confiscated and burned.

The distraught Acosta subsequently remained at home, in near-total isolation from family and fellow Jews. Yet, even then, he would not desist from pressing on in his embrace of "right reason." Moreover, he began to question the very bedrock of Judaism. "I began to ask myself," he wrote, "whether the law of Moses should be considered the law of God. . . . At length I came to the conclusion that it was nothing but a human invention . . . that it contained many things contrary to the law of nature." No religion, he added in his notebook, was reasonable that could set brother against brother. He would continue to reject it, whatever the cost.

But fifteen years passed in a quarantine that eventually became soul-destroying. "I began to reason with myself," Acosta wrote in his despair. "What can it profit me to spend all my days in this melancholy state, isolated from the society of this people . . . especially since I am a stranger in this country without . . . even any knowledge of its language?" In fact, Acosta, a widower, had fallen in love again. The young woman evidently returned his affection, but to no avail. They could not marry. No rabbi would perform the ceremony. Repeatedly, Acosta's fiancée begged him to recant. And, in the end, he did. Arrangements were made for his brother Joseph to inform the rabbis and parnassim that he, Uriel Acosta, had returned to Judaism, that he was prepared to confess his errors and live as a true Jew. After interminable discussions, the elders finally consented. A document of confession was drawn up, Acosta signed it, and he was duly received back into the community. On the following Sabbath, he attended synagogue. Called to the reading of the Torah, he was emotionally embraced afterward by the congregants.

The reconciliation endured barely a single month. One day Acosta inadvertently committed a violation of the Jewish dietary code, and he was informed upon. Brought again before the rabbinical court, he was warned that he could avoid the dreaded cherem only by entering the synagogue dressed in black mourning garb, acknowledging the magnitude of his crime, then submitting to public scourging and prostration at the feet of the congregation. Was Acosta prepared to accept this penance? He was not. Whereupon the *bet din* reimposed its ban of excommunication. As Acosta departed the courtroom, the assembled crowd of Jews spat on him. His fiancée ended their engagement.

He was again alone. Without legal recourse, Acosta watched helplessly as his brothers preempted the largest part of the family capital, leaving him only a pittance. Seven more years passed in impoverishment, solitude, and recurring bouts of illness. No one would attend him. Acosta sensed that his resistance was failing. Evidently there was no alternative; he would give in. In 1640, he allowed himself to be led back to the Esnoga— and to public degradation. The great synagogue was filled when Acosta was paraded down the aisle, garbed in black, carrying a black taper. Mounting the stage, he was handed a long scroll of recantation. This he read off tonelessly, confessing to his sins and errors. He was then stripped and tied to a pillar. A bailiff of the congregation set about inflicting thirty-nine lashes on the unfortunate penitent. Acosta did not cry out. But neither was his ordeal over. After dressing, he was ordered to prostrate himself at the entrance of the synagogue. Here the entire congregation passed over his body, some kicking him. Acosta remained rigid, still not crying out. Only then was the cherem removed.

The experience destroyed him. Jotting down the last pages of his *Exemplar Humanae Vitae,* he wrote:

> O shameless race of men! O detested fathers! . . . Now let anyone who has heard my story judge how decent a spectacle it was to see an old man . . . stripped naked before a large assembly of men, women, and children and be scourged . . . to [see] his own brothers . . . joining . . . with his persecutors and indifferent to the great affection with which I always loved them.

"The Law of Moses [has] brought only discord to human society," he concluded. The rabbis were "advocates for a fraud that . . . make them a prey and slaves of men." Upon finishing his testament, Acosta prepared to enact a private drama. Carrying a brace of dueling pistols to his brother Joseph's home, he entered the house, aimed the first gun at Joseph, fired, and missed. He aimed the second pistol at his own head, fired, and did not miss. He was fifty-five.

Uriel Acosta's religious doctrines were far from coherent. Nevertheless, he was enshrined centuries later as a martyr in the battle against religious intolerance. The German dramatist Karl Ferdinand Gutzkow produced two works on the theme: *Der Sadduzaeer von Amsterdam* (1834), a novella, and later the five-act tragedy *Uriel Acosta* (1846). Gutzkow's dramatic interpretation subsequently inspired a Hebrew version by Shlomo Rubin (1856), and Abraham Goldfaden's late-nineteenth-century Yiddish adaptation for the New York stage, with musical accompaniment. Possibly the three best-known modern works on the man remain Israel Zangwill's sketch in *Dreamers of the Ghetto* (1898), Charles Reznikoff's play *Uriel*

Acosta (1921), both of them idealized portraits, and the Habimah Theater's perennial version of Rubin's work. The tormented figure of Uriel Acosta manifestly still resonates in the Jewish imagination.

Benedictus the Heretic

In the year Acosta died, 1640, Baruch Spinoza was eight years old. Born in Amsterdam, he was the son and grandson of former Portuguese marranos. His father, a successful merchant and active member of the Amsterdam Jewish community, provided the youngster with every advantage of Hebrew and secular education. Then, in 1654, the elder Spinoza died and the son's circumstances changed dramatically. A stepsister claimed the bulk of the substantial legacy. Although the court decision favored him, Baruch Spinoza preferred not to create a family scandal. He allowed the stepsister to keep nearly everything, asking for himself only a modest annuity. It was a magnanimous gesture but an impetuous one. His growing intellectual independence would have been better served by financial security.

By the early 1650s, as it happened, Spinoza was beginning to question traditional Judaism. Some of his iconoclasm doubtless was acquired from Christian acquaintances, particularly Francis van den Enden, a respected classical scholar who operated a local secondary school. Through van den Enden, Spinoza was introduced to neo-scholasticism, and the "new" philosophy of René Descartes. Yet an even more decisive influence was the skepticism already gestating beneath the surface of Jewish life. Uriel Acosta's earlier ordeal attested to the fact. So did the appearance of *Praeademitae,* a severely rationalist critique of religion, just published in Amsterdam by Isaac La Peyrère, a Jewish apostate. By 1656, Spinoza's Jewish companions also included Juan de Prado and Daniel de Ribera, rationalists who provoked controversy by questioning whether Moses actually wrote the Torah or if Mosaic law took precedence over natural law. Under pressure from the community, Ribera and Prado retracted their challenges and apologized. Not so Spinoza. Instead, he began relentlessly pressing the same issues.

At this point, Spinoza may not have intended an irretrievable break from the community. He attended the synagogue as late as 1655, even making a modest donation. But he would not refrain from his campaign of inquiry. To the pleas and threats of communal elders he turned a deaf ear. Nor was he given pause by their warning that heresy was an offense to the Dutch no less than to the Jews. At last, in July 1656, Amsterdam's rabbis and parnassim moved decisively against Spinoza. Citing his "abominable blasphemies" and "monstrous acts," they invoked a cherem upon him:

> Cursed be he when he riseth up, cursed be he when he goeth out, and cursed be he when he cometh in. May the Lord never pardon him, may the anger and wrath of the Lord rage against this man, and bring upon him all the curses that are written in the Book of the Law.

The elders then took care to inform the Dutch authorities of their dutiful concern for civic rectitude.

As in the case of Uriel Acosta, the ban of excommunication precluded all human contact, and specifically the opportunity to earn a living among one's fellow Jews. Spinoza was acutely aware of this fact. In a written clarification, therefore, he sought to prove that he was not formally renouncing Judaism, merely seeking to "explicate" it. But at the same time, in an apparent gesture of ideological independence, he latinized his first name to Benedictus. Leaving Amsterdam, then, he settled eventually in Voorburg, near The Hague. There, comparatively remote from Jewish scrutiny, he turned to lens-grinding for a livelihood, and to his studies and writing for intellectual satisfaction.

It was in this initial period of self-exile, during the late 1650s and early 1660s, that Spinoza produced a number of short philosophic works, including a commentary on Descartes and the first book of his *Ethics*. Virtually all were written under pseudonyms or were circulated as handwritten manuscripts. In whichever form, they evoked attention in learned circles. Before long, Spinoza's intellectual acuity, enhanced by his kindly, artless disposition, won him a growing coterie of prestigious admirers. Leibnitz corresponded respectfully with him. In 1673 the Palatine Elector invited Spinoza to accept the chair of philosophy at Heidelberg, with the proviso that he agree not to disturb the established religion. The prince of Condé offered Spinoza a pension, on condition that he dedicate his next work to Louis XIV. Both offers were politely declined.

The declination evinced Spinoza's commitment equally to political and to intellectual freedom. In 1672, he reacted in shock to the public lynching of Jan de Witt, Grand Pensionary of the Republic, a gallant constitutionalist and freethinker. Afterward, intent on defending De Witt's ideas against tyrants, both secular and religious, Spinoza embarked upon his *Tractatus Theologico-Politicus*. In precise, elegantly nuanced Latin, this magisterial work adopted a carefully calibrated political stance. On the one hand, it expressed support for an idealized form of republican democracy. On the other, revealing a characteristically Jewish suspicion of mob rule, the *Tractatus* conceded that submission to "just" authority often was preferable to "agitation and rebellion." Yet Spinoza's central purpose in the *Tractatus* was to expose the dead hand of false religious beliefs. Thus, in evaluating biblical texts, he argued that the Torah could not have been the product of Moses, nor could the books of the Prophets have been written by their putative authors. In any case, none of the events or laws appearing in the Bible should be accepted literally, but instead as a reflection of the limited worldview of early Israelites writing for their time. These accounts at best might be regarded as parables or morality tales; any other interpretation would serve only to perpetuate error and confusion.

The notion hardly was revolutionary. The great Maimonides had made essentially the same case in his *Guide for the Perplexed.* In seventeenth-century Amsterdam, however, philosophic speculations were not limited to an austere, literate elite, as in the twelfth-century Islamic-Mediterranean world, or insulated from possible wider ramifications. The Jewish and Protestant religious establishments, if not the public at large, could hardly ignore Spinoza's threat to scriptural literalism. The *Tractatus* appeared unsigned, but its authorship was not a secret. Soon after its appearance, therefore, Jewish and Dutch clerics alike excoriated Spinoza with a ferocity directed at few men in the then brief history of the United Provinces. The Classis of the Reformed Church appealed to the government, and the government in turn went through the motions of forbidding the book's sale. Yet the Netherlands was too effervescent in its liberalism by then to foreclose the open movement of ideas, any more than the open movement of capital. The *Tractatus* circulated freely, albeit under false title pages, going through five editions in five years.

And Spinoza, for his part, continued to forge on in his rationalist campaign. In 1674, he completed the *Ethics,* possibly his most original metaphysical work. It was surely his most forthright analysis of the role of God. Until its appearance, most philosophers had accepted the notion of mankind functioning as a separate, autonomous kingdom within God's all-encompassing imperium. Spinoza now offered the innovative theory that the universe comprised one divine, indivisible empire. Under this interpretation, everything was a modification, or mode, of God, functioning according to the necessity of His own nature. God, therefore, could not have divided, or delegated, any portion of His realm specifically to the care of man; and the good man, although he loved God, would not expect God necessarily to hold him in special regard. The vision was uncompromisingly rationalistic, even somewhat chilling. To be sure, Spinoza was not prepared to repudiate certain basic Jewish themes. The unity of God was one of these. Like Maimonides, he rather patronizingly favored a metaphorical interpretation of the Bible, and the notion that it was socially important for man both to know and to love God. It is indisputable, nevertheless, that the Judeo-Christian notion of God's interplay with man no longer functioned in his system. As Harry Wolfson has described Spinoza's role: "Benedictus is the first of the moderns. Baruch was the last of the medievals."

By the time he had transcribed his principal ideas, Spinoza already was in an advanced stage of silicosis, a disease contracted during his years as a lens-grinder. In 1677, he died. According to his written instructions, his manuscripts were collected and organized for publication. So it was, posthumously, that his *Ethics,* his *Tractatus Theologico-Politicus,* his *On the Improvement of Understanding,* as well as his Hebrew grammar and his essay on the rainbow, were officially published. With the passage of time, Spinoza's views came to influence Voltaire and other eighteenth-century French *philosophes,* and later German Romantics like Goethe, Schlegel, and Herder, as well as the English poets Coleridge and Wordsworth. Indeed, the man's reputation grew uninterruptedly as one of history's authentic heroes of freethinking and modern thought, and surely as one of the monumental philosophers of Western civilization.

With some exceptions, Orthodox Judaism continues to regard Spinoza as a threat. But such modern Jewish thinkers as Hermann Cohen, Leo Strauss, and Mordecai Kaplan accepted his views as the basis for a more universalistic Judaism. Israel's prime minister David Ben-Gurion, himself a learned philosopher manqué, once proposed that the cherem on Spinoza be formally repealed. Whether the ban stands or not, however, Spinoza endures as the greatest Jewish philosopher since Maimonides and as a paradigm of Sephardic intellectualism in its uniquely sinuous and accommodating vision of the relationship between God and man.

Afterglow and Revolution

By the eighteenth century, the Netherlands had fallen behind Great Britain as the leading maritime power of Europe. Gradual, at times imperceptible, the decline nevertheless was irreversible. Dutch Jewry shared in the protracted malaise. In the heyday of the mid- and latter 1600s, the privileged inner sanctum of their elite capitalists had tended to neglect commerce in favor of finance. Thus, many Jews had preferred to live off their income from the East and West India companies. But those enterprises now were all but in default. Other Jews had invested heavily in the stock exchange, and as a consequence also paid the price in the attrition of major industrial and commercial ventures. Meanwhile, tradesmen—still the majority of Jews—experienced Holland's commercial demise even more acutely. By the mid-1700s, nearly half the Esnoga's three thousand congregants were reduced intermittently to accepting relief.

By then, too, the Sephardim had been inundated by a wave of impoverished immigrants from other regions of Europe. While Amsterdam Jewry in the eighteenth century had grown to ten thousand people, comprising some 5 percent of the city's population, more than two-thirds of these were Ashkenazim from either Germany or the Ukraine. Moreover, the numbers of newcomers would continue to increase as circumstances in Eastern Europe deteriorated. Inhabiting their own slums, wearing clothes markedly different from those of their neighbors, the immigrants spoke Yiddish and practiced the menial ghetto trades of clothes dealing and peddlery, vocations long since disdained by the Sephardim. No contact of any kind existed between the two Jewish communities. Writing in 1762, Isaac de Pinto, a banker and economist, assured the duke de Richelieu that

> [t]he Portuguese and the Spaniards, who have the honor of being descendants of the tribe of Judah . . . have never mingled, through marriage, association, or in any other way, with the children of Jacob known under the name of *Tudusques,* Italian, or Avignonese Jews.

Notwithstanding this and other antiseptic protestations of dissimilarity, it was the influx of Ashkenazim that remarginalized the Sephardim within Dutch society. In 1795, while the Ashkenazim had grown to twenty thousand, the Sephardim had stabilized at barely three thousand. Increasingly, it was the tatterdemalion immigrants whom most Dutch Gentiles identified with all Jews. In their economic redundancy, their hunger-based desperation, the Central and Eastern Europeans evoked only ill will. The distaste this time was based not on theology but on sociology.

At the initiative of municipal authorities, therefore, obsolete restrictions on Jews were gradually revived. These included bureaucratic delays and gratuitous extra payments for business licenses and marriage registrations, together with eccentric and demeaning oaths before magistrates and law courts. The confluence of humiliations further exacerbated the Jews' sense of abasement and moral degradation. But so did the endless zealotry of parnassim and rabbis within the Sephardic community itself. In bad times as well as good, the synagogue functionaries maintained their traditional power to assess and levy communal taxes, to impose fines and punishments, including the dreaded cherem—in short, to bedevil their people's collective and personal lives. These were the blackest days of Dutch Jewry.

Suddenly, a force majeure intruded. It was the French Revolution, and specifically the French revolutionary army, which invaded the Netherlands in 1793 and in the next year and a half overran the country. Operating as the puppet "Batavian Republic," the new Dutch provisional government then issued a declaration, proclaiming that "[a]ll men are . . . equal, all are eligible to all offices and services." Traditionally, most of the nation's Jews pledged their loyalty to the now fugitive House of Orange. Among the Sephardim, however, an educated minority gave serious attention to the promise of full equality. Indeed, if the French regime were to be a model, political emancipation would liberate Jews not least of all from the tyranny of their own communal elders. So it was, as French troops marched into Amsterdam in 1795, that a small group of Sephardic veterans welcomed them as liberators. They proceeded then to form a society, "Felix Libertate," with the purpose of mobilizing the Jewish community on behalf of the revolutionary regime. The reaction of the parnassim and rabbis was precisely the opposite. They feared the secularism and assimilationism implicit in the French revolutionary model. Even more, they feared the loss of their fiscal and juridical authority. That concern was justified. In September 1796, the National Assembly of the Batavian Republic proclaimed full and equal citizenship for the Jews of the Netherlands. Two years later, Jewish communal autonomy was dissolved.

It was never revived. Even following the return of the House of Orange in 1813, few changes were made in the Jews' new and equal status. Their political liberty survived. So did their communal emancipation. The anachronism of their inbred corporate autonomy expired for good and always. Meanwhile, as the nineteenth century progressed, the Netherlands itself regained a certain moderate prosperity, albeit this time less as an overextended empire than as a small, thrifty, neutralist country. Dutch Jews shared in the rewards of the nation's peaceful commercialism. By the early twentieth century, with their population growing steadily, perhaps two-thirds of Dutch Jewry, Ashkenazim and Sephardim alike, had once again achieved a modest but comfortable embourgeoisement in business and the professions. By then, too, liberalism had triumphed in Dutch public affairs, a chastened and softened Calvinism in the nation's religious ethic. The Jews accordingly savored an extended second honeymoon with their Gentile neighbors.

Farewell and Reembrace

In 1940, their presence in the Netherlands was calculated at 140,000 souls, of whom 30,000 were refugees from Hitler's Third Reich. Of the entire combined population, not more than forty-three hundred were Sephardim. Nevertheless, it was the ancestry of this minuscule group that became the object of a particularly bizarre episode of the Nazi Holocaust. In October 1941, a year and a half into the German occupation, the Jewish population was quarantined, then obliged to register in preparation for relocation to Poland. At the same time, the SS published a summary of those to be exempted from deportations. As elsewhere in Europe, the list included Jews married to Gentiles, together with their children and other *mischlingen.* In the Netherlands, however, a newer category of exemptions was added. This was "Portuguese Jews without Eastern Ashkenazi European blood." Of marrano ancestry, such people conceivably were more of Iberian than of Jewish stock. The problem was to verify the proportion of Jewish blood in each of the forty-three hundred. It was a daunting task, and indeed, for the Nazi bureaucracy, soon an overwhelming one.

So it was that the SS "Jewish expert" in the Netherlands, Hans Callmeyer, sought the advice of other authorities. Two of these were German professors who sent Callmeyer a report allegedly confirming the Iberian—non-Semitic—roots of the Sephardim. Another German academician attributed to the Sephardim a substantial admixture of West Gothic blood. A well-meaning Dutch professor argued that skull measurements proved that "so-called Portuguese Jews" could not by any stretch of the imagination be classified as Jews. Throughout 1942, even as these investigations were being conducted, Jewish deportations were proceeding uninterruptedly. Nearly half the tiny Sephardic group were among those shipped off to Auschwitz. By February 1943, as the SS rounded up the last five thousand Dutch Jews, only four hundred Sephardic families remained. By the summer, three hundred of these had been shipped off to the "privileged" concentration camp at Theresienstadt. Here, too, the majority perished. Altogether, between 1941 and 1945, over 110,000 Jews in Holland were "relocated." Of the 30,000 who survived, 21,000 were émigrés who had fled the Netherlands before the German occupation.

The Jewish community's postwar revival was very slow. By the late twentieth century, its population had stabilized at barely twenty-seven thousand, among a Dutch population of fourteen million. Nevertheless, from the moment of their liberation and return, the survivors enjoyed the unalloyed goodwill of the Dutch government and people. In vivid contrast to the nations of Eastern Europe, or even of Austria and France, their homes and shops were returned to them almost immediately. In 1953, a law was passed in parliament allocating the equivalent of $7 million to recompense Jews for their untraceable chattels and securities. Later, with its share of German reparations money, the Netherlands government was able to provide an additional $5 million to Jewish survivors, including those living in Israel.

In its mellower, contemporary version, this record of solicitude evokes the flinty toleration of Holland's seventeenth-century Calvinist forebears. Today, visitors to Amsterdam's old Joodenbuurt pass a heroic statue of a dockworker on Jonas Dam Mayerplein, itself a square named for a Jew, between the massive Ashkenazic Great Synagogue and the original Sephardic Esnoga. It is a monument to local stevedores who displayed almost unimaginable courage in walking off their jobs to protest the Nazi roundup of some four hundred young Jews in the area. Later, transport workers and others joined the strike. Elsewhere in the city, three bridges on the Weeperstraat memorialize Dutch rabbis who perished in Auschwitz. The Anne Frank House is a national museum. Anne's statue stands in the Jankserhof. There is an Anne Frank School in Amsterdam, an Anne Frank Square in Utrecht. Memorials to "relocated" Jews, usually bearing Hebrew and Dutch inscriptions, are found in all the larger cities. Spinoza House in The Hague is also a national monument.

Nowhere else in Europe are representatives of church and state, often the royal family, as likely to attend Jewish community functions. In recent decades, three mayors of Amsterdam have been Jews. Admiration for Israel has been deep, at times passionate. During the 1967 Six-Day War, thousands of young people conducted a sympathy march in Amsterdam for Israel, and hundreds offered their services to the Israeli embassy in The Hague. The 1973 Yom Kippur War produced an identical outpouring of solidarity.

In March 1958, while living in Israel, I entered into correspondence with the Netherlands Cultural Foundation on behalf of a scholarship program then being established for overseas students at Brandeis University. "It will be a privilege for our students to attend Brandeis," the director assured me. "We Dutch are reared on the Bible, you know. For us, the Jews are God's holy people." Responding to this gracious lady, I discerned a modest symbolism in our correspondence. She was writing me from her office on Amsterdam's Jozef Israëls Lane, named for an eminent

Dutch Jewish painter. I was responding from my apartment on Tel Aviv's Rembrandt Street, named for a rather more famous Gentile one.

Even now, it is in the seventeenth-century portraits by the Old Master of Joodenbreestraat 4 that all and everything is yet said of the Dutch, and of the little people to whom they extended an initial wary asylum, and an eventual openhearted brotherhood.

CHAPTER XIV

THE EMISSARIES

The Lost Tribes

In September 1644, a West Indian merchant vessel dropped anchor at the port of Amsterdam. Among its disembarking passengers was a rather wild-eyed Spaniard, Antonio de Montezinos, who was returning to Europe after nearly a decade of fortune seeking in Latin America. Montezinos in fact was a marrano whose original name was Aaron Levi. Back safely in Amsterdam, he hurried to meet with Rabbi Menasseh ben Israel and other Jewish leaders. To them now he recounted an extraordinary story. Some two years earlier, Montezinos explained, while prospecting in the Ecuadorian region of New Granada, he and a group of fellow explorers had traveled by mule from Puerta de Honda to the distant province of Papián, in Peru. They were accompanied by several Indian guides. As their small party made its way through the Cordillera range, a blizzard unexpectedly stopped them short. Huddling then for shelter in a cave, the Indians muttered repeatedly that the storm was God's punishment upon the Spaniards "for their treatment of a holy people." Eventually the snowfall abated, and the travelers resumed their journey.

Several weeks afterward, upon returning to Ecuador, Montezinos was arrested by the Inquisition for suspected judaizing. It was in prison, mulling over the Indians' comments during the storm, that he vowed to search out the "holy people" should he ever regain his freedom. Fortunately, he did not have long to wait; the Inquisition released him for lack of evidence. Thereupon Montezinos located his Indian guides and entreated them to conduct him to the "holy people." When they hesitated, he explained that he himself was a member of that community. Astonished and awed, the Indians hesitated no longer. Three days afterward, they set out with Montezinos for the distant northern side of the Cordillera range. The trek required a fortnight of hard travel. Finally, upon reaching a small clearing at the edge of a forest, the guides halted and loosed a series of whistles.

After several minutes, a quartet of Indians emerged. Suspicious at the presence of Europeans, the forest dwellers conferred at length with the guides in their own language. It was then that they were apprised of Montezinos's identity. Overwhelmed with joy, the Indians repeatedly embraced their "brother." With great excitement, too, they recited the Hebrew *Sh'ma* prayer for him. The entire group then set off for a nearby village. There, with the guides serving as interpreters, the tribal elders gave Montezinos the gist of their story. They were descendants of the Lost Tribe of Reuben, they explained, and had lived in this jungle for centuries. It had always been their dream to reestablish contact with the main body of the Jewish people. Now, at last, upon receiving their brother, that dream could be realized. It was their most cherished wish to be thoroughly instructed in the principles of their ancient faith. Would their brother now dispatch emissaries to them? Montezinos, deeply moved, gave his solemn promise to try. He departed for Europe soon afterward, and upon reaching Amsterdam wasted little time in describing his adventure to the local Jewish leadership.

Montezinos's listeners were enthralled. No one doubted his story. Its details were far too compelling. Nor did any need to be reminded of the prophecy contained in the books of Daniel and Zachariah. Once the Children of Israel were dispersed to the four corners of the earth, it avowed, the moment would be ripe for their ingathering again in Zion. Here now, in the fourth and last corner, in distant Latin America, a remnant of Israel apparently had been discovered. Was the messianic era at hand? The notion hardly was an exotic one in the world of the Diaspora. For over a hundred years, after all, that world had been thoroughly impregnated by the *Zohar* and the Lurianic kabbalah. Its susceptibility to redemptionist apocalypticism soon would explode in the mass hysteria of the Shabbatean movement. Like other Dutch Sephardim, even Rabbi Menasseh ben Israel was not immune to these messianic impulses.

Neither, for that matter, were substantial numbers of fundamentalist Protestants. On both sides of the North Sea, in the Netherlands and in England, these literalists inhabited a Bible-centered world. With their divines and evangelicals, they were caught up in an eschatological euphoria as they awaited the Fifth Monarchy, the glorious restoration of the Kingdom of Israel, which alone would portend the Second Coming of Christ. Like the Jews, they accepted as an essential precondition of that restoration an initial dispersion of the Chosen People to the farthest reaches of the earth. Thus, Petrus Serrarius, a Dutch physician-philosopher, argued in his *Assertion du Règne de Mille Ans* (1656) that the dispersion could be verified by actively "seeking out" the Lost Tribes of Israel.

Even as the Montezinos report became known, its account of the recently discovered Indians was viewed as the penultimate phase in the odyssey of dispersion and return. Among Protestant fundamentalists, it soon became legitimate speculation that the New World's Indians were none other than the Lost Tribes. In 1648, a Norfolk preacher, Thomas Thorowgood, published a volume, *Jews in America, or the Probability That the Indians Are Jews.* John Dury, a Scot born in Holland, was similarly shaken by the Montezinos report. Writing Menasseh ben Israel, he inquired if the learned rabbi concurred in the identity of the Indians.

At first, Menasseh hesitated. Yet, under persistent questioning, he finally acknowledged that Montezinos's Indians might indeed belong to one of the Lost Tribes. For Thorowgood, that tentative endorsement was approbation enough. In 1660, the Norfolk minister issued a new edition of his book, supplemented with additional data confirming the Indians' identity as Jews; and John Dury, in turn, wrote a supportive foreword for Thorowgood. Quaker William Penn, swept up in the excitement, also professed to discern "incontestable" Jewish practices among the Indians of his own New World colony. The theory would persist in America as late as the nineteenth century, and among the Mormons even later. In seventeenth-century England, meanwhile, the preface of Edward Winslow's *The Glorious Progress of the Gospel among the Indians in New England* (1649) cited the confirmation of "a great Dr. of the Jewes, now living in Amsterdam." Other Puritan divines then and later were dispatching letters "to the learned Jew Menasseh ben Israel of Amsterdam," "the most respected and learned of the Jewes," suggesting that discovery of the Lost Tribes surely mandated the immediate conversion of the Jews, to hasten the Redemption.

"A Man of the Highest Utility"

The man to whom these European pietists were turning for enlightenment and confirmation was the son of Portuguese marranos. Menasseh's father, Joseph Soeiro Nuñes, had been imprisoned briefly by the Lisbon Inquisition and left financially ruined. The son, Manoel Dias Soeiro, born during his parents' flight from Portugal to Holland in 1604, did not become Menasseh ben Israel until the family name was hebraized in the Netherlands. Afterward, displaying a precociousness approaching genius during his talmudic studies, Menasseh was ordained at the age of seventeen. Upon assuming the pulpit of Neve Shalom synagogue in 1633, then marrying a distant relative, a member of the renowned Abravanel family, he evidently was well launched upon a distinguished career and an even more distinguished social life.

Yet the talented young rabbi was a curious mixture. His approach to Judaism appeared conventionally Orthodox. Indeed, Menasseh sat on the rabbinical court that excommunicated Uriel Acosta. At the same time, his independence of temperament, his insistence on freedom of the pulpit, more than occasionally affronted his lay parnassim, who retaliated by freezing his salary. In his frustration, Menasseh in 1641 applied for the position of senior rabbi at Recife, in Dutch Brazil. But his reputation for unflinching independence preceded him. The Recife Jews selected another candidate. Even then, Menasseh was not without alternatives. During the late 1630s, he had established one of the first Jewish printing presses in Amsterdam. It was a profitable enterprise. In later years, the firm turned out beautifully printed and widely admired Bibles and other works of Jewish content in Hebrew, Spanish, and Portuguese. As a man of protean energy and talents, the Amsterdam rabbi also found time to publish a wide variety of his own books and articles. One of them, a Portuguese-language manual, *Thesouro dos Dinim,* proved indispensable for the hundreds of returning conversos who needed a handbook of basic Jewish rites and rituals.

Perhaps of even more enduring value among Menasseh's endless succession of publications were his *Conciliador* (1632), *De termino vitae* (1634), and *Piedra gloriosa* (1655), treatises that lucidly and eloquently interpreted Judaism for the Gentile reader. None of these works was particularly original, but Menasseh displayed uncommon skill in bringing together a vast assortment of passages from numerous sources—Hebrew, Greek, Latin, Spanish, Portuguese, the Church Fathers as well as Jewish scholars—to defend Jewish unitarianism against Christian trinitarianism, Jewish free will against Calvinist predestination. Altogether, a rabbi who could engage in discourse on equal terms with learned non-Jews was a revelation to the Gentile world. Over the years, Menasseh even became something of a cult figure among Christian intellectuals and theologians. Many corresponded with him, debated with him, questioned him on points of Judaism.

From the Netherlands, then, and increasingly from England, growing numbers of these Christian interlocutors set out to visit Menasseh at his home. In short order, they were captivated by his charm. "He was of middle Stature, and inclining to Fatness," an English contemporary recalled of him. "He always wore his own Hair which (many years before his Death) was very Gray, so that his Complexion remained . . . fresh, his

Demeanor Graceful, and Comely, his Habit plain and Decent. He Commanded an aweful Reverence which was justly due to so venerable a Deportment." Rembrandt painted him. The jurist Hugo Grotius wrote of Menasseh that "he is a man of the highest utility both to the state and to the advancement of knowledge." Fully sharing this evaluation were theologians, bishops, and philosophers in Germany, Sweden, Bohemia. No man of his time did more to endow his people with dignity in Protestant Europe.

For nearly five years, however, Menasseh had taken no initiative in evaluating the Montezinos report. Uninterested in lending credence to conversionary interpretations, he preferred simply to respond to the queries of others. Yet by 1649 it began to dawn on the Amsterdam rabbi that another, nonconversionary purpose might be served. "I know not," he wrote later, "but that the Lord . . . might have design'd, and made choice of me, for bringing about this work." The work Menasseh had in mind was not simply verification of the Jews' dispersion but assurance of their welcome. These were precisely the years when England's burgeoning maritime and colonial power was threatening the Netherlands' role as an international carrier. In 1651, London issued the first in a series of Navigation Acts that were intended to foreclose use of Dutch vessels in the transport of British cargoes. The Jews of Amsterdam all but lived and died by that immense import-export traffic. For these people, a new lease on their economic future would have been resettlement in England, a nation plainly emerging as the fulcrum of world trade.

Menasseh ben Israel had that future much in mind as early as 1650 as he produced a new booklet, *Spes Israel* (The Hope of Israel). Published initially in Latin, the essay soon was followed by translations in Spanish, Hebrew, English, and Dutch. The rabbi's premise was fascinating. It was the straightforward assertion that Montezinos's recently discovered Indian community was indeed one of the Lost Tribes of Israel. Menasseh continued then by tracing evidence of Jews elsewhere in the world, including Asia and even Central Africa. Recharting much of the terrain already staked out by Protestant millenarians, he reaffirmed the biblical prophecies in the books of Daniel and Zechariah that the people Israel, upon being fully scattered throughout the planet, would at last reclaim their ancestral land. One corner of the earth had yet to fulfill the preliminary dispersion, however—England. If only Jews could be introduced into that green and pleasant land, the Diaspora would be completed, and the Messianic Deliverance could begin.

There was no need for Menasseh to raise or reject the issue of a Second Coming. He had genuflected to England sufficiently for his purposes. The rabbi's preoccupation, after all, was the fate and security of his own people, not of Christendom. Lest his purpose remain in any sense obscure, Menasseh dedicated his tract to England's parliament, whose "favour and good will" on behalf of the Jews he now expressly solicited. As it developed, the impact of Menasseh's appeal was possibly more far-reaching than he could have foretold. Moses Wall, a millenarian and friend of John Milton's, produced the English version. It was hardly less than a sensation. The booklet went through three editions in three years. Menasseh was gratified. Nevertheless, he sensed that millennialist enthusiasm alone was hardly a national policy. Was there not also a more pragmatic, "realistic" basis for anticipating Jewish settlement in England?

Strangers in Angleterre

By the thirteenth century, as many as four thousand Jews may already have lived on the island. Dating back to Norman times, they were a French-speaking community, a trading community, and they played a characteristically important economic role in an agricultural land. There is speculation that King Henry I may even have extended them a charter of protection. It was Crusading fanaticism that doomed their future. In 1290, Edward I responded to public sentiment by ordering the Jews out. Most returned to France. A few stayed on, however, and others intermittently made their way back from the Continent. Some were merchants, some were moneylenders, a few were physicians. Following the 1492 Spanish Expulsion, they were joined by two to three hundred marranos, and eventually by perhaps three times that many Portuguese New Christians, including several who were prominent in international commerce. Thus, in the early 1500s, the great marrano trading house of Diogo Mendes opened a branch in London, and Beatriz da Luna Mendes and her family paid a short visit to England in 1536 en route from Portugal to Antwerp. It was also the custom of Christopher Fernandez, a local Mendes agent, to meet Portuguese spice-ships reprovisioning at Plymouth and to warn any marranos on board of possible dangers awaiting them in Flanders. In 1544, the Spanish government got wind of this activity and immediately protested to Henry VIII. The king in turn ordered the arrest of "certain persons suspected to be Jews." The little community dispersed.

Again, the hiatus was comparatively brief. Fourteen years later, ascending the throne, Elizabeth I encouraged "foreign merchants" to settle in England. Inevitably, several dozen New Christians were among the early arrivals. By the end of the queen's long reign, their numbers had reached some one hundred. It was plainly less than dramatic growth, for in the latter sixteenth century, most of Portugal's convertido émigrés were drawn to the Ottoman East or to Amsterdam. And once James I, a rigid High Anglican, began his reign in 1603, orders went out to expel all suspected judaizers among the "Portuguese merchants." Barely two dozen managed to remain on secretly. Even among this remnant, however, a few managed to cast long shadows. One was Antonio Fernandez (Abraham Israel) Carvajal, a Portuguese-born convertido. Earning a fortune as an importer in Madeira, Carvajal had intended to explore new opportunities in Provence. But stopping off in England in 1633, he was intrigued by the commercial potential of London, and summarily transferred his base of operations there. Twenty years later, in a clandestine three-way operation, Carvajal was importing Spanish silver bars at an annual rate of one hundred thousand pounds in return for a wide variety of English-manufactured exports. Luxuriating in his wealth, riding fine horses, collecting armor for his mansion, Carvajal was widely known in London as "the Great Jew."

In 1655, a baptized Jew, Paul Isaiah, eager to convert all marranos to Christianity, proclaimed his certain knowledge that Jews resided in London and "have their Synagogues and there exercise Judaism." It was true. Jewish religious services were indeed being conducted in a private home on Creechurch Lane, and a second congregation may also have been meeting intermittently in the city. England's ideological climate had changed by then. Although hostility toward Jews had by no means vanished, it hardly compared to the more rampant fear and hatred of Catholics. Moreover, the innovative notion of religious liberty was emerging in England as an integral feature of the Protestant struggle against Catholic oppression, then of sectarian resistance to the Protestant establishment. Even as Baptists, Anabaptists, Quakers, and other dissenting subcommunities experienced persecution, whether at the hands of Anglican clerics or Presbyterian dissenters, the cry went up for a freedom of conscience that would embrace all religions.

It was in this tumult of sectarian contention, as early as 1614, that a Jacobite, Leonard Busher, submitted to King James I his proposal for "Religious Peace, or a Plan for Liberty of Conscience," including freedom of conscience for Jews. The tract underwent a timely reprinting in 1646. Others who embraced the tolerationist cause by then were the proto-Baptists Samuel Richardson and Roger Williams. Williams recently had founded a settlement in New England based on freedom of conscience. In 1644, he published a celebrated essay, "Bloody Tenent of Revolution," rejecting with particular horror the very notion of ill-treating the "People of God." A year later, Hugh Peters, one of Oliver Cromwell's army chaplains, similarly advocated that "strangers, even Jews, [be] admitted to trade and live with us."

Then, in December 1648, a sizable collection of Protestant dissidents united behind Thomas Pride in the "purge" that ended Presbyterian domination of the House of Commons and ushered in the Puritan Commonwealth. The tolerationists among this phalanx now had high hopes. Indeed, anticipating a new policy of religious liberalism, their Council of Mechanics voted in favor of "a toleration of all religions whatsoever, not excepting Turkes, nor Papists, nor Jewes." To this sentiment, the Council of Army Officers added its own endorsement. Yet more time would have to pass before the notion could evoke serious resonance. In 1649, Charles I was beheaded, and in the shocked aftermath of the execution Cromwell and his associates were disposed to proceed more cautiously on issues of social change.

There was another approach, however, that offered possibilities for the Jews. It was the one Menasseh ben Israel had discerned early on, and that had animated his *Spes Israel.* From his personal acquaintance with the extensive collection of English dissidents then living in Amsterdam, he was keenly aware that no people in Europe, not even the Dutch, were more obsessed by Scripture than were these émigré fundamentalists. Indeed, fixation with the Old Testament had burgeoned with particular vibrancy following publication of the King James "authorized" version in 1611. Both in England and on occasional visits to the Netherlands, English Hebraists like John Selden, Edward Pocock, and John Milton shared their knowledge of the Bible with one another. Some among them actually sought to live according to the Levitical law, and even secretly practiced circumcision. A few, like Robert Everard "the Leveller," publicly called themselves Jews. Others departed for Amsterdam and were received formally into the synagogue. At the very least, they shared in a growing eschatological anticipation of the Second Coming of Christ, and of its indispensable prelude, the universal dispersion—and then restoration—of the Jews.

For most Protestants, there remained a second caveat. Dispersion and restoration ideally should be accompanied by Jewish conversion. Millenarians like Isaac Pennington, George Fox, and Margaret Fell Fox wrote tracts making this point. But first things first. In the cauldron of messianism, the admission of Jews into England was accepted as an indispensable preliminary step. As it happened, no one articulated the conviction with greater fervor than Henry Jessey. The man was an eloquent spokesman for the Jacobite Church, parent congregation for a group of London dissidents that later would evolve into the Baptist denomination. A faith-healing mystic, closely associated with the Fifth Monarchy Men, Jessey was shaken to his depths by Menasseh's *Spes Israel.* Thus, from 1650 on, seized by a millennialist passion, he became a typhoon of sermonizing and tractating: the Lord was about "to roare aloud from Heaven . . . to rouze us up out of present great security." Above all, Jessey was fascinated by the eternal role of the Jews, which he described in a small volume, *The Glory of Ieuhdah and Israel* (1653). There could be no Second Coming without their conversion, he acknowledged, but the initial priority was their return to Zion, and, before that, to England. Jessey was fortified in his campaign by John Dury, Nathaniel Homes, Jonathan Cartwright, John Sadler, Edmund Spencer, and other redemptionists, all strenuously preaching, writing, petitioning in favor of Jewish admission.

If the largest number of these exhortations still favored conversion to Christianity as a requisite for the Jewish presence in England, other pamphlets seemed to allow leeway for compromise. Edward Nicholas, in the fifteen-page *An Apology to the Right Honourable Nation of the Jews, and All the Sons of Israel,* suggested a new flexibility. "God hath exceedingly blessed this Empire above all others," he wrote, ". . . so that now [it behooves] . . . that we all show ourselves compassionate, and helpers of the afflicted Jews, and . . . repeal the severe [expulsion] laws made against them." The pamphlet caused much stir.

The early 1650s represented high tide in the Cromwellian interregnum. The atmosphere seemed hopeful for a chiliastic gesture. Soon, then, Parliament took up a petition dispatched by Joanne Cartwright and her son Ebenezer, who had lived in Amsterdam as Baptists, requesting formal abrogation of Edward I's 1290 Statute of Banishment. The proposal in fact was merely one of the scores that were floating about Westminster by then. The spate of activity was by no means gratuitous. Recently, the issue of Jewish admission had evoked the attention of none other than the Lord Protector himself, Oliver Cromwell.

A Visitor from Amsterdam

Ironically, Cromwell displayed little personal interest in the utopianist fantasies of the Fifth Monarchy Men or other millenarians. If he favored toleration, it was for Protestant Christians of his own persuasion. Nevertheless, understanding well the importance of a thriving export economy for his nation, he grasped precisely the role of Jews in the Spanish, Portuguese, and Levant trade. He was acquainted with the New Christian merchants Antonio Fernandez Carvajal (p. 310) and Simon de Cáceres, and with their leadership in that commerce. He saw only gain in a Jewish mercantile presence on English soil. As late as 1651, however, Cromwell believed that the issue of Jewish admission could be settled quietly, without governmental initiative. In that year, he had proposed a treaty of coalition to the Netherlands. Under its terms, all inhabitants of the United Provinces ipso facto would have acquired in England the same residency and economic privileges they enjoyed at home.

When negotiations on the proposal broke down, Parliament subsequently enacted the first in the series of Navigation Acts intended to exclude Dutch vessels from Britain's colonial carrying trade. But early in 1651, when hopes for the Anglo-Dutch coalition still were high, Cromwell had dispatched a negotiating mission to The Hague. It was led by Chief Justice Oliver St. John, a man who happened to be a staunch advocate of religious freedom. During a recess in the discussions, St. John and his fellow envoys journeyed to Amsterdam to visit the renowned Menasseh ben Israel. The meeting took place in Menasseh's synagogue. There the Englishmen were much taken by the rabbi's gentle demeanor and rich erudition. It was they who now urged him to make formal application to London for Jewish readmission.

Once Anglo-Dutch negotiations collapsed, the Jewish issue had to be postponed. Nevertheless, in 1653, St. John and his colleagues ventured to raise the notion of Jewish admission directly with Cromwell. The Lord Protector was receptive. Indeed, to enhance the prospect's chances, he devised an approach of his own. Menasseh ben Israel should be invited to England, where he would personally sell his people's case to Parliament and public. Cromwell thereupon issued an official directive, authorizing "Menasseh ben Israel, a rabbi of the Jewish nation, well respected for his learning and good affection to the State, to come from Amsterdam to these parts." English consuls were to give Menasseh and others whom he would select "favourable entertainment" en route. It was a tantalizing invitation, virtually unprecedented except for those issued by Turkey's Sultan Mehmet II and Tuscany's Duke Cosimo de Medici (p. 76 and p. 230). Yet Menasseh hesitated to accept it. Local feeling against England was high at that moment. Among Dutch Jews and Christians alike, Menasseh might have been seriously compromised had he undertaken a mission to London. For the time being, he postponed his departure.

It was Cromwell who would not permit the venture to lapse. Colonial issues were much on his mind. Lately, too, the Lord Protector had become heavily dependent for advice on Simon de Cáceres, the London marrano who had developed extensive trading connections in the West

Indies. At Cáceres's suggestion, Cromwell in April 1655 dispatched to Barbados a marrano physician, one Abraham de Mercado, with his son Raphael. From this base, the Mercados were charged with exploring the possibility of colonizing the recently acquired former Spanish territory of Jamaica. The immigrants Cromwell had in mind were Jewish fugitives who lately had fled Portuguese Brazil (p. 357). Prospects for their settlement appeared encouraging. The Mercados' recommendation was affirmative, and so was Cáceres's. To those Jews, then, who would agree to take up residence in Jamaica, Cromwell offered full civil rights, even the promise of major land grants. The Lord Protector's gesture represented the first step in negotiating a Jewish return to English soil.

Yet the task of winning public support for Jewish settlement in England proper would be a more formidable one. To achieve this feat of diplomacy, the presence of Menasseh ben Israel himself was now indispensable. The famed rabbi was still hesitant. But Cromwell had an ally. It was Menasseh's son, Samuel. The young man had arrived in London as early as 1653 to explore the lay of the land. Now, a year and a half later, in May 1655, Samuel was informed that the Lord Protector wished him to return to Amsterdam forthwith and persuade the esteemed rabbi to come over. Samuel was more than eager to comply. During his stay, he had been much impressed by England's possibilities for his fellow Jews. Upon reaching Amsterdam, therefore, he made a convincing case with his father. Finally, in September 1655, Menasseh duly sailed for England, accompanied by Samuel and three other local rabbis who insisted upon sharing the honor of the mission with him.

The delegation reached Plymouth in three days. Arriving in London at the end of the week, the entire group was lodged as guests of the Lord Protector in a handsome abode opposite the New Exchange. The accommodations bespoke Cromwell's personal interest in the mission. At the same time, Manoel Dormido, a local New Christian, put Menasseh in touch with London's tiny group of marrano businessmen. The rabbi thereupon conducted Rosh HaShanah services for them. Finally, Menasseh prepared to get down to diplomacy. His first task was to submit his petition for Jewish readmission. Indeed, he had written and translated the document into English even before departing Holland. It was entitled: "To His Highnesse the Lord Protector of the Commonwealth of England, Scotland, and Ireland, the Humble Addresses of Menasseh ben Israel, a Divine, and Doctor of Physick, in behalfe of the Jewish Nation."

Fortunately for his readers, Menasseh avoided the rather apocalyptic theories of his original *Spes Israel*. This time, he argued his case almost entirely on the grounds of political and economic utility:

Three things [he wrote], if it please your Highnesse, there are that make a strange Nation well-beloved amongst the Natives of a land where they dwell: . . . Profit they may receive from them; Fidelity they hold towards their Princes; and the Nobleness and Purity of their Blood [a characteristic Sephardic transposition of limpieza de sangre].

Now when I shall have made good, that all these three things have been found in the Jewish Nation, I shall certainly persuade your Highnesse, that with a favourable eye . . . you shall be pleased to receive again the Nation of the Jews.

In his disquisition, Menasseh shrewdly emphasized his people's mercantile contributions to their host societies, the intensity of their devotion to their rulers. Accounts of ignoble behavior were based upon false reports, he insisted. "[T]he Jews indeed have reason to take care for their own preservation, and therefore will not go about by such wayes to make themselves odious to Princes and commonwealths, under whose Dominions they live." Menasseh concluded then with the forthright request for open Jewish immigration and settlement.

The petition was rather too frontal for royalists and High Churchmen. Neither did it appeal to London's merchants, who were fearful of Jewish competition. Each of these camps now launched its own vigorous countercampaign. Rumors were circulated that the Jews had offered to buy St. Paul's Cathedral and the Bodleian Library, that the Lord Protector was prepared to hand over the customs concessions to them. The notion of proselytizing Jews was illusory, argued the opponents. Rather than become Christians, the Jews would "stone Christ to death." Their alleged profitability was a myth; they would suck all financial gain from good Christians. Faced with this avalanche of hostility, even the millenarians who had offered Menasseh encouragement over the years were now intimidated into silence. Prospects for Jewish admission seemed as bleak as before the rabbi's journey.

Once again, it was Oliver Cromwell who took the initiative. In November, he personally tabled the readmission petition before the Council of State, endorsing it in his own language: "That the Jews deserving it may be admitted into this nation to trade and traffic and dwell amongst us as Providence shall give occasion." Plainly, the Lord Protector wanted swift action. His recommendation was dispatched to a committee, and the committee reported back the following morning. Its members were by no means irredeemably hostile to the Jews. They simply declared themselves legally unqualified to advise the Council of State. It was their suggestion, rather, that the Council itself summon a gathering of representative citizens to "ascertain the views of the Nation." Cromwell accepted the proposal on the spot. Within thirty-six hours, his advisers drew up a list of "representative personages," and the Council promptly invited this group to meet two weeks later, in mid-December.

Convening at Whitehall in the Council Chamber, the representative personages included government ministers, justices, lord mayors, aldermen, senior military commanders, theologians and divines, including the president of Magdalen College, Oxford, and the canon of Christchurch College, Cambridge. To decide the issue of the Jews, in fact, Cromwell had summoned one of the most notable conclaves in the history of the Puritan Commonwealth. He and his advisers also had taken care to select members known specifically for their tolerationist views. Thus, at the outset, the judges among the assembly confirmed that no law forbade Jews to return to England. Under their interpretation, Edward I's original Statute of Banishment of 1290 was an exercise of the royal prerogative over his personal "chattels," not an Act of Parliament. Cromwell was gratified. "If it be lawful," he asked, "then upon what terms is it meet to receive them?"

The matter was not to be that easily resolved. Over the next twenty days, the assembled notables learned that they could not function in isolation from public opinion. The hostility of Anglican clerics was particularly fierce. Dire warnings were issued of a "judaizing heresy," possibly even of "Moloch worship," in England. Hardly less emphatic was the reaction from commercial circles. In an ill-advised gesture, the Council of State had agreed to open the assembly's final session to the public, and among the mob now crowding into Whitehall were numerous small tradesmen. Many had been worked to a frenzy by William Prynne's recent pamphlet *A Short Demurrer to the Jewes' Long Discontinued Remitter into England,* a harshly antisemitic document. Taken aback by the spectators' shouts and imprecations, the businessmen in the Whitehall Assembly now changed course, favoring a ban on Jews, at least in the principal retail trades, and the imposition of special licensing fees for Jews. The argument raged into the night.

By the early morning hours, Cromwell, who had been present for most of the session, recognized that his entire scheme was crumbling. Summarily adjourning the conclave, he announced that he and his Council of State would make the decision on their own. The Lord Protector thereupon departed the chamber in a towering passion. Yet, as matters developed, he would secure little satisfaction even from the Council of State. Shaken by the tumult in the recent assembly, the Council also proved unexpectedly timid and declined to make a recommendation. Another fortnight passed. It was late January 1656. Cromwell himself remained ominously silent.

During these weeks, Menasseh ben Israel was not idle. Here the role of his close adviser, Henry Jessey, proved crucial. More than any man, it was this impassioned millenarian who stage-managed the rabbi's visit, who established contacts and made appointments for him with public and private figures alike. Thus, under Jessey's guidance, Menasseh sallied forth from the apartment placed at his disposal in the Strand, meeting politicians, divines, intellectuals, anyone who might help him reach his goal. He conferred with Ralph Cudworth, Regius Professor of Hebrew at Oxford; Henry Oldenburg, future secretary of the Royal Society; the Countess of Ranelagh; Cotton Mather, the New England missionary who was then on a return visit to London; Jean d'Espagne, minister of the French Reformed Church. On one occasion, Menasseh dined at Cromwell's table, the Lord Protector making special provision for the rabbi's dietary needs. In all his conferences, Menasseh invariably proved captivating in his unobtrusive wisdom and gentle persuasiveness.

Meanwhile, Cromwell moved to resolve the status of the Jews on his own. It was in March 1656 that London's diminutive settlement of marranos timorously asked his permission to worship at last as avowed Jews. The Lord Protector's response was immediate and affirmative—provided the agreement was not bruited about, and the Jews conducted their services "discreetly" in private homes. Yet only a few days passed before news of the "secret agreement" began circulating in London's mercantile and clerical circles. There were sullen mutterings. Cromwell was unperturbed. Indeed, he soon turned to the Jewish issue even more forthrightly. England's intermittent conflict with Spain recently had erupted again, and the Council of State routinely proclaimed all Spanish funds, merchandise, and shipping as lawful prizes. In March, one Antonio Rodrigues Robles, a wealthy marrano importer, suffered the confiscation of all his stock including two of his vessels anchored in the Thames. Robles appeared to be legitimate prey. He was a member of the "Portuguese Nation," after all, and Portugal remained linked to the Spanish monarchy. The rest of London's New Christian minority was equally at risk.

Robles was not the man to accept his fate lying down. Aware of the Lord Protector's goodwill, he appealed to the Council of State for restitution. He was not an enemy national, he insisted, but a "Portuguese of the Hebrew nation." It was an unprecedented acknowledgment of Jewish identity. Once committed, moreover, Robles took the initiative, launching into a graphic account of his life's experience, of the agony he and his kin had endured at the hands of the Inquisition. His father had died under torture, he explained. His mother had been permanently crippled. Other family members had been "relaxed" at the stake or sentenced to the galleys. Invoking the historic English tradition of asylum to "afflicted strangers," Robles then intimated that mistreatment of Jews would be equivalent to introducing the dreaded Inquisition into England itself. Thereupon, other prominent New Christians also threw off their disguises and submitted affidavits endorsing Robles's petition.

In May 1656, the Council of State ordered the restoration of Robles's property. The man was no Portuguese, the Council acknowledged, but rather a fugitive Jew, a victim of the Inquisition, and thus entitled to remain in England unmolested. So, evidently, were other identified Jews. At no time did the Council issue a law or ordinance defining the new status of these people. If Jewish circumstances were evolving almost by intimation and indirection, the technique was characteristically English. Plainly, the Council's decision owed much to Cromwell. In June, the Lord Protector acted more decisively yet, pressing the Council to allow the Jews full privileges of residency, worship, and trade "on an equality" with other citizens. The recent marranos, for their part, were obliged only to worship privately, to abstain from all religious controversy or proselytizing activities. The Council agreed. Interestingly enough, the measure was never recorded in law. All reference to it was torn from the Council minute book, and only private accounts have left the historical evidence.

If the little Sephardic community was relieved and gratified by the compromise, Menasseh ben Israel was not. Nor did he disguise his indignation. Quarreling bitterly with London's Jews, he exhorted them to insist on nothing less than a parliamentary act of full citizenship. They were not interested. By then, in fact, they were no longer interested in Menasseh's presence. He had fulfilled his role, and his persistence now threatened to disrupt an entirely tolerable new state of affairs. They wanted him gone. Yet the rabbi was unable simply to return to his Amsterdam pulpit. In some measure, Dutch Jews shared the Stuart sympathies of Dutch Christians. Menasseh's negotiations with the English Commonwealth thus supplied his parnassim with their long-desired pretext for terminating his incumbency. He was stranded.

Deserted by his former London admirers, Menasseh soon used up the last of his funds. One can only imagine the mortification with which a distinguished spiritual leader, a former eminence of Dutch Jewry, now wrote Cromwell for help. The Lord Protector, he explained, was "the lone succoror of my life in this land of strangers." And Cromwell, with admirable generosity, duly provided the rabbi a gift of twenty-five pounds, and in March 1657 supplemented that gift by granting an annual pension of one hundred pounds. But somehow the annuity never materialized, and Menasseh soon was reduced to begging his bread from local Jews. Then, in September, his son Samuel, who had remained with him during his stay in England, died of a kidney ailment. Swallowing the final remnants of his pride, Menasseh cajoled a few last pounds from Cromwell, then booked passage to Amsterdam. He departed with the corpse of his son. En route home, exhausted and penniless, he died of heart failure at the age of fifty-three.

Anglo-Gradualism and Jewish Status

England's tiny Jewish nucleus survived both Menasseh's death and, a year later, Cromwell's. Ironically, the compromise of July 1656 turned out to be their good fortune. In its initial stage, the arrangement had disturbed the nation comparatively little, thus permitting later governments discreetly to connive at the Jews' presence. Had Menasseh fully realized his appeal for guaranteed, formal status, England might have been deluged by a substantial immigration of destitute Ashkenazic Jews, particularly from the recent Ukrainian massacres. Instead, public attention hardly was aroused by the thirty or forty comfortable Jewish merchants and their families residing in mid-seventeenth-century London.

Cromwell's gentle, ineffectual son Richard held office as Lord Protector for just over a year, until 1659. Unwilling to tamper with his late father's compromise, he ignored occasional petitions to expel the Jews. It was also the approach of the restored monarchy after 1660. Charles II was entirely opposed to religious oppression, and not least of all in the case of the Jews. Better than many of his royal contemporaries, the king appreciated the Jews' mercantile value. While in exile in Holland, Charles had enjoyed congenial dealings with Jewish financiers. Augustino Coronel—the marrano Nuñes da Costa—was the intermediary who secured a major loan on his behalf from Afonso VI of Portugal. Afterward, in 1660, Coronel followed Charles to England, where he served as Portugal's consular and financial agent. It was he who negotiated the impecunious king's marriage to the wealthy Princess Catherine of Bragança, in 1662. Gratefully, Charles knighted Coronel.

The king proved equally generous to England's professing Jews. He approved their periodic "denization," a limited form of naturalization secured through private parliamentary bills. In 1664, the Conventicle Act came into force, nominally banning all religious congregations other than the Church of England's. Although the measure was aimed at Catholics and Christian nonconformists, it evoked consternation among the little

Sephardic colony. Charles II then had his Privy Council reassure the Jews in writing that they would enjoy "the same favour as formerly they have had, so long as they demean themselves peaceably & quietly with due obedience to [the king's] Lawes & without scandall to his government." The letter was a significant one. It represented the first official confirmation that the Jews might live and worship freely in England.

Well before then, in fact, in 1657, they had already purchased their former rented premises on Creechurch Lane and transformed the house into a permanent synagogue. Seven years later, the congregation brought over its first rabbi, Jacob Sasportas, from Amsterdam. At the outset, public worship evidently did little for the Jews' public image. In 1664, Samuel Pepys visited the Creechurch Lane synagogue. It was the festive holiday of Simchat Torah, a time specifically of merrymaking. Pepys was repelled:

> Lord! to see the disorder, laughing, sporting, and no attention, but confusion in all their service, more like brutes than people who know the true God, would make a man foreswear ever seeing them more.

Pepys could not have grasped that the synagogue was less a religious congregation in the English sense than an ethnic community, still largely administering its own laws and even levying its own taxes. Although without government imprimatur of any kind in England, the communal arrangement survived well into the eighteenth century and functioned also as the model for Jews in British colonies as diverse as Kingston, Jamaica, and Newport, Rhode Island—even as Amsterdam's Esnoga served as the model for the Jews of London.

In 1699, their numbers growing, the little Anglo-Jewish community set about erecting a permanent synagogue in Bevis Marks, barely down the road from Creechurch Lane. The building still exists and is still used. A functional rectangle, spacious enough to accommodate some five hundred worshippers, it is ventilated by plain arched windows. Its paneling, Ark railing, pews, central pulpit, warden's box, and canopy are all of dark oak, severe and dignified. The austerity is relieved only by six brass candelabra (four of them provided by Amsterdam's Esnoga), by low-hanging lamps emerging from gilded rosettes in an ivoried ceiling, by door frames adorned in gold garlands and fluted wooden columns of green and cream.

During its very construction, Bevis Marks in some measure evidenced the normalizing status of Britain's Jews. Some years earlier, in 1685, the community had reacted in alarm to the death of Charles II. Throughout his twenty-five-year reign, the Restoration monarch had never failed to protect them. By contrast, his Catholic brother, James II, made little effort to inhibit occasional revived outbursts of anti-Jewish agitation. The era was an uncomfortable one. Mercifully, it was also brief. For the Jews, the Revolution of 1688–89 opened a particularly happy chapter. Indeed, the expedition that provoked James's flight, and the ascension to the throne of Willem of Orange and his wife, Mary Stuart, was substantially financed by Dutch Sephardim. Francisco López Suasso advanced Prince Willem the munificent sum of two million crowns, interest-free. Francisco de Córdoba, acting on behalf of Isaac Pereire, supplied bread and foraged food for Willem's army.

It was entirely a fitting gesture, therefore, as construction began on the Bevis Marks synagogue in 1699, for Princess Anne to offer the congregation a present on behalf of her family. It was an oak beam from a vessel in the Royal Navy. Anchored to a rafter in the synagogue's roof, the solid joist became an appropriate talisman of Anglo-Jewish security. During the late seventeenth century, Protestant England emerged as a coveted haven for nearly a thousand Spanish and Portuguese conversos, and for twice that many identified Jews who arrived directly from Amsterdam. Most of them were businessmen anxious to circumvent the Navigation Acts by operating directly within the British trading ambit. Others followed. By 1700, England's Jewish population had grown to six thousand, including an influx of several hundred families from Leghorn, Italy.

The newcomers wasted little time in developing trade links with the kinsmen they had left behind. In the import-export trade, they operated as shippers, brokers, financiers, bullion and diamond merchants. Some became contractors to the armed forces. In 1688, the Anglo-Dutch firm of Machado and Pereire supplied William III's army in Ireland. Joseph Cortissos provisioned the earl of Peterborough's expeditionary force in Spain in 1705. Solomon de Medina became principal contractor to the duke of Marlborough's army during Queen Anne's War of 1707–11. Denied entrance to the bar, many Sephardim became notaries and legal scriveners. Others became physicians (a profession less distinguished than law in those days). Fernando Mendes had been physician to Charles II's family; Jacob de Castro Sarmento, to the Portuguese embassy. Yet most Jews were petty retail businessmen. Indeed, many were quite poor, especially the several thousand North African berberiscos and European Ashkenazim who arrived early in the eighteenth century. The charity rolls of the Bevis Marks congregation soon were stretched to the limit. In 1733, the synagogue board was obliged to cooperate with the government in shipping at least forty of its indigents to General Oglethorpe's Georgia plantation.

By the mid-eighteenth century, Ashkenazim comprised a majority of

England's fifteen thousand Jews. In their frequent poverty and cultural deprivation, these unprepossessing immigrants evoked a new upsurge of anti-Jewish sentiment. Thus, in 1753, public outrage induced Parliament to revoke its recently passed Naturalization Act, which granted foreign-born Jews the right of participation in local and county government. "Such a fury was reigning against [the Jews]," acknowledged Thomas Chitty, Lord Mayor of London, "that I feared violence in the streets." Although transitory, the episode was frightening enough to impel the organization of a joint Sephardic-Ashkenazic "vigilance" committee. In later years, the body evolved into the Board of Deputies of British Jews, Anglo-Jewry's spokesman to the "outside" world.

A Convoluted Pathway to Respectability

Well into the mid-1800s, any participation in England's political life, let alone aspiration to national political leadership, would have appeared unthinkable for an alien and still unpopular minority. Nevertheless, in the decades that followed, one member of the "race," Benjamin Disraeli, precociously overcame every obstacle of suspicion and bigotry to become arguably England's greatest prime minister of the nineteenth century. It was Disraeli's father who unwittingly launched his son's public career by having him baptized in the Church of England. With his family's money behind him, the younger Disraeli first came to the public's attention as a belletrist. Beginning with *Vivien Grey* in 1826, he turned out a series of well-received satirical novels on English public life. During the next few years, still producing books and articles, titillating society with his wit, bejeweled fingers, and flamboyant green velvet attire, Disraeli moved temperamentally and ideologically closer to the Tory party.

It was as a Tory, in 1837, that he eventually won election to the House of Commons. Four years later, rejecting his party's drift toward a bourgeois orientation, Disraeli became leader of the Young England movement, a group of maverick conservative politicians intent on rallying poorer voters away from their traditional alignment with the middle classes and into a new association with throne, church, and aristocracy. In 1852, as chairman of this faction, Disraeli successfully orchestrated the Tory return to power. With Lord Derby serving intermittently as prime minister, Disraeli himself occupied the second billet as chancellor of the exchequer and party leader in the House of Commons. Upon Derby's retirement in 1868, Disraeli enjoyed a brief stint as successor prime minister. Finally, in 1874, he managed to win the prize on his own in a resounding popular electoral victory. "The oriental," as his political enemies mocked him, now plainly had become respectable. During his six years in office, Disraeli shepherded through Parliament a program of enlightened factory and welfare legislation that was unprecedented in European history.

The man's achievements in foreign policy were more impressive yet. They were based forthrightly on Disraeli's idealized vision of the British Empire as the stronghold of peace and civilization. India was the pearl of that empire, and Disraeli's acquisition of controlling shares in the Suez Canal, in 1875, with the financial help of the Rothschilds, guaranteed Britain swift and economical maritime access to the mighty Indian subcontinent. A year later, Disraeli climaxed his imperial achievement by having Queen Victoria proclaimed Empress of India. Victoria, in turn, anointed Disraeli earl of Beaconsfield. At the same time, to protect Britain's Mediterranean lifeline, the prime minister remained vigilant in checking Russian expansion through the Balkans. The strategy led to a memorable diplomatic triumph at the Congress of Berlin in 1878. Indeed, the coup transformed Disraeli into a national hero, evoking cheers such as rarely had been heard by a returning British statesman.

Were these accolades bestowed on a Christian or on a Jew? On a marrano? Disraeli's mother's family was descended from Leghorn Jews who may have been either Sephardic or Italian. His father's family unquestionably were Sephardim who had fled Castile to settle first in North Africa, then in the Papal States, ultimately in England. Disraeli's career in many ways was suggested by that of his father, Isaac, who derived his principal income from a family import-export business but regarded himself essentially as a litterateur. By the standards of his time, Isaac Disraeli apparently was a decent enough poetaster and a respectable magazine writer. His relationship with his own Bevis Marks synagogue was similarly unexceptionable. Then, in 1813, the congregation's board decided that he was suitable for the office of parnas—president. Courteously, he declined; communal service held no interest for him. Whereupon the board fined him forty pounds. An acrimonious correspondence ensued, and persisted on and off for nearly four years. In 1817, Isaac Disraeli resigned from the synagogue in a huff, then afterward impetuously had his children baptized.

Yet in the case of Benjamin, Jewish ancestry was imprinted as indelibly upon his consciousness as upon his features. There was no way to escape the identification, and least of all as a member of the Tory party with its emphasis on "good" family lineage. Could that which was inescapable, then, possibly be exploitable? A man of imagination might yet find ways to transform an otherwise ineradicable ancestral blemish. Benjamin Disraeli assuredly was that man. An incurable romantic, he set about embellishing a compensatory vision of his "aristocratic" Jewish descent. In an autobiographical note, he boasted that his Hebrew ancestors "assumed the name of d'Israeli, a name never borne before or since by any other family, in order that their race might be forever recognized." In the parliamentary election of 1847, opposed by a member of the duke of Cavendish's family, Disraeli boldly proclaimed his own provenance as superior to that of the Cavendishes. "Fancy calling a fellow an adventurer," he mused on another occasion, reacting to an ethnic slur, "when his ancestors were probably on intimate terms with the Queen of Sheba."

It was in his novels even more than in his political career that Disraeli gave widest rein to his racial fantasies. *Alroy* was perhaps the most revealing of these works. Published in 1833, soon after Disraeli visited the Holy Land, it was based on an actual twelfth-century Jew, Menachem ben Solomon al-Ruhi, who lived in the Azerbaijani region of the Caucasus Mountains. The historical "Alroy" was believed to have rallied his fellow mountain Jews in revolt against their Moslem overlords, only to be treacherously murdered by his own father-in-law. Reworking the slender evidential record, Disraeli transformed Alroy into the son of a Prince of the Captivity. Visiting Jerusalem, exploring the Tomb of the Kings, the young warrior encounters the ghost of Solomon, who enjoins him to restore the independence of the Jewish people and their ancient glory. Alroy rises to the challenge, gathers his Jewish soldiers behind him, overthrows the Moslem yoke, sweeps through the Holy Land and much of western Asia. Then, tragically, the gallant commander is overthrown in battle. Upon refusing to save his life by embracing Islam, he is executed. The tale was not unlike numerous other lush oriental romances of the time. Yet this one rather transparently identified Disraeli himself with the proud, "aristocratic" Jewishness of the legendary warrior chieftain.

An identical racial bombast is evident in Disraeli's "Young England" political satires: *Coningsby* (1844), *Sybil* (1845), and *Tancred* (1847). In *Tancred*, the eponymous young hero, once again scion of an aristocratic family, prefers to "find himself" before standing for Parliament. To that end, he sets out on the path of his Crusading ancestors to seek inspiration from the "genius" of Semitic stock. After a series of improbable adventures, Tancred acquires insight into the sovereignty of the "common Father" during a climactic ascent of Mount Sinai. Turgid in plot and rhetoric, the novel abounded in improbable speculations on Jewish wisdom, genius, vision.

So, however, did all Disraeli's writings, even his obiter dicta and conversations. For him, the central theme was the unique "racial" aristocracy of the Jews, and thus, by intimation, of himself as a bearer of that pedigree and as an equal, thereby, to any mandarin in the Tory party. "All is race—there is no other truth," declares the character Sidonia in *Coningsby.* "Progress and reaction are but words to mystify the millions. . . . All is race" (*The Life of Lord George Bentinck,* 1852). When Lionel de Rothschild (appearing and reappearing in Disraeli's novels as Sidonia) became a father, Disraeli's letter of congratulations typically expressed the wish that the new son "will prove worthy of his pure and sacred race." "What did you talk about last night?" a friend asked Baron Lionel, meeting him in town the day after he entertained Disraeli. "The race, as usual," was his gloomy reply. In *Endymion* (1880), the novel of Disraeli's old age, Ambassador Serius provides the valedictory observation that race "is the key to history. . . . There is no race gifted with so much tenacity [as the Jews], and with such skill in organization."

If for Disraeli the Jews remained the creative leaven in every land, that role was manifest perhaps most of all in England. "Vast as are the obligations of the whole human family to the Hebrew race, there is no portion of the modern population so much indebted to them as the British people." And that people, in consequence, owed the Jews political emancipation. Indeed, beyond all others, the Tories were obliged to recognize "the Jews . . . [as] a race essentially monarchical, deeply religious, and essentially Tories." It was nonsense, of course. The Liberals were the party that admitted Jews to Parliament in 1858, and the Jews ever after remained their dutiful protégés. To his fellow Tories, the "oriental" in his posturing was never more than a glittering parvenu.

A Frontal Pathway to Respectability

Ultimately, it was not Benjamin Disraeli, the exotic illusionist of Jewish genius, but Moses Montefiore, the bulldog champion of Jewish rights, who served a distinctly more austere purpose for the English conscience. Among his fellow Jews, first and foremost, no individual in Montefiore's time evoked a comparable veneration. For a series of impoverished and persecuted Jewish communities extending from Europe to North Africa to Asia, it was he who played an often decisive role as philanthropist-protector. A common Jewish aphorism in the nineteenth century, as in the Middle Ages, stated: "From Moses to Moses, there was none unto Moses"—that is, from the original Moses the Lawgiver to Moses Maimonides, and now to Moses Montefiore, no Jew could compare in stature.

Born in 1784 into an affluent Leghorn family that had immigrated to England several decades before, Montefiore became one of the earliest

Jews to be admitted to the London stock exchange. He flourished mightily as a bullion broker. As early as 1824, at the age of forty, he was wealthy enough to retire from active business and devote all his energies and the bulk of his fortune to his fellow Jews. In that effort, no cause was dearer to Montefiore than restoration of a Jewish presence in the Holy Land. He made his initial visit to Palestine in 1827, the first West European Jew to venture the pilgrimage in modern times. It was still a long and rather dangerous journey in those days, but Montefiore and his redoubtable wife, Judith, undertook it in the spirit of piety. Upon arrival, he, Judith, and his entourage of advisers and servants set about dispensing charity to Jerusalem's impoverished Orthodox remnant. Eventually, Montefiore would make six trips to the Holy Land, the last in 1875 when he was almost ninety-one. On each occasion, he was tendered the reception normally extended visiting royalty. For all his largess, too, Montefiore distributed his funds selectively. His favored projects were printing presses, flour mills, and farm villages—essentially ventures that offered Jews the opportunity to support themselves. Several of these enterprises ultimately succeeded.

Between journeys to Palestine, Montefiore was endlessly on the move in behalf of threatened Jewish communities elsewhere. His first diplomatic mission, in 1840, was to rescue eleven Jews of Damascus who had been imprisoned for the alleged ritual murder of a local Catholic priest. To Jews in the West, who had witnessed their people's recent steady progress toward emancipation, this "Damascus Affair" was an ominous throwback to medievalism. Whereupon, under Montefiore's leadership, a delegation of prominent French and British Jewish spokesmen journeyed to Alexandria, seeking the personal intervention of Mehemet Ali, khedive of Egypt-Syria. Montefiore's resourcefulness in mobilizing the resident European ambassadors to his cause proved decisive; Mehemet Ali eventually ordered the prisoners' release. The Jewish world greeted the news with transports of joy. Montefiore was extolled in proclamation, verse, prose, and prayer as the Jewish grand seigneur, the incomparable protector of his people's welfare.

In truth, no corner of the Diaspora was too remote for the great man's solicitude. In 1842, the tsarist government announced that "state security" required that some one hundred thousand Russian Jews be transported from their homes near the Austrian and Prussian borders deeper into the Russian interior. Although a four-year grace period was allowed, enforced migration would have meant economic ruin for the uprooted Jews. In 1846, therefore, Montefiore climaxed a long diplomatic campaign of appeal and remonstration by personally embarking for St. Petersburg. Received by Tsar Nicholas I and his cabinet ministers, the renowned Jewish emissary delivered a passionate entreaty in defense of his people. Long discussions followed. In the end, Nicholas agreed to cancel the planned transplantation. Accordingly, as Montefiore made his way back through the vast Jewish hinterland of western Russia, he was received again in every community as a king, a liberator, a new messiah.

The "messiah's" forays were not always successful. His personal intercession with the Vatican in 1848 on behalf of the Mortara family of Bologna, whose son Edgardo had been abducted by papal police (p. 234), failed to secure the boy's release. A visit to Romania in 1867 produced little improvement for that country's substantial Jewish minority. But Montefiore's effort in 1863 to ameliorate the political and economic conditions of Moroccan Jewry may have been the apotheosis of his career. Then seventy-nine years old, he embarked with his wife and retinue of advisers on a long, heroic trek by horse and mule across one hundred twenty miles of Moroccan desert-and-mountain terrain. Upon reaching the then capital of Fez, he was tendered a dazzling official reception, replete with a six-thousand-man honor guard and a royal banquet. The venture concluded successfully when the sultan of Morocco offered a personal pledge of better treatment for "his" Jews. Once again, the Jewish world was agog at Montefiore's amalgam of saintly compassion and tenacity of will.

The man's gravamen invariably was that of the self-respecting Jew. On all his missions and pilgrimages, whether to Alexandria, Rome, St. Petersburg, or Fez, he insisted on bringing with him a personal Jewish cook and kosher kitchen utensils. Over six feet tall, dignified of manner, he dealt self-assuredly with monarchs and ministers as the spokesman for a distinguished people. Little wonder that his fellow Jews hung on his every accomplishment, his every pronouncement, as if it came from the original Moses. On the occasion of Montefiore's one-hundredth birthday, in 1884, his town of Ramsgate was profusely beflagged, and all schools and shops were closed. Ninety constables were mobilized for the thousands of arriving visitors, many of whom traveled on specially chartered trains. Montefiore died in 1885, just short of his one-hundred-first birthday.

In the end, however, Moses Montefiore's achievements reflected less his own heroic exertions than the solicitude of the British establishment. As early as 1830, Montefiore was presented to King William IV by the duke of Norfolk, the first peer of the realm. Montefiore's wife, Judith, was presented to the queen by the countess of Albemarle. That same year, he was elected a member of the Athenaeum, the most exclusive club in London. Was this escalating progression of courtesies and honors evoked by virtue of his ancestry, or in spite of it? A year before, unanimously elected sheriff of Middlesex (he would soon also be elected sheriff of Kent), Montefiore had explained his inability to attend the inaugural banquet, which was scheduled for the eve of Rosh HaShanah. The dinner committee instantly changed the banquet date. In 1837, upon the accession of Victoria to the throne, Montefiore as president of the Board of Deputies of British Jews led a deputation to the coronation. Kneeling to pay the young queen homage, he himself then was unexpectedly favored with knighthood. Moreover, as a special gesture to him, the queen had arranged for the word "Jerusalem" to be sewn on Montefiore's ceremonial pennant of baronetcy. Was the knighthood a compensation for the man's Jewishness, or a consequence of it?

In advance of Montefiore's initial visit to Palestine in 1827, and on each of his five later journeys there, the Foreign Office directed all British consular officials along his scheduled route to extend to him the utmost in diplomatic protection and personal solicitude. In 1840, Whitehall let it be known that Montefiore's rescue effort for the Jews of Damascus was a matter of great importance to the British government. Indeed, before his departure for the Near East, Sir Moses was granted a private audience with Queen Victoria, to signify her personal concern for the success of his mission. And when at last the prisoners were released, Victoria solemnized Montefiore's triumph by granting embellishments to his baronet's coat of arms, "in commemoration of these his unceasing exertions on behalf of his injured and persecuted brethren in the East and the Jewish nation at large."

In 1846, to forestall the transplantation of Russian Jewry, Montefiore brought with him to St. Petersburg letters of commendation from Prime Minister Peel and Foreign Secretary Aberdeen. Hardly less than formal démarches, the documents emphasized London's official concern—and proved decisive in assuring the success of Montefiore's mission. Afterward, too, Victoria celebrated his achievement by transforming his knighthood into a hereditary title. In 1863, Montefiore returned from his exhausting Moroccan odyssey to a public "reception of appreciation" tendered by the lord mayor of London. Among the two thousand guests— most of them non-Jews—was Prime Minister Gladstone, the featured speaker.

Four years later, Gladstone offered Montefiore a peerage. The honor, which Montefiore graciously declined for reasons of age, did not spring full-blown from the prime minister's brow. It had been suggested by Ashley Cooper, seventh earl of Shaftesbury. The quintessence of obdurate Torydom, Shaftesbury was the last man one would have taken for a philosemite. In earlier years, he had relentlessly opposed the Jewish struggle for admission into the House of Commons. But in 1867 it was he who sent to Gladstone a note of almost obsequious contrition:

> All that [struggle for Jewish emancipation] is now passed away, and let us now avail ourselves of the opportunity to show regard to God's ancient people. There is a noble member of the house of Israel, Sir Moses Montefiore, a man dignified by patriotism, charity, and self-sacrifice, on [whom] Her Majesty might graciously bestow the honour of the Peerage. It would be a glorious day for the House of Lords when that grand old Hebrew were enrolled on the lists of the hereditary legislators of England.

"A glorious day for the House of Lords." England in the 1860s was approaching the meridian of its wealth and power. Awestruck at their developing good fortune, its people were keenly aware that their island, lacking even grain for sustenance, had managed somehow to dominate the markets of five continents, even to plant the Union Jack on four of them. Surely, therefore, it was freedom that had provided the little country with its matchless eminence in international affairs. However defined by conservatives or liberals, it was toleration in all its permutations, respect for all creeds and sects, that at long last had won universal recognition as the wellspring of British vitality, the source of the nation's envied stature throughout the civilized world. The climate of that pluralism had repeatedly to be tested, then, and endlessly reconfirmed. Who better than a Jew to serve as weathervane?

CHAPTER XV

THE VANGUARD OF
A NEW WORLD

The Royal Cosmographers

It is appropriate that Lisbon's Maritime Museum, housing the memorabilia of Europe's earliest overseas explorers, stands on the north bank of the Tagus River. Portugal lacks a window on the Mediterranean. With the Tagus, however, a vast, deep-flowing estuary, as wide as the Mississippi or the Nile, its people have always faced outward, away from the classical centers of European civilization, westward toward the untamed Atlantic and southward to an Africa that for centuries also remained largely unfathomed for Europeans.

The nation's first tentative venture outside the Peninsula began in 1415 with King João I's conquest of Ceuta, in North Africa. Directing the campaign, Prince Enrique, João's third son, was stunned by the loot that fell into his hands. The treasure included not only slaves, ivory, and ostrich feathers from Saharan Africa in the south, but gold, silver, jewels, tapestries, and exotic spices from the Indies to the east. Plainly, more information was needed of this fecund hinterland, and specifically of the Asia that lay beyond. To acquire that knowledge, Prince Enrique then assumed personal responsibility for additional exploration. Upon returning home, he uprooted himself from cares of state in Lisbon and transferred his headquarters to Sagres, on Cape St. Vincent, the southwesternmost tip of Portugal. Here Enrique—later known as Prince Henry the Navigator—assembled the most talented group of geographers and astronomers he could recruit, both from his own country and from other nations. Together, they charted a series of historic expeditions.

The initial objective was to probe the African coast. In that undertaking, Enrique's vessels combed the Gulf of Guinea and the mouth of the Congo. But at the same time, veering wide around the West African littoral into the Atlantic, Portuguese mariners also discovered Madeira and the Azores. In later years, well after the prince's death, they also identified the Cape Verde Islands. Later yet, in 1488, while plying the identical leeward route, Bartholomeu Dias was blown across Africa's southern cape and found himself off its east coast. Could a sea highway, then, be open to India? The prospect was confirmed barely a decade later when Vasco da Gama, also sailing the Cape of Good Hope route, led the first Portuguese fleet across the Indian Ocean. Following in his wake, other Portuguese mariners established trading posts in Asia, the Spice Islands, and the Moluccas. So it was that Prince Enrique's initial vision was fulfilled. Portugal now dominated European commerce to the Far East.

Today, it is a rather moving experience to revisit Sagres, where the mighty adventure began. All that remain at the desolate "sacred promontory" are a spray-flecked lighthouse and the crumbled skeleton of a fortress-barracks. It was precisely this citadel that functioned as the original work- and living-space for Enrique's collection of astronomers, geographers, and navigators. In addition to Portuguese natives, the men gathered here included Castilians, Catalans, Italians, Germans, Scandinavians, Greeks, Berbers, Arabs. And there were Jews. Of these, by far the greatest at Sagres was "Mestre Jacome." Originally known as Judah Crescas, he was the talented son of Abraham Crescas, who himself was widely renowned as the ablest cartographer of the fourteenth century. Both men were products of Majorca.

Over the years, this largest of the Balearic Islands, with its substantial Jewish population of between two and three thousand (before 1391), had nurtured a truly distinguished collegium of merchant mariners, navigators, and mapmakers. Their knowledge was drawn from personal acquaintance with the existing trade routes, and, more extensively, from information shared among friends and relatives throughout the Diaspora. It was thus a logical move for Prince Juan of Aragón to appoint Abraham Crescas, doyen of Majorca's renowned fraternity of Jewish cartographers, as Master of Maps and Compasses, and in 1376 to commission him to execute the most detailed and complete terrestrial map within his power. Crescas and his son Judah set to work.

The project required fully two years. It showed. A vast tryptich, mounted on twelve wooden leaves to fold like a screen, the *mapamundi* displayed the principal known oceans and seas, the totality of southern Europe, North Africa, the Orient—including, for the first time, the entire Indian subcontinent—together with all existing information on regional geography and topography as collated from existing data, the reports of mariners, and Jewish correspondents. In breadth, detail, and accuracy, nothing like the Catalan Atlas (named for its sponsor, Juan of Aragón-Catalonia) had ever been produced. "Never have we seen so fair a map," cried the prince when it was delivered to him. Years later, he generously presented the atlas as a gift to France's King Charles VI, and it remains now a valued possession in the Bibliothèque Nationale in Paris. A facsimile may also be viewed in the Catalan Maritime Institute in Barcelona.

Abraham Crescas died in 1387. Judah inherited both his reputation and his clientele, as well as his former patron, now King Juan. Yet the old relationship did not endure, not after the mass pogroms of 1391. Indeed, the savagery terrorized Judah Crescas into baptism. Gratefully, then, he accepted Henry the Navigator's invitation to Portugal in 1416. All but openly resuming his Jewish identity as Mestre Jacome, Judah Crescas served as first director of Sagres's nautical laboratory. It was according to his guidelines that the institute's cartographers and navigators subsequently charted the prince's audacious new expeditions.

Other Jews, both professing and convertido, eventually shared in the heady adventure of exploration. For all seafarers, navigational accuracy remained the cardinal objective. Mariners who sailed below the equator moved beyond sight of the North Star, and consequently were left helpless to determine their latitude. It was to surmount this obstacle that Portugal's João II appointed a commission in 1481 led by Joseph Vecinho, a Castilian Jewish astronomer-mathematician. Four years later, Vecinho set out personally on a voyage to devise a technique of measuring latitude not by the North Star but by the height of the sun at midday. He accomplished the feat by recording the sun's path off the coast of Guinea. The achievement, while significant, in fact was based upon an earlier coup. This was the *Almanach perpetuum,* published seven years before by Vecinho's former professor at the University of Salamanca, Abraham Zacuto. In the end, therefore, perhaps Vecinho's most enduring achievement was his role in bringing his mentor to Lisbon in 1492.

Zacuto was an authentic giant of the Renaissance era of discovery. A professing Jew, richly versed in biblical and talmudic lore, he had studied astronomy at Salamanca, where he himself subsequently became a renowned teacher. It was in Salamanca, in 1478, that Zacuto produced a series of magisterial astronomical treatises, of which incomparably the most important was his Hebrew-language *HaChibur HaGadol* (The Great Essay). Later translated into Latin as the *Almanach perpetuum,* then republished in Castilian, Portuguese, Italian, and German, Zacuto's tables of celestial position at last permitted sailors to ascertain their latitudes even without recourse to the sun's meridian. The feat won Zacuto an exalted reputation. Indeed, even the Spanish Expulsion Decree of 1492 interrupted his career only minimally. Through Joseph Vecinho's initiative, he was able to cross into Portugal, where he forthwith accepted appointment as court astronomer to João II.

In Lisbon, Zacuto was consulted extensively by Vasco da Gama before the latter's voyage to India in 1496. Strongly favoring the project, the great astronomer provided da Gama with an improved version of the old Greek astrolabe, fashioned from copper rather than wood. The device proved so indispensable to the navigator, together with the Majorcan maps and Zacuto's *Almanach,* that references to it appear in Luiz Vas de Camões's 1572 epic poem of Portugal, *Os Lucíadas.* Other mariners were equally indebted to Zacuto. At the Archives of the Indies in Seville, Columbus's personal copy of the *Almanach* is still preserved, together with marginal notations in his own hand.

However epic their contributions, Jewish astronomers in Portugal were not spared Manoel I's forced conversion of 1497. Joseph Vecinho instantly submitted. Under the name Diogo Mendes Vecinho, he continued his scientific work for the Crown. So did Pedro Nunes, professor of mathematics at the University of Coimbra, whose *Treatise on the Spheres,* first published in Lisbon in 1537, opened the way for Mercator's research and thus for an entirely new generation of spherical cartography. But apostasy was unacceptable for a person of Abraham Zacuto's intense Jewish commitment. With his son Samuel, the great astronomer fled Portugal for North Africa. Although twice imprisoned by pirates en route, the two finally managed to reach Tunis in 1504. There Abraham Zacuto subsisted as a private tutor in mathematics and astronomy. There, too, at last, he completed a long-delayed work of the heart. It was the Hebrew-Aramaic *Sefer Yuchasin* (The Book of Relations), an ingenious history of Jewish law as portrayed through biographies of ibn Daud, Maimonides, and other historic talmudic scholars. In 1513, finally, Zacuto was to be found in Jerusalem, teaching in a rabbinical seminary—and compiling yet another almanac, in Hebrew, on biblical meteorology. And it was in Jerusalem, two years later, that he died in relative obscurity.

The Imperial Conversos

The Archives of the Indies, a massive stone edifice on Seville's Avenida Queipo de Llano, is the principal historical repository for Spain's exploration and conquest of the New World. Within, a regal marble stairway ascends to a vast L-shaped gallery. Here, on shelves of Cuban mahogany, some four hundred thousand documents are ranked, filed, and indexed. Locked away in air-conditioned storage, too, are the charts, account books, logs, letters, and memoirs of Christopher Columbus.

Jewish filiopietists, as well as several non-Jewish historians, have speculated that the "Admiral of the Ocean Sea" was a Jew. They note that his Spanish name, Colón, was a not uncommon one in Hebrew tradition; that his father was a weaver, one of the few trades open to Jews in his native Genoa; that his mother, Susanna Fonterossa, was the daughter of Jacobo Fonterossa and granddaughter of Abraham Fonterossa. The hypothesizing has been extensive, and Columbus himself doubtless was responsible for much of it. His letters in the Archives drop tantalizing hints: "I am not the first admiral of my family, let them give me whatever name they please; for when all is done, David, that most prudent king, was first a shepherd and afterward chosen King of Jerusalem, and I am a servant of that same Lord who raised him to such a dignity." In his ship's log, Columbus makes frequent references to the Hebrew Bible, to Jerusalem, to Moses, David, Abraham, Isaac, and Sarah. He computes the age of the world according to the Jewish calendar: ". . . and from the destruction of the Second Temple according to the Jews to the present day, being the year of the birth of Our Lord 1481, are 1413 years." In discussing the mines of the New World, he observes: "Our Lord, who rescued Daniel and the three children, is present with the same wisdom and power as He had then." In his last will and testament, Columbus asks that one-tenth of his income be given to the poor; that a dowry be provided for poor girls "in such a way that they do not notice whence it comes"—a characteristically anonymous technique of Jewish philanthropy.

Today, however, most scholars dismiss the rather poignant effort to judaize Columbus. They prefer to focus on the overwhelming, thoroughly documented role of Jews in the great mariner's voyages of discovery. In Lisbon, Columbus knew and consulted Joseph Vecinho, Martin Behaim, and other astronomer-navigators of the royal court. It was Vecinho who presented Columbus with a Castilian translation of Zacuto's astronomical tables. Later, Zacuto himself also met Columbus, and endorsed his proposed Atlantic expedition. "[T]he distant Indies," Zacuto acknowledged, "can be reached through [Columbus's] enterprise, though it is hazardous." Not the least of those hazards was the absence of funding. For Columbus, none could be found in Portugal. He moved on to the Spanish court in Andalusia.

There he was received sympathetically by the small group of converso royal officials, among them Juan Cabrero, Gabriel Sánchez, Juan de Colomba, Alfonso de la Caballería, and Luis de Santángel. It was the latter who emerged as particularly vital to Columbus's expedition. Chancellor of King Fernando's household, comptroller-general of Aragón, and an immensely wealthy tax-farmer on his own account, Santángel was in a unique position to exert influence at court. Personally, he favored Columbus's Atlantic venture and recommended it to his ruler. When the king was not forthcoming, Santángel arranged three separate audiences for Columbus with Castile's Queen Isabel. Both men made a strong case. Indeed, as an additional inducement, Santángel offered to advance 1.4 million maravedis of his own. Finally persuaded, the queen—and her husband—then supplied the rest of the funds. Santángel's crucial intermediary role would not be forgotten. It was to him that Columbus sent off the first report of his discovery after returning from his initial Atlantic voyage.

In underwriting the expedition, the royal couple depended upon more than Santángel's participation. April 29, 1492, the day Columbus received authorization to equip his fleet, was also the day the Edict of Expulsion was publicly announced in several of the larger Spanish cities. The timing was not coincidental. For the Catholic Monarchs, the anticipated revenues of forfeited Jewish property represented a substantial "down payment" on Columbus's venture. Indeed, the two events were linked to the final moments of joint departure. "After the Spanish monarchs had expelled all the Jews from all their kingdoms and lands," Columbus recorded, "they commissioned me to undertake the voyage to India with a properly equipped fleet." The scheduled date of sailing, August 2, was also the deadline for Jewish departure. Scores of vessels, with thousands of Jews packed into their holds, congested Palos de la Frontera, the maritime inlet of the Gulf of Cádiz. Here, too, Columbus gathered his fleet of three little caravels.

The tumultuous "ethnic cleansing" provided Columbus with more than his funds. At least part of his crew were conversos. Among them were Alfonso de la Calle, a bursar, who eventually settled in Hispaniola. Rodrigo Sánchez of Segovia, a surgeon, was a relative of Aragón's treasurer, Gabriel Sánchez. Another surgeon, Maestro Bernal of Tortosa, only recently had escaped the clutches of the Inquisition. Luis de Torres was a Jew who had accepted baptism just in time to sign on with Columbus's fleet. As a multilingual "oriental," Torres was regarded as a likely interpreter to the "oriental" potentates of the Indies. Later, he sought government permission to remain on the island of Cuba as royal agent, and his appeal was granted, along with a pension. Meanwhile, in gratitude for Columbus's discovery of the Indies, the Catholic Monarchs in 1493 authorized the great mariner to set sail again for the New World. To fund the second expedition, however, the royal court pounced on all remaining Jewish wealth—all unsold land and homes and unredeemed certificates of indebtedness; all chattels, precious metals, jewels, gold and silver utensils, even synagogue artifacts. The expropriation would generate 6 million maravedis, four times the amount available for the initial voyage. This time, the Admiral of the Ocean Sea departed in style.

It is a fact of history that Columbus's four voyages achieved only a precarious foothold in the New World. Another half-century of exploration and conquest was required for others to secure Spain's vast empire, and to structure the sheer magnitude of terrain into the three manageable viceroyalties of New Spain (Mexico, Central America, the Philippines), New Castile (Peru, all of South America except Brazil and the Guineas), and New Granada (Panama, Colombia, Venezuela, Ecuador). Colonization in those years took precedence over trade as an imperial objective. To foster that settlement, the Crown offered the inducement of great landed *encomiendas* to loyal soldiers and farmers and shared profits for the prospectors, engineers, and overseers of South America's boundless silver mines. Ostensibly, the constraints of limpieza de sangre excluded New Christians from these ventures, or even from settlement in Spanish America. Yet conversos aplenty found ways to emigrate to the New World. Spain's notoriously venal bureaucracy was quite prepared to sell permits of exemption. For the right price, ship captains were equally willing to disembark New Christian passengers at secret inlets along the Gulf of Mexico south of Veracruz, or on the Honduran coast.

Indeed, the infiltration of conversos became something of an influx once the Spanish throne assumed its rule over Portugal in 1580. As on the Peninsula itself, the transmigration of Portuguese New Christians to the Americas came to be known as the *penetración portuguesa*. The process was infinitely facilitated by Felipe III's Royal Pardon of 1601, and Pope Clement VIII's Papal Pardon three years later. Secured through massive bribes (p. 178), the decrees opened a window of new opportunity for conversos in Spanish America. They exploited it to the hilt. In the early seventeenth century, between three and five thousand Portuguese New Christians may have departed for the New World. They anticipated important commercial inducements overseas, and they were not disappointed. In New Spain, as many as two thousand conversos settled in Mexico City, Guadalajara, Vera Cruz, Puebla, and Guatemala City. In New Castile, approximately the same number of New Christians resided in Lima, Potosí, Tucumán, and Córdoba. By the 1630s, hardly a town in the Spanish Empire did not shelter at least a scattering of conversos, some of whom migrated as far as New Mexico and Florida.

Their vocations were no less diverse than in Europe. Among the conversos there were numerous artisans—shoemakers, spice-makers, tailors. Others were ranchers. Several New Christians were priests. One was a bishop. There were converso military officers. The mayor of Tecali was a New Christian. Yet, as in Europe, most Sephardim gravitated toward commerce. Several became managers of silver mines. Others were gem- and food-dealers. They played their traditionally decisive role in the import-export market, including the slave trade. Altogether, New Christians were as prominent in the Americas as in Spain, Portugal, or the Netherlands. Cuba's governor Pedro de Valdés may have exaggerated in 1605 in reporting to Felipe III that the "Portuguese on the island have . . . all the money . . . in their hands. . . ." Nevertheless, the early 1600s unquestionably was their best period in the New World.

The Family Carvajal

It was also an evanescent moment, bracketed by an oscillation of inquisitional malevolence. In March 1589, Luis de Carvajal, governor of the New Kingdom of Léon, a three-hundred-thousand-square-mile fiefdom in northern Mexico, was arrested at the behest of the Inquisition and by personal order of the viceroy of New Spain. Portuguese-born, Luis de Carvajal y de la Cueva, "el Conquistador," was descended from a family of eminent businessmen and royal functionaries. While still a young man, he served as comptroller of the Cape Verde Islands. Subsequently, as admiral of a naval armada based in Tampico, Mexico, he led his squadron in a series of important victories over British and pirate interlopers. His reward was the governorship of León. In that capacity, "el Conquistador" discovered several important new deposits of silver and established a chain of new towns. No public official could have served his Crown more loyally or productively. As it happened, Carvajal was of partial New Christian descent. So was his wife, Guiomar. Yet the government was prepared to overlook this blemish in a man of such prodigious talents and achievements. He was even permitted to bring over some one hundred members of his extended family, although his wife chose to remain in Spain.

Personally, Carvajal was the devoutest of Catholics. As a young man, he had studied for a short period in a seminary. Yet a substantial minority among the three or four thousand other conversos in New Spain appear to have been marranos. Their knowledge of Judaism unquestionably was vestigial. None knew Hebrew, none possessed Jewish books or even the dimmest familiarity with the classical Jewish liturgy. Hardly any even remembered the principal Jewish holidays except for Yom Kippur and

Passover. Nevertheless, whenever possible they observed the Sabbath by bathing and changing their linen. They also avoided pork. Remarkably, too, whatever the degree of their observance, few of these crypto-Jews appeared to be in danger. Inquisitional activity in the Americas was unsystematic in those early years, the initiative left essentially to local bishops and various Dominican and Franciscan monks. Even following appointment of an Apostolic Inquisitor for New Spain in 1515, any investigative effectiveness was undermined by local jealousies and jurisdictional squabbles. Indians and blacks, in any case, were exempted from scrutiny. Even among Europeans, the hunt initially concentrated on blasphemers and bigamists. Well into the sixteenth century, fewer than twenty-five cases of judaizing are recorded among six hundred heresy trials, and only two of these resulted in burnings. The presence of conversos hardly was a secret to the royal administration, but neither was their value to the empire.

Then, in 1571, the Suprema at last persuaded the zealous Counter-Reformationist Felipe II to introduce the Holy Office into Spanish America. Emphasis henceforth was shifted from haphazard blasphemy trials to "freeing the land, which has become contaminated by Jews and heretics, especially of the Portuguese nation." From then on, a smokeless chimney on the Jewish Sabbath, a festive family dinner at Passover time, a worn or hungry look on Yom Kippur, was enough to induce the Inquisition to pounce. It was in these years that Governor Luis de Carvajal became more vulnerable. Unknown to him, his sister Francisca and her husband, Francisco Rodríguez de Matos, both of whom he had brought to Mexico, were committed judaizers. So were eight of their nine children and most of their nephews and nieces. The single exception was a son, Gaspar de Matos, who became a Dominican priest. Living in Mexico City, earning a decent livelihood as merchants, the family managed to observe the principal Jewish holidays and fasts (however imprecisely) as well as the Jewish dietary laws. Upon the death of their father, the sons and daughters camouflaged their activities more effectively yet by adopting the name of their illustrious uncle, Carvajal.

In 1589, however, the judaizing activities of an older daughter, Isabel, became too flagrant to ignore. She was arrested. Within the next two days, the Inquisition's constables and bailiffs descended on the rest of the family. Of the sons and daughters living at home, only two eluded capture. It was then that the governor himself was taken into custody. Outraged, Luis de Carvajal protested his innocence. Although lately aware of Isabel's activities, he insisted that he had been planning soon to denounce her. The Inquisition rejected the argument. Even Carvajal's distinguished public record could not secure his release, and he was remanded to prison for trial. As for the other defendants, the mother, Doña Francisca—the governor's sister—was savagely tortured. Soon she confessed everything put in her mouth, implicating all her children, nieces, nephews, and in-laws. Most of the others then collapsed under torture or terror, even the entirely innocent priest, Fray Gaspar.

It was at this point, early in 1590, after months of imprisonment, that the third son, Luis de Carvajal—a namesake of his famous uncle and henceforth known as "el Mozo," the Younger—emerged as spiritual leader of the family. Like all conversos in sixteenth-century New Spain, he possessed only limited knowledge of the ancestral religion. Ironically, it was his command of the Vulgate, and of Catholic devotional literature with its numerous Old Testament references, that transformed him into the family's most learned and vigorous judaizer. Luis was intensely, even euphorically, immersed in that effort when suddenly he was arrested and thrown into Flat House, Mexico City's grim inquisitional prison. There, in his dank cell, the young man affirmed his loyalty by using an old pair of scissors to perform on himself the excruciating and dangerous operation of circumcision. From then on, no torture could shake his commitment. While admitting his own Judaism, and even giving public lip service to contrition, Luis flatly refused to implicate other family members—although, unknown to him, they had already confessed.

At an auto de fe in February 1590, the inquisitional tribunal pronounced sentence on the Carvajals. A posthumous punishment was imposed on the late Don Francisco, whose remains were exhumed and publicly burned. Inasmuch as all the prisoners had declared contrition, however, their punishment was less than draconian. Doña Francisca and Isabel were sentenced to life penance in a convent, Marina and Catalina were given two years in a convent, twelve-year-old Leonor was given one year, while ten-year-old Ana was consigned to indeterminate penance in the home of a "reliable" Catholic family. Gaspar the priest was spared prison in favor of life service at a monastery. Penance for the younger Luis was three years in a seminary.

It was Governor Luis de Carvajal himself, finally, who endured perhaps the most traumatic sentence of all. Found guilty of "abetting and protecting" judaizers, he was stripped of his office and estate, condemned to six years of exile from New Spain, then remanded to his cell for transport back to the homeland. It is likely that Carvajal preferred not to survive in shame and guilt. His premonitory farewell was implicit in a verse later found by his warden:

Adiós España, tierra bonita,
tierra de la consolación.

Four months into his imprisonment, still awaiting transfer to Spain, the disgraced governor perished of undetermined causes.

The Carvajal tragedy acquired a more somber dimension yet in the aftermath of trial and sentencing. Two brothers had managed to elude the Inquisition: Miguel had gone underground in Madrid, while Baltasar, hiding in various safe houses, eventually stole out of Mexico and traveled south to Nicaragua. There he sought out a converso shipmaster at Puerto de los Caballos, who agreed to carry him to Spain. Weeks later, arriving in Madrid, Baltasar contacted his brother Miguel, who "purchased" his anonymity and safety. In Mexico, at the same time, a brother-in-law, Antonio Díaz de Cáceres, managed to elude the Inquisition long enough to secure passage on a vessel departing Acapulco. Three months later, he reached Manila, only to discover that even in the Philippines the Inquisition was on the lookout for him. He reboarded ship and proceeded on to Macao, capital of Portugal's eastern empire, then still ruled jointly with Spain. But in Macao, too, almost incredibly, an inquisitional warrant was out for Cáceres's arrest. He was seized and imprisoned. Again, money changed hands. He was allowed to escape once more, negotiating passage on still another vessel. This one carried him back to Mexico. And in Mexico City, the very eye of the hurricane, Cáceres actually managed for a while to resume his life, unrecognized.

During these same years, other members of the Carvajal family were duly fulfilling their penitential sentences in convents, monasteries, mission hospitals. The Carvajals in fact were less than penitent. Each was intent on maintaining at least symbolic links with Judaism. The focus of that revived effort was none other than the home of Antonio de Cáceres—doubtless the last place the Inquisition would have suspected a judaizing cell. At night, as their proctors slept, family members stole out of convents and hospices to meet in the Cáceres attic. Here again, young Luis de Carvajal emerged as leader. With much imagination, he organized a private *colegio* of studies in Judaism, even composed new liturgical works, conducted prayer sessions, led psalm-singing to the accompaniment of a guitar. Under his guidance, the little cell soon became the clandestine headquarters for other marranos in Mexico City, and then elsewhere throughout New Spain.

At last, in February 1595, a spy penetrated the *colegio* and incriminated the entire family. They were imprisoned again immediately. None could have entertained any illusions about their fate by then. Luis himself was caught up in fantasies and visions—biblical patriarchs and matriarchs appeared before him in the guise of long-dead friends and relatives, enjoining him to acknowledge his Judaism openly, to sustain his family's morale. This he tried to do. A friendly warden supplied him with pen and paper and offered to smuggle his notes to his mother and sisters. Luis then hurled himself into a fever of writing. A characteristic message reads:

> My precious ones . . . remember the sacrifice of the saintly Isaac. When he was bound, how obediently he awaited the thrust of the knife. [Remember] the faith of his saintly father, our patriarch, Abraham . . . [t]he dangers confronting the saintly Moses . . . the wandering of our holy father, Israel, of David and all the [later] saints. . . . [G]reat is the joy that will be placed upon our heads through all eternity. . . . Leonor, my dearest—whom I love, as I do all [my sisters] like darling Rachels . . . since you are nearby, send me songs [to let me know] whether you are alone. . . . What do you suppose my Lord God will do with our little [sisters] Anica [Ana] and Mariana . . . and our sister Isabella, the poor widow? Oh, my darling flock.

Typically intermingling Judaic and Christological themes, Luis reminded his mother and sisters that in paradise they would tread soft fields, luxuriate in scented orchards, delight to the thrum of a harp and the click of castanets. He produced some twenty letters in this vein. None was ever delivered—except to the Inquisition.

Under torture, the womenfolk recanted all heresies. Not so Luis. On December 6, 1596, he left his testament: "I happily bring to an end the course of my present life, bearing living faith in Your divine promise of salvation through Your infinite mercy . . . of resurrection in the company of our sainted patriarchs, Abraham, Isaac, and Jacob." The next day began the most elaborate auto de fe thus far held in Mexico. Thousands of spectators witnessed the long procession, replete with the traditional column of elaborately costumed clergy and public officials, the melancholy queue of sanbenito-and-miter-attired prisoners. The familiar routine of prayers, sermons, and sentence-reading followed. Among the forty-five accused judaizers, the Carvajals represented nearly half. Not all were present. Baltasar and Miguel were safe in Europe. Gaspar had not been rearrested. But among the file of prisoners were Doña Francisca, Luis, and five of his sisters—Isabel, Mariana, Ana, Catalina (wife of Antonio Díaz de Cáceres), and Leonor—together with their husbands and several children. All but Mariana and Ana were sentenced to immediate relaxation. A girl of sixteen, Ana was consigned again as a penitent to the custody of a Catholic family.

The next day, the condemned were sent off to the quemadero, the burning ground. More dead than alive, Doña Francisca and her daughters agreed to embrace the church. They were accordingly garroted, and only their corpses were burned. Luis spurned reconciliation and was burned alive. Reporting on the executions to the Suprema, a Fray Contreras offered an undisguised eulogy:

> [Luis] was always such a good Jew and he reconciled his understanding, which was very profound and sensitive, with his highly inspired divine determination to defend the Law of God—the Mosaic—and to fight for it. I have no doubt that if he had lived before the Incarnation of our Redeemer, he would have been a heroic Hebrew and his name would have been as famous in the Bible as are the names of [other biblical heroes].

For the next four years, Mariana de Carvajal languished in prison. Alternating between lucidity and disorientation, she was judged not yet sane enough to undergo relaxation. Instead, she was subjected to the "cure" of prolonged beatings and whippings. In 1601, during a final period of clarity, Mariana confessed her heresy and the Inquisition declared her punishable. In a mass auto de fe of that year, she was garroted and her corpse burned.

With the decimation of the Carvajals and their *colegio,* the Inquisition apparently had wiped out all significant judaizing activities in New Spain.

The Great Conspiracy

The assumption was premature, of course. King Felipe III's and Pope Clement VIII's pardons of the early seventeenth century had allowed New Christians to replenish their ranks in the Americas. Yet the newcomers' essentially Portuguese background did not endear them to other colonists, still less as they thrived mightily in this golden age of free movement and free enterprise. Then, in 1640, Portugal broke free from Spanish rule, and with renewed virulence Spain's Inquisition in Mexico was soon again in hot pursuit of alleged Portuguese judaizers. By midcentury, the number of arrests exceeded two hundred. The succession of trials eventually reached a climax in April 1649 with the single most elaborate auto de fe in the history of New Spain.

It was described in much detail by Fray Mathias de Bocanegra, a member of the inquisitional entourage. Brilliantly re-created by Professor Martin Cohen, the friar's account captures the atmosphere in Mexico City: the bells tolling mournfully, the vast retinue of magnificently uniformed state and clerical officials winding its way through the streets of the capital, the human remains carried in twenty-three boxes for posthumous burning, the one hundred six accused prisoners in sanbenitos embroidered with flames, demons, and serpents and wearing grotesque mitre-like hats. The final setting, in the city's largest public square, near the governor's palace, included stages, tiers, bleachers, lush velvet coverings and pennants and heraldic standards. The scene glittered in a pomp and brilliance that manifestly were intended to remind its eighteen thousand onlookers that the sovereign dignity and prestige of Spain extended to the farthest reaches of its empire. Fray Mathias, for his part, discerned a less secular purpose in the extravaganza:

> This day is very pleasing to God because the very holy Mexican Tribunal has consecrated on its altars . . . that the Faith is revindicated, religion applauded, errors corrected, heresy refuted, truth acclaimed, Christ triumphant, and our law victorious.

Sixty-seven of the accused were burned in effigy. Twelve others were relaxed at the stake, among them an entire family—father, daughter, and two sons. The father, Tomás Treviño de Sobremonte, may have been, after Luis de Carvajal el Mozo, the most captivating figure among the marranos of New Spain. Nobly born and wealthy, he combined aristocratic Spanish pride with unshakable commitment to Judaism. And like Luis, he met his end with a dignity so monumental that it appeared in a Mexican folk poem of the nineteenth century:

> The Jew's turn came, he was the first
> to be burned alive on account of his
> sacrilegious acts.
> It is said that when he was tied
> to the rough steel pile
> and when the red flames of the fire
> were all around him, he shouted
> to his executioners with a mad voice:
> "Throw on more wood, you wretches,
> because I am paying for it."

Among the eleven remaining victims who were relaxed was none other than Ana de Léon de Carvajal, Luis's youngest sister. Arrested half a century after having been "penanced" to a Catholic family, Ana now was found guilty of relapsing. It mattered not that she was sixty-four years old and suffering from an illness that probably was terminal cancer. As Fray Mathias explained: "She was . . . very punctual in the observance of the Sabbath. . . . [Afterward,] even though she was a prisoner, this wicked old lady fasted and prayed day and night and commended to the God of Israel all the other Jews who were imprisoned." Ana was burned alive. With her death, in the holocaust of 1649, ended the fragile legacy of crypto-Judaism in New Spain. Although two other marranos were burned in 1659, and one in 1699, no further trace of judaizers, or scarcely of conversos, could be found in Mexico.

They had long since moved elsewhere on the continent. Indeed, members of the "Portuguese nation" had arrived by the many hundreds in New Castile (Peru, essentially) during the early 1600s. Encouraged by the Royal Pardon, and the vast mineral wealth of the interior, these Sephardim settled predominantly in Lima. By then, the Peruvian capital was a raucous boomtown, so unruly in its heterogeneity of settlers that Cervantes once described it as "a refuge and shelter for Spain's desperados, an asylum for fraudulent bankrupts, a safe-conduct for murderers, a cover-up for gamblers . . . a lure for loose women . . . and a special remedy for failure." An influx of conversos here was not likely to have fazed the Spanish viceroyalty. If the newcomers eventually provoked a reaction, the cause was not attributable to their suspected judaizing but to their wealth.

Thus, in 1619, when Captain Manuel de Frías, the Inquisition's regional procurator, dispatched a memorandum protesting the deluge of New Christians, he observed ruefully: "[T]hey belong to the rich and influential merchants, who are highly expert in all kinds of merchandise and Negro slaves." Another official report, in 1636, asserted that New Christians controlled the entire merchant marine, that "pure" Castilians had no chance of competing with them. The converso mercantile role in Lima was assuredly vast. Even today, the street opposite the former viceroy's palace is known as Calle de los Judíos. "[From] brocade to sack-cloth," suggests the historian H. C. Lea, whose *Inquisition in the Spanish Dependencies* draws extensively from local records,

> from diamonds to cumin-seed, everything passed through their hands; the Castilian who had not a Portuguese partner could look for no success in trade. . . . They would buy cargoes of whole fleets with the fictitious credits which they exchanged, thus rendering capital unnecessary, and would distribute the merchandise throughout the land by their agents, who appeared likewise Portuguese.

As in Spain itself, it was the visibility and affluence of the New Christians that proved their undoing.

For decades, the Inquisition gave them only intermittent attention. Earlier, in 1595, ten alleged citizens were paraded in an auto de fe, four of whom were relaxed at the stake. In 1600, fourteen judaizers were sentenced and two were burned. In 1605, twenty-eight were sentenced, three burned. Yet as news of Felipe III's and Clement VIII's pardons reached the New World, the quest for judaizers subsided in New Castile. Three quiescent decades followed. Then, in the summer of 1635, the Inquisition launched one of the major purges in Latin American history. The episode began on a Saturday in June, when Antonio Cordero, a young New Christian in Lima, was tidying up the warehouse of his employer, a carpet manufacturer. Several customers dropped by, but Cordero informed them that he was unable to transact business on a Saturday. Reports of the comment eventually reached the Inquisition, and Cordero was brought in for questioning. Under torture, he soon revealed the identities and activities of an extensive network of marranos. In the following weeks, sixty-four people were arrested and charged with judaizing. Thus began the sequence of events known as *La Complicidad Grande* (The Great Conspiracy) of colonial Peru.

The ensuing arrest or flight of nearly four hundred prominent conversos, and the sequestration of their property, soon plunged New Castile into serious economic disruption. To settle matters quickly, the Inquisitors organized their trials with unusual dispatch, completing them in an unprecedented three years. It was extensive use of torture that did the job. One prisoner had his arm torn to pieces. Another, a woman, died of her ordeal. The sixty-three remaining defendants were all convicted and sentenced at a spectacular auto de fe of January 1639. Eleven were relaxed. A twelfth, who had committed suicide during the trial, was burned in effigy.

Two of the victims were of more than passing importance. Manuel Bautista Pérez was the single wealthiest man in Lima, the owner of two silver mines and two vast plantations. He was also leader—"el Gran Capitán"—of the marrano community in New Castile. Although tortured, Pérez heroically refused to disclose information about his brethren. When the pain became unendurable, he attempted suicide, repeatedly plunging a homemade knife into his stomach, but he survived. Afterward, in his cell, he exhorted a fellow prisoner who had confessed, his brother-in-law Sebastián Duarte, to repudiate his confession. Duarte did so, and paid with his life at the stake. When a fellow victim, the surgeon Tomé Cuaresma, cried out for mercy just before his pyre was lit, Pérez gave him a commanding look and the surgeon fell silent. "El Gran Capitán" then went to his own death so proudly that even the Inquisitors were moved.

Ironically, the most celebrated of all the victims of 1639, Francisco Maldonado de Silva, a physician, was not part of the Great Conspiracy. His mother was probably an Old Christian. His father, Diego Nuñez de Silva, also a physician, was a converso, possibly even a marrano. Yet it was not the father who transformed the younger man into a judaizer. While still a resident at the Santiago hospital in Chile, Maldonado happened to pick up the volume *The Wars of the Lord* by the Spanish Jewish apostate Abner of Burgos (p. 41). Published originally to expose the errors of Judaism, the book had the reverse effect on the young doctor. It impelled him to question the very foundations of Christianity, and ultimately to embrace his ancestral religion. He confirmed the decision by circumcising himself.

Practicing medicine in Lima afterward, Maldonado diligently observed the Sabbath and fast days. He also remained in active communication with other marranos. Remarkably, he continued undetected. His mistake, in 1627, was his attempt to convert his two sisters. Both women were horrified, and immediately denounced him to the Inquisition. Maldonado then was arrested, torn away from his pregnant wife and young daughter, imprisoned, tortured. He would not repent or incriminate others. Rather, for twelve years, in a fetid cell and isolated from the world, he managed to compose several tracts in defense of Judaism, using rags for paper, a chicken bone for a quill, and coal dust for ink. With rope fashioned from corn silk, Maldonado succeeded occasionally in guiding these writings from his window grate to the cell below, with entreaties for other prisoners to hold on. In his fervor, too, the doctor allowed his hair and beard to grow in the manner of a biblical Nazarite and even began calling himself "Eli Nazareno." Finally, on the day of the historic auto de fe of January 1639, Maldonado ecstatically joined ten martyrs of the Great Conspiracy at the stake.

The trauma of the Great Conspiracy far exceeded trial and punishment by the Inquisition. Beyond disrupting commerce in New Castile for several years, it shattered any remaining hopes for a revived Jewish presence in Peru and Chile, as in Mexico and Central America later. Few additional trials of suspected judaizers were held. Few were needed. Nor were they required in the Caribbean Basin. One sizable auto de fe was staged in Panama in 1614, but none of the prisoners was relaxed. Of the handful of conversos who remained in Spanish America by the latter part of the seventeenth century, hardly any were crypto-Jews. Most of their fellow marranos had been burned. The rest had been hounded into permanent flight, either to the West Indies or to North America. In the Spanish Empire, as in the Spanish homeland, the long, poignant struggle of vestigial Judaism now flickered out at last. When it revived again, two and a half centuries later, the flame no longer would be Sephardic.

CHAPTER XVI

THE END OF THE
INHABITED EARTH

The Sugar Barons

In April 1500, six weeks after departing Lisbon en route to India, a Portuguese naval expedition led by Admiral Pedro Alvares Cabral inadvertently veered westward off the Cape of Good Hope and landed on the hitherto undiscovered northern coast of Brazil. Making the most of his navigational error, Cabral immediately took possession of the uncharted wilderness in the name of his king, Manoel I. At least one member of the admiral's crew, as it happened, was a *cristão novo,* a New Christian. His original name remains unknown, but his odyssey was memorable, even in the often surrealistic history of the Jewish dispersion. A Portuguese mercenary, the young man had served as naval fleet captain for Sabayoj, the Arab ruler of Goa, India. It was in Goa, on a February morning in 1498, that he made a courtesy call on Vasco da Gama, discoverer of the sea route to India, whose own fleet was anchored nearby. But instead of greeting this European warmly as a fellow Portuguese, da Gama ordered him seized as a spy.

Under torture, the prisoner then attempted to explain that he was not a spy at all but a Jew whose family had come to Portugal originally from Granada. Da Gama was not appeased. Rather, he carried his prize back to Portugal and obliged him to undergo baptism—duly to be reborn as "Gaspar da Gama." Soon afterward, Gaspar was put on display before King Manoel I. The young man's dignity of bearing quite impressed the king, who promptly ordered him freed. Several months later, Gaspar was even put to good use: he was dispatched as an interpreter on Admiral Cabral's expedition to India, which resulted in the accidental landing in Brazil. It was Gaspar da Gama's subsequent account of the voyage and discovery that has remained ever after a classic of the literature of exploration.

Still another cristão novo in this early period of Portuguese empire was Fernão de Noronha. As chairman of a consortium of New Christian investors, Noronha obtained the first royal concession in the Brazilan province of Bahía. He made the most of the opportunity. In return for tax exemption, for a monopoly of the province's resources and its slave trade, Noronha and his fellow concessionaires dispatched ships and settlers to Brazil at their own expense in 1503, then brought over a flotilla of troops and supplies to construct Bahía's principal fortress. Noronha also found time to discover an island close to the Brazilian coast that henceforth would be known as Ilha de Fernão de Noronha. King Manoel was not unappreciative of these achievements. In 1504, he ignored the homeland's rules on limpeza de sangue to appoint Noronha a knight of the Crown and *donatário* (lord) for life of his namesake island.

Virtually all early colonists were on the qui vive for a swift payoff in the New World. Yet none was more preoccupied with instant security than Portugal's beleaguered handful of convertido expatriates. Thus, Duarte Coelho, son of the Portuguese astronomer-navigator Gonçalo Coelho, became the earliest European to cultivate sugar in Brazil. Appointed donatário of the province of Pernambuco, Coelho established the New World's first sugar mills on his own vast plantation. A number of the skilled workmen he and his brother-in-law imported from Portugal were also New Christians. Their presence seemed an anomaly at first. In theory, Brazil was out of bounds for cristãos novos. Yet even during the earliest period of colonial settlement, Sephardim plainly were coming over by the scores, possibly by the hundreds.

Nor were their origins a secret. With the Crown intent on consolidating its holdings in Goa, Macao, Ceylon, and Angola, as well as Brazil, it was inevitable that cristãos novos should also quietly be enlisted in the cause of empire. Early in the seventeenth century, Felipe III's Royal Pardon and Clement VIII's Papal Pardon similarly opened the door for an even more substantial Sephardic presence in the New World. Afterwards, in a multi-racial frontier nation, New Christians fitted without difficulty into local European society. By 1620, Brazil's white population was estimated at forty-four thousand; cristãos novos may not have represented more than a thousand of these, but they comprised at least 15 percent of all European settlers in the struggling little frontier towns of Bahía, Olinda, Rio de Janeiro, and Recife.

By 1600, too, as sugar became Brazil's most lucrative export, planters and refiners emerged as Portuguese America's preeminent capitalist magnates. Some one hundred twenty sugar mills were in operation by then, and approximately one-fifth were owned and largely operated by cristãos novos. Salvador Correia exported sugar in his own ships to his agents in Lisbon. Other New Christians exported to relatives in Hamburg and Amsterdam. It was an international network still unavailable to Old Christian refiners.

The sugar barons were never other than a minority among their own people, however. Most Sephardim were wholesale and retail merchants. Some operated general import-export houses. Still others were teachers, lawyers, physicians, writers, poets. Bento Teixeira Pinto, author of the *Prosopea* (Emphatic Discourse), Brazil's first epic poem, and Ambrósio Fernandes Brandão, author of *Diálogos das Grandezas do Brasil*, a famed early history, both were convertidos. With singular indifference to the homeland's constraints of limpeza de sangue, New Christians in this frontier world soon were making their way even into the colonial administration. Diogo Lópes Ulhoa served as counsellor to the governor of Bahía; Antonio Mendes de Oliveira, as Bahiá's royal treasurer. Others were magistrates, notaries, priests.

Most New Christians arrived for economic, not religious purposes. Reared as Catholics, long out of contact with the Jewish tradition, they tended to marry into other European castes and disappear from the Jewish rolls. Nevertheless, as in Europe, a marrano nucleus evidently survived longer among Portuguese Sephardim than among their Spanish counterparts (p. 170). In Pernambuco, judaizers were a particularly vigorous element among the Sephardic colonists. Diogo Fernandes and his wife, Bianca, the first known marranos in Brazil, sustained a clandestine synagogue in the town of Camaragibe. The historian Brandão almost certainly was a judaizer. A number of these people circumcised their sons, and observed Jewish dietary laws and other Jewish ceremonies and customs. With extensive leeway for maintaining ancestral customs, few of them bothered to take precautions beyond occasional bribes to local officials.

The cristãos novos were functioning on borrowed time, however. In Portugal, the existence of an overseas marrano community was the subject of growing concern. So it was as well in Spain, where King Felipe II, upon bringing Portugal under his rule in 1580, was intent on extending the restrictions of limpieza de sangre both to that kingdom and to its dependencies abroad. The process took time. In Portugal itself, we recall, the Inquisition had not been introduced until 1537. And now, even under pressure from Madrid, the Portuguese remained unenthusiastic about establishing an inquisitional tribunal for Brazil. In 1580, the Lisbon Suprema delegated its authority overseas to a *visitador,* an itinerant local bishop. The usual litany of offenses and rules of procedure were in force here, from grace periods to secret informers. Yet defendants had to be transported back to Portugal for trial and sentencing. It was a cumbersome, inefficient system. To be sure, even a limited campaign against heretics in Brazil produced occasional successes. During the 1590s, members of a half-dozen prominent families were turned in and shipped to Portugal, among them Afonso Mendes, chief surgeon in Bahía, together with his wife and four children.

In that same decade, moreover, a new and larger *visitacão* arrived in Recife, capital of Pernambuco province and center of Brazil's thriving sugar industry—and of its thriving New Christian sugar barons. Several of the latter now were identified as judaizers by former servants or slaves. Evidently they cleaned their homes on Friday or refrained from work on Saturday. Typical was the case of Ana Rois, an elderly widow who had arrived in Recife with her husband in 1557. Now, thirty-six years later, settled in Bahía with her children and grandchildren, Donha Ana was suddenly arrested. Queried and threatened by the inquisitional visitador, she acknowledged that such foods as pork and wild game did not "agree" with her; that on Friday nights she had placed her hands upon the heads of her grandchildren because she remembered her mother performing the rite. Ana Rois's sons and daughters were exonerated, but she herself was dispatched to Lisbon for prosecution. Awaiting trial, she died in prison, and her corpse was burned in effigy. Over the turn of the century, the notorious visitador Heigor Furtado de Mendonça turned up a number of eminent sugar mill owners, landowners, and merchants. The writers Ambrosio Brandão and Bento Teixeira Pinto also were among those denounced and arrested. Teixeira was carried back to Lisbon for trial. Sentenced to life imprisonment, he died of tuberculosis in his cell in 1600.

These occasional successes notwithstanding, the Inquisition in Brazil hardly was comparable to the reign of terror inflicted on Mexico and Peru. It produced considerably fewer arrests and even fewer convictions. Furtado de Mendonça's twenty-seven-year visitacão did not so much as cover its expenses. In 1628, Lisbon dispatched still another visitador, Marcos Teixeira. He managed to turn up 134 suspects. Of these, however, only five were shipped back to Portugal for trial. If the record was less than spectacular, the explanation was not to be attributed simply to the absence of inquisitional tribunals in Brazil. Rather, their absence bespoke a lack of doctrinal fervor in Portuguese America. For all its vastness, Brazil remained an isolated imperial foothold. On its land frontiers, the great jungle behemoth was still outflanked by more densely inhabited Spanish possessions. From the sea, it was still threatened by the Dutch fleet. Despite all of Madrid's pressures and threats, then, a nation with Portugal's modest demographic resources was not yet prepared to jeopardize its single viable outpost in the New World.

A Dutch Interlude in the Tropics

Officially, Lisbon claimed a monopoly over Brazil's vast exports. Unofficially, the bulk of the munificent Brazilian sugar crop went not to Portugal but to the Dutch Netherlands. By 1620, through bribery of local officials and the assistance of New Christian agents, some fifty thousand chests of Brazilian sugar were reaching Amsterdam each year. It was this clandestine trade, in turn, that fueled the growth of Amsterdam's great sugar-refining industry. From Amsterdam, it is recalled, the finished product was reexported to England, France, and the Baltic nations. Indeed, the sheer profitability of the commerce was a major factor in the establishment of the Dutch West India Company, in 1621. Privately financed but government supported, the venture was launched specifically to gain control of the tantalizing Brazilian sugar crop. To ensure its success, the States General awarded the company an official charter of monopoly for the American trade, together with assurance of full military support and the right to appoint its own administration for any territory it conquered and settled. In the spring of 1624, a Dutch naval flotilla consisting of twenty-six vessels, four hundred guns, and three thousand troops sailed for Brazil. Among the personnel were approximately a dozen Jews, a few to serve as interpreters.

The armada reached Bahía on May 9 and easily intimidated the little Portuguese garrison into surrender. Yet the company had won a deceptive victory. It failed to provide enough manpower to sustain a Dutch presence. Within the year, the Spaniards and Portuguese jointly mounted their own expedition of reconquest, and in May 1626 their landing force of five thousand men easily overwhelmed the West India Company's outpost. Chastened by this early misstep, the Dutch subsequently chose to concentrate their efforts on a prize far greater than Bahía. It was the northern province of Pernambuco, and its five satellite provinces, a region that comprised the very heartland of Brazil's sugar industry. Here, then, in 1629, the West India Company launched its single most formidable military effort, a vast armada comprising fifty-six vessels, eleven hundred guns, and over seven thousand men. In February 1630, the fleet and its disembarking army easily invested Recife, the skeletal little capital of Pernambuco.

Before landing, to soften any possible resistance, the Dutch commander had sent word to the local authorities that "[the] liberty of Spaniards, Portuguese, and natives, whether they be Roman Catholics or Jews, will be respected. No one will be permitted to molest them . . . in matters of conscience or in their private homes." The promise was honored, although with qualifications. Members of the Jesuit Order were expelled, their missions closed. The Dutch Reformed Church henceforth became the state religion. But for the cristãos novos, the change in circumstances was entirely propitious. They were sought out now by the expedition's principal guide, Antonio Dias Paparrobalos. A New Christian, and a former inhabitant of Recife, Paparrobalos had emigrated to Holland, resumed his identity as a professing Jew, and sailed back with the West India Company flotilla to help win over his convertido friends and neighbors. It was specifically to these people that the company now made good its pledge of religious freedom. Very soon, large numbers of Sephardim began openly returning to Judaism—much to the outrage of the Portuguese Old Christian majority.

In 1636, Johann Maurits of Nassau, a collateral relative of the Netherlands statthalter, arrived to take up his responsibilities as governor-general of the six northern provinces of Dutch Brazil. A vigorous, imaginative administrator, Maurits wasted little time launching into an extensive program of public improvements, constructing roads, bridges, hospitals, and schools, establishing a series of public markets and assay offices, instituting a rigorously honest judicial system. The dynamic new mercantile ambience was all but tailor-made for Pernambuco's Jews. So grateful were they to Maurits that, upon expiration of his first term of office, they successfully petitioned the company in Amsterdam to extend his stay. Meanwhile, their own numbers in Brazil increased steadily. Jews were arriving not only from Portugal and Spain, but from Italy, Turkey, North Africa—above all, from the Netherlands. By 1644, an estimated 1,450 Jews were settled in Recife, comprising two-fifths of the town's European civilian population. The number equaled that of the Jewish population in Amsterdam.

They thrived. Buying up numerous abandoned Portuguese sugar mills at auction, at least a dozen Jewish newcomers became instant sugar barons. A far greater number emerged as financiers of the sugar industry, as brokers and exporters. In Pernambuco, too, Jews revived their historic vocation of tax-farming. Moses Navarro, who had arrived with the invading fleet in 1630, paid 55,000 guilders for Pernambuco's sugar-tax concession. Other substantial tax-farmers were Benjamin de Pina and Duarte Saraiva. Over the next quarter-century of Dutch rule in Brazil, fully 60 percent of the tax-farming business was in Jewish hands. Jews also appear to have been extensively represented in the slave trade. It was the practice of the West India Company to import slaves and sell them at public auction for cash. Well experienced in such transactions, Jews were among the preeminent buyers. In turn, they resold the slaves to sugar-plantation owners on credit, payable at the next harvest. With their solid command of the Portuguese and Dutch languages, Jews similarly became indispensable middlemen between the two communities in a wide variety of business negotiations. Pernambuco's retail trade was overwhelmingly Jewish. So palpable was Jewish commercial eminence in Brazil that the Dutch traveler Johann Nieunof, who roamed the country during the 1640s, later reported:

> Among the free inhabitants of Brazil, those of the Jewish nation were the most extensive in number, many of whom had transplanted themselves there from the Netherlands. They concerned themselves principally with business, in which they conducted a vast traffic beyond the rest of our people. They operated numerous sugar mills, and in Recife built dignified homes.

Their affluence was not universally admired. "They reside mostly in Recife and know how to become masters of the entire business of trade," complained one observer. "For the most part they are involved in business," wrote another, "which would have been advantageous to Brazil, had the trade been confined within the rules of ordinary business and not reached such extravagances and excesses." As early as 1637, a group of veteran Portuguese settlers petitioned the company to expel the Jews, or at least ban them from the retail and brokerage trade for reasons of "sharp practices, trickery, [and] frequent bankruptcy." And when sixty-six merchants repeated the appeal in 1641, bitterly criticizing "this cheating and dishonest race," Governor-General Maurits himself supported the request in a personal letter to Amsterdam. Three years later, ironically, the Jews of Recife, who remained unaware of Maurits's private bias, thanked him for his endless solicitude on their behalf, even offered him an annual stipend of three thousand guilders if he would remain on. He graciously declined.

The Jews' appreciation for their governor in fact was merited. If they had not yet won complete political and social equality, it was under Maurits's stewardship that they achieved the fullest plenum of religious and community rights. Ostensibly, they were to conduct their worship in private. By 1636, however, a synagogue already existed in Recife, as well as rudimentary congregations in nearby Paraíba and Mauricia. A year later, the Jews of Recife chartered a cemetery plot. In the decade that followed, invitations went out to the famous Rabbi Isaac Aboab da Fonseca, one of the two religious leaders of Amsterdam's Esnoga, and to the respected Amsterdam scholar Moses Raphael d'Aguilar. Both men arrived in 1642, Fonseca to assume the pulpit of the Recife congregation, d'Aguilar of the neighboring Mauricia congregation—thereby becoming the first rabbis in the New World. As in Europe, all professing Jews were subject to the regulations, judgments, and assessments of their congregational boards. The company enforced these decrees. In practical fact, then, Jews in Brazil sustained a communal autonomy at least as broad as in Holland itself.

A Brazilian Farewell

In 1640, after sixty years of uneasy political union with Spain, the Portuguese Crown declared itself independent once again. Accordingly, it was at this point, disentangled from Spain's armistice agreements with the Netherlands, that Lisbon was free to redirect its attention to its lost colonies in Brazil. It thought it had a chance to recoup. The Dutch had left a rather thin military presence in the New World following their occupation of Pernambuco. Indeed, for the Netherlands, the Brazilian venture was always a commercial rather than an imperial undertaking. Obsessed with financial profit, the West India Company had not bothered to enlist local cooperation by dealing humanely with Indians, mestizos, or black slaves. As the Portuguese saw it, internal unrest against Dutch rule might well be exploited for purposes of reconquest.

The effort was launched as early in 1642. From their enclave in Bahía, the local Portuguese authorities directed an insurrection of their own settlers in the nearby, Dutch-ruled town of Maranhão. The uprising was entirely successful. Within two years, Lisbon was able to appoint a governor for the entire Maranhão province. Moreover, throughout 1644 and 1645, bands of slaves who had suffered cruelly at the hands of the West India Company rampaged on through the Dutch-ruled hinterland. Soon they were joined in unlikely alliance with the Portuguese inhabitants. In an even unlikelier association, the rebels actually received a substantial quantity of their funds and equipment from local New Christians. By 1644, doubtless intimidated by the Portuguese majority, Brazilian cristãos novos provided not less than 17 percent of locally raised financial contributions. And from 1649 on, New Christians in Portugal itself supplied much of the capital to charter vessels and hire mercenaries for a more substantial military offensive in Brazil.

The Portuguese campaign began to pay off. As early as 1645, it forced

Dutch settlers and militiamen back from their provincial outposts in Pernambuco toward their central redoubt in Recife. Jews were among the defenders—many more than among the Portuguese rebels. Swept up in the common resistance, a number were killed in battle. Others were captured. On one occasion, thirteen of these prisoners were executed on the spot for treason against their former Portuguese rulers. The brutality of the retaliation so unnerved Recife's Jews that they now frantically sought assurance of protection from the Netherlands government. In response, the States General, always sensitive to the importance of Jewish financial and military support, issued an unequivocal directive to company officials in Recife:

> The said Supreme Government . . . in Brazil shall favor and be of service to the aforesaid Hebrew nation on all occasions according to, and as their loyalty and valor deserve, and also in all cases let them enjoy the results thereof without in any manner making or observing . . . any greater or lesser distinction or division between them and those of our other nationals, not doubting that the said [Hebrew] nation will thereby more and more be animated and encouraged to further the service in this state and that of the puissant West India Company.

From a seventeenth-century Christian government, this *Patentate Onrossa* (Honorable Patent) was an unprecedented commitment on behalf of the Jews. Indeed, it represented the first governmental policy statement on Jewish rights in the Americas.

In this case, it came too late. Tightly congested, Recife's Dutch enclave by 1646 was surrounded by far larger numbers of Portuguese colonists and black irregulars. The settlers eventually were reduced to slaughtering their milk cows and oxen, even their horses. The neighboring Indian tribes and most of the slaves were defecting to the enemy en masse. Over the next three years, Dutch Brazil was reduced to a wasteland. The Jews, sharing in the destitution and starvation, experienced an additional ordeal—the terror of possible capture and execution, or shipment back to Portugal and trial before an inquisitional tribunal.

The tragedy already was in progress. A memorable episode was that of Isaac de Castro, a nineteen-year-old seized outside Bahía in 1645 and carried off to Portugal two years later. He had come to Dutch Brazil in 1641 and lived there as a practicing Jew. In Recife, however, after killing a man in a duel, Castro had fled to Portuguese Bahía. There he practiced Catholicism in public but remained a Jew in private. Under torture in Lisbon, the young man admitted all, but noted that he had been born a

Jew and thus legally was exempt from the inquisitional charge of judaizing. The tribunal was unconvinced. It offered Castro the choice of reconciliation with the church or death. He chose death. The relaxation was performed in December 1647, before a huge crowd that included members of the royal family. Amid the flames, the young prisoner cried out the Hebrew words *Eli, Adonai Tzva'ot* (My God, the Lord of Hosts). Widely reported, the Castro sacrifice shook a Jewish world already deeply scarred by the Inquisition. In Amsterdam, where the martyr's parents still lived, a communal memorial service was held. Poems and obituaries were composed to his memory. Menasseh ben Israel alluded to the case in his *Spes Israel.*

There were other, comparable tragedies, and for some years they intensified the determination of Recife's Jews to avoid surrender. But resistance was a vain hope. In January 1654, the end came when representatives of the Governor's Council signed a document of capitulation. They had been offered honorable terms by General Francisco Barreto de Menezes, the Portuguese military commander. No one would be obliged to abandon his home, Barreto assured the Dutch authorities, neither Christian nor Jew; and if the citizens of Recife chose to leave, they would be allowed three months to liquidate their assets. A large-spirited man, the Portuguese commander was prepared even to make several of his own vessels available for transporting emigrants to other South American or Caribbean ports.

The one exception to those assurances were former New Christians. Regretfully, Barreto acknowledged that these individuals would become "subject to the Holy Inquisition, wherein I cannot interfere." The Jews had known it would come to this. Even earlier, in the last months before surrender, many of them had sought to flee the town, and a number had managed to board coastal schooners. With harsh incomprehension of the terrifying fate awaiting these people at the hands of the Inquisition, Calvinist preachers attacked them savagely as "rats leaving a sinking ship." In any case, not all of the departing Jews actually escaped. Several of their vessels foundered, one off the Isle of Wight, causing the death of at least one hundred passengers.

By January 1654, barely six hundred Jews remained in Brazil to join the official exodus. Of these, a few risked staying on as marranos. They confronted a grim future. The surrounding economy was in ruins, and the Inquisition was always on the hunt. During the years following Portuguese recapture of the northern provinces, local bishops continued to function as visitadores, with the right to dispatch suspected crypto-Jews to Portugal. The number of victims was not large—fewer than ten throughout the entire second half of the century. Yet denunciation of judaizing was ceaseless. In the early eighteenth century, moreover, there occurred an unexpected upsurge of arrests and extraditions. The discovery of gold in Brazil had attracted numerous adventurers into the mining areas. Many were of convertido background and thus fell under instant suspicion and surveillance. From 1707 on, by order of Bishop Francisco de São Jeronimo, serving then as the Inquisition's commissioner in Rio de Janeiro, some two hundred Brazilian cristãos novos were arrested and shipped back to Lisbon. There they underwent the notorious autos da fé of 1709 and 1711. While few of the defendants were burned, most were sentenced to prison terms and all had their property taken. Indeed, so extensive was the chain reaction of arrests, prosecutions, and confiscations in these years that it gravely disrupted Brazil's production and export of sugar and trade with Europe.

Zealotry in Brazil finally guttered out by the mid-eighteenth century, together with a comparable relaxation in Portugal itself. Yet the witch-hunt had more than fulfilled its purpose. Judaizing had long since ended. Brazilian New Christians by then were Old Christians. They confronted no remaining vocational barriers. Many attained distinguished positions in the economy and administration. They moved, and married, smoothly within the nation's European society. Their issue extended from Recife as far north as present-day New Mexico and Texas, and intermingled with every Portuguese- and Spanish-speaking community in the New World. But their footprints as Jews had long since disappeared.

A Caribbean Interlude

Among Recife's departing six hundred Jews, the majority returned to the Netherlands. Yet approximately two hundred remained in the Americas to seek asylum beyond reach of the Spanish and Portuguese Inquisitions. Here it was that the West Indies became an initial port of call. Several dozen refugee families made their way to the French islands of Martinique, Guadeloupe, and Saint-Dominique (Haiti). At first, these outposts would have appeared unlikely sanctuary. As recently as 1615, King Louis XIII had reconfirmed the banishment of Jews from French soil. But the law was hardly applied even in France itself (p. 199), and in the colonies no serious attempt ever was made to enforce it. Periodic orders for expulsion simply were ignored. To provincial governments, the Jews' experience in sugar and their connections in international trade were not to be forfeited easily. By the mid-eighteenth century, as a result, the French West Indies' two or three dozen Jewish families had essentially achieved freedom of settlement and worship. The latter in fact was less important to them than the former. Over the years, most of these colonists took Catholic spouses and allowed their Jewish identification to lapse.

A still likelier refuge was the British West Indies. Barbados and Jamaica were havens of choice for the Recife fugitives, although in later years scatterings of Jews also appeared in Nevis, Tobago, St. Lucia, Antigua, and St. Kitts. By the early eighteenth century, as many as a thousand Jews may have settled throughout this Protestant-dominated archipelago. Indeed, they arrived not only from Brazil and elsewhere in Latin America but directly from Spain, Portugal, and the Canary Islands, from Bordeaux and Bayonne, from Amsterdam and London. At first, they enjoyed no particular legal status. Yet they encountered little difficulty in establishing residence or doing business. By then, it was axiomatic that Jewish entrepreneurialism served a useful mercantile purpose.

By the early 1700s, even little Nevis contained seventy-five Jews, a quarter of the island's white population. Some two hundred and fifty Jews lived in Barbados, operating their own shops and their own synagogue in the "capital" of Bridgetown. For years, they were subjected to occasional discriminatory taxes, denied the right to own slaves, even to testify in criminal cases. But otherwise they traded and worshipped as they pleased. Gradually, too, they won a certain respect, even social acceptance, for their public-spiritedness and generosity to charitable causes. "Sir," reported the governor of Barbados to the chairman of the British Board of Trade in 1786, "this despised . . . but peaceable, loyal, and, I will add, venerable people, still remember, as they were commanded, the affliction of their forefathers in the land of Egypt."

Jamaica, ruled by Spain until 1654, was the largest of Britain's West Indian possessions. Even under Spanish rule, its white population intermingled extensively with New Christians. Thus, when the British conquered the island, their commander noted that approximately half the European settlers were "Portugals." One of these "Portugals," Captain Campoe Sabbatha, guided the invading British fleet into Kingston Bay. Granted full rights of settlement by Oliver Cromwell, and later by Charles II, the island's professing Jewish population by 1735 numbered eight hundred out of a European population of twenty-five hundred. Settling in Port Royal, Spanish Town, Montego Bay, and Kingston, Jews here experienced no constraints of any kind in business or worship. Christian merchants occasionally petitioned to limit their numbers, but to no avail. As early as 1671, Sir Thomas Lynch, the Jamaican governor, stated the official position bluntly: "His Majesty cannot have more profitable subjects than the Jews and the Hollanders, for they have great stocks and correspondence. . . . One cannot find any but Jews who will adventure their goods or persons to get a trade."

Government solicitude paid off. By the late eighteenth century, England conducted a third of its seaborne trade with its colonies. The West Indies were preeminent in that traffic, and the Jews of Jamaica were the preeminent traders of the West Indies. As importers-exporters, planters, and vanilla-curers, their role in the archipelago's economy was all but decisive. Many other Jews were retailers; still others, physicians and translators. Only a few were very wealthy, but most were comfortable. Edward Long, describing the island in 1770, summarized the position of the Jews in the British West Indies altogether:

> It must be acknowledged . . . that these people have shewn themselves very good and useful subjects upon many occasions. When the French invaded this island . . . they opposed the enemy with great courage. Their knowledge of foreign languages, and intercourse with their brethren, dispersed over the Spanish and other West Indian colonies, have contributed greatly to extend the trade and increase the wealth of the island. . . . [They display] a very solid attachment to the interest and security of Jamaica, which they consider as their home.

Like the Jews of Barbados and Nevis, those of Jamaica erected handsome synagogues, five of them in Kingston alone. Although not recognized as an autonomous entity in the continental tradition, the Jews here operated their own cemeteries, schools, charitable funds, ritual baths, and abattoirs, all with a full professional staff of rabbis, cantors, teachers, kosher butchers, and other functionaries. They managed also to negotiate a series of toleration edicts and charters that offered them "endenization" as British citizens under the Naturalization Act of 1740. By the mid-eighteenth century, in fact, the Jews of the British West Indies may well have been the freest Jews on earth.

Yet that status was closely approached by their kinsmen under Dutch rule. The largest number of Brazil's departing Sephardim returned forthwith to the Netherlands. The next largest, however, found refuge in Dutch territories much closer at hand. In the undeveloped Caribbean Basin, the Dutch West India Company would turn away no prospective—non-Catholic—immigrant, least of all survivors of the recent siege of Recife. So it was that the territory of Surinam attracted possibly two hundred of the Recife Jews. Nestled into the South American littoral off Brazil's northern shoulder, this lush, tropical savanna emerged as one of the Netherlands' most substantial New World outposts in the 1600s. As its economy developed, Jews began arriving from Brazil and Europe alike. Their numbers reached at least a thousand by the eighteenth century, most of these in Paramaribo, the capital, where they comprised almost half the European population. A 1730 survey revealed twenty-five Jewish plantation owners. Twice that many were sugar brokers. More than a hundred were slavers, while scores of others were peddlers of horses and cattle; still others, importers of spices and manufactured articles. They prospered greatly and lived in elegant mansions in Paramaribo's Jooden Savanna.

In Surinam, too, as in Dutch Brazil earlier, Jews were entirely free to charter cemeteries, organize congregations and schools, build synagogues. Their autonomy in fiscal and juridical matters was so extensive that they functioned virtually as a self-governing enclave under Dutch rule. Their neighbors preferred it that way. The Jews were never a popular minority. In Paramaribo they were denied the right to hold public office, to practice law, or to serve as notaries. Yet here as elsewhere in the Netherlands West Indies, their basic security was never in question. It was not prejudice that ultimately eroded the Jewish foothold in Surinam. By the latter 1700s, a succession of slave insurrections drove hundreds of white families into flight. Jews were among them. A century later, in a population of 350,000, Jews barely numbered 400, and less than half that by the eve of World War I. Today, scarcely two dozen Jewish families remain.

The Jewish presence in Curaçao is rather more substantial. Here approximately seven hundred Jews can still be found, in business, the professions, government. Here, too, remains the oldest functioning synagogue in the Western Hemisphere. Yet the enclave today is less than half the size of a community that once was the largest in the New World. The Jews' initial choice of settlement was apt. An island of some three hundred seventy square miles off the coast of Venezuela and possessing a superb natural harbor, Curaçao functioned as the Dutch West India Company's principal naval and commercial entrepôt in the Americas. As early as 1649, five years before their flight from Recife, twelve Jewish families departed Brazil to settle here. Three years later, they were joined by fifty more. Curaçao's governor, Pieter Stuyvesant, had little use for them. In a letter to company headquarters in Amsterdam, Stuyvesant described the Jews as "a crafty and generally treacherous people in whom not much confidence must be placed," and warned that "time must show whether we shall succeed well with this nation."

The auguries did not appear favorable. Rather than cultivate the soil, the early Jewish settlers displayed a marked propensity for smuggling cattle. Together with not a few Gentiles, they illegally imported horses from New England, then secretly transported the animals to enthusiastic buyers elsewhere in the Caribbean. The traffic enraged Stuyvesant. Impulsively, he prohibited Jews from owning slaves, an indispensable source of labor in those years. The ban might well have extended to Jewish settlement altogether, but in 1654 an arriving group of two dozen Recife fugitives resumed their former vocations as sugar and tobacco planters. Soon, their expertise proved as valuable here as elsewhere in the Caribbean. Stuyvesant's early restrictions were slowly lifted. The newcomers were permitted to acquire slaves, cattle, and eventually a two-mile residential stretch of their own along the Willemstad seacoast. As in Amsterdam, the enclave was known variously as the Jooden Quaertier or the Joodenbuurt.

Over the years, as their numbers grew and their economy diversified, Jews emerged as Curaçao's leading merchant-shippers, transporting their products to other islands or direct to Holland. It was risky business. Spanish, Portuguese, British, Dutch, and pirate seamen preyed on one another in the Caribbean. Indeed, Spanish corsairs were especially on the lookout for Jewish vessels, which were known to pay hefty ransoms for cargoes and crews. A number of Jewish importers thus were intercepted with their ships, carried off to Jamaica (then under Spanish rule), thrown into inquisitional prisons, and tortured. Most eventually were ransomed, but some met death at the hands of their captors. It was all the more extraordinary, in view of these dangers, that Jewish shipowners continued in this vocation without a single interruption. Many actually insisted on giving their ships Jewish names. British Board of Trade documents of 1721 assert that "nearly all the navigation of Curaçao is in the hands of the Jews who even equip privateers to defend themselves against pirates and other interlopers."

By the mid-eighteenth century, the Jews of Curaçao numbered fifteen hundred souls and comprised half the island's European population. They also formed the single largest and wealthiest Jewish community in the Western Hemisphere. Here, as elsewhere in the Dutch Caribbean, they lived a full, rich community life, maintaining two handsome synagogues, two schools, a wide range of social service organizations whose rules and regulations were determined by the Esnoga in Amsterdam. They celebrated their festivals with much splendor, their weddings and funerals with pomp and circumstance. As befitted their number and wealth, they also contributed munificently to Jews elsewhere in the Americas, to victims of plagues and other misfortunes, to incipient communities requesting funds for synagogues. So it was in the Americas that Curaçao's Jewish minority became the mother Jewry for a cluster of other fledgling Diaspora settlements.

A Foothold in the Mainland Wilderness

And it came to pass, in the year 5414 [1654], that the Portuguese
returned, and from the Dutch took their land by force. And God had
mercy on His people, and gave it favor and grace in the eyes of the
mighty ruler Barreto. . . . And he gave permission to our brethren
. . . to return to our country here [the Netherlands]. And all our people
went down to the sea in sixteen ships, and set sail.

From his home in Amsterdam, the chronicler, David Franco Mendes, was
describing the recent exodus of his fellow Jews from Brazil. Most of their
sixteen vessels reached friendly ports without event. But one of them was
intercepted by a Spanish frigate. Its crew anticipated turning the captive
Jews over to the Inquisition. Almost at the last moment, however, a
French gunboat arrived on the scene and liberated the prisoners, carrying
them on to safety in Florida, then under French rule. Still another refugee
vessel, the Dutch schooner *Valck*, departed Recife in February 1654 with
a refugee cargo of approximately one hundred Dutch Gentiles and three
dozen Jews. The ship's initial destination was the French island of Martinique. En route, however, the *Valck* was similarly intercepted by a
Spanish privateer and forced to drop anchor in Spanish Jamaica. The
Inquisition promptly incarcerated the former New Christians on board,
while the rest of the passengers were detained "pending further inquiry."
Only the last-moment intercession of the Netherlands government, in
May 1654, secured their release.

Among the twenty-three identified Jews permitted to depart were four
men, six women, and thirteen children. Their interim stopover was Cape
St. Anthony, on the western tip of Cuba. Upon arrival, the refugees sought
to negotiate additional passage for New Amsterdam, the Dutch West
India Company's outpost in North America. Eventually, after protracted
haggling, they reached agreement with the captain of the French barque
Sainte Catherine, who consented to transport them for the exorbitant fee of
twenty-five hundred guilders, nine hundred to be paid in advance. In
midsummer, then, the *Sainte Catherine* headed north. Nearly six weeks
later, the vessel rounded the tip of Manhattan Island and sailed into the
mouth of the Hudson River. Here it dropped anchor at the little fortress-
town of New Amsterdam, capital of mainland New Netherlands.

The twenty-three fugitives on the *Sainte Catherine*, in fact, were not the
first Jews to set foot in this ramshackle village. Occasional Jewish traders
from Dutch Brazil and the Netherlands Antilles had passed through in
earlier years. One of these, Jacob Barsimson, a young Ashkenazi, had

arrived directly from Europe less than a month before the Recife passengers and was among the group of onlookers who witnessed their landing. It could not have been a happy sight. When the refugees failed to produce the balance of their passage money, the irate captain obtained a court order to attach their furniture. And when a public auction did not cover the debt, two of the Jews were promptly clapped into the stockade. There they remained until October, when kinsmen in Amsterdam finally dispatched the needed funds.

The ordeal of the Recife immigrants had only begun. Thus far, they had subsisted on handouts provided by Jacob Barsimson, and by one Solomon Pietersen, who may also have been a Jew. But winter was coming and the newcomers would require shelter and hot meals. At the last moment, Dominie Johannes Megapolensis and his colleagues of the local Dutch Reformed Church provided a few hundred guilders, for the "Jews have come weeping and bemoaning their misery." The churchmen in fact were influenced less by Christian charity than by the expectation that the refugees would soon be gone. New Amsterdam's resident governor was none other than Pieter Stuyvesant. Earlier, it is recalled, as governor of Curaçao, "Peg Leg Piet" had been exasperated by the local Jewry's incorrigible preference for commerce over farming. Having failed to keep these people out of Curaçao, he would now try his luck with the West India Company board again. Thus, in his letter to Amsterdam, Stuyvesant asked permission

> to require [the Jews] . . . to depart, praying most seriously in this connection, for ourselves as also for the general community of Your Worships, that the deceitful race—such hateful enemies and blasphemers of the name of Christ—not be allowed further to infect and trouble this new colony.

Before a reply could arrive, still another contingent of Jews—five families and three unmarried males—disembarked in New Amsterdam, in March 1655. They had sailed direct from Holland. Neither indigent nor obsequious, the newcomers made clear their intention of organizing a congregation. The prospect was altogether too much for Johannes Megapolensis. Adding his appeal to Stuyvesant's, the dominie warned, in his letter to the church Classis in Amsterdam, that

> as we have here Papists, Mennonites and Lutherans among the Dutch, also many Puritans or Independents, and many Atheists and various other servants of Baal . . . who conceal themselves under the name of Christians, it would create still greater confusion if the obstinate and immovable Jews came to settle here.

Yet these obstinate and immovable Jews were not without contacts of their own. In a petition to the West India Company board, their kinsmen in Amsterdam noted that "the Jewish nation in Brazil have at all times been faithful and have striven to guard and maintain that place, risking for that purpose their possessions and their blood." The Amsterdam Jews then added, meaningfully:

> Your Honors should also please consider that many of the Jewish nation are principal shareholders in the Company. . . . [Moreover] as foreign nations (viz., England, even France) consent that the Jewish nation may go to live and trade in their territories, how can your Honors forbid the same . . . to [the] Portuguese nation who reside . . . [in] a Dutch territory that needs people for its increases?

The petition incorporated every humane and mercantilist argument likely to touch the board's conscience and self-interest, and it registered. Stuyvesant was instructed now to allow the Jews to settle and trade in the New Netherlands, on condition that "the poor among them shall not become a burden to the deaconry or the Company, but shall be supported by their own nation." Twice more, the governor ventured a protest. Each time, he was rebuffed. It was not possible to bar the Jews, explained the board in its firm and final directive, without "diminishing the population and stopping immigration. . . . You may therefore shut your eyes, at least not force people's consciences, but allow everyone to have his own belief, as long as he behave quietly and legally, give no offense to his neighbors and does not oppose the government."

The foothold was secured. Well, then, might David Franco Mendes conclude his account of his people's exodus from Brazil:

> [A]nd God led [the Jewish nation] to their destination to . . . [the Netherlands] . . . except one ship which the Spaniards captured on the high seas. And God caused a savior to rise unto them, the captain of a French ship . . . and he rescued them from out of the hands of those who had done violence to them and oppressed them, and he conducted them until they reached the end of the inhabited earth called New Netherlands.

CHAPTER XVII

THE LONG ROAD HOME

A Spark Flickers in Iberia

Leaving Portugal, I am not permitted to forget that this little nation remains on the threshold of the modern world. From Oporto, the journey by rail to Madrid is less than a straightforward one. It requires a change of trains in Lisbon, disembarkation at the border town of Entremonte, a trek to the nearby travel agency for a reissuance of tickets, a stiff fee for the tryptich of new documents, a two-hour stopover until the arrival of the Talgo, the Spanish bullet train. If there is progress in this endearing land, it moves in delayed-action time frames.

Sitting on the depot bench, I contemplate a delayed-action Jewish time-frame. It is the fate of Artur Barros Basto's struggle to revive the sleeping settlement of marranos in Portugal's northern Estrela Mountain region. The campaign had a belated sequel, and the second time around an Ashkenazi was the catalyst. Isser Steinhardt, born in Lisbon to Polish-Jewish parents, eventually moved to Israel, where he worked in a Hadera factory and freelanced as a local correspondent for several Portuguese newspapers. On a return visit to Portugal in 1963, worshipping at the Lisbon synagogue, Steinhardt happened to meet two marranos from Belmonte. It was Yom Kippur, and the men explained that they had emerged on this holy day to express gratitude for God's help in a private family matter. To Steinhardt's queries, they acknowledged that at least three hundred of their friends and relatives in the north similarly maintained a cautious Jewish allegiance.

Fascinated by their account, Steinhardt asked the men if he might accompany them home. They hesitated. He persisted. Finally, they consented. Several days later, the three traveled north together. Once reaching Belmonte and meeting the little marrano community, Steinhardt was given a cordial welcome. It soon became clear that the earlier campaign

of Barros Basto and the Pro-Marrano Committee had, after all, not been
in vain. The group's knowledge of Jewish tradition was no longer entirely
vestigial. Families observed the Sabbath and the principal Jewish holidays. On Passover, they baked their own unleavened bread. Although a
priest performed the last rites on their dead, relatives observed the seven-
day Jewish mourning period. Marriages, publicly solemnized in church
by a priest, were conducted according to Jewish ritual in the privacy of the
home. Perhaps most important, the Belmonte marranos this time did not
instantly flee to the shadows upon being identified. Rather, over the years,
Steinhardt kept in touch with them from Israel. Frequently, he sent them
religious artifacts and literature.

And in April 1983, two decades after that initial meeting, the Israeli
Knesset members Yosef Nahmias and Rabbi Menachem Hacohen flew to
Portugal to develop their own contacts with the Estrela Mountain crypto-
Jews. The visitors hoped to explore chances of forging links with the
marranos, possibly even of bringing them to Israel. Discussions were not
easy. The Portuguese-born Steinhardt in a sense had been a kinsman, but
these aggressive Israeli newcomers evoked little response. Soon afterward,
therefore, Steinhardt himself returned to Portugal and spent a number of
months reviving the confidence and trust of his old friends. Still later in
1983, a certain limited breakthrough was achieved. Israel's Sephardic chief
rabbi consented to drop any *halachic*—legal-religious—objections against
receiving the Belmonte marranos into the Jewish mainstream, should they
decide to settle in Israel and undergo an intensive course of instruction.
Thereupon, eighteen of the villagers finally dropped their hesitations and
accepted an invitation to visit Israel as guests of the Jewish Agency. They
found the experience a moving one. While still noncommittal about immigration, the crypto-Jews agreed to remain in communication with the
Israelis, to accept literature about Judaism and Israel, even to participate
in future visits back and forth. Those exchanges have since taken place.
More than sixty years have passed since the marranos' initial awakening.
Does Barros Basto yet live?

I, too, sit in that immemorial Portuguese time-warp, until the Talgo
finally arrives to carry me across the Spanish frontier—and into modern
Europe. The passing Mancha is a revelation. In 1947, on my first visit, as
a student, this flat tableland was a baked-clay aridity. Now its irrigated
fields are green, speckled with golden baled cubes of harvested wheat.
Eight hours later, I arrive in a Madrid almost equally unrecognizable. My
memories are of a threadbare and hungry capital, its population reduced
by the Civil War and World War II blockade to less than a million. Only
the thousands of fugitive Nazis had money to spend in those years. Now

I encounter a dazzling metropolis of four and a half million, a high-tech, high-fashion city of magnificent boulevards, gleaming skyscrapers, luxurious shops, pulsating cabarets.

At my hotel, off the Puerta del Sol, I ask directions to Calle Balmes. "Ah, the synagogue!" exclaims the clerk. With practiced fingers, he traces the route for me on a map. My destination is near the intersection of Calle Balmes and Calle de la Santa Trinidad (a nice touch). The synagogue center is a subdued, bronze-colored edifice of three floors, its windows laced with steel bars, its heavy wooden main entrance embossed with metalwork of Israeli design. Pressing the buzzer and identifying myself, I am admitted by a security guard in a bulletproof plastic cubicle, equipped with a closed-circuit television screen. The return of Jews to Spain plainly is not quite yet a casual matter.

It began almost imperceptibly, and New Christians definitely were not part of the process. The Inquisition had purged the country thoroughly. Nevertheless, in the 1840s, a few dozen Provençal Jewish merchants and financiers arrived intermittently for business. Their presence was ignored. Over the years, it was gradually augmented by other foreign Jewish tradesmen and agents. Some opened offices and rented apartments in Madrid. In the 1850s, conducting religious services in the privacy of their homes, they sought and received permission to charter their own cemetery. In 1869, following a political coup that drove the reactionary Isabel II from the throne, a new constitution was promulgated, and one of its innovations was a guarantee to non-Catholics of "freedom from molestation." By the early twentieth century, therefore, perhaps two thousand Jews were living in Spain. Divided almost evenly among Madrid, Seville, and Barcelona, most were Sephardi tradesmen, essentially refugees from the Balkan Wars. Yet several among them were Central European Ashkenazim, and of these a few were bankers and engineers. Ignacio Bauer, an Alsatian Jew, served as an influential financial adviser to King Alfonso XIII.

They were all safe. By then, it was open knowledge that Jews were living and praying and being buried in Spain; that they were engaged in Jewish philanthropic activities, even funding a Zionist society. The nation was modernizing. In Spanish intellectual circles, interest was reviving in Sephardic Jewry as carriers of Hispanic culture. A research institute, Casa Universal de los Sefardís, was established in Seville shortly before World War I, as well as a chair in Semitics at the University of Madrid. The prognosis for Jewish communal revival seemed excellent, and not least of all under the "benign" dictatorship of Prime Minister Miguel Primo de Rivera, from 1923 to 1930. Primo de Rivera genuinely admired the Jews, their commercial talents, their intellectual acumen. At his initiative, in 1924, the Cortes issued a law restoring Spanish citizenship to all "descendants of the exiles of 1492," wherever they lived. It was a breathtaking gesture, even if largely a symbolic one. Others would follow. In 1931, once the Bourbon regime was overthrown in favor of a republic, local Jews of all backgrounds were extended full and equal status as Spanish citizens. Later, the country's doors were opened to German Jewish refugees from Nazism. By 1935, approximately six thousand Jews were living in the country. As a belated token of respect for the Jewish strand in Hispanic culture, the government that year officially celebrated the eight-hundredth anniversary of the birth of Maimonides. Elaborate state and academic festivities marked the occasion.

"El Benefactor"

The idyll of toleration ended with the Spanish Civil War. Beyond the nearly two thousand foreign Jews who fell in battle as members of the International Brigade, several hundred resident Jewish Loyalists suffered execution or imprisonment at Falangist hands. A majority of Spain's Jews simply fled the country. For the less than one thousand who remained, all earlier guarantees of religious liberty were abrogated. The synagogues of Madrid and Barcelona were closed, and Jewish religious worship was forced underground. With the outbreak of World War II, moreover, Francisco Franco adopted an undisguised stance of pro-German collaboration. The nation's tiny Jewish remnant henceforth maintained a fearful, tremulous vigilance, never certain when the sword of Damocles might fall. It was known that Hitler was pressing Franco to apply the Nuremberg racial laws in Spain.

Nevertheless, despite the Falangist regime's periodic diatribes against "Jewish bolshevism," and occasional cases of police brutality, no government measures were directed specifically against Jews. Nor were Jewish refugees from Hitler's Europe singled out for discrimination. In 1940, with the fall of France, thousands of French Jews who crowded into the Vichy Zone joined other non-Jewish fugitives in applying for Spanish visas, at least for transit purposes. Madrid's policy was harsh: applicants were required to hold official Vichy exit permits as well as documents authorizing permanent refuge elsewhere. Yet, even then, no distinctions were made between Jews and Gentiles. In the next two years, some thirty thousand Jews were among the much larger number of non-Jews who entered Spain and continued on to Lisbon, and eventually to sanctuary beyond Europe. Less than five hundred Jews remained in the country longer than three to four weeks.

In September 1942, however, the period of legal rescue through Spain ended. Under German intimidation, Vichy canceled all exit permits for Jews, and Madrid in turn denied the necessary transit documents. Two months later, the German Wehrmacht flooded into Unoccupied France and the hunt for Jews immediately gained new scope and momentum. In their terror, the fugitives resorted to illegal crossings into Spain, hiring guides to lead them along secret trails through the Pyrenees. Most of the illegals were caught. Few actually were sent back to France, but all were consigned to Spanish internment camps. By the end of the year, approximately seven thousand Jews were impacted into these bleak compounds, together with an even larger number of non-Jews. They subsisted under near-starvation conditions, and the often brutal antisemitism of their fellow internees. It was not until February 1945, with Nazi Germany near collapse and the likelihood imminent of Allied retaliation, that the Spanish government allowed Jews out of the camps. Only then was the Joint Distribution Committee permitted to lodge the refugees in Madrid and Barcelona hotels and provide for their food and medical care.

Altogether, the Falangist regime displayed little interest in the fate of European Jewry. Yet one group of Jews actually thought it discerned a glimmer of compassion. As far back as 1924, we recall, Primo de Rivera had initiated an omnibus grant of citizenship to the "descendants" of Spanish Jewry. Even Generalissimo Franco displayed a certain respect for the Jewish heritage. In 1940, he authorized the establishment of a Sephardic Studies Center in the capital, and a full Institute of Semitic Studies at the University of Madrid. During the war, pinning their hopes on these tentative gestures of approbation, Sephardic Jews from Marseilles to Salonika frantically entreated local Spanish consuls for immigration documents. Madrid vetoed all such appeals. Only after the tide of the war shifted, in 1943, did the Spanish government grudgingly relax its transit ban for those Jews who could prove their bona fides under the Primo de Rivera law.

In any case, less than a thousand could. Throughout the Balkans and Vichy France, isolated groups of Sephardim occasionally managed to win Spanish asylum. The condition was assurance that the Allies later would accept them in North Africa or Malta. On rare occasions, Jews even of non-Sephardic ancestry secured the intercession of local Spanish consuls. In the summer of 1944, as the Nazi deportation of Hungarian Jewry reached its crescendo, approximately twenty-eight hundred Jews remained in Budapest under the mantle of "Spanish citizenship." Some one hundred Jews in Romania and Bulgarian Macedonia escaped death employing the same poetic license.

This meager record of rescue notwithstanding, Madrid in the postwar years diligently set about reclaiming the goodwill of liberals and Jews. Its purpose was the entirely pragmatic one of winning membership in the United Nations. To that end, the Franco government in 1949 could even make the noteworthy observation that "Spain, imbued with its universal Christian spirit of love for all the races on earth, contributed to the rescue of Jews, and acted more for spiritual than for merely legal or political reasons."

The synagogue on Calle Balmes actually is two synagogues. The principal sanctuary, on the main floor, is spacious. On an upper level, a modest chapel is available for private family ceremonies. Here a bearded youngish man is stacking metal chairs. Beneath his prayer shawl, a shirttail hangs out in back, a quivering paunch in front. Food particles cling to his lower lip. I introduce myself in primer-book Castilian. The man's own Spanish is pidgin. We switch to Hebrew. He does better, although with a distinctly Ashkenazic accent.

"The name's Yitzchak," he explains. "I represent the Lubavitcher movement here." Not merely an Ashkenazi in this land, but a Chasid!

"You're from the States, then?" I inquire.

"Right. Brooklyn. Williamsburg."

We continue our chat in English. It turns out that Yitzchak has been in Spain for nine years. He lives nearby with his family, and his world is confined almost exclusively to synagogue and apartment. "We don't mingle with the Gentiles," he boasts. A small boy wanders in, pale and skullcapped. Yitzchak addresses him in Yiddish. The boy responds in kind. "The third of my eleven children." Yitzchak smiles proudly. "We speak only *mame-loshn* [mother's tongue] in our family." One foot rooted in garlic and chicken soup, the other in sanctimonious ignorance, Yitzchak is an intriguing variant of Jewish revival in Spain. I wonder what Maimonides, ibn Ezra, Judah Halevi, or others of the Golden Age's austere humanists would have made of this gelatinous mess. Or whether Spain's political and social landscape can yet absorb a self-fulfilled caricature of the "uncouth" Ashkenazi.

It can. It has for decades. Initially, Spain's postwar approach to the Jews was ambivalent. For at least a decade and a half, the nation's press and pulpit continued to disseminate anti-Jewish propaganda. Yet as early as July 1945, bowing to Allied pressures, Madrid enacted a series of laws that once again guaranteed non-Catholics the right—privately—to conduct religious services. The legislation at least ended the juridical limbo in which the approximately one thousand Jews (and some thirty-five thousand Protestants) had lived under Franco since the fall of the republic.

Cultural gestures of friendship also were forthcoming. One of its earliest manifestations was the renewed support given the Arias Montano Institute, established by Spain's ministry of education as early as 1940. Located in a rather nondescript office building on Madrid's Calle Duque de Medinaceli, the enterprise is named after the sixteenth-century bibliophile and Hebraist who assembled Felipe II's renowned library at the Escorial. Over the years, its collection of Sephardica has grown to twenty thousand books and journals. Arias Montano also publishes its own quarterly, *Sefarad*. During the late 1950s and early 1960s, in a typically mingled gesture of cultural solicitude for the Sephardic heritage and political anxiety for Jewish and Western goodwill, the Franco government arranged an imposing exhibition of documents on the Golden Age of Spanish Jewry. Additional courses in Hebraic and Semitic studies were introduced at the universities of Madrid, Barcelona, and Granada. A ten-day symposium was conducted on the status of Sephardic culture throughout the world. A postage stamp was issued, engraved with the likeness of Toledo's renowned fourteenth-century El Tránsito Synagogue.

In June 1967, the climate for Spain's Jews changed more decisively yet. After nearly two years of painstaking study and discussion, the Cortes approved a law on religious freedom that accepted "religious liberty as a fundamental right of the dignity of the human person." Henceforth, non-Catholics were entitled to worship in public, affix identifying plaques on their synagogues and churches, form religious associations, publish religious literature, even hold any public office except that of chief of state. The law was a cataclysm for Fascist Spain. During these years, too, a group of Jewish communal spokesmen and liberal Catholic clerics privately established the Amistad Judeo-Cristiana, a Catholic-Jewish friendship society. Thanks to the Amistad's persistence, school textbooks and press editorials were purged of antisemitic bias. Altogether, by the mid-1970s, Jews appeared to be as secure on the Iberian Peninsula as anywhere in Western Europe.

Restoration and Redemption

Avenida Castellana is Madrid's Fifth Avenue. The nation's financial movers and shakers operate out of its bronze-and-glass buildings. Here, in a fifteenth-floor suite, graced with the last word in electronic office equipment, Maurice Toledano directs his industrial-commercial empire. Behind his desk are autographed photographs of King Juan Carlos, Queen Sofía, Prime Minister Felipe González. A handsome, well-spoken man in his mid-thirties, Toledano is pure Sephardic. His ancestor, Rabbi Daniel Toledano, left Castile in the Great Exodus of 1492. Moving eventually to Salonika, the rabbi was among the first in a long line of talmudic scholars who laid down the juridical guidelines for Jewish communities throughout the Balkans. As recently as the 1940s, when the family had long since moved on to Tangiers, numerous Toledanos continued to be revered as "chief rabbis of Castile."

Other family members went into trade. From his offices in Tangiers, Moshe Toledano, Maurice's grandfather, conducted an extensive import-export business with the Spanish mainland. It was a favorable base of operations. Nominally ruled by the sultan of Morocco, Tangiers functioned under Spanish protection and flourished as a semiofficial free port. By the mid-twentieth century, nineteen thousand Jews had migrated there and to its sister community of Tetuán. Most of them were Sephardim whose first language was a Maghreb version of Ladino, whose second was French, and whose third, increasingly, was Castilian. Their relations with Spain were close. Even during the period of Franco's wartime collaboration with Hitler, it was not unheard of for Moroccan Jews to study at Spanish universities.

With the emergence of Morocco to independence in the 1950s, six or seven thousand Jews from Tangiers and Tetuán moved directly on to metropolitan Spain (and a few hundred others opted for Portugal). Samuel Toledano, son of the late Moshe, was one of these. Although obliged to leave much of his estate behind, he had already developed extensive business contacts in Madrid. Within four years, he revived his fortunes in the Spanish capital as a manufacturer of sewing machines and, later, television sets and other electronic communications equipment. Samuel Toledano's son, Maurice, Oxford-educated, helped guide Toledano Enterprises to a central position in Spain's communications industry.

Meanwhile, Jewish immigration from both Spanish and French Morocco continued to grow, reaching some ten thousand by 1975. That year Francisco Franco died. After three and a half decades of Falangist rule, Spain reverted, gingerly, to a constitutional monarchy under Juan Carlos de Borbón. Indeed, in May 1978, a new national constitution was adopted by popular referendum. A key provision guaranteed "freedom of ideology, religion and worship for individuals," and proclaimed for the first time that "there shall be no state religion." Not since 1931 had Jews been as solidly assured of their protected status in Spain. Today, at least thirteen thousand of them are resident in the country, a number larger than the Jewish population of Austria or Denmark. Of these, approximately six thousand live in Barcelona, three thousand in Madrid, an additional thousand along the Costa del Sol, from Malága to Gibraltar. Scattered smaller groups are to be found inland and on the island of Majorca.

Most Spanish Jews are businessmen. Many share Maurice Toledano's lifestyle. Settled comfortably in a choice Madrid suburb, he and his Tangiers-born wife send their three children to the Jewish day school. Maurice is president of the Calle Balmes congregation. His father, Samuel, president of the Federation of Spanish Jewish Communities, helped organize that congregation and fund construction of its synagogue, the first in Spain since 1492. Dedication services for the building took place in 1969. It was still the Franco era. Yet the government ensured that its leading ministers and senior church officials were present for the occasion. Since then, the day school has gone up, and later a second one. In Barcelona, with its much larger Jewish population, communal life has been substantially more active than in Madrid. Its synagogue center functions in a comfortable middle-class neighborhood on Calle Porvenir. A rather muted five-story building, it offers facilities for classrooms and other cultural and recreational functions. Its day school is attended by nearly half of Barcelona's Jewish children.

Jewish security and vitality in Spain have also reflected the personal solicitude of the royal family. As early as February 1976, King Juan Carlos tendered a warm reception to visiting delegates of the World Sephardic Federation. Three months later, Queen Sofía attended a Sabbath service at the Madrid synagogue. It was a shrewd genuflection to Western liberal opinion, for it occurred on the eve of the royal couple's visit to the United States. Indeed, the gesture was trumped two years later when Israel's Sephardic chief rabbi, Ovadia Yosef, attended the dedication of Madrid's new Jewish day school. Invited to the royal palace, the elderly rabbi arrived with a motorcycle escort and received a welcome normally accorded a visiting head of state. Following the reception, the king and queen personally escorted Rabbi Yosef to his waiting limousine. In 1990, climaxing a long series of symbolic gestures, the Spanish government awarded the nation's most prestigious honor, its Príncipe de Asturias prize, to the World Sephardic Federation. The citation emphasized Sephardic Jewry's role in upholding and preserving the Spanish language and culture, thus serving as "the wandering Spain" in all the corners of the earth. The entire Jewish world resonated with pride, for the Príncipe de Asturias award is the Spanish world's Nobel prize. Nowhere by then could the "new" Spain have found a more committed ambassador of goodwill than Diaspora Jewry.

Except Israeli Jewry. For decades, the relationship between Spain and Israel had been querulous. Francisco Franco's postwar ambition to succeed Mussolini as "protector of Islam" led him to flirt with the Arab League, to acquiesce in the latter's campaign of diplomatic quarantine against Israel. Yet throughout the 1950s and 1960s Madrid cooperated with the Jewish Agency by offering transit facilities in the huge migration of Moroccan Jews to Israel. During the 1956 and 1967 Middle East wars, Madrid extended consular protection to some one hundred "Sephardim" of Egypt, enabling them to leave that country. And Israel was prepared to reciprocate. Earlier, it had joined other democratic governments in blocking Spain's membership in the United Nations. But in 1975, Jerusalem dropped its opposition.

In these same years, trade, tourist, and shipping contacts grew steadily between the two countries. Only diplomatic relations were lacking. Indeed, Spain remained the single Western nation to deny Israel official recognition. Its rationale was the need for Arab oil. But the argument would not fly after the Egyptian-Israeli peace treaty of 1979. By then, Madrid's efforts to secure full membership in the European Community were becoming more urgent. At last, in the spring of 1986, Prime Minister González announced the establishment of diplomatic ties with the Jewish state. Several months later, Shmuel Hadas, member of a veteran Israeli Sephardic family, presented his ambassadorial credentials to King Juan Carlos. Six years after that, on the five-hundredth anniversary of the Expulsion Decree of 1492, Israel's president Chaim Herzog arrived in Spain on a state visit. Amidst the pageantry of governmental and royal receptions, the most poignant moment of the ceremonies was the joint visit of Herzog and King Juan Carlos to the Calle Balmes synagogue. The king, wearing a skullcap, addressing his Israeli guest, the congregation, and the Jewish world at large, asked "forgiveness" for the "cruel and unjust" events of five centuries earlier.

"The apotheosis of the Jewish experience in modern Spain?" I asked Maurice Toledano.

He nodded his head toward a photograph behind his desk. I recognized his father, Samuel. Dressed in a morning coat, as befitted the president of the Federation of Spanish Jewish Communities, the elder Toledano was standing next to a taller man, also frock-coated. This was Minister of Justice Antonio Oriol. The two were examining a leather-bound document.

"The date was December 16, 1968," explained Maurice, "still well within the Franco era. Minister Oriol was presenting my father a government proclamation formally revoking the Catholic Monarchs' Expulsion Decree of March 1492." For several moments, the younger Toledano allowed me to savor the magnitude of the event. "My ancestor Daniel Toledano was on one of the first vessels carrying Jews out of the realm," he continued. "Now, after five centuries, here was a modern Spanish government officially notifying another Toledano that the Jews were a 'legal' presence in Spain once more. A few years later, when my own first son was born, I named him Daniel. It was a matter of closing the circle, so to speak."

A "Sleeping" Settlement

Not everyone would agree. For other Jews, even for other Sephardim, home would always be elsewhere. In Jerusalem's old Jewish Quarter, a compact enclosure lying within the medieval Old City, the thread of this people's continuity is discernible less in memorialized landscapes than in a quartet of restored Sephardic houses of worship. Best reached via St. Stephen's Gate, the more impressive of the four are the Istanbuli and Eliahu HaNavi synagogues. The former is Turkish; the latter, Italian. In the aftermath of Israel's recapture of the Old City in 1967, both these modest stone edifices were salvaged from their decrepitude under Hashemite occupation. In their original sixteenth- and seventeenth-century incarnations, they had boasted sumptuous tapestries, plush maroon upholstery, gold-leaf moldings and cornices. The decor has not been restored. Yet like the Nachmanides Synagogue, circa 1680, sheltered in a modest declivity only a few hundred feet away, and the even older neighboring Ben-Zakkai Synagogue, dating back to 1615, the buildings at least are "purified"—repaired, refurbished, whitewashed, even electrified.

There have been more vivid talismans of historical continuity. Among the best known for many years was Moshe Castel, one of modern Israel's most renowned artists (p. 127). Whether in traditional oils or in his later métier, melted basalt, Castel's work uniquely evokes the hushed, pietistic atmosphere of pre-Ashkenazic Palestine. So does his family history. His forebears shared in the mass 1492 exodus from Castile, whence they acquired their family name. Rabbis and scholars, immersed in the apocalyptic speculations of their generation, they, too, were among the mystics resolved to fulfill the divine commandment implicit in the catastrophe. They would return to the Holy Land.

The Castels settled in Gaza. For the next three centuries, they sustained their vocation as rabbis in that town. But in 1799, as in 1492, the family was uprooted by a force majeure—in this case, Napoleon Bonaparte. Jews and Arabs alike fled the invading French army. The Castels escaped to Hebron. One of Palestine's four "holy cities," together with Jerusalem, Tiberias, and Safed, Hebron was venerated as the birthplace of King David, as the grave site of the Patriarchs Abraham, Isaac, and Jacob. Here the Castels settled in as rabbis and communal leaders. During the late nineteenth and early twentieth centuries, Moshe Castel's uncle, Rabbi Meir Castel, served as chairman of the Sephardic community of Hebron. In 1929, however, he was among the scores of Jews who were murdered there in an Arab nationalist uprising. Survivors of that massacre departed the town to the last soul.

Moshe Castel's father, Rabbi Yehuda Castel, brother of the slain rabbi, relocated with his family to the Bukharan quarter in the New City of Jerusalem. The rabbi's life prefigured his son Moshe's career. A distinguished Hebraist and scholar, he was also a renowned aesthete, a composer of Hebrew melodies and calligrapher of Torah scrolls. His legacy to his son was a rich one. From every wall of the family home, works of oriental art and design greeted Moshe Castel's eyes. The music that filled his ear was a blend of medieval Iberian and modern Bukharan. The amalgam was characteristic. If the Sephardim of Moshe Castel's circle— parents, relatives, friends—steadfastly maintained their own ritual and dialect, they had long since become immersed in a neighborhood that was a microcosm of the Jewish Orient.

The acquaintances Moshe Castel greeted as he walked with his father through the blackened stone roadway of the Bukharan quarter often were as swarthy as Arabs. Some actually were descended from the original Jewish inhabitants of antiquity. Others were *mustarabin,* Jews of nearby Arab lands, or *moghrebim,* equally orientalized Jews from Morocco. Still others were tiny, nut-brown Yemenites from southwestern Arabia, or *bucharim,* slow-speaking Jews from Asian Russia, wearing elaborately patterned skullcaps and cassocks. Many of these passersby greeted Rabbi Yehuda with bows. The boys understood the significance of the gesture. All but inundated by new waves of Ashkenazim, the non-Europeans were becoming a minority in Jewish Palestine. Yet within the oriental community, at least, the understanding was clear: the Sephardim were still respected aristocrats, still the court of last resort in communal affairs.

Their role mattered. By the mid-nineteenth century, Ottoman *Tanzimat* reforms and improved communication were opening vistas of economic progress for the Holy Land. Palestine's imports and exports were rising steadily, at an annual rate of between 6 and 8 percent between 1825 and

1875. That burgeoning commerce, in turn, spurred completion of a railroad between Jaffa and Jerusalem in 1892, a line that functioned in its turn as a branch of the Hejaz Railroad, then under construction. With the widening traffic, a nucleus of local go-betweens emerged to serve such inland centers as Jerusalem and Safed and the coastal ports of Jaffa and Haifa. Most tended to be Armenians, Greeks, and Sephardic Jews, Levantines who enjoyed widest familiarity with European languages. For the Sephardim, of course, a network of kinsmen in other lands was an old story. In Palestine now, serving as dragomans—translators and agents—for local branches of European companies, they usually enjoyed the latter's capitulatory (extraterritorial) protection, and thus were exempted from local taxes. With the often considerable savings accumulated through this advantage, moreover, the Sephardim gradually were able to venture into business on their own. Often, they invested in land. Some of them opened small banks. But occasionally, as incipient developers, they would bid on public works projects.

The Amzalek family is a case in point. Joseph Amzalek, born in Gibraltar in 1799, of Moroccan Sephardic ancestry, flourished initially as a smuggler of contraband to nearby Spain. After the Napoleonic Wars, he fulfilled a lifelong ambition by settling in Jerusalem's Old City. There he augmented his comfortable estate by serving as a private mortgage banker. Maintaining a spacious home with a private synagogue, Amzalek also became a generous philanthropist and a respected member of the local community council. Over the years, he was able to marry off his children to other prominent Sephardic families. They followed his lead as venture capitalists. His son Chaim moved to Jaffa, where he invested extensively in orange groves, banks, import-export houses, and thrived. Chaim's daughter Esther in turn was betrothed in her early teens to Eliyahu Navon, son of Jerusalem's Sephardic chief rabbi and nephew of several eminent Jerusalem merchants. Through his wife's family, Eliyahu Navon developed extensive social and business connections with leaders of the Moslem community and was so well regarded by the local Turkish aga that he was invariably included in welcoming committees for visiting potentates and statesmen.

It was Eliyahu Navon's son, Joseph, born in 1852, who elevated the Navon and Amzalek family fortunes to a new plateau. After attending a Jerusalem talmud torah, the youngster was sent off to a Parisian lycée for his secular education. Upon his return at the age of twenty, Joseph Navon bought a partnership in the Ashkenazi-owned Frutiger Bank in Jerusalem. Under his managing direction, the bank several years later purchased control of the German Duisberg Company, Jerusalem's largest trading house. With the extensive capital leverage at his disposal, Joseph Navon then proceeded to negotiate a government concession to build Palestine's first railroad line, the Jaffa-to-Jerusalem route (p. 377). Later, for an enormous profit, he sold out his controlling interest to the French company that completed the project. Altogether, Joseph Navon's eminence as a business and communal leader in Palestine was unsurpassed. Sultan Abdul Hamid II awarded him the honorific title of bey. The French government inducted him into the Legion of Honor.

Other Sephardic families played comparable roles in fostering the Palestinian economy. Among them, in Jerusalem, were the Eliashars, Meyouhases, and Valeros; in Jaffa and Tel Aviv, the Moyals, Chelouches, Recanatis, and Carassos. Manifestly, there were also Ashkenazim, from Simon Lämel to Edmond de Rothschild, whose investments proved crucial in nurturing the growth of Jewish Palestine. Yet none of these Europeans lived in the Holy Land. The Sephardim invested their families as well as their funds.

"Our families never let us forget our pedigree," recalls Shaul Nahmias, a former chief of the Israel National Police. "We really had nothing to do with those wild-eyed Ashkenazi newcomers. In those pre–World War I days, every neighborhood in Jerusalem lived its own life." Nahmias's family shared the "Saidoff Compound" with dozens of other Sephardic clans. They worshiped in the Be'er Ya'akov synagogue, a spherical, Turkish-style structure where prayers were intoned in Hebrew and Ladino. "My family and friends used to call the Ashkenazim 'them,' " Nahmias reminisces. "If a Sephardi boy came to fetch me, my parents would tell me, 'David was here looking for you.' But if an Ashkenazi boy called, my parents would say, 'An Ashkenazi boy was here to see you.' " It was a telling aperçu. In early-twentieth-century Palestine, the Sephardim maintained virtually no contact with the "uncouth" Ashkenazim, and still less with the latter's frenetic Zionist politics. Nahmias's family, after all, were businessmen of the old Sephardic Levantine school. They dealt with such littoral affairs as insurance, banking, and sea freight. In their extensive negotiations with Arabs, Turks, Greeks, and other East Mediterranean interlocutors, the least of their interests was in political ideologies. For them, it was satisfaction enough to be living in the Holy Land. "Our main talent was for accommodation," Nahmias explains. "We knew how to get along with the Turkish and Arab authorities, and later with the British authorities. We were not looking for political confrontations."

But, in the end, there was no way even for Sephardim of Nahmias's background to avoid the challenge of political Zionism. During the early

1920s, while still a teenager, he was drawn to the romantic dynamism of the "Boy Scouts Legion." It was essentially a Zionist youth group, and from its ranks membership in the *Haganah,* the Jewish underground defense movement, was an inevitable next step. Although young Nahmias continued the family business tradition, working in an insurance company, even becoming a branch manager at the precocious age of twenty-two, he made time to continue his Haganah activities. Every member was needed, particularly during the 1929 and 1936–39 Arab uprisings. "Perhaps our involvement was not really nationalism after all," muses Nahmias. "By the 1920s and 1930s, it was simply a question of self-defense."

With the outbreak of World War II, Nahmias volunteered for the British army and he was accepted immediately. Valuing his credentials as an experienced executive and a fluent Arabic speaker, the British put him in charge of a company of Arab recruits. Later, during the 1942 crisis of al-Alamein, Nahmias was given command of a unit of four hundred Palestinian Jewish troops and dispatched to the Western Desert. The battle action was heavy, his company's performance estimable. Following Rommel's withdrawal, in 1943, Nahmias and the Palestinians were transferred from Egypt to Italy. As members of the newly organized Jewish Brigade, they participated in the landing at Salerno beach. Although they suffered heavy casualties, the Palestinians continued their offensive up the Italian peninsula until the final German surrender, in May 1945.

The Brigade's most crucial role in Europe began only then. It was entirely unofficial, even illegal. This was to help organize the secret transmigration of European Jewish survivors from their displaced persons camps in Central Europe to the Mediterranean coast—and, eventually, through the British naval blockade to Palestine. "For the refugees," Nahmias recalls, "it must have been strange to encounter a Jew like me, who did not speak 'Jewish,' that is, Yiddish. Actually, for most of them it was a meeting with a new kind of Jew, a *Frank* [Ashkenazic slang for Sephardi]. But this *Frank* was a major in the British army, and without his help they could not get to the Land of Israel." The "new" Jew in fact was the oldest Jew of all. More than all others, it was he over the centuries who had maintained his people's foothold in the Holy Land.

The Shock of Modernity

There were more recent *Franks.* Indeed, Jews of oriental-Sephardic background comprised a majority of Israel's immigrants in the postindependence years. Hitler had disposed of the rest. Few of the newcomers were classic Iberian "aristocrats," as it happened. They had endured the vicissitudes of life in North Africa and the Near East too long. Nor was their lot in Israel an easy one. Marginally housed, underemployed, they languished for years as the nation's underclass. Periodically, too, they vented their frustrations in raucous public outbursts, even in violence. Thus, in July 1957, a barroom brawl in Wadi Salib, a mixed Arab-Sephardi-oriental Haifa slum, erupted into a two-day explosion of public vandalism that left scores of police and civilians injured. Afterward, in hearings before a Knesset commission of inquiry, one witness after another testified to the discrimination suffered by non-Ashkenazim in housing, employment, education—in social status. Sobered then by the chasm opening in Israeli society, the Labor government embarked on a "crash" program to upgrade education in slum neighborhoods, to provide the Sephardim-orientals with better employment and housing opportunities. Over the years, the program registered a certain limited success.

Less easily corrected was the unflattering stereotype of the non-Ashkenazim. Even the nation's leading figures betrayed residual ethnic preconceptions. As minister of education, Abba Eban could state in an address that "one-half of our population comes from nations which, since the decline of Islamic culture, have had no educational history or environment." Labor Minister Golda Meir once publicly asked: "Shall we be able to elevate these immigrants to a suitable level of civilization?" President Yitzchak Ben-Zvi, a scholar of oriental Jewish history, could refer in his book *The Exiled and the Redeemed* to these "lost and forlorn tribes." Until the mid-1960s, the Israeli school syllabus emphasized the Ashkenazic heritage, with extensive courses in European Jewish history and literature.

In the 1960s and 1970s, however, the non-Ashkenazim no longer were prepared to await the dispensations of the Europeans. Their most vocal advocates included such unruly elements as the "Black Panthers," groups of volatile young demonstrators from Jerusalem's underprivileged Musrara quarter. In clamorous rallies, the Black Panthers made known their determination to win a place in the sun for their people. But, in fact, rather less noisily, their people already were achieving recognition in the vital arena of politics. Reflecting their demographic preponderance, the non-Europeans were negotiating choicer slots for themselves on the (dominant) Labor party's Knesset list, winning significantly larger numbers of city council seats and mayoralties in local elections. And, finally, in a classic revolution of rising expectations, the Sephardim-orientals abandoned the Labor party altogether. It was their defection to the right-wing Likud bloc in the Knesset election of 1977 that helped Menachem Begin become prime minister.

Political changes alone guarantee no transformation in self-image. Moreshet, a training program of "young leadership for Sephardic communities," is sponsored by the World Zionist Organization. Ostensibly, the purpose of the program is to remind Sephardic youth in the Diaspora of their once glorious heritage. More functionally, it seeks to bring these teenagers to Israel for a year's sojourn. I visit Moreshet's headquarters in the Old City of Jerusalem. It is a combination dormitory-classroom center, formerly part of the Sephardic Chief Rabbinate's office complex. Here youngsters of "Sephardic background" from Europe and the Western Hemisphere gather to attend lectures and symposia. I chat with four or five of the students as they loll about, anticipating the lunch bell. They are from Argentina and Uruguay. Spanish is their language, all right, and that is the extent of it. Even so, the intention is honorable.

It is the brainchild of Yitzchak Navon. A heavyset, bespectacled man in his early seventies, effervescent and ingratiating, Navon is a paradigm of the Sephardic experience. His ancestors shared in the exodus from Spain, settled in Turkey, then moved to Jerusalem in the seventeenth century (the genealogy has been traced, authenticated, and publicized to a fare-thee-well by Navon's sister, Mazal Navon Linenberg). His grandfather was a petty merchant. His father, born in the Old City, directed a soup kitchen, taught Hebrew and Jewish studies. Yitzchak Navon, like his parents and seven brothers and sisters, grew up speaking Ladino at home and Arabic with his wide assortment of Arab acquaintances. Later, at the Hebrew University, he specialized in Arabic and Islamic culture.

The man's career henceforth was devoted exclusively to public service. In 1946, Navon was appointed Jerusalem area commander of the Haganah's Arabic-speaking section. Following Israel's war of independence, he was dispatched as his nation's first consul to Argentina and Uruguay, easily making the transition from Ladino to Castilian. Three years afterward, he was called home to serve as political secretary to Foreign Minister Moshe Sharett, and subsequently to Prime Minister David Ben-Gurion. During his free hours, Navon also devoted a considerable literary talent to the reconstruction of his Sephardic heritage. In 1968, his *Romancero Sefardi,* a theatrical presentation of Ladino secular and religious songs, achieved wide popular success. In 1971, his *Bustan Sefardi,* a Hebrew-language drama based on the folklife of Jerusalem's old Sephardic families, won comparable praise.

In effect, Yitzchak Navon's determination to salvage his people's image and self-esteem reverses the pattern of their once legendary cultural narcissism. As late as the 1930s, in Jewish Salonika, that self-appraisal remained a mirror image of Christian Spain's limpieza de sangre. Thus, in his

Histoire des Israélites de Salonique (1935), Joseph Nehama defined the chasm between his fellow Sephardim and Jews of other lands:

> The Sephardi looked down from on high upon the poor little Jew from the north, accustomed to misery and oppression, who cringed, sought to make himself inconspicuous by clinging to the wall, who had always lived behind closed doors and windows . . . always ready to flee, with his bundle and his wanderer's staff.

For Nehama, there was no language "nobler and more harmonious" than the Sephardi's "Castilian" tongue. Even during his own generation, numerous Sephardim continued rather touchingly to adorn their signatures with the Hebrew letters *samech tet*—s.t.—for *sefardi tahor,* "pure" Sephardi.

It was all compensatory bombast, of course. With their numbers shrunken by 1939 to barely a million among sixteen million Jews worldwide, followed by the wartime deracination of their proudest communities, and finally the massive, belated transplantation to Israel of their impoverished and poorly educated cousins from North Africa and the Near East, the image of the *sefardi tahor* had become obsolete, even illusionary. It was inevitable, then, within Israel's Ashkenazic establishment, that the very term *sefardi* should be equated with the disheveled berberiscos of Casablanca and Tunis, with a culturally deprived lumpenproletariat that clung to the lower tiers of the nation's economy, and tended to erupt in street demonstrations. One of Navon's compelling missions, then, in his career as a writer and later as minister of education was to reacquaint his own people—and Israelis of all backgrounds—with Sephardic Jewry's dazzling humanistic legacy.

The Challenge of Humanism

That heritage never was more critical than in the 1970s and 1980s. Ironically, it was the very period in which Sephardic-oriental Jews were beginning to achieve a certain economic security and political leverage. Yet it was also in these years that they confronted an unanticipated sequence of ideological pitfalls. By then, Israel's Orthodox parties had long suspected the existence of a high-assay lode of religious fundamentalism among the non-Ashkenazic communities. They were not wrong. Nowhere was the proof more vivid than in the western Negev development town of N'tivot. Here, even now, a dense enclave of synagogues, prayer rooms, and administrative offices functions as headquarters for a spiritual domain ruled by one Baruch Abuhatzeira, known to his fellowers as the "Baba Baruch."

In his native Marrakech, the Baba Baruch's father, Rabbi Israel Abuhatzeira, was widely revered as a gentle, otherworldly, even saintly man. Thus, when the family joined the great migration of Moroccan Jews to Israel in the 1950s, the elder Abuhatzeira continued to minister to his flock on a purely spiritual basis. Not so the son. Upon completing his rabbinical studies in Jerusalem and being ordained, Baruch Abuhatzeira began capitalizing on the family name to build a political career. Indeed, he rose to the position of deputy mayor of N'tivot within a year, and was pegged as a future star in the otherwise Ashkenazi-dominated National Religious party. A few obstacles remained, however. In 1977, returning from a vacation in Paris, Abuhatzeira was intercepted at Ben-Gurion Airport bringing in several thousand black-market French francs. He was fined. Later that year, he was arrested, indicted, and convicted for accepting a bribe from a contractor, for passing false documents, and for embezzling funds raised from the sale of municipal lands. Yet even as Baruch Abuhatzeira was serving his seven-year term, his cousin, Rabbi Aharon Abuhatzeira, who on his own had risen to chairmanship of the National Religious party, was ensconced in the Begin cabinet as minister of religions. Soon afterward, however, Aharon Abuhatzeira similarly was convicted of embezzlement—in his case, from a trust fund he had managed before joining the government.

Did these derelictions undermine the credibility of the Abuhatzeiras with their North African followers? Not likely. Baruch was released on parole after four years. Soon afterward, in 1983, with the death of the aged and venerated Rabbi Israel Abuhatzeira, the son appeared before the huge funeral procession to lay claim to his father's mantle. Subsequently, as the "Baba Baruch," he mobilized local Sephardic officials and overseas Sephardic donors in support of his burgeoning N'tivot complex of synagogues, seminaries, cemeteries, and other ostensibly charitable institutions. Since then, reigning over his emergent empire, the Baba Baruch has held court daily, listened to the pleas of the ill and desperate, accepted contributions, and faith-healed at a self-proclaimed cure rate of 85 percent. Doing good, Abuhatzeira also does very well. He owns several handsome villas, purchases new automobiles each year and takes expensive European vacations. His tens of thousands of followers are not daunted.

"It's frightening," acknowledges Yitzchak Navon. "In the classical Sephardic tradition, religious study always was combined with openness to reason, to culture, to the arts and sciences. That was the tradition of Maimonides, after all."

Navon's memory is selective. Among his forebears, there were anti-Maimunists, kabbalists, Shabbateans, and other mystics, even plain and simple charlatans. Yet it is incontestable that Jewish religious philosophy was an innovation specifically of Iberian Jewry. The point has been emphasized by spokesmen for the World Sephardic Federation, a body founded in the 1960s with Yitzchak Navon's active participation. At Navon's initiative, too, the federation leadership in recent decades has taken on the challenge of religious fundamentalism within the Sephardic world. "It's almost a contradiction in terms," insists Jacque Khafif, a Brazilian and a federation vice-president. "There was a time when that kind of fanaticism was exclusively an Ashkenazic characteristic. Superstition, yes," he admits, doubtless alluding to the Abuhatzeira phenomenon, "but fanaticism, intolerance . . ." He shakes his head.

It was presumably to confirm the distinction between the two communities that, in 1981, North African members of the National Religious Party broke away to establish their own faction, Tami, an acronym signifying Religious Movement of Eastern Jews. Did the secession prefigure a certain ideological moderation? It did not. Rather, by 1984, borrowing from the unloveliest precedents of Ashkenazic zealotry, Tami produced an even more implacable splinter offshoot known as Shas (Sephardic Torah Guardians), this one a Sephardic counterpart to the Ashkenazim's ultrafundamentalist Agudat Israel party.

"Why are all the Sephardic rabbis wearing black coats these days?" laments Stephen Shalom, a New Yorker and also a federation vice-president. "This is not our tradition. When I asked a religious leader from Morocco why he wears a black coat and not his traditional ceremonial robes, he said, 'They won't let me.' . . . The people who have taken over the Sephardic rabbinical seminaries are turning out robots, not thinking people."

"It's one of our gravest challenges," admits Yitzchak Navon, still finessing such "aberrations" as the excommunications of Uriel Acosta and Baruch Spinoza. "Fanaticism was a quality we once identified with those closed-minded, close-windowed Jews from the north. In our tradition, a man's relation with God was his own business. All our teachers preached tolerance. Unlike the Ashkenazic rabbis, they didn't feel it necessary to dress in black as proof of their piety." Here Navon has a point. "Our teachers shared our joys. We were an open people, a Mediterranean people, open to the sun, to the sky, to color, to the tactile pleasures of the world around us. We were open to knowledge. To life."

Are the Sephardim open to non-Jews? More specifically, to their cousin Ishmael—the Arabs? It seems unlikely. In the political earthquake of Israel's 1977 election, it was more than social resentments that turned Israel's non-Ashkenazim away from Labor and into the camp of Menachem Begin's hawkish Likud bloc. In recent centuries, the Easterners' families and forebears often had suffered acute deprivation under Moslem rule. Nothing in their experience would have induced them to trust Arab intentions, or to part with augmented territorial frontiers. After 1967, too, when thousands of West Bank and Gaza Arabs became commuting laborers in Israel, Sephardic contact with these kinsmen of their former persecutors aroused old grievances. Ensconced vocationally a rung above the Arabs, Sephardic and oriental Jews developed a "poor white" mentality, and with it a vested interest in the territorial status quo.

"Begin undoubtedly appealed to our darker side," concedes Navon, "but there is also another side. And after the events of recent years, we're beginning to catch glimpses of it again."

The "events" Navon has in mind are the long paralysis in negotiations on Palestine after the initial peace treaty with Egypt; the ill-fated 1982 Lebanon invasion, with its attendant Lebanese Christian massacres of Palestinians in the Sabra and Shatila shantytowns; above all, the upsurge of *intifada* violence among the Arabs of Gaza and the West Bank. By the 1990s, the mood in Israel was one of fatigue, of impatience with the chauvinism and militant territorialism that had cost the nation dearly in lives and economic resources. This time, the Sephardim increasingly shared in that mood. Indeed, they made the fact plain by their extensive defection back to Labor in the 1992 Knesset elections, and their acceptance of autonomy negotiations with the Palestine Arabs a year later.

Yitzchak Navon has long been prominent among the "doves" of his people. "In the Jerusalem of my childhood," he explains, "friendship with our Arab neighbors was a given. As youngsters, we played together in the street. My father was a frequent guest in Arab homes, and they in ours. I remember him saying to one of his closest friends, Raghib Bey al-Nashashibi: 'The Turks were here and they went away. The British are here and they will go. Only we, Jews and Arabs, will remain.' " In October 1980, Navon repeated those words in Cairo. It was the aftermath of the Egyptian-Israeli peace treaty, and Navon was addressing the People's Assembly, Egypt's parliament. In fluent, luminous Arabic, he dazzled, electrified his audience with a speech at once complimentary and conciliatory, invoking the common heritage of Moslem and Jew, their shared higher ideals of respect for God, wisdom, family, charity. Whether in Andalusia, the Maghreb, or the Middle East, the two civilizations once had nurtured and refined those values in common terrain.

It was also the message Navon earlier had transmitted to another assembly, this one in his own country. Since 1965, he had sat in the Israeli Knesset. Emerging as one of the Labor party's brightest stars, he had served as deputy speaker of the Knesset for seven years, as chairman of its crucial Defense and Foreign Affairs Committee for four more. In tribute then to the man's intellectual brilliance and transparent integrity of character, the Knesset in September 1978 elected Yitzchak Navon president of the State of Israel. The first Sephardi to be accorded the honor, it was he, possibly more even than the Toledanos of Spain, who at long last had negotiated his people's endlessly tormented and improbably vibrant odyssey of return.

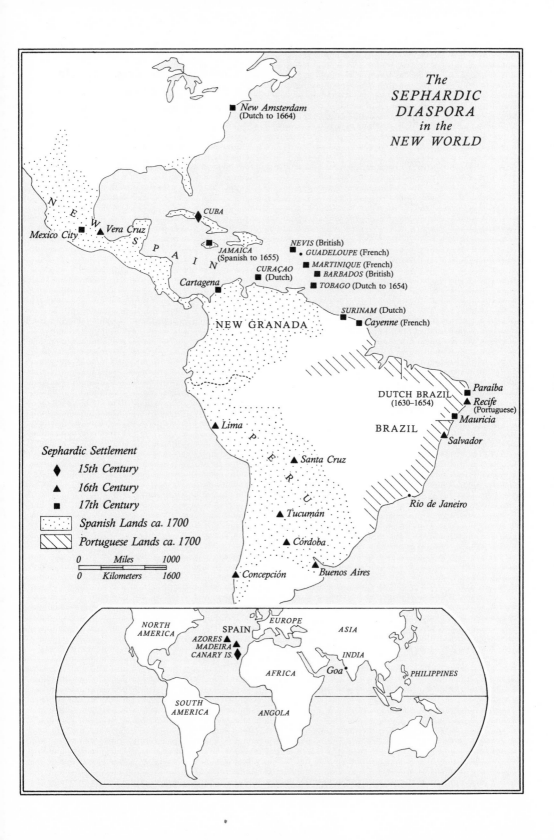

The
SEPHARDIC
DIASPORA
in the
NEW WORLD

■ New Amsterdam
(Dutch to 1664)

*N
E
W
S
P
A
I
N*

Mexico City ▲ *Vera Cruz*

◆ CUBA

NEW GRANADA

■ JAMAICA
(Spanish to 1655)

CURAÇAO
(Dutch)

■ *Cartagena*

NEVIS (British)
• GUADELOUPE (French)
■ *MARTINIQUE* (French)
■ BARBADOS (British)
■ *TOBAGO* (Dutch to 1654)

SURINAM (Dutch)
■ Cayenne (French)

DUTCH BRAZIL
(1630–1654)

■ *Paraíba*
▲ *Recife*
(Portuguese)
■ *Mauricia*

BRAZIL

▲ Lima

*P
E
R
U*

▲ *Santa Cruz*

▲ *Salvador*

Sephardic Settlement

◆ 15th Century

▲ 16th Century

■ 17th Century

⋮ Spanish Lands ca. 1700

╱ Portuguese Lands ca. 1700

▲ *Tucumán*

Rio de Janeiro

▲ *Córdoba*

0   Miles   1000

0   Kilometers 1600

▲ *Concepción*   ▲ *Buenos Aires*

NORTH
AMERICA

EUROPE

SPAIN

ASIA

AZORES ▲
MADEIRA ▲
CANARY IS. ◆

INDIA

Goa •

PHILIPPINES

AFRICA

SOUTH
AMERICA

ANGOLA

*Acknowledgments are limited to poetry and extended quoted transla-
tions from English-language publications. Comparable ascriptions to
authors in other languages normally appear in the text.*

CHAPTER I

page 8   "Send a carrier pigeon . . .": Israel
Zinberg, ed., *A History of Jewish
Literature: The Arabic Spanish Period*
(Cleveland, 1972). Bernard Martin,
tr.

9   "Your [king]": Norman Stillman,
The Jews of Arab Lands
(Philadelphia, 1979). Bernard
Lewis, tr.

12   "Old Moses": Zinberg, *History.*

12   "At the dawn I seek thee": Israel
Davidson, ed., *Selected Poems of
Solomon Ibn Gabirol* (Philadelphia,
1952).

13   "But if she hath been defiled":
Ibid.

14   "Why should I grieve": Solomon
Solis-Cohen, ed., *Selected Poems of
Moses Ibn Ezra* (Philadelphia, 1934).

14–15 "Ye deaf": Ibid.

15   "Would that after my death":
Israel Efros, ed., *Judah Halevi as
Poet and Thinker* (New York, 1941).
Israel Zangwill, tr.

15   "The sun is on thy face": Ibid.

16   "Lo, sun and moon": Zinberg,
History.

16   "My heart is in the East": Ibid.

17   "like an Ethiopian woman": Nina
Salaman, ed., *Selected Poems of
Jehudah Halevi* (Philadelphia, 1924).

28   Maimonides inscription: Jacob S.

Minkin, *The World of Moses
Maimonides* (New York, 1937).

CHAPTER II

29   Moses ibn Ezra lament: Yitzhak
Baer, *A History of the Jews in
Christian Spain,* vol. 1
(Philadelphia, 1961).

31–2 Spanish doggerel: J. M. Hillgarth,
The Spanish Kingdoms, vol. 1
(London, 1976).

CHAPTER IV

80   Praise for Doña Gracia: in Martin
A. Cohen, ed., *Samuel Usque's*
Consolation for the Tribulations of
Israel (Philadelphia, 1977).

82   Eulogy for Doña Gracia: in Cecil
Roth, *The House of Nasi: Doña
Gracia* (Philadelphia, 1977).

CHAPTER V

96   Ladino ballads: in Moshe Lazar,
ed., *The Sephardic Tradition: Ladino
and Spanish Jewish Literature* (New
York, 1972).

CHAPTER VI

131   Translation from Bar-Yosef's *The
Enchanted City:* Howard M. Sachar,
Aliyah: The Peoples of Israel
(Cleveland, 1961).

CHAPTER VII

151   Lament for Jews of Salonika: Isaac
Jack Levy, ed., *And the World
Stood Silent: Sephardic Poetry of the
Holocaust* (Urbana, Ill., 1989).

CHAPTER VIII

171–2 Transcription of Inquisitional
torture: H. C. Lea, *A History of the
Spanish Inquisition* (New York,
1906–07).

190   Castro's evaluation of returning
conversos: in Yosef H. Yerushalmi,
From Spanish Court to Italian Ghetto
(New York, 1971).

CHAPTER IX

195   Extract from Germaine Mouette's
description of Maghreb Jewish life:
cited in Norman Stillman, *The Jews
of Arab Lands* (Philadelphia, 1979).

208   Mendes-France's bitter
recollection: cited in Abram L.
Sachar, *A Host at Last* (Boston,
1976).

CHAPTER X

214–15 "A tower of strength": Jacob S.
Minkin, *Abrabanel and the
Expulsion of the Jews from Spain*
(New York, 1938).

224   "O how I long and yearn": Ibid.

CHAPTER XIII

282   Gedenck-Klanck loyalty oath:
Simon Schama, *The Embarrassment
of Riches: An Interpretation of Dutch
Culture in the Golden Age* (New
York, 1987).

290   *Parnassim*'s injunction against
relapsos: Yosef Kaplan, *Jews and
Conversos: Studies in Society and the
Inquisition* (Jerusalem, 1981).

CHAPTER XV

341   Luis de Carvajal's message to his
family: Seymour B. Liebman, *The
Enlightened: The Writings of Luis de
Carvajal el Mozo* (Coral Gables,
Fla., 1967).

342   "[Luis] was always such a good
Jew": Ibid.

342–3 Bocanegra account of Mexican
auto de fe: Martin A. Cohen, ed.,
*The Martyr: The Story of a Secret
Jew and the Mexican Inquisition in
the Sixteenth Century* (Philadelphia,
1973).

343   Treviño's defiance: Seymour B.
Liebman, *The Jews in New Spain*
(Coral Gables, Fla., 1970). Enrique
Rivas, tr.

BIBLIOGRAPHY

This compendium is arranged by topic. Some works are listed, as appropriate, under more than one chapter. Readers seeking additional general works on the Sephardim should consult— beyond virtually any and all books by Cecil Roth—Jane S. Gerber's excellent *The Jews of Spain: A History of the Sephardic Experience* (New York, 1992), Yosef H. Yerushalmi's luminous *From Spanish Court to Italian Ghetto* (New York, 1971), and two rich collections: Haim Beinart's *The Sephardi Legacy* (2 vols., Jerusalem, 1992) and R. D. Barnett's and W. M. Schwab's *The Sephardic Heritage: Essays on the History and Cultural Contribution of the Jews of Spain and Portugal* (2 vols., London, 1971; Grendon, 1989).

CHAPTER I: UNDER ANDALUSIAN
SKIES

Ashtor, Eliyahu. *The Jews of Moslem Spain.* 3 vols. Philadelphia, 1973.

Assis, Yehuda. "Sexual Behavior in Medieval Hispano-Jewish Society." In *Jewish History: Essays in Honor of Chinen Abramsky,* ed. A. Rapaport-Albert and S. J. Zipperstein. Leiden, 1988.

Barnett, R. D., and W. M. Schwab, eds. *The Sephardic Heritage: Essays on the History and Cultural Contribution of the Jews of Spain and Portugal.* Vol. 1. London, 1971.

Baron, Salo W. *Essays on Maimonides.* New York, 1941.

———. *A Social and Religious History of the Jews.* Vols. 5, 8. New York, 1958.

Brann, Ross. *The Compunctious Poet: Cultural Ambiguity and Hebrew Poetry in Muslim Spain.* Philadelphia, 1986.

Brody, Heinrich, ed. *Selected Poems of Jehudah Halevi.* Philadelphia, 1952.

Cambridge History of Islam. Vol. 1. Cambridge, U.K., 1970.

Davidson, Israel, ed. *Selected Poems of Solomon Ibn Gabirol.* Philadelphia, 1952.

———. *Thesaurus of Medieval Jewish Poetry.* New York, 1970.

Dozy, Reinhart. *Spanish Islam.* London, 1913.

Efros, Israel. *Judah HaLevi as Poet and Thinker.* New York, 1941.

Fox, Marvin. *Interpreting Maimonides.* Chicago, 1990.

Friedenwald, Harry. *The Jews and Medicine.* Vol. 1. Baltimore, 1944.

Glick, Thomas F. *Islamic and Christian Spain in the Early Middle Ages.* Princeton, N.J., 1979.

Goitein, S. D. *Jews and Arabs: Their Contacts through the Ages.* New York, 1974.

———. *A Mediterranean Society.* Vol. I. Berkeley, Calif., 1967.

Goldstein, David. *The Jewish Poets of Spain, 900–1250.* Harmondsworth, U.K., 1971.

Grünebaum, Gustav E. von, ed. *Medieval Islam: A Study in Cultural Orientation.* Chicago, 1966.

Halkin, Abraham. *Crisis and Leadership:*
The Epistles of Maimonides.
Philadelphia, 1985.
———. "Judeo-Arabic Literature." In
The Jews, ed. Louis Finkelstein. 4th
ed. Vol. 3. New York, 1971.
———. "The Judeo-Islamic Age." In
Great Ages and Ideas of the Jewish
People, ed. Leo Schwarz. New York,
1956.
Hartman, David. *Crisis and Leadership:*
The Epistles of Maimonides.
Philadelphia, 1985.
———. *Maimonides: Torah and*
Philosophic Quest. Philadelphia, 1976.
Heschel, Abraham J. *Maimonides.* New
York, 1982.
Hyman, Arthur, ed. *Essays in Medieval*
Jewish and Islamic Philosophy. New
York, 1977.
Idel, Moshe. "Jewish Thought in
Medieval Spain." In *The Sephardi*
Legacy. ed. Haim Beinart. Vol. 1.
Jerusalem, 1992.
Katz, Solomon. *The Jews in the Visigothic*
and Frankish Kingdoms of Spain and
Gaul. Cambridge, Mass., 1937.
Kayser, Rudolf. *The Life and Times of*
Jehudah Halevi. New York, 1949.
Leaman, Oliver. *Moses Maimonides.*
London, 1990.
Millás Vallicrosa, J. M. *Solomon ibn*
Gabirol como poeta y filósofo. Madrid,
1945.
Minkin, Jacob S. *The World of Moses*
Maimonides. New York, 1937.
Morag, Shelomo. "The Jewish
Communities of Spain and the
Living Traditions of the Hebrew
Language." In *The Sephardi Legacy,*
ed. Haim Beinart. Vol. 1. Jerusalem,
1992.
Nyld, A. A. *Hispano-Arabic Poetry.*
Baltimore, 1941.
Pines, Shlomo, and Yehuda Yovel, eds.
Maimonides and Philosophy. Boston,
1986.
Romano, David. "The Jews'
Contribution to Medicine, Science,
and General Learning." In *The*

Sephardi Legacy, ed. Haim Beinart.
Vol. 1. Jerusalem, 1992.
Salaman, Nina, ed. *Selected Poems of*
Jehudah Halevi. Philadelphia, 1924.
Scheindlin, Raymond. *Wine, Women and*
Death: Medieval Hebrew Poems on the
Good Life. Philadelphia, 1986.
Sáenz-Badillos, Angel, and Judit
Tarragona Borrás. *Poetas hebreos de*
al-Andalus (siglos X–XII): Antología.
Madrid, 1990.
Shwarz, Zvi. *The Social and Political Ideas*
of Maimonides. Jerusalem, 1983.
Singer, Charles. "Science and Judaism."
In *The Jews: Their History, Culture,*
and Religion, ed. Louis Finkelstein.
4th ed. Vol. 2. New York, 1971.
Solis-Cohen, Solomon, ed. *The Selected*
Poems of Moses Ibn Ezra. Philadelphia,
1934.
Stillman, Norman. *The Jews of Arab*
Lands. Philadelphia, 1979.
Twersky, Isadore, ed. *A Maimonidean*
Reader. New York, 1972.
———. *Studies in Jewish Law and*
Philosophy. New York, 1982.
Weinberger, Leon. *Jewish Prince in*
Moslem Spain: Selected Poems of
Samuel ibn Nagrela. University, Ala.
1973.
Ye'or, Bat. *The Dhimmi: Jews and*
Christians under Islam. Rutherford,
N.J., 1985.
Zinberg, Israel. *A History of Jewish*
Literature: The Arabic Spanish Period.
Cleveland, 1972.

CHAPTER II: THE RISE AND FALL OF
CONVIVENCIA

Amador de los Ríos, José. *Historia social,*
política y religiosa de los judíos de
España y Portugal. Madrid, 1973.
Atienza, Juan G. *Guía Judía de España.*
Madrid, 1979.
Baer, Yitzhak. *A History of the Jews in*
Christian Spain. 2 vols. Philadelphia,
1961.
Barnett, R. D., and W. M. Schwab, eds.
The Sephardic Heritage: Essays on the

History and Cultural Contribution of the Jesus of Spain and Portugal. Vol. 1. London, 1971.

Baron, Salo W. *A Social and Religious History of the Jews.* Vols. 7, 13, 15. New York, 1969, 1973.

Beinart, Haim. "The Jews in Castile." In *The Sephardi Legacy,* ed. Haim Beinart. Vol. 1. Jerusalem, 1992.

Brody, Heinrich, ed. *Selected Poems of Ibn Ezra.* Philadelphia, 1945.

Burns, Robert I. *Moslems, Christians and Jews in the Crusader Kingdom of Valencia.* Cambridge, U.K., 1984.

Cantera Burgos, Francesco. *Sinagogas de Toledo, Segovia y Córdoba.* Madrid, 1973.

Caro Baroja, Julio. *Inquisición, brujería y criptojudaísmo.* Barcelona, 1970.

Carpenter, Dwayne E. *Alfonso X and the Jews.* Berkeley, Calif., 1986.

Castro, Adolfo de. *Historia de los judíos en España.* Madrid, 1847.

Chazan, Robert. "The Barcelona Disputation of 1263, Missionizing and Jewish Response." *Speculum* (1977).

———. *Daggers of Faith: Thirteenth-Century Christian Missionizing and Jewish Responsa.* Berkeley and Los Angeles, 1987.

Cohen, Jeremy. *The Friars and the Jews: The Evolution of Medieval Anti-Judaism.* Ithaca, N.Y., 1982.

Epstein, Israel. *Responses of R. Solomon ben Adreth of Barcelona (1235–1310) As a Source of the History of Spain.* London, 1925.

———. *Studies in the Communal Life of the Jews of Spain.* New York, 1968.

Glick, Thomas F. *Islamic and Christian Spain in the Early Middle Ages.* Princeton, N.J., 1979.

Grayzel, Solomon. *The Church and the Jews in the Thirteenth Century.* Philadelphia, 1933.

Hillgarth, J. M. *The Spanish Kingdoms, 1250–1516.* 2 vols. London, 1976.

Idel, Moshe. "We Have No Kabbalistic Tradition on This." In *Rabbi Moshe*

Nachmanides, ed. Isadore Twersky. Cambridge, Mass., 1983.

Metzger, Therese, and Mendel Metzger. *Jewish Life in the Middle Ages.* Secaucus, N.J., 1982.

Millás Vallicrosa, J. M. *La poesía sagrada hebraicoespañola.* Madrid, 1940.

Navarro Peiro, Angeles. *Narrativa hispano-hebrea.* Madrid, 1988.

Neumann, Abraham A. *The Jews in Spain.* Vol. 1. Philadelphia, 1942.

Sarachek, J. *Faith and Reason: The Conflict over the Rationalism of Maimonides.* Williamsport, Pa., 1935.

Schechter, Solomon. *Studies in Judaism.* Philadelphia, 1896.

Sebastiá, J. Doñata, and J. R. Magdalena Nom de Deu. *Three Jewish Communities in Medieval Valencia.* Jerusalem, 1990.

Septimus, B. *Hispano-Jewish Culture in Transition.* Cambridge, Mass., 1982.

Wolfson, Harry A. *Crescas' Criticism of Aristotle.* Cambridge, Mass., 1971.

CHAPTER III: THE LONG GOOD-BYE

Adler, Elkan. *Auto-de-Fe and Jew.* London, 1908.

Alcalá, Angel, ed. *Jews and Judeoconverts of Spain: The Expulsion of 1492 and Its Consequences.* New York, 1992.

Aridjis, Homero. *1492: The Life and Times of Juan Cabezón of Castile* [a novel]. New York, 1991.

Assis, Yom Tov. "The Jews in the Crown of Aragon and Its Dominions." In *The Sephardi Legacy,* ed. Haim Beinart. Vol. 1. Jerusalem, 1992.

Baer, Yitzhak. *A History of the Jews in Christian Spain.* 2 vols. Philadelphia, 1961.

Barnatan, Marcos Ricardo. *La Kabala.* Barcelona, 1974.

Beinart, Haim. "The Great Conversion and the Converso Problem." In *The Sephardi Legacy,* ed. Haim Beinart. Vol. 1. Jerusalem, 1992.

Bernadette, M. J. *Hispanic Culture and*

Character of the Sephardic Jew. New York, 1982.

Braunstein, Baruch. *The Chuetas of Majorca: Conversos and the Inquisition of Majorca.* Scottdale, Pa., 1936.

Cohen, Martin A. "The Sephardic Phenomenon: A Reappraisal." *American Jewish Archives* (spring–summer 1992).

Gampel, Benjamin R. *The Last Jews on Iberian Soil: Navarrese Jewry, 1479–1498.* Berkeley, Calif., 1989.

Gutwirth, Eleazar. "Towards Expulsion: 1391–1492." In *Spain and the Jews: The Sephardi Experience, 1492 and After,* ed. Elie Kedourie. London, 1992.

Hroch, Miroslav, and Anna Skybova. *Ecclesia Militans: The Inquisition.* London, 1988.

Kamen, Henry. "The Expulsion: Purpose and Consequence." In *Spain and the Jews: The Sephardi Experience, 1492 and After,* ed. Elie Kedourie. London, 1992.

———. *Inquisition and Society in Spain.* London, 1983.

———. *Spain 1469–1714: A Society in Conflict.* New York, 1983.

Kaplan, Yosef. *Jews and Conversos.* Jerusalem, 1984.

Kedourie, Elie, ed. *Spain and the Jews: The Sephardi Experience, 1492 and After.* London, 1992.

Langhurst, John E. *The Age of Torquemada.* Lawrence, Kans., 1962.

Lea, Henry C. *A History of the Inquisition.* Vol. 1. New York, 1906.

Meyuhas-Ginio, Alisa, ed. *The Mediterranean World After 1492: Jews, Muslims and Christians.* London, 1992.

Minkin, Jacob S. *Abrabanel and the Expulson of the Jews from Spain.* New York, 1938.

Netanyahu, Ben-Zion. *Don Isaac Abravanel: Statesman and Philosopher.* Philadelphia, 1968.

———. *The Marranos of Spain.* Millwood, N.J., 1973.

Neumann, Abraham A. *The Jews in Spain.* Vol. 2. Philadelphia, 1944.

Peters, Edward M. *Inquisition.* New York, 1988.

Quesada, Miguel. "Questions and Fallacies Regarding the Number of Jews in Spain in 1492 and Those Who Left." In *Jews and Judeoconverts of Spain: The Expulsion of 1492 and Its Consequences,* ed. Angel Alcalá. New York, 1992.

Raphael, David, ed. *The Expulsion, 1492 Chronicles.* North Hollywood, Calif., 1991.

Trend, J. B., ed. *Isaac Abravanel.* Cambridge, U.K., 1937.

CHAPTER IV: OTTOMAN DAWN

Angel, Mark. *The Jews of Rhodes.* New York, 1978.

Argenti, P. R. *The Religious Minorities of Chios.* Cambridge, U.K., 1967.

Aster, A., ed. *The Itinerary of Benjamin of Tudela.* New York, 1927.

Baron, Salo W. *A Social and Religious History of the Jews.* Vol. 18. New York, 1979.

Bornstein-Makovetsky, Leah. "Sephardic Communities in the Ottoman Empire from the Sixteenth to the Eighteenth Centuries." In *The Sephardic Heritage.* Vol. 2, *The Western Sephardim,* ed. R. D. Barnett and W. M. Schwab. Grendon, U.K., 1989.

———. *The Structure of Law-Courts in the Sixteenth and Seventeenth Centuries in the Communities of the Ottoman Empire.* Ramat Gan, Israel, 1972.

Bowman, Steven. "The Arrival of the Sephardim in the Ottoman Empire." In *Jews and Judeoconverts of Spain: The Expulsion of 1492 and Its Consequences,* ed. Angel Alcalá. New York, 1992.

———. *The Jews of Byzantium, 1204–1453.* Birmingham, Ala., 1985.

Braude, Benjamin, and Bernard Lewis, eds. *Christians and Jews in the Ottoman Empire.* 2 vols. New York, 1982.

Dobrinsky, Herbert C. *A Treasury of*

Sephardic Laws and Customs. New York, 1986.

Franco, Moïse. *Essai sur l'histoire des israélites de l'empire ottoman.* Paris, 1897, 1980.

Galanté, Abraham. *Histoire des juifs d'Anatolie.* Vol. 1 Istanbul, 1937.

——. *Histoire des juifs d'Istanbul.* 2 vols. Istanbul, 1941–42.

——. *Histoire des juifs de Rhodes.* Istanbul, 1935.

——. *Histoire des juifs de Turquie.* 9 vols. Istanbul, 1937.

Goodblatt, M. *Jewish Life in Turkey in the Sixteenth Century As Reflected in the Legal Writings of Samuel de Medina.* New York, 1970.

Grünebaum, Gustav E. von, ed. *Medieval Islam: A Study in Cultural Orientation.* Chicago, 1966.

Isaacs, A. Lionel. *The Jews of Majorca.* London, 1932.

Juhasz, Esther. *Juifs sépharades de l'empire ottoman.* Jerusalem, 1989.

——, ed. *Sephardic Jews in the Ottoman Empire.* Jerusalem, 1966.

Levy, Avigdor. *The Sephardim in the Ottoman Empire.* Princeton, N.J., 1992.

Merriman, Roger B. *Suleiman the Magnificent, 1520–1566.* Cambridge, Mass., 1966.

Netanyahu, Ben-Zion. *Don Isaac Abravanel: Statesman and Philosopher.* Philadelphia, 1968.

Porter, David. *Constantinople and Its Environs.* Vol. 1. New York, 1835.

Rodrigue, Aron. "The Sephardim in the Ottoman Empire." In *Spain and the Jews: The Sephardi Experience, 1492 and After,* ed. Elie Kedourie. London, 1992.

——, ed. *Ottoman and Turkish Jewry: Community and Leadership.* Bloomington, Ind., 1992.

Roth, Cecil, *The House of Nasi: Doña Gracia.* Philadelphia, 1977.

——. *The House of Nasi: The Duke of Naxos.* Philadelphia, 1946.

Sapirstein, Marc. "Martyrs, Merchants and Rabbis: Jewish Communal Conflict as Reflected in the Responsa on the Boycott of Ancona." *Jewish Social Studies* (winter 1981).

Shmuelevitz, A. *The Jews of the Ottoman Empire in the Late Fifteenth and Sixteenth Centuries.* Leiden, 1984.

Trend, J. B., ed. *Isaac Abravanel: Six Lectures.* Cambridge, U.K., 1937.

Werblowsky, R. J. Zvi. "R. Joseph Caro, Solomon Molcho, Don Joseph Nasi." In *The Sephardi Legacy,* ed. Haim Beinart. Vol. 2. Jerusalem, 1992.

Wittek, Paul. *The Rise of the Ottoman Empire.* London, 1971.

Yaari, A. *HaDefus HaIvri b'Kushta* [Hebrew Printing in Constantinople]. Tel Aviv, 1967.

Zinberg, Israel. *A History of Jewish Literature: The Jewish Center of Culture in the Ottoman Empire.* Cleveland, 1974.

CHAPTER V: TURKISH SUNSET

Angel, Marc D. *La America: The Sephardic Experience in the United States.* Philadelphia, 1982.

Benbassa, Esther. *Un Grand Rabbin sepharade en politique, 1892–1923.* Paris, 1990.

Braude, Benjamin, and Bernard Lewis, eds. *Christians and Jews in the Ottoman Empire.* 2 vols. New York, 1982.

Cardozo, Abraham Lopes. "The Music of the Sephardim." In *The World of the Sephardim,* ed. David da Sola Pool et al. New York, 1960.

Cohen, Hayyim J. *The Jews of the Middle East, 1860–1972.* Jerusalem, 1973.

Dobkowski, Michael N., and Isidor Wallimann. *Genocide in Our Time: An Annotated Bibliography.* Ann Arbor, Mich., 1992.

Dobrinsky, Herbert C. *A Treasury of Sephardic Laws and Customs.* New York, 1986.

Epstein, M. *The Ottoman Jewish Communities and Their Role in the*

Fifteenth and Sixteenth Centuries.
Freiberg, 1980.

Franco, Moïse. *Essai sur l'histoire des Israélites de l'empire ottoman.* Paris, 1897, 1980.

Galanté, Abraham. *Histoire des juifs d'Anatolie.* Vol. 2. Istanbul, 1939.

———. *Histoire des juifs de Turquie.* 9 vols. Istanbul, 1937.

Gerber, Haim, and Jacob Barnai. *Yehudei Izmir b'Mea Shanah Tishah-Esrei* [The Jews of Izmir in the Nineteenth Century]. Jerusalem, 1984.

Goodblatt, Morris. *Jewish Life in Turkey in the XVI Century: As Reflected in the Legal Writings of Samuel de Medina.* New York, 1952.

Grunzweig, Bedrich. "Istanbul." *Present Tense* (summer 1977).

Guroian, Vigen. "The Politics and Morality of Genocide." In *The Armenian Genocide: History, Politics, Ethics,* ed. Richard G. Hovannisian. New York, 1992.

Haboucha, Reginetta. "The Popular Literature of the Sephardim." In *Jews and Judeoconverts of Spain: The Expulsion of 1492 and Its Consequences,* ed. Angel Alcalá. New York, 1992.

Hacker, Joseph. "The Sephardim in the Ottoman Empire in the Seventeenth and Eighteenth Centuries." In *The Sephardi Legacy,* ed. Haim Beinart. Vol. 2. Jerusalem, 1992.

HaCohen, D'vora, and Menachem HaCohen. *One People: The Story of the Eastern Jews.* New York, 1969.

Harris, Alan C. "The Jews of Turkey." *Jewish Digest* (November 1967).

Heyd, Uriel. "The Jewish Communities of Istanbul in the XVII Century." *Orient* (autumn 1951).

Hovanissian, Richard G. *The Armenian Genocide in Perspective.* New Brunswick, N.J., 1986.

———, ed. *The Armenian Genocide: History, Politics, Ethics.* New York, 1992.

Inalcik, H. "Jews in the Ottoman Economy and Finances." In *The Islamic World: Essays in Honor of Bernard Lewis.* Princeton, N.J., 1984.

Jerusalmi, Isaac. "Ladino: The Language of Judaism and Daily Speech." In *Jews and Judeoconverts of Spain: The Expulsion of 1492 and Its Consequences,* ed. Angel Alcalá. New York, 1992.

Juhasz, Esther, ed. *Sephardic Jews in the Ottoman Empire.* Jerusalem, 1966.

Lazar, Moshe, *The Jews of Islam.* Princeton, N.J., 1984.

———. ed. *The Sephardic Tradition: Ladino and Spanish Jewish Literature.* New York, 1972.

Lewis, Bernard. *The Emergence of Modern Turkey.* London, 1961.

Levy, Avigdor. *The Sephardim in the Ottoman Empire.* Princeton, N.J., 1992.

Mirsky, Aharon. "Hebrew Literary Creation." In *The Sephardi Legacy,* ed. Haim Beinart. Vol. 1. Jerusalem, 1992.

Molho, M. *Histoire des israélites de Castoria.* Salonika, 1938.

Nachmani, A. *Israel, Turkey, and Greece: Uneasy Relations in the Eastern Mediterranean.* London, 1987.

Nathan, Naphtali. "Notes on the Jews of Turkey." *Jewish Social Studies* (December 1964).

Papo, Joseph M. *Sephardim in Twentieth Century America.* San Jose, Calif., 1987.

Rodrigue, Aron. *French Jews, Turkish Jews: The Alliance Israélite Universelle and the Politics of Jewish Schooling in Turkey, 1860–1925.* Bloomington, Ind., 1990.

Romero, Elena. "Literary Creation in the Sephardic Diaspora." In *The Sephardi Legacy,* ed. Haim Beinart Vol. 2. Jerusalem, 1992.

Rubin, Barry. *Istanbul Intrigues: A True-Life Casablanca.* New York, 1989.

Sachar, Howard M. *The Emergence of the*

Middle East, 1914–1924. New York, 1969.

Shaw, Stanford J. *The Jews of the Ottoman Empire and the Turkish Republic.* 2 vols. New York, 1991.

———. *Turkey and the Holocaust: Turkey's Role in Rescuing Turkish and European Jewry from Nazi Persecution, 1933–1945.* New York, 1992.

Shmuelevitz, A. *The Jews of the Ottoman Empire.* Leiden, 1984.

Vyronis, Speros, Jr. "A Critical Analysis of Stanford Shaw's *History of the Ottoman Empire and Turkey, Vol. 1.*" *Institute for Balkan Studies* (1983).

———. "The Turkish State and History." *Institute for Balkan Studies* (1991).

Weiker, Walter F. *Ottomans, Turks, and the Jewish Polity: A History of the Jews of Turkey.* Lanham, Md., 1992.

Zinberg, Israel. *A History of Jewish Literature: The Jewish Center of Culture in the Ottoman Empire.* Cleveland, 1974.

CHAPTER VI: THE MYSTICAL LAND

Aster, A., ed. *The Itinerary of Benjamin of Tudela.* New York, 1927.

Barnai, Jacob. "Blood Libels in the Ottoman Empire of the Fifteenth and Sixteenth Centuries." In *Antisemitism throughout the Ages,* ed. S. Almog. Oxford, 1988.

Cohen, Amnon. *Economic Life in Ottoman Jerusalem.* Cambridge, U.K., 1989.

———. *Jewish Life under Islam: Jerusalem in the Sixteenth Century.* Cambridge, Mass., 1984.

Cohen, R., ed. *Vision and Conflict in the Holy Land.* Jerusalem, 1987.

Dan, Joseph. "The Emergence of the Messianic Theology in the Thirteenth Century Kabbalah in Spain." In *Occident and Orient: A Tribute to the Memory of A. Scheiber.* Leiden, 1988.

David, Avraham. "Demographic Changes in the Safed Jewish Community of the Sixteenth Century." In *Occident and Orient: A Tribute to the Memory of A. Scheiber.* Leiden, 1988.

———. "The Spanish Exodus in the Holy Land." In *The Sephardi Legacy,* ed. Haim Beinart. Vol. 2. Jerusalem, 1992.

Fine, Lawrence. *Safed Spirituality.* New York, 1984.

HaCohen, D'vora, and Menachem HaCohen. *One People: The Story of the Eastern Jews.* New York, 1969.

Hirschberg, H. Z. "The Oriental Jewish Communities." In *Religion in the Middle East,* ed. A. J. Arberry. Vol. 1. Cambridge, U.K., 1969.

Idel, Moshe. *Kabbalah: New Perspectives.* New Haven, Conn., 1988.

———. "Spanish Kabbalism After the Expulsion." In *The Sephardi Legacy,* ed. Haim Beinart. Vol. 2. Jerusalem, 1992.

———. *Studies in Ecstatic Kabbalah.* Albany, N.Y., 1988.

Patai, Raphael. *The Jewish Mind.* New York, 1977.

Rossof, David. *Safed: The Mystical City.* Jerusalem, 1991.

Sachar, Howard M. *Aliyah: The Peoples of Israel.* Cleveland, 1961.

Schechter, Solomon. *Studies in Judaism.* Philadelphia, 1896.

Scholem, Gershon. *Major Trends in Jewish Mysticism.* Jerusalem, 1941.

———. *The Origins of the Kabbalah.* Philadelphia, 1987.

Silver, Abba Hillel. *A History of Messianic Speculation in Israel.* Boston, 1959.

Sirat, Colette. *A History of Jewish Philosophy in the Middle Ages.* Cambridge, 1985.

Ta-Shma, Israel M. "Rabbi Joseph Caro and His *Beit Yosef.*" In *The Sephardi Legacy,* ed. Haim Beinart. Vol. 2. Jerusalem, 1992.

Vilnay, Zev. *Legends of Galilee, Jordan, and Sinai.* Philadelphia, 1976.

Werblowsky, R. J. Zvi. *Joseph Karo: Lawyer and Mystic.* Oxford, 1962.

———. "Shabbetai Zevi." In *The Sephardi Legacy,* ed. Haim Beinart. Vol. 2. Jerusalem, 1992.

Yerushalmi, Yosef H. *Zachor: Jewish History and Jewish Memory.* Seattle, 1982.

Zinberg, Israel. *A History of Jewish Literature: The Jewish Center of Culture in the Ottoman Empire.* New York, 1974.

CHAPTER VII: THE MESSIAH OF THE AEGEAN

Ashkenazi, Tova. *Salonika HaYehudit* [Jewish Salonika]. Jerusalem, 1960.

Ashtor, Eliyahu. *Levant Trade in the Later Middle Ages.* Princeton, N.J., 1982.

Aster, A., ed. *The Itinerary of Benjamin of Tudela.* New York, 1927.

Barnett, R. D., and W. M. Schwab, eds. *The Sephardic Heritage: The Western Sephardim.* Vol. 2. Grendon, U.K., 1989.

Baron, Salo W. *An Economic History of the Jews.* Jerusalem, 1975.

Barzilay, Isaac. *Between Reason and Faith: Anti-rationalism in Italian Jewish Thought, 1250–1650.* The Hague, 1967.

Benveniste, David. *Kehilot HaYehudim b'Yavan* [Jewish Communities in Greece]. Jerusalem, 1979.

Ben-Zvi, Itzhak. *The Exiled and the Redeemed.* Philadelphia, 1957.

Calbo, Comparo. *Cuentos de los rabinos.* Madrid, 1991.

Emmanuel, I. S. *Histoire des Israélites de Salonique.* Paris, 1936.

Gaon, Haham S., and M. Mitchell Serels, eds. *Sephardim and the Holocaust.* New York, 1987.

Hirschberg, H. Z. "The Oriental Jewish Communities." In *Religion in the Middle East,* ed. A. J. Arberry. Vol. 1. Cambridge, U.K., 1969.

Lazar, Moshe, ed. *The Sephardic Tradition: Ladino and Spanish Jewish Literature.* New York, 1972.

Levy, Isaac Jack. *And the World Stood Silent: Sephardic Poetry of the Holocaust.* Urbana, Ill., 1989.

Mazur, Belle D. *Studies on Jewry in Greece.* Athens, 1935.

Meyuhas-Ginio, Alisa, ed. *The Mediterranean World after 1492: Jews, Muslims, and Christians.* London, 1992.

Molho, M., and J. Nehama. *In Memoriam: hommage aux victimes juives des nazis en Grèce.* 3 vols. Salonika, 1948–53.

Nehama, Joseph. *Histoire des Israélites de Salonique.* 7 vols. Paris, 1935–79.

Patai, Raphael. *The Vanished Worlds of Jewry.* New York, 1980.

Scholem, Gershon. *Major Trends in Jewish Mysticism.* Jerusalem, 1941.

———. *The Messianic Idea in Judaism.* New York, 1971.

———. *Sabbatei Sevi: The Mystical Messiah.* Princeton, N.J., 1971.

Sciaky, Leon. *Farewell to Salonica.* London, 1946.

Silver, Abba Hillel. *A History of Messianic Speculation in Israel.* Boston, 1959.

Sirat, Colette. *A History of Jewish Philosophy in the Middle Ages.* Cambridge, U.K., 1985.

CHAPTER VIII: AN IBERIAN EPITAPH

Adler, Elkan. *Auto de Fe and Jew.* London, 1908.

Alcalá, Angel, ed. *Jews and Judeoconverts of Spain: The Expulsion of 1492 and Its Consequences.* New York, 1992.

———. *The Spanish Inquisition and the Inquisitorial Mind.* Boulder, Colo., 1987.

Aguinis, Marcos. *La gesta del marrano.* Buenos Aires, 1992.

Barnett, R. D., and W. M. Schwab. *The Sephardic Heritage.* Vol. 2, *The Western Sephardim.* Grendon, U.K., 1989.

Baron, Salo W. *A Social and Religious History of the Jews.* Vols. 13, 15, 18. New York, 1969, 1973.

Beinart, Haim. "The Conversos and Their Fate." In *Spain and the Jews:*

The Sephardi Experience, 1492 and After, ed. Elie Kedourie. London, 1992.

————. *Los conversos ante el Tribunal de la Inquisición*. Madrid, 1983.

————. "The Conversos in Spain and Portugal in the Sixteenth to Eighteenth Centuries." In *The Sephardi Legacy*, ed. Haim Beinart. Vol. 2. Jerusalem, 1992.

————. "The Return of Jews to Spain after the Expulsion." In *Jews and Judeoconverts of Spain: The Expulsion of 1992 and Its Consequences*, ed. Angel Alcalá. New York, 1992.

Belgrado Merchant, Luis. *La judería, la inquisición y la Santa Hermandad.* Ciudad Real, Spain, 1907.

Benardete, Mair José. *Hispanic Culture and Character of the Sephardic Jews.* New York, 1982.

Bonfil, Robert. "The Legacy of Sephardi Jewry in Historical Writing." In *The Sephardi Legacy*. Vol. 2. Jerusalem, 1992.

Braunstein, Baruch. *The Chuetas of Majorca: Conversos and the Inquisition of Majorca.* Scottdale, Pa., 1936.

Cohen, Martin A., ed. *Samuel Usque's Consolation for the Tribulations of Israel.* Philadelphia, 1977.

Esteban, Fernando Díaz. "Jewish Literary Creation in Spain." In *The Sephardi Legacy*, ed. Haim Beinart. Vol. 2. Jerusalem, 1992.

Estrugo, J. M. *El retorno a Sefarad.* Madrid, 1933.

————. *Los sefardíes.* Havana, 1958.

Eymeric, Nicolau. *Manual de inquisidores.* Barcelona, 1974.

Fernández, María Angeles. "Inquisitorial Criteria of Marrano Detection: Cryptojews in Andalusia in the Sixteenth Century." In *Jews and Judeoconverts of Spain: The Expulsion of 1492 and Its Consequences*, ed. Angel Alcalá. New York, 1992.

Ford, I. M., ed. *Letters of John III, King of Portugal, 1521–1557.* London, 1931.

Glaser, E. "Portuguese Sermons at Autos-da-Fé." *Studies in Bibliography and Booklore* (spring 1955).

Goitein, S. D. *A Mediterranean Society.* Vol. 2. Berkeley and Los Angeles, 1988.

Herculano de Carvalho e Araujo, A. *History of the Origin and Establishment of the Inquisition in Portugal.* Palo Alto, Calif., 1926.

Hroch, Miroslav, and Anna Skybova. *Ecclesia Militans: The Inquisition.* New York, 1988.

Kamen, Henry. *Inquisition and Society in Spain.* London, 1985.

————. *Spain 1469–1714: A Society in Conflict.* London, 1983.

Kaplan, Yosef. *From Christianity to Judaism: The Story of Isaac Orobio de Castro.* Oxford, 1989.

————. *Jews and Conversos.* Jerusalem, 1984.

Lea, Henry C. *A History of the Inquisition in Spain.* Vol. 1. New York, 1906.

Lindo, Elias H. *The History of the Jews of Spain and Portugal.* New York, 1979.

Livermore, H. V. *A New History of Portugal.* Cambridge, U.K., 1946.

Melammed, Renee Levine. "Judaizing Women in the Inquisitional Records." *Proceedings of the Conference on Sephardic Studies.* College Park, Md., 1991.

Moore, Kenneth. *Those of the Street: The Catholic Jews of Mallorca.* South Bend, Ind., 1976.

Netanyahu, Ben-Zion. *Don Isaac Abravanel: Statesman and Philosopher.* Philadelphia, 1968.

————. *The Marranos of Spain.* Millwood, N.J., 1973.

Pérez, Lorenzo. *Los anales judaicos de Mallorca.* Palma de Majorca, 1974.

Peters, Edward M. *Inquisition.* New York, 1988.

Porcel, Baltasar. *Los chuetas mallorquines.* Barcelona, 1970.

Romano, David. "The Jews' Contributions to Medicine, Science, and General Learning." In *The*

Sephardi Legacy, ed. Haim Beinart.
Vol. 1. Jerusalem, 1992.

Roth, Cecil. *A History of the Marranos.*
Philadelphia, 1941.

———. *The House of Nasi: Doña Gracia.*
Philadelphia, 1946.

———. *The Inquisition.* New York, 1964.

Schlouschz, N. *HaAnusim b'Fortugal*
[The Converts in Portugal].
Jerusalem, 1932.

Selke, Angela S. *The Conversos of
Majorca.* Jerusalem, 1986.

Sicroff, Albert. *Los estatutos de limpieza de
sangre: controversias entre los siglos XV
y XVII.* Madrid, 1979.

Toaff, Ariel, and Simon Schwartzfuchs,
eds. *The Mediterranean and Jewish
Banking, Finance, and International
Trade (XVI–XVIII Centuries).* Ramat
Gan, Israel, 1989.

Vacandard, E. *The Inquisition.* New
York, 1924.

Wolf, Lucien. *Jews in the Canary Islands.*
London, 1926.

Yerushalmi, Yosef H. *From Spanish
Court to Italian Ghetto.* New York,
1971.

———. *The Lisbon Massacres of 1506.*
Cincinnati, 1970.

CHAPTER IX: THE POISONED
EMBRACE

Abitbol, Michael, ed. *Judaïsme d'Afrique
du Nord aux dix-neuvième et vingtième
siècles.* Jerusalem, 1980.

———. *Les Juifs d'Afrique du Nord sous
Vichy.* Paris, 1983.

Ansky, Michael. *Les Juifs d'Algérie du
décret Crémieux à la libération.* Paris,
1960.

———. *Yehudei Algeria* [The Jews of
Algeria]. Jerusalem, 1968.

Arberry, A. J., ed. *Religion in the Middle
East.* Vol. 1. Cambridge, U.K., 1969.

Aster, A., ed. *The Itinerary of Benjamin of
Tudela.* New York, 1927.

Barnai, Jacob. "The Jews of Spain in
North Africa." In *The Sephardi*

Legacy, ed. Haim Beinart. Vol. 2.
Jerusalem, 1992.

Baron, Salo W. *A Social and Religious
History of the Jews.* Vol. 18. New
York, 1973.

Ben-Ami, Issachar. *Yehudei Maroc* [The
Jews of Morocco]. Jerusalem,
1975.

Benbassa, Esther. *Un Grand Rabbin
sepharade en politique, 1892–1923.* Paris,
1990.

Benguigui, Georges, Josiane
Bijaoui-Rosenfield, and Georges
Lévitte. *Aspects of French Jewry.*
London, 1969.

Bensimon-Donath, Doris. *L'Evolution du
judaïsme marocain sous le protectorat
français: 1921–1956.* Paris, 1968.

———. *Immigrants de l'Afrique du Nord
en Israël.* Paris, 1970.

Berg, Roger, Chalom Chemouny, and
Franklin Didi. *Guide juif de France.*
Paris, 1971.

Blumenkranz, Bernhard. *Histoire des juifs
en France.* Toulouse, 1982.

Chouraqui, André. *Les Juifs d'Afrique du
Nord.* Paris, 1953.

———. *La Saga des juifs en Afrique du
Nord.* Paris, 1972.

Cohen, Hayyim J. *The Jews of the Middle
East, 1860–1972.* New York, 1973.

Corcos, David. *The History of the Jews of
Morocco.* Jerusalem, 1976.

Derogy, Jacques, and Edouard Saab. *Les
Deux Exodes.* Paris, 1968.

Deshen, Shlomo. *The Mellah Society:
Jewish Life in Sherifian Morocco.*
Chicago, 1989.

———, and Walter P. Zenner, eds.
Jewish Societies in the Middle East.
Washington, D.C., 1982.

Elgraby, Jordan. "The Sephardic
Community of Paris." *Present Tense*
(summer 1983).

Friedenwald, Harry. *The Jews and
Medicine.* Vol. 2. Baltimore, 1944.

Gerber, Jane S. *Jewish Society in Fez.*
Leiden, 1980.

Gilbert, Martin. *The Jews of Arab Lands:
Their History in Maps.* London, 1976.

Goitein, S. D. *Jews and Arabs: Their Contacts through the Ages.* New York, 1974.

———. *A Mediterranean Society.* 2 vols. Berkeley and Los Angeles, 1967, 1988.

HaCohen, D'vora, and Menachem HaCohen. *One People: The Story of the Eastern Jews.* New York, 1969.

Harari, Yosef. *Toldot Yehudei al-Magreb* [History of the Jews of the Maghreb]. Tel Aviv, 1973.

Harris, André, and Alain de Sedoury. *Juifs et français.* Paris, 1979.

Hirschberg, H. Z. *A History of the Jews in North Africa.* Vols. 1, 2. Leiden, 1981.

Jonas, André. *Jews in Arab Countries.* London, 1971.

Landau, Jacob. "Bittersweet Memories: Memoirs of Jewish Emigrants from Arab Countries." *Middle East Journal* (spring 1981).

———. *The Jews in Nineteenth Century Egypt.* New York, 1969.

Laskier, Michael M. *The Alliance Israélite Universelle and the Jewish Communities of Morocco, 1863–1962.* Albany, N.Y., 1983.

———. *The Jews of Egypt, 1920–1970.* New York, 1992.

———. *North African Jewry in the Twentieth Century.* New York, 1993.

Loeb, Isadore. "Un Convoi d'éxiles d'Espagne: Marseilles en 1492." *Revue des Etudes Juives* 1 (1984).

Malino, Frances. *The Sephardic Jews of Bordeaux: Assimilation and Emancipation in Revolutionary and Napoleonic France.* University, Ala., 1978.

Malka, Elie. *Essai de folklore des israélites du Maroc.* Paris, 1976.

Marrus, Michael, and Robert O. Paxton. *Vichy France and the Jews.* New York, 1981.

Martin, Claude. *Les Israélites algériens de 1830 à 1902.* Paris, 1936.

Memmi, Albert. *La Terre intérieure.* Paris, 1976.

Nahon, Gérard. "Spanish and Portuguese New-Christians in France, XVIth and XVIIth Centuries: Literary Circles." In *Jews and Judeoconverts of Spain: The Expulsion of 1492 and Its Consequences,* ed. Angel Alcalá. New York, 1992.

Nataf, Félix. *Juif maghrebin.* Paris, 1978.

Patai, Raphael. *The Vanished Worlds of Jewry.* New York, 1980.

Sabille, Jacques. *Les Juifs de Tunisie sous Vichy et l'occupation.* Paris, 1954.

Sachar, Howard M. *Diaspora: An Inquiry into the Contemporary Jewish World.* New York, 1985.

———. *Egypt and Israel.* New York, 1981.

Segev, Shmuel. *"Ma'avak Yachkin": HaAliyah HaSodit shel Yehudei Maroc l'Yisrael* ["Operation Yachkin": The Clandestine Emigration of Moroccan Jewry to Israel]. Tel Aviv, 1984.

Serels, Mitchell M. "The Arrival and Settlement of First Generation Spanish Jews in Morocco." In *Jews and Judeoconverts of Spain: The Expulsion of 1492 and Its Consequences,* ed. Angel Alcalá. New York, 1992.

Singer, Charles. "Science and Judaism." In *The Jews: Their History, Culture, and Religion,* ed. Louis Finkelstein. 4th ed. Vol. 2. New York, 1971.

Stahl, Avraham. *Toldot Yehudei Maroc* [The History of Moroccan Jewry]. Jerusalem, 1966.

Stillman, Norman. *The Jews of Arab Lands.* Philadelphia, 1979.

———. *The Jews of Arab Lands in the Modern Period.* Philadelphia, 1991.

Szajkowski, Zosa. *Jews and the French Revolutions of 1789, 1830, and 1848.* New York, 1970.

———. "Population Problems of Marranos and Sephardim in France, from the Sixteenth to the Twentieth Century." *Proceedings of the American Academy for Jewish Research* (1958).

Tessler, M. A., and L. L. Hawkins. "The Political Culture of Jews in Tunisia and Morocco." *International Journal of Middle Eastern Studies* (February 1980).

Trigano, Shmuel. *La République et les juifs.* Paris, 1982.

Yetiv, Itzhak. "Marseilles Jewry at the Crossroads." *Dispersion and Unity* (1963).

Zafrani, Haim. *Les Juifs du Maroc: Vie sociale, économique et religieuse.* Paris, 1972.

CHAPTER X: THE JEWS OF
RENAISSANCE

Adler, Israel. "Art Music in the Italian Ghetto." In *Jewish Medieval and Renaissance Studies,* ed. Alexander Altman. Cambridge, Mass., 1967.

Amram, David W. *The Makers of Hebrew Books in Italy.* London, 1988.

Baron, Salo W. *A Social and Religious History of the Jews.* Vol. 13. New York, 1969.

Bedarida, Guido. *Ebrei d'Italia.* Leghorn, 1952.

Bonfil, Robert. "The Arrival of the Spanish Refugees in Italy." In *Jews and Judeoconverts of Spain: The Expulsion of 1492 and Its Consequences,* ed. Angel Alcalá. New York, 1992.

———. *Gli ebrei in Italia nell'epoca del rinascimento.* Florence, 1991.

———. "The History of the Spanish and Portuguese Jews in Italy." In *The Sephardi Legacy,* ed. Haim Beinart. Vol. 2. Jerusalem, 1992.

———. "How Golden Was the Age of the Renaissance in Jewish Historiosophy?" *History and Theory* (1989).

Cooperman, Bernard D. "Venetian Policy towards Levantine Jews and Its Broader Context." In *Gli ebrei a Venezia.* Milan, 1987.

———, ed. *Jewish Thought in the Sixteenth Century.* Cambridge, Mass., 1983.

Curiel, Roberta, and Bernard Cooperman. *The Ghetto of Venice.* London, 1990.

D'Ancona, Levi. "The Sephardi Community of Leghorn (Livorno)." In *The Sephardic Heritage.* Vol. 2, *The Western Sephardim,* ed. R. D. Barnett and W. M. Schwab. Grendon, U.K., 1989.

Ehrlich, Israel. *Italyah: P'rakim b'Toldot HaKehilot HaYehudiot* [Italy: Chapters in the History of the Jewish Communities]. Tel Aviv, 1974.

Fortis, Umberto. *The Ghetto on the Lagoon: A Guide to the History and Art of the Venetian Ghetto.* Venice, 1973.

———. *Jews and Synagogues: Venice, Florence, Rome, Leghorn: A Practical Guide.* Venice, 1973.

Malkiel, David J. *A Separate Republic: Venetian Jewry, 1607–1621.* Jerusalem, 1991.

Meyuhas-Ginio, Alisa, ed. *The Mediterranean World after 1492: Jews, Muslims and Christians.* London, 1992.

Milano, Attilio. *Storia degli ebrei in Italia.* Turin, 1963.

———. *Storia degli ebrei italiani nei Levante.* Florence, 1973.

Milburn, A. R. "Leone Ebreo and the Renaissance." In *Isaac Abrabanel: Six Lectures,* ed. J. B. Trend. Cambridge, U.K., 1937.

Miskimin, Harry A. *The Economy of Later Renaissance Europe, 1460–1600.* Englewood Cliffs, N.J., 1969.

Morais, Sabato. *Italian Hebrew Literature.* New York, 1928.

Netanyahu, Ben-Zion. *Don Isaac Abravanel: Statesman and Philosopher.* Philadelphia, 1968.

Patai, Raphael. *The Jewish Mind.* New York, 1977.

Ravid, Benjamin. *Economics and Toleration in Seventeenth-Century Venice.* Jerusalem, 1978.

Reisz, Matthew. *Europe's Jewish Quarters.* London, 1991.

Rivkin, Ellis. *Leon de Modena and the Kol Sakhal.* Cincinnati, 1952.

Roth, Cecil. *A History of the Jews in Venice.* New York, 1930.

———. *A History of the Jews of Italy.* Philadelphia, 1946.

———. *The Jews in the Renaissance.* Philadelphia, 1959.

———. *The Last Florentine Republic.* Vol. 2. London, 1968.

Ruderman, David. *Kabbalah, Magic, and Science.* Cambridge, Mass., 1989.

———. *The World of the Renaissance Jew: The Life and Thought of Abraham ben Mordecai Farissol.* Cincinnati, 1981.

Schechter, Solomon. *Studies in Judaism.* Philadelphia, 1896.

Shulvass, Moses A. *The Jews in the World of the Renaissance.* Leiden, 1973.

Simonsohn, Shlomoh. *A History of the Jews in the Duchy of Mantua.* Jerusalem, 1977.

Sirat, Colette. *A History of Jewish Philosophy in the Middle Ages.* Cambridge, U.K., 1985.

Toaff, Ariel, and Simon Schwartzfuchs, eds. *The Mediterranean and Jewish Banking, Finance, and International Trade (Sixteenth–Eighteenth Centuries).* Ramat Gan, Israel, 1989.

Trend, J. B., ed. *Isaac Abravanel: Six Lectures.* Cambridge, U.K., 1937.

Twersky, Isadore, ed. *Studies in Jewish Law and Philosophy.* New York, 1982.

Wirszubski, Chaim. *Pico della Mirandola's Encounter with Jewish Mysticism.* Cambridge, Mass., 1959.

Yerushalmi, Yosef H. *From Spanish Court to Italian Ghetto.* New York, 1971.

Zinberg, Israel. *A History of Jewish Literature: Italian Jewry in the Renaissance Era.* Cincinnati, 1974.

CHAPTER XI: ITALIAN TWILIGHT

Barzilay, Isaac. *Between Reason and Faith: Anti-rationalism in Italian Jewish Thought, 1250–1650.* The Hague, 1967.

Bassani, Giorgio. *The Garden of the Finzi-Continis.* London, 1965.

Bonfil, Robert. "The Jews of Romagna." *Pa'amin* (1989).

Cannistraro, Philip V., and Brian R. Sullivan. *Il Duce's Other Woman.* New York, 1993.

Carpi, Daniel. *Dappim l'Cheker HaShoah v'HaMered* [Investigations into the Holocaust and the Revolt]. Jerusalem, 1968.

Falconi, Carlo. *The Silence of Pius XII.* Boston, 1970.

Felice, Renzo de. *Storia degli ebrei italiani sotto il fascismo.* Turin, 1963.

Furbank, P. N. *Italo Svevo.* Berkeley, Calif., 1966.

Hellman, Peter. *Avenue of the Righteous.* New York, 1980.

Hughes, H. Stuart. *Prisoners of Hope: The Silver Age of the Italian Jews.* Cambridge, Mass., 1983.

Levi, Primo. *Survival in Auschwitz.* New York, 1961.

Lottman, Herbert. "Venetian Ghetto." *Present Tense* (winter 1974).

Michaelis, Meir. *Mussolini and the Jews.* Oxford, 1978.

Morley, John F. *Vatican Diplomacy and the Jews during the Holocaust, 1939–1942.* New York, 1980.

Patai, Raphael. *The Vanished Worlds of Jewry.* New York, 1980.

Poliakov, Leon, and Jacques Sabille, eds. *Jews under the Italian Occupation.* Paris, 1955.

Pullan, Brian. *The Jews of Europe and the Inquisition of Venice, 1550–1670.* Oxford, 1983.

Roth, Cecil. *A History of the Jews of Italy.* Philadelphia, 1946.

Sachar, Howard M. *Diaspora: An Inquiry into the Contemporary Jewish World.* New York, 1985.

Stille, Alexander. *Benevolence and Betrayal: Five Italian Jewish Families under Fascism.* New York, 1992.

Toaff, Ariel, and Simon Schwartzfuchs, eds. *The Mediterranean and Jewish Banking, Finance, and International Trade (XVI–XVIII).* Ramat Gan, Israel, 1989.

Valabrega, Guido. *Ebrei, fascismo, sionismo.* Urbino, 1974.

Zucotti, Susan. *The Italians and the Holocaust.* New York, 1987.

CHAPTER XII: A BALKAN SEPHARAD

American Jewish Congress. *Jewish Communities of Eastern Europe.* New York, 1967.

Arditi, Benjamin J. *Yehudei Bulgaria b'Shanot HaMishtar HaNatzi* [Bulgarian Jewry in the Years of the Nazi Occupation]. Cholon, Israel, 1962.

Auty, Phyllis. *Yugoslavia.* New York, 1965.

Baron, Salo W. *A Social and Religious History of the Jews.* Vol. 18. New York, 1983.

Bartov, Hanoch. *Dado: Forty-eight Years and Twenty Days.* Tel Aviv, 1981.

Canetti, Elias. *Auto-da-Fé.* New York, 1982.

————. *The Tongue Set Free.* New York, 1982.

Chary, Frederick B. *The Bulgarian Jews and the Final Solution.* Pittsburgh, 1972.

Freidenreich, Harriet Pass. *The Jews of Yugoslavia.* Philadelphia, 1979.

Gaon, Solomon S., and M. Mitchell Serels, eds. *Sephardim and the Holocaust.* New York, 1987.

Grünwald, Kurt. *Turkenhirsch: A Study of Baron Maurice de Hirsch, Entrepreneur and Philanthropist.* Jerusalem, 1966.

Kerner, Robert J., ed. *Yugoslavia.* Berkeley, Calif., 1949.

Koen, Albert. *Le Sauvetage des juifs en Bulgarie, 1941–1944.* Sofia, 1977.

Lazar, Moshe, ed. *The Sephardic Tradition: Ladino and Spanish Jewish Literature.* New York, 1972.

Levy, Isaac Jack. *And the World Stood Silent: Sephardic Poetry of the Holocaust.* Urbana, Ill., 1989.

Loker, Zvi. "Spanish and Portuguese Jews amongst the Southern Slavs: Their Settlement and Consolidation during the Sixteenth, Seventeenth, and Eighteenth Centuries." In *The Sephardic Heritage.* Vol. 2, *The Western*

Sephardim, eds. R. D. Barnett and W. M. Schwab. Grendon, U.K., 1989.

Luria, Max A. *A Study of the Monastir Dialect of Judeo-Spanish.* New York, 1930.

Mazur, Belle D. *Studies on Jewry in Greece.* Athens, 1935.

Mézan, S. *Juifs espagnols en Bulgarie.* Paris, 1925.

Michaelis, Meir. *Mussolini and the Jews.* Oxford, 1978.

Molho, M. *Histoire des israélites de Castoria.* Salonica, 1938.

————, and J. Nehama. *In Memoriam: hommage aux victimes juives des nazis en Grèce.* 3 vols. Salonika, 1948–53.

Oren, Nissan. "The Bulgarian Exception: A Reassessment of the Salvation of the Jewish Community." *Yad Vashem Studies* (1968).

Patai, Raphael. *The Vanished Worlds of Jewry.* New York, 1980.

Poliakov, Léon, and Jacques Sabille, eds. *Jews under the Italian Occupation.* Paris, 1955.

Schner, Zvi, ed. *Extermination and Resistance.* Vols. 1, 2. Jerusalem, 1958.

Sitton, David. *Sephardi Communities Today.* Jerusalem, 1985.

Stoianovich, Traian. *A Study in Balkan Civilization.* New York, 1967.

Tamir, Vicki. *Bulgaria and Her Jews.* New York, 1979.

Zucotti, Susan. *The Italians and the Holocaust.* New York, 1987.

CHAPTER XIII: A CALVINIST JERUSALEM

Aciman, André A. "Was Spinoza a Heretic?" *Commentary* (August 1990).

Angel, Mark. *Voices in Exile: A Study in Sephardic Intellectual History.* Hoboken, N.J., 1991.

Arkin, Marcus. *Aspects of Jewish Economic History.* Philadelphia, 1975.

Barnett, R. D., and W. M. Schwab, eds. *The Sephardic Heritage.* Vol. 2, *The*

Western Sephardim. Grendon, U.K., 1989.

Baron, Salo W. *An Economic History of the Jews.* Jerusalem, 1975.

———. *A Social and Religious History of the Jews.* Vol. 15. New York, 1974.

Blau, Joseph, et al., eds. *Essays [by Salo Baron] on Jewish Life and Thought.* New York, 1959.

Bloom, Herbert I. *The Economic Activities of the Jews of Amsterdam in the Seventeenth and Eighteenth Centuries.* Williamsport, Pa., 1937.

Bodian, Miriam. "Amsterdam, Venice and the Marrano Diaspora in the Seventeenth Century." In *Dutch Jewish History,* ed. Joseph Michman. Jerusalem, 1989.

———. "The Shaping of *Converso* Identity in Early Modern Europe." *Proceedings of the Conference on Sephardic Studies.* College Park, Md., (1991).

Boxer, C. R. *The Dutch Seaborne Empire, 1600–1800.* New York, 1965.

Cohen, Martin A., ed. *Samuel Usque's* Consolation for the Tribulations of Israel. Philadelphia, 1977.

Fuks, L., and G. Fuks-Mansfeld. *Hebrew Typography in the Northern Netherlands.* Vol. 1. Leiden, 1984.

Gans, M. H. *Memorboek: The History of Dutch Jews from the Renaissance to 1940.* Baarn, Netherlands, 1977.

Israel, Jonathan. *European Jewry in the Age of Mercantilism, 1550–1750.* Oxford, 1983.

———. "Sephardi Immigration into the Dutch Republic." *Studia Rosenthaliana* (1989).

———. "The Sephardim in the Netherlands." In *Spain and the Jews: The Sephardi Experience, 1492 and After,* ed. Elie Kedourie. London, 1992.

Kaplan, Yosef. "The Intellectual Ferment in the Spanish-Portuguese Community of Seventeenth Century Amsterdam." In *The Sephardi Legacy,* ed. Haim Beinart. Vol. 2. Jerusalem, 1992.

———. "The Social Functions of the 'Herem' in the Portuguese Jewish Community of Amsterdam in the Seventeenth Century." In *Dutch Jewish History,* ed. J. Michman. Jerusalem, 1981.

———, et al., eds. *Menasseh ben Israel and His World.* Leiden, 1989.

Katz, David S. "The Abendana Brothers and the Christian Hebraists of Seventeenth-Century Amsterdam." In *Essays in Modern Jewish History,* eds. Francis Malino and Peter Cohen. London, 1982.

Meyer, Michael A., ed. *Ideas of Jewish History.* Detroit, 1987.

Michman, J., ed. *Dutch Jewish History.* Jerusalem, 1981.

Morgenstern, Susan W., and Ruth S. Levine. *The Jews in the Age of Rembrandt.* Rockville, Md., 1982.

Parker, Geoffrey. *The Dutch Revolt.* Ithaca, N.Y., 1977.

Patai, Raphael. *The Jewish Mind.* New York, 1977.

———. *The Vanished Worlds of Jewry.* New York, 1980.

Peters, Edward M. *Inquisition.* New York, 1988.

Polak, Jack. "The Sephardim of Holland and the Holocaust." In *Sephardim and the Holocaust,* eds. Solomon Gaon and M. Mitchell Serels. New York, 1987.

Presser, Jacob. *The Destruction of the Dutch Jews.* New York, 1967.

Reisz, Matthew. *Europe's Jewish Quarters.* London, 1991.

Revah, J. S. *Spinoza et le Dr. Juan de Prado.* Paris, 1959.

Roth, Cecil. *A History of the Marranos.* Philadelphia, 1941.

———. *The Life of Menasseh ben Israel.* Philadelphia, 1945.

Roth, Leon. *Spinoza, Descartes, and Maimonides.* New York, 1924.

Schama, Simon. *The Embarrassment of Riches: An Interpretation of Dutch Culture in the Golden Age.* New York, 1987.

Shulvass, Moses A. *From East to West.* Detroit, 1971.

Stengers, L. J. *Les Juifs dans les Pays-Bas au moyen âge.* Brussels, 1950.

Wolfson, Harry A. *The Philosophy of Spinoza.* Cambridge, Mass., 1958.

Yovel, Yirmiyahu. *Spinoza and Other Heretics.* 2 vols. Princeton, N.J., 1990.

CHAPTER XIV: THE EMISSARIES

Arkin, Marcus. *Aspects of Jewish Economic History.* Philadelphia, 1975.

Barnett, R. D., and W. M. Schwab, eds. *The Sephardic Heritage.* Vol. 2, *The Western Sephardim.* Grendon, U.K., 1989.

Baxter, S. B. *William III and the Defense of European Liberty, 1650–1702.* London, 1966.

Goodman, P. *Moses Montefiore.* London, 1925.

Hyamson, Albert. *The Sephardim of England.* London, 1951.

Israel, J. I. "Menasseh Ben Israel and the Dutch Sephardic Colonization Movement." In *Menasseh ben Israel and His World,* eds. Yosef Kaplan et al. Leiden, 1989.

Jones, Pamela Fletcher. *The Jews of Britain.* Gloucestershire, U.K., 1990.

Kaplan, Yosef, et al., eds. *Menasseh ben Israel and His World.* Leiden, 1989.

Katz, David S. *Philosemitism and the Readmission of the Jews to England, 1603–1655.* Oxford, 1982.

Lipman, V. D., ed. *Three Centuries of Anglo-Jewish History.* London, 1961.

Loewe, Louis., ed. *The Diaries of Sir Moses and Lady Montefiore.* 2 vols. London, 1890.

Mechoule, Henri. "Menasseh ben Israel." In *The Sephardi Legacy,* ed. Haim Beinart. Vol. 2. Jerusalem, 1992.

Nahon, S. U. *Sir Moses Montefiore.* London, 1965.

Newman, Aubrey. "The Sephardim in England." In *Spain and the Jews: The Sephardi Experience, 1492 and After,* ed. Elie Kedourie. London, 1992.

Roth, Cecil. *Benjamin Disraeli: Earl of Beaconsfield.* Philadelphia, 1952.

———. *Essays and Portraits in Anglo-Jewish History.* Philadelphia, 1962.

———. *A History of the Jews in England.* Oxford, 1964.

———. *The Life of Menasseh ben Israel.* Philadelphia, 1934.

———. *Magna Bibliotheca Anglo-Judaica.* London, 1937.

Schorsch, Ismar. "From Messianism to Realpolitik: Menasseh ben Israel and the Readmission of the Jews to England." *Proceedings of the American Academy of Jewish Research.* New York (1978).

Segre, Renata. *The Jews in Parliament.* 2 vols. Jerusalem, 1986.

Wolf, Lucien. *Essays in Jewish History.* London, 1932.

———, ed. *Menasseh ben Israel's Mission to Oliver Cromwell.* London, 1901.

Woolf, M. "Foreign Trade of London Jews in the Seventeenth Century." *Transactions of the Jewish Historical Society of England* (1975).

CHAPTER XV: THE VANGUARD OF A NEW WORLD

Adler, Elkan. *Auto de Fe and Jew.* London, 1909.

Amler, Jane Frances. *Christopher Columbus's Jewish Roots.* Northvale, N.J., 1992.

Baron, Salo W. *A Social and Religious History of the Jews.* Vols. 12, 15. New York, 1967, 1973.

———. *An Economic History of the Jews.* Jerusalem, 1975.

Becker, Lavy. "Jews in the Caribbean." *World Jewry* (October 1971).

Böhm, Günter. *Los judíos en Chile durante la colonia.* Santiago, 1948.

Boorstin, Daniel. *The Discoverers.* New York, 1983.

Boxer, Charles R. *The Church Militant*

and Iberian Expansion, 1440–1770. Baltimore, 1978.

Cohen, Mario E. "What Spanish-America Lost: The Impact of the Expulsion on Its Cultural and Economic Backwardness." In *Jews and Judeoconverts of Spain: The Expulsion of 1492 and Its Consequences,* ed. Angel Alcalá. New York, 1992.

Cohen, Martin A., ed. *The Jewish Experience in Colonial Latin America.* 2 vols. Waltham, Mass., 1971.

———. *The Martyr: The Story of a Secret Jew and the Mexican Inquisition in the Sixteenth Century.* Philadelphia, 1973.

Elkin, Judith Laikin. *The Jewish Presence in Latin America.* Boston, 1987.

———. *The Jews of the Latin American Republics.* Chapel Hill, N.C., 1980.

Isaacs, A. Lionel. *The Jews of Majorca.* London, 1932.

Israel, Jonathan I. "The Sephardi Contribution to Economic Life and Colonization in Europe and the New World." In *The Sephardi Legacy,* ed. Haim Beinart. Vol. 2. Jerusalem, 1992.

Kayserling, Meyer. *Christopher Columbus and the Participation of the Jews in the Spanish and Portuguese Discoveries.* New York, 1906.

Kohut, George A. "Jewish Martyrs of the Inquisition in South America." *Proceedings of the American Jewish Historical Society* (1894).

Lea, H. C. *The Inquisition in the Spanish Dependencies.* New York, 1908.

Lebeson, Anita. *Jewish Pioneers in America, 1492–1848.* New York, 1931.

Lewin, Boleslao. *Mártires y conquistadores judíos en la América Hispánica.* Buenos Aires, 1954.

Liebman, Seymour B. *A Guide to Jewish References in the Mexican Colonial Era, 1521–1821.* Philadelphia, 1964.

———. *The Enlightened: The Writings of Luis de Carvajal el Mozo.* Coral Gables, Fla., 1967.

———. *Jews and the Inquisition of Mexico.* Lawrence, Kans., 1974.

———. *The Jews in New Spain.* Coral Gables, Fla., 1970.

Marcus, Jacob R. *The Colonial American Jew, 1492–1776.* Vol. 1. Detroit, 1970.

Parry, J. H. *The Spanish Seaborne Empire.* New York, 1966.

———. *Trade and Dominion: The European Overseas Empires in the Eighteenth Century.* New York, 1971.

Postal, Bernard, and Malcolm Stern. *A Tourist's Guide to Jewish History in the Caribbean.* New York, 1975.

Roth, Cecil. *The Jewish Contribution to Civilization.* London, 1938.

Selka, Angela S. *The Conversos of Majorca.* Jerusalem, 1988.

Sicroff, Albert. *Los estatutos de limpieza de sangre: controversias entre los siglos XV y XVII.* Madrid, 1979.

Sitton, David. *Sephardic Communities Today.* Jerusalem, 1985.

Sola Pool, David de. *An Old Faith in a New World.* New York, 1955.

———. *Portraits Etched in Stone: Jewish Settlers, 1681–1831.* New York, 1952.

Stampfer, Joshua, ed. *The Sephardim: A Cultural Journey from Spain to the Pacific Coast.* Portland, Oreg., 1987.

Toribio Medina, Jaime. *Historia de la inquisición de Lima.* 2 vols. Lima, 1956.

Twinam, A. "From Jew to Basque: Ethnic Myths and Antiqueño Entrepreneurship." *Journal of Inter-American Studies* (February 1980).

Wiznitzer, Arnold. "Crypto-Jews in Mexico during the Sixteenth Century." *American Jewish Historical Quarterly* (spring 1962).

Zimmels, H. J. *Ashkenazim and Sephardim.* London, 1958.

CHAPTER XVI: THE END OF
THE INHABITED EARTH

Andrade, J. A. P. M. *A Record of the Jews in Jamaica from the English Conquest to the Present Time.* Kingston, Jamaica, 1941.

Arkin, Marcus. *Aspects of Jewish Economic History.* Philadelphia, 1975.

Boxer, Charles R. *The Dutch in Brazil, 1621–54.* New York, 1957.

——. *The Dutch Seaborne Empire, 1600–1800.* New York, 1965.

——. *Four Centuries of Portuguese Expansion, 1415–1825.* New York and Berkeley, Calif., 1969.

——. *The Portuguese Seaborne Empire, 1415–1825.* New York, 1975.

Davis, Nicholas N. *Notes on the History of the Jews in Barbados.* New York, 1909.

Emmanuel, Isaac S., and Suzanne A. Emmanuel. *A History of the Jews of the Netherlands Antilles.* 2 vols. Cincinnati, 1970.

Israel, Jonathan I. "The Sephardi Contribution to Economic Life and Colonization in Europe and the New World (Sixteenth–Eighteenth Centuries)." In *The Sephardi Legacy,* ed. Haim Beinart. Vol. 2. Jerusalem, 1992.

Kaplan, Yosef. "The Curaçao and Amsterdam Jewish Community in the Seventeenth and Eighteenth Centuries." *Dutch Jewish History* (winter 1982).

Karner, Francs P. *The Sephardics of Curaçao.* Assen, Netherlands, 1969.

Levy, Emma Fidanque. "The Fidanques: Symbols of the Continuity of the Sephardic Tradition in America." *American Jewish Archives* (spring–summer, 1992).

Loker, Zvi. *Jews in the Caribbean.* Jerusalem, 1992.

Metz, Allan. " 'Those of the Hebrew Nation . . . ': The Sephardic Experience in Colonial Latin America." *American Jewish Archives* (spring–summer 1992).

Novinsky, Anita. *Cristãos Novos da Bahía.* Rio de Janeiro, 1972.

——. "The Persistence of Cryptojudaism in Portugal and Brazil." In *Jews and Judeoconverts of Spain: The Expulsion of 1492 and Its Consequences,* ed. Angel Alcalá. New York, 1992.

Sachar, Howard M. *Diaspora: An Inquiry into the Contemporary Jewish World.* New York, 1985.

Stern, Malcolm. "Portuguese Sephardim in the Americas." *American Jewish Archives* (spring–summer 1992).

Swetschinski, D. M. "Conflict and Opportunity and 'Europe's Other Sea' ": The Adventure of Caribbean Jewish Settlement." *American Jewish History* (winter 1982).

Weinstein, Rochelle. "Stones of Memory: Revelations from a Cemetery in Curaçao." *American Jewish Archives* (spring–summer 1992).

Wiznitzer, Arnold. "The Exodus from Brazil and Arrival in New Amsterdam of the Jewish Pilgrim Fathers, 1654." *Publications of the American Jewish Historical Society* (December 1954).

——. *Jews in Colonial Brazil.* New York, 1960.

Yerushalmi, Yosef H. "Curaçao and the Caribbean in Early Modern Jewish History." *American Jewish History* (December 1982).

Zucker, Norman, and Naomi Zucker. "Survivors on a Desert Island: Curaçao." *Present Tense* (summer 1977).

CHAPTER XVII: THE LONG ROAD HOME

Alan, Ray. "Spanish Anti-Semitism Today." *Commentary* (August 1964).

Aronsfeld, C. C. *The Ghosts of 1492: Jewish Aspects of the Struggle for Religious Freedom in Spain, 1848–1976.* New York, 1979.

Atienza, Juan. *The Jewish Guide to Spain.* Madrid, 1979.

Avni, Haim. *Spain, the Jews, and Franco.* Philadelphia, 1982.

Azancot, Leopoldo. *La novia judía.* Barcelona, 1977.

Baron, Salo W. *An Economic History of the Jews.* Jerusalem, 1975.

Ben-Arieh, Yehoshua. *Jerusalem in the Nineteenth Century.* Tel Aviv, 1989.

Ben-Rafael, Eliezer. *The Emergence of Ethnicity: Cultural Groups and Social Conflict in Israel.* Westport, Conn., 1982.

Bensimon-Donath, Doris. *Immigrants d'Afrique du Nord en Israël.* Paris, 1970.

Ben-Zvi, Yitzchak. *Eretz Yisrael v'Yehudehah Tachat HaShilton HaOtomani* [The Land of Israel and Its Jewish Settlement under Ottoman Rule]. Jerusalem, 1963.

Bunis, David M. *Sephardic Studies: A Research Bibliography.* New York, 1981.

Caro Baroja, Julio. *Los judíos en la España moderna y contemporánea.* Madrid, 1978.

Cohen, Amnon. *Economic Life in Ottoman Jerusalem.* Cambridge, U.K., 1989.

Cohen, S. "The Sephardic Condition." *New Outlook* (January–February 1979).

Darin-Drabklin, Haim. *The Other Society.* New York, 1963.

Deshen, Shlomo, and Moshe Shokeid. *The Predicament of Homecoming: Cultural and Social Life of North African Immigrants in Israel.* Ithaca, N.Y., 1974.

Díaz, Adolfo S. "Spain's Wandering Jews." *America* (July 1951).

Díaz-Más, Paloma. *Sephardim: The Jews from Spain.* Madrid, 1992.

Dutter, L. E. "Eastern and Western Jews: Ethnic Divisions in Israeli Society." *Middle East Journal* (autumn 1977).

Elazar, Daniel. *The Other Jews: The Sephardim Today.* Glencoe, Ill., 1989.

Eliachar, E. "The Sephardi Non-Presence." *New Outlook* (January–February 1977).

Gerber, Haim. *Ottoman Rule in Jerusalem, 1890–1914.* Berlin, 1984.

Glass, Joseph B., and Ruth Kark. *Sephardi Entrepreneurs in Eretz Israel: The Amzalak Family, 1816–1918.* Jerusalem, 1991.

Goldstein, Amy D. "The Development of Spanish-Israeli Diplomatic Relations." Ph.D. diss., University of Michigan, 1988.

Haddad, Hezkel M. *Yehudei Artzot Arav v'Islam* [The Jews of Arab and Islamic Lands]. Tel Aviv, 1983.

Inbar, Michael, and Chaim Adler. *Ethnic Integration in Israel.* New Brunswick, N.J., 1977.

Kohn, Moshe. "Hidden Persuasion." *Jerusalem Post.* November 25, 1983.

Krausz, E., and M. Bar-Lev. "Varieties of Orthodox Religious Behavior." *Jewish Journal of Sociology* (July 1978).

Landau, Jacob. "Bittersweet Memories: Memories of Jewish Emigrants from Arab Countries." *Middle East Journal* (spring 1981).

Lissak, Moshe. *Social Mobility in Israel Society.* Jerusalem, 1969.

Melamed, Aharon. *No'ar b'Metsukah* [Youth in Distress]. Haifa, 1983.

Nataf, Felix. *Juif maghrebin.* Paris, 1978.

Patai, Raphael. *Cultures in Conflict.* New York, 1961.

Perlmutter, Amos. "Cleavage in Israel." *Foreign Policy* (summer 1977).

Polner, Murray. "Report from Madrid." *Present Tense* (winter 1980).

Raphael, Chaim. *The Road from Babylon.* London, 1985.

Rejwan, Nissim. "The Myth of the Black Panthers." *New Middle East* (October 1971).

Sachar, Howard M. *From the Ends of the Earth: The Peoples of Israel.* Cleveland, 1964.

———. *A History of Israel since the Yom Kippur War.* New York, 1987.

Selzer, Michael. *The Outcasts of Israel: Communal Tensions in the Jewish State.* Jerusalem, 1965.

Shamir, Shimon. *The Laws of Egypt: A Mediterranean Society in Modern Times.* Boulder, Colo., 1987.

Sitton, David. *Sephardic Communities Today.* Jerusalem, 1985.

Smooha, S. "Ethnic Stratification and Allegiance in Israel: Where Do Oriental Jews Belong?" *Il Politico* (1976).

Stillman, Norman. *The Jews of Arab Lands Today.* Philadelphia, 1991.

Swirski, S. "The Oriental Jews in Israel: Why Many Tilted toward Begin." *Dissent,* no. 1 (1984).

Weingrod, Alex. *Israel Group Relations in a New Society.* New York, 1965.

———. *The Saint of Beersheba.* Albany, N.Y., 1990.

Ysart, Federico. *España y los judíos en la Segunda Guerra Mundial.* Barcelona, 1973.

INDEX

Grateful acknowledgment is made to the following for
permission to reprint previously published material:
Behrman House, Inc.: Excerpts from poem translated by
Israel Zangwill, from *Judah Halevi as Poet and Thinker*,
edited by Israel Efros (Behrman House, Inc., 1941);
excerpts from *Abrabanel and the Expulsion of the Jews from Spain*
by Jacob S. Minkin (Behrman House, Inc., 1938).
Reprinted by permission.
Jewish Publication Society: Verse excerpt translated by
Bernard Lewis from *The Jews of Arab Lands* by Norman Stillman
(Jewish Publication Society, 1979); verse selections from
Selected Poems of Solomon Ibn Gabirol, edited by Israel
Davidson; verse selections from *Selected Poems of Moses
Ibn Ezra*, edited by Solomon Solis-Cohen; verse excerpt
from *Selected Poems of Jehudah Halevi*, translated
by Nina Salaman. Reprinted by permission.
KTAV Publishing House, Inc.: Excerpts from *A History
of Jewish Literature*, edited by Israel Zinberg,
translated by Bernard Martin (World Publishing Co., 1972).
Reprinted by permission.
University of Miami Press: Excerpt from *The Enlightened:
The Writings of Luis de Carvajal el Mozo*, edited
by Seymour Liebman (University of Miami Press, 1967).
Reprinted by permission.

A Note About the Author

Born in St. Louis, Missouri, and reared in Champaign, Illinois, Howard
Morley Sachar received his undergraduate education at Swarthmore and
took his graduate degrees at Harvard. He has taught extensively in the
fields of Modern European, Jewish, and Middle Eastern history, and lived
in the Middle East for six years, two of them on fellowship, the rest as
founder-director of Brandeis University's Hiatt Institute in Jerusalem. Dr.
Sachar has contributed to many scholarly journals and is the author of
eleven previous books: *The Course of Modern Jewish History* (1958), *Aliyah*
(1961), *From the Ends of the Earth* (1964), *The Emergence of the Middle East,
1914–1924* (1969), *Europe Leaves the Middle East, 1936–1954* (1972), *A History of
Israel: From the Rise of Zionism to Our Time* (1976), *The Man on the Camel*
(1980), *Egypt and Israel* (1981), *Diaspora* (1985), *A History of Israel: From the
Aftermath of the Yom Kippur War* (1987), and *A History of the Jews in America*
(1992). He is also the editor of the thirty-nine-volume *The Rise of Israel: A
Documentary History*. Based in Washington, D.C., where he serves as
Charles E. Smith Professor of History at George Washington University,
Dr. Sachar is a consultant and lecturer on Middle Eastern affairs
for numerous governmental bodies, and lectures widely throughout
the United States and abroad. He and his family live in Kensington,
Maryland.

A Note on the Type

This book was set in Calisto, a
typeface designed by Ron Carpenter
in 1987 while working for the
Monotype Corporation in
the United Kingdom.

Composed by ComCom, a
division of Haddon Craftsmen,
Allentown, Pennsylvania
Printed and bound by
The Haddon Craftsmen,
Scranton, Pennsylvania
Maps by George Colbert
Designed by Anthea Lingeman